ACCRINGTON & DISTRICT 1927 -1934.

THE COTTON CRISIS & THE MEANS TEST.

BY

JIM AINSWORTH

Published by Hyndburn & Rossendale Trades Union Council

1997

Copyright Jim Ainsworth 1997

ISBN 0 9523496 1 2

Typeset by Jim Ainsworth

Printed and Published by Hyndburn & Rossendale Trades Union Council.

Secretary: Peter Billington
10 East Crescent, Accrington, Lancashire.

Dedicted to the memory of Ken Slater and all the other local socialists, who spent their lives working for the betterment of the working class of this district.

CONTENTS.

Details of the Author.   Page No
Acknowledgements.
Map of North East Lancashire 1927 -1934
Foreword. Peter Billington, Secretary Hyndburn & Rossendale TUC.
Preface

Chapter 1   The Trades Disputes & Trade Unions Act.   1
  The Campaign Against the Bill.   1
  Mr. C.R. Buxton's Speech.   3
  Mr. C.R. Buxton's Attack on Mr. Edwards MP.   10
  Mr. Robert Blatchford's comment from the past.   13
  The National Minority Movement.   15
  The Reaction to the Act.   16
  Comments on the effects of the Act.   17
  Comments on similar legislation enacted since 1979.   19
  References.   22

Chapter 2   The Cotton Industry.   23
  Organisation: Weaving.   23
  Organisation: Spinning.   23
  Organisation: General.   23
  Organisation: Dyeing.   24
  1927 - The Park Mill Dispute, Accrington.   25
  8th. Annual Procession & Sports Day, Accrington TCLP.   27
  Fining.   27
  The Death of Mr. J.C. Parker J.P.   30
  1928 - The Dispute in the Dyeing & Finishing Trades.   38
  The Accrington & Rishton Weavers' Blackpool Excursions.   41
  Sir David Shackleton Guest Speaker.   41
  1929   46
    Death of Gt Harwood Weavers' Secretary, Mr. Hesmondhalgh.   48
  The Lockout Begins.   54
  The Decision of the Arbitration Board.   58
  Hours of Work.   61
  1930   65
  Death of Gt Harwood Weavers' Sec., Mr. John W. Hudson.   65
  The Appointment of Mr. J.W. Sunderland.   68
  The Strike at Bury's Union Mill.   71
  The Cotton Report is Published.   75

Domestic Service for Unemployed Female Labour.	80
The Employers Prepare to Institute the More-Looms-System.	82
1931 - The More - Looms Dispute Lockout.	86
Work is Resumed.	96
The effect of the Indian Boycott & the arrival of Mahatma Gandhi in North East Lancashire.	98
1932	116
Angry Scenes at Gt Harwood - Police Escort for Scab Labour - Mounted Men Scatter Crowds of Thousands.	116
The Vine Mill Dispute, Oswaldtwistle.	123
Preference Share Schemes.	128
The Deteriorating Situation in Rishton.	131
Messrs. W.F. Chambers, Ellesmere No.1 & No.2 Mills.	133
Church Bank Mill, Church.	134
Gt Acc. Scab Labour Travelling to Burnley & Haslingden.	135
Preparation for Action Against the Employers Decision to Abrogate Agreements.	136
The Cotton Strike.	146
The Spinners'.	159
Further Court cases.	162
Reinstatement.	163
The Rishton Weavers' Secretary Sentenced to Serve Time in Strangeways Prison.	167
1933	183
The Employers' efforts to get an Earlier Start to the Day.	183
The Mass Demonstration in Gt Harwood.	186
The Death of Mr. Peter Williamson, Pres. of Gt Harwood Weavers'.	188
Local Authority Support for Government Intervention in the Cotton Industry.	191
1934	193
Presentation to Mr. Arthur Dawson.	195
The Death of Mr. William Hughes.	196
The New Wages and Hours Agreement.	196
The Death of Mr. Jonathan Ashworth J.P.	200
Conclusion.	200
References.	204
Chapter 3 **The Engineering Industry, Brick Manufacturing and Mining.**	**206**
The Accrington & District Engineering Allied Trades Federation.	206
The Amalgamated Engineering Union.	207

The General & Municipal Workers Union.	223
Accrington, Altham & Rishton Branches of the LCMF.	235
The Death of Mr. Harry Smith.	267
References.	271

Chapter 4   Unemployment & the Means Test.   273

Wal Hannington & the NUWM.	273
1930	279
Margaret McCarthy & the 1930 Hunger March to London.	280
The Attitude of Mr. Tom Snowden M.P.	282
1931	284
Tom Snowden's Belated Conversion to the Cause of the Unemployed.	285
Communists March to Moorlands.	287
NUWM Demonstration in Gt Harwood.	287
The March from Gt Harwood to Clayton-Le-Moors.	289
The March from Gt Harwood to Rishton.	289
NUWM Demonstration in Accrington.	290
NUWM March from Gt Harwood to Accrington - Arrests Made.	291
Gt Harwood Demonstrator's Court Case.	294
NUWM March from Gt Harwood to Rishton.	296
Communists March to Moorlands.	296
1932	298
1933	310
Lancashire Hunger March to Preston.	313
1934	316
Councillor Constantine Defeats Councillor Slack in a heated County Council Election.	318
References.	327

Chapter 5   The Political Situation.   329

1927 - Accrington TCLP and the ILP - Charles R. Buxton.	329
Workers' Control.	331
UDC Elections.	333
Oswaldtwistle's First Labour Chairman.	334
Accrington Borough Elections	335
The Russian Connection.	336
1928 - UDC Elections.	339
The Departure of Mr. Buxton.	340
The Opening of the Blackburn Road Labour Hall.	344
Mr. Tom Snowden Selected.	345
Labour Procession and Field Day.	348

The Maxton / Cook Initiative.	348
Accrington Borough Elections.	351
1929 - The UDC Elections.	352
Presentation to Mr. Buxton.	353
The General Election.	354
Mr. Ramsay MacDonald's Visit-Recollections of Accrington.	355
The Labour Party Field Day.	357
The Labour Party Trip to Bingley.	358
Accrington Borough Elections.	358
Accrington's First Labour Alderman - Mr. W.A. Lambert.	358
Accrington Labour Party's Bazaar.	359
1930 - The UDC Elections.	359
The ILP.	360
New Borough Magistrates.	361
Mr. Tom Snowden's Defence of the Government.	361
Accrington NUR's Presentation to its Secretary.	362
The Labour Party Field Day.	362
Accrington Borough Elections.	363
1931- Mr. James Maxton MP's Visit to Accrington.	364
The County Council Elections - UDC Elections.	369
The Crisis.	370
The General Election Cont.	377
The Death of Mr. J.C. Breare. Secretary Oswaldtwistle Labour Party.	381
Accrington Borough Elections.	381
Accrington's First Labour Mayor - Councillor Constantine.	381
Maxton and the ILP's Disaffiliation.	382
Tom Snowden's Speech at Rishton.	383
Alice and Wallace Haines.	384
Accrington TCLP's Sale of Work.	384
1932 - New Magistrates.	385
UDC ELections.	386
The Mayor's Illness. - The Labour League of Youth.	387
The ILP. - Accrington Borough Elections.	388
The New Labour Candidate - Mr. Frederick George Burgess.	389
1933 - The Death of Mr. Bert. J. Lee.	390
Major Clement Attlee MP Speaks in Accrington.	390
The UDC Elections.	391
Clayton-Le-Moors Labour Party Presentation.	392
Rishton Labour Party Rally.	392

	Accrington Borough Elections.	392
	The Labour Party Bazaar.	392
	Oswaldtwistle Labour Party League of Youth.	393
	1934 - The County Council Elections.	394
	The UDC Elections.	394
	Mr. Manny Shinwell at Accrington.	395
	New Magistrate - Mrs. Susannah Holgate.	395
	Church & Oswaldtwistle Lab. Party Picnic.- Mr. M. Walsh	396.
	Oswaldtwistle UDC By-Election. - Accrington B. Elections.	397
	The Oswaldtwistle Clarion Cycling Club.	397
	The Fascist Threat.	398
	Mr. Bill Haworth.	401
	Conclusion.	403
	References.	404
Chapter 6	Thoughts on Society's Improvement.	**406**
	References.	418
Appendix 1	Election Results.	**420**
Appendix 2	Labour Party Officials.	**431**
Appendix 3	Sir Oswald Mosley - The New Party - The BUF.	**436**
Appendix 4	Trade Union Officials.	**438**
Appendix 5	The Gold Standard.	**450**
Appendix 6	Useful thoughts for the Labour Party front bench.	**453**
Bibliography		**456**

DETAILS OF THE AUTHOR.

Jim Ainsworth was born in 1947 and is married with two stepdaughters. He attended school at St. Mary's RC Oswaldtwistle and Holy Family RC Accrington. Having served an engineering apprenticeship at Howard & Bullough Ltd Accrington, he worked as a fitter and draughtsman in the local engineering industry.

In 1968, free from the constraints of his apprenticeship, he joined in the adventurous lifestyle of the time and travelled overland through Europe, Turkey, Iran, Afghanistan and Pakistan.

Later he attended Salford University and Huddersfield Polytechnic as a mature student, gaining a BA [Hons] in Politics & History, and a Post-Graduate Certificate in Education. For the last 14 years he has been employed as a business studies lecturer at Manchester College of Arts and Technology.

During the period 1971-1974 he was a Labour councillor on the old Accrington Borough Council and the Chairman of the Blackburn & Accrington branch of the Draughtsmans & Allied Technicians Association [now MSF]. In 1982 he was the last Secretary of the now defunct Accrington CLP, and in 1983 became the first Secretary of the new Hyndburn CLP, relinquishing the office one year later.

Previous publications:

"Accrington 1926." Pub. by Hyndburn Trades Council 1994. 219 pages. £9.50 Available from Mr. Peter Billington, 10 East Crescent, Accrington, Lancashire.

"The North Western Provincial [Whitley] Councils - The First 75 Years - A Celebration." Awaiting Pub.

ACKNOWLEDGEMENTS.

I wish to thank the following:

1. Hyndburn & Rossendale Trades Council for asking me to write the book.
2. The Staff of Accrington Library Local History Section.
3. The 'Accrington Observer' for permission to extensively use their material.
4. Alice Haines for her many correspondences and allowing me to interview her.
5. The late Ken Slater without whom, there wouldn't have been a 'Left' in Accrington.
6. Both Mr. Roland Hagan and the late Mr. Bob Campbell for giving me an interview.
7. The late Mr. James Dunn.
8. The late Margaret McKay [nee McCarthy] for responding to my correspondence and to her daughter Morag McKay for her contribution to the book.
9. Edmund and Ruth Frow, and Alain Kahan of the Working Class Movements Library, Salford,
10. Michael Hindley MEP

In addition the author and publishers also wish to apologise for any inadvertent infringement of copyright and have sought to keep within the publishers convention in the use of some recently published secondary sources. In every case, the documents have been fully attributed.

MAP OF NORTH EAST LANCASHIRE.

During this period Accrington Parliamentary Division comprised of Accrington Municipal Borough and the Urban District Councils of Oswaldtwistle, Church, Rishton, and Clayton-Le-Moors. Huncoat amalgamated with Accrington in 1929.

In 1974 all the above were included in the new Hyndburn Borough Council and Hyndburn Parliamentary Constituency, together with Great Harwood UDC and AlthamParish.

NORTH EAST LANCASHIRE RAILWAY SYSTEM 1926
Accrington Parliamentary Division comprised of Accrington Municipal Borough and the Urban District Councils of Oswaldtwistle, Church, Rishton, and Clayton-le-Moors.

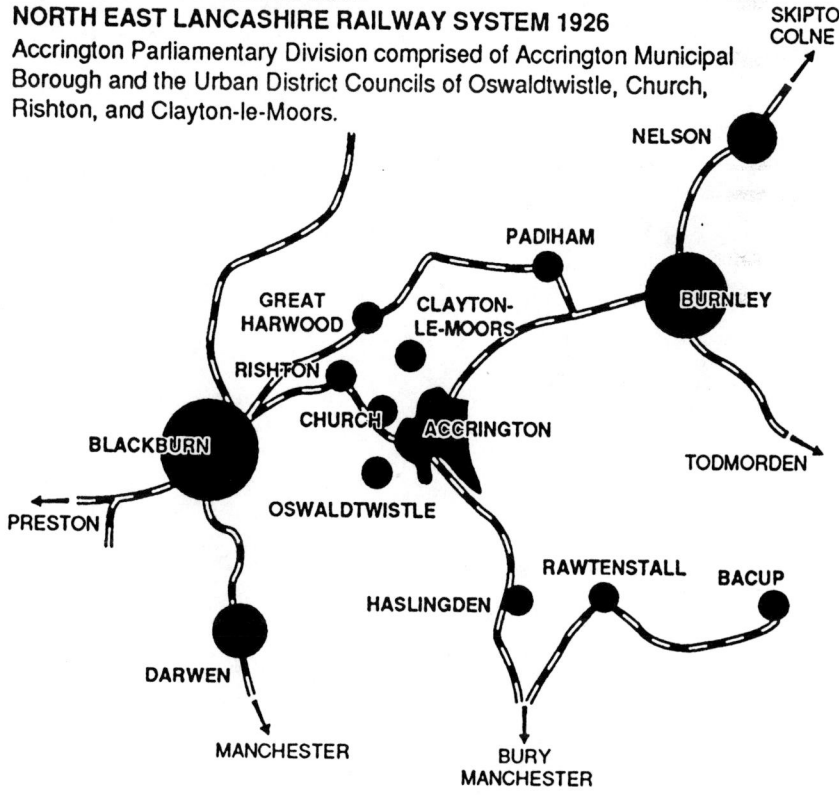

Map taken from 'Industry and Prudence: A plan for Accrington'. Published by the Borough of Accrington, 1950. Page 8.

CENSUS.

	1931	**1951**	**1991**	**% Drop 1931-51**
Accrington	42991	40685	32741	5.5%
Altham	902	677	1484	2.5%
Church	6187	5200	6056	16%
C-L-M	7909	6825	6151	14%
Gt. Harwood	12789	10739	10557	16%
Oswaldtwistle	14218	12130	14629	14.5%
Rishton	6633	5800	6772	12.5%
Hyndburn	91629	82056	78390	10.5%

FOREWORD.

The period of economic depression between the two World Wars struck a massive blow at the idea that the unchecked free market could be relied on to correct high levels of unemployment. The depth and persistence of the slump meant that this was no ordinary period. Things were not going to get better by just waiting for the economic cycle to turn upwards again.

Even worse, for those who believed that it was harmful to intervene in "natural" movements of the economy, the long years of poverty and unemployment in the industrial nations were heightening the chance of social unrest and revolution. This had happened elsewhere. The old bogey of imported continental revolt returned to haunt the establishment in Britain.

Free market economic policies could not answer the question of what needed to be done to break out of the slump. The Labour Government of 1929-31 accepted that the only options available to it were those justified by conventional economic thinking. In doing so, it came to a dead end. The "National Government" which followed, carried on the work of its predecessor. At the time, the TUC and Labour Party never accepted that the lesson of this was that the Tory policies of the National Government were the continuation of those of Ramsay MacDonald's Labour Government

Jim Ainsworth's "Accrington & District 1927-1934" is a reminder of what happens when the labour and trade union movement accepts the ideology of the free market. The consequences were very real for local workers. Government intervention in the economy to create employment was a long time coming for those who had spent years out of work living on demoralising pittances hedged around with demeaning conditions. It is a tribute to the Lancashire textile workers that they stood out in taking mass strike action in defence of their wages and conditions during this period.

Then, as now, the arguments for common ownership and the direction of the economy in the interests of working people were as powerful as ever. The long discredited economics of the free market may have returned to favour in the hierarchy of the labour and trade union movement but its fragility is there for all to see in the period covered by this book.

Peter Billington
Secretary, Hyndburn & Rossendale TUC

PREFACE.

This book is the sequel to 'Accrington 1926.' In that volume I gave a brief national picture of the events that affected Accrington economically and politically during the 7 year period following the First World War. An in-depth look, was then undertaken of the happenings and the characters involved in the stormy year of '26.

The period under investigation here can be objectively described as a period of even greater turmoil and militancy than had gone immediately before. Lancashire was the scene of industrial unrest during this entire period and historians have tended to ignore this fact. The reason for this is that being confined to the textile areas of Lancashire, it just did not have the national impact in the limited media channels of the day. People in London and Glasgow, unless they were politically active, would have known little about the cotton crisis.

Although describing events in Greater Accrington, this volume can be read as a history of the industrial unrest in Lancashire as a whole. As such it is probably the first book to be devoted entirely to this subject.

With regards to textiles, the main problem was the result of stock market speculation in 1920. Mills were bought and sold at 8 times their pre-war value and by the late '20's the owners were left in a position of negative equity. A similar, but even worse position than that faced by a million householders today. Eg. Stone Bridge Mill, Oswaldtwistle: 1920 value £80,000 - 1933 value £1,400. Mill owners basically wanted 'blood, sweat and tears' from their operatives in order to maintain the lifestyle to which they had become accustomed. It was hoped by the employers, that this effort by the workforce would be undertaken whilst being paid slave wages.

How wrong they were. The normally moderate textile employees put up an amazingly spirited resistance to the mean hearted actions of the owners.

This whole period was one of depression due to the adherence by the various Governments, whether Conservative, Labour, or National, to laissez-faire, free market economics. If they had fully adopted the ideas of Keynes and funded massive public work schemes, instead of half-heartedly sanctioning small scale projects, events might have had a happier ending. As it was, the schemes initiated were of no use to the cotton operatives, engineers and miners of Lancashire.

Of course the middle of the road approach of Keynes was not the solution advocated by the local Labour Party, ILP and Communist Party activists. They, to differing degrees, wanted the overthrow of capitalism and the establishment of Socialism. Tony Blair's New Labour Party will not like to be reminded of the Socialist speeches made by Labour Party mainstream supporters of that time. For instance: At the 1932 TUC Annual Conference held in Newcastle, Mr. W. Slynn of the Great Harwood Weavers, a man who stood as the Trades and Labour candidate in the local UDC Elections of 1928, 1930 and 1934 said:

> "My position is this, that as a Socialist inside the Trade Union Movement, inside the Co-operative Movement, and inside the Labour Party, fighting for the overthrow of the present system, I do not take the view that I will never again take up armaments for the simple reason that if I am forced into the position of having to defend the class to which I belong..... I am prepared to do it..... It will not be our fault; we are striving inside the three movements mentioned to prevent the possibility of the class to which we are opposed forcing us into that position..... At the same time, if we are Socialists let us face up to the issue and let us prepare ourselves for the sacrifices which may be forced upon us in the near future if we are to transfer this system from capitalism into Socialism, which I believe every man and woman here, is working for in the future." [1]

Strong words, but the above remarks were not the comments of an ultra leftist. In 1934 'The First Workers Government' written by G.R. Mitchison was published. This succeeded in propagandising the idea that the transformation to Socialism would depend on sharp and decisive action to combat the risk of civil war with the Establishment. It advocated a future Labour Government immediately passing an Enabling Act, under which the economy could be nationalised, wealth distributed and Socialism instituted as quickly as possible. Indeed Clement Attlee himself said:

> "The moment to strike is the moment of taking power, when the Government is freshly elected and assured of its support. The blow struck must be a fatal one and not merely designed to wound and turn a sullen and obstructive opponent into an active and deadly enemy." [2]

The above comments were a justifiable reaction to the 'out and out' class war being waged by the Establishment. The most blatant evidence to support this contention is the 1931 National Government's Budget. Out of every 20s. [£1] of Government spending, 9s. 2.5d [46p] went on paying War Debt, whilst only 6d. [2.5p] was spent on the Unemployed.

The War Debt was in the main a confidence trick on the British people. During the First World War a number of War Loans were raised. The terms of these transactions was scandalous in the extreme. Banks were prepared to lend money to potential subscribers to the loan at 3% interest, whereas the

Government was prepared to pay that subscriber at least 4%. As an ILP pamphlet of the time says:

"Had I applied, say, for £20,000 of War Loans, I should have had to put up no margin, no money, no securities. It would have cost me a penny stamp for the covering envelope and no more." [3]

Subscribers to the loan were in a similar position to the Lloyd's Names of today, who for years had to put up no capital and who received envelopes every year containing a big fat cheque for doing nothing. Many of these names now face bankruptcy due to bad assessments by underwriters. The subscribers to War Loans should have experienced a similar ending to their yearly financial windfalls in 1931, rather than the Government introduce the 'Means Test.'

The truth is, and it needs stating loudly, that there was simply no need whatsoever for the setting up of the 'Means Test.' Unemployment pay could have been doubled if action had been taken to hit the speculators on the War Loans. My Grandparents, Mother and Father, and all my other relatives need not have suffered the deprivations they experienced at that time.

Similarly today, society can easily produce enough food, clothing, housing, household furnishings and appliances, pensions, educational opportunities, health services etc. for all the people of Great Britain. There is ample for everyone, but the capitalist system refuses to sanction such an idea. It would also help if the above could be produced in an environmentally friendly manner. Remember that Karl Marx warned us in 'Capital' in 1867:

"Moreover, every advance in capitalist agriculture is an advance in the art, not only of robbing the worker, but also of robbing the soil; .....Capitalist production, therefore, is only able to develop the technique and the combination of the social process of production by simultaneously undermining the foundations of all wealth - the land and the workers." [4]

In the Hans Anderson story 'The King Wore No Clothes' the little boy can see through the lies perpetuated by the ruling class, just as Socialists have over the past century. Why can't Tony Blair and New Labour see this truth ?

REFERENCES.

1. 64TH ANNUAL TUC CONFERENCE, NEWCASTLE 1932. PP. 355/356
2. Addison, Paul. "The Road To 1945." Pub. Quartet Books. 1977. p. 48
3 Tait, Frederick. "The Jugglers of Finance are Bleeding the Nation White." Pub. ILP. London. 1932. p.5 to 15.
4. Marx, Karl. "Capital Vol.1." Pub. J.M. Dent. London 1957. pp. 547/548

Chapter One

The Trades Disputes & Trade Unions Act.

THE CAMPAIGN AGAINST THE BILL.

Due to the T.U.C. leaderships' betrayal of the working class at the end of the General Strike, the employers and their Tory Government were able to complete the rout of the trade unions by bringing into law the 'Trades Disputes and Trade Unions Act'. This Bill wended its way through Parliament and became an Act by September 1927. The T.U.C. went through the motions of having a platform campaign against the injustices inherent in the Act, but after their disgraceful actions during 1926 the potential for building up a nationally successful active opposition had been thwarted.

Locally the politically conscious membership attempted to bring the terrible situation to the attention of the workers and indeed an energetic programme of activities was embarked upon.

The Great Harwood Weavers' Association ordered their delegates to the National Council of the Amalgamation to support the Central Committees resolution against the 'Trade Union Bill'. [Minutes of their Meeting of April 20th 1927.]

The 'Observer' had a piece on the Accrington T.C.L.P. monthly General Management Committee Meeting held on Wednesday April 20th, which had a good attendance. The Executive Committee had been given the task of arranging a conference on the Bill, with the purpose of focusing public opinion on its harsh contents. It does not appear to have succeeded in arranging such a conference; it seems to have left this to the various Trade Federations to organise. The Meeting did however pass a resolution which was very similar to that which would be carried at the Textile Trades Federation Meeting on the 22nd April. This resolution was forwarded to Mr.Hugh Edwards the Liberal M.P.

The 'Observer' reported that a meeting of delegates of the textile trade unions in the Accrington Parliamentary Division had been held on April 22nd at the Weavers Institute in Oswaldtwistle. Mr.Peter Hart, Secretary of the Accrington Textile Trades Federation had presided over a good attendance. At the end of the meeting the following resolution had been carried.

"1.That the Bill as a whole be unanimously opposed.2.That this meeting of the Textile Trades Federations of Accrington, Church and Oswaldtwistle, Clayton-le-Moors and Rishton, comprising the whole of the textile unions in the Accrington Parliamentary Division emphatically protests against the Governments' Trades Disputes and Trade Unions Bill, believing that it is inimical to the interests of trade unions and is of such a repressive character as to endanger their industrial activities, which have been obtained at great sacrifice, and we therefore ask you in all seriousness to oppose the passage of this Bill into law."

The resolutions were sent to Mr. Edwards M.P. and were signed by; Messrs. Peter Hart and J.R. Emmett, Accrington, Messrs. J.T. Wolstenholme and Edward Reeder, Church and Oswaldtwistle, Messrs J.W. Hope and Philip Wilkinson, Clayton-le-Moors, and Messrs. J. Ashworth and S. Gregory, Rishton.

At the Quarterly Meeting of the Accrington branch of the General and Municipal Workers Union held at Jacob Street School on Thursday 21st April, according to the Minute Book, the following resolution was moved and seconded from the body of the hall and was again forwarded to Mr. Edwards M.P.

"That this general meeting emphatically protests against the provisions of the Trades Disputes and Trade Unions Bill brought before Parliament by the Government, as a menace to the legitimate aspirations and activities of the workers organisations and calls for its total rejection."

At their meeting of April 27th the Great Harwood Weavers agreed to be represented at the conference to be held at Blackburn to protest against the Trades Disputes Bill, by four delegates plus their Secretary Mr. Hesmondhalgh.[Minute book]

The District Committee of the Amalgamated Engineering Union at its meeting of April 28th requested all its branches representing over 2,400 members, to send resolutions to Mr.J.H. Edwards M.P. asking him to oppose the Government's Trades Disputes Bill both by speeches and by voting against the Bill in the House of Commons. They instructed their Secretary Mr. Chalmers to write to Mr. Edwards requesting him to "define in writing his attitude to the Trades Disputes Bill". It was also agreed that the full membership of the D.C. would attend the conference on this issue, called by the National Joint Trade Union Defence Committee, to be held on May 7th.

The A.E.U. - D.C. Minute book also mentions asking the Engineering Allied Trades Federation to arrange a demonstration and to ask all other unions to co-operate in such a venture, but there is no evidence confirming that such an action took place.

MR. C.R. BUXTON'S SPEECH.

On Saturday April 30th at 7.30pm. the Independent Labour Party at their rooms, 87 Back Blackburn Road, Accrington presented a lecture by Mr. C.R. Buxton, Labour Prospective Parliamentary Candidate, entitled "The Governments' Attack on Trade Unions". This speech was repeated on Sunday May 1st at 7.00pm on Accrington Market Ground when the meeting was held under the auspices of Accrington T.C.L.P. The highlights of Buxton's speech are printed below.

"Since the Tory Government came into power there had been many attempts to injure the workers cause. They had had a number of separate Bills brought forward by private members with regard to trade unionism; they had had attacks upon the unemployment insurance scheme, upon the national health insurance scheme, the cutting down of social expenditure and of educational expenditure, but they were now seeing something which was more important than any of these, because it was an attack, not on this or that privilege or advantage which had been gained by the workers, but on the machinery whereby they had gained those advantages and the machinery whereon they must rely for any further gains in the industrial field. If the weapon of trade union organisation was broken or blunted it would damage their power to make progress in any direction. If the workers had established themselves in any way in a strong position, it had been in the main through the gradual building up of the trade union movement. He did not mean for a moment that they had not used the political weapon as well, but the trade union weapon stood as, it were behind the political weapon and represented the great force that was necessary to be created before the weapon of Parliamentary and of political action could be effectively used ."

An Act of Industrial War

"Was it not a strange thing that at the very time when the leadership of the Tory Party had been making strong appeals, sometimes eloquent appeals, almost tearful appeals for industrial peace, and had been urging that employers and workers should agree to co-operate and work together in harmony, that they should come forward with a Bill which was the very contrary, the very negation of the whole idea of industrial peace. It was an act of industrial war. We hear a great deal about the class war. My view of the class war is a very clear one. Class war is not a thing that we wish for; a class war is not a thing that I advocate, but it is a thing which already exists whether we like it or not. It may, perhaps, be an exaggeration to call it a war, but if by war we mean a conflict between the interests of one class and the interests of another class, who can possibly deny that that conflict and that struggle is going on in our midst? The whole object of Socialism is to do away with that war, to bring it to an end on a basis of justice and peace, every man reaping the due reward of his labour. But in the particular case of this Bill it is the employing class and the middle class, in the broadest sense of the word, which is committing an act of class war. This Bill is the strongest and clearest example of class war you can possibly have. It is an act which is designed to cripple the workers in the very means by which they carry on their activities, and it does not lie in the mouths of those who represent the leaders of industry, or the middle class of the nation to accuse our party of waging class war when they themselves are bringing forward the strongest possible example of the class war".

No Mandate for the Bill

"With what right did the Government bring forward the Bill? Suppose at the last election the leaders of the Tory Party, and for aught he knew, the leaders of the Liberal Party as well, had said they intended to bring forward a Trade Union and Trade Disputes Bill, which would cripple the powers of the trade unions and make it more difficult for them to carry on their work, did they think for one moment they would have got one quarter of the support they did? Instead, they put forward a different pretext-the Bolshevist scare and the Red Letter, misleading a great proportion, not only of the middle and upper classes, but of the workers as well. They realised now what a false pretence it was. The Government had no mandate whatever from the people of the country, and least of all from the workers to introduce so fundamental an attack upon the position of the workers as embodied in this Bill."

Un-English and Unfair

"What could be more un-English, asked Mr. Buxton, than to take from a man's hands the only weapon with which he could defend himself, and to choose the moment when the workers were weak owing to the efforts they made last year and when their resources were at the lowest to try to deal them a deadly blow. It was contrary to the whole English sense of fair play; it was contrary to the English sense of what was sporting; it was hitting below the belt; and he could not but believe that the people of this country as soon as they realised what was intended and entailed by this Bill would by a great majority turn against the Government. Even though there might be a temporary triumph for the Government it would be a very temporary one indeed, and on the very first opportunity that the people could express themselves it would be found that the Government, in bringing forward this Bill, had gone too far, had prepared a noose for its own neck, and would suffer very much, from the electoral point of view, in the long run."

The Freedom of the Individual

"He supposed the chief excuse put forward by the advocates of this measure in its defence was that trade unionism was a tyrannical affair; that it did not allow freedom for the individual and did not allow him to choose whether or not he would contribute to a political fund after a ballot had gone in favour of that contribution. He was one of those who believed very strongly in freedom and that people should not be ordered about more than was necessary in the public interest, but there were certain things done by men when they formed themselves into large organisations which must limit the freedom of certain individuals, otherwise they could not form an effective organisation at all. Whatever else the trade union movement was, it was thoroughly democratic in its origins, in its development and in the whole structure of its organisation, and throughout the whole of the movement it was a matter of the majority ruling and not the minority."

"Mr. Buxton proceeded at some length to describe the position to which trade unionism had attained, and the obstacles which had been overcome prior to the introduction of the present Bill, mentioning incidentally that out of a total expenditure of nearly £11 millions on the trade unions in 1925, only a little over £100,000 was spent on political work and agitation of a political character. If anyone wanted industrial peace, they had better have left things as they are."

Room for Political Prejudices

"Describing the main proposals of the Bill he dealt first with the question of 'illegal strikes', and quoting the words in the Bill asked how difficult it would be for anyone to decide whether a strike was one that was going to injure 'a substantial portion of the community'. The words were so vague and wide that a magistrate or judge could practically decide according to his own feelings. There was nothing definite to go by, and the Bill left room for the political prejudices of judges and magistrates to operate. He emphasised the point that while every kind of sympathetic strike, at any rate on any large scale, was rendered illegal on the part of the workers, there was nothing whatever to render illegal a lockout on the part of the employers."

"Mr. Buxton next referred to the Clauses relating to the protection of the 'blackleg' and to picketing. On the latter point he said it was very difficult to draw an exact line between what was proper and was not proper in the matter of picketing, but Parliament in the past had done its best to define it, and to lay down what was meant, and it would have been far better to let well alone, and to let the system that everybody understood continue than attempt to restrict it by new definitions which would practically make any kind of picketing impossible."

Cruel and One-Sided

"The Bill provided that instead of a man who objected to the political levy from trade union funds having to send in his objections in writing, it should be the other way round, and every single man or woman who wanted to contribute to the political levy would have to send in a special form filled up to that effect. They could imagine what a terrific business that would be in a large union with hundreds of thousands of members. All these were difficulties put in the way with the simple object of making it more difficult to use the funds of the unions for political work. And it became all the more unreasonable and all the more cruel and one-sided when they realised that the political organisations to which the employers belonged had no such limitations at all. The funds contributed by the trade unions to the Labour Party were the main proportion of the financial strength of the Labour Party, and this attempt by one party to damage the financial position of another party was peculiarly hard and cruel when they considered that the Labour Party, at least so far as trade union funds were concerned, did everything in the open, whereas the other parties raised much of their money from political transactions behind the scenes, from people who paid large sums of money to get titles and secret gifts."

"Other proposals in the Bill referred to by Mr. Buxton were those dealing with civil servants and employees of local authorities and the provisions regarding injunctions against the funds of trade unions. Summarising the main provisions of the Bill, he repeated that the measure was no sudden thought, but a deeply laid scheme to injure the whole power of the working-class movement. That was why the movement was united as one man in resisting the attack, and determined, if ever the Bill became law, to wipe it off the Statute Books at the earliest possible opportunity."

THE CAMPAIGN CONTINUED.

On May 4th. the Great Harwood Weavers declared that they would send delegates to, the conference to be held in Manchester called by the United Textile Federation Unions Association re: Trades Disputes and Trade Union Bill.[Minute Book]

The Accrington G.M.W.U. at its branch meeting of May 5th. endorsed its Secretary's action in arranging for delegates to attend the Blackburn Conference on the Trade Unions Bill to be held on May 7th.

On May 7th. the 'Observer' published the following letter:

Dear Sir,

It is indicated in the papers that the Member for Accrington, Mr. J. H. Edwards voted in favour of the Trade Union Bill.

I am therefore directed to issue a challenge to Mr. Edwards to come to Accrington to defend his action in public debate on the Market Ground with Mr. Dawson, Lancashire District Secretary of the National Union of Textile Workers.

Yours faithfully

B. Ledwick

Branch Secretary

National Union of Textile Workers

There is no evidence to hand to show that he ever took up the challenge.

At their meeting of May 8th. the Great Harwood Weavers agreed to deliver circulars printed by the Amalgamation regarding the Bill to all their members within the week.

The 'Observer' reported the proceedings of a further Special Meeting of the Textile Trade Federations within the Parliamentary Division held on Thursday 12th. May with Mr. P. Hart, Secretary of the Accrington Spinners Association, presiding over a good attendance. After a long and considered discussion the following resolution was carried:

"That this meeting of the Textile Trade Federations covering the Accrington Parliamentary Division strongly protests against the attitude of the Member for Accrington, Mr. J. Hugh Edwards, in not even acknowledging the letter sent from this Federation on April 22nd. asking him to oppose the Trades Disputes and Trade Unions Bill, and are of the opinion that at least he ought to have given some reasons why he intended to vote with the Government against the unanimous wishes of the textile workers of this constituency."

The 'Observer' reported that the proposed open-air protest meeting to be held on Sunday the 15th. of May on Accrington Market Ground, under the auspices of Accrington T.C.L.P., had to be transferred to the Covered Market in Peel Street because of the unfavourable weather conditions. The governments attack on trade unionism, the workers only practical defence against unscrupulous employers, ensured that 400 people gathered to voice their opposition.

The high spot of the campaign took place in Accrington Town Hall on Wednesday evening May 25th. This Mass Meeting was convened by the United Federation of Trade Unions in the Accrington Parliamentary Division. The attendance was over 400 and was chaired by Mr.J.R. Emmett, Secretary of the Accrington Weavers. The speakers included the former Labour M.P.'s Mr.W.J. Tout J.P. and Mr.Charles Dukes J.P. The other supporting speakers were Councillors R.I. Constantine J.P., W.A. Lambert of the G.M.W.U., and J. Baron of the Miners, plus other trade union representatives. The following contributions were reported in the 'Observer';

"Mr. Emmett said the Bill was generally known as the 'Blacklegs Charter'. It might have been more easily swallowed by trade unionists a hundred years ago, when about 70% of the workers of the country could neither read or write. A Bill of this character was nothing more than an insult to every intelligent trade unionist. The Government were making much of what they were pleased to call intimidation, but if the Government were anxious to stop intimidation, why did they not tackle the real intimidators, the employers?.....Under the Bill a strike could not be entered upon without fear of the law courts. It was a Bill in favour of the minority and not the majority. Briefly referring to Mr.Hugh Edwards M.P. who voted in favour of the Bill, he said they now knew where Mr. Edwards stood."

"Mr. A.E. Naesmith of the Weavers Amalgamation, moved a resolution of protest, which stated that the objects of the Bill were unjust and would seriously hinder the industrial activities of trade unionists, and, further, was of such a repressive character that they called upon all their members to render an unswerving opposition to the

Bill. In formally moving the resolution, he described the Bill as an iniquitous measure."

"Mr. Harry Smith, of the Accrington Miners' Association, briefly seconded, remarking that....what they had to do was to concentrate, not only on the industrial field, but also on the political field."

"Mr. Charles Dukes, speaking in support of the resolution, said that bad as the Bill might be when it became an Act, it would not accomplish what the Government desired - to make trade unions impotent. He urged upon them to get rid of any pessimism, because if they were determined the Government could do very little with them. There were 5 million trade unionists in the country, who with their families, represented about 1/2 the people of the country. The Bill would seriously inconvenience them, and it would make the timid in their ranks hesitate, but it would not stifle their aggressive spirit. Dealing with the motive of the Bill, he said if they got into a state of panic over it they could expect the Government to give effect to it in accordance with the spirit of those who were behind and designed the Bill. Personally, he did not believe the Bill was going to have the effect which the Government thought, and when the Labour Government was again returned to power it would be their first duty to reverse such an iniquitous measure. Today they were living in a world in which nothing counted but organised effort, but no leader feared the employer; he feared his own men. The Bill was evidence of the weakness of their own movement. It was an attempt of the other side to prevent that growth which their opponents knew they had lost. The other side did not go to football matches, picture palaces and dog races. No they put first things first, and he only wished trade unionists would do the same. [Applause]"

"Mr. W.J. Tout, said it had been generally agreed by the opponents of the Bill that it was designed to cripple trade unionism industrially and politically..."

Tout is then credited with saying the following heavily blinkered quote concerning Ramsay MacDonald and the 1924 Labour Government.

"Answering the question as to why they had got the Bill, he said two things had happened during the last few years. In 1924 Labour for the first time in the history of the political life of this country, assumed the reins of office. Prior to then it had been a favourite cry and criticism by all the Winston Churchill's that Labour was unfit to govern and could not govern, and that if-ever it got the chance it would prove its inability. The result was that many trade unionists had fear in their hearts and thus delayed the time for Labour to have the opportunity of governing. But in 1924 Labour did, in fact, occupy the Front Benches of the House, and never in the history of this country had Liberal or Tories produced a Prime Minister of the calibre of Mr.Ramsay MacDonald - Not merely members of the Labour Party, but the whole of the thinkers of the wide world, recognised that Mr. MacDonald in his capacity as Foreign Secretary was preparing a pathway to permanent peace the world over, and no one recognised that better than the Liberals and the Tories. No two men ever equalled in capacity, knowledge, and honesty, Mr. MacDonald and Mr. Philip Snowden, who had control during the Labour Government. It was shown that not merely had Labour the capacity to govern, but that Labour had the capacity to govern better than any of its predecessors. Their opponents today were chiefly concerned about that ever happening again." [I hope that he was reminded of this speech when MacDonald and Snowden finally joined the Tory camp in 1931]

"The second thing that had happened was the so - called General Strike of 1926. He was proud to have lived through the strike, and he was proud to have seen the exhibition of solidarity and identity of interests which was displayed. The present Bill was designed in order to prevent a repetition of a sympathetic strike. The miner, railwayman, docker, when they came to their senses would realise that there was a community of interests. They could not be prevented from taking that intelligent conception of their political responsibility, an activity which pointed to a surer method of bringing about their industrial emancipation." [Applause]

"The resolution was enthusiastically carried."

"During the evening the Accrington and Church Co-operative Male Voice Choir gave a number of selections, under the conductorship of Mr. J. Hallworth."

MR. C.R. BUXTON'S ATTACK ON MR. EDWARDS MP.

The I.L.P. held a further Public Meeting on the Market Ground, Accrington, on Sunday May 29th. at 7.00p.m. The Speakers were Mr. C.R. Buxton and Mr. J.W. Moor from Rochdale and the subject was 'The Fight on the Trade Unions Bill'. The meeting was presided over by Mr. Bill Haworth who in later years became the successful Communist Convener of the Howard and

Bullough Works Committee.

Mr. Buxton described the Trades Union Bill as:

"The most serious attack that had yet been made upon the rights of the workers....If that weapon [of trade unionism] was disarmed, or weakened as it was meant to be, then the standard of living would go down again. The great attack had had a wonderful effect on the Labour movement. It was not simply an attack on the Labour Party, and it was not simply a movement on the political side. The principal object was to weaken the Labour movement on the industrial side, and therefore one of the great effects of the Bill was that it appealed to the trade unionist who was not a politician. The trade unionist who was not a politician felt that his dearest rights were being attacked by the Trade Unions Bill and the result was that there was greater unity with the Labour movement and those people."

"Another serious point.....was that it was an act of class war; it was a definite attempt of one class to injure the privileges of another, a definite attempt by the more powerful and the more firmly established class to injure the poorer and weaker....He believed such extreme action was not looked on with favour by the British public, he believed ....that the British public outside the ranks of Labour itself would condemn the Government for such an action when they got the opportunity."

"The serious thing so far as Accrington was concerned, continued Mr. Buxton, was that their M.P. Mr. Edwards, had now definitely come out on the side of reaction, on the narrowest side of the section of the employing classes and on the side of out and out Toryism. He had voted for the Trades Unions and Trades Disputes Bill. Up to this time Mr. Edwards had been rather cautious and when such questions came up he had tried to give the idea that he had a mutual sympathy with the worker, that he had a tender place in his heart for the interests of the worker. When there was any question which was clearly directed against the working class he generally took care not to be there at the moment when the vote was being taken and not to give a vote. As they knew on many occasions he abstained from voting....Mr. Edwards was no longer sitting on the fence; he had definitely and openly taken sides with the narrowest section and the narrowest views of the employing class....There would now be a clearer issue to face at the next election than what they had at the last.....He believed they would find at the next election that the workers would no longer be taken in in the way they had been in the past, and would realise that the fight was between the Tory-Liberal or whatever he ought to call him and the Labour candidate. A straight issue between reaction on the one hand and Labour on the other."

"Mr. Edwards had not only taken the stand against Labour, but it was worth noting also that he had taken his stand against Liberalism. Those who had been Liberals in the past had believed, he thought, that Mr. Edwards had some sympathy with Liberalism. He was supposed to be a member of the Liberal Party, but now in the fight for the Trade Union Bill he had come out against Liberalism also. He did not say that the Liberal Party were entirely united on that subject....but the great majority of the Liberal Party had taken the opposite line and voted against the Bill......Mr. Edwards had disassociated himself from the bulk of the Liberal Party. How that would effect the Liberal followers in the constituency he was not able to say. If they did not feel he had betrayed their Liberal Party he could only say they must be very weakened in their Liberalism, if they were prepared to take it lying down. That however, was a matter for them not for him."

THE CAMPAIGN CONTINUED.

On Tuesday May 31st. a meeting organised by the United Federation of Trade Unions was held in the Primitive Methodist School, Rishton. The 'Observer' reported that a moderate attendance heard Mr.J. Ashworth, Secretary of the Rishton Weavers, Mr. Andrew Naesmith, Assistant Secretary of the Weavers Amalgamation, and Mr. Arthur Dawson, Secretary of the National Union of Textile Workers. Mr. Fred Hodgson, of the Rishton Miners Association proposed a resolution protesting against the Trades Disputes and Trade Unions Bill which was carried.

On Wednesday June 1st. another meeting was held under the auspices of the United Federation of Trade Unions at the Town Hall Clayton-le-Moors which was presided over by Mr. T. Bulcock of the Overlookers Association. The speakers included Miss Mary Quayle of the Transport Workers Union, Mr. Cephas Speak J.P., of Bolton, Mr. J.W. Hope, Secretary of the Clayton-le-Moors Weavers Association, Mr. J.R. Emmett J.P., Secretary of the Accrington Weavers Association and Mr. W.T. Hindle, Secretary of the Overlookers Association.

The local Council had been critical of what they termed a political meeting being held in the Town Hall. Indeed, Mr. Bulcock went out of his way to say it was not a political meeting because if it was, some members of the platform would not have attended. He said that it had been called simply to deal with the Trades Union Bill and how it would affect the workers. Apparently quite a substantial number of local trade unionists especially in the Urban Districts lived in a state of false consciousness in which they could happily take an active part in the running of their union and at election times vote in an anti-trade union manner for the class enemy. The Overlookers were particularly prone to this disorder.

MR. ROBERT BLATCHFORD'S COMMENT FROM THE PAST.

As long ago as 1893, Robert Blatchford, had pointed out this inconsistency in the thinking of the backward elements within the trade union movement. In 'Merrie England', a book which sold over 700,000 copies within the year, he said:

"The older unionists think that Trade Unionism is strong enough in itself to secure the rights of the worker. This is a great mistake. The rights of the worker are the whole of the produce of his labour. Trade Unionism not only cannot secure that, but has never even tried to secure that. The most that Trade Unionism has secured, or can ever hope to secure for the workers, is a comfortable subsistence wage. They have not always secured that much, and, when they have secured it the cost has been serious. For the great weapon of Unionism is a strike, and a strike is at best a bitter, a painful, and a costly thing.

"Do not think that I am opposed to Trade Unionism. It is a good thing; it has long been the only defence of the workers against robbery and oppression; were it not for the Trade Unionism of the past and of the present, the condition of the British industrial classes would be one of abject slavery. But Trade Unionism, although some defence, is not sufficient defence......

"The Capitalist, is the stronger. He holds the better strategic position. He can always outlast the worker, for the worker has to starve and see his children starve, and the Capitalist never gets to that pass. Besides, capital is more mobile than labour. A stroke of the pen will divert wealth and trade from one end of the country to the other; but the workers cannot move their forces so readily.

"One difference between Socialism and Trade Unionism is that whereas the Unions can only marshal and arm the workers for a desperate trial of endurance, Socialism can get rid of Capitalism altogether. The former helps you resist the enemy, the latter destroys him.

"I suggest that you should join a Socialist Society and help to get others to join, and that you should send Socialist workers to sit upon all representative bodies.

"The Socialist tells you that you are men, with men's rights, and with men's capabilities for all that is good and great......

"The Socialist begs you to form a party of your own......

"To be a Trade Unionist and fight for your class during a strike, and to be a Tory or a Liberal and fight against your class at an election is folly." [1]

Mr. Bulock unfortunately had not accepted this truth and continued to promulgate the Liberal interpretation of events by saying the following:

"The Trade Unionists had had a heritage left to them by their predecessors who had to fight hard in years gone by to establish their rights. Were they going to be so indifferent that they would not use any effort to retain that heritage?

"If they were they must not complain whatever happened in the future. In his opinion the reason why the Bill was being brought forward was because there was an extreme element in the trade union on the one hand, and on the other there was apathy amongst the members that enabled the Government to play as they were doing. So long as the trade unions were divided they had no power."

This obvious gibe at the so called 'extreme element', namely the National Minority Movement [See end of this section] showed a lack of understanding of the situation prevailing at the time. The wages and conditions of better days, could not be regained by a timid appeasement to the demands of the various militant Employers Federations, who wanted a stringent set of laws that would shackle the unions in any forthcoming disputes. And those Disputes were definitely coming. His remark about 'apathy amongst the members' could only be blamed on the moderate leaderships betrayal at the end of the General Strike.

After a short speech Mr. W.T. Hindle moved the following, which was carried:

"That this public meeting emphatically protests against the Governments Trade Disputes and Trade Unions Bill, believing that the objects of the Bill are unjust and will very seriously hinder the industrial and political activities of trade unions and is of such a repressive character that it will call upon all our members to render unswerving opposition to the Bill."

In the course of a lengthy address Miss Mary Quayle speaking of the

Clauses in the Bill which concerned the political levy of the trade unions said:

"There was no control or interference in regard to the party funds of any other parties. They had never interfered with Mr. Lloyd George's million pound fund, nor with the party chest of the [Tory Party]. They had criticised them, of course, because they in their movement and the Labour Party wanted to make England a clean place for people to live in. They did not want it besmirched by the sale of honours. The reason the Government were interfering with the political chest of the Labour Party was because their party, the working class party were becoming intelligent and they were beginning to think, and the capitalist classes did not want them to do that."

THE NATIONAL MINORITY MOVEMENT.

The National Minority Movement was founded under Communist control on August 23rd and 24th 1924.

"The name signified that its members were the organised minority within the large movement of the working class." [2]

The National Minority Movement's aims and objectives were:

"To organise the working masses of Great Britain for the overthrow of capitalism, the emancipation of the workers from the oppressors and exploiters, and the establishment of a Socialist Commonwealth; to carry on a wide agitation and propaganda for the principles of the revolutionary class struggle..... and against the present tendency towards social peace and class collaboration and the delusion of the peaceful transition from capitalism to socialism; to unite the workers in their struggles against the exploiters." [3]

THE CAMPAIGN CONTINUED.

The Annual Meeting of the Accrington and District Textile Trades Federation was held at the Weavers Institute on Thursday 16th. June. The 'Observer' reported that a long discussion took place on the Trades Disputes Bill and a unanimous resolution denouncing it was passed.

The Half Yearly Report of the Church and Oswaldtwistle Weavers was printed in the 'Observer' of June 18th. It describes the Government's Trades Disputes Bill as:

"The latest and most reactionary evidence of consistent and uncompromising hostility of the present Government towards the working class movement and the workers organisations"....and declares it to be "A distinct class measure intended to cripple the trade union movement by taking away the workers right to strike"....It appealed to the membership to present "unswerving opposition to the Bill."

At the Monthly Conference of the L.C.M.F. held at the Miners Offices, Bolton on Saturday 18th. June, the following resolution was carried;

"We call upon our National Executive Committee to ask the T.U.C. and Labour Party Executive Committee to immediately arrange a conference of National Trade Union Executive Committees and delegates from Trades Councils in order to review the whole position up to date and face the uncertainty of the Anti-Trade Union Bill becoming law, and decide the necessary steps in order to prevent the Bill becoming operative."

At the Accrington Weavers, Winders and Warpers Associations Annual Meeting held on Saturday June 25th., the 'Observer' reported that the Trades Disputes and Trades Union Bill had been high on the agenda and that a resolution had been carried against it.

At Great Harwood Trades Council held on Monday June 27th.

"It was decided to support the No More War Movement in their objection to Clause 1 of the Trade Union Bill which it was stated, would result in making it an illegal step for trade unionists to refuse to use their labour for war purposes."

On July 21st. at their Annual General Meeting held in Jacob Street School, Accrington, the usually moderate G.M.W.U. carried the following confrontational resolution:

"That this meeting of the Accrington branch is of the opinion that the union should not administer the provisions of the proposed Trades Disputes and Trade Unions Act and that the General Council should not propose to alter the Rules for that purpose." [Minute Book]

THE REACTION LOCALLY TO THE ACT.

By the autumn, however, the unions were preparing to come to terms with the Act. At the Accrington G.M.W.U.- Clay [Brickworks] Shop Stewards meeting of August 25th. Bro. Riding gave an outline of the union's proposed policy regarding a campaign to maximise the collection of the Political Levy [Union Minute Book]. Indeed, on September 14th. a Special Meeting had been arranged for G.M.W.U. members as a whole, to be informed of this policy.

At the L.M.C.F. Monthly Conference held at the Miners Offices,

Bolton on Saturday September 10th. the following resolution No.26a. submitted by Burnley branch was carried;

> "Having regard to the serious position of Trade Unions arising out of the New Trade Union Act, the Federation do refuse to operate the Act in its present form, and further that this Federation do not revise the rules of this Federation to bring it in conformity with the Act. Same to be forwarded to the Miners Federation of Great Britain."

Lancashire were the only coalfield in favour of not operating the Act, when the matter was discussed at the National Executive Committee Meeting [L.C.M.F. Minutes Saturday October 8th.]. The Minutes of that date confirm;

> "That Minute 26a. be not confirmed and that this L.C.M.F. fall in line with the political policy of the M.F.G.B."

By passing the above the L.C.M.F. accepted the need to put their backs into obtaining the maximum number of their members signatures on Political Fund Contribution Cards.

Further evidence that trade union objectives had now centred on the need to collect as many endorsements for paying the political levy as possible, is found in the Minute Book of the Great Harwood Weavers of November 9th. which states:

> "That circulars re. Trades Disputes and Trade Unions Act and cards for signature be taken out on Monday next and collected on Tuesday."

This is obviously a reference to the collection of acceptance forms for the future payment of the political levy.

On Saturday, January 14th. 1928, the 'Observer' published details of the Rishton Weavers Half Yearly Report. Extracts are printed below:

> "The failure of the Government to legalise the 48 hour working week is a great betrayal to the workers and there could be no stronger reason required and no other reason should be necessary, why every member should sign the contracting-in form for payment of the Political Levy. We are glad to say we have had a good response from our members and the number of members who have signed the contracting-in forms is even greater than we expected, and we have also reason to believe that the same applies to the other districts in the Amalgamation, and to the trade unions in other industries, so that the Governments attempt to cripple the political power of the trade union movement is likely to be a failure."

COMMENTS ON THE EFFECTS OF THE ACT.

Commenting on the events outlined in this Chapter, Allen Hutt says;

"In 1927 the Trades Disputes and Trade Unions Act [the 'Blacklegs Charter'] was placed on the Statute Book. Not only general strikes but sympathetic strikes, even when purely industrial in aim, were made illegal. A clause without precedent suggested that it might be a criminal offence for persons not actually in employment to refuse to accept employment on an employer's terms. Anyone leading or participating in an 'illegal' strike was liable to fine or imprisonment [up to two years, on indictment], while union funds were made liable for civil damages, thus removing the immunity conferred by the Act of 1906. Mass picketing was forbidden and ordinary picketing hamstrung by a blanket definition of 'intimidation'. Civil Service unions were forbidden to affiliate to the T.U.C., or the Labour Party. Trade Unionists who blacklegged were protected against any disciplinary actions by their unions. A blow was struck at the unions' political activity by changing the existing legal arrangements regarding political levies. Instead of objectors to the political levy having to 'contract out', its supporters now had to 'contract in'. The Act was appropriately summed up as :

"The most reactionary example of British labour legislation placed on the statute book since the evil Combination Laws of 1799-1800.....a crudely framed piece of restrictive class legislation." [4]

This was of course until the Tories repeated all of the above actions of class warfare during their last 18 years of reactionary Government. It is really annoying that a significant number of working class people, who had enjoyed full employment until 1979, were taken in by Tory lies and propaganda. The Trade Union Movement is the only means of defence that the workers have, and to vote into power a trade union bashing Tory Government, as many workers have done over the last 18 years, was an act of kamikaze dimensions. If they had only read their history, they would have seen the depths of despair that such backward looking policies would inevitably bring.

The immediate effect of the 1927 Act was to reduce the Labour Party's income from its trade union affiliates by a third. However, the Act inadvertently, from the Governments point of view, strengthened the union leaders support for the political path of action and therefore their support for the Labour Party. The contents of the Act were resented as an infringement of their privileges secured over decades of hard fought campaigning. The T.U.C. leadership, although moderate politically, were determined to have the Act consigned to the dustbin of political history.

"They were not successful in this for almost 20 years, but in the meantime the somewhat battered relationship between the unions and the Labour Party was strengthened by their resolve." [5]

COMMENTS ON SIMILAR LEGISLATION ENACTED SINCE 1979.

Over the last 18 years the Government created, as a deliberate act of policy, the mass unemployment that we see today. This mass unemployment has obviously had the fully intended effect of reducing trade union militancy. Secondly, as if such actions were not sufficient for capitalists to exploit the situation to the full, the Government introduced legislation to remove the constitutional rights that unions had enjoyed since the Second World War. They backed this up by using the courts to impose crippling financial penalties for any union, or individual, who dared to raise their head above the parapet by advocating action in support of the workers position.

Ken Gill, whilst General Secretary of M.S.F., wrote in Socialist Campaign Group News, October 1989, the following which was taken from his speech at that years T.U.C.;

"The International Labour Organisation [the United Nations body charged with overseeing human rights at the workplace] states that the policies of the British Government are a serious breach of civil liberties and are undemocratic. A judgement normally reserved for dictatorships, or banana republics."

"Britain is now at the bottom of the European league table for trade union rights....The law is being used to effectively outlaw official strikes,....Our problem, and society's problem, is that workers action will be increasingly challenged in the courts, it will be more difficult to resolve the initial dispute, and more difficult to organise effective action. But difficult is not impossible."

"The T.U.C. can play a bigger role in explaining the issues, in organising public support, in political campaigning for just laws, in raising financial and moral support."

"But Congress House has its limitations - solidarity has to come from the grass-roots. It is our job to encourage it. We cannot turn our backs on working people in dispute. We cannot say we would like to help but the law will not let us. If we take this approach, we can be sure that they will introduce more legal shackles. They will ban Public sector strikes. They will make unofficial action official and then prosecute us."

"These are the lessons of history. When the movement takes determined action then the official solicitor unlocks the gates of Pentonville. [Reference to the 5 dockers gaoled under the Industrial Relations Act, who were freed from Pentonville Prison after the intervention of the 'Official Solicitor' in 1972] When we are immobilised for whatever reason, then the Tories and the judges will attack workers' rights even more. You cannot just wait for a Labour government - if we don't mobilise public support, we will not get a Labour government, certainly not a Labour government which restores democratic rights."

Unfortunately, the leaderships of individual trade unions, the T.U.C. and the Labour Party have in the main, sat back and watched the unrelenting attacks made against the working class and their trade unions and done very little about it. I have heard it said that ' their silence has been deafening'.

Britain in 1997, is in an economic shambles, the late Tory Government's economic policies and strategies have been proved to be bankrupt, and this, if nothing else, nails the lie that it was trade union militancy that was the root cause of Britains economic decline.

The Labour Party leadership has got to change course and argue for a strong trade union movement as a prerequisite for making the world of work more democratic, fairer and safer. This is a necessity in order to counter - balance, what has always been the case, the enormous powers wielded as a matter of course, by the C.B.I., the various Employers Federations and individual employers.

Socialists must again argue for the restoration of trade union rights in order to increase the bargaining power of trade unions. Indeed, the Third Socialist Conference of 1989 advocated the following action to restore the legal protection of trade unions and their funds;

"* End the legal provisions which entitle the courts to sequestrate union funds;

* reintroduce immunities for trade union officials and members against legal actions by employers;

* make secondary picketing legal;

* allow votes on potential industrial action and the election of officials to be held at workplace meetings, rather than by postal ballot.

In addition, there must be a package of positive, enabling rights for trade unionists which go beyond present conceptions of collective bargaining. Such positive rights package should at a minimum consist of;

* rights to information from employers, at least as strong as those originally proposed - before the multi-nationals forced them to be weakened - by the Vredling directives;
* the legally enforceable right to consultation and negotiation over issues such as pricing policy, product development, research and marketing strategy, new technology, and other investment plans; as well as positive rights in the traditional areas of collective bargaining.
* legal backing for forms of worker control, including the transformation of privately owned companies by a vote of the workforce.

It is vitally important that full resources are provided to improve and extend education and training for the maximum number of trade unionists. This will require:

* more generous support from public funds for trade union educational institutions.
* grants without strings to establish trade union and community resource centres throughout Britain; these should have access to the technical facilities of universities, so that trade unions have the back-up to develop positive bargaining positions on new technologies; they should also provide facilities for trade unionists to learn foreign languages.....

It is vital that the trade union movement should adapt itself to the exigencies of the 1990's and beyond, not by adopting the use of credit cards, but by modernising itself to meet the challenge posed by;

* the Governments attack on the legitimacy of the trade unions;
* the sweeping changes in the composition of the workforce;
* the spread of new decentralised forms of work, including the spread of homeworking and sub-contract work.

Only by taking radical action and adopting a more political and social role can the unions begin to organise low paid service workers, casualised and part-time workers and at the other end of the scale, the scientific and administrative workers and those working on a self-employed basis, all of whom make up such a large proportion of the new workforce."

It is essential that the above steps are enacted by the Labour Government, otherwise the unjust society created by the Tories, where millions of people are suffering acute social and economic depravation, will continue to exist. To not legislate, in the manner described above, will perpetuate the most reactionary and most authoritarian anti-trade union legislation seen anywhere within the European Union. The present legislation belongs to the Victorian era, because as we have seen in this Chapter; even the 1927 Act, hated as it was at the time, did not hit at trade union rights as much as those enacted by the Tory Government over the last 18 years.

REFERENCES

1. Blatchford, R. 'Merrie England'. Pub. Journeyman Press, London 1977, p. 92 and 93
2. Murphy, J.T. 'Preparing for Power'. Pub. Pluto Press 1972. p.217
3. Martin, Roderick. 'Communism & the British Trade Unions 1924-1933: A Study of the National Minority Movement.' Pub. Oxford UP 1969. p.37
4. Hutt, A. 'British Trade Unionism: A Short History'. Pub. Lawrence and Wishart, 1975. p. 114 and 115
5. Pelling, H. 'A History of British Trade Unionism'. Pub. Pelican, 1971. p. 187 and 188

CHAPTER TWO

THE COTTON INDUSTRY

ORGANISATION: WEAVING.

National negotiations on wages, hours, etc, were conducted between the unions, [through the Northern Counties Textile Trades Federation - NCTTF] and the employers [through the Cotton Spinners and Manufacturers Association - CSMA]. However, many mills were not members of the CSMA and tried to establish worse pay and conditions than had been nationally agreed.

The NCTTF comprised the following Amalgamations of trade unions:
1. Lancashire Amalgamated Tapesizers' Association,
2. Amalgamated Tapesizers' Friendly Protective Society,
3. General Union of Lancashire and Yorkshire Warpdressers' Association,
4. Amalgamated Association of Beamers, Twisters and Drawers,
5. General Union of Associations of Loom Overlookers,
6. Amalgamated Weavers' Association, and
7. Amalgamated Textile Warehousemen's Association.

ORGANISATION: SPINNING.

National negotiations on wages, hours, etc, were conducted between the unions, through the Executives of the 'Cardroom Amalgamation' and the 'Spinners' Amalgamation', and the employers, who went under the name of the Federation of Master Cotton Spinners' Associations - FMCSA.

The trade union amalgamations involved, were the National Association of Card, Blowing, and Ring Room Operatives, and the Amalgamated Association of Operative Cotton-Spinners and Twiners

ORGANISATION: GENERAL.

Each district had its own local Textile Trades Federation. EG. Church & Oswaldtwistle; Accrington & District; Great Harwood; Rishton; and Clayton-Le-Moors. Surprisingly each of these Federations included representatives of all the above affiliated trade unions. Therefore we had the situation of Cardroom Workers' and Spinners' representatives working locally with their counterparts in the Weavers' and Overlookers' Associations, etc.

If a dispute arose in a mill, the local Textile Trades Federation officials were called in to settle the problem. A shop steward system, such as operated in the engineering industry, did not exist within the mills. In effect, locally, the various full time Weavers' Secretaries, were normally the first to be involved in negotiations, due to them having a majority of members in most mills.

In addition to the above, there existed the United Textile Factory Workers' Association - UTFWA, which had an Executive and which also held an Annual Conference [usually at Blackpool]. This could best be described as a Textile Unions' TUC. Delegates from both the Northern Counties Textile Trades Federation and the Cardroom and Spinners' Amalgamations attended. Issues of a political significance were debated over a two day event. EG. 'The Means Test'; 'The 40 Hour Week'; 'The League of Nations' etc.

The textile unions which affiliated to the Labour Party nationally, did this through the UTFWA. This body supported union MPs. financially, and was also the various unions' means of taking an active part in international textile conferences and associations.

The various local Weavers' Associations, were affiliated to the Amalgamated Weavers' Association, which had its National Headquarters in Accrington.

ORGANISATION: DYEING.

The main union locally was the National Union of Textile Workers. This and five other unions were affiliates of the Joint Dyers' Societies. This latter body negotiated nationally with the relevant Employers' Association.

1927

On New Years Day 1927 at the Labour Party's Tea and Concert in the Co-operative Assembly Rooms Accrington, Mr. Emmett, the Accrington Weavers' Secretary, delivered a pessimistic speech to the 300 in attendance. Two mills Oak Vale and Scaitcliffe had been closed over Christmas week. Two days previously Bramley Street Manufacturing Company's Milnshaw/Albion Mill containing 200 looms had just closed down for an indefinite period and another 4 mills were standing idle.

THE PARK MILL DISPUTE, ACCRINGTON

An atmosphere of gloom and depression prevailed. During the spring and the summer of 1927, the cotton unions had put all their efforts into combating the Government's Trade Unions and Trades Disputes Bill. Meanwhile pressure was being exerted by the owners regarding the conditions of service worked by their employees. This eventually resulted in an unofficial strike at Park Mill from Tuesday August 9th until Monday August 15th. The mill contained 900 looms and 270 weavers were affected. The 'Observer' reported:

"The point of difference between the management and the weavers is in regard to the scraping of looms, a contentious question .....The weavers maintain that they are not compelled by any rule or custom to scrape looms, and hold that reasonable cleaning of the machinery is quite ample, especially when it is remembered that in other branches of the cotton industry employees are paid extra for cleaning......At present Park Mill is closed down, and a strike or lockout arising out of such a cause has never before been known in the history of the cotton trade in Accrington.....Mr. Emmett, said: "In the early part of the summer pressure was brought to bear upon the weavers by the manager to scrape the looms, and he went so far as to get specially made scrapers for each weaver. He also began to have all the accumulated dirt taken off the floor of the shed, and this created a lot of feeling amongst the weavers, owing to the stench, which was nearly unbearable. This has kept going on and some of the weavers scraped each of their looms, while others did not. Finally, a deputation of the weavers saw me and insisted on the Association taking the whole matter up. Under the circumstances, seeing that the majority of the weavers had already done the scraping, the committee of the Association advised the other portion of the weavers to do the same, provided the firm would see that the accumulated dirt on the floor was got up by themselves, and that the weavers were not asked to do it. Doing this work was conditional upon the firm considering some kind of compensation when the job was finally completed".

"The firm were pressed to consider this suggestion before the July holidays, but there was a point blank refusal to give any consideration to the matter at all. Eventually the weavers, one after the other did the scraping until, when the July holidays arrived every loom in the mill had been scraped. In the holiday week the firm had no doubt, been looking over the looms, and in their view a certain number of the looms had not been scraped satisfactorily."

"On Friday last, eleven of the weavers were sent for and informed that the scraping had not been done satisfactorily and that it would have to be done in a proper manner, otherwise they would get their unemployment cards. This created some feeling in the shed, which developed on Tuesday morning, when a further number of weavers - eight or nine- were spoken to in the same way as the eleven on Friday."

"The whole thing came to a head on Tuesday noon owing to another lot of weavers being sent for and complained to in regard to this scraping. On the return of these particular weavers to the shed they informed their colleagues of what had occurred, and they decided not to put up with it."

"I heard of the matter and went to the mill to see if there was any possibility of squaring the trouble up. I saw Mr. Seddon, and his point of view was that as the workpeople had come out unconditionally they must return unconditionally before he would discuss the matter. I met the workpeople in the mill yard and informed them that they had to go back unconditionally, and a resolution was passed that they would return to work on the Wednesday morning if the firm would receive a deputation that day to discuss the whole matter. I told Mr. Seddon the conditions they were prepared to go back to work on, and he said they would have to return unconditionally or he would shut off the boilers."

"I conveyed that message to the workpeople, and they refused unanimously to accept the terms of resuming. I then advised them to go home."

On Wednesday morning the wages were paid as usual, but the mill did not resume work.

"It is an unofficial strike," added Mr. Emmett, "but the firm seems to think there is no grievance. A queer thing in the textile trade now is that the weavers are the only people who don't get paid for cleaning. If people want to make old looms into new ones by having them scraped they should be willing to give extra pay. The mill has been running 40 or 50 years, and I have no doubt the looms are in a bad state as far as cleanliness is concerned,......"

In order to expedite matters the Accrington Weavers' Association placed an advertisement in the 'Observer' inviting all union members employed at Park Mill to a Special Meeting to be held on Sunday afternoon, August 14th. at 3.00pm at the Picture House, Church Street. The attendance of nearly a 100% was presided over by Mr.J.T. Davenport, President. Mr. J.R. Emmett J.P. presented a lengthy report in which he explained that he had been in contact with the Employers Association's Secretary, regarding the matter. He recommended a return to work on Monday morning in order to allow a joint meeting to take place within the week between the Employers' Association and the Weavers' Union. The workers agreed to a return to work but the results of the joint discussions were not printed in the local press.

8th. ANNUAL PROCESSION & SPORTS DAY, ACCRINGTON TCLP.

Whilst the above events were taking place the weavers and other trade unionists had been looking forward to a day of fun at the 8th. Annual Procession and Sports Day, organised by the Accrington Trades and Labour Party.

On Saturday August 6th., the Accrington Weavers' had placed an advertisement in the 'Observer' as follows:

"Trades and Labour Party Annual Procession and Demonstration Saturday August 13th.,1927. All members of the above Association are cordially invited to take part in the Procession and are asked to meet the officials outside the Weavers' Offices Wellington Street on the above date at 1.15 prompt. Children can accompany parents.

J.R. Emmett Secretary"

The demonstration, which was favoured with ideal weather, attracted 5,000 marchers. The Observer's report of the proceedings refers to the good muster of textile workers who followed their union banners. Heading the Weavers' contingent were Messrs. J.T. Davenport, J.R. Emmett, E. Richardson, (Insurance Clerk) and A. Lloyd. (Treasurer).

FINING

At their regular meetings with the cotton employers, the Weavers' Amalgamation had tried for many years to have the system of fining abolished. However, the 'Observer' of September 20th.,1927, reported that the employers had again refused the union's request. Mr.J.C. Parker J.P., Secretary of the Weavers' Amalgamation, said:

"We cannot possibly think of accepting the employers' letter as the final word on this question. The agitation against the fining system has been going on in the weaving industry longer than most people realise. I can remember forming one of a local deputation to the local employers more than 30 years ago. This considered reply will make no difference so far as we are concerned. Sooner or later the fining system will have to go. It is about the last remnant of the old days when 9 year old half-timers were herded into the mills at six in the morning."

Mr.J.R. Emmett J.P. said :

"He was astonished at the attitude the employers had taken up. We are the only people on earth who get fined. There is very little fining done now, and I am sure they can't submit the statement, that they cannot do without it. For instance there are many mills at which there have been no fining for years, but sometimes a mill runs for a month or two without a fine being imposed on the weaver and then there are several in succession. One can hardly understand the attitude the employers have taken up."

Mr. Andrew Naesmith J.P. again referred to the detestable system of fines on weavers. In an address at Clitheroe on Tuesday January 22nd. 1929, reported in the 'Observer', he commented on the recent decision of the High Court which had supported the legality of the fining system. He said:

"We are determined to pursue this matter to the bitter end. We believe we have justice on our side. We consider our contention fair and reasonable, and we ask for the support and encouragement of members, strengthening us in our conviction that whether we succeed of fail in the courts, we are going to see this matter through. I am hopeful that we shall succeed."

"Nothing had been so fruitful as the fining system in bringing about bad relationships and disputes in the industry. It had caused strikes and had resulted in young men and women shortening their lives. Not long ago, 11,000 operatives in one town became idle for seven weeks because of a dispute respecting fining. Clearly there was deep resentment against the injustice of the system. All over the country there was objection to the practice....."

"The intelligent employer within the county is recognising the justice of our claim. Already 30% of the employers have voluntarily relinquished this system in their mills, and many of them have told me that the standard of cloth and the discipline in their mills are quite as high, if not higher, than when fines where imposed. Weavers are not in the habit of wilfully making faults in their cloth. They do their best with the material at hand, and having done that they expect when the cloth is placed on the table in the warehouse to have consideration given to all the circumstances under which it was produced."

"There are two methods of ending this system. One is the

industrial way, by withdrawing labour. We can utilize the industrial weapon as much as we like in order to stamp out this hated system. That is a costly and a vicious method, and nobody wants to adopt it except as a last resort. The other method is the legal way, and that is the one we propose to follow. It has been ruled that the employer is entitled by law to make deductions from weavers' wages as compensation done to his property - his cloth. We cannot allow the decision to remain where it is......"

"The time is coming when the word will be given that we must march forward in a demand, not only to extend our wages, but to secure such improvements in the condition of our factory life as will make them sweeter and better than they have ever been before."

The Accrington Weavers' Half Yearly Meeting of Tuesday June 17th. 1930, at the Co-operative Assembly Rooms, Oak Street, was presided over by the President Miss Lena Worsley. In her opening remarks she referred to the recent success in the Chancery Court in regards to 'Fining' for spoiled work. She stated that the Amalgamation took the view that they had won the case, and that unless the case was reversed on appeal to the House of Lords, the decision should be binding in law and 'fining' would become a thing of the past. ['Observer' June 21st. 1930]

The case referred to by Lena Worsley was that of Thomas Sagar against his employer Messrs H. Ridehalgh & Sons, Nelson. The union was represented by Hon. R. Stafford Cripps, K.C. and Mr. Neville J. Laski, K.C. On May 6th. 1930, Mr. Justice Farwell in the Chancery Court, London, decided that the action of the employer was illegal.

However, the employers appealed and on December 9th.1930 the verdict was overturned.

The union sought the help of the T.U.C. with a view to taking the case to the House of Lords, but counsels advice in June 1931 advised against such an appeal. Hopwood says:

"Thus the fining question was left - in an unsatisfactory position." [1]

THE COTTON CRISIS, CONTINUED

The parochial nature of working class organisations, as indeed of all political groupings within the parliamentary boundary, is highlighted by the following event. The Saturday 'Observer', 15th. October, 1927, reported that:

"The proposed amalgamation of the 3 Textile Federations of Accrington, Church & Oswaldtwistle, and Clayton-Le-Moors, has not matured, and the position remains to-day as it was at the beginning of the year. [This was decided at a] meeting held on Monday evening at the Weavers' Institute, Oswaldtwistle.....It will be recalled that 6 months ago when the Federations met to consider the question of amalgamation, opposition was raised by the Church Overlookers, and the Oswaldtwistle Twisters and Drawers. Since then, these 2 societies have held independent meetings, with the result that the opposition to amalgamation was as strong as ever at Monday's meeting. The result was that the meeting was further adjourned 'sine die'."

THE DEATH OF Mr. J.C. PARKER J.P.

Saturday 5th. November, 1927, was a day of sadness for the Weavers' Amalgamation; they lost the services of Mr.J.C. Parker J.P., their General Secretary, of 210 Whalley Road, Clayton-Le-Moors, who died suddenly at the age of 63 years.

When he was 9 years old, he had been sent to work at the Canal Mill, Clayton-Le-Moors, to learn the trade of weaving. In July 1892 at the age of 27, he was elected as the representative of Albion Mill to the Executive Committee of the Clayton-Le-Moors Weavers' Association. One year later in November 1893, he was appointed President. From December 1895, until April 1919, he held the position of Secretary. He then went on to become the Assistant Secretary of the Weavers' Amalgamation, whose offices were in Accrington, and in March 1925 was appointed its General Secretary.

The 'Observer' reported that in 1903 the Clayton-Le-Moors Weavers' Association became affiliated to the Accrington and District Trades Council and Mr. Parker was elected President of that organisation from 1905 to 1907. Later he was one of those responsible for setting up a local Trades Council at Clayton-Le-Moors, and he held the position of Secretary until 1919. At the same time he was instrumental in forming the Clayton-Le-Moors Textile Trades Association in 1906 and was its Secretary until 1919.

"Nominated by the local Weavers' Association, he was returned at the head of the poll to the Clayton-Le-Moors Urban District Council in 1903. He served on the Council until 1921, 18 years without a break, and at each election he received the highest number of votes. He held the position of Chairman of the Council from 1915 until 1917."['Observer' 8th. November 1927]

In April 1911 he was appointed a Justice of the Peace. The funeral cortege was over a quarter of a mile in length.

The position of General Secretary to the Weavers Amalgamation was taken by Mr. Andrew Naesmith.

THE COTTON CRISIS CONTINUED.

Meanwhile, everyone could see that events were going from bad to worse, and the future of the cotton industry looked as bleak as any other major industry. Knowing that this was so, local activists used all available material to promote debate about improving the lot of the common man. Bill Brotherton, a future Labour Alderman of Accrington, utilized the thoughts of the Liberal economist John Maynard Keynes as a means of getting the message across that things could be changed for the better, if only radical socialist ideas were put into practice. His letter to the 'Observer' published on Tuesday, November 29th. 1927 is printed below.

"Dear Sir,

"The cotton industry is sick and the Liberal economist, Mr. Keynes has been saying nasty things about it. His powerful indictment follows closely the Socialist criticism not only of the cotton trade, but all our staple industries. Coal is bankrupt; agriculture goes from bad to worse; engineering cannot pay a living wage."

"I do not propose to recapitulate the points made by Mr. Keynes. What we socialists are primarily concerned about is the way out. Mr. Keynes after showing up the pitiable attempts of the cotton kings to meet the situation, goes on to point out the remedy. He says no one has yet propounded a fourth alternative to the 3 original alternatives of bankruptcy, cartelization, or combines. There is a fourth alternative; that is the socialization of the industry. This involves the complete reorganisation of the industry as a national service; the elimination of uneconomic concerns and present day competition and overlapping; the compulsory reduction of capitalisation and the abolition of brokers and middlemen; the creation of a State buying agency with a view to steady buying and the stabilization of prices; and lastly, the securing of an international cotton control and international labour standards."

"Socialism seeks to introduce order into the cotton industry. Gambling only benefits the few fortunate winners. Are the workers to be always the victims of this haphazard system? The answer rests with them. Let them work and vote for Socialism ,which means common sense and science, in place of chaos and anarchy."
Yours,

William Brotherton
30 Craven Street
Accrington

1928

On Saturday evening January 14th. 1928, a presentation to mark the 25 years service as Secretary of the Church and Oswaldtwistle Weavers', Winders', and Warpers' Association, was made to Mr. J.T. Wolstenholme J.P. He received a solid gold Waltham watch, heavy gold albert and gold pendant and a smoking cabinet. Mr. F. Coleman presided over a gathering of 700 in Oswaldtwistle Town Hall.

When he began doing, the job membership stood at 2,394 and this rose to 5,186 at the outbreak of war in 1914. In 1918 the figure stood at 4,000 rising to 4,600 in the boom year of 1920. With the depression however, membership now stood at 3,094.

In his address to the gathering Mr. Naesmith, Secretary of the Amalgamation, referred to the proposal to reduce wages and increase working hours. He assured them that their trade union officials would do all they could to protect the interests of the cotton workers. (Observer January 17th.1928)

The Rishton Weavers' Half-Yearly Report, dealt with the Governments attitude towards the 48 hour week. It said:

"With regards to any attempt on the part of the employers to seek a reduction in wages or an increase in working hours, we are quite sure such an attempt will meet with the most strenuous resistance of all sections of operatives in the cotton trade."

"When fully employed the wages of our members are small and not in proportion to the wages of people engaged in other trades who are not called upon to exercise anywhere near the same skill."

"With regard to the proposal to increase working hours, this seems ridiculous when we know that there have been, and still are scores of mills stopped altogether and others on short time, and there are thousands of cotton operatives either unemployed, or underemployed at the present time. To ask for longer hours when they cannot find full work for a 48 hour week appears absurd. .....We feel sure that the Amalgamation will have the full support of all our members in resisting to the uttermost any attempt to either reduce wages or increase working hours."('Observer' January 14th.1928)

At the actual meeting which took place on Monday 16th., January, a resolution was also passed recording a vote of thanks to Mr. J.H. Whittaker who was one of the pioneers of the society. He had held office as a member of the committee, collector, or auditor for over 40 years.('Observer' January 17th.1928)

On Sunday afternoon January 15th., 1928, at the Picture House, Accrington, Mr. A.J. Cook, the Secretary of the Miners' Federation of Great Britain spoke to a large audience, "the spacious building being packed to overflowing." He was supported by Mr. John McGurk, President, Lancashire and Cheshire Miners' Federation, Mr. Tinker M.P., and Councillor Baron, Secretary of the Accrington Miners Association. The speeches although aimed at restoring confidence to the mine workers after their experiences of 1926, alluded to the crisis facing the cotton workers. The 'Observer' reported as follows:

"Mr. McGurk said the object of the meeting was to impress upon the workers in every industry in Accrington the necessity of 100% organisation and the necessity for political action.....He insisted that trade unionism and politics were inseparable. In connection with the cotton industry a demand had been put forward for a reduction in wages and longer working hours. He reminded them that during the dispute in the mining industry in 1926, they were told that there was a loss of 5 1/2 d per ton on coal produced in Lancashire and Cheshire, and that that loss could, if the miners accepted a reduction in wages and worked longer hours, be turned into a profit of 6d per ton, and that 5d of the latter would go into the pockets of the miners. That statement was issued in 1926 as a 'cold fact', and the people were gulled with it, and when 'our own people were gulled with it you cannot wonder at tacklers getting gulled with it too.' He hoped, however, that the cotton weavers and tacklers would not be gulled with the story of the employers that if they would work longer hours and accepted a reduction in wages there would be prosperity in the cotton trade. He hoped the experience of the miners would be a lesson for the cotton operatives."

"Mr. Cook, who was accorded a warm reception, opened by saying, "It is my lot, it seems, to be a centre of storm. It is the lot of most of you to be connected with the two industries, cotton and coal, and these are the orphans of the storm"....

"In striking fashion he charged the audience with being responsible for the mess the country was in, in that they returned a Tory Government to power. "Today," he remarked, "ignorance is a crime; you have no right to be ignorant".....

"He recounted a conversation with Lord Rhondda, in which the latter advised him that the worker must produce more if he wanted more; that the worker could not have two pounds worth of value to share unless they created it. That theory was sound if in producing more there would have been a distribution that was equitable as a result of the increased production. It was in Lancashire that capitalism was born and developed, and in Lancashire there had been more financial juggling than anywhere. Sir Charles Macara had been giving colossal instances of financial gambling in the cotton industry and of watering stock."....

"Coal and cotton made Great Britain the workshop of the world. Coal and cotton, unless soundly controlled by different mentalities, would cease to be British industries......The experience of the miners was the classical example to the cotton industry. Lord Beaverbrook, he said, had at long last realised that working longer hours and reducing wages was ruinous to the country, and was demanding the trustification of the coal industry.".....

"He hoped the demand to reduce wages and increase working hours in the cotton industry would be resisted by the whole of the trade union movement, the Labour Party and the people, after they had seen the suicidal results of the insane policy of the coal owners."

The local operatives got the chance to hear the Communist view of the cotton crisis at the Accrington Discussion Class on Sunday evening January 22nd. 1928, when Mr. T. Bright of Manchester spoke to a moderate attendance. The report is printed below:

"About 3 weeks ago the Master Cotton Spinners' Federation and the Manufacturers' Association issued a report in which they..... gave a very gloomy picture...... They came forward with definite proposals that sacrifices would have to be made in the form of a reduction in wages of 12.5%, - 25% on the list price. Then they had the audacity to suggest, in addition, an increase in the working day from 48 hours to 52.5. Having given further thought to the matter, they now came forward with the abrogation of the present cleaning time agreement which, so far as he could understand, would mean an additional 2.5 hours per week so far as the operatives were concerned. Due to the policy of fining in the textile industry the operatives would be compelled to keep the machinery cleaner in order that the manufactured goods should not be spoiled....... Their arguments were that the keen foreign competition and the large amount of interest on loans and overdrafts demanded by the bankers were responsible for the decline in the industry. But they even went further, they also came forward with a definite proposal that pressure should be brought to bear on the present Tory Government to reduce expenditure as far as social service was concerned, or to reduce payment on such things as unemployment benefit......."

"Mr. Bright next criticised the trade union officials for assisting in peace discussions with the employers. The employers....would take no notice of the trade union officials. The only notice they would take was 'Are the workers going to fight ?' They could take it from him that the proposals by the employers was not bluff, but behind this there was a serious attempt to reduce wages and increase the working week."

"Mr. Bright's solution was 100% trade unionism in the mills, in each of which a committee should be formed. He advocated the institution of committees for each locality and one negotiating body for the whole of Lancashire. Pressure should be brought to bear also upon the union executive to secure a special meeting of the full management committee to consider the position of the textile workers."

The cotton crisis was mentioned by Mr. C.R. Buxton, Parliamentary Labour Candidate, at an I.L.P. public meeting held at the Primitive Methodist School in Rishton, on Tuesday 24th. January 1928. The 'Observer' reported his contribution as follows:

"Mr. Buxton said a threat was now being made by the employers' organisations in the cotton industry to reduce the wages and lengthen the hours. He was astonished when he first read the proposals, coming from such a responsible body of employers - astonished that such audacious proposals should be made at such a time as this, when wages were at an appalling low level, when they took into account the short-time working and the unemployment. The average earnings in the cotton industry throughout the whole county were not more than 36s per week. It was proposed to lengthen the hours at a time when the mills could not find employment enough for the operatives for the hours they now worked. The proposal was of a most reactionary character."

"One of the things they blamed the present Government for was their utter indifference to the hours of labour of the working people. There was at least one thing they might have done and that was to ratify the Washington Convention for the universal 48 hour week, but they had not done that, and the fact that Great Britain was lagging behind in that respect was used by almost every other country for not ratifying conventions. He hoped there would be a most strenuous resistance to any such proposals and resistance to even discuss them by the workers, and that they would point out that there were many other ways in which the industry might be saved. Bad organisation through capitalism, the utter failure to read the modern lessons of the times, trying to run industry on the old competitive system - those things might be done away with without laying sacrilegious hands on the wages of the workers. It was high time a proper impartial enquiry was made into the cotton industry, like the one that was made into the mining industry. He would support such an enquiry."

On Saturday, January 28th., the 'Observer' printed extracts from the Clayton-Le-Moors, Weavers' Association's, Half Yearly Report. This read as follows:

"We affirm that the remedy for bringing about a change for the better in the cotton trade, is to obliterate the speculators who are a menace to the manufacturers and the trade generally as a whole and in reconstruction in relation to mill finance, such as share capital, which is, in some instances at 6 times higher than pre-war value; efficient organisation and attention to changing fashions and varying market needs."

"A reduction of wages and an increase in working hours is no remedy for bad trade. These things will not reduce the cost of production. They will increase the cost for two reasons. Lower wages reduce the physical efficiency of the workers, and their productivity is lessened. Lower wages reduce purchasing power and the demand for commodities. In manual labour there is a point beyond which it is not economical to continue work; that the physical energy begins to flag, and the production falls off."

"There is a decided movement in foreign countries towards shorter hours. Britain alone is standing in the way of ratification of the Washington Hours Convention. If hours are increased in this country, it will certainly encourage a retrograde movement all over the world."

"There is no boon which the trade unionist has won for the workers which they should guard so zealously as the shorter working day."

"In the words of Sir Charles Macara, the speculators have forced up the price of cotton on a years output of the cash crop by about £300,000,000. No industry can stand such a burden as that. Let the cotton employers deal with that scandal before they talk about reducing wages and increasing hours."

The 'Observer' stated that a meeting had taken place of the Accrington Weavers on Monday 30th. January 1928, to discuss a report compiled by Mr. J.R. Emmett, the Secretary, on the question of the proceedings regarding working hours and wages.

"A unanimous feeling was manifested that the Weavers' Amalgamation should strongly oppose any suggestions in the direction of increasing hours and reducing wages. As a means of propaganda, it was decided to issue leaflets throughout all the mills in the district, and to make a special appeal to new unionists. It was stated that since the employers announcement regarding wages and hours the membership of the Accrington branch has increased by 60."

A short report appeared in the 'Observer' of Saturday, February 4th.,1928, of the conference held between the cotton trade employers and the representatives of the textile trade unions at Manchester the day previously. The discussion centred on the employers proposals for an extension of the working week and a reduction in the piece price list. The meeting had broken up without agreement, or any arrangements for a further meeting.

"The trade union representatives reiterated their demand for a statutory inquiry into the whole ramification of the cotton industry, but we understand that the employers definitely refused to agree to being jointly responsible for requesting the Government to set up this public inquiry."

"The operatives refused to enter into discussions on the subject of an increase in working hours and a reduction in wages."

The 'Observer' reported a speech made by Mr. Andrew Naesmith, at Haslingden Public Discussion Class on Sunday evening February 19th., 1928. His subject was 'Cotton Problems', and at the outset he accused the Government of a lack of interest towards the industry's condition, saying that its attitude was that the industry must work out its own salvation. He said:

"Between 80-85% of what we produce is for export trade. The cotton industry maintains well over half a million people, and its exports amounted to 20-25% of the total national exports....."

"For a long period under employment had been a cause of upset in the cotton trade, and now there was unemployment. The need for cotton goods still existed. What had arisen was inability to supply our goods at prices the consumers of other countries could pay......"

"With a view to rehabilitating the industry the employers had recently tabled certain proposals. Among these proposals they laid down that the merchanting system that had been operative in the industry from its inception was chaotic. The operatives' representatives had been amazed that for so long a parasitical class had been allowed to live at the expense of the producer without performing any real and necessary function. The firms doing well today, were those who did their own merchanting of cloth and handling their own materials. The specific proposals of the employers, however, were that the wages of the operatives should be reduced 25% on the piece price and the working hours increased by 4.25 hours."

"If the operatives accepted those proposals the....effect upon mill prices would be infinitesimal, and there would be no assurance that what decrease there was would be passed on to the consumer. The decreased cost might be used to cut losses or to increase profits. Along those lines there was no solution of Lancashire's problems. Those problems were inherent within the industry. There were enormous wastages and inefficiencies that had got to be removed. The operatives must equip themselves for the changes that were bound to come, and from which they would get a more just reward for their labour."

It was announced in the 'Observer' March 3rd., 1928, that Mr. Andrew Naesmith, of 202 Haywood Road, Accrington, General Secretary of the Weavers Amalgamation, had been made a magistrate.

DISPUTE IN THE DYEING & FINISHING TRADES.

Meanwhile, disputes were also taking place in the dyeing and finishing trades. The 'Observer' of June 9th., reported:

"The intention of the National Union of Textile Workers', and other unions in the Joint Dyers' Societies numbering six altogether, to hand in notices this week to enforce their claim for 25% advance in wages pending such time as piece work rates are put into operation, has not been carried out. As stated last week, notices had been prepared to be handed in at Messrs. F. Steiner and Company's works Church, and Foxhill Bank and Grimshaw's Plantation Mill, Accrington, but on Wednesday the local officials received instructions to withhold the notices."

"The decision followed upon a meeting of the Executives of the six unions at Bradford on Wednesday. They were unable to agree on a common policy and finally the National Union of Textile Workers' decided to secede from the Joint Dyers' Societies....."

"The National Union of Textile Workers comprised workers in the cotton warp and hank section and the Huddersfield trade - about 1,000 in Bradford, 2,000 in Huddersfield and between 3,000 and 4,000 in Lancashire. Mr. Rushworth, the Secretary of the Amalgamated Dyers', said that the vote by the majority of the unions for the re-opening of negotiations truly reflected the feeling of the union branches, and that the five unions preferred arbitration to striking, if arbitration became necessary."

An article appeared in the 'Observer' of June 12th. updating the situation. A joint conference had been held in Manchester between the unions and the employers organisations and prospects for a settlement appeared bright. The unions had put forward proposals for an agreement which the employers appeared interested in.

Meanwhile the National Union of Textile Workers had handed in notices of strike action which would expire at the end of the week. However, their Executive Committee was still prepared to meet the employers for the purposes of negotiating a settlement.

The employers stated that they were also prepared to negotiate and it would appear that an agreement was reached because no further mention of the dispute is made in the local press.

THE COTTON CRISIS CONTINUED.

At the Annual Meeting of the Accrington Weavers' Association held on Tuesday June 12th., at the Co-operative Assembly Rooms, Oak Street, a decision was made to celebrate their 70th. Anniversary with a trip to Blackpool in September. The 'Observer' reported:

"Miss Lena Worsley, President, referring to the past history of the Association said that when it was formed the working hours were 12 per day, and employees were working without a break for 6 hours. When they considered that with the conditions which prevailed at the present time they could see the benefits they had received. It was in 1874 before the 10 hour day became operative in England. The Particular Clause, which was of great benefit to them, was won after hard fighting, and in more recent times the half-timer system in the mills had been abolished. Since their last half-yearly meeting they had all been interested in hours and wages, and it was a significant coincidence when they remembered that their union was formed to improve conditions and deal with hours of labour, that the matter should come up at a time like that."

"The committee, during the last few months, had had a very anxious time both in regard to hours and wages, 'but', she added, 'I am glad to say that common sense has prevailed in Lancashire, and for a time this thing that they tried to put into operation will not be. But, I venture to say at the same time that if you had not had a Weavers'

Amalgamation and a United Textile Factory Workers' Association you would have been on longer hours to-day.' (Hear, Hear.)"

The meeting also decided to arrange for a presentation to be made to their Secretary, Mr. Emmett, to commemorate his 21 years service to the Association.

An interesting item appeared on the agenda, concerning the re-election of Miss Margaret McCarthy to the committee. As an active Communist Party worker, Margaret had just returned from a visit to the Soviet Union and I feel sure that her activist brand of politics would not have seen favour with her colleagues on the executive. The 'Observer' reported that:

"The re-election of Miss Margaret McCarthy as a member of the committee was proposed, but it was stated that she did not at present work in Accrington, and Miss Worsley, on being asked to give her ruling, said she thought it was only right that as an Accrington and District Weavers' Association the members of the committee should work in Accrington. If Miss McCarthy resumed work at a mill in Accrington the committee had always power to co-opt her if she was nominated by members."

The 'Observer' June 26th., reported the death of Mr. George Robert Richardson aged 66 years, of 125 Whalley Road, Accrington, sick pay steward and treasurer to the Accrington Weavers' Association. Formerly a weaver at Heifer Bank Mill he was officially connected with the society for over 40 years.

The 'Observer' July 7th., announced that Mr. George F. Kilshaw had been appointed as clerk to the National Health Insurance section of the Association in succession to Mr. Richardson. Mr. Kilshaw was 26 years of age and formerly a weaver at Bury's Fountain Mill.

Splendid weather greeted the annual procession and field day organised by the Accrington Trades and Labour Party on Saturday 14th., July 1928. The event was held on a field off Burnley Road beyond the reservoir, where a political meeting took place. The guest speakers were Mr. C.P. Trevelyan M.P. for Newcastle and Mr. Tom Snowden, the newly appointed prospective Labour Party candidate for Accrington.

"The National Union of Textile Workers were led by a group of children of members bearing 'N.U.T.W.' worked in flowers, followed by a tableaux of young children on a lorry bearing the inscription 'Labour's Hope is the Rising Generation'......"

"The Accrington Weavers' Association had the largest turnout.....were led by the Read and Simonstone Band and their banner, beneath which was a pretty group of children holding flowers.Their section numbered about 300 in all. The officials in front were Miss

Worsley, President, Messrs J.R. Emmett, Secretary, F. Cunliffe J.P., A. Lloyd and G.F. Kilshaw. Mr. T. Davenport acted as marshall."

THE ACCRINGTON & RISHTON WEAVERS' BLACKPOOL EXCURSIONS.

SIR DAVID SHACKLETON GUEST SPEAKER.

The highlight of the year, as far as the Accrington Weavers' Association was concerned, took place on Saturday September 8th. Nearly 5,000 members and friends visited Blackpool, to commemorate their 70th. anniversary. It was stated to be the largest single party which had ever left Accrington on a picnic. The 'Observer' reported that:

"Seven special trains, each capable of carrying 750 passengers, were utilized,.....The first train left Accrington at 10.50 a.m., practically all the employers having acceded to the Weavers' Association's request that the mills should stop at 10.00 a.m., so that the employees might not be too rushed, and from that time until the departure of the 7th. train at 12.50 p.m. Accrington station presented a busy scene.... The officials travelled in 2 saloons on the last train...."

"The only depressing feature of the day's proceedings was the weather....for at Blackpool rain was falling heavily and this state of affairs continued with only slight cessation from the time of arrival until the departure between 9.00 p.m. and 10.30 p.m....."

"Chief officials of the Association and certain invited guests from kindred organisations partook of tea at the Arcade Cafe, about 120 being present, and opportunity was taken to make the presentations to Mr. and Mrs. Emmett [for his 21 years service as Secretary]......"

"The presentation was made by Mr. F. Cunliffe J.P. The baby grandmother clock was handed over to Mr. Emmett at Accrington, and on Saturday he received the gold watch at the formal proceedings."

"Both presents bore the following inscription: "Presented by the Accrington and District Weavers' Association to Mr. J.R. Emmett J.P., in recognition of his 21 years unremitting service as Secretary. September 6th 1907 - September 8th. 1928......"

"Miss A. Kirkham J.P. presented Mrs. Emmett, on behalf of the officials of the Society, with a silver cake basket."

The toast to the 'Accrington and District Weavers' Association on the attainment of its seventieth birthday' was proposed by Sir David Shackleton, a past President of the Association. The 'Observer' reported:

"Looking back, he did not remember an occasion on which he felt prouder of the honour of being called upon to take part in a ceremony in connection with trade union work. Since he joined the Society, 45 years ago, he had gone through many changes and had had many experiences. He recalled that he was married in August 1883. His wife was already a member of the Society; he was not, but she enroled him as a member the same week-end."

"The early days were somewhat trying. I look back upon them now with a certain amount of indifference, but at the time they were certainly difficult. My 17 weeks compulsory unemployment without unemployment benefit has never left my mind. I think about it often, but I am pleased to know I have had some part in Parliament and in Government service to remove from the minds of unemployed persons to-day the terror of being out of work and nothing coming in at all.(Hear, Hear.) I hesitate to feel what would have happened to me in those days if my wife had not been earning on 3 looms at Park Mill 18s. a week to keep us both."

"But he was pleased to say they lived over it and got through, and he hoped they had helped to improve things for those who have followed them.....He remembered the Association meeting in Albion Street over an entry, long before the time they met in Wellington Street. He was only a young fellow then, remarked Sir David, but they were early training days and he had to thank the Weavers' Association of Accrington for the start they gave him. That experience gave him the first chance to step into an official position at Ramsbottom in the year 1893, and from there to other positions later on.....One other thing he was connected with when he left Accrington was the calculations classes, and he had been pleased to know that the work of his then was appreciated by the scholars. He took the responsibility of teaching them the calculations of weaving prices, as he believed it was a proper thing that the weavers of the town should take an active interest in the prices and calculations under which they were working. In those days there was no Particulars Clause and all sorts of dodges had been resorted to in order to find out what they were doing...."

[Sidney and Beatrice Webb, state in their 'History of Trade Unionism 1666-1920' p679 that Section 24 of the Factory Act 1891 provides, as regards textile manufactures, that the employer shall supply every worker by the piece with certain particulars as to the quantity of work and rate of remuneration for it.]

"Referring briefly to matters of a more general nature. Sir David said that two years ago the trade union movement in the country went through a bad time. The miners' dispute and the general strike cost the trade union movement a tremendous amount.... and he was afraid they had many years to go before they recovered all they lost in those terrible weeks....."one thing that was costly...was the set back we got in the trade union laws. You know I had some responsibility as the Member for Clitheroe for the 1906 Trades Disputes Act. The position we secured by that Act of Parliament was such that I was proud of it myself and I know the movement was generally. And it was a serious regret to me .....that out of that trouble [the Government] set back the clock as regards the trade union position under the law of this country.....I hope the time will come when it will be recovered." [Applause]

"On Sir Davids' suggestion, three hearty cheers for the health of the Accrington Weavers' Association were given."

David Shackleton was the Darwen Weavers' Secretary, when as the Labour Representation Committee candidate, he was returned to Parliament unopposed in the 1902 Clitheroe Bye-election. The Parliamentary Division included the town of Nelson at that time.

During the Edwardian era, there emerged two groups of working class representatives in Parliament, namely the Labour Party Group and the Trade Union Group, the latter being nicknamed the 'Lib/Labs'.

In Parliament, during the T.U.C's. Trades Disputes Bill which would have reversed the Taff Vale judgement, all hostilities between the two groups were suspended. United action was necessary for the issue at stake was the preservation of Trade Union funds. Shackleton was one of the Labour members appointed to serve on the Standing Committee, to which the Bill had been referred. The Bill was eventually withdrawn, but the following year the Liberal Government introduced a similar Bill which Shackleton helped to pilot through the House.

Shackleton succeeded in maintaining a good relationship between the two Labour Groups and eventually on July 7th. 1908 he presided at the first official meeting of the two groups which numbered 58 members.

In addition to being an M.P. he was elected President of the Weavers' Amalgamation in May 1906, a position he held until December 1910, when he resigned due to taking up a permanent appointment with the Board of Trade. He was an outstanding Edwardian Trade Union leader.[2]

However, the following statement by Shackleton made whilst standing for a local council seat at Lytham St. Annes, reported in the 'Observer', October

9th. 1928, showed how much he had moved to the right.

"In the course of his speech, he flatly denied that he was a Socialist. How in the world that had got into the head of anybody, he said, he did not know. Up to leaving for London and entering Government service, his life had been spent as a trade union leader for the weavers of Lancashire. He had never been a member of, or subscribed to the Socialist programme."

On Saturday October 6th., the Rishton Weavers' Association also celebrated their Jubilee with a trip to Blackpool. It was Rishton's biggest ever organised trip, with 3,063 members and friends enjoying the ideal weather conditions. Three trains made the journey, the first setting out at 12.20 p.m. and the last at 12.50 p.m.. No formal gathering had been arranged, the trippers being free to choose their own amusements. The 'Observer' stated "that they had spent an enjoyable half day and evening was evidenced by the tired but happy expressions of the picnickers when they assembled at the station for the journey home." They returned to Rishton at 1.20 a.m. on Sunday morning.

The officials, members of the committee and the collectors of the Accrington Weavers' Association, enjoyed a delightful outing to Cockerholme and Blackpool, on Sunday October 14th. The 49 strong party left Avenue Parade in two coaches at 1.00 p.m. They were entertained at Mr. J.R. Emmett's expense, to an excellent tea at the Manor House, Cockerholme. At Blackpool, due to the heavy rain, the party did not alight from their coaches. They drove along the front enjoying the illuminations and eventually arrived back in Accrington at 10.30 p.m.

THE COTTON CRISIS, CONTINUED

At the 1928 Labour Party Conference held during the first week of October in Birmingham, the following resolution became Party policy:

"A Labour Government would take in hand the deplorable situation in the Cotton Industry."

"The Labour Party, recognising evils to which over-capitalisation, speculation and excessive cost of distribution and defective organisation have given rise, has unsuccessfully pressed for a Government Inquiry into the problems which confronts the industry."

"A Labour Government would carry into law its factory and other labour measures for immediate improvement of working conditions and would institute a searching investigation with a view to working out a policy for the restoration of the prosperity of the trade."

Mr. Ramsay MacDonald, Party Leader, said:

"We accept this. Of course we may just do a bit of redrafting, but everything that is here will be put in."[Conference Minutes]

On Sunday October 28th., Mr. Andrew Naesmith J.P. gave a speech on the 'Cotton Trade Difficulties', at a meeting organised by the I.L.P. in the Stanley Supporter's Club Rooms. The meeting was presided over by Bill Haworth, [later to become the Communist Convenor of Howard and Bullough Ltd.] of Oswaldtwistle. Mr. Naesmith is reported in the 'Observer' as saying:

"One of the factors was unquestionably the mad gambling and speculation of 1919 and 1920 that was indulged in by financiers and speculators on that side of the industry, and no matter what the cost was efforts must be made to readjust the financial position of those mills that were refloated on watered capital."

"Another effort the industry must make was that of amalgamation in order to secure centralized control and policy and the elimination of all forms of waste that arose from the individualistic basis upon which the industry was run today...."

"The employers had only attempted to solve their problems by curtailment of production, control of prices, proposed reductions in wages and another increasing of working hours. These did not touch the fringe of our difficulties at all, as the problems confronting us were inherent within the industry, which required reorganisation on a scientific basis, modernising our machinery, utilizing co-operative methods for marketing our products, such as was done in Japan and Belgium; and so enabling us to meet the newer methods employed by the newer industries in other countries who were our chief competitors."

The 'Observer', November 27th., published a section of the Half-yearly Report of the Accrington Weavers' Association. It stated:

"The prolonged depression in the cotton industry tenaciously clings to us, and we look around, at times almost despairingly, for signs of a trade revival....."

"An undesirable measure has recently been before Parliament, namely the prolongations of an Act, one section of which enables the Home Secretary to authorise the employment of women and young persons on the two shift system. The measure was first enacted in 1920, the justification advanced for the particular section being that it was merely an emergency provision, which should not operate after 1926. Two years in excess of that period have elapsed and still the iniquitous measure is extended. Its renewal is a serious matter for Lancashire textile operatives who realise the potential evils it engenders, among which is the demoralising effect upon home-life, and the difficulty of proper supervision over factory conditions. It is a retrograde step in labour legislation, which our members should strenuously oppose, and the most effective means of so doing is by returning those to Parliament at the general election next year, who are truly representative of the workers interests."

1929

The 'Observer' February 2nd. 1929, published extracts from the Clayton-Le-Moors Weavers' Association's Half Yearly Report as follows:

"The year 1928 has been one of real disaster so far as the cotton workers of Clayton are concerned. Mills have been closed down and under employment has been rampant during the year. Finally, machinery has been taken out of at least 3 mills, namely: Providence, Albert, and Hyndburn, thereby causing many operatives to seek work in other districts, this being a real hardship to persons who had formerly worked at the above mentioned mills, in some instances from 20 years and upwards."

The Accrington Weavers' Association held a presentation night at Watsons Restaurant on Wednesday evening February 20th. to commemorate the 35 years service as Auditor of Mr. John Jackson Mills. 90 officials and friends were present to see him receive a wallet containing a sum of money. The guest speaker was Mr. Andrew Naesmith, who said:

"There is a greater need to-day for our trades union organisation. There never was a time in the history of our industry when so many deep rooted problems and changes were taking place......."

"We have in front of us today an industry which is languishing unto death. One cannot tell what is going to be the machine that weavers will be running in ten years time in this country. There are such mechanical inventions as the Northrop loom, the Vickery-Stafford loom, the Whittaker automatic loom, the Terry loom, and two or three other different types of looms that are now practical propositions; and there is certainly no weaver here who can be certain that the looms you are running today will in ten years time be the looms you are running then. If you can visualise an ordinary four-loom weaver today with probably ten looms, twenty looms, maybe, perhaps, if I am not too imaginative, forty looms, in ten or twenty years time, you can quite understand the tremendous difference that that is going to make to the life and well-being of the weavers of Lancashire. These changes are here. It is no good closing our eyes to them. The time has gone by for us imitating the ostrich, burying our head in the sands, thinking the winds and the storms and the dangers will pass us by and leave us where we are. We cannot be so foolish. These changes are here, and being here it is your concern and mine to try and understand them, study their implications, ascertain their potentialities and possibilities, and doing that, try and guide these changes of mechanical lines in such a way that while it means less work actually for weavers through the improved mechanical appliances we obtain at the same time in wage remuneration a higher standard of life than we are getting today."

"In conclusion, Mr. Naesmith urged them to think about those things, that each of them could pay their contribution towards the policies they would formulate and operate, so that in times of adversity, as well as of success, they could keep a united front and proceed on that unbroken march towards obtaining a higher rate of wages, a better and a sweeter life, and an opportunity to enjoy the gifts that God had endowed them with."

This speech proves that the General Secretary had given much thought to the future technological development of the industry and could therefore genuinely throw off any attacks from the employers, which might have suggested a Luddite mentality in the stated policies of the Weavers' Amalgamation. Indeed, the actions of the employers would suggest that it was they who were living in the past, and watching the industry die in front of their eyes.

An objective observer however, might also pass the comment that the trade union leadership were being too moderate, in that they had not formulated a policy for the nationalisation of the industry. In addition, it 'sticks out a mile' that they were being too reasonable with the employers, and we know from past experiences [eg. The end of the General Strike.] that such a strategy only 'ends in tears'.

In February, 1929, the Textile Workers' Minority Movement, the Communist Party Pressure Group, published a 20 page pamphlet entitled 'The Struggle of the Lancashire Textile Workers'. It had been compiled by 6 activists including Margaret McCarthy, who emphasised her connection with the Accrington Weavers' Association in its Foreword. The following paragraph shows that there was an alternative policy available:

"It is clear that the workers in the cotton industry can no longer rest on the hope that the good and prosperous times of the past will return. Throughout Lancashire the economic depression during the past eight years has brought poverty and bitter want into the homes of the workers. Unemployment, short time, bad material, and terrible under-employment in the weaving sheds, all these things are showing themselves in the lives of the men and women in every town and village. The cotton workers are finding that they must take a firm stand, and fight - otherwise the aim of the employers to beat the 'competition' of the 'coolie' will be achieved. The prospects before the cotton workers are, on the one hand, to follow the old and useless policy of co-operation, and the weak-kneed leadership of the friends of the employers, and so find themselves back in the dreadful days when the workers of Lancashire toiled in the mills from 6 a.m. for very low wages, or, on the other hand, they can fight against the attacks of the employers, sweep aside the leaders who are standing in the way, and adopt [in the place of the friendship of the cotton masters] the unity of the workers nationally and internationally......"

"In the face of the present attacks the cotton workers must rally their forces in the mills, and join with the Cotton Workers' Minority Movement which is conducting a struggle against capitalist rationalisation and worse conditions in the cotton industry."

The 'Observer' March 2nd., reported that the Clayton-Le-Moors Weavers' Association had nominated Mr. John William Hope, their Secretary, as a Trade Union Candidate in the U.D.C. election. On Monday March 25th., he became a member of the Council when he came second in a contest of nine candidates; four being elected.

DEATH OF GREAT HARWOOD WEAVERS' SECRETARY

A Special Meeting of the Great Harwood Weavers' Association had to be held on Sunday March 10th., due to the death of their Secretary, Mr. Hesmondhalgh. Their Minute Book states:

"2. It was resolved that the Central Committee of the Amalgamation have an invitation to be represented at the funeral and that the whole of the local committee be invited."

"3. That Districts be invited to send representatives."

"4. That the Trades Council and the Textile Trades Federation be invited to send representatives."

The Blackburn Times reported that Great Harwood had lost its "strong silent man of Labour." Apparently he was a man that shunned the limelight, preferring the media of the conference table instead.

Mr. Hesmondhalgh was 63 years of age, and lived at 2 Railway Terrace, in the township. He had left school at the age of ten and entered Victoria Mill as a half timer. After working in the capacity of committee man and later as President, he became the Secretary of the Weavers, Association 28 years ago. He was also the first President of the local Trades and Labour Council, holding the office from 1905 until his death. He was also the first Labour member of the Urban District Council, a seat he had held since 1903, except for a break of 2 years. This led to him becoming the first Labour Chairman of the Council. His wife, two sons and a daughter survived him. ['Blackburn Times' March 16th.1929]

At the Committee Meeting of March 20th., it was agreed that applications be invited for the position of Secretary. On April 23rd., 1929, a Special Committee Meeting interviewed the 3 short listed candidates, namely; Messrs. Kay, of Colne; Walsh, of Wigan; and Hudson of Nelson. All 3 candidates addressed the Committee, after which, it was resolved that Mr. J.W. Hudson be recommended to the position of Secretary. This was endorsed at a Special Members Meeting held on April 25th.

THE COTTON CRISIS, CONTINUED

Accrington was the venue for a special conference of officials and representatives of the textile unions, on Wednesday evening 1st. May 1929, at the new Labour Hall. It was held under the auspices of the United Textile Factory Workers' Association, and was presided over by Mr. J. Helm J.P., Assistant Secretary of the Amalgamated Weavers' Association. Mr. T.H. Richardson of Salford, Mr. Tom Snowden, Prospective Labour Candidate, and Mr. J.R. Emmett J.P., the local Weavers' Secretary made speeches. The Primary purpose of the meeting was to rally the textile workers of the constituency behind Mr. Snowden. Mr. Richardson said:

"I want to make a statement that I don't think has been made before. It is this; that since 1920, the loss of wages to the cotton operatives of Lancashire has been no less than £100 million. They were often told that the cotton trade was in bad straits, but the cotton trade never made more money in the whole of its history than it made in the last nine or ten years."

"Mr. Richardson emphasised this by pointing out that the bank clearings in Manchester last year of £681 millions were twice as much as the bank clearings of Birmingham, Bradford, Bristol, Hull, Leeds,

Leicester, Newcastle, Nottingham and Sheffield put together. Cotton was the most important export trade in the country and one person in five got his living by it directly or indirectly. If the cotton trade was going to give a bad time for 600,000 operatives and a good time for a handful of shareholders and directors, it was time the many got busy and began to talk about the few....."

"There were 8,000 managers and directors to look after the Lancashire cotton trade, and he would say without any fear of contradiction as a man who knew what the cotton trade was, that he could sell all the yarn in Manchester on Friday with the assistance of six clerks. Anybody knew it could be done without those superfluous people. A dying industry could not afford to carry those people about. They had got to go and co-operation would shift them....."

"Mr. Richardson spoke of the decreased use of cotton in England, and submitted that whilst people in Lancashire were waiting for orders there were millions of people in our country going about ill-clad. If the man who made cotton goods had a little more money to spend he might spend a little more on the things he made during the day."

"The speaker suggested rationalisation as a means of getting out of the difficulty. 'Rationalisation,' he said, 'was only another term for order in industry. It would squeeze out those gentlemen who trotted about the boards at the Manchester Exchange, and at one fell swoop would wipe out 400 directors. In other words it would become a system of co-operation, concerns would buy their supplies of various requirements through a central buying agency and it would do away with all the surplus men. There would be a direct selling agency....."

"There would be a lot of men thrown out of work by rationalisation; that was inevitable. Inefficient mills would be closed and for a period there would be great difficulties, but he thought that by a sound system of unemployment policy, by a curtailing of entrants into the industry at one end and pensioning old workers at the other end at a decent pension of £2 per week, as suggested by the Turner/ Melchett conference, he felt sure they could get over the worst consequences of unemployment through rationalisation."

".......He believed that the cotton trade would save itself when the cotton operatives of Lancashire had a political conscience and understood that Parliament could not only help but could be compelled to help immediately they woke up and sent the right people to the House of Commons." [Applause]

Mr. Emmett backed up Mr. Richardson's ideas by saying the following:

> "There are too many middlemen and directors, and he thought everybody must agree it was time there was something done to bring about some kind of reorganisation. They had too many parasites living on the cotton trade, and no industry could stand that. He did not think there was any industry in the world with the number of parasites living on it that they had in the cotton trade. People were making money who had never seen a loom or a spindle, and while that state of affairs went on the cotton trade would go lower and lower. He believed there was no alternative to the resolution which he proposed ":

> "This conference welcomes the support of the Labour Party to the policy advocated on behalf of the cotton trade, and pledges itself to support the Labour candidates at the next election."

The 'Observer' 1st. June, reported that Tom Snowden had gained the Accrington Parliamentary seat for the Labour Party, defeating Mr. Hugh Edwards, Liberal by 2,226 votes.

The Church and Oswaldtwistle Weavers' Association's Half Yearly Report, published in the 'Observer', June 15th., again paints a gloomy picture.

> "In reviewing the state of the cotton trade since we issued our last report, we regret to say that another mill in our area has closed down, namely, Brookside Mill and this now makes a total of 1800 looms being idle. Church Bridge Mill has been gutted and the looms broken up, and Bridge Street Mill has been sold, with the result that the looms are being removed in order to allow the new owners [Messrs. Hepworth and Webster, lithographic printers] to install their own plant."

At their meeting reported in the 'Observer', June 22nd., the Secretary, Mr. Wolstenholme, announced his resignation after 26 1/2 years service. His place was taken by Mr. W. Hughes, the former Assistant Secretary.

Meanwhile the Committee of the Great Harwood Weavers' Association at their meeting of June 19th. agreed that:

> "In view of the proposed reductions of wages threatened by the employers in the cotton trade, this Association calls upon the government to immediately institute an enquiry into the best methods of improving them, in accordance with the demands for such an enquiry by the cotton operatives." [Minute Book]

The Accrington Weavers' Association's Half Yearly Report backs up the ideas stated at the Special Conference held in the Labour Hall, on May 1st. 1929.

> "The position of the industry is truly critical, and no vested

interests should be allowed to stand in the way of its recovery. Why then, can we not have, as the Textile Unions and the Labour Party have so persistently advocated, a full impartial Government inquiry into the entire ramifications of the industry, when all the facts and figures would be brought into the daylight of publicity, and a scheme of re-organisation ultimately evolved for the eradication of chaos, and suffering, and the substitution, therefore, of industrial peace and prosperity?"

At their meeting, reported in the 'Observer' June 22nd., a further attack by the employers on the working conditions of the operatives was considered. The employers just wanted more and more from the workers whilst giving less in return. It would appear that they wanted an extra 15 minutes weaving for no extra money. During the Saturday morning shift, the mill engines had kept going until 11.45 a.m. instead of the 11.30 a.m. shut down. Mr. Emmett's advice was as follows:

"We don't want any trouble", said Mr. Emmett, "but we think it is one of the meanest things the employers could attempt to do -[Hear, Hear]- and our weavers can kill it the very first week if they will only do what they ought to do. That half hour from 11.30 to twelve o'clock is supposed to be for cleaning purposes and what I want you to do - and to inform others to do on Saturday - is at 11.30 to stop your looms and begin cleaning. The engines won't run the Saturday following if you will only do that the first week......"Pointing out that the introduction of sweepers had probably something to do with the matter, Mr. Emmett said that at two or three mills in Oswaldtwistle the weavers paid about 3d a loom for cleaning, and he supposed the employers came to the conclusion that they could run until 11.45 a.m. If one employer could do a certain thing an employer in another place thought he was justified in doing the same. In Accrington last Saturday, two firms with 4 or 5 mills ran until a quarter to twelve."

"Mr. Emmett again urged all weavers to stop their looms at 11.30 on Saturday. If it was possible, they did not want any trouble at present, because they were going to be in trouble before very long whether they wanted it or not. They all knew that the employers were considering a reduction in wages because trade was ruined and everything was going worse, and the only thing that would save it [from the employers point of view] was the employees working 25% off the list price. The employers knew as well as he did that if they insisted on a reduction in wages there would be a fight."

The Great Harwood Weavers conducted a ballot. The question asked was:
"Are you prepared to cease work rather than submit to a reduction of the Standard Piece List Price Rates by 25%?"
The result was:

In favour of ceasing work	Against	Spoiled
3,943	249	58

In the Amalgamation as a whole 96.17% were in favour. [Minute Book July 10th.]

On Tuesday July 16th. the 'Observer' Editorial stated:

"As everyone anticipated the Operative Spinners' Amalgamation the first of the three big textile unions to take a ballot on the question of ceasing work on July 27th. rather than accept the proposed reduction of 12.82% has voted solidly for a stoppage. The votes against acceptance were 97.45%.

"There can be no doubt that the ballots now being taken by the Weavers' Amalgamation and the Cardroom Amalgamation will be equally divisive. The attitude of both employer and the operatives affords exceedingly little hope of any accommodation between the two sides. And yet no one - except perhaps Lancashire's foreign rivals - wants to see a lockout, and it would be a great relief to see a compromise reached...........it would be strange indeed if a Labour government were to let a situation such as is now developing go by default."

The Operative Spinners' Amalgamation held a representative meeting in Manchester on Monday August 5th. 1929, to receive the result of the district meetings on the question of empowering the Executive "to negotiate the best terms possible, such terms, when obtained, to be submitted to a special representative meeting."

The delegates representing all the districts voted by a show of hands not to empower the Executive to negotiate. No future meeting was arranged.

In the summer of 1929, the Egyptian and American sectors of the spinning industry and both the home and export sectors of the weaving side experienced a slump in trade. The employers demanded that their request for a wage reduction of 25% off list prices and an increase in hours to 52.5 per week be accepted by the operatives.

Andrew Bullen writes:

"The request was essentially an hours one because some employers at least believed wages were already too low and the extension of the working week would cheapen production without lowering the operatives living standards. The operatives' leaders were always ready to discuss ways of making the industry more profitable and were already taking part in joint discussions to bring this about, but on these proposals for hours and wages there was outright rejection. If the employers wanted to attack not only the operatives wages but their quality of life again, they would have to do it by force." [3]

THE LOCKOUT BEGINS

This the employers did, when on July 27th.1929, they announced a lockout of any operative not willing to accept the new terms.

At a Special Committee Meeting of Great Harwood Weavers held on July 29th, the following was agreed:

> "1. The representatives reported that all the mills were stopped and therefore 100% were out in accordance with the decision of the ballot.
>
> 2. That we be represented at the Special General Council Meeting at Bury on Tuesday 30th. July, by R. Wardell, J. Dunn, J. Birchett and the Secretary.
>
> 3. That we congratulate the Central Committee on their stand in the recent negotiations with the employers and that we support the request for the dispute to be submitted to an Industrial Court." [Minute Book]

On August 1st.,a Special Meeting for the entire membership was held in the Mercer Hall, Great Harwood, at 2.00p.m.. There was a crowded attendance and the members were addressed by Councillor P.L. Taylor of Preston. He spoke on the cotton situation and was thanked for a splendid address. The Secretary reported the deliberations of the Special Amalgamation Meeting, held at Bury, Tuesday 30th. July, which included the details of the negotiations with the employers. It was resolved:

> "That we accept the report, and endorse the action of the Central Committee, in refusing to negotiate a reduction of wages and asking for the dispute to be submitted to arbitration."

In Accrington, Church, and Oswaldtwistle, the workers were on holiday but the mills were closed to them on Monday August 5th. The 'Observer', August 3rd., reported that all the 10 mills in Rishton were idle and that the Weavers' Association were distributing benefits to their 1,900 members. In Clayton-Le-Moors, the lockout was being enforced at the four mills in the town that had remained running.

The paper further announced that the Prime Minister, Ramsay

MacDonald, had appointed a Committee of Inquiry, to look into the operation of the cotton industry. The Committee comprised:

Mr. William Graham, President of the Board of Trade [Chairman],
Mr. A. V. Alexander, First Lord of the Admiralty,
Sir Alan G. Anderson, Director of Messrs Anderson, Green, and Co. Ltd.
Mr. Joseph Jones, Secretary of the Yorkshire Mine Workers' Association, and
Sir William McLintock, of Messrs. Thompson, McLintock and Co., Chartered Accountants.

The Committee's terms of reference were:

"To consider and report upon the present condition and prospects of the cotton industry, and to make a recommendation as to any action which may appear desirable and practicable in order to improve the position of this industry in the markets of the world."

The 'Observer', August 6th., reported that at Accrington; Albion, Wellington, Royal, and Perseverance [Huncoat] Mills, the employers had agreed to pay the old rates and so remained open. 600 operatives were employed at these mills.

The majority of mills however, were not prepared to pay the old rates, and so the operatives refused to enter the sheds. Blacklegs went into one or two mills, accompanied by jeers from the pickets, but at none of these establishments did the engines run very long, as none of the union members resumed work. Altogether, not counting the mills regarded as permanently closed, 23 mills were stopped in the town.

Long queues stretching from the union's offices in Wellington Street, back into Cotton Street, lasted all Monday morning as members waited to have their cards checked and numbered to facilitate the payment of stoppage benefit on Thursday and Friday. This amounted to £1 for trade scale members and 18s. for death scale members.

Mr. Emmett said:

"Our people know how things stand, and they are all standing loyal, which I felt sure they would do. There is no fear of any dissension in our ranks in Accrington, either amongst the weavers or any of the operatives in the textile trades, including overlookers, twisters, tapers, warehousemen, etc."

At Church and Oswaldtwistle, a couple of mills did not open, the owners realising the strength of feeling amongst the operatives. However, at Paddock Mill, 20 of the 70 weavers accepted the wage cut and went into work. The owners also managed to cajole a tackler, a twister and a warehouseman to join them from the firms other factory, Fern Mill at Duckworth Hall. By noon the situation had become general knowledge and the police, a number of pickets and a hostile crowd assembled. By 4.30 p.m. a crowd of over 1,000 had assembled outside the mill in Moscow Mill Street. When the engines stopped at 5.15 p.m. the group of weavers were greeted with abusive shouts. The 'Observer' reported that:

> "Mr. Westwell, the head of the firm, placed his car at the disposal of a few of the weavers who lived in the Spring Hill district, and the car went off to cries couched in approbious(sic) terms. A section of the crowd followed the car, and assembling round the homes of the weavers indulged in lusty hooting, but the presence of the police prevented further demonstrations."

> "Two young women weavers who live near Oswaldtwistle Town Hall were followed by another large section, who hooted them all the way. They too were escorted by police constables."

The firm decided that due to the reaction of the crowd, the mill would not open on the Tuesday.

The area covered by the Church and Oswaldtwistle Weavers' Association included 4 mills that had been closed for some considerable time, and these contained 1,794 looms. Until Monday, 13,651 looms were normally worked. Approximately 4,000 adult workers were affected by the dispute and of these 3,300 were members of the Weavers' Association and 357 members of the Spinners' Union. Payments of stoppage benefit were paid at the Weavers Institute on Wednesday and Thursday starting at 9 a.m. and continuing straight through until 7 p.m.

At Clayton-Le-Moors no operatives were working and every mill was standing idle. The Clayton-Le-Moors Weavers' Association had 1,300 members.

A further Special Meeting of all the members of the Great Harwood Weavers was held in the Mercer Hall on Wednesday August 14th. 1929, at 2.00 p.m. The members were addressed by Mr. W.J. Tout J.P., and members of the Central Committee of the Amalgamation, who spoke on the Cotton Inquiry. At the end of the Meeting the Secretary moved the following recommendation:

> "That we pay benefits to all our members up to and including August 24th. 1929 [On account of the Holidays] whether the dispute is ended or not."

Mr. W. Slynn seconded and it was carried unanimously. There were 1,200 present and after the meeting, members danced until 5.30 p.m.

'The Cotton Lockout Special', issued by the Communist Party's Manchester District Committee, a double sided A3 size newspaper priced 1/2d, dated August 14th, 1929, contained this prophetic article:

> **"The Arbitration Swindle Is Being Prepared.**
> **Fellow-Workers, Beware!**

"The leaders of the unions have declared their willingness to put the dispute to arbitration. This is the cue to the employers. Already the deputy-chairman of the Lancashire Cotton Corporation has declared for arbitration. The other employers' reply is expected to-day."

"This means our complete betrayal. We cotton operatives stand simply for no reductions. It is a foregone conclusion that arbitration will involve a cut. Fellow-workers, stand firm against the trickery of arbitration."

In the 'Cotton Lockout Special' dated August 17th, 1929, the headline was:

Arbitration Betrayal Now A Fact.

"At last it has taken place as we Communists confidently predicted. The cotton textile workers have been betrayed. Thursday's meeting, marked, in the words of the Manchester Guardian, with 'much friendliness,' 'extreme cordiality,' 'cheerfulness and immense relief' between 'masters and men,' decided upon arbitration......"

"But, and this is the most important thing - not only have the trade union officials betrayed the workers at this point, but it is practically decided that in future all major questions of disputes which threaten to lead to a stoppage of the mills shall be referred to arbitration. What is more, MacDonald's henchman, Sir Horace Wilson, has proposed the establishment of a permanent joint committee, under an 'independent' chairman, in order to facilitate this......"

The front page also had an article concerning Accrington:

Accrington Workers Welcome Communist Lead.

"Meetings held at Accrington during the week have seen great approval given to the Communist Party. At one meeting a group of Labour Party supporters were asked to put forward their case when the speaker had finished. The way in which the Labourites dodged the issue and fled from the meeting caused great amusement in the crowd. These Labour Party Goliaths, while refusing to question or debate on the Communist policy, have yet threatened to hold a meeting some days hence, 'when you Communists aren't there!'"

The lockout lasted for 3 weeks. On the 19th. August work was resumed at the old wage rates awaiting arbitration. The employers had accepted arbitration after pressure had been exerted by the Ministry of Labour and the Prime Minister; and the unions were happy to go to arbitration because they thought they had an excellent case to put before the Arbitration Board.

Practically all the cotton operatives returned to work in the Accrington District. Of 23 mills closed down, two mills, Messrs. W. F. Chambers and Sons, Ellesmere and No.2 Victoria Mills failed to re-open. The reason given was that the firm had some warps out at those mills.

Mr. J.R. Emmett said to the 'Observer':

"There is a fairly general feeling of satisfaction amongst the operatives at the way in which the lockout has been cleared up."

Commenting on the probable outcome of the arbitration process he said:

"We believe our case is sufficiently strong to show that nothing can be gained to trade by reducing weavers wages. If nothing results out of this except a settlement of wages, it will, in my opinion, be a very poor end to the whole thing. I hope something in the shape of re-organisation will show itself either from the arbitrators' report, or the Commission which has been set up. There has been probably £2,000,000 spent in connection with the dispute by the employers and the operatives combined, but if some scheme of re-organisation is produced it will be money well spent. On the other hand if nothing but the question of wages is settled and the cotton trade is allowed to drift as it has been doing, it will simply have been money wasted."

The sound financial position of the Accrington Weavers' Association was not seriously affected by the payment of £7,000 in benefits during the dispute. Half of this amount was refunded from the Weavers' Amalgamation.

The mills that had been working prior to the dispute at Clayton-Le-Moors, opened their doors, but it was estimated that it would take a week or two to re-instate all the operatives.

A full resumption of work did not take place at Church and Oswaldtwistle. Hippings Vale Spring Mill, and the Commercial and Stanhill Mills of T. Bradley Ltd., did not re-open. A notice on the door of Hippings Vale abruptly stated that "This mill will not resume on Monday morning August 19th." No mention was made about when it would re-open. In the case of Commercial and Stanhill Mills notices stated that they would re-open on the 26th. August.

THE DECISION OF THE ARBITRATION BOARD

On the evening of August 22nd. 1929, the Board of Arbitration gave its award, which deeply shocked the weavers side. All reasonable people had thought that the award would come down in favour of the weavers. The weavers knew that previous reductions had not resulted in a recovery within the industry and they believed, correctly, that the reduction under discussion would not produce an upturn in trade. Even on the employers own admission the reductions were not sufficient to alter the trading position. The weavers had been convinced that any arbitrator who seriously considered the case would reject any reductions in wages and in addition would recommend a reorganisation of the way the industry was run. Andrew Bullen says:

"Even when it was discovered that the chairman of the Arbitration Board was ex-Conservative M.P., Mr. Justice Rigby-Swift, who had been responsible for the gaoling of prominent communists, their belief in the eventual outcome favouring them was unshaken. Unfortunately, their faith proved to be totally unfounded, and any idea of the usefulness or fairness of Arbitration lost completely. Mr. Rigby-Swift, who hadn't made a note during the proceedings, suddenly stopped the hearing on the second day and asked the two sides to settle it themselves by compromising on the amount of a reduction, he undertaking to make the Award of the Court what they agreed."

"After all," he said, "you do not want us five strangers to settle it for you."

"The weavers were stunned, their well reasoned case it was being suggested was to be ignored in favour of the crude method of splitting the difference. Unable to agree to the Chairman's proposal, they called for a properly considered award by the Court based on the facts, but forced to continue the hearing, Rigby-Swift merely imposed what he'd suggested the two sides should agree. Wages were to come down by half the amount the employers had asked for, irrespective of the merits of the case." [4]

The 'Observer' August 24th., stated that the reduction represented a wage cut of 1s.3d. in the £, rather than the 2s.6.5d that the employers had demanded. The reduction amounted to a saving of £60,000 per week from the wage bill of the 500,000 operatives affected.

Mr. Andrew Naesmith, said that he was very sore about the result, and that if he said anything else, it might not help matters. The 'Observer' quoted Mr. J.R. Emmett, as saying:

"I am very dissatisfied with the award. I expect the biggest part of our members will be sorely disappointed, because I think they realise that their wages were as low as it was possible for anybody to live off decently. It will be a bitter disappointment to all our people because we fully expected that weavers', winders', and warpers' wages would not be affected in any shape or form. How on earth they are going to improve anything with it, I don't know. I am satisfied that this reduction in wages will have a bad effect on the operatives in the sense that it will discourage them...... In all fairness, we shall have to accept the arbitration, seeing that we have put our signatures to it, but what troubles me is that nothing appears to have come out of the arbitration which is likely to improve matters. If the trade is to be allowed to go on and drift as it has been doing this last few years - well, all this money that has been spent is going to be simply wasted."

Referring to Mr. Justice Rigby-Swift's Statement, "that the Board of Arbitration were not charged with the reorganisation of the industry, a task which had been undertaken by the Sub-Committee of Civil Research," Mr. Emmett commented:

"There is no doubt that the whole industry wants reorganising from top to bottom. There are too many people living out of the cotton trade who know nothing about it except being able to make a living out of it. When you can manufacture a yard of cloth, say, for 1s., and pay all the expenses and wages and have a decent profit for the employer, and when that yard of cloth is sold in London at 4s.11d, and 5s. - what we are anxious to know is where that 3s.or 4s. margin goes between leaving the mill and landing in the houses of the consumer. There might have been something to say for the reduction if our people had all been in full work, but seeing that we have - I think it is safe to say - 60% of our workpeople earning nothing like full wages, and no chance of earning full wages, the reduction is a bitter disappointment."

Asked if he thought the reduction in wages would have the effect of improving trade, Mr. Emmett replied:

"I don't think it will make an iota of difference, and I think the majority of the employers know that it won't. There will have to be something different altogether to that before they can hope to sell their cloth any cheaper. There are too many people between manufacturer and consumer to do any good, and the amount of the reduction will be swallowed up long before any benefit which it might give can reach the consumer and the manufacturers know it, if they would only speak their mind."

In the Accrington District Messrs. W.F. Chambers and Sons', Ellesmere No.1 and No.2 Mills, together with Messrs. T. Haworth and Sons', Scaitcliffe Mill had been closed all week.

At the Great Harwood Weavers' Association's Quarterly Meeting held on September 11th. 1929, Minute 7 states:

"There was a general expression of dissatisfaction at the terms of the award of the Arbitration Court, and it was eventually resolved:

"That this meeting of members of the Great Harwood Weavers', Winders' and Beamers' Association, expresses its profound dissatisfaction at the terms of the award of the Court of Arbitration, that we consider the wages of weavers, winders and beamers were already low, and we therefore instruct our committee to promote or support any attempt to immediately improve the wages of our members." [Minute Book]

The 'Observer' of the 28th. September, carried a report of the Rishton Weavers' Association meeting at which dissatisfaction was expressed with the terms of the award from the Court of Arbitration.

The Textile Minority Movement published a further pamphlet in early 1930 entitled 'Women and the more Loom System'. In this document is a scathing attack on the Arbitration Courts and the Labour Government:

"In our difficulties many of us eagerly looked forward to the coming of the 'second Labour Government' as a means of overcoming our difficulties. The Labour Party had stated prior to the General Election that there was no need for Lancashire workers to suffer wage reductions. Many workers thought in May 1929 that if the Labour Party were successful in the General Election, and a Labour Government was set up, that our conditions would be very much improved. Within one month after the Labour Government was formed, and the ink hardly dry on the Labour Party leaflets promising no wage reductions, the cotton employers posted lock-out notices demanding 12.5% wage cuts. One of the first acts of the new government was to break its solemn promise to Lancashire workers, by setting up an Arbitration Court, which inflicted heavy cuts in our wages. This same government has attacked the workers in other industries in the same way......[They] have all suffered reductions in wages and worsened conditions as a result of Labour Government Arbitration."

HOURS OF WORK

The 'Observer' of Saturday, November 16th. reported that the Accrington and District Cotton Employers' Association wanted to alter the hours worked by their operatives. They wanted a 7.00 a.m. start instead of the existing 7.45 a.m. and they had issued ballot papers in order to move progress on the matter. The suggested hours were as follows:

                7.00 a.m. - 8.30. a.m.   7.00 a.m. - 8.30 a.m.
Week-days 9.00 a.m. - 12.30 p.m. Saturdays 9.00 a.m. - 11.15 a.m.
                1.30 p.m. - 5.15 p.m.   11.15a.m.-11.45 a.m.[For cleaning]

On Tuesday November 19th. the 'Observer' reported that the North East Lancashire Card and Blowing Room Operatives' Association had passed the

following resolution:
"that we recommend our members to vote against the employers suggestion of a 7.00 a.m. start and in favour of the present working hours."

The result of the ballot, taken by the Textile Trades Federation among the cotton operatives of Accrington, Clayton-Le-Moors, and Church and Oswaldtwistle, respecting the proposal of the Employers' Association were printed in the 'Observer' of November 30th. Only 333 operatives voted in favour and 7,551 voted against. In other words an adverse vote of 96%. The result was forwarded to the Employers for their further consideration. This issue crops up again at the end of 1932, and the beginning of 1933.

THE COTTON CRISIS, CONTINUED

Mr. Andrew Naesmith made a speech at Colne, on Monday evening December 2nd. In it he explained that the Amalgamation was trying to get included in the new Bill, introduced by Miss Margaret Bondfield, the Labour Minister, a clause which would give compensation for under employment. The 'Observer' went on :

"Mr. Naesmith said the feeling of textile operatives today was very sore and very strong. The feeling emanated from the deep sense of injustice which gripped them all at the miserable earnings textile operatives were getting for their services to the industry. They had lately had a cut of 6.41% from their wages, which was granted by the Arbitration Court,..... He made bold to say that the increase in production had not materialised; that there were looms now idle that were idle before the reduction in wages; and that before the end of this year there would be still more looms stopped in consequence of the depression and contraction which was taking place within the industry. The only effect of the Arbitration Court award had been to impoverish textile operatives without having stimulated or increased the demand for textile cloth which they were all so anxious to produce."

Under Employment

"In addition to the problem of unemployment from which they were suffering, there was still the more pressing problem of under-employment, which every weaver at some time or other experienced. He did not know of anything in the incidence of their work-a-day life that was so harassing, and caused so much feeling and resentment, as being on the employers' premises 48 hours a week, and at the end of it only having 50, 75, or 80% of their normal wages. The declared policy of textile weavers was to make an effort to obtain equity and justice, and to remove this problem from their work-a-day life. They were making two approaches with that end in view. They had approached the Minister of Labour with a view to her inclusion in her Bill, which was going through the Committee Stage in the House of Commons, of Clauses that would enable textile operatives so affected to receive some benefit from the State...... So far as weavers were concerned, they were determined that within the scope of insurance legislation there should be some Clauses that would ensure for them certain benefits from unemployment insurance and compensate them for periods of under-employment.[Applause]"

Employers Responsibility

"They said that whilst there was legislative responsibility on any Government to compensate citizens and workers who suffered in the way that textile operatives were doing, an equally grave responsibility rested upon the employers. The latter had a contract with them which was binding on both sides. The employers' responsibility was to see that the looms which they contracted to run, and which belonged to them, should be supplied with warps and weft in order that weavers could fulfil their functions, and at the end of a week, on a calculated price of the cloth woven, they would get a declared amount of money. They wanted to say to the employers that where a weaver was on their premises 48 hours a week there should be at the end of that time a 48 hour wage. It was not sufficient, either from the standard of equity, justice, or common sense, for weavers to come out at the end of 48 hours with 50% of their normal earnings. That condition ought to be ended, and ended quickly. He only hoped that there was going to be behind them sufficient public opinion and informed judgement that would strengthen their hands in order that they could, with reasonable arguments and with the conviction of the justice of their case, persuade, or force, if necessary, the employers to concede them some compensation as a charge upon the industry for the loss that the workers sustained in consequence of their looms and machinery being stopped."

Light & Common Sense

"Mr. Naesmith asked: "Is it not time a little light and common sense is thrown upon this problem of ours?"...... They could not expect men and women outside the county to understand properly what was going on in Lancashire. He knew there were some towns in the county where the distress, poverty, and misery was as great as in any of the mining villages or towns of the country, and the sooner the nation and the public was roused to a consciousness of their actual conditions the better it would be for all men and women within the State. **This business was not the concern of the workers only; it was the concern of those who employed them and who owned the means of production. It was the business of Cabinet Ministers and Parliament, who were responsible for the scientific organisation of society."**['Observer' December 7th]

The Half Yearly Meeting of the Accrington and District Weavers' Association was held on Tuesday the 10th. December at the Co-operative Assembly Rooms, Oak Street. The chief item under discussion was the Weavers' Amalgamation Ballot on whether to strike in support of a 25% wage increase. Mr. Emmett had this to say:

"Dealing with the preliminary matters, Mr. Emmett said that after the publication of the Arbitration Courts decision the officials would not have been as much upset about it if they had thought it would have had a tendency to improve trade. The cut, although it was big enough, would not have been felt to the extent that it was being if everybody was on full work, but, unfortunately in Accrington they had nearly 50% of their members who were not having full work."

"Referring more particularly to the Amalgamation's application for a 25% advance in wages, Mr. Emmett said that one could see things were not quite as favourable as they might be for a strike. They were all anxious to have a fight for better wages, and they knew their wages as weavers were very low indeed, but when they were talking about a strike they had to consider where they were going, and whether there was any possibility of winning. The people who had studied the cotton trade minutely must come to the conclusion that sooner or later the cotton trade would have to be re-organised. It could not keep on as it was now for ever. During the past 5 years they had had 5,800 looms stopped in Accrington, probably never to start again, and there was a likelihood of more looms being stopped before very long...... There were a lot of mills running to-day that were not worth running, and if those could be closed down, and provision made for the people who were going to be thrown out of work, it might benefit the industry. If something was not done in that direction those mills were automatically going to close down, with no provision whatever made for the workers, except being thrown on the Labour Exchange."

Accrington Resolution Turned Down

"They did not know what the Government Cotton Enquiry,

which was being held at present, would bring forth. They hoped it would do something to help to put the cotton trade on a business-like footing. Every effort should be made to try to put it on a financial and sound basis, and if a strong committee of employers' and operatives' representatives could meet and a reasonable scheme put to them, he believed it would be possible to come to some understanding. The Accrington Weavers' Association, said Mr. Emmett, had sent a resolution to the Amalgamation asking for the question of the 25% advance in wages, and the question of a 'fall back' wage of 7s. 6d. per loom on looms standing idle, to be adjourned until the report of the cotton enquiry was issued, but the motion was lost."

Money Required In Future

"The Accrington Weavers' Committee had studied the question of the ballot from every stand-point, and they believed the members ought not to vote for a strike at the present moment. They believed there would come a more opportune time,....... Whilst they were prepared to do everything possible to try to get an increase in wages to the benefit of their members, they realised that if they spent all their money on this particular occasion the time was not very far distant when they would need the same money to spend in another direction. Within a very few months they would be faced with all sorts of ideas about automatic looms. When automatics came there were going to be some big changes, and if they had no money behind them they could not help to direct those changes."

Attitude Of Other Sections

"Referring to the doubtful attitude of other sections of the trade in the event of a strike, Mr. Emmett said: "If we had to say definitely we should come out on strike it is very questionable whether the other sections would be unanimous in coming out along with us. And if they did not, things would soon get into chaos. The officials of your Association will vote unanimously against a strike, and we are anxious that you should do the same."['Observer' December 14th. 1929]

1930

THE DEATH OF MR. JOHN W. HUDSON

At the Great Harwood Weavers' Special Meeting of January 8th. 1930, the President made reference to the serious condition of the Secretary's health and it was resolved:

"to convey to his wife and daughter their earnest hope for an early and complete recovery to health and strength and a speedy resumption of his normal activities."[Minute Book]

However, on January 12th., the Committee heard the Chairman announce the death of their Secretary, John W. Hudson, and as a token of respect to his memory all stood in silence. The minutes read as follows:

"1. That we tender to J. Cross our appreciation of his work during the illness of our Secretary.

2. That E. Hothersall and T.H. Seed act as temporary secretaries, and that their remuneration be £3 per week.

5. That we arrange and finance the funeral of our late Secretary.

6. That all officials be invited to attend and be paid for lost time.

8. That we ask the management of the mills to arrange to stop for a short time to enable members to pay a last tribute to our Secretary."

At their Committee Meeting of January 13th. 1930, it was decided to invite the Social Democratic Federation to be represented at Mr. Hudson's funeral.

On Saturday January 18th., the 'Observer' ran the following report of the funeral together with biographical details:

"Mr. Hudson only served 9 months [In his capacity as Secretary]. He died of pneumonia at his home 29 Arthur Street, Great Harwood, on Sunday. He was 38 years old."

"Before succeeding the late Mr. Hesmondhalgh at Great Harwood, Mr. Hudson held a responsible clerical post with the Nelson Weavers' Association. He was originally a member of the Weavers' Association in his native town of Padiham, where he was also a worker on behalf of the Social Democratic Federation. He moved to Nelson at the beginning of 1920 and became identified with the I.L.P. acting as Educational Secretary and Organiser of the Burnley and Nelson Federation."

"In 1921, Mr. Hudson was elected to the Executive of the Nelson Weavers' Association, and in 1924 contested Southfield Ward in the Labour interest, being defeated by 43 votes. For 12 months he was the Chairman of the Nelson Labour Party."

"In 1925 he organised a campaign for the Nelson Weavers' Association against non-unionists, and subsequently was engaged in organisation work for the Textile Trades Federation at Barnoldswick and also in Manchester."

"Striking scenes marked the funeral of Mr. Hudson at Great

Harwood on Wednesday. The main streets were lined with people, and 4 mills closed during the progress of the funeral, whilst in other factories permission was given to those operatives who desired to attend, to absent themselves from work."

"The hearse was preceded by about 100 persons, including representatives of the Weavers' Association office staff at Great Harwood, Nelson Weavers' Association, Great Harwood I.L.P., Manchester Weavers' Association, Great Harwood S.D.F., Great Harwood Trades and Labour Party, Great Harwood Textile Trades Federation, Great Harwood Overlookers' Association, North Lancashire Labour College, Blackburn Division of the I.L.P. Council, Great Harwood Textile Warehousemen and Padiham Weavers' Association. There was also a strong deputation from the Amalgamated Weavers' Association."

"The service in the house was conducted by Councillor R. Bland of Nelson I.L.P. and Mr. E. Sandman M.P. for Kirkdale and Chairman of the No.9 I.L.P. Council conducted the last rites at the graveside.."

THE COTTON CRISIS, CONTINUED

Meanwhile in the same issue of the 'Observer', happier news for the weavers was forthcoming with the announcement that Mr. Jonathan Ashworth of 102 Harwood Road, Rishton, and Secretary of the Rishton Weavers' Association had been appointed a Justice of the Peace.

The decision of the Arbitration Court of August 1929, had caused the weavers great resentment. Many activists in other districts organised resolutions of protest which were debated by the General Council of the Amalgamation during September 1929. Some wanted the Amalgamation to secede from the Northern Counties Textile Trades Federation and the United Textile Factory Workers' Association. However, the proposal to apply for an immediate 25% increase was eventually accepted.

Negotiations were entered into with the employers on November 12th 1929, when the application for an increase of 25% in list rates, plus a fall-back rate of 7s. 6d. for any stopped looms was made. A negative reply was received, which then caused the General Council to take a ballot of its members regarding strike action. The attitude of the Accrington Weavers Executive Committee which was against strike action was overwhelmingly defeated in the national ballot. The result published in the 'Observer', Tuesday January 28th. 1930 was as follows:

For Strike Action	92,142
Against	43,531
Returned Blank	8,523
Spoiled Papers	173
Papers Not Returned	19,631

Even though a clear majority supported strike action the General Council decided that action would not be taken for the time being.

On February 4th., the 'Observer' reported the retirement of Mr. Robert Kay, the General Secretary of the North East Lancashire Card and Blowing Room Operatives and Ring Spinners Association. His resignation took effect from March 15th., which was his 70th. birthday. He had completed 18 years service in the post. Practically all of his working life had been associated with the Association. The meeting accepted his resignation with regret and placed on record their high appreciation of his past services

His successor, reported in the 'Observer' March 15th., was Mr. Herbert Potts, of 11 Esther Place, Bacup. He was originally from Denton, and although only 29 years of age, he had been President of the Bacup Association for the previous 10 years. He was the first Secretary of the Bacup Borough Labour Party and he had served the Stacksteads Labour Party, resigning both positions in November 1929.

Mr. Potts remained as secretary to the union until 1942, when it became known that he had been fraudulently converting money from the union into his own pocket. He was up on 5 charges of fraudulent conversion of Association money all in 1941, and there was a further charge of falsification of accounts on December 31st. 1940. He had stated that the worth of the local Association was £3,158..11s..9d., whereas in fact it was nil. He had been taking the money over a period stretching back to 1934. He was given a sentence of 18 months imprisonment. ['Observer' 18th. April 1942]

APPOINTMENT OF MR. J.W. SUNDERLAND

At the Great Harwood Weavers meeting of January 29th., the following advert was compiled, which was to appear in the Daily Herald, The Cotton Factory Times, and the Local Journal.

"Weavers Association, Town Hall Street, Great Harwood. Applications are invited for the position of Secretary from members or officials of any Society connected with the Weavers' Amalgamation. Applicants to state age, experience, or any other qualification, and apply in own handwriting to Mr. P. Williamson, President, at the above address, not later than first post 17/2/30. Wages £5..5s. per week. Applications to be endorsed 'Secretaryship'."

At their meeting of February 18th., it was resolved:

"That we allow 5s. plus expenses to the eleven candidates sitting for examination and that Mr.Naesmith be appointed examiner and be paid £1 for his services."

The meeting of February 25th. agreed that Messrs. Sunderland, Titherington and Thornton be invited to appear before the Committee at 7.00 p.m. Thursday February 27th. At that meeting, the three candidates addressed the Committee and it was resolved:

"That we recommend to the Quarterly Meeting of the Members that Mr. J.W. Sunderland of Todmorden be appointed Secretary of the Association."

The Quarterly Meeting of March 5th. endorsed the Executive's decision and Mr. Sunderland commenced work on March 17th. 1930. The Union bought the property 29 Arthur Street for £470 and rented it out to the Secretary at the weekly rental of 11s.9d. inclusive of rates. [Minute Book April 2nd.1930]

THE COTTON CRISIS, CONTINUED

On March 25th., the 'Observer' reported the death of Mr. J.W. Ogden, President of the Weavers' Amalgamation. He was a resident of Heywood but he worked in the Amalgamation's Head Office, in Accrington. At their meeting of July 16th., the Great Harwood Weavers arranged for a framed photograph of Mr. Ogden to be hung in their Headquarters.

On Saturday March 29th, the General Council of the Weavers' Amalgamation decided to oppose the introduction, or continuance of the 8 loom system. An experiment using this system was to end in Burnley on Monday 31st. March. The resolution unanimously adopted by 165 delegates from 38 districts read as follows:

"That this General Council meeting having heard the report of the proceedings on the Burnley experiment, is convinced that the 8 loom system would not bring about the object which the employers had in view when the subject was introduced and our co-operation invited."

"The economics of the question have revealed that, whilst an increased individual wage was possible, a serious reduction in the family income would ensue and considerable displacement of labour, would take place."

"The Council are impressed with the statement of the President of the Board of Trade, and await with interest the report of the inquiry."

"The Committee therefore instructs the Central Committee not to enter into any agreement on this subject, and calls upon the different district associations to oppose its introduction or continuance, and promises the financial support of the Amalgamation to any district which may be involved in a dispute."

The 'Observer' reported the explanation given by Andrew Naesmith of the position. The employers argued that the diminution of trade had taken place in the grey goods area, where Far Eastern competition had seriously affected Lancashire exports. He continued:

"The employers came along and said; 'Let us revise our methods of production, and in that revision there will be a lowering of production costs to enable us to cheapen our goods on the market, stimulating demand, and tending to increase the possible volume of exports. That would help in increasing the available work for the mills that are now idle and the looms that are not running to-day.'"

"By acquiescing in this we should impoverish ourselves, and there is no guarantee that we should benefit the merchants and the middlemen to our general impoverishment."

The 'Observer' said:

"The decision of the Amalgamation may have vital consequences to the whole of the cotton industry, for were the employers to persist in their endeavours to secure the general adoption of the 8-loom system, and this resulted in a definite stand being taken by the weavers, the spinning section would be affected and sooner or later a general stoppage would result. This would mean the throwing out of employment of 500,000 Lancashire cotton operatives."

"The next move, it is stated, is likely to be the employers, who are expected to meet at an early date to review the position."

Apparently, the Weavers' Amalgamation were later to go back on their above decision and allow the experiment in Burnley to continue until the Graham Report was published. According to a further pamphlet published by the Textile Minority Movement, entitled 'Fight the Eight Looms':

"Here, although there was a ballot in March 1930, which resulted in a vote of 20 to 1 against the 8 loom system, this has been deliberately flouted; workers are not even allowed to discuss it, in fact, when a special meeting was called to discuss the matter, these [trade union] officials locked the doors and called the police."

At the Great Harwood Weavers' Meeting of April 11th., it was decided:

"That out of £50 granted for the presentation, we purchase a Grandfather Clock and a pocket wallet to be suitably inscribed and presented to Mr. Williamson, President, along with the balance of the money remaining. The presentation to be made by the Secretary at Concerts to be arranged for May 6th. in Mercer Hall, Great Harwood and May 7th. in the Whalley Co-operative Hall."

The position was becoming progressively worse. The 'Observer' April 19th. 1930, announced that 11,128 persons were unemployed in the Accrington District. With regards to Clayton-Le-Moors the 'Observer' April 26th. said:

"Canal Mill has been the only mill working in Clayton-Le-Moors this week, and only half the operatives employed there have had full work. Clayton is rapidly becoming a town of unemployed people and is suffering severely in consequence."

The situation ensured that a strong representation from Accrington attended the Annual Conference of the United Textile Factory Workers' Association held in Blackpool on the 5th. and 6th. May. The delegation comprised of Mr.J.R. Emmett, Accrington Weavers, Mr.J.H. Duxbury, Secretary of the Accrington and District Overlookers' Association, Mr.R. Armistead, Secretary of the Warehousemen's Association, Mr. Edward Thorn, Secretary of the Accrington and District Spinners' Association, and Mr. Herbert Potts, Secretary of the North East Lancashire Card and Blowing Room Operatives.

THE STRIKE AT BURY'S UNION MILL

A further crisis arose on Monday May 12th. 1930, when a 6-loom system of working was introduced on an experimental basis at Messrs. John Bury and Company's, Union Mill, Pickup Street, Spring Hill, Accrington. The proposal was that a weaver should run 6-looms at a standing wage of 7s. per loom or £2..2s. per week, with the weaver being solely employed at the weaving process. The carrying of weft, removing 'cuts' and oiling being done by labourers. A total of 18 weavers had been chosen to take part in the scheme.

Later, that evening, a shop meeting was held at the nearby St. Mary's School, Oswaldtwistle, to consider the position. This meeting was presided over by Mr. Ormerod, President of the Oswaldtwistle Weavers' Association. The position was explained by Mr. Hughes, Secretary of the Oswaldtwistle Weavers , Mr. J.R. Emmett, Secretary of the Accrington Weavers and Mr. Helm, Assistant General Secretary of the Weavers' Amalgamation. Both the two local secretaries were in attendance because the mill was situated on the borders of each district and the presence of Mr. Helm showed how much importance this possible dispute had to the Amalgamation as a whole. The meeting unanimously agreed not to resume work, if the experiment continued. Mr. Ormerod, explained that communications had been going on between the firm and the union for over a month on the question of 6-loom working, but the union had not agreed to the conditions proposed by the management. The 'Observer' reported the union as saying:

" that the average earnings per loom at Union Mill were over 9s. per week, which meant that a 4-loom weaver was receiving about 38s. or 39s. per week, whereas under this scheme it was proposed to pay 42s. for running 6-looms. The union officials were not opposed to schemes being tried for the benefit of the trade, but they objected to this scheme mainly on the ground of the insufficiency of the wage offered."

"One of the causes of dissatisfaction among the operatives at Union Mill was the displacement of a number of young operatives, but that, of course was inevitable."

The firm did not back down and so a strike took place. Of the 300 weavers only 6 entered the mill on Tuesday morning. The 'Observer' May 17th.,1930, reported Mr. Hughes as saying:

"The proposal involves a reduction in the piece rate prices on which weavers wages are based and is a direct violation of the agreement between the Weavers' Amalgamation and the Cotton Spinners and Manufacturers' Federation as to the uniform list price for weaving..... The firms offer of 42s. for 6-looms was a violation of all wages agreements. The compensation offered in the way of relieving the weaver of many duties previously done by the weaver was not commensurate with the increased work entailed in running 6-looms."

"The scheme had been considered by the Weavers' Amalgamation, who refused to sanction it, hence the firm by introducing it had precipitated the strike."

"We appealed to the firm to delay their action until the publication of the findings of the Government Commission which has been conducting an inquiry into the trade, but our appeal was made in vain."

"There were many other points which would arise from the experiment as proposed at Union Mill. The operatives feared that the 6-loom weavers would receive preferential treatment, to the disadvantage of the remainder of the operatives. For instance, in the event of 'playing for warps' it would be the weavers on fixed wages who would be kept fully employed. Again, if more than one loom required the services of the 'tackler' at the same moment doubtless the looms run by the 6-loom weavers would be first to be attended to. Such matters would adversely affect the earnings of the other weavers."

"He agreed that under the scheme the 6-loom weavers would be relieved of certain duties, but that would only make their work more monotonous. "That is the position as it appears to us," added Mr. Hughes. "We are not wanting to get at loggerheads with the firm, and would like the job to be settled amicably as soon as possible."

On Thursday evening May 15th. 1930, the two Textile Federations of Accrington, and Church and Oswaldtwistle, at a joint meeting passed the following resolution unanimously:

"That this joint Federation gives its fullest support to the weavers in the action they have taken in regards to the 6-loom experiment at John Bury and Company's Union Mill."

Strike pay was issued at the respective weavers offices on Friday 16th. May.

Work resumed at the mill on Monday, May 26th. 1930, with the firm agreeing to withdraw the experiment until after the publication of the Graham Report. The following notice was posted on the mill gate, Friday 23rd. May.:

"This mill will re-open at 7.45 a.m. on Monday next. It has been decided to suspend temporarily the 6-loom per weaver experiment. The reasons for doing this are:

"1. That we are not prepared to meet additional monetary losses on the cloth from the warp in the loom through cancellation, or penalties for late deliverers, which in the present disturbed market conditions would assuredly result if the stoppage continued."

"2. To see what agreements are entered into regarding the 8-loom scheme after publication of the Graham Report."

"For J. Bury and Company Limited"

"A.E. Haworth"

The 'Observer' stated that after the strike began on the 13th. May, the firm tried to transfer some of its warps to their mill at Great Harwood, but the Weavers' Union in that town, decided that the warps would be 'blacked'. Negotiations started during the middle of the week, and this resulted in a meeting of the operatives at the Oswaldtwistle Weavers' Institute on May 23rd. Mr. Hughes explained the situation, after which it was unanimously agreed to return to work on Monday the 26th. Mr. Hughes is reported in the 'Observer' as saying:

"The settlement was perfectly amicable to both sides, and that the good relationship that had always existed between the Union and the firm would be in no way jeopardised by the occurrence."

THE COTTON CRISIS, CONTINUED

The Great Harwood Weavers' Minute Book stated on May 21st. that Mr. J.W. Sunderland had been given permission to take leave of absence for any mid-week cricket matches, subject to him rearranging his office work. Mr. Sunderland was one of the best amateur cricketers in the Lancashire League.

The 'Observer' of June 14th. 1930, painted an even gloomier picture. The figures on the Unemployment Register at the Accrington Employment Exchange which included Church and Oswaldtwistle had reached 13,863.

In Oswaldtwistle, Rose Mill was closed down with the few unfinished warps being transferred to the firm's Rhoden Mill. Only 13 mills remained open, with no fewer than 10 factories containing over 7,000 looms standing idle. The report ended by saying:

"The district would welcome the advent of new industry."

A similar story was reported at Rishton, were 6 mills had been idle during the week.

In the same newspaper the Accrington Weavers', Half Yearly Report was published:

"The prolonged depression in our industry continues to cause profound anxiety, and we are naturally alarmed at a condition of affairs which is marked by the unemployment of so many of our members, due to the stoppage of many mills,and the serious under employment which necessitates our members working the full number of hours for reduced wages. The statistics recently released by the Ministry of Labour make very harrowing reading. Behind these figures lies a tale of suffering and misery that makes the stoutest of hearts quail at the financial failure of one firm after another....."

"Whatever the causes of this appalling position may be, the effects are clearly apparent, and we as trade unionists are prepared to assist in any reasonable manner, sound proposals for effecting some improvement....."

"We are patiently awaiting the report of the Government Inquiry into the cotton industry. From it we hope that enlightenment will be forthcoming, and the acknowledged difficulties not withstanding, that some tangible alleviation of the position will result. This has been our hope for some time past."

At the actual meeting held on Tuesday June 17th, the Secretary, Mr. Emmett J.P., went on to mention the two-shift system. He said that whether they agreed to it or not, Higham's were going to introduce a two-shift system using male labour only. He was of the opinion that it would be better to have some input into it's setting up, rather than have no say and leave the mill to become non-unionist.

At the Rishton Weavers' Half Yearly Meeting held on Monday June 16th. 1930, Mr. J. Crossley, the President welcomed the news that the system of 'fining' had been abolished.

On Tuesday evening June 24th., the Church and Oswaldtwistle Weavers' Half Yearly Meeting expressed the following foreboding comments:

"One thing is certain, and that is, that we shall have to be more united in order to oppose any lowering of wages which may be offered in any suggested new schemes."

On Saturday July 19th. 1930, the 'Observer' reported a record number of 14,289 persons receiving unemployment benefit in the Accrington District. This did not include Clayton-Le-Moors, Rishton, or Great Harwood.

THE COTTON REPORT IS PUBLISHED

Saturday the 12th. July 1930, saw glorious weather favouring the Annual Field Day of the Accrington Labour Party. The event was held in a field off Burnley Road and it was a pronounced success. The speaker was Mr. Tom Snowden M.P. who during the course of his speech stated that the Cotton Report had just been published. Before I quote Mr. Snowden's comments on this issue I will attempt a summing up of the situation up to this point.

In the summer of 1929 a minority Labour Government had been elected. Unfortunately, although Labour was the largest Party, they had to depend on support from the Liberals to have a majority of votes in the House. The similarities between the policies of both the Conservative and Liberal Parties did not hold out too much hope of Labour being successful in effecting economic and social change in favour of the working class.

The cotton operatives and workers in general, expected a radical turn round in Government thinking, particularly in regards to policies to alleviate unemployment. Indeed, the textile workers of Lancashire had played an important role in achieving the Labour Party's success at the election. For instance, locally Labour had gained Accrington, Blackburn, Rossendale, and had held Burnley. Much of this success could be put down to Labour promising a Government enquiry into the cotton industry as a whole. Alan and Lesley Fowler believe however, that:

"The cotton union's campaign for an enquiry, had a

fundamental weakness because unlike the miners who were demanding the nationalisation of the mines, they had no alternative strategy for their industry. Their great weakness was that they relied upon the employers for policies for the industry." [5]

We have already seen that in July 1929 the operatives suffered a lockout, with the result that an Arbitration Board decision forced them to accept a 12.5% reduction on the wage list. This set-back brought an end to the unity between the spinning and the weaving sections of the union movement, because the spinners were at that time more moderate in their demands. The Weavers leadership found itself under mounting pressure from its left-wing to improve the lot of the cotton weaver.

As the various local Weavers' Associations press releases testify, the Amalgamation had pinned everything on the Government enquiry making logical, sensible recommendations for a thorough re-organisation of the industry, particularly on the distribution, selling, marketing and exporting side. They also hoped that the enquiry would directly blame the employers for the industry's problems and not themselves, who had merely adopted a defensive posture which had in effect left the weaver suffering a substantial drop in living standards.

The report however, was disastrous, a 'right kick in the teeth'. Little was put forward that would help transform the industry on a scientific basis and move it away from the traditional methods that had patently failed. However, all the report seemed to suggest was a policy of rationalisation which merely sided with the employer and the 'more-looms system'. It was not what was expected with a Labour Government in office and Tom Snowden M.P. could only bluster his way through his comments on the report. His thoughts as expressed at the Labour Party Field Day are as follows:

> "They had just had presented to them the Cotton Report, an interesting report, the speaker continued. The cotton industry was in a different position to most other industries. That Report did not reveal anything new; it simply stated what was known during the past ten or fifteen years. It made certain suggestions, not exactly of a constructive character. Unless and until the industry not only employers but employees, got together for the one purpose of trying to do something of a nature and character that would uplift the industry there was little hope for the Lancashire cotton trade."

> "One of the suggestions was that there should be 8-looms to a weaver. He did not think that the employees would resist the consideration of 8-looms to one weaver on the condition that they were going to have a say in the future on how the industry was to be run. If

there was to be rationalisation in the cotton or in any other industry, then those who were kept in work must try to realise that they had difficulties in common with those out of work, or the unemployed were going to be cast on the scrap heap. He asked those in work to have the same regard for those out of work, and urged operatives to so organise themselves that it would be co-operation not only in name but in reality....."

"He appealed to them to carry on the good work and assured them that the Prime Minister [Ramsay Mac Donald] and his colleagues would not let them down."

My initial comment is that I wouldn't have liked to have seen the position if Mr. MacDonald had let them down, according to Snowden's criteria. The Labour Cabinet had not exactly helped the weavers, they had in fact collaborated in 'putting the boot in.'

The July issue of the 'Ministry of Labour Gazette' reported:

"Severe depression continued in all sections of the industry; employment was even worse than in May, and much worse than a year ago. The holidays at Whitsuntide were extended in most of the principal centres. The percentage of insured workpeople unemployed, including those temporarily stopped, as indicated by the unemployment books lodged at Employment Exchanges, was 42.2% at 23rd. June 1930, as compared with 39.1% at 26th. May 1930, and with 13.7% at 24th. June 1929."

Commenting on the above, the 'Observer' July 26th. 1930, said that:

"Out of 53 weaving mills in the Accrington district only 6 worked during Whit week; 23 were closed permanently or for an indefinite period, and the remainder were stopped for an extended holiday."

The 'Observer' August 9th. 1930, published Tom Snowden's review of his first year as Accrington's Labour M.P.. Snowden gives the impression that he felt "The Labour Government had emerged from a most difficult year of office with added prestige."

With regards to the cotton industry, he said:

"The constructive part of the Labour Government is to be found in the £95 million work schemes, which will provide 380,000 persons with work for one year. This I know is poor satisfaction to the cotton operatives and engineers in Lancashire....."

"......One would like to have dealt with the Cotton Report, but having taken up so much space, [on Work Schemes, the National Economy, and attacking the previous Government] I will save this for the future." [**He then went on a three week holiday**]

The above shows that Snowden was just not in touch with the real world. He could just as well have been the representative for the planet Pluto, as for downtown Accrington. His epistle to the constituents of Accrington after one year as their representative should have concentrated on the problems affecting the cotton industry. This means that at that particular time he should have, at least, re-affirmed his support for the cotton unions demands for an entire re-organisation of their industry, and he could have started this by attacking the recommendations of the Cotton Report.

In 'Fight the Eight Looms' pamphlet, the Textile Minority Movement had this to say:

> "We must take note that the Labour Government Graham Committee not only recommends definite steps of how to improve the Cotton Industry at the expense of the workers, but it directly threatens that if any section is antagonistic to the particular recommendations, that the Labour Government will ask Parliament for special powers to deal with them. This means that if necessary the Government will be prepared to take action against the workers who are determined to fight the more looms system by trying to drive them back to work on the bosses' terms by means of arbitration [either voluntary or compulsory], and in this they will receive the assistance of the trade union officials."

Indeed, the trade union officials helped the bosses by expelling militant members from the unions in Burnley, Blackburn and Barnoldswick. Of course it will not surprise the reader to learn that all the expelled members were organised in the Textile Minority Movement.

THE COTTON CRISIS, CONTINUED

On Saturday August 30th. 1930, the registered unemployed in the Accrington District stood at 14,187; Saturday September 20th, 14,584; Saturday October 4th. 15,807. [Figures do not include Rishton, Great Harwood. or Clayton-Le-Moors] The September unemployment figures for Accrington taken from the Guardian and reported in the 'Observer' were Men 40%; Women 58.9%; Juveniles 34.5%; an overall total of 46.7%.

The mass unemployment, the set back of the Cotton Reports's findings, and the class-war being waged incessantly by the local mill owners in their attack on their operatives wages and conditions, appears not to have been realised by the leadership of the Overlookers' and the Tape Sizers' Societies. These two organisations in collaboration with the Accrington and District Mill

Managers actually organised a series of joint visits and lectures for the winter months. The first visit arranged for Saturday October 18th. was to Messrs. Hacking and Co. Ltd., Textile Machinists, of Bury; and the first lecture was on Tuesday October 28th. entitled 'Present day problems in the cotton industry.' The fee for the winter session was 2s. This sort of activity appears to be nothing short of fraternising with the class enemy.

The 'Observer' November 1st. 1930, reported that the funeral had taken place on Wednesday of Mr. Joseph Rushton of 24 Dryden Street, Clayton-Le-Moors, who was one of the pioneers of the Clayton-Le-Moors Weavers' Association, he was 84 years of age.

On Monday, November 3rd., the Labour Party suffered a big slump in their vote in the Accrington Borough elections. They only managed to keep their stronghold of Spring Hill, which they won unopposed.

The 'Observer' of November 15th., reported the Manager of the Employment Exchange remarking on the seriousness of the industrial situation. He stated that a third of the employable capacity of the cotton industry in Accrington and District had been destroyed by the scrapping of looms and the closing of sheds which had taken place over the previous two years.

In his speech at the Discussion Class on November 9th. 1930, Mr. Tom Snowden M.P. in a reference to the Cotton Report said that it held out some hope on reorganisation, and he even said:

"Upon Whose Lines?-Upon the lines of the owners of the machinery. Cotton operatives were not consulted about it at all."

However, instead of attacking the unfairness of the Report, he went on to hold up his hands in total bewilderment and say:

"The Government could not determine the cotton, worsted or engineering trades. They could not go to China, India, or South Africa, and say to the people there that they had got to take these goods. The Government was absolutely helpless in the matter. The Government said they had had no part in industry up to the present, and industry had been left to others and was in such chaos that apart from exercising their influence with banks they could do nothing."

This statement by Snowden showed that he had given up the fight. He had asked for and received the votes of the cotton operatives at his election; and he had over the years made speeches on the socialisation of industry, but when it came to action in support of the working class, he was not forthcoming. As the Member of Parliament for a cotton constituency, he should have been at the forefront of the agitation for Government intervention which would have helped improve the conditions of the operatives. If the Tories and their Liberal allies refused to back-up Labour legislation to do this, then all well and good, the electorate could blame both the Conservative and Liberal Parties for their poverty stricken predicament.

By maintaining the status quo, to try to woo the more liberal capitalists, the Labour Party and indeed Snowden himself were sowing the seeds of their own destruction. The workers could not see how the Labour Party was helping them, all they witnessed around them after one year of a Labour Government was growing unemployment and a growing crisis in the textile industry. O.K. there was a world slump, Capitalism was in a desperate crisis, but surely this was just the time to propose a radical capitalist solution offered by Keynes, or to propose what many people expected of a Labour Government, namely a Socialist solution to the problem. Unfortunately, no radical solution was offered.

The 'Observer' November 29th. 1930, printed extracts from the Accrington and District Weavers' Half Yearly Report:

"It is now nearly six months since the Report of the Government Inquiry was published and we still await the application of the recommendations contained therein, or of the removal of other obstacles to trade resuscitation with which the report did not deal. The weaving employers appear to be obsessed with the belief that the principal way to salvation lies in the introduction of a scheme of more looms per weaver, and have accordingly submitted details of a scheme which removes restrictions on the number of looms a weaver shall attend, and is accompanied by a complete revision of the basis of calculating weaving prices."

"We are not prepared to condemn summarily any suggestions which are made irrespective of their origin, for we are fully alive to the urgent necessity for sound reorganisation. Nevertheless we are convinced that any scheme which involves reductions in rates should be applied only after every other avenue towards industrial recovery has been thoroughly explored. During the last few years the wages of weavers have been several times reduced and we fail to discern any improvement in the volume of trade which has resulted. This forces us to the conclusion that to lower the remuneration of the operatives is not a sound economic policy, but may on the contrary be glaringly uneconomic, because of the consequent loss of purchasing power."

DOMESTIC SERVICE FOR UNEMPLOYED FEMALE LABOUR

Rishton Weavers' Association's Half-Yearly Report brought to the attention of the public the behaviour of the officials employed at the Employment Exchanges in requiring unemployed young women and girls, whose normal occupation was as cotton operatives, to take up employment as domestic servants.

"Whilst there can be no objection to cotton operatives taking up such work if they choose, we think it is unreasonable to ask them to undertake such work against their will and desire, and especially when they are temporarily stopped and have good reason to expect that they will again be employed in their normal occupations when trade improves. Whilst we can admire Miss Bondfield, Minister of Labour, for her courage in defending the action of the officials in her department, we think she is wrong in the attitude she has taken up on this question. There can be no question as to the strong resentment the action has caused throughout the cotton trade."

The attitude of the Labour Government on this question is really astounding. Miss Bondfield's reaction, when hearing that officials were taking it upon themselves to stop unemployment benefit if female cotton operatives refused work as domestic servants far away from home, should have been one of total condemnation. She and the Labour Government would not have been in power but for the votes of the cotton operatives. The operatives expected to be treated with dignity and respect, not treated like feudal serfs, especially by a so-called Socialist Government. Miss Bondfield had taken no cognizance of the ideas of female equality whatsoever, but had taken to heart the wishes of the Treasury and the exploiters of labour. Her actions were unhelpful and disappointing.

At their Half Yearly Meeting the Rishton Weavers' showed their anger by passing a resolution condemning the actions of the Employment Exchange officials, and by sending their protest to Miss Bondfield and to Mr. Tom Snowden M.P.

The Clayton-Le-Moors Weavers' at their Half Yearly Meeting, reported in the 'Observer' of December 20th. 1930, also condemned the Government's action regarding domestic service.

In Great Harwood the Weavers' Association had been fighting the case of 14 unemployed mill girls. They had only recently found themselves in such a position and refused to take up domestic service in Blackpool, when offered the work at the local Labour Exchange. They were then immediately refused benefit. ['Blackburn Times' January 10th. 1931]

Twenty three years later, Margaret McCarthy still felt disgust at this tactic used by the Labour Exchanges. In her book 'Generation in Revolt' she said the following:

"The authorities tried to tackle the unemployed problem among the women by attempting to force us into training centres for domestic service. We were shepherded into lecture rooms at the Labour Exchanges and there talked to about the prospects of employment open to us in domestic service. This we bitterly resented: 'service' to the independent Lancashire factory girl was a form of employment deeply tainted with the stigma of genuine servitude. No self-respecting girl would go into service. More important, 'service' was a non-insurable occupation, and we were quite convinced that the authorities were opening these avenues to us, not from the least concern about our poverty and our problems, but merely as a means of getting us off the register and washing their hands of all responsibility for us." [6]

THE EMPLOYERS PREPARE TO INSTITUTE THE MORE-LOOMS SYSTEM

Over 200 members attended the Accrington Weavers' Half Yearly Meeting held at the Co-operative Assembly Rooms, Oak Street, on Tuesday 2nd. December. Mr. F. Cunliffe J.P., said that:

"It might mean, that the present proposals of the employers were going to bring the weavers of this country to the state of slaves" [Hear, Hear.]

"He believed that in a certain capitalist Press they were told not to buy wheat from Russia because it was got by slave labour. He was going to say now in connection with the new proposals of the cotton employers that nobody ought to buy cotton if it was going to be produced under the conditions which the employers sought to impose." [Hear, Hear.]

The Secretary, Mr. Emmett J.P. expressed the opinion that the least said at that time the better, because the 8 and 6 loom systems had not yet been introduced in the district. The 'Observer' reports him saying:

"They did not want to make a scene about it and encourage the employers to introduce the systems. He was rather afraid that they might make the mistake of doing that if they were not careful. Everybody in their organisation was opposed to 8 looms, because everybody knew that it was a physical impossibility to run 8 looms."

"On Saturday, November 29th. the proposals of the employers were turned down. The Central Committee of the Amalgamation had decided......that if there was to be a system of 8 or 6 looms there must be a standing wage for the weaver....[They] refused to meet the employers, on the grounds that they said the employers must not talk about changing the uniform list unless they said they were prepared at the outset to give the minimum wage. They held that if the weavers worked all the week, no matter how many looms, they were entitled to a weeks wage."

"The employers formulated a list of their own.....The Central Committee had a full delegates meeting and by an almost unanimous vote decided that no further negotiations take place with the employers on this list. In doing that, they let themselves in for a very serious position.....He thought they could assume that there would be trouble before the end of January."

On Friday December 5th. 1930, the Central Committee of the Cotton Spinners' and Manufacturers' Association at their meeting in Manchester decided to give one months notice to the operatives, that the more-looms-per-weaver-system would commence on Monday January 5th. 1931.

The 'Observer' December 13th. 1930, published interesting items from the Rishton Weavers' Association's Half Yearly Report. With regards to the more-looms-to-a-weaver the report states:

"It appears to us that the employers have not had the courage to seek a straight forward reduction in weavers' wages, but are trying to achieve the same end in a very subtle way."

The report compares the present list prices with those for the 6, 8, and 10 looms system. Under the 6 looms the weaving price would be 10% below; under the 8 looms it would be 30% less; and under the 10 looms it would be 42% less than the present uniform price list. The report continues:

"We claim that a skilled weaver, if his, or her, services are required for 48 hours per week, should be paid a wage for 48 hours per week. Under the proposals there is nothing to prevent an employer from saying he is on the 8 looms-to-a-weaver system, or the 10 looms-to-a-weaver system, and yet at the same time the weaver having a less number of warps in and the wages being paid on the less number of looms production. In view of this and other objections, we cannot agree to accept the employers proposals."

THE COTTON CRISIS, CONTINUED

The 'Observer' December 13th. 1930, published extracts from the Church and Oswaldtwistle Weavers' Half Yearly Report. Their comments on the more-looms-to-a-weaver are printed below:

> "With respect to the running of more looms [8 or 10] this is a farce in face of the number of complaints we receive with regard to the poor quality of material at present in use. Our members find it difficult to run 4 looms at the present time, so the running of more looms would have to be met by a far better class of material and this will not be supplied because it will be argued that the employers cannot make it pay with the quality of to-day let alone paying for a better class of yarns."

On Thursday December 18th. the Church and Oswaldtwistle Weavers' Association held a mass meeting in Oswaldtwistle Town Hall, which was addressed by Mr. J.P. Riding of Stockport and Mr. Helm, Assistant General Secretary of the Weavers' Amalgamation. The meeting pledged itself to resist the employers intentions to introduce the system with its new piece price lists and to support the committees of the local Associations and the Amalgamation in any steps they may take to deal with the matter.

Meanwhile, the Unemployment figure reported for the area covered by Great Harwood, Rishton, and Clayton-Le-Moors had reached 7,690.

The General Council of the Weavers' Amalgamation met on Saturday 20th December in Manchester with delegates representing 38 towns. It met to consider the action of the employers who had issued instructions to managers to post notices at all mills, informing weavers, not required after January 5th. 1931, of their dismissal. After the meeting a union leader said:

> "An employer may, from today, give seven days' notice to individual weavers that their services will not be required when the new system is introduced, and will be able to allot eight looms, instead of four as at present, to any weaver as he desires. Operatives will not know whether they are to be dismissed or even given more looms to operate. Time will show what the employers intend to do."

In the days following this meeting the various districts all held mass meetings of their members in order to prepare a defence against the employers actions. Mr. Andrew Naesmith was the principal speaker at a meeting in Rishton on Monday December 22nd. 1930. A resolution pledging resistance to the employers intentions to introduce the system of more looms to the weaver with its new piece price list was adopted. The 'Observer' reported:

> "Mr. Naesmith said the problem was one of the greatest that had ever confronted weavers, and it presented all kinds of difficulties and complications.....After referring at length to the Burnley experiment, Mr. Naesmith proceeded to say that those new piece price lists marked an enormous change in the traditional practice that

obtained in Lancashire. These lists with their various systems of 6, 8 and 10 looms, meant a complete abrogation of the uniform list....."

"The new proposal put each individual employer in the position of being the list maker. It gave each individual employer the right to say what list he would apply and how his wages would be paid. And it created by inference, and would create by practice, all the chaotic conditions that existed in Lancashire before there ever was a uniform list of weaving prices. The new list struck a deadly blow at many of the Clauses of the uniform list that had given allowances for the extra work and care the weaver put into his work."

"There was a multitude of things which employers had made up their minds they were not going to pay for. And this list which they had designed had been formulated on the basis of paying as little as they possibly could for as much work as could be got from the weaver for the price offered........"

"They not only wished to safeguard the operatives......but they also wished to save the honest employers [who gave their] operatives a square deal. [They wished] to save them from those who would take advantage of the market."

"Then there should have been a minimum wage proposal. The weavers contracted to run for the employers so many looms per week, and were entitled to a wage for being there." [Applause]

"Then there was the inevitable displacement of labour by these proposals. Where were the 'others' going to get work? Who was to be discharged? Who was to determine which weaver was to be retained and which not retained?.....Mr. Naesmith concluded by saying that he believed industry required re-organisation to enable them to enter world markets with a reasonable chance of success."

At Clayton-Le-Moors on the same night Mr. Helm, Assistant Secretary to the Amalgamation, addressed a meeting of weavers in the Town Hall. He was supported by Mr. J.W. Sunderland, Secretary of the Great Harwood Weavers'. The meeting unanimously supported a motion to support the Amalgamation in any steps they might take to deal with the matter.

The 'Observer' reported that Mr. Emmett was again receiving a gift from his membership, this time for the attainment of his 60th. birthday. At an excellent supper in the Weavers Offices, Accrington, Monday December 29th. 1930, he was presented with a pipe by Miss Lena Worsley, President, and Miss Annie Kirkham J.P.

1931

On Friday January 2nd. 1931, a joint meeting of the representatives of the operatives and the employers was held at the Cotton Manufacturers Association, but this broke up without any change in the position. The 'Observer' stated that there was no likelihood of the more-looms experiment being adopted in Accrington, Church, Oswaldtwistle and Rishton. At Clayton-Le-Moors, however, Canal Mill the only mill still running, out of 11 in the township, had indicated that weavers would be asked to work 8 looms on Monday January 5th. 1931. Mr. Hope, Secretary to the Clayton Weavers, had informed the management of the mill, that a strike would be declared if the threat was put into operation.

THE MORE-LOOMS DISPUTE LOCKOUT

The Tuesday 'Observer' January 6th, announced that the cotton dispute had started with 3,500 Burnley Weavers withdrawing their labour. At Canal Mill, Clayton-Le-Moors one young woman operative started work on 8 looms and was allowed to work quite peacefully during the day, but a meeting held that evening in the Town Hall decided to cease work immediately.

On Friday January 9th, the Central Committee of the Spinners' and Manufacturers' Association, decided to ask all mills to close their doors on Saturday, January 17th. 1931, unless the dispute was settled. This was in response to the decision of the Northern Counties Textile Federation at their meeting the night before, in which they reiterated their support for the Weavers' Amalgamation and the Burnley Weavers in particular.

On the second day of the lockout the weavers were issued with the following ballot paper to which they were asked to declare Yes or No:

"Whether you are in favour of empowering the Central Committee to negotiate with the representatives of the employers' organisations upon variations in the piece-price-lists for the more-looms-to-a-weaver system which the employers intend to introduce gradually, and its extension, jointly controlled, provided that satisfactory safeguards such as fall-back wages and minimum wages can be assured."

The membership of the local Weavers Associations were stated as being;

Accrington and District	3,460
Church and Oswaldtwistle	2,850

Clayton-Le-Moors   1,420
Rishton   1,935

The situation in Accrington on day one of the lockout was as follows: Still Working; Messrs. Higham's Woodnook Mill [440 looms]

Industrial Mill, Baxenden [897 looms]

Messrs. Worsley's 3 hard waste mills, Alliance, Rising Bridge and Victoria. [The stoppage did not affect the hard waste section at that stage] Closed down; Melbourne Mill, Fountain Mill, Peel Mill, Helene Mill, Ellesmere No.1 and No. 2 Mills, Oak Vale Mill, Union Buildings Mill, and Queens Mill. All other mills had been closed prior to the stoppage.

In Church, the only mills that had been working, Church Bank, Providence and Albion were closed. Canal Mill, a hard waste mill, was expected to reopen that week.

In Oswaldtwistle, Rhoden and Rose Mills remained open together with the 3 hard waste mills of Clifton, Fern, and Paddock. Stanhill Ring Spinning Mill and Vine Spinning Mills also continued working. The mills closed were Three Brooks, Rhyddings, and Commercial. Bury's Union Mill actually in Accrington, but included in the Church and Oswaldtwistle area, was also locked out.

In Rishton only Albert Mill continued to run, all other operatives being locked out. ['Observer' January 10th.1931]

In Clayton-Le-Moors on Thursday 22nd. January, 700 members of the Weavers' Association crowded into the Town Hall to discuss their financial situation. The committee's recommendation to cut part of the benefit of unemployed members in order to make possible payments to the 300 eligible for lockout benefits was carried unanimously.

On Saturday, January 24th. the result of the ballot was declared in the Central Office of the Weavers' Amalgamation at Accrington, as follows:

Against Negotiating Powers Being Given   90.770
For   "   "   "   "   <u>44,990</u>
Majority Against   45,780
85.5% Poll

Mr. Andrew Naesmith issued the following statement:

"There appears to be much controversy about the proposal that has been put to the weavers on the ballot paper. Various observations are being made concerning the wording of the paper and the way in which the position was put. The ballot paper was very clearly and carefully drawn up. The Executive of the Amalgamation had to find the mind of its members upon both the acceptance of the principle of more-looms-to-a- weaver and the employers' proposed conditions governing each of the particular systems that had been submitted in the employers letter of October 31st."

> "The result of the ballot has unmistakenly demonstrated that the weavers generally throughout the whole of the districts of the Amalgamation do not want the more-looms-to-a-weaver system and neither are they prepared to give to their Executive, powers to negotiate with the representatives of the employers organisations on wages and conditions."

> "The Executive do not understand the ballot vote as a lack of confidence or trust, but rather is it a revelation to their minds that under no circumstances do the operatives desire to run more than the ordinary number of looms, and consequently are not prepared to give authority for negotiations to take place upon something which they do not want."

Accrington Weavers' Secretary, Mr. J.R. Emmett, had complained in the 'Observer' of January 24th. that the ballot had been badly worded and hinted that he was in favour of negotiations. It would appear that his views were absorbed by the Accrington Weavers because a slight majority voted in favour.

In Accrington the union had divided its members into two groups for payment purposes; those receiving unemployment pay from the Employment Exchanges and those who would be receiving lockout pay only. He said:

> "Those who are receiving from the Exchange get less lockout pay than others who are not. A weaver who is receiving 15s. or 17s. a week from the Exchange, cannot reasonably hope to get £1 on the top of that, whilst others receive £1 only."

At a Labour Party meeting in Accrington on Sunday 25th. January, Mr. Tom Snowden M.P. again showed his conservative attitude to the whole affair. Instead of standing up and expressing a radical alternative to improve the lot of the cotton operatives, Snowden just half-heartedly uttered comments roughly in favour of appeasement to the employers. [One of which, he was.] The local weavers had all the right in the world, to consider themselves badly let down by their Labour Parliamentary Representative. He is actually quoted in the 'Observer' January 27th. as saying that he:

> "Frankly confessed that he did not see how M.P.'s could interfere in the dispute with any advantage to the workers."

He further commented that they should have put their trust in their union leadership, and ended by stating that:

> "The outlook indeed was very black."

Snowden as the representative of thousands of cotton workers, should have been putting forward positive ideas on the subject that the minority Labour government could have brought before Parliament. He should have been encouraging them to strive for a better future, but instead he asked them to accept a system that forced them into either harder work and poverty, or unemployment and near starvation. The man was not exactly a working-class hero.

A more supportive speech was made by Mr. J.W. Sunderland, Secretary of the Great Harwood Weavers, at the Rishton I.L.P. Rooms on Sunday evening January 25th. He said:

"In the course of the development of the industry, circumstances such as the nature of the employment, the nature of the product, and the physique of the operative all tended to make 4 looms the normal complement to a weaver. He wanted to stress that point at the beginning, because the number of looms which a weaver normally tended in Lancashire had not been fixed by a trade union nor by the employers. It was what might almost be called the natural result of almost a century's experience."

"It had been said that the employers were following out practices commenced in America.....it would appear from the development of that idea that what they had in mind was a definite change from the idea of running the looms as fast as they could to running them more slowly and getting the weaver to tend more than 4 looms. From the Burnley experiment there had evolved the employers' more-looms-to-a-weaver proposals....."

"Referring to the 20 to 1 vote in Burnley against continuing the 8 looms experiment, Mr. Sunderland said they would appreciate that it was this decision, largely arising out of the experience of the operatives in Burnley, which strengthened the minds of the leaders of the operatives in other Lancashire districts against a further introduction of the more looms system."

"It was quite easy to imagine that many of the people who voted for the 8 looms' system were people who had good reasons for believing that the extension of the system would not affect them."

"They [the audience] must know that many people, through their experience of long depression, through fear of a lockout itself, would vote in favour of a resumption of negotiations."

"The subject matter of the dispute had been given prominence in the daily press, and the pros and cons had been argued out by both sides. Meetings had been held in all districts, hence they could not accept the criticism that the weavers did not know what they were voting about....."

"The ballot vote was 2 to 1 'against'. <u>At last the leaders of the trades' union movement in Lancashire had got a mandate,</u> which

definitely approved of the action they had taken hitherto in this matter."
['Observer' January 27th.1931]

On Great Harwood, Town Hall Square, on Wednesday afternoon, January 28th. 1931, Mr. Saklatvala, ex-Communist M.P. addressed a crowd of around 500 on the cotton question. Mr. Mullighan presided. ['Blackburn Times' January 31st. 1931]

At an Accrington and District Weavers' Concert held in the Labour Hall, Blackburn Road, on Wednesday January 28th. 1931, Mr. Emmett J.P. continued with his lukewarm support by saying:

> "It seems a great pity that the mills of Accrington should be closed down on the 8 loom question, when the system had not been, and under present conditions, probably would never be attempted in this district.....The Weavers' Amalgamation were not opposed and never had been to weavers running any number of automatic or semi-automatic looms, provided, of course, a reasonable wage was guaranteed to the weaver at the week-end."

The Central Rank and File Strike Committee, organised by the Textile Minority Movement, issued a leaflet from their headquarters at 4, Old Hall St. Burnley, which was distributed amongst cotton operatives. The leaflet correctly predicted forthcoming events:

> "The action of the Employers' Federation locking out all workers in the manufacturing side of the industry, now extends the struggle against the More Loom system to 200,000 workers."

> "The Employers, with the support of the Labour Government and T.U. Officials, in attacking the workers in the weaving section of the industry, are only making the first series of attacks which are recommended for immediate operation, in the Graham Committee Report."

> "The weavers are attacked first on the More Looms issue. In this struggle, the Union Officials are making desperate attempts at negotiations. In the Ballot that has just been taken, they even descended to lies and misrepresentation to secure powers to negotiate. They have with deliberate intent issued a Ballot Paper in which they tried to delude the workers to give them powers to negotiate for the More Looms, on the basis of false promises of Safeguards, a Fall Back wage, Minimum Wage, etc, which the employers have repudiated in authorised press statements."

> "In other sections of the industry the Union Officials make no effort to support the weavers. They, along with the Weavers' Officials and employers, hope to settle the dispute in favour of More Looms."

> "The Labour Government which betrayed us in the 1929 struggle, and which initiated and inspired attacks on all sections of workers, is all out to assist the employers in enforcing the Graham Committee recommendations."
>
> "These recommendations mean attacks upon the workers in every section of the industry. They have sent their Ministry of Labour Officials to put the More Looms by means of negotiations. They are even now taking steps to prepare 'Arbitration'....."
>
> "In face of the attacks being made upon us by the employers, calls upon all cotton workers to come out on strike now, establishing a united struggle with the Weavers......"

On Tuesday January 27th. the Prime Minister Ramsay MacDonald, issued an invitation to the employers and unions to meet the Minister of Labour and himself at separate conferences in London, on Thursday January 29th. The delegates from the Weavers' Amalgamation were Messrs. J. Hindle, L. Bates, W.J. Tout M.P. and Mr. A. Naesmith. The separate meetings continued with the P.M. and his colleagues until 5.30 p.m. on Friday evening, when the negotiations were broken off. As the Weavers' Chairman, Mr. Hindle left Downing Street, he said:

> "I should say that it amounts to a breakdown. We have finished as far as the present conversations are concerned."

At the same time, the employers issued the following statement:

> "All the employers in the manufacturing section of the cotton industry are requested to keep their mills closed until further notice."
>
> ['Observer' January 31st.1931]

By attending these meetings with the Government, the union leadership had blatantly disobeyed the decision of the ballot which had withdrawn their negotiating powers regarding the More-looms question. Any claim by the Amalgamation's Executive to the contrary was nothing more than out and out lies; the discussions had had the eventual aim of ending the dispute with an agreement between the two sides incorporating an acceptance of the More-looms principle. Indeed the 'Observer' February 3rd. reported that prior to the negotiations breaking down:

> "The operatives had offered to allow the trial to take place at three mills in three different towns, but the employers insisted that it should take a wider field and suggested 4 mills spread over 6 towns."

This undemocratic action by the union leadership obviously caused a reaction and this resulted in a rebel delegation, that more accurately presented the weavers aspirations, going to the House of Commons. The action originated at the Nelson Discussion Class on Sunday evening February 1st. During the course of the discussion the idea of sending a delegation to put forward the Weavers' case to the Cabinet gathered momentum. Later a hurried meeting of the Nelson Weavers' Association took place and it was agreed that the delegation should comprise of Mr. George Brame, Secretary of the Clitheroe Weavers, Mr. Zeph Hutchinson, Secretary of the Bacup Weavers, Mr. J. Spedding, Nelson Weavers' President, Mr. Alvery Barker, Secretary of the Skipton Weavers plus 5 other members of the Nelson Executive Committee. The group as a whole were closely connected with the I.L.P.[7]

Their objectives were to ensure that the Cabinet were made aware in no uncertain terms, that the Amalgamation had no mandate to negotiate as they had been doing; and secondly to urge them to re-organise the industry under a form of Government control. This they hoped to achieve by meeting the Minister of Health, Mr. Arthur Greenwood M.P. for Nelson and Colne, and who had been involved in the failed negotiations.

Mr. Andrew Naesmith immediately issued the following statement from the Amalgamation's headquarters in Accrington:

"It is to be regretted that an unofficial deputation, so far as is known, from 4 divisions of the Amalgamated Weavers' Association, have seen fit to interfere in the present dispute. This is a matter that concerns the whole of the district associations included in this Amalgamation, and the authority is vested in the General Committee, who are the representative officials elected by the members to deal with the whole question."

Well he would say that, wouldn't he?

The North East Lancashire Textile Minority Movement meanwhile, issued a leaflet condemning the Weavers' Amalgamation's conduct of the affair. This contained the following advice:

"Fellow Weavers,

"In the interests of capitalist profits an understanding has been arrived at between the Labour Government, the Employers and Trade Union officials to force the eight or more loom system upon us."

"Negotiations are about to take place, not on the question of whether there shall be more looms per weaver, but on the new piece price list, based upon eight or more looms. The trade union officials, who consented behind our backs to the 8-loom experiment, deliberately deceived us. They intended it to be a permanency. That is why they ignored our ballot vote. Further proof of their treachery was the payment of backpay to 8-loom weavers [after the employers had refused] out of our Union funds. In order to draw our attention away from the issue of more looms, our officials will no doubt be prepared to haggle at some length with the employers over the new Pick List."

"This sham fight over the new list will only be a smoke screen, behind which they will co-operate to get the more loom system generally introduced.""Fellow Weavers, we must not allow ourselves to be deceived again."**Our fight is against the more loom system, and for the retention of the Standard Piece Price List as at present in operation.** The position is very serious."

"We must prepare at once for action! Against the united front of the Government, the Employers and Trade Union Officials, we must organise the United Class Front of the workers against this sinister attack."

Meanwhile, only a slight change in the local position occurred. In Accrington and District all the hard waste mills, with the exception of Perseverance, Huncoat, which closed down on Thursday February 5th. in accordance with a decision made by the Hard Waste Employers' Association, resumed work on Monday February 9th.

Tanpits and Albion Mills belonging to the Antley Manufacturing Company containing 1,400 looms recommenced on Monday 2nd. February on the old terms.

In Rishton, Wheatfield Mill employing 200 operatives reopened on the old terms on Thursday February 5th. Three out of the ten mills in the township were now running on the old rates leaving about 1,300 weavers and winders still locked out.

The rebel delegation succeeded in seeing their M.P., Mr. Arthur Greenwood, Minister of Health and went on to address a joint meeting of Lancashire Labour M.P's. and the Parliamentary I.L.P. group. A resolution carried at this meeting was placed on the order paper of the House of Commons but did not get debated. According to Alan and Lesley Fowler:

"It was claimed that never before had the Lancashire Weavers' case been so eloquently stated in the House of Commons."[8]

On their return, the rebel delegation organised a series of mass meetings which were very successful. Indeed 10% of Nelson's population, over 3,000 people, turned up to hear their report, thereby demonstrating the strength of feeling against the proposed new system.

The 'Observer' reported that on Saturday February 7th. the Central Committee of the Amalgamation spent over 4 hours discussing the situation and finally voted by 114 to 49, against giving the Committee the power to negotiate for a scientific experiment of the more-looms-to-a-weaver system. They also refused to give the Central Committee the power to proceed with a ballot of the membership upon the question of a scientific experiment of the more-looms-to-a-weaver system. After the meeting Mr. Andrew Naesmith was forced to say:

"The feelings and opinions in the districts as expressed by the delegates were stronger than at the commencement of the lockout, and in no uncertain fashion did they indicate that they were not prepared to allow their Central Committee to negotiate with the employers proposals."

Attempts to discipline the rebel delegation came to nothing because it was pointed out that it would have been hypocritical for the General Council to force such an issue, when they themselves had disregarded their own ballot.

Prior to the meeting a lively demonstration took place by members of the Communist led 'Central Rank and File Strike Committee', [Textile Minority Movement] who were as opposed to the rebel delegation as they were to the Central Committee. The following are some passages from their leaflet;

"The officials twisted the words on the ballot paper to secure a vote in favour of negotiations. But, we workers saw through the deception and refused the power to negotiate by a smashing majority. But these 'super-democrats' had hardly counted the votes than they were negotiating with the employers on the basis of 'more-looms'."

"They want you to endorse this treachery. They want you to become their partners in the crime of arranging a deal with the employers to secure the introduction of the 'more-looms' system as a permanent part of the cotton industry. Refuse to be used as pawns in this treacherous game."

"Nor should you be deceived by the words of the I.L.P. members of the recent delegation to London. You must know that the raising of false issues, such as the Labour Government setting up a Cotton Control Commission composed of representatives from the unions, the employers, and the Government is directed towards creating a 'smoke-screen' to cover up all the moves now being made to betray us. Such a proposal could only mean in practice - control of we cotton workers in the interest of capitalist rationalisation." ['Observer' February 7th.1931]

In 'Fight the Eight Looms' pamphlet, the Textile Minority Movement said:

"The trade union officials say that they are in the most critical period which has ever faced the Weavers' Amalgamation, or, in other words, how can they appear militant in the eyes of the workers, and at the same time help the boss to extend the more loom system."

"This is their problem."

"We have seen that they are **not against** the more loom system in principle, but at the moment are putting up a sham pose to deceive the weavers on the question of the fall back wage. Whether the Fall Back Wage is conceded or not there will still be drastic cuts in wages and employment."

"The fall back wage negotiations will mean nothing to the weavers in face of the application of the more-looms-per-weaver system. In fact, this is only a manoeuvre to hoodwink the workers and to divert their attention away from the real fight which is against the more looms system."

"The Minority Movement is mobilising the weavers for the fight against the more looms, and for a £2 per week minimum wage for all cotton workers, which will give a guarantee to all workers against their present impoverishment."

On Tuesday 10th. of February, Union Mill, Accrington, opened up for its 280 operatives on the old rates.

In Church, work resumed at Church Bank Mill at the old rates, giving work to its 350 workpeople. With Providence and Albion Mills reopening a few days earlier, this meant that the three Church mills working before the lockout were back at work.

In Oswaldtwistle, Vine No.4 Mill reopened on Monday February 9th. joining Rhoden and Rose Mills as the three mills in operation in the district.

In Clayton-Le-Moors however, Royal and Commercial Mills which hadn't run since 1929 posted up new price lists.

The 'Observer' Saturday February 14th 1931, announced the ending of the Cotton Lock-out, the abandonment of the More-Looms experiment, and the mills re-opening on Monday February 16th.

After a meeting of the Executive of the Weavers' Amalgamation in Manchester Friday 13th. February, Mr. Andrew Naesmith issued the following statement:

"The Central Committee welcomed the decision of the representatives of the employers to lift the lockout and discontinue the Burnley experiment, and express the hope that means will be devised by joint consultation for machinery to become operative that will prevent a recurrence of such events as has led to this dispute."

"The Central Committee are instructing all their district associations to recommend the members to present themselves for work in the mills when they re-open on Monday morning."

Mr. J.R.Emmett J.P. Secretary of the Accrington Weavers, expressed his satisfaction that the lock-out was over, but went on to say:

"We have all along felt that in towns like Accrington where there was no question of 8 loom working in the mills, it was deplorable that the whole of the mills should be closed on such an issue. It was the most curious dispute I have ever been connected with and was leading us nowhere."

Mr. Emmett seems to have been as much out of touch with the views of the average operative as the Weavers' Central Committee had been. I agree with the following analysis of the situation made by Alan and Lesley Fowler:

"The Rebel Delegation had inflicted a highly effective blow to the Amalgamation leadership's plans to call off the dispute. The employers' tactic was to force the weavers to give their leaders power to negotiate an agreement but the Rebel Delegation only illustrated how clearly that leadership had neither control over events nor the confidence of the members."

"The Delegation convinced the employers that the aims of the lockout could not be achieved quickly and they called off the lockout. The pretext was an appeal by Lord Derby for an end to the dispute during the London Textile Exhibition, but the reality was that many individual employers were already asking workers back and one local employers federation, Skipton, had announced the end of the lockout in their area. All this persuaded employers to end the lockout and also to end the More Looms experiment at individual mills in Burnley. The mills re-opened on 13th. February a total capitulation to the Union."

"The weavers had a far greater victory than many might have expected given the unfavourable economic climate. It represented the greatest industrial victory for labour since the defeat of 1926. The More Looms System, as later events were to show, did not have a great deal to offer the majority of employers while the consequences of a prolonged lockout was potentially disastrous. Even so the astonishing victory in the depths of depression reflected the solidarity of Weavers and their determination not to have the More Looms System."[9]

WORK IS RESUMED

The 'Observer' of February 17th., reported no apparent difficulties being encountered with the resumption of work. In Accrington, Bury Brothers, Fountain Mill which had been stopped for a week prior to the lockout reopened. It was accepted that in ordinary weaving sheds 7,500 looms were working and that a further 1,250 looms devoted to hard waste manufacture were also operating. The total of 8,750 looms working meant that less than half the number operating pre-cotton slump were now in full production. However, the position had at times been a lot worse.

At Church the three weaving sheds at which work was being carried out before the lockout had already restarted the previous week.

At Oswaldtwistle the two mills which were closed during the lockout Three Brooks and Rhyddings were reopened.

At Clayton-Le-Moors, Canal Mill, which had tried to introduce the more-looms system, was reopened, making it the only working mill in the township.

At Rishton 8 of the 10 mills were running and two which failed to reopen had been closed for a considerable time.

Just as news of the end of the lockout was being welcomed, another section of the industry, the dyeing trade was facing an employers proposal for a reduction in wages. The unions stated that they would resist such an attempt.

The unemployment figures given in the 'Observer' February 21st. showed 8,460 totally unemployed and 5,390 temporarily unemployed, making a total of 13,850 for the Accrington Employment Exchange, which included both Church and Oswaldtwistle.The figures for the Great Harwood Exchange which covered Rishton and Clayton-Le-Moors, gave a total of 7,625. Therefore the official unemployment figure for the area now covered by Hyndburn Borough Council was 21,475.

On Wednesday February 18th. the General Management Committee of the Accrington Trades Council and Labour Party sent the following to the Weavers Amalgamation:

"That we send our heartiest congratulations to the Weavers' Amalgamation on the victory gained in forcing the masters to withdraw the lockout notices, believing that it will give a greater impetus to other unions, such as the railwaymen's and engineers' to fight against the recent ruthless attack of the employers to reduce the workers' standards of living."

On Monday March 16th 1931, India Mill at Church, containing 1,000 looms, which had been standing idle for over 12 months, reopened with 300 looms 'gaited' up immediately. In the same issue of the 'Observer' it was also reported that Commercial Mill in Oswaldtwistle also reopened with 75 weavers being given 2 looms each, with the assurance that each would be provided with material for running one or two more looms during the week.

On Wednesday March 18th., Mr.E. Grimshaw, of Lock Street, aged 74 years, Treasurer of the Church and Oswaldtwistle Weavers died at his home. He had originally been elected Auditor in 1903 and had been the Treasurer since

1916.

The 'Observer' March 24th. reported a new strike over the More-Looms System in Burnley. This again brought conflict as well as depression of trade into the forefront of the operatives minds. Although the Weavers had won a significant victory against the employers, their success had a major drawback for the future of the workforce. The defeat had weakened the credibility of the Employer' organisation and this was not in the interests of the Weavers. Individual firms having left their Association did not feel obliged to operate the joint agreements; they could undercut existing price lists and attempt to introduce the more-looms system. This resulted in the Amalgamation having to fight for the enforcement of agreements at more non-federated firms, where the operatives felt much more vulnerable to being undercut by the army of unemployed, many of whom were not trade unionists.

We must remember that the employers were fighting for less than half of what had been the normal trade. Some employers demanded that their operatives bought shares in the company. Years later this was judged to be illegal, but any scheme giving the slightest of advantage to an employer over the competition became fair game. The employers federation only controlled 60% of the looms at the best of times, but in 1931 nearly all the trade could be completed by rogue firms.

Rogue firms, however, depended on a standard rate otherwise they wouldn't gain any benefits if a free for all existed. Similarly it was only beneficial to operate more-looms if every other company was still operating 4 looms. Firms were in effect trying to cheapen production by paying less remuneration to their employees, in order to merely make sure that they maintained their orders, not gain new orders. The Weavers' Amalgamation found itself in a new type of crisis, in trying to maintain the County Agreement.[10]

On the 8th. April 1931, the 80,000 operatives in the dyeing trade accepted a 5% reduction in wages. The employers had asked for a 15% cut but following considerable negotiations a 5% cut was agreed, and this came into operation on May 1st. This meant a reduction of 2s..5d. per week for male workers above 21 years of age.

On Thursday evening April 30th,1931, the Textile Trades Federations, of Accrington, Church and Oswaldtwistle, and Padiham met in Accrington to consider the dispute at Messrs Ashworth Bros. Perserverance Mill, Hapton, as it affected each district. The 'Observer' reported that resolutions were adopted and that they hoped the dispute could be brought to a satisfactory conclusion.

THE EFFECT OF THE INDIAN BOYCOTT AND THE

ARRIVAL OF MAHATMA GANDHI IN NORTH EAST LANCASHIRE

The Lahore Congress, of the Indian Congress Party, at the end of 1929 had adopted the policy of Complete Independence for India and in order to achieve that aim it launched a programme of Civil Disobedience, including non-payment of taxes. Gandhi explained that he would rather be defeated rather than allow a violent victory.

"I would welcome even utter failure with non-violence unimpaired, rather than depart from it by a hair's breadth to achieve a doubtful success." [Quoted in the 'Times', May 8th.1931][11]

R.Palme Dutt writes:

"Thus on the eve of rising mass struggle Gandhi proclaimed the fight on two fronts, not only against British rule, but against the internal enemy in India. This conception of the fight on two fronts corresponds to the role of the Indian bourgeoisie, alarmed as it sees the ground sinking beneath its feet with the growing conflict of imperialism and the mass movement, compelled to undertake leadership of the struggle, despite the 'mad risk', in order to hold it within bounds and seeking to conciliate both with the magic wand of 'non-violence'. However, 'Non-violence', was 'one-way non-violence'. It was 'non-violence' for the Indian masses, but not for imperialism, which practised violence to its hearts content - and won the battle....."

"When it became clear that the power of the mass movement was exceeding the limits set it, and that the authority of Gandhi, who had been left at liberty, was in danger of waning, on May 5th. 1930, the Government arrested Gandhi. The official justification for the arrest was stated in the Government communique:

"While Mr. Gandhi has continued to deplore these outbreaks of violence, his protests against his unruly followers have become weaker, and it is evident that he is unable to control them.....Every provision will be made for his health and comfort during his detention."

"The response to the arrest was shown in the wave of hartals and mass strikes all over India.....Imperialist repression was limitless. Ordinances followed one another in rapid succession, creating a situation comparable to martial law. In June 1930 the Congress and all its organisations were declared illegal.....

"Nevertheless, the power of the movement during 1930,

exceeded every calculation of the authorities, and growing in spite of repression, began to raise the most serious alarm in the imperialist camp, which already found open expression by the summer of 1930, especially in the British trading community, who were hard hit by the boycott [of British goods]. This was especially noticeable in Bombay, where was the centre of strength of the industrial working class, where repression was most severe, but where the movement was strongest, and again and again held possession of the streets, despite repeated police charges, in mass demonstrations which the Congress leaders vainly begged to disperse, and in which the red flags were conspicuous besides the Congress flags, or even predominated......"

"The British business men in Bombay joined with the Indian business men, through the Millowners' Association [with a one third European element] and the Chamber of Commerce, in demanding immediate self-government for India on a Dominion basis".....

"Thus a situation of 'defeatism' and 'demoralisation' bordering on panic, despite all the bluster and repression, was beginning to show itself on the imperialist camp; and it became essential for imperialism at all costs to negotiate a settlement".....On the basis of this mutual alarm [of both British Imperialism and the Indian bourgeoisie] there was the possibility of a settlement - against the Indian people."

"On January 20th. 1931 MacDonald as Prime Minister made the declaration at the Round Table Conference:

"I pray that by our labours India will posses the only thing which she now lacks to give her the status of a Dominion among the British Commonwealth of Nations - the responsibility and the cares, the burdens and the difficulties, but the pride and the honour of Responsible Self-Government....."

"On January 26th. 1931 Gandhi and the Congress Working Committee were released unconditionally.....Prolonged negotiations followed. On March 4th. 1931 the Irwin-Gandhi Agreement was signed, and the struggle was declared provisionally suspended."

"The Irwin-Gandhi Agreement secured not a single aim of the Congress struggle. Civil disobedience was to be withdrawn. Congress was to participate in the Round Table Conference, which it had sworn to boycott. Not a single concrete step to self-government was granted.....Freedom of boycott of foreign goods was to be allowed - but not 'exclusively against British goods'. not 'for political ends', not with any picketing that might be regarded as involving 'coercion, intimidation, restraint, hostile demonstrations, obstruction to the public.'"

"[However,] the maximum gain was the right to peaceful boycott of foreign goods...[And] the fact that the British Government had been compelled to sign a public Treaty with the leaders of the National Congress, which it had previously declared an unlawful association and sought to smash."

"[In reality] all the aims of complete independence and no compromise with imperialism, so loudly proclaimed at Lahore, had gone up in smoke.....Congress was now reduced to accepting the Round Table Conference, which it had previously refused."[12]

Gandhi set sail from India on August 29th. 1931, as the sole delegate of Congress to the second Round Table Conference in London.

Protests in North East Lancashire against the rapidly disappearing Indian market started off with a reactionary gathering of both the unions and employers at Blackburn on Tuesday April 28th. 1931.

The employers and the operative's leadership united to protest against the economic policy of the Government of India and the boycott and picketing policy directed against Lancashire goods by the Indian National Congress Party. More than 3,000 people representing all sections of the cotton trade crowded into King Georges Hall, Blackburn, where the Mayor of Blackburn, Alderman Luke Bates, Secretary of the Blackburn Weavers' Association and Secretary of the Northern Textile Trades Federation presided.

The tone of the speeches was one of outrage that subjects of a British Colony could behave in such a way against the Imperial master. I will limit myself to the remarks made by Mr. Andrew Naesmith which were of a relatively milder construction.

Mr. Andrew Naesmith J.P., said that in 1913 exports to India had averaged 2,508 million yards; in 1927, 1,652 millions yards; in 1928, 1,541 million yards; in 1929, 1,374 million yards; and in 1930, 778million yards. This he stated, made it a problem for operatives as well as employers.

Although India possessed 350 mills with 174,992 looms and 9 million spindles with a further 50 million spinning wheels and 2 million handlooms; their total production could not possibly meet the normal requirements of the country.

The 'Observer' reported Naesmith as saying that:

"Since the war, there had arisen, and expanded, various forms of organisation which were propagating intense national feeling to-day under the guise of political activity, and using that organisation for economic and industrial ends."

"Gandhi was continually avowing that his object was the total extinction of the markets of Lancashire cotton piece goods. Here was a case of history repeating itself in the reformer, animated with high ideals and noble aspirations creating an organisation he could not possibly control, and which was being exploited by other people to enrich themselves."

"The progressive rise in the rate of import duty had had a crippling effect. Now at 20%, it almost prohibited the sale of cloth in India. It was intended for our degradation and industrial death."

"The Government pleaded that they could not interfere because what was known as the Fiscal Autonomy Convention gave India fiscal independence. That was not true. The convention was not part of the constitution. It had no standing in law, and, in point of fact Parliament, through the Secretary of State for India, had statutory authority and responsibility."

"The Bombay millowners and the Indian Government had raised the tariff on the plea that they wanted revenue, but in doing so they were almost starving the goose that laid the golden egg. The argument was advanced that the boycott of British goods was tantamount to a 'Support Home Industries' plea, but the analogy was false. The boycott was accompanied by intimidation, coercion, and violence against all who refused to support it, not to say that it was mainly directed against the goods of one particular country, and that country our own."

"The economical fallacies of the Swarajists were mediaeval in principle and diabolical in intention. For a man to talk in these modern days about the creation of art and craftsmanship at the spinning wheel and at handlooms was 'the most high-falutin balderdash' that could be uttered by anybody who claimed to know anything at all of the economic development of people and country."

Representatives of the Chamber of Trade and Commerce gave support, but when two Communists tried to make themselves heard, they were ignored.

After more reflection on the problem, the attitude of the union leaders became one of constructive understanding.

On Thursday May 14th. 1931, a special meeting of the Accrington and District Textile Trades Federation was held at the Weavers' Institute to consider a letter from the Overlookers' Society regarding the deplorable position in which the cotton trade found itself. At the end of the meeting the 'Observer' reported that the following resolution was passed:

"That this Federation, comprising all the operatives and textile organisations in Accrington and district, calls upon Mr. Tom Snowden

M.P., the Labour M.P. for the Accrington Division, to exert every possible endeavour to urge upon the Government the necessity for immediate and bold action being directed towards the improvement of the present deplorable state of the cotton industry. We believe that high import duties against Lancashire goods and the economic boycott in India are militating substantially against the recovery of trade. We, therefore, urge that no effort should be spared by the Government in endeavouring to quickly effect amicable relations with India....."

On Sunday June 7th. 1931, a public meeting was held in the Labour Hall, Accrington, on the subject "The Cotton Industry and India," at which the guest speaker was Mr. W.J. Tout M.P. for Sowerby Bridge and a member of the Central Committee of the Weavers' Amalgamation. Mr.J.R. Emmett J.P. presided.

Mr. Emmett commented that 3 years ago nearly 3,000 looms in Accrington made cloths for the Indian market, but today it was questionable whether any cloth woven in Accrington was destined for India. He went on to say:

"The Tory advocates, Winston Churchill, Douglas Hacking and a few more, were continually preaching the iron hand in India. He thought they could honestly say that the reason for this boycott existing today was because of what was done by former governments prior to the Labour Government taking office. We were now suffering the results of the iron hand, and it would certainly take some time to overcome it. He liked the idea of what Ramsay MacDonald said at Blackpool last Tuesday. The way to open the Indian market is to establish political tranquillity between India and ourselves, and give India the sense that she is having a fair deal and sympathetic approach."

Mr. Tout assured the audience that since the import duties on cotton cloths to India were increased, Mr. Tom Snowden M.P. had been in regular contact with the Secretary of State for India, Mr. Wedgewood Benn. He had impressed on him the need to prevent these duties being imposed.

Mr. Tout was of the opinion that these duties had mainly been imposed at the behest of, and in the interests of, the Bombay millowners and were against the interests of the Indian peasants. He also reminded the audience that it was not a Labour Government that had given India the Right to impose these duties.

With regards to what the Lancashire cotton industry was to do in the present situation, he urged the drastic reorganisation of its selling methods. He stated that the organisations responsible for disposing of the cotton cloth to India added up to 100% on to the price. He said:

"The organisation of the cotton trade, the policy of drift which had been followed, had allowed more parasites and a more expensive distribution and purchase of raw materials than any other industry in the world."

In answering a question Mr. Tout denied that conditions were worse in India since the Irwin-Gandhi Agreement. He believed that it was no longer a political boycott, but an economic boycott. However, he thought it would take some time to recover from the former. The Indians had not promised to encourage the consumption of British cloth, they had promised to merely reduce the intensity of the boycott.

On Saturday June 27th. Mr. Stanley Awberry, of South Wales, Secretary of the Transport and General Workers Union at Barry Docks was adopted as prospective Labour Candidate for the Clitheroe Division at a meeting held in Great Harwood. During his acceptance speech, reported in the 'Observer', he said:

"That the people who were shouting most about the Indian boycott were the very people who had sent machines across and put their money in factories, thus competing with Lancashire in the cotton goods there. 'Why did they do this?', he asked. 'Not because they love the Hindu, or the worker of Lancashire, but because they can make greater profit by exploiting the Hindu than by exploiting you'.

"The boycott was the result of the past foreign policy towards India, because we had refused to stretch out the hand of goodwill and friendship..... There was still a potential market in India, if they raised the standard of living of the Hindu."

According to the 'Observer' July 25th. 1931, Mr. H. Potts, Secretary, of the Accrington and District of the North East Lancashire Card and Blowing Room Operatives Association, in his Half Yearly Report, stated:

"According to press reports employers were preparing for another attack upon the cotton operatives in the form of reduced wages and longer hours. This was sure to be resisted."

"Already the operatives had made great sacrifices, always under the impression that a revival in trade would follow and the time had now arrived when operatives had the right to expect employers to prove that every avenue whereby the cost of production could be reduced had been explored before they were again expected to accept worse conditions. Underpaid foreign workers were often used as arguments against the better paid workers and it was hoped that the proposed visit to Lancashire of Mr. Gandhi, whereby he would obtain close contact with the suffering of cotton operatives, would help to convince this leader that the workers of any country could ill afford to be antagonistic towards each other and also that by raising the standard of living of the Indian workers - and there appeared to be plenty of scope for improvement, - a great service would be rendered to a noble cause."

On Wednesday September 23rd. 1931, over 1,000 people packed themselves into the Mercer Hall, Great Harwood, to hear Mr. Andrew Naesmith address a meeting organised by the local Weavers' Association.

He mentioned the severity of the unemployment situation within the cotton industry and referred to the fact that Britain was only carrying out 1/6th. of the trade with India, that they had achieved the previous year. He went on to say:

> "India presented a remarkable problem, but if there was one thing he was keenly anxious about it was that a just settlement to the differences existing between us and India might be arrived at by sane and sensible efforts....."

> "We do not fear the legitimate aspirations of the Indian people to dominion status, or even self-government. We would welcome a large measure of dominion status being given to them. It is right that they should determine their own destinies. But this Indian question is not being assisted by the policy that is being exercised upon us. This policy is one of creeping paralysis, and if we are not mighty careful it means industrial decay and death."

On Friday 25th. and Saturday the 26th. of September, Mr. Gandhi visited the Greenfield Mills at Spring Vale, Darwen. He stayed at the home of Mr. Charles Haworth the firms welfare officer. Before going to Darwen, Mr. Haworth, a Quaker, had been actively associated with the Accrington Society of Friends. Through this association a group of Nonconformist ministers from Accrington were invited to talks with Mr. Gandhi and the 'Observer' printed an outline of their conversation on Tuesday September 29th.:

> "Our first question was whether the movement he represented had its roots in national and racial antagonism. This he strenuously denied. His people were not free and there was of necessity an element of nationalism in it; but his mind was towards a world wide brotherhood, an internationalism of common service. He wanted to make India free so that they could make their contribution to the common civilisation of the world....."

> "Then we asked him his attitude towards machinery.....[He said] his attitude to machinery was that the machine must be the servant and not the master.....he believes machinery is making millions of people unemployed to-day.....He feels it, is essential to have spinning

by hand in the interests of the Indian villages.....He himself enjoyed using a sewing machine.....but it must not be the sort of machine that got people into mills and factories. He was not out for setting Indian industry against British industry. If the Indian mills obstructed the freedom of India's millions they would have to go. He made it perfectly clear to us that he was not against British trade as such, but against machine civilisation, from which he believes India's people are suffering at present. He also said that the machine must not be used for the benefit of a small group against the welfare of the greater portion of society....."

"Our whole impression is that in Gandhi there is a man who has no hostility to English people. He is anxious to establish his own people to make their contribution to the world. There was no suggestion of bitterness in his attitude, but a desire that all peoples should prosper and live a life full, spacious and worthwhile."

Mr. Gandhi's itinerary after speaking to the above included a visit to the Mayor of Darwen, a conducted tour of Greenfield Mill where crowds of people gave him a hearty reception, a visit to Edgeworth to interview cotton employers and trade unionists including Mr. Andrew Naesmith, and to end the day he went to Heys Farm, West Bradford, to be entertained by associates of Greenfield Mill.

During a quiet Sunday at West Bradford, he interviewed a number of cotton operatives from Great Harwood, Clayton-Le-Moors, Blackburn, and Clitheroe. In the evening he set off by road to Manchester where he caught a train to London. His route took him through Clayton-Le-Moors and Accrington at around 10.20 p.m. Although it was not officially known that he would be passing through the locality, a good number of people were on the streets at the time expecting to see the Mahatma and so were not disappointed.

The 'Observer' October 13th. printed a report of the local textile deputation's interview with Mr. Gandhi which was presented to the Clayton-Le-Moors Textile Trades Federation. The deputation had consisted of 4 from Great Harwood, 4 from Blackburn, 2 from Rishton and 2 from Clayton-Le-Moors. The report back was given by Mr. H. Potts.

The deputation was introduced to Gandhi by Mr. J.W. Sunderland, who pointed out that the Lancashire textile operatives were not antagonistic towards him and the Congress Party. Indeed the operatives had responded magnificently, towards the Indian Famine Fund. An explanation of the situation prevailing in Rishton and Clayton-Le-Moors was given, in which they gave the example of 5 of the 10 mills in Rishton being closed through the Indian boycott. In the case of Clayton only one out of the eleven mills in the town was now working due to the boycott. The 'Observer' report is as follows:

"Mr. Gandhi agreed that, in comparing the atmospheric conditions of his country with those of Lancashire, coupled with the cost of living, it was, to some extent, reasonable to say that Lancashire people were almost as badly off as his unfortunate people."

"[The deputation stated] that what ever had happened in the past as regards legislation concerning India, the working classes of Lancashire were quite innocent. They should not be held responsible for that state of affairs....."

"Their concern was that their people should not be reduced to a low standard of living, but they hoped it would be possible to raise both peoples to the standard which Lancashire people once enjoyed. The deputation asked that the boycott might be removed where ever possible, in fairness to their people, so that those of Lancashire might be able to work and live."

"In his reply Mr. Gandhi said.....He was entirely in sympathy with the unfortunate Lancashire people, now that, he recognised the poverty which existed. He said that previously he had been in conversation with what he termed our experts, and that they agreed that the loss of Lancashire trade to India totalled 15% and he could only attribute 3% to the boycott, and remarked that the main problem in Lancashire was world production."

"The deputation pointed out that in Clayton-Le-Moors and some of the areas directly affected, the loss was much greater than 3% and Mr. Gandhi agreed."

"Mr. Gandhi, said that the boycott was not on British goods alone, but on all foreign cloth. The reason it had developed into a Lancashire boycott was that his people considered themselves morally at war with this country, and it had become a sin to touch Lancashire goods, and an open market for Japan and other countries with whom India was of course at peace had been created. For the time being at any rate India would require one-third of her cotton cloth importing, and if a peaceful settlement could be obtained he was prepared to advise his followers to give preferential treatment to Lancashire. This would only be a kind of temporary measure until such times as India could produce sufficient for herself. In the meantime he advised the deputation that Lancashire should be considering reorganisation to meet the changed conditions brought about by this world competition. If we could persuade the Dominions to take Lancashire cloth, it would considerably assist Lancashire trade....."

"Mr. Potts told the 'Observer' representative that according to

Mr. Gandhi's point of view, Lancashire would not be able to obtain any preferential treatment other than a peaceful settlement of the Round Table Conference would enable him to give. Mr. Gandhi's point of view was that if he could go back to his people and say that they had been treated with some justice, then he could influence them to give Lancashire a free hand, and he could almost guarantee that Lancashire would have the whole of the third of the trade necessary to India until they could clothe themselves. If they in Lancashire considered that a peaceful settlement could be obtained without affecting their interests they ought to bestir themselves and bring all the pressure to bear that they could in that direction, so that their people could be found employment."

With Gandhi back in India hoping that there would be no need to renew the struggle and saying that he would do all in his power to promote peace, the reality of the situation was totally different. Imperialism was embarking on an attack on Congress. On January 4th. 1932, Gandhi was arrested together with all the Congress leadership; Congress itself was declared illegal, and censorship was imposed throughout the country. By March 1932, over 120,000 arrests had been made, together with the accompanying wholesale violence. The final end came to the struggle in May 1934, when the All-India Congress Committee was allowed to meet at Patna to end civil disobedience unconditionally.

On Sunday March 20th. 1932, Tom Snowden attacked Maj. Procter the Conservative M.P. for Accrington, in a speech at the Labour Hall, on Blackburn Road. He said:

"In a recent speech, Maj. Procter glorified, to his shame, the fact that Gandhi was locked up in India. I don't know whether the Hon. Member has read much history, or not; he may know a little about Judeah, [Apparently Procter could speak Hebrew] but he will learn more about India if he lives for the next 15 years. De Valera was locked up and now he is Prime Minister of the Free State of Ireland. Although Gandhi is locked up, there will be no extensive trade in India until he is released. Gandhi is a prophet. I am not afraid of saying, after seeing and hearing Gandhi on 3 occasions, that he is something more than a prophet, he is a seer, and he knows what he is talking about."
['Observer' March 22nd. 1932.]

A point not brought out in the speeches at the time, which directly affected cotton imports into India, was the increasing poverty of the Indian people. In 1914 the per capita consumption of machine made cotton cloth was nearly 14 yards, whereas in 1929 this had dropped to 12 yards. Freda Utley states:

"It is this fact of increasing poverty among the vast peasant population of India which affects Lancashire far more than increased production by the Indian mills or increasing Japanese competition."[13]

However, the Indian cotton mills, which in 1914 produced 25% of the country's needs were producing 75% by 1935. At the same time the export of British goods to India dropped from 1,452 million yards in 1928 to only 334 million yards by 1937.

The statistics for British exports to India, not just cotton goods, fell from 63% in 1913, to 35% in 1932. Subsequently due to the Ottawa preferential measures, imposed despite Indian protests, this figure rose to 40% by 1935, but it sank back to 38.5% by 1937.

The days when Lancashire could depend on a captive Indian market were over for good.

THE COTTON CRISIS, CONTINUED

Returning to the situation existing in the Accrington district, the 'Observer' reported that on Monday 1st. June, 1931, the Clayton-Le-Moors Weavers' Association, held a special meeting at which it was decided to sanction a scheme for one instalment of unemployment benefit to be paid at the rate of 5s., 3s.9d., and 2s.6d, according to the scale of contributions paid. On Friday 5th. June, an almost continuous stream of members queued up to receive the benefit at the Associations offices, where over £300 was paid out. For some months past, the Association had only been paying out benefit at half the official scale.

At the Rishton Weavers' Associations Half Yearly meeting held on Monday 15th. June, a resolution was sent to Miss Bondfield, the Minister of Labour and to Tom Snowden M.P. condemning the interim report of the Royal Commission on Unemployment Insurance, but I discuss this further in the next Chapter.

On Saturday July 11th., 1931, the 'Observer' reported the closing down indefinitely of Scaitcliffe Mill, Accrington. This brought the number of looms being worked in Accrington to only a third of those worked five years before.

On Saturday August 8th., the General Council of the Weavers' Amalgamation referred to the districts the request of the CSMA for a reopening of negotiations on the more-looms question. On Thursday 13th. August, a representative meeting of the Amalgamation held in Manchester heard the response of the districts, and authority was given to the Central Committee to meet the employers and discuss the question. This was the first time the general body of weavers had authorised their Central Committee to negotiate with the employers on the more-looms-to-a-weaver system.

In Accrington both employers and weavers appeared to be agreed that it was not possible for the weaver to run any more looms without automatic attachments. A weavers official told the 'Observer' that if the employers were prepared to install automatic machinery he thought it would be possible to come to an understanding with them.

On Monday August 24th.,1931, the minority Labour Government resigned office. More will be written on this subject in Chapter 4.

On Saturday September 5th., the 'Observer' reported that attempts at a settlement of the more-looms negotiations between weavers and employers had reached deadlock. In an official statement it was explained that the two sides were unable to agree on the amount of the minimum wage to be assured under the system.

On Monday September 7th., Messrs. W.F. Chambers and Sons Ltd., the owners of Daisy Hill and Spring Mills, Rishton; India and Primrose Mills, Church; and Victoria and Ellesmere Mills, Accrington; forwarded the following letter to their Rishton workforce for them to sign:

> "We the undersigned, agree to work for Messrs W.F. Chambers and Sons Ltd, at Daisy Hill or Spring Mill, Rishton, on a 6 loom basis, with a reduction on current rates of 20%, which would enable us to earn about 45s. per week, provided the above firm are prepared to co-operate with us as regards the closing down of engines, and similar arrangements as are applying at Burnley."

The 'Observer' said that 90% of the weavers previously employed at the two mills had signed the letter. The two mills had been closed for two months. Operatives at the firms Church mills were concerned because of the possibility of the company transferring work from Church to Rishton.

The response of the Rishton Weavers Association to the letter was to expel two women weavers who had canvassed support for the petition. Mr. J.W. Ashworth J.P., Secretary of the Rishton Weavers' Association was reported in the 'Observer':

> "We have not heard a single word of complaint, on the contrary all have agreed that we have taken the right course. Many who signed did so under protest. They were told that those who signed first would be the first to get work, and, seeing others signing, they added their signatures. The two weavers made no approach whatever to the Association. They did it absolutely on their own."

> "Mr. Ashworth added that immediately he heard of the petition he posted a notice outside the Weavers' Association office in Cliffe Street, stating that it was against the rules of both the Weavers'

Amalgamation and the local association to work on a six-loom basis at a wage not in accordance with the uniform list, and that the action of the weavers would be strongly resisted."

"The Central Committee of the Weavers Amalgamation," added the notice, "are at present in negotiation with the Central Board of the CSMA on the more-looms-per-weaver system, and the action of these weavers does not strengthen the efforts of the Central Committee to get the best terms possible for the weavers....."

"Mr. Ashworth went on to say that things were really worse than they thought before they saw the letter. They understand that the proposal agreed to a wage of 45s. per week, but at a reduction of 20% on the list prices which would earn 45s., the weavers might not earn 30s."

Following on the above, the 'Observer' September 19th, reported that at Britannia Mill, Rishton, operatives had agreed to a management proposal to spend 10% of their wages on preferential shares. After this had become general knowledge in the township the same deal was offered to the weavers at Albert Mill. This was further followed by a similar proposal from the owners of Wheatfield Mill.

"Mr. J.W. Ashworth told an 'Observer' reporter that the weavers who were at work were so afraid of losing their employment that they were prepared to agree to almost anything. Any other agreement, apart from the Sir Amos Nelson scheme, would have to come through the Weavers' Amalgamation. If each mill was allowed to make its own arrangements the whole county would be upset."

On Wednesday evening September 16th., the Great Harwood Weavers' Association, at their Quarterly Meeting, held at the British School, condemned what was going on at Rishton. In the 'Observer' Mr. J.W. Sunderland declared that:

"Weavers who accepted reduced wages thereby created a price list which must inevitably be reflected in the current wages negotiations by the central bodies. It was almost certain that their action would result in worse conditions being obtainable by the operatives' leaders. He appealed to the members to preserve that unity of purpose which Great Harwood trade unionists had always shown, and which had resulted in such beneficial conditions for the operatives in the district, by remaining solid in their attitude towards individual agreements."

The same issue of the paper reported that the unemployment figure for Accrington, Church and Oswaldtwistle was 14,037. In addition the 'Blackburn Times' reported that the figure for Great Harwood, Rishton and Clayton-Le-

Moors, was 7,906. This made an area total of 21,943.

At the 1931 Annual T.U.C. held at Bristol during the second week in September, Mr. A. Dawson [Textile Workers Accrington] spoke from the rostrum supporting the principle of holidays with pay for all workers.

The Central Committee of the Weavers' Amalgamation met on Tuesday September 22nd. after which Mr. Naesmith said that whilst they were prepared to met the employers at any time to discuss the more-looms system, they could not see how this could be done at present. The employers had not approached them on the subject and there had been no indication that their attitude had changed.

On Wednesday September 23rd., as already mentioned in connection with Mr. Gandhi and the Indian boycott, over 1,000 people packed into Mercer Hall, Great Harwood, to hear Mr. Naesmith issue a strong appeal for all cotton operatives to resist attempts on the part of individual employers to reduce wages.['Observer' September 26th. 1931]

On Sunday September 27th. at a mass meeting of weavers at Burnley, Mr. Naesmith said that the announcement that Britain had come off the Gold Standard should make a contribution towards the recovery of the textile industry. ['Observer' September 29th. 1931]

The 'Observer' October 20th. reported that Victoria Mill, Rishton had been bought by Messrs Joshua Hoyle and Company Ltd., Bacup, who intended to restart the mill at some future date. The mill which had been closed since August, contained 1,084 looms and employed 600 operatives.

It was also reported that Ellesmere Mill, Accrington, had reopened after two and a half months closure. The firm employed around 200 operatives.

On Monday October 26th., the workpeople of Stanhill Ring Mill, Oswaldtwistle, started work at 6 a.m. despite union officials trying to persuade them otherwise. The company had requested its workers to attend for 55.5 hours rather than the usual 48 hours to enable them to fulfil orders. At the workplace only 7 workers voted against in a ballot. The 'Observer' reported that officials from both the Weavers' Union and the Cardroom Workers' Union had held meetings with the operatives at which those present had voted unanimously against working such hours.

Mr. W. Hughes, Secretary of the Church and Oswaldtwistle Weavers', said that;

> "The operatives had not willingly consented to start work at 6.00 a.m. and that they would not have started, but for the persuasive efforts and influence of the manager. Whilst a number of operatives were standing outside the entrance hesitating whether to start or not, they were reminded that it was 'nice and warm inside' and also that they

should know 'which side their bread was buttered on.'"

The unions were not against the operatives working longer hours to complete 'just the odd order', but were opposed to a permanent return to the 10 hour day, which this case appeared to be. The extension of hours at Stanhill Ring Mill lasted until November 1932.

On Wednesday November 4th., a notice was put up at Highams, Woodnook Mill, Accrington, intimating that those who desired could begin work at 6.30 a.m. rather than 7.45 a.m.. The following morning Mr. J. R. Emmett J.P., Secretary of the Accrington Weavers' and his Assistant Secretary, Mr. George Kilshaw, together with a number of pickets posted themselves outside the mill. The 'Observer' reported that many of the weavers turned up for work at the earlier hour, but that the majority remained outside until 7.15 a.m., when they entered the building in order to take their breakfast.

Later in the morning the management held a meeting with Mr. Emmett, and agreed to withdraw the notices.

At Premier Mill, Great Harwood, the management posted a notice that stated that the workers wages would be reduced by 20% on the present price list, from Friday November 6th. One thousand operatives were addressed by Mr. A. Naesmith and Mr. J.W. Sunderland and a resolution was passed to resist the wage cut.

The firm stated that unless wages were cut, they would have to close the mill which was one of only 7 mills operating in the township. The town had started the depression with 22 working mills.

After union management negotiations the notice of reduction of wages was withdrawn for one month.

On Tuesday November 24th., Victoria Mill, Rishton, reopened.

The 'Observer' December 12th., published extracts from the Rishton Weavers' Association Half Yearly Report:

> "Whilst there appears to have been some improvement in certain sections of the trade since this country went off the gold standard, the improvement has not been felt to any great extent in this district....."

> "During the past six months the question of more-looms-to-a-weaver has again been very prominent. The matter has been fully discussed at meetings of the Amalgamation, and the Central Committee were authorised to endeavour to formulate a list to apply when weavers were engaged on six or eight looms. This was presented to the employers for consideration recently, and has been somewhat summarily rejected. Owing to the conditions prevailing in many districts through prolonged unemployment, employers in various mills

have commenced to run their mills either on the more-looms-to-a-weaver system or are working at prices less than those provided under the uniform list. Every effort has been made in these districts to prevent this occurring. It is regrettable, though perhaps understandable, that the weavers in these places have agreed to work under those conditions, and so undermine the position taken up by the Amalgamation. We are quite confident it could not have been done but for conditions prevailing as a result of the long period of trade depression....."

Prospect of severe struggle

"There is every prospect that we may again be involved in a severe struggle to preserve the wages and conditions of members from attack by the employers. The employers in the spinning section of the industry have given one months notice to abrogate the Hours and Wages Agreement made in 1919. This is the agreement which provides for a 48 hours working week. It seems strange that at a time when there are so many mills stopped and there is not enough trade to employ all the spindles for a 48 hours week, that the employers should seek to increase working hours. The reduced working week was the only benefit the cotton operatives gained as a consequence of the war, and it is quite certain that they will never agree to go back to pre-war hours or the early morning start. The employers on the manufacturing side do not appear as yet to have decided to join the spinning employers to seek longer working hours, but according to press reports at the time of writing the Employers' Central Committee are recommending to their local associations that they should authorise them to give one months notice to terminate all wages agreements. We assume that this is being done to help those who wish to go on a more-looms system and at the same time to reduce wages of those weavers who remain on the ordinary number of looms in the same proportion. The uniform list of prices for weaving has been in existence for a great number of years, and we think on the whole has operated fairly. We can only assume that the employers will have something to propose to take its place. We are confident that the weavers will not be agreeable to accept any proposals that are likely to lead to reduced wages, as the wages are too low already for the work they are called upon to perform. We have said in previous reports and again we repeat, that if economies have to be achieved in costs of production, they can and ought to be sought in other directions than in reducing the already meagre wages of the weavers. We wonder what is being done to implement the report of the Government Committee of Enquiry into the cotton trade. We think the employers would find a more fruitful field for considering reducing costs of production in that report than in attacks on weavers wages."

The same issue of the 'Observer' published the following from the Church and Oswaldtwistle, Weavers' Half Yearly Report:

"At some mills in the district, schemes have been started with a view to helping the firms to carry on, but in our opinion these schemes are purely a reduction in wages. In three instances the firms are asking for a return of 5% of wages earned, and although the employers say that this is being done voluntarily, unless the employee does return the 5% he is not allowed to remain at work and this in effect means that the voluntary is compulsory. As an Association we do not approve of these schemes because they give an unfair advantage to the firm which adopts such procedures against employers who would not stoop to such methods. At another mill a scheme has been adopted on a basis of a deduction from wages to buy shares in the company, and yet another mill has instituted a return to the 55.5 hour week. All these happenings have been dealt with by the Committee and are still being followed up."

In the same issue, the 'Observer' reported the Accrington Weavers' Half Yearly Meeting, held at the Co-operative Assembly Rooms, Oak Street, on Tuesday 8th. December, 1931. Miss Helena Worsley, the President, informed the meeting that some members of the Committee had attended a special meeting of the United Textile Factory Workers' Association the previous Saturday and had pledged their support to do all in their power to keep the 48 hour week. She claimed that the 48 hour week was the only good thing to come out of the First World War.

In a general look at the situation existing in Accrington, Mr. Emmett said that rogue firms were leaving the Employers' Association, thus making it impossible for decent employers to exist. He knew of women working six looms and predicted that their health would break down as a result. He mentioned operatives handing back a percentage of their pay to their employer. However, he warned the reactionary employers that the Committee was fully aware of their behaviour and that sooner or later, "it would have to be stopped, if it cost everything the Association possessed."

On Wednesday December 16th., Mr. Andrew Naesmith opened the Sale of Work at the Labour Hall, Accrington. The 'Observer' reports as follows:

"I will be doleful, and prophesy this, that 1932 will be far worse than 1931 has been, and 1931 has been worse than 1930. It is no use you being deluded, and false hopes being created in your minds. It is about time that people stripped language of all its embellishments, and told men and women the truth about things. We shall have to go through the mill, make no mistake about it. It is inevitable and the problem for you and I is how can we reduce the hardships and unpleasantness of it all to an absolute minimum....."

"He urged them to maintain their organisation, and he believed that during the next few years, black as the immediate future was, they would emerge from it stronger, healthier and wealthier people than they were at this moment."

1932

The 'Observer' January 5th., reported that the Weavers' Amalgamation had met the previous afternoon to discuss the negative result of their meeting with the employers the week before. That meeting had ended in the employers refusing the weavers request for a 50s. per week minimum wage. The Amalgamation sent a letter asking for a further meeting with the employers.

On January 9th., the 'Observer' printed the Quarterly Report of the Clayton-Le-Moors Weavers' Association. It repeated all the bad news contained in the reports from adjacent districts but appeared more optimistic than the others, stating:

"The reports to date are that there is a more hopeful sign of an understanding being arrived at on the 'more-looms' question, and it is expected that both sides will meet at an early date."

On the same page, however, it was reported that the management of Canal Mill, Clayton-Le-Moors, the only working mill in the township, had requested a 6 a.m. start for a period of one month. After discussions with the local Textile Trades Federation the firm agreed to withdraw its demand.

ANGRY SCENES AT GREAT HARWOOD - POLICE ESCORT FOR SCAB LABOUR - MOUNTED MEN SCATTER CROWDS OF THOUSANDS.

Grange Mill, Blackburn, were in dispute with the Blackburn Weavers' Association and in order to keep the mill working the owners Messrs. Birtwistle and Fielding had recruited 40 blackleg weavers from the unemployed of Great Harwood, and were ferrying them to work and back by omnibus. The 'Observer' reported:

"The hostility of a large body of the cotton operatives of Great Harwood to their fellow operatives [blacklegs], has increased in intensity and led to amazing demonstrations, necessitating the presence of a large number of police and the introduction into the town of a number of mounted police."

"On Monday evening 11th. January.....a crowd of some thousands had gathered on and around the Market Square, and a Jazz Band, played lively tunes in the centre of the crowd."

"The bus was met at the boundary by mounted police and a police motor patrol. When it reached the Market Square there was loud booing and hissing, and cries of 'Traitors' and 'Blacklegs'......"

"The escort passed up Church Street accompanied by loud jeering. Each operative was escorted to his or her home by policemen, and the mounted men and other officers lined up in Church Street to prevent the crowd from getting near the operatives. The mounted men had to go onto the footpath to press back the crowd."

"Supt. Pagett made an appeal to the crowd to disperse. Some responded, but others pressed round the police, particularly the mounted men, jeering and shouting at the tops of their voices."

"Several times the police advanced on the crowd, pressed them back, and then re-formed. The Jazz Band played incessantly. For half an hour the temper of the crowd was uncertain, but eventually the patient work of the police had the effect of sending most of the crowd home, though a large number remained....."

"Similar scenes have been enacted nightly and on Wednesday evening the demonstrators became so menacing in their attitude towards the operatives [blacklegs] that the mounted police found it necessary to charge the crowd."

"The bus went past the Market Place, where over 5,000 people had assembled - up Church Street, and into Cattle Street, a quieter part of town, but it was followed by hundreds. Immediately the weavers alighted the crowd made a rush. The police present were reinforced by a detachment about 100 strong from the Market Square. The foot constables formed a cordon behind the mounted men, who eventually succeeded in pressing the crowd back and clearing the thoroughfares....."

Arising out of the demonstrations, the 'Observer' January 23rd., 1932, reported that John Loynd, of 2 St. Cecilia Street, Great Harwood, appeared before the magistrates at Blackburn, County Police Court, on January 20th. He was charged with using violence towards Mary Alice Shaw, of 51 Gladstone Street, "With a view to compel her from doing an act which she had a legal right to do," and also for "conducting himself in a manner likely to cause a breach of the peace." The offence was caused at 6.10 p.m. on January 12th. The defendant was represented by Mr. Riley of the Great Harwood Weavers' Association.

"Mr. Riley, said the defendant was certainly a weaver, but had no interest in the dispute. Although it had been causing a great commotion every night for at least 14 days, defendant had never been present before the night in question. He was one of the curious people who went there to see what was going on. Defendant stood with his brother opposite the corner of the British Legion offices. Defendant had told him [Mr. Riley] that a mounted officer went practically on the footpath driving people back, and he ran across the street. He may have banged against someone in doing so, but so far as striking the woman to attempt to compel her not to work - that had not occurred. If the man had been a picket of the Weavers' Society, he [Mr. Riley] could not pretend to appear for him and argue that he did not commit the offence, but he was a man who happened to rush across the street out of the way of the mounted police....."

"The defendant, John Loynd, said on the evening in question the mounted police went on the footpath and drove people away. He rushed across Cattle Street, and the next he knew a policeman was taking him up Cattle Street. He did not know Mrs. Shaw, or any of the people who worked at Grange Mill. When the policeman came he denied striking the woman, and said he was evading the mounted police....."

"Richard Loynd, brother of the defendant, said when they were stood in the street there was no thought of hostility. When the bus came the next thing they knew a horse went on the footpath and drove him down Church Street and his brother into Cattle Street. He did not see his brother strike anyone....."

"Francis Bolton, weaver, of 23 Gladstone Street, said the mounted police went on the footpath to disperse the crowd. Loynd ran across Cattle Street, and the next thing he knew a policeman had hold of the defendant.....he [witness] thought the policeman was just getting him out of danger."

Perhaps the most significant witness was the husband of the alleged victim, Mr. James C. Shaw, tailor, who said that his wife "had alighted from the omnibus, but he did not see anything happen, apart from his wife stumbling."

Unfortunately, for John Loynd, he found himself in front of Major Trappes-Lomax, Chairman of the Magistrates, who found the case fully proved. He was fined 40s. and costs in the first case, and 20s. and costs in the second case. Major Trappes-Lomax said:

"I want to point out to those concerned that for conduct of this sort people are liable to a few months' imprisonment. I hope the public will take this as a warning of what may happen if they don't behave."

It would appear that John Loynd was just in the wrong place at the wrong time.

The 'Observer' January 30th. 1932, reported that a further court case hearing took place on Wednesday January 27th. This time, Samuel Stott, of 24 Princess Street, and Richard Eatough of 44 James Street, both of Great Harwood, were fined 20s. each in each of two cases, and ordered to pay 10s. costs for "wrongfully and persistently following cotton operatives with a view to compelling them to abstain from following their employment at Grange Mill." The 'Observer' stated that the blacklegs:

"Included Maria Hindle and Fred Slater, who with five other people lived in the St. Huberts Road district and were escorted by a detachment of police. Thirty people, led by Stott followed the weavers shouting, 'Blacklegs' and 'Scabs.' Stott repeatedly looking back to the crowd and gesturing to them to follow. When a police officer spoke to Stott he said 'I shall go where I want Sergeant.'"

"Stott, pleaded not guilty, said he was on the Market Square shortly before 6 o'clock on January 19th. when a committee which had been set up told him there was a meeting that night, and asked him if he had brought his account books. He said he would go home for them. When he reached St. Huberts Road, he saw that a crowd had collected, and he was walking along when a sergeant came up and told him that if he persisted in following the people he would 'book' him. 'I have never been at the head of any people', he said. Joseph Ainsworth of Queen's Street, Great Harwood corroborated....."

"In the other case Supt. Pagett stated that the circumstances were similar to the first, except that they took place on January 20th. Evidence was given that Eatough was at the head of a crowd following the weavers. Eatough denied that he was following the workpeople.....[and] called corroborative evidence."

Again the Chairman of the Magistrates was Major Trappes-Lomax, who advised people to refrain from such conduct.

The Great Harwood Weavers' Half Yearly Report, stated that operatives from the township who had taken the places of weavers on strike at Grange, Wesley Fold, Gorse Bridge, and Shakespeare Mills in Blackburn:

"Have committed an unpardonable sin, and have made the name of Great Harwood **STINK** in the nostrils of trade unionists in Lancashire."

Later in the year, workers from Great Harwood and Clayton-Le-Moors were also strike breaking at Sun Mill, Clitheroe. A small group of Great Harwood men attempted to hold a meeting on Greenacre Street recreation ground in order to appoint a strike committee for the dispute, but the police gave them a warning saying that they would be reported. ['Observer' June 11th. 1932]

THE COTTON CRISIS, CONTINUED

On Tuesday January 12th. the 2,000 strong Accrington Branch of the National Union of Textile Workers held a special meeting in the Co-operative Assembly Rooms where they were addressed by their General President, Alderman Sir Ben Turner and their District Secretary, Councillor Arthur Dawson.

On the same evening, the Clayton-Le-Moors, Weavers' Association at their Half Yearly Meeting nominated Mr. J.W. Hope, their Secretary, as candidate in the U.D.C. elections.

On Friday January 15th., the Central Committee of the Weavers' Amalgamation, met after the employers had refused to reopen negotiations as long as the Amalgamation insisted upon:

"The formation of a piece price list which will give the weaver working 48 hours and running the full compliment of looms a wage of not less than 50s. per week."

They issued the following important statement:

"We are inevitably forced to the conclusion that the employers are relying upon the economic and industrial conditions of the operatives for enforcing the more-looms-to-a-weaver system at their own terms."

"The employers are thinking that there is more to gain by proceeding through district action rather than negotiating a county agreement on this question. In addition, we are hearing many statements from our members which indicate that intimidatory methods are being used upon the operatives to compel them to accept the employers terms."

"It is a fatal mistake to think that the morale of the weaving operatives is so low that any condition can be imposed upon them."

"The principles contained in Clauses 1 and 2 [proposed by the Amalgamation] are not by any means as revolutionary as the employers have given the public of Lancashire to understand. Fundamentally, the operatives say that in changed processes of cotton cloth production, the well-being and the earnings of the weaver should be adequately safeguarded and in their judgement this cannot be done satisfactorily unless a form of guaranteed wage is provided such as is contained in the first clause of our proposals."

"Our own list on simple cloths would give a weaver a wage of 50s. 11d. per week of 48 hours on 8 looms. The employers proposals, the same factors operating, would give a wage of 49s."

"The difference between us is not in so many pence, but in the fact that we say to the employers: 'Guarantee the wage that should be earned because we are not satisfied that all the factors calculable in ascertaining the wage on a piece-price list basis will operate at mills throughout the county."

"If our Clause 1 was admitted it would at once tend to raise the standard of mill efficiency and discourage continuation of production at inefficient mills." ['Observer' January 16th. 1932]

The 'Observer' of Tuesday January 19th., printed the following statement made by Mr. Andrew Naesmith:

"The action contemplated by many firms in the Burnley area to institute the more-looms-per-weaver system, without the consent of the local weavers association or of the Amalgamation, is likely to lead to a first-class crisis in the industry."

"It [the General Council of the Weavers' Amalgamation] calls upon operatives to offer unrelenting opposition to any proposals that are made, and if need be to act upon the advice that is given by their district associations on behalf of the whole Amalgamation."

A preference share scheme was put into operation at Vine Spinning Mills on January 29th.1932. This is explained more fully later, in a section on the ensuing Vine Mill dispute.

The 'Observer' January 26th.1932, announced that Mr. Herbert Potts, General Secretary of the North East Lancashire Cardroom Association in his Half Yearly Report had said:

"We earnestly appeal to all our members to resist any attempt to lengthen hours or reduce wages and thereby support the action of your trade union representatives to preserve the only material advantage obtained for the operatives since the Great War."

On Friday February 5th., the Northern Textile Trades Federation decided to call a strike at mills in the Burnley district that were breaking the agreements by working the more-looms system, longer hours, or paying lower wages than uniform lists. The strike was to begin on Monday February 8th.

At the A.G.M. of the Accrington and District A.E.U. Shop Stewards meeting, held on Sunday morning February 7th., a resolution supporting the Burnley Weavers strike was passed unanimously.

The A.G.M. of the Accrington and District Textile Trades Federation discussed the question of the possible amalgamation of the three local Textile Trades Federations. The 'Observer' February 20th., reported that the meeting had decided to ask the Church and Oswaldtwistle, and the Clayton-Le-Moors, Federations, to seriously consider the matter with a view to holding a joint conference in the near future. Nothing appears to have become of the suggestion.

On Tuesday February 23rd., it was announced that Mr. J.W. Sunderland, Secretary of the Great Harwood Weavers had been appointed a J.P.

On March 8th., after five breakdowns the joint committee of representatives of the Cotton Spinners' and Manufacturers' Association and the Operative Weavers' Amalgamation, reached a partial agreement. It related to the weaving of plain cloth on the 6-loom-system, and did not include a fall-back rate. The Amalgamation had asked for a fall-back wage of 35s., whether a weaver was running 6 looms or less. The proposals had to be considered by the Central Committee of the Amalgamation and then placed before the General Council. They in turn would refer it back to the district associations for their comments, prior to a final decision by the General Council.

The operatives of Woodnook Mill, Accrington, were asked by their management to accept a 12.5% wage cut, which they reluctantly agreed to at a management organised meeting. However, after being urged by their unions, the Joint Operative Spinners and Cardroom Association, they reversed their previous decision and declined the firms proposals. ['Observer', March 12th.1932]

The partial agreement on the more-looms question was discussed for 4 hours by the 500 delegates representing 40 districts of the Weavers' Amalgamation, on Saturday March 12th., at the Textile Operatives Hall, Bury. It was learned, that the general feeling was hostile to the agreement and that acceptance by the General Council was improbable.['Observer', March 15th.1932]

On March 16th. 1932, the Quarterly Meeting of the Great Harwood Weavers' Association endorsed the partial agreement and sanctioned its representatives to vote for the recommendation. [Minute Book]

On Saturday March 19th., the General Council of the Weavers' Amalgamation rejected the partial agreement made by the Negotiating Committee of the Central Council of the Amalgamation and the C.S.M.A., on the question of the piece rates to be paid to the operatives working 6 looms. The operatives were opposed to any scheme which did not provide an adequate fall-back wage. The employers had offered a fall-back wage of 28s., whereas the weavers had demanded 35s. The meeting was attended by 160 delegates representing the 38 district associations and the voting was 83 votes against acceptance of the Negotiating Committees recommendations, with 73 in favour. Mr. Naesmith said:

> "That for the moment, so far as the General Council and the district associations are concerned, the whole matter is ended. This is not a very optimistic outlook." ['Observer' March 22nd.1932]

On Monday March 21st., the operatives at Moscow Mill, Oswaldtwistle, run by Enfield Manufacturing Company commenced work at 7 a.m. after receiving a directive from the management. This action had been previously postponed after representations had been made to the company by the local Weavers' Association. However, all the operatives without exception presented themselves at the appointed time. A few pickets protested, but they were ignored. A number of unemployed weavers had also turned up in readiness to commence work if the opportunity arose. The hours normally worked in Church and Oswaldtwistle were 7.45 a.m.- 5.30 p.m. with a midday lunch break of one hour. With the 7 a.m. start, the operatives had a half-hour stoppage for breakfast, one hour stoppage for lunch and finished work at 5.15 p.m. ['Observer' March 26th.1932]

The Firm later extended the finishing time to 5.30 p.m., making it a 50 hour week. [according to the 'Observer' April 23rd. 1932.]

On Wednesday March 30th., the former employees of Royal Mill, Clayton-Le-Moors, held a meeting in the warehouse and agreed to work for the Company, if the mill re-opened, for a reduction in wages of 12.5%. The mill contained 1,000 looms and had employed 350 people, but it had been closed since December 1929. ['Observer' April 2nd.1932]

On Monday April 4th., at the monthly meeting of the Church and Oswaldtwistle branch of the Twisters, Beamers, and Drawers Association, held at the Weavers Institute, the General Secretary, Mr.J. Stott of Bury, presented a timepiece to Mr. W. Bentley who had just resigned as Secretary after 15 years service. Mr. T. Briggs presided. ['Observer'April 9th.1932]

The spinners and cardroom operatives at the Accrington Cotton Spinning Company's, Woodnook Mill, returned to work on Monday April 4th., after being on strike against a 12.5% reduction in wages since March 21st. The firm had agreed for the operatives to return at the usual trade union agreed rates of pay.

THE VINE MILL DISPUTE, OSWALDTWISTLE

The 'Observer' January 26th. and 30th.1932, reported that employees of Vine Mills, Oswaldtwistle, were being forced to take up preference shares in the Company, or face the prospect of the mill closing. These were to be purchased by weekly contributions, based on 12.5% of their wages, or 2s. 6d. in the £.

Members of the Spinners and Cardroom Operatives employed by the firm met at the Weavers Institute to fully discuss the project. It would appear that they thought the firm 'had them over a barrel' and so when the management organised a ballot the result was:

> For acceptance of the scheme 264
> Against 4

The scheme was put into operation immediately, on pay day, January 29th. but the operatives were far from happy with the situation.

The Operative Spinners' Amalgamation and the Cardroom Workers' Amalgamation called a meeting of the operatives employed at Vine and Brook Spinning Mills, Oswaldtwistle, at the Weavers' Institute, on Wednesday March 16th., regarding their weekly payments towards investment in their companies. Operatives had signed the following form:

> "Having heard the scheme put forward by directors of......................at meetings held...................., I am in favour of contributing equal to 12.5% of my wages to a loan account in the company on the following conditions:-
> "1. Interest to be paid at the rate of 7% per annum, less income tax, payable half-yearly in August and February.
> "2. All repayments of such loan to be entirely at the discretion of the directors."

The operatives decided to discontinue the practice after hearing the views of their union leaders. However, on Thursday the Company Secretary, of Vine Spinning Company, addressed a meeting of the workforce, after which they voted in favour of continuing the scheme. On Friday March 18th., 96% of the workers made their weekly contributions. Vine Spinning Mill contained nearly 200,000 spindles.

At a meeting held on Friday evening April 8th., the operatives of Vine Mills, members of the Operative Cotton Spinners and Cardroom Workers' Amalgamation, voted to go on strike rather than accept the Company's preference share scheme. The 260 operatives were addressed by Alderman Johnson Secretary of the East Lancashire area of Operative Cotton Spinners' Union; Mr. T. Gradwell, Chairman of the Blackburn Province; Mr. S. Potts, General Secretary of the North East Lancashire Card and Blowing Room Operatives; Mr. E. Reeder, Secretary of the Oswaldtwistle Spinners' Union; and Mr. R. Armistead, Secretary of the Warehousemen's Union. The appearance of such a high profile set of trade union leaders, showed how much they viewed the significance of the employers action. ['Observer' April 12th.]

On Friday April 15th., 100 operatives walked through the picket lines and the mill was reopened. Mr. Harry Boothman, General Secretary of the Operative Spinners' Amalgamation said:

> "We cannot agree to the suggestion that such a scheme is not a trade union matter. In our view it amounts to a reduction in wages of 12.5%, and no such scheme can be brought into operation without having its effect on other manufacturers as well as upon the operatives. Indeed, complaints have already been made by firms that they are losing customers through action of this kind."
>
> "As to the contention that no pressure has been brought to bear on the operatives at the mill, if handing the wages in two packets, one containing 87.5%, and the other 12.5% to be returned, is not pressure, it is difficult to say what it is."

A dozen pickets had been on duty all week, with little resulting disorder. On Tuesday April 12th. a number of women attempted a demonstration and followed a few of the blacklegs home, screaming abuse at them. On Wednesday evening, a huge crowd was in position to heckle and boo, but the police prevented any hostile demonstration. ['Observer' April 16th.1932]

On Saturday April 16th. the Company posted the following notice:

> "A scheme is in operation at these mills whereby employees are contributing to the purchase of preference shares to enable the concern to run during these difficult times. We require a limited number of workpeople in all departments and preference will be given to all persons employed prior to April 11th., 1932." [A. Holden, Secretary]

The notice had the effect of raising the temperature of the dispute. The number of pickets were increased and these were visited by Alderman Johnson and Mr. E. Reeder. However, despite their efforts three more spinners and a number of boys walked through the picket line to join the scab labour. ['Observer' April 19th.1932]

In the week up to April 23rd. there were no unruly scenes, but considerable feelings existed against the blacklegs. On Wednesday April 20th., those on strike attended a meeting at the Weavers Institute, Lock Street, Oswaldtwistle. ['Observer' April 23rd.1932]

On Monday April 25th., with the strike entering its third week, a considerable number of pickets assembled, reinforced by sympathisers and the union's leadership. In the evening crowds gathered but were kept on the move by the police. ['Observer' April 26th.1932]

Herbert Potts wrote a letter to the 'Observer' answering a letter published previously, which had attacked the strikers. An edited version is printed below:

"The attitude of individual employers making arrangements with their operatives, does not relieve the present depression in trade, but produces a state of guerrilla warfare which gives unscrupulous employers the opportunity to take advantage of the present economic position of the operatives by instituting a lower standard of living, and consequently employers who honour agreements made by collective bargaining find themselves severely undercut in price when marketing their commodity."

"During the boom period operatives were not invited to share in the plunder which took place at that time and which to a large extent is responsible for the present deplorable state of affairs. But we now find the management of the Vine Spinning Company initiating a scheme whereby the operatives purchase preference shares by giving back 12.5% of their earnings - upon which interest would be paid at the rate of 7.5% should a profit be made....."

"May I point out that the operatives are simply endeavouring to preserve the present standard of living of themselves and their dependants.....At the moment one can see preparations being made for another attack upon wages and conditions, which if successful, will further reduce the standard of life of the textile operatives and I venture to suggest that a reduction of the purchasing power of the operatives does not provide a solution to the problem which is before the textile trade of Lancashire."

"In conclusion I would remind 'Looker On' of an old saying which is still frequently used. 'Even a worm will turn when crushed under an iron heel.'"

Herbert Potts,
General Secretary, Card, Blowing and Ring Room Operatives Association.
24 Avenue Parade
Accrington

At the end of the third week, the management reported that 60% of the machinery in Numbers 3 and 4 Mills were up and running and that they did not intend to recede from that position. On Thursday April 28th. the operatives on strike distributed leaflets appealing for the support of all trade unionists in their fight against the employer. ['Observer' April 30th.1932]

On Tuesday May 3rd., the Vine management posted the following notice:

"All workpeople who have not returned to work will be repaid their contributions, to the preference shares by applying to the mill on Friday next at 2 p.m."

This influenced some of the strikers to return to work due to the finality of the terms. Indeed the management stated that they now had as many mules running as they had prior to the strike. In response to the notice, the operatives who held by the decision of the union by remaining on strike presented themselves on Friday afternoon to receive monies owed, together with their health insurance cards. This latter action was another gesture on the part of the firm to indicate that they would not be re-engaged. They were mostly men and women of mature years, who had long years of service at the mill. ['Observer' May 7th.1932]

On May 9th., the strikers gained a victory at the Court of Referees at Accrington Employment Exchange, when their claim for unemployment benefit was upheld. They had contended that the share scheme was a compulsory one and therefore a breach of the wages agreement. The Court decided that they had not lost their employment by reason of a trade dispute and that they were entitled to unemployment pay. ['Observer' May 10th.1932]

After six weeks the pickets were still on duty, but the mill was operating normally. The strikers made a hostile demonstration outside the homes of two strike breakers but otherwise no unruly scenes occurred. Disappointment was felt by the strikers when benefit was not forthcoming at the local Employment Exchange. They were informed that they would have to wait another week before payment was made. ['Observer' May 21st.1932]

On May 27th., the strikers received their first out of work pay at the Employment Exchange. However, they did not receive the full amount due to them under the decision of the Court of Referees from April 11th. ['Observer' May 28th.1932]

As the strike entered its 12th. week on Monday June 27th., all the strikers turned up to support the pickets who had been on duty throughout the dispute. The blacklegs were jeered when they left the mill and a few heated altercations took place. ['Observer' June 28th.1932]

On Monday July 18th., the strike entered its 15th. week, with all the striking operatives assembling outside the factory gates as the blacklegs were leaving. A silent demonstration took place. Pickets continued to man the gates and the strikers continued to draw State unemployment benefit and trade union strike pay. ['Observer' July 19th.1932]

The next mention of the Vine Spinning Mill was in the 'Observer' of August 30th. This said that a notice had been posted stating that the mill was closed until further notice. Ever since the strike started in the weaving section at

Burnley and other towns, the mill had been on short time working.

Later in this Chapter, I will record the events of a cotton strike throughout Lancashire, the result of which determined that the operatives had to accept a 1s. 6.5d. in the £ reduction in wages. Following the settlement of the strike on the weaving side, Vine Mills reopened on Wednesday October 5th., with the pickets still on duty. Unfortunately for the strikers they had been in receipt of unemployment benefits for 26 weeks and had to transfer onto transitional benefit determined by the 'Means Test'. ['Observer' October 8th. 1932]

At the Vine Spinning Mill, the management still refused to accept the agreement. Instead of 2s. 6d. being deducted to purchase preference shares, they now deducted 11.5d. in the £ for such purchases, but being a blackleg workforce they had to accept the situation. ['Observer' November 12th. 1932.]

I can find no further mention of this dispute, but the mill closed in December 1932 due to lack of trade. They opened temporarily for the occasional weeks work in October 1933. ['Observer' 28th. 1933]

Vine Mills consisted of 4 distinct factories. Mills No.1 and No.2 closed down in 1934, but the rest of the complex continued until 1968.

PREFERENCE SHARE SCHEMES

In addition to the preference share scheme introduced at the Vine Mills, other local employers took up the idea.

The 'Observer' of July 18th. and July 25th. 1931, reported that the Church and Oswaldtwistle Weavers' Association Committee were not in agreement with the operatives buying shares in Messrs T. Houghton [1920] Ltd., Rhoden and Rose Mills. However, the workforce rather than face unemployment voted by 98% to agree to the company's scheme.

The Preferential Share Scheme at Rhoden and Rose Mills, Oswaldtwistle, came into force on Friday August 14th. 1931. The operatives had to contribute 2s.6d. in the £ from their earnings and the sums thus contributed were placed to the credit of the operative and preference shares in the firm were then allotted. The mills contained over 2,000 looms and when fully running provided work for over 600 operatives.

At a meeting of the operatives held on October 3rd. 1932, a resolution was passed to the effect that the firm be asked to reduce the contributions to 1s. in the £. This was due to a wage reduction of 1s. 8.5d. in the £ having been agreed. The company reluctantly acceded to the request.['Observer' 8th. October 1932]

In September 1933 the firm again requested that the subscriptions should be increased to 2s.6d in the £. At a first meeting of the operatives held in Holy Trinity School the request was declined. However, the management did not like their attitude and asked them to meet again and agree to the scheme. This second meeting duly took place on Thursday September 7th.1933. It was stated that a great many of the workers abstained from voting, being opposed to both schemes, however, a majority voted in favour of increasing their payments to 2s.6d in the £. ['Observer' September 9th. 1933]

At Rishton, as already stated, the management at Britannia Mill, Albert Mill and Wheatfield Mills had proposed that their workforce as a condition of employment had to agree to spend 10% of their wages on buying preference shares.['Observer' September 19th.1931]

Steven Swann mentions an 'operatives as shareholders' scheme being in operation at Hellene Mill, Accrington, also in September 1931.[14]

I have commented on the dispute caused by the preference share scheme at Vine Mills throughout 1932.

The employees of Brook Spinning Company's, Stonebridge Mills, Oswaldtwistle, containing 42,192 mule spindles reluctantly agreed to invest 12.5% of their weekly wages with the firm as loan capital, bearing interest to be paid at fixed intervals. ['Observer', March 5th.1932]

With regards to the taking up of shares by operatives at Industrial Mill, Baxenden, the owners wanted cash-up-front. It was suggested that overlookers pay £20 and that if there were a few members of one family at least £50 would have to be invested before employment would be given. Of course, as in all these schemes 2s.6d. in the £ would be deducted from their weekly wages. ['Observer', March 12th.1932]

The next report on the Industrial Mill scheme was in the 'Observer' of June 4th. 1932, when it was stated that a number of weavers had commenced work on Monday May 30th. The mill had been closed since August 1931 and a new company had been formed. The weavers subscribed 50s. per loom and continued to have 12.5% of their wages deducted weekly towards the purchase of preference shares in the company. The warehousemen and other workers had to subscribe a similar proportion of their earnings towards the scheme.

The mill continued to run on a 'self-help' scheme until November 1934. It contained 897 looms and roughly 300 workpeople were affected. ['Observer' 10th. November 1934] Industrial Mill, Baxenden was taken over in 1935 by W. Holland Ltd. 'confectionery manufacturers and bakers'.[15]

The former workpeople of Commercial Mill, Oswaldtwistle, [Closed in 1931 and which contained 712 looms] were called to a meeting on Monday March 14th. 1932, to discuss the setting up of a new company. The suggestion was that each weaver should invest capital in the proportion of £8..10s. per loom, with overlookers contributing £50. The meeting was adjourned for one week to allow time for the workers to consider the situation. ['Observer' March 19th. 1932] Further attempts were made in June to get the scheme off the ground. ['Observer' June 18th 1932] However, nothing came of the idea and the owner Mr. Hamer sold the mill and machinery. ['Observer' October 3rd. 1933] The building was partially demolished in late 1933. [16]

The Great Harwood Weavers' Association in their Quarterly Report read out at their Meeting in the British School, March 8th. 1933, stated the following:

> "We understand that Clayton Street Mill is expected to open shortly and that Operatives are being invited to lend certain sums to the Firm. The practice is deeply lamented by your Committee for good and valid reasons. We have no desire to interfere with the way our members invest their savings, that is their own business entirely, but we do say emphatically **that the investment of money should not be a condition of employment.** It is a dangerous precedent and must lead to the concentration of unemployment amongst the poorest operatives. Our Industrial magnates have made a sorry mess of their job when we are led to a state of things which calls for such a deplorable means of raising capital."

The Half Yearly Report of May 1933 remarked that the mill had reopened to operatives prepared to loan money in exchange for work. The work offered was paid upon the 'Six looms basis' although most of the work carried out used the traditional four looms. This combination of deteriorating conditions led the Committee to advise their members not to accept employment at Clayton Street Mill.

Operatives were also invited to take up preference shares at Stanhill Ring Spinning Mill by contributing 1s. in the £. ['Observer' May 20th. 1933]

Swann states what the operatives at the time thought about these schemes:

> "That these shares proved useless - with workers exchanging them for packets of cigarettes - confirms how such decisions [to agree to take part in such schemes] were based less on rationalised choice than on the fear of the lay off."[17]

In 1969, Hopwood commented on the preference shares scheme scam as follows:

> "In the case of Ada Kenyon v The Darwen Cotton Manufacturing Co. Ltd., the firm had obtained contributions from the operative's wage each week, authorised by documents which had been

signed in 1932, after the conclusion of the 1932 stoppage of work. The plaintiff left the firm's services in January 1935, and the amount she had contributed to share capital from her wages, £9 18s 3d., was claimed from her late employers. Judge Peel gave a very lengthy written Judgement after the hearing in the Blackburn County Court, in which he found in favour of the employers. This judgement was unsatisfactory, and at once an appeal was lodged, on the advice of Sir William Jowitt, K.C. The appeal was heard in the Court of Appeal on 14th February, 1936, by Lord Justices Slesser and Scott and Mr. Justice Eve. After considerable argument the appeal was allowed, and success therefore crowned our efforts in this case."[18]

From the above it can be read that the employers regarded the schemes to be in effect a permanent wage cut. In the document signed by the operatives at the beginning of their schemes, the phrase:

"All repayments of such loan to be entirely at the discretion of the directors."

was intended, in no uncertain terms, to mean that no repayments would ever be made to those taking part. Hopwood gives no figures as to the number of operatives who got their investments back, but I bet it was an insignificant number.

THE COTTON CRISIS, CONTINUED

On Saturday April 16th. 1932, the 'Observer' reported that Three Brooks Mill, Oswaldtwistle, was starting a shift system. This involved two shifts from 6 a.m. until 2 p.m., and 2 p.m. until 10 p.m. with operatives changing the shifts on a weekly basis. Women were given permission to work the shifts, but not the juveniles under 18 years old. The scheme required an additional 60 weavers. The local weavers' association did not look with favour on the shift system, but did not make any active objection.

Meanwhile, in Accrington, Lodge Mill and Rising Bridge Mill, Baxenden, closed down for the week and Union Street Mill closed indefinitely. Park Mill having been closed for 3 weeks opened on a temporary basis for one week only.

THE DETERIORATING SITUATION IN RISHTON

On Wednesday April 27th., Albert Mill, in Rishton, became the first mill in the township to cut 12.5% off the uniform price list, or 7.5% off wages.

Half the 220 operatives attended a meeting organised by the Rishton Weavers' Association in the evening, when it was decided to resist the reduction. However, on the Thursday morning, in spite of a large crowd gathering, 100 operatives were working by breakfast time. This must have caused a sense of defeat amongst the strikers because by Friday all the operatives were back at work. Mr. Ashworth, the Weavers Secretary, stated that because his members had returned to work, there was little the union could do to improve the situation. He also warned that there was every likelihood that more mills in Rishton would attempt to impose these cuts. ['Observer' April 30th.1932]

At the Annual Meeting of the United Textile Factory Workers' Association, representing half a million operatives, at Blackpool, Mr. W. Thomasson, in his Presidential Address warned all operatives to avoid making individual wages and hours agreements. He said:

> "The making of individual agreements can only end in disruption and destruction, and the action of such workers is suicidal, and calls for emphatic condemnation." ['Observer' May 3rd.1932]

A mass meeting of the workers employed at Victoria, Wheatfield, Bridgefield, and Britannia Mills was held at the Empire Pictures, Rishton, on May 9th. These mills were following the lead set by Albert Mill, in demanding a wage cut of 1s. 4.75d. in the £. Half the workforce of around 900 attended the meeting and each was given a ballot paper to vote for or against a strike. The Weavers' Association issued the following statement after the meeting:

> "In spite of the fact that a majority vote has been secured, it is of such a nature that immediate action will not be taken, and it is referred to the Central Board for their consideration." ['Observer' May 10th.1932]

On Tuesday May 10th., the Central Committee of the CSMA, decided to give one months notice that they were abrogating the Hours and Wages Agreement with the unions. The 1919 Agreement reduced working hours from 55.5 to 48 and gave an advance in list price rates of 30%.

The position was discussed by the Central Board of the Northern Counties Textile Federation, at Blackburn, on Thursday May 12th. at their meeting which had originally been called to discuss the situation prevailing in Rishton. After the meeting Mr. E. Duxbury, the Chairman said that a meeting of the combined executives of the amalgamation connected with his organisation would be called as soon as possible. He said that the Rishton position had been discussed but that it was now merely a part of the whole general position and no [specific] action was being taken in regard to it ['Observer' May 14th.1932]

MESSRS W.F. CHAMBERS, ELLESMERE No. 1 & No. 2 MILLS

The whole situation was going from bad to worse. On the same day the owners of Ellesmere No. 1 and No. 2 Mills, Accrington, stated that they were proposing a further 5% wage cut and making an hour's earlier start in the morning. For some months the 400 operatives had been returning 5% of their wages in packages as a gift to the firm and a partial 6 loom system had been in operation. On Friday morning a deputation of trade union officials were told that no one from the management was available for talks. Mr. Emmett, Accrington Weavers Secretary, said:

"There had been previous reductions there, but the Union had not interfered because they felt that sooner or later some county agreement would be arrived at. The new developments, however, meant that the reductions would now be equal to 2s. in the £."

The firm stated that:

"The position was quite simple. These mills were in competition with firms on the lower basis of wages, who were securing the orders." ['Observer' May 14th.]

On Wednesday May 18th., the new terms of employment were applied and at 6.45 a.m. instead of 7.45 a.m., nearly all the operatives, with the exception of a small minority walked through the picket line made up of trade union officials. Stood next to the picket line were the head of the firm Mr. W.F. Chambers J.P. and his two sons. The operatives held a meeting under the auspices of the Accrington Textile Trades Federation at the Old Band Club on Friday May 20th., at which they decided to resume work only on the conditions applying before May 18th. In reality however, Mr. Emmett accepted that only 21 workers were on strike and these were now 'signing on'. He went on to say:

"Mr. Chambers could not think that because he ran his mills for longer hours other manufacturers would stand still. He would simply be bringing in longer hours all round and so aggravating the situation, for there would be still fewer orders to be got. If any change was required the need was for shorter hours all round."

"Mr. Emmett said that even among the people who were working there was a good deal of dissatisfaction, but the difficulty in getting other work, together with the Means Test and Anomalies Regulations had led to the fear of losing their employment."

"Mr. Chambers was probably arguing that he was finding employment, which was better than the dole, but he was finding employment at a terrible cost, inasmuch as he was trying to introduce conditions which would eventually bring people down to the lowest level." ['Observer' May 21st.1932]

On Monday May 23rd. the firm's two mills in Church, Indian and Primrose Mills containing over 1,000 looms, were asked to accept similar conditions to those imposed at Ellesmere Mills. On Wednesday evening a joint meeting of the operatives at both mills attended a meeting at which trade union leaders urged them not to work on the terms offered, but by Friday all the operatives were at work on the new terms. Later, on Friday evening the operatives met again together with Church residents working at the Ellesmere Mills. This took place in the Co-operative Rooms, Church, and were addressed by Messrs. W. Hughes, J.R. Emmett, R. Armistead and G. Kilshaw. Following the speeches, the meeting passed,

> "This meeting pledges its loyal and active support to the operatives at Ellesmere Mills, Accrington, in resisting the unfair attack on hours and wages, and further agree to a joint meeting with the operatives employed at the Accrington mills."

The above meeting took place as a result of a meeting held on the Wednesday, organised by the Accrington and District Textile Trades Federation, at Unsectarian School, Cotton Street. The situation at Ellesmere Mills was the topic of the meeting, and it was agreed that owing to many of the operatives residing in Church and Rishton, meetings would be arranged in those townships. The places of the 18 workers who refused to accept the new terms had been filled. ['Observer' May 28th.1932]

The next mention of this dispute was in the 'Observer' of August 13th., when it was reported that the 18 workers were still on strike. The dispute became part of the general cotton strike later in the month.

CHURCH BANK MILL, CHURCH

On Wednesday May 11th., Church Bank Mill, Church, posted a notice stating that wages would be cut by 10% [2s. in the £]. A shop meeting of the 350 operatives was held on Thursday, at which a resolution was passed against accepting the reduction with only one dissentient. ['Observer' May 14th.1932]

The unions met the management on Saturday May 14th. after which the management posted up an amended notice stating in effect that wages would now only be reduced by 1s.4d. in the £. The officials reported back to the operatives at noon Saturday, at Church Kirk. Over 250 of the 350 attended the meeting where it was agreed unanimously not to accept the amended terms, which were to come into operation on the following Wednesday. ['Observer' May 17th.1932]

In view of the collapse of strike action in other mills, considerable interest was focused on the events at Church Bank Mill. The Whitsuntide holidays being over, the operatives assembled outside the factory and were directed by the pickets to Church Kirk School, where a meeting was held. This action allowed the union to get its message across and only a handful of operatives entered the mill. On Thursday, however, the strike collapsed, after a large number of out of work weavers from Rishton and Clayton-Le-Moors put in an appearance. The operatives feared that they might be displaced and lose their work and so they reluctantly went into the mill. ['Observer' May 21st.1932]

GREATER ACCRINGTON SCAB LABOUR TRAVELLING TO BURNLEY & HASLINGDEN

At this stage I will relate the activities of local blacklegs travelling to adjacent districts during the summer of 1932.

On June 13th. the operatives of Syke Mill, Haslingden, unanimously rejected their employers insistence of a 6.25% wage reduction and over 160 weavers went on strike.

During the last week of June large crowds gathered in Melbourne Street Bus Station, Accrington, where pickets awaited the arrival of buses from Burnley and Haslingden. This was to counter the actions of blackleg weavers, who had been travelling to Rosegrove Mill, Burnley and Syke Mill, Haslingden, where strikes were in progress.

Apparently 32 local weavers were working in Burnley, including some from Clayton-Le-Moors and Great Harwood. These latter scabs, avoided the pickets by leaving the bus at the Griffin Hotel, Huncoat, and then walking over Whinney Hill. ['Observer' June 14th. 1932]

On July 4th. violent scenes occurred at Syke Mill when 4 special buses containing Accrington workers arrived. At Acre, en route for the mill, locals threw stones at the buses, breaking 5 windows.

At the Accrington Borough Council Meeting, held on July 4th, Councillor Dawson, Labour, asked a series of questions relating to the use of buses involved in the Syke Mill dispute.These were as follows:

"1-Is it a fact that our traffic arrangements with the Ribble Bus Co. prevent them from running services to the south of the borough other than their express services to Manchester, which services involve limited and agreed stops?

"2-Is the Chairman of the Transport Committee aware that the Ribble Bus Co. are running four buses between Accrington and Syke Mill, Haslingden?

"3-Is the Chairman aware that passengers are being set down in parts of the borough which are not agreed stopping places for the Ribble Bus Co.?

"4-Have any steps been taken to prevent the Ribble Bus Co. from carrying out this practice? If not, what assurance can the Chairman give us that steps will be taken to prevent this practice?

"5-Can the Chairman give us any information whether these buses, the indicators of which on arrival in Melbourne Street are altered from 'Private' to 'Duplicate', are included in the pooling arrangements existing between the Accrington Corporation and the Ribble Bus Co.?

"6-Can the Chairman of the Transport Committee tell us on whose authority the bus leaving Lang Bridge's has been deflected from its original route for the purpose of picking up strike-breakers at Pickup Street, Accrington."

Coun. Dawson, having read out his questions asked to move the suspension of Standing Orders so that he could draw the attention of the Council and the public to the unauthorised services being operated by the Ribble Bus Co. This was seconded by Alderman Lambert, Labour, but the motion was defeated by 13 votes to 9. At that point Coun. Dawson asked for a record of the votes to be recorded in the Minutes. These were as follows:

"For - Alderman Lambert, Councillors, Walsh, Baron, Lord, Dawson, Pilkington, O'Connor, Leaver and Howson.

Against - Aldermen, Barlow, Waddington, Higham and Rawson, Councillors, Moorhouse, Slack, Robinson, Lancaster, Tetlow, Platt, Priestly, Higham and Wilkinson." ['Observer' July 5th. 1932]

The blatant bending of the rules, in order to give succour to their fellow capitalist mill owners, over the border in Haslingden, only brought shame on the reactionary rulers of Accrington. Coun. Dawson and his mates knew full well that the result of the vote was a foregone conclusion, but the 'Observer's' policy of reporting Council debates on its front page meant good publicity for the workers cause.

PREPARATION FOR ACTION AGAINST THE EMPLOYERS DECISION TO ABROGATE AGREEMENTS

On Thursday 19th. May, at a meeting of the executives of the various amalgamations within the Northern Counties Textile Trades Federation, it was agreed to ballot the membership on whether to strike against the employers decision to abrogate the hours and wages agreement. ['Observer' May 21st.1932]

The Weavers Amalgamation's General Council recommended their members to vote for strike action on this first question. The ballot papers, however, contained a second question which was to cause some confusion later on. In this the members were asked to vote for or against: "Are you in favour of your officials negotiating with the employers?" ['Observer' May 24th.1932]

In a speech at Colne on Monday May 23rd., Mr. Andrew Naesmith explained how it was not the operatives fault that the industry was in crisis. The employers shortsightedness in their determination to abrogate all agreements on June 11th. had accelerated individual employers demands to cut wages and lengthen hours. He repeated the weavers undoubted claim that economies could be made elsewhere, other than by attacking the standard of living of the workers. He then gave a brief survey of the situation countywide:

"If they looked at the county geographically they would find that in the South, Manchester, Hyde and Ashton-under-lyne areas, where unemployment had been very bad, the employers, through the poverty and distress of their operatives, had secured breaches of the agreements. They found a solid belt of operatives between Manchester and Bury who were still adhering to agreements. Immediately on the fringe of the Rossendale Valley they also found breaches taking place, and straight through Haslingden, Accrington and then diverting through Church, Clayton-Le-Moors, Great Harwood, Rishton, Blackburn and Darwen, they found a large number of mills which had departed from existing agreements. In Padiham, Burnley, Nelson, Colne, Barnoldswick and Skipton there had, as yet been very few departures from the agreements."

He ended his speech by saying:

"The Government concerned with the problem were apparently baffled by it. It seemed to him that it would be more statesmanlike to urge the claims for a reduction in hours....."

"Last year the employers received an advantage when the county went off the gold standard, and they benefited to the extent of 25%. Now we had got tariffs, and despite all this the trade had gone worse. The sooner the Government took cognizance of the position and condition in Lancashire, before it had gone too far, the better for all concerned." ['Observer' May 28th.1932]

On Monday June 6th., the result of the cotton ballot was announced at Blackburn by the Northern Counties Textile Trade Federation as follows:

For Withdrawal of labour	88,603
Against withdrawal of labour	24,493
For negotiations with the employers	63,279
Against negotiations with the employers	29,967

The result was referred to the various executives within the Federation.

The Accrington Weavers' Association's Half Yearly Report stated the following:

"We are inclined to the belief that the cotton industry is, at the moment in a hopeless tangle. The long continued abnormal unemployment experienced by the operatives, the drastic changes in Unemployment Insurance, and the rigorous application of the 'Means Test', seems to have given encouragement to a section of the employers to introduce all sorts of violations of the wages and hours agreements, which, if left to go unchallenged will eventually bring the standard of life of cotton workers down to the lowest possible level. Though abrogation of all agreements by the Cotton Employers' Association does not take effect until June 11th., 1932, we find the more unscrupulous of them feverishly endeavouring to make their sheds into 'blackleg' shops before the date stated....."

"We cannot allow industrial anarchy to prevail in the cotton trade, and it must and can only be thwarted by sensible arrangements and agreements being arrived at between operatives and employers organisations."['Observer' June 11th.1932]

The Church and Oswaldtwistle Weavers' Half Yearly Report had this to say:

"In almost all mills in this area the agreements have been broken already, and it appears to us that we have had a repetition of the 1914 fiasco, when a foreign nation was accused of making agreements into scraps of paper. The privilege to scrap agreements does not now belong to the foreigner, but to a class of people much nearer home."

"The individual agreements which are being made by our people are all against sound reasoning and can only lead to the worst of conditions being imposed, and further these firms will, like Oliver Twist, come back for more, and the trouble will be that honest firms will be dragged into the gutter with the bad firms."['Observer' June 11th.1932]

The Rishton Weavers' Report contained similar sentiments, as did the Great Harwood and Clayton-Le-Moors Reports.

To give some idea of the situation existing in Great Harwood, Prospect Mill, Delph Road Mill, and Deveron Mill had all been in dispute over reductions in wages at some time or other during May and June 1932. Pickets had been placed at all these mills plus three others. However, it was decided to accept defeat on the issue and the pickets were withdrawn on July 8th. [Minute Book] After the decision had been made to withdraw the pickets, Church Street Manufacturing Company's Mill, Wellington Mill, Victoria Mill, and York Mill all cut their wages with the operatives reluctantly accepting the situation.[Minute Book]

At the Great Harwood Quarterly Meeting, however, Mr. J.W. Sunderland J.P. said:

"The dissatisfaction of the weavers at the wording of the ballot had been fully justified by the way members had voted. Votes cast in favour of the withdrawal of labour had largely been cancelled by votes in favour of negotiations. It was impossible to estimate correctly the desires of operatives on the question. Some thought negotiations ought to be entered upon before the withdrawal of labour, and others thought labour should be withdrawn first and then give the Amalgamation Executive power to negotiate terms of settlement." ['Observer' June 11th.1932]

At the Central Board of the Northern Counties Textile Federation, held at Manchester, Monday June 13th. it was decided to hold another ballot, in order to clear any confusion. The following two questions were to be asked with the operative replying to one question only:

"1. Are you in favour of strike action?

2. Are you in favour of negotiations?" ['Observer' June 14th.1932]

The Accrington and District Textile Trades Federation held a mass meeting at the Picture House, Church Street, Accrington on Sunday June 12th. which was addressed by Mr. A. Naesmith J.P., Mr. J.R. Emmett J.P. and Mr. W. Hughes. Mr. H. Potts of the Cardroom Operatives Association presided over a meeting that was not largely attended.

Members of the Lancashire Textile Minority Movement distributed leaflets outside the meeting urging operatives to carry out strike action in order to enforce the continuance of the old agreements.

"Mr. Emmett said: If anyone had told him two or three years ago that their Lancashire people would stand this, he would have called them ignoramus - he could not possibly have believed it - but knowing the trend of events and what had happened in the last few years, the very severe unemployment their people had to face, and the great difference the 'means test' had made to them, one could really forgive a number of their people for the weakness they were displaying at the moment."

"Accrington had been fairly free from these reductions up to now. One employer, Mr. Chambers [Ellesmere Mill] had led the way, and unfortunately, through the circumstances, as they stood at the moment, he was able to attain his object.....They knew when Mr. Chambers introduced this idea that it would not stop at his mill....."

"They were now faced with a similar position at six other mills in the town - Peel Mill, Queen Mill, Haworth's Melbourne and Scaitcliffe Mills, Oak Vale and Bury Bros' Fountain Mill. They knew there was a lot of dissatisfaction in those mills, but that dissatisfaction was not shown in the attendance that afternoon....."

"But somebody has got to put up a fight somewhere; this thing cannot go on indefinitely....."

Mr. W.Hughes, said:

"One thing which he regretted was that most of the shop meetings he had attended and most of the mills where they had taken strike action had been ruined by youngsters who, in the main did not value what other people had won for them. They were a great stumbling block, and he hoped the youngsters would realise that this was their battle as well as that of the older people....."

Mr. Naesmith, said:

"The hall ought to have been packed to the doors. If men and women whose livelihood was dependent upon the wages they earned were not sufficiently interested in the condition under which they worked and the wages they received to attend a meeting of that description, all he had to say was 'God help us all; we are unable to help ourselves.' If that meeting had been called in other parts of Lancashire there would have been a seething mob of men and women half an hour before the meeting began, but in Accrington where they had a Weavers Association for over 70 years, and side by side with that, the growth of other organisations, to see 150 or 160 people gathered together out of well over 2,000 to determine the policy that affected them all the following morning, well nigh broke ones heart."

He ended by saying:

"The rehabilitation of their industry was not going to come through cuts in wages. It could only come through a scientific examination of the industry, and bringing all their minds and gifts to bear upon how they could rectify the flaws and the faults in the structure of their industry, in order that their costs of production could become competitive."

The following resolution was carried with only one dissentient:

"That this meeting of textile workers of Accrington and

District declares its emphatic protest against the posting of notices of wage reductions at the various mills, and definitely decides to do everything possible to resist such reductions....." ['Observer' June 14th.1932]

The leaflets given out to those who had attended the meeting, by the Lancashire Textile Minority Movement, was probably entitled 'A Call To Action'. This contained the following message:

"After years of continuous wage cuts, after reducing unemployment benefit, after subjecting both the employed and the unemployed workers to the despicable robbery of the **'means test'**, after cutting tens of thousands of married women off benefits, and after robbing the workers by means of rising prices, the capitalists are preparing further attacks upon the working class."

"The Lancashire Cotton Bosses are determined to impose **longer hours, less wages,** and the **more looms system** upon the cotton workers. In order to carry out their plans, the Bosses have decided to try to divide the ranks of the workers, by holding off the attack upon the spinners and cardroom operatives, and to go forward with the attack against the weavers."

".....The workers' reply to this manoeuvre of the Bosses must be **'One out, All out'**

".....The Trade Union leaders are assisting to the fullest extent this drive of the Cotton Capitalists. These men who have constantly betrayed us in the past, i.e., the arbitration swindle of 1929, the flouting of ballot votes against the 8 looms, constant meetings in secret with the Bosses, expulsion of all militant workers from the Unions, etc., are part of the enemy forces, and at the present time are the greatest asset of the employers in stifling the militancy of the workers and allowing the Bosses to introduce worsened conditions."

"Fellow workers, we must learn from past experience. Take no notice of the so-called 'Left' local officials [referring to the I.L.P.] who say that all that is necessary is to bring pressure to bear on the Union leaders and to put these so-called 'Lefts' in their places."

"Victory can only be assured by taking control from these men and placing it in the hands of the Committees elected by the rank and file in the workshop."

"We therefore call upon all Textile Workers to rally behind the **Minority Movement** which is leading the fight around the slogans of:

"1. AGAINST THE 8 OR MORE LOOM SYSTEM.
2. AGAINST THE LONGER WORKING DAY.

3. NOT ONE PENNY OFF WAGES.
4. RETENTION OF THE PIECE PRICE LIST."

At the Half Yearly Meeting of the Accrington Weavers' Association held at the Co-operative Rooms, Oak Street, Tuesday June 14th., there was a large attendance. The main topic of discussion was the action to be taken on Wednesday morning June 15th., and this resulted in the following resolution being carried with only one dissentient:

"That this members' meeting decides that they are definitely opposed to the suggested wage reductions, and they recommend that deputations be formed at every mill tomorrow where this reduction is being put into operation, to consult with the firm with the object of trying to persuade them to post-date notices until after the next ballot. In the event of them failing, the Society recommends them to come out on strike." ['Observer' June 18th.1932]

The 'Observer' June 25th., reported that in Church and Oswaldtwistle, approximately 100 people were on strike at Messrs J. Bury's, Union Mill, Spring Hill, but that all other operatives had accepted the wage reductions in some form or another.

In the Accrington District the operatives had gone into work, where that was possible, but Higham's Woodnook and Warburton's Lodge Mills were closed all week due to bad trade. A similar situation existed in the other districts.

The result of the cotton ballot was declared on Friday June 24th. at a meeting of the Central Board of the Northern Counties Textile Trades Federation as follows:

For a strike	78,437
For negotiation	61,742

The 'Observer', June 25th., commented that it was regarded as certain that in Nelson and Burnley they would have voted for a strike because wages had not been reduced in those districts. On the other hand the Blackburn and Greater Accrington Districts, having had their wages reduced, had probably voted for negotiations to take place.

On Monday June 27th., the Central Board of the Textile Trades Federation issued the following statement:

"In view of the figures disclosed by the ballot vote this Central Board finds itself unable to agree to enter into negotiations so long as the conditions laid out by the Employers' Association remain.

"These conditions which commit the operatives to a reduction in wages before they enter into negotiations, create a difficulty which ought to be removed. A better atmosphere should be created in order to remove the chaos now existing in the industry."

In other words a deadlock situation had been reached. This was to remain the case until Thursday July 14th., when the Central Committee of the Weavers' Amalgamation at a meeting in Accrington, decided in favour of reopening negotiations with the employers. The object being to secure a new uniform agreement on wages and conditions. The resolution adopted which was sent to the Central Board of the Federation read as follows:

"That we recognise that the absence of agreements between the general body of employers and operatives is bringing about conditions in the industry disastrous to both sides. We are, therefore, prepared to meet the employers in order to discuss the conditions under which an agreement can be made, fixing the rates of wages and conditions to be applied to the whole, of the industry." ['Observer' July 16th.1932]

On Monday July 18th., the Central Board of the Northern Textile Trades Federation agreed to meet the employers to endeavour to arrange a new wages and hours agreement. ['Observer' July 19th.1932]

This attitude of compromise did not go down well with more militant areas. The Committee of the Nelson Weavers' Association passed the following resolution:

"We call upon the Central Committee of the Amalgamated Weavers' Association to withdraw the whole of its members throughout the county until such time as the uniform list of weaving prices is re-established." ['Observer' July 23rd.1932]

On Friday July 29th., at their first meeting, the employers opened the negotiations by asking for a 30% reduction on the price list, equal to about 16% in wages, or just over 3s. in the £. The meeting was adjourned. ['Observer' July 30th.1932]

Meanwhile in Burnley there was an amazing response to the Burnley Textile Trades Federation's call for strike action against the cuts on Monday 25th. July. Over 15,000 operatives heeded the call and on Tuesday, following noisy demonstrations and disturbances, more mills closed. So widespread was the dispute, that the police were unable to provide cover at every mill. 50 police had to be drafted in from Manchester. By Wednesday evening every mill in Burnley was shut, with over 25,000 workers in dispute. ['Observer' July 30th.1932]

The position locally, in view of the Burnley strike, was considered by the Accrington Weavers' Association on Tuesday night August 2nd., but it was decided to defer any action until a decision was taken by the General Council of the Weavers' Amalgamation. ['Observer' August 6th.1932]

The Amalgamation met on August 3rd., where they received a full report of the negotiations with the employers, discussed the resolution from Nelson Weavers' Association calling for an industry wide strike, and a further resolution from its own Central Committee. The result was that all power and authority was placed in the hands of the Central Committee to do as they thought fit. ['Observer' August 6th.1932]

The negotiations continued in Manchester on Friday August 5th, but after 6 hours the conference was adjourned. The employers had dropped their demand to a wage cut of 25% off list prices, or 2s. 9d. in the £., whereas the unions were only prepared to a reduction of 12.5%, or 1s. 4.5d. in the £. ['Observer' August 6th.1932]

On Thursday August 11th., a Central Committee recommendation calling for a strike was placed before the General Council of the Weavers' Amalgamation. The meeting representing 36 districts was attended by 155 delegates. The Central Committee's recommendation which was unanimously approved by the meeting read as follows:

> "In view of the breakdown in negotiations and the unsatisfactory attitude of the employers, the Central Committee recommends a general stoppage of the industry for the restoration of agreements with regards to list prices, and the reinstatement of operatives brought out on strike."

The general strike of weavers was to be delayed for a week, in the hope of enlisting the support of the Northern Counties Textile Trades Federation, which embraced the other trade unions concerned in the industry. ['Observer' August 13th.1932]

At a specially called General Committee meeting of Great Harwood Weavers' Association on August 11th., and at a Special Members Meeting on August 16th., [400 members present] a resolution in support of a County Strike to maintain full list wages and to secure the reinstatement of operatives previously brought out on strike, was passed unanimously.[Minute Book]

The Great Harwood Weavers' wasted no time and immediately set up a strike committee, which set about printing leaflets aimed at each of the mills still running in the township.[Minute Book]

On Monday August 15th., at a meeting in Blackburn, the Northern Counties confirmed the decision of the Weavers' Amalgamation to call a general strike within the industry. The following official statement was issued:

> "This Central Board is of the opinion that any further attempt to continue the cotton industry without satisfactory agreement with regard to wages and conditions can only end in disaster to both employers and operatives."

> "We regret that the employers refuse to reinstate those

operatives who have withdrawn their labour in order to maintain agreements then in existence. We offered to recommend certain proposals with regards to wages but have found the employers determined to reduce wages by an amount which we regard as unreasonable. "

"In those circumstances we have no alternative but to recommend the withdrawal of all operatives unless the employers meet us in a more reasonable manner."

The resolution adopted by the meeting read:

"That in the event of there being no alteration in the situation by Saturday August 20th., we give notice that labour be withdrawn on Saturday August 27th." ['Observer' August 16th.1932]

On Friday August 19th., Mr. Andrew Naesmith warned that an immediate strike might be called if the concentration of police protecting imported blackleg labour in the Burnley district was not stopped. He said:

"If the police are going to continue to concentrate on Burnley, the only effective way the operatives have of replying is to spread the dispute instantly so that the concentration will have to be broken."['Observer' August 20th.1932]

At Oswaldtwistle Town Hall, on Sunday August 21st. delegates of the combined Textile Trades Federations of Accrington, Church and Oswaldtwistle, and Clayton-Le-Moors, unanimously endorsed the decision of the Northern Counties Federation to call upon their membership to answer the strike call on Saturday August 27th.

The meeting also arranged for three mass meetings of the operatives to run simultaneously on Thursday evening August 25th., in the Town Halls of Accrington, Oswaldtwistle and Clayton-Le-Moors.

The membership of the local districts prior to going into the dispute were Accrington 3,300; Church and Oswaldtwistle 2,850; Rishton 1,796; Clayton-Le-Moors 1,359; and Great Harwood 3,926. ['Observer' August 23rd.1932]

All the mass meetings held in the various Town Halls on the Thursday passed resolutions pledging the workers to loyally respond to the county strike call. All the meetings had large attendances and were characterised by unanimity and enthusiasm. Over 1,000 persons were present in Accrington Town Hall, over 800 attended at Oswaldtwistle and at Clayton the 'Observer' stated that it was a well attended meeting. ['Observer' August 27th.1932]

On the evening of August 26th., three days of discussion between the employers and union representatives, under the neutral chairmanship of Alderman Titt, Deputy Lord Mayor of Manchester, came to deadlock. Alderman

Titt issued the following official statement:

"I regret to inform you that the attempt to obtain a settlement of the difficulties in the manufacturing section of the cotton industry has failed. It has been found impossible to find accommodation on the difficult question of reinstatement."['Observer' August 27th.1932]

With regard to the reinstatement of the strikers who had refused to work under the new conditions, even the 'Observer' came out in their support:

"Accrington has something just over a hundred operatives who left their looms as a protest against wage cuts and whose places were taken by others who were prepared to accept the lower rates of pay. Throughout the whole of the industry there are between two and three thousand operatives similarly situated - roughly 2% of the total number of operatives who will be brought to a standstill by a strike....."

"It would have brought ample reward had it been agreed that these people should be taken back with the least possible delay, and that in the meantime they shall not suffer financial loss because of the loyal action they took at the behest of their leaders. It would be infinitely the better way to reach some such terms than to plunge Lancashire into the throes of a disastrous strike."['Observer' August 27th.1932]

On Sunday August 28th., a Mass Meeting organised by the Rishton Textile Trades Federation, was held at the Empire Pictures, Rishton, and a large number of cotton operatives unanimously decided to strike on Monday morning. The meeting presided over by Mr. J. Looms [that's what the 'Observer' said,] was filled to overflowing and all present enthusiastically supported the decision to strike. Mr. Carey Hargreaves, Secretary of the Nelson Weavers' Association, Mr. H. Beardwood J.P., Secretary of the Blackburn Overlookers' Association and Mr. J.K. Bailey J.P., Secretary of the Darwen Weavers' Association were the guest speakers. ['Observer' August 30th.1932]

THE COTTON STRIKE

On the first day of the strike, the response in North East Lancashire went practically solid for the stoppage, with Burnley and Nelson being totally closed. At Accrington at the end of the first day, the following mills were stopped:

	Number of operatives
Bury Bros,' Fountain Mill	500
Peel Mill	500
Queens Mill	340

Messrs Haworth's, Melbourne Mill	280
Messrs Worsley's, Mills, Baxenden	400
Oak Vale Mill	296
Hellene Mill	300
Park Mill	100
Chambers', Ellesmere Mill	350
John Bury and Son's, Union Mill	<u>280</u>
Total	3346

Of the above Oak Vale opened, but the engine stopped at 9 a.m. due to only a handful of workpeople turning up. Crowds of over 1,000 strong demonstrated outside Chambers' Ellesmere Mill where under 100 operatives were blacklegging. On the arrival of Mr. Chambers his car became surrounded and at lunch time two rushes were made by the crowd at the scab labour. This resulted in the mill closing down at 4 p.m.

At Bury's Union Mill, a large crowd had assembled and the blacklegs were booed and jeered. Police had to keep a way clear for the scabs to walk into the mill unmolested. Again the mill closed at 4 p.m.

At Park Mill 30 strike breakers were at work but at lunch time a demonstration of over a thousand which filled Park Street from end to end, put the fear of God into them. The mill closed at 4 p.m. A similar number had gone into work at Hellene Mill, but this also closed at 4 p.m.

Mills still running	Number of operatives
Higham's, Woodnook Mill	200
Warburton's Lodge Mill	100
Perserverance Mill, Huncoat	100
Industrial Mill, Baxenden	<u>300</u>
Total	700

Industrial Mill, Baxenden, had apparently been allowed to remain open until Wednesday with the union's agreement.

At Church, the pickets and strikers turned up in force especially at Messrs. Chambers' Indian and Primrose Mills, where very few entered the sheds. At Albion and Tanpits Mills belonging to the Antley Manufacturing Company, the mills closed at lunch time. At Church Bank Mill, the pickets reported that only a few operatives resumed work. Only at Canal Mill was the strike not a success, the majority turning into work.

At Oswaldtwistle, Moscow Mill, reported a dozen strike breakers and the mill shut at lunch time. At Rose and Rhoden Mills the majority went into work through the picket line. At Three Brooks Mill, were the employees throughout the depression had enjoyed continuous employment at full standard rates of pay, the union officials were agreeably surprised that so few of the operatives entered the mill.

However, at Clifton Mill, Paddock Mill, Stanhill Mill, and Fern Mill, the operatives all walked through the picket lines. At Rhyddings Mill 25 operatives had blacklegged. Vine Spinning Mill management stated that the mill would be closed until further notice.

The General Secretary of the Overlookers' Association, Mr. Duxbury of Bury, visited Oswaldtwistle in an attempt to get the Church and Oswaldtwistle branch to reverse their anti-strike decision.

At Clayton-Le-Moors the response to the strike call was poor. Only Canal Mill with 200 operatives and Claymore Mill with 150 operatives, were normally working in the township. At Canal Mill the operatives were waiting for a lead from the overlookers and when it became known that they had entered the factory earlier than usual, they all went into work except for four loyal members of the union. At Claymore Mill all the workers became strike breakers.

At Rishton over 2,000 operatives were on strike with only two mills attempting to remain open. At Daisy Mill, owned by Messrs W.F.Chambers and Sons, 35 blacklegs were working in the morning, but after enduring a storm of hissing and booing at lunch time, they had decreased in numbers. At Wheatfield Mill, 17 operatives did not heed the strike call and the mill closed later in the day.

At Great Harwood, Mr. J.W. Sunderland was 'fairly pleased with the situation. If the people on strike remain loyal we should rescue a stoppage at the other mills.' At a Special Committee Meeting held on August 29th, 1932 the Minutes state:

> "1. That we report a magnificent response to our call for strike action. York, Wellington, Victoria and Palatine Mills were practically stopped......only a comparatively few operatives working at Britania, Prospect and Deveron. Nearly all members were out at Whalley and Sabden. Not more than 200 members working throughout the district."

At a further Special Meeting held on August 30th. the Minutes state that the unions position was strengthening in Great Harwood.

However, the 'Observer' reported that nearly all the mills were open, with between 20% and 50% strike breaking. The main body of the Overlookers' Association waited outside a mill in the centre of the town at lunch time and persuaded members to join the strike and a number of other operatives stayed out. There were many scenes of noisy behaviour as scabs left the factories. ['Observer' August 30th.1932]

At the end of the first week, the situation remained the same in Accrington. However, pickets had been placed at Industrial Mill, where the management continued to work the mill after giving the union a definite promise to close on Wednesday night. Of the 180 workforce over 100 blacklegged. A mass demonstration took place as they left the factory in the evening.

At Oswaldtwistle, where the majority of operatives had ignored the strike call, Tuesday saw the local pickets and demonstrators numbers swollen by contingents of strikers from Accrington and Rishton. The plan of campaign was to target one mill at a time. Rose and Rhoden Mills were selected for special attention and at 5.30 p.m. over a thousand demonstrators surrounded Rose Mill and these were faced by 20 police constables and 2 mounted policemen. When the operatives came out the police had difficulty maintaining order, terrific booing and jeering took place and a few blows were struck. Many of the blacklegs were 'cowed with terror.' The 'Observer' reported:

> "The situation was distinctly ugly, as a section of the crowd were seething with anger and excitement. What had been intended as a demonstration against the workers, turned into a demonstration against the police. Every time they moved the 'booing' became terrific, and not only were many of the young folks filled with fright, but all were anxious as to what might happen."
>
> "There was another ugly scene when.....two of the foremen appeared. As they walked along Commercial Street the crowd closed in towards them booing them,.....Two officers seized one young man demonstrator, and there was a rush towards them by a group of men and women, evidently intent on rescuing the man. For a minute they swayed to and fro, but other constables ran to the assistance of the two police officers, and eventually, after explanations and admonitions the police released the man.....The excitement spread further afield and stories were told of fighting in at least two streets...."['Observer' September 3rd.1932]

The above proceedings were observed by Councillors O'Connor and Howson of Accrington. Scenes such as the above had not been seen in Oswaldtwistle since the strikes of 1878.

The following morning, the management decided to take notice of the townships strength of feeling and closed the mills, sending 700 strike breakers home.

At Three Brooks Mill, there were mild demonstrations on Tuesday, but on Wednesday, the owner decided that the wise course of action was to close the mill down.

The same situation came about at Paddock, Clifton, Stanhill and Rhyddings, all closing on Wednesday. This meant that all the mills in the urban part of town were closed and so on Thursday the pickets concentrated on Fern Mill at Duckworth Hall, but this continued to run. Three other small mills in the township, but which were in the Blackburn Weavers' Association area, continued to run. These were two mills at Belthorn and one at Knuzden.

Oswaldtwistle Mills closed at the end of the first week:

	Number of looms
Rhoden	1,263
Moscow	991
Rose	848
Three Brooks	833
Rhyddings	691
Paddock	348
Stanhill	312
Clifton	118

At Church, all the mills had closed by Tuesday, except for Canal Mill. Huge crowds assembled and the intensity of the booing was terrific, resulting in the firm closing the factory down on Thursday.

Church Mills closed at the end of the first week:

	Number of looms
Church Bank	1,048
Union [Accrington]	1,024
Indian and Primrose	1,000
Albion	704
Providence	647
Canal	327

Over 3,000 members of the cotton unions were on strike in Church and Oswaltwistle, and to these must be added a number of non-unionists. Non-unionists who came out on strike on Monday, were given the opportunity of joining the union and receiving half-pay benefits, but this offer was not extended beyond that day.

At Clayton-Le-Moors, the strike became 100% on Tuesday evening, after intensive picketing caused too few operatives to enter the mills, and the management closed them down.

At Rishton, the strike had been a complete success with about 2,500 operatives out. Of these, 1,800 were members of the Rishton Weavers' Association.

On Friday September 2nd., Mr. Tom Snowden, the former Labour M.P. for Accrington, forwarded a letter of encouragement to Mr. J.R. Emmett which contained one guinea, together with the promise of a further guinea one weeks hence. He said:

"I hope you will all bear up through it all" ['Observer' September 6th. 1932]

At the end of the second week events remained unchanged in Accrington, except that the Industrial Mill, at Baxenden, had closed on Saturday afternoon, September 3rd., following intensive picketing. Higham's Mill, Lodge Mill and Perseverance Mill, Huncoat, remained running. The town remained quiet during the day, but in the evenings crowds gathered to listen to the Communist speakers on the Market ground.

In Oswaldtwistle, Stanhill Mill, reopened on Monday, September 5th. The police apparently prevented crowds from assembling in the vicinity of the mill, the wet weather being a valuable ally to them in achieving their objective. ['Observer' September 10th.1932]

At the 1932 Annual T.U.C. held at Newcastle, September 5th. to 9th., Mr. W. Slynn, of the Great Harwood Weavers during a debate on disarmament said the following:

> **"My position is this, that as a Socialist inside the Trade Union Movement, inside the Co-operative Movement, and inside the Labour Party, fighting for the overthrow of the present system......."**

> **"Let us prepare ourselves for the sacrifices which may be forced upon us in the near future if we are to transfer this system from Capitalism into Socialism which I believe, every man and woman here, is working for in the future."** [Conference Minutes]

'The Cotton Strike Leader', published by the Cotton Strikers Solidarity Movement, September 10th 1932, contained a report of a Delegates Conference of 121 strikers elected at meetings in Haslingden, Blackburn, Rochdale, Crawshawbooth, Rawtenstall, Earby, Barnoldswick, Accrington, Bacup, Oswaldtwistle, Preston, and Great Harwood, which was held in the Co-operative Hall, Burnley on September 7th. [Jim Garnett was in the Chair]

> "The Conference was permeated with a splendid infectious spirit of militancy and enthusiasm. Every delegate from the strike front, and every one straining every nerve to gain a smashing victory."

> "It was the first time in the history of Lancashire cotton struggles that such a united rank and file gathering had ever been organised."

On Monday September 12th., two mills restarted in the Greater Accrington area, namely Canal Mill, Church, and Industrial Mill, Baxenden, but they were not sufficient to make any material difference to the situation.

At Canal Mill, the firm were continuing to pay the full standard rates of wages. All but six operatives had returned and the firm had posted a notice saying that operatives who had not returned by Tuesday September 13th., would be considered to have left their employment. The pickets on duty, including Mr.

W. Hughes, Church and Oswaldtwistle, Weavers' Secretary, had their names and addresses taken with a view to prosecution under the Trades Disputes Act. The police prevented crowds gathering at the mill and whenever people stood together they were asked to move on.

On Tuesday afternoon, the Church and Oswaldtwistle Weavers, held a crowded meeting in Oswaldtwistle Town Hall, at which Mr. W. Hughes, together with Mr. Helm, Assistant Secretary to the Weavers' Amalgamation, "strongly appealed to the weavers to stand firm and continue the strike until a satisfactory solution was reached."

However, on Wednesday, Clifton Mill, Moscow Mill Street, Oswaldtwistle, employing about 60 workpeople reopened, but continued to pay standard wages. ['Observer' September 17th.1932]

'The Cotton Strike Leader' published by the Cotton Strikers' Solidarity Movement, on September 17th. 1932, contained an article by a striker from Great Harwood. It is reprinted below:

"Government Intervention In Great Harwood"

The position in Great Harwood seems to be very illuminating to we workers at the present. The drafting of mounted police and foot police is arousing the suspicion that the employers are going to start a mill or mills, but the Textile Trade Federation have given no lead, nor have they even started a protest movement against this action of the State."

"But in Sabden, where a mill has been flooded, they have given them permission to start."

"In Sabden the police used the most filthy kind of language, irrespective of whether they where women or children, when we workers of Great Harwood rambled in the village, and a horse trampled on a woman worker."

"But these police, who deliver summonses in the street, who attend working-class meetings, try to overawe us, and try to stop we workers from organising or, when organised, try and stop us workers from being effective, are let come in the town without a protest."

"The 'Daily Herald' wanted Government intervention, but the workers have seen Government intervention in Great Harwood before. The police - horse, mounted and mobile - were used when the mass pickets protested against workers going to Blackburn to work at the Gorse Mill."

"The tactics of the Government can be defeated, and the Textile Trade Federation know it. For every trick of the police the workers know a hundred, but we workers will have to do it ourselves.

Protest meetings, sending workers into other towns to get support - this question should be raised at every meeting in the country, resolutions of protest in every union branch."

"The workers in Great Harwood should also rally round the Provisional Strike Committee, which is composed of strikers and unemployed workers, so that at the conclusion of the dispute the question of conditions in the mill shall not be as bad, but that they must be improved."

"Only in this way are we workers ourselves going to make life bearable. Alvery Barker said he was sure of Skipton, but in Harwood it was all out by Tuesday. It took the mass pickets longer at Skipton, but we must go forward to more successes. Mass picketing will keep all out."

T.U. Officials Strike Breaking.

"On the 31st. of August the local Textile Trades Federation organised a demonstration to Sabden in order to encourage the workers to come out on strike. They were successful in their object on the same day."

"It must be remembered that the workers at this period were very militant."

"Within one week the employer at one of these mills approached the local weavers' officials to ask them if they could open one of the mills, owing to heavy rains having wet the warps."

"The employer said he would stop the mill when the warps were dry."

"The T.U. officials agreed to the employer' request, and the mill opened up again."

"What puzzles me is, Who is going to decide when the warps will be dry?"

"This mill is still running, thanks to our obliging T.U.officials. That is one individual mill agreement."

Now For The Next.

"On September 8th. heavy rain again made a good excuse for the bosses of 'Victoria Mill' Great Harwood, to come forward and ask to restart this mill, to weave up all the wet weft, etc."

"To-day, Monday, September 12th., a meeting has been called by T.U. officials of the workers employed at this mill to consider whether this mill shall open."

"The T.U. officials favour reopening."

"One thing stands out plain to we workers. We are all striking for a county agreement, and here are our local officials arranging for individual agreements and agreeing to them."

"Our slogan should be, 'Not a picking stick to wag, nor another inch of rag, until we've got our old agreement back again."

In Accrington at the start of the 4th. week, Monday September 19th., Messrs Bury Bros. Fountain Mill, Portland Street, was reopened. Out of a total workforce of 500, 16 weavers and 30 winders were prepared to strike break. None of the overlookers, or tapers presented themselves. A dozen police officers prevented the large crowds from getting near the mill gates. ['Observer' September' 20th.1932]

The weaving shed was again closed on Wednesday, September 21st., after demonstrations and 'followings':

"One woman was accompanied by a crowd, said to number about 200 people. She took refuge in a house on the way, and did not reach home until 7.45 p.m."['Observer' September 24th. 1932]

All other mills remained closed except for the 3 hard waste mills and Industrial Mill, Baxenden.

In Oswaldtwistle, on Monday September 19th., Rose, Rhoden, and Paddock Mills reopened. This meant that all the mills in Oswaldtwistle which were running prior to the strike were now back at work except for Moscow Mill and Rhyddings Mill. The 'Observer' made the following comment about the Oswaldtwistle weavers:

"Oswaldtwistle is surely in a unique position in respect of the number of weavers who have resumed work whilst the strike is in progress, and it is evident that the trade union spirit is less strong in Oswaldtwistle than in most weaving centres." ['Observer' September 24th.1932]

Extra police had been drafted into the township with orders to stop any crowds gathering, especially in the vicinity of any mills.

In 'The Cotton Strike Leader', September 24th., a letter from 'Great Harwood' regarding Victoria Mill was published:

"On Saturday, while selling our paper, I asked a worker who I know if he would buy one. The worker worked at the Victoria Mill, where arrangements between the Boss and Unions had been made to weave up the weft damaged by floods. He replied he hed nowt. I said, hed nowt and working?"

"Worker: Now, and I dornd agree withum starting Victory, though we are on standard wage."

"Myself: Why?"

"Worker: Because we are aw out to-gether, and we should aw

go back to-gether, and another thing I'll tell th,' they reduced wages at Victory same as anyweer else. They didn't ask us er't union if they could either."

"I've only eleven shillings to draw this week, and there's three kid's, and 7/6 o' thad for rent, and I understood that this were a feight to stop separate agreements, and while we were out the question of aw rotten goings on in shed would be took up."

"Myself: But hesta nod fun out yet, thad whad they say and whad they mean and do are two different things, they only called aw out because workers in other towns were coming out on their own."

"Worker: They aw want to ged together, and then summat will be done."

"Myself: They will nod ged um together anymore than at present, but into midst of a strike, you give way to individual agreements, doin' things nod because yo' want, but because they know if lead be gi'n by union, and some aw loyal, tothers follow, frightened a being picked at, lessons were learnt in Harrod this year about individual mill agreements. But thee and tothers hev remedy in your own hands."

"Worker: Whad's thad?"

"Myself: By joining th' Cotton Strikers Solidarity Movement."

"Worker: I've never heard o' thad before. Whd's it for?"

"Myself: It aw workers in't town getting together and making unions whod they should be, fighting organisation of the dissatisfied and class-conscious workers."

"Worker: By gum, id's wods needed."

The same paper also carried a report of a meeting of women strikers held in the Burnley Spiritualist Hall on September 21st. Amongst the 64 delegates were representatives from Great Harwood.

In Rishton, Messrs W.F. Chambers and Sons, Daisy Hill Mill, reopened on Tuesday September 20th. All those 'blacklegging' were non-unionists and a hostile crowd awaited them in the evening. Demonstrations continued on Wednesday, but it was on Thursday evening when the real trouble started. A large body of extra police had been drafted into the town and mounted police were used to actually clear the streets.

Following this confrontation a protest meeting of over 2,000 people demonstrated on the 'sands'. The meeting was addressed by the Weavers' Secretary, Mr. J. Ashworth J.P. and the following resolution was passed:

"That this mass meeting protests strongly against the excessive drafting of outside police in the district, and that we are of opinion that the situation does not warrant such action and has a tendency to create disorder rather than prevent it."

The 'Observer' reported:

"We consider it an insult to the village to bring these police here," declared Mr. Ashworth.....addressing the large crowd. Rishton was a quiet, peaceful village, and throughout the whole of his experience he had never known mounted police to be called into action. They had had many strikes and lockouts, but there had never been such a situation as had arisen that evening, due to the drafting into the town of outside police.....Prior to Thursday, the local police had handled the situation admirably, and no scenes of any description had been witnessed."

A Special Meeting of Rishton U.D.C..

"was called on Thursday evening to discuss the matter, and a sub-committee was formed. [This] waited upon a member of the firm in an endeavour to persuade them to close the mill."

Councillor B. Ainsworth, Conservative, the Chairman of the Council was informed by Messrs. W.F. Chambers and Sons that the mill would close on Friday afternoon. This information was immediately conveyed to the local Textile Trades Federation who then withdrew their pickets. ['Observer' September 24th.1932]

On Saturday September 24th., it was stated that following these scenes the police had served three summonses, including one on Mr. J. Ashworth, for alleged persistent following of operatives as they left work. I will reproduce the 'Observer' reports of the subsequent trials later in the Chapter.

The firm of Messrs. W.F. Chambers and Sons appear to have been the most aggressive employer in the whole of Greater Accrington. They seem to have gone out of their way in trying to cut wages, worsen conditions and in attacking their organised workers, in Accrington, Church and now latterly in Rishton. Today, an observer of the situation might come to the conclusion that the firm had really stepped out of line, and that their actions were threatening to cause serious social upheavals in the township, the effects of which would be permanent if not stopped quickly. This was obviously the analysis arrived at by the Conservative dominated Rishton District Council, who wasted no time in demanding that the Firm close their mill instantly.

As early as September 5th. the Ministry of Labour had concluded that the time was ripe to intervene in the dispute. They did this by sending a communication to both sides, who after considering the initiative allowed a conference to be convened on September 13th. This was held at the Midland Hotel Manchester over several days. On Thursday September 22nd. an agreement was reached for a wages reduction of 1s. 8.5d. in the £., and on

Saturday an agreement was reached on the question of re-instatement of sacked operatives. These terms had to be ratified by the individual organisations, which was forthcoming and work was resumed on Wednesday September 28th. According to the 'Observer' the terms of the settlement were:

"Rights of operatives who struck against breaches of agreement established. Reinstatement to be effected within two months.
Wage reductions of 1s. 8.5d. in the £.
Collective arrangements restored.
Agreements which were abrogated restored.
Observation of agreements by the responsible organisations ensured.
Amendment of rules relating to displacement of workers.
Permanent conciliation committee with independent chairman.
Committee to interpret the rules in event of wage rate dispute.
More-looms-per-weaver [wages and conditions] referred to new conciliation for settlement within two months.
New conciliation arrangements to remain in operation for three years."

Andrew Bullen says:

"The so-called 'Midland Agreement' was regarded by those who took part in the negotiations, as a milestone in the history of industry. For the operatives outside the Conference Hall, a less warm reception awaited the news that approximately half the employers' demanded wage cut had been accepted with the issue of reinstatement barely papered over. Those weavers in Nelson and Colne who hadn't before the strike been on a reduction, feeling particularly aggrieved. The settlement did, however, make some attempt to fulfil the hopes that Leggett [the Chief Conciliation Officer from the Ministry of Labour] had voiced for a new commitment towards industrial peace and the reform of procedures to that purpose. Whereas before, the exhaustion of the joint rules meant a climb down or action, now a Conciliation Committee would be appointed with an independent chairman with powers to arbitrate. As for the rest of the settlement, for the most part it was a collection of auspicious promises. It was true the County Agreements on hours and wages [with reductions], were restored, but only the promise to examine the question of how to stop firms breaking them. Similarly on 'more-looms', the Midland Agreement didn't provide a final settlement, only the commitment to reopen negotiations within a period of 2 months. Neither problem was really any nearer a solution, as the weavers were to find out."[19]

On the front page of 'The Cotton Strike Leader'. of September 21st. 1932, Jim Garnett, Secretary of the Cotton Workers' Solidarity Movement, published a letter that he had sent to Mr. F.W. Leggett. It is printed below:

"On Saturday, September 17th, the second Conference of Cotton Strikers convened by the Cotton Workers' Solidarity Movement at which 127 delegates were present, representing 17 towns and elected by Strike Committees, Strike Relief Committees, Mass Meetings, etc., decided to appoint a negotiating committee on their behalf and instructed the said Committee to attend this week's negotiations at the Midland Hotel, Manchester."

"We would point out to you that this negotiating committee is the only official body representing the desires and wishes of the strikers, which has been expressed in numerous Ballots, Trade Union General Meetings and finally by strike action."

"Our Conference was definitely of the opinion that the meeting now taking place in this Hotel do not give expression to the opinions and desires of the strikers."

"We therefore present ourselves as the accredited negotiators on behalf of the strikers and demand the right to be present at this week's negotiations."

"On behalf of the Cotton Workers' Solidarity Movement,"

J. Garnett, Secretary."

Leggett would not negotiate with the Communist controlled Solidarity Movement, and so the workers were 'sold out' by their union officials. 'The Cotton Workers' Leader' of October 22nd., analysed the situation facing the operatives as follows:

"The recent betrayal of the T.U. Officials in the great weavers strike, and the 1929 sell out, must give all trade unionists food for thought."

"How could these Labour Leaders, Naesmith, Tout, Hindle, Bates, Bell, Whittam, and many others sit together with the employers, and the representatives of the National Government in the Midland Hotel and give us 'More Looms', 'Wage Cuts',etc., which we were bitterly opposed to?

"It was because we have not taken sufficient interest in our T.U's in the past, have not built up our own movement inside to fight against their rotten policy, and thus won the masses of members to our point of view, and thus took the authority out of the hands of these officials who are the agents of the employers in our midst."

"Instead of us workers using the Union as a battering ram against the attacks of the employers, we find now that actually the employers have used the Union [by the help of the officials] to drive us back into the mills on their terms."

In Accrington, Mr. J.R. Emmett appeared happy at the turn of events. Speaking on the day before final ratification, he said that he hoped the terms would be accepted by all concerned in the right spirit. He thought that the two sides could quickly get together to arrange for the reinstatement of sacked workers. His optimism in this regard was to be proved false. In Accrington those dismissed amounted to 125 operatives. 19 of these were employed by Messrs. Chambers and Sons' Ellesmere Mill and the other 106 at Messrs John Bury and Company's Union Mill. ['Observer' September 27th.] All the mills restarted after the ratification.

At Rishton, one of the districts to vote against the ratification, all the mills which were running prior to the strike recommenced operations on Wednesday morning. There was no reinstatement question in Rishton.

In Church and Oswaldtwistle District, the news was welcomed due to the fact that the reduction of 1s. 8.5d. in the £. agreement, was less than many had been enduring previous to the strike. All the mills in Oswaldtwistle restarted, except Moscow Mill and Rhyddings Mill, which reopened the following Monday. A question of reinstatement, however, arose at Rhoden and Rose Mills, where blackleg weavers had been given the looms of the strikers. The numbers affected were between 50 and 60. All the mills at Church reopened on the new terms. ['Observer' October 1st.1932]

A deputation of weavers addressed the Great Harwood Weavers Association's Executive Committee on September 26th. and expressed their views forcibly that they should oppose the ratification of the Midland Agreement at the Special General Council Meeting of the Weavers' Amalgamation the following day. The Committee, however, resolved that their delegates Messrs. Cooper, Bibby, Hothersall and J.W. Sunderland be given a 'free hand'. [Minute Book]

THE SPINNERS'

On Friday September 2nd., the Spinners' Amalgamation Executive issued ballot papers to their members, asking if they were prepared to strike rather than submit to a 25% cut in standard piece price list rates.['Observer' September 3rd.1932]

The result was :   30,999 in favour of strike action
                       1,518 against.

The employers immediately announced that they were postponing for one month, the reductions. However, Mr. H. Boothman, General Secretary of the

Operative Spinners' Amalgamation, stated that strike action would take place at any mill which attempted to bring in the reduction. ['Observer' September 10th.] Locally, members of the union had been on strike at the Vine Spinning Mill, Oswaldtwistle, since April and the blacklegs had been laid off during the last week of August due to the cotton crisis.

A conference was held between the Employers' Federation and the Operative Spinners' and Cardroom Amalgamation, in Manchester on September 19th. The meeting was adjourned with the employers demanding 2s. 2.25d. in the £ reduction and the unions offering 9.86d. in the £.

On October 31st. the spinners at Woodnook Mill, Accrington, went on strike in accordance with the decision of the Operative Cotton Spinners' Amalgamation, which on Saturday October 29th. had rejected the wages agreement previously signed by their officials. Over 100 operatives were affected. ['Observer' November 1st.1932]

Alan Fowler describes the situation in the spinning section as follows:

"The Cardroom and Spinners' Executives both accepted the principle of a wage reduction, but talks were adjourned until after the Weavers' dispute had ended.....Negotiations in spinning were resumed in October with the help of the Ministry of Labour.....Frank Leggatt, who had played a key role in the settlement of the weaving dispute, acted as chairman. He was keen to introduce a new conciliation system into spinning similar to the one introduced in weaving, believing that without conciliation machinery the cotton industry would continue in conflict, and he skilfully arranged the agenda to leave the most contentious matter of wages until the end. Agreement was found on the question of extending the industry's collective negotiating machinery, and the question of reinstating the 48 hour week. The majority of time was spent discussing wages, but finally the two Amalgamations were persuaded by the F.M.C.S.A. to accept a reduction of 14.5% off the wage list, which was effectively a wage reduction of 7.5%....."

"The relief expressed in the press about the agreement was short lived when a Special Representative Meeting of the Spinners' rejected the agreement by 84 votes to 38.....The Meeting agreed to a ballot of the members. Boothman defended the agreement on the grounds 'that a reduction of wages has been in the air for a time, certainly for not less than two years, and to have staved it off for so long must be regarded as no mean achievement.' As a consequence of the Meeting's decision, the employers locked out the spinners.....The ballot showed a majority to reject the agreement, but the 60% vote for strike action fell short of the 80% required under the Amalgamation's rules....."

"Though the dispute lasted for only one week, it was the last major strike in British industry until the Second World War."[20]

'The Cotton Workers' Leader' November 5th. 1932, reported the situation as follows:

"The shop meetings and the delegates at the Spinners Amalgamation Council meeting last Saturday, turned down the 'Midland agreement' and called the strike."

"The T.U. leaders immediately planned to sabotage the delegates decision by manoeuvres around the ballot just announced."

"The Council decision, which meant strike action, represented the demands of all workers in the industry. We have been on strike for a week; we are out to smash the slave agreement."

"The T.U. officials put aside our 20 to 1 and 15 to 1 ballots against wage cuts several weeks ago. They prevented us from coming out on strike in a common fight against wage cuts alongside the weavers."

"They entered into negotiations with the employers under the chairmanship of Leggett, the National Government's representative, they agreed to a 1s.6 1/2d. in the £1 wage reduction and a lengthening of the working week through their '48 hours week' agreement. They have agreed to a Conciliation Board to prevent us from taking any strike action in the mills for the next three years."

"It is significant that they made this agreement with Leggett just at the moment when the National Government are planning to still further apply the Means Test, and also increase tariffs, which will mean higher prices for us with lower wages."

"At Shop Meetings, Branch Meetings, Mass Meetings and at the Spinners Council last week, we repudiated, Boothman & Co and their Slave Agreement."

This week they have manoeuvred to get round our decisions and to get us back at work on the Slave Agreement terms."

"They and the employers press have made every effort to split our ranks by trying to develop a gulf between Piecers and Spinners. They have tried to raise the 'Communist bogey' about 'trouble makers', when they themselves make the trouble with their 'Midland Agreement'."

"On Saturday they order a return to work, although we have voted by 20,252 to 13,553 to continue the strike. This means that they are imposing their decision in the name of a small minority

against the big majority; the will of one upon two."
"**We have turned them down once already - we must turn them down again on Monday by continuing the strike.**"

Of course, the strike was over once the union leaders had called it off, but it was nothing short of out and out collaboration with the class enemy on their part. It might have been in the union rule book that an 80% vote in favour had to be obtained in order to call a strike, but the operatives were already on the streets, locked out for a week. A 50% + 1 vote in favour of its continuance should have been sufficient to have kept the workers out.

FURTHER COURT CASES

Following the outcome of disturbances at Delph Road Mill, Great Harwood, on August 30th., Sarah Wells (45) Beaconsfield Street, and Mary Aspinall (32) 36 Gladstone Street, both of Great Harwood, appeared before Major Trappes-Lomax, at Blackburn County Police Court, Saturday 10th., September.

It was stated that a crowd 500 strong had been booing and jeering, when the police tried to escort Margaret Heap into the mill. The police alleged that the two defendants rushed at Miss Heap and kicked her.

Mr. T. Holden, defending said that he had:

"Persuaded his clients against their wishes to plead guilty. Two defendants had already been sent to the Quarter Sessions, and as these women with family responsibilities to be borne with tightened belts, he did not want them to undergo two months' suspense of waiting for trial. His clients strenuously denied the offences but on his advice now pleaded guilty."

The Court fined them both £20, or 3 months imprisonment and in addition they were also fined £2 and £1..2s..6d. witnesses expenses with two months in which to pay. Today we can only look at the Courts' action with amazement. The two women in question would have earned less than £2 per week at the best of times, which meant that the Major had in effect fined them more than 3 months wages. Think of what that involved in reality; it meant working in a mill for 48 hours per week [52 hours if the employers got their way] for a period of over 13 weeks, and receiving no money in return. What were their families supposed to live on during that time? The Court's decision was, to say the least,- 'unhelpful to the working class cause.'

However, some people in the township were prepared to redress the balance in favour of those sentenced so harshly. The defendants had their fares and subsistence in Blackburn paid for by the Great Harwood Weavers' Association, and a committee made up of Mrs. Hallworth, Messrs. Wardell, Harrison, and Taylor, was appointed to raise subscriptions to pay their fines. [Minute Book September 7th. and 14th.]

On Tuesday October 11th., at the Preston Sessions, Richard Rutter (46) was fined £20 with one month to pay for 'intimidation and following'. On Thursday October 13th., Thomas Wardell (41) was also found guilty of 'intimidation' but received the relatively lower fine of £5. Both cases related to the events of August 30th. at Delph Road Mill. ['Observer' October 15th.1932]

REINSTATEMENT

On October 5th. officials of the Accrington Weavers' Association met the local Employers' Association to discuss the urgent question of reinstatement. The employers diplomatically stated that they would do all they could to get the operatives concerned back into work, but this did not include a commitment to sack the 'scab' labour taken on during the strike. Without this policy being enacted, it was obvious that the employers were going to adopt a prolonged campaign of victimisation against the people concerned. Nothing in the operatives favour came out of the meeting.

On October 6th. Messrs. Chambers' Ellesmere Mill sent for all their 17 strikers en bloc. There had been 19 but one had been taken on and another had found work elsewhere. The Mill took their names and addresses and hinted that there might be work for two or three in one weeks time. In reality the firm knew the names and addresses of the people concerned; they were just emphasising that they were the masters and the operatives were the slaves who should do as they were told.

The formality of taking the names and addresses of strikers was also carried out at the other Accrington Mill with a similar problem. This was Messrs. John Bury's Union Mill, where around 100 people were involved. ['Observer' 8th. October 1932]

In the 'Observer' October 22nd., Mr. Emmett was reported to have stated that only 18 of the strikers had been reinstated up to that time.

With regards to Church and Oswaldtwistle, the 'Observer' November 12th. stated that:

> "A number of weavers who came out on strike in October are still awaiting to be absorbed in their former places as agreed upon in the terms of the settlement."

The Half Yearly Report of the Accrington Weavers' Association contained the following paragraph:

"On the question of reinstatement of operatives, we cannot see, as yet, that there has been that spirit of goodwill displayed by the employers that we naturally expected. True, there have been a few already reinstated, but the majority of them in this district are still unemployed, with very slight prospects before them, unless there is a speeding up on the part of the employers to re-engage them."

The Accrington Weavers held their Half Yearly Meeting on Tuesday December 6th. and Mr. Emmett said that 84 of their members required reinstatement after the struggle [some of the 100 operatives at Bury's Union Mill were members of the Church and Oswaldtwistle Weavers'] and 30 had since been reinstated, leaving 54 still receiving strike pay. He went on to say that their Association had carried out their part of the agreement to the letter, but the 'sacking of all the knobsticks'[the strike breakers] should be the only course of action open to the employers to keep their side of the agreement, but they refused. In conclusion Mr. Emmett said:

"So far as we are concerned, you can take it for granted that we are going to fight to the last ditch to have everyone of our members reinstated, and I am asking for your sanction to continue paying those people who were so loyal." This was approved. ['Observer' December 10th.1932]

The Half Yearly Report of the Church and Oswaldtwistle Weavers states:

"When the settlement of the strike took place a gentlemans agreement was arrived at with regard to reinstatement, but we cannot say that this has been honoured with the alacrity that was expected, and at the time of writing we still have a large number of members awaiting reinstatement."['Observer' December 17th.1932]

The Rishton Weavers' Association repeated this theme in it's Half Yearly Report:

"When the dispute was settled we, along with the operatives in other districts, certainly expected that within a period of 2 months the whole of the displaced operatives would have been reinstated, or re-absorbed, in employment."

"Three months have passed and there are still almost 2,000 members of associations affiliated to the Northern Counties Textile Trades Federation who have not been reinstated. We think we are justified in expecting the employers to honour the Midland Agreement and to show goodwill referred to in the agreement by speeding up the process of reinstatement." ['Observer' January 7th. 1933]

At Accrington Town Hall, Thursday January 19th. 1933, a joint meeting took place between the employers and the Textile Trades Federations of Accrington, and Church and Oswaldtwistle. The Federations stated that 85 weavers in the area were still awaiting reinstatement, 20 weeks after the strike had been settled. The employers again repeated their promise to do something about it, but would not agree to sacking the strike breakers.

The situation was similarly discussed at Blackburn, between the employers and the Textile Trades Federations of Blackburn, Great Harwood and Clitheroe. Over 150 workers had not been reinstated in Great Harwood. Again no specific action to remedy the situation was forthcoming from the employers. ['Observer' January 21st. 1933]

During the last week of January and the first week of February 1933, the area suffered an influenza outbreak. Mr. Emmett stated that the depletion of weavers in some mills had allowed the temporary reinstatement of some victimised operatives, but he expected these people to be back on the union books when the epidemic was over. He also continued to complain about the lack of goodwill on the part of management. ['Observer' February 4th. 1933]

The Accrington Trades Council and Labour Party, at their General Management Committee meeting held on February 15th., discussed the reinstatement problem and decided to call a special meeting on the subject on Sunday February 26th. ['Observer' February 18th.1933]

On Saturday February 25th. the matter was discussed at the Central Board of the Northern Counties Textile Trades Federation at a meeting in Accrington, where it was decided to make another request to the CSMA for further talks on the issue. ['Observer' February 28th. 1933]

At Great Harwood, the Report written for the Quarterly Meeting of the Weavers' Association, which took place in the British School on Wednesday March 8th 1933, had this to say:

"There are still a few members who have not been started at Prospect, Judge Walmsley, and Sabden Mills, but it is at Premier Mill where we are having most difficulty. At the time of writing there are still 35 of these victimised persons who should be working at this Mill.....If we were not observing the conditions of an agreement we should find the full force of public opinion in Great Harwood and Lancashire directed against us. In an endeavour to preserve peace and to secure justice is it too much to ask that some independent local body with influence will assist us in persuading the Premier Mill Company to toe the line? We have been unable to fix up an interview with these employers and they have gently but firmly turned down a similar request from the Central Board of the Northern Counties Textile Trades Federation. When one or two sides won't meet the other, negotiation is impossible." [Minute Book]

The reinstatement problem was still unsettled when the Accrington Weavers' produced their Half Yearly Report in May 1933. Mr. Emmett said:

"Although we have done better in this respect than some other districts, we have still a number of members on our books whom we could easily have absorbed before now, if only the spirit of goodwill which we naturally expected on the conclusion of the Midland Agreement had been displayed by the employers." ['Observer' May 27th. 1933]

At the actual Half Yearly Meeting, the Accrington Weavers' President, Lena Worsley, stated that there were still 21 operatives still awaiting reinstatement. ['Observer' June 3rd. 1933]

The position in Church and Oswaldtwistle was outlined in their Half Yearly Report. It said:

"We still have a large number of operatives who have not, as yet, been reinstated, and unless something is done to implement the Midlands Agreement it would appear that the employers will just reinstate one or two operatives at long intervals." ['Observer' June 17th. 1933]

In their Half Yearly Report of December 1933, they still complained of members failing to be reinstated. ['Observer' December 16th. 1933]

In fact 40 members of the Church and Oswaldtwistle Weavers' Association were still receiving full benefit up to 2 years after the dispute. The 'Observer' reported that the Weavers' Amalgamation decided that all strike pay in respect of the 1932 dispute should cease, and the local association decided to prolong the payments for a further two months period. [Observer' August 25th. 1934]

The affected operatives rebelled against this decision and obtained the necessary number of signatures to force the committee to hold a special meeting of members. This was held on Tuesday August 28th. 1934, at the Oswaldtwistle Town Hall. 150 members attended out of a membership of around 2,000 and by a vote of 80 to 49 forced the committee to continue the strike pay, minus the 7s 6d contributed by the Amalgamation. In effect, this meant that in many cases the operatives continued to receive 16s 6d per week. [24s - 7s 6d] ['Observer' September 1st. 1934]

Reinstatement was an issue that the unions failed to win and it was only one of the collection of promises in the Midland Agreement that the employers failed to comply with. The campaign after 12 months, became submerged in a more general fight against the Breaches of Wages and Hours Agreements, which included complaints against the workings of the More-Looms System. This latter campaign will be discussed later.

RISHTON WEAVERS' SECRETARY SENTENCED TO SERVE TIME IN STRANGEWAYS PRISON

As already mentioned, Mr.J. Ashworth J.P. and two others had been issued with summonses by the police, for alleged persistent following of blacklegs as they left work at Daisy Hill Mill.['Observer' September 24th. 1932]

The due process of law followed its course and Thomas Sanderson, weaver, of 53 Commercial Street, Rishton, and Mr. Jonathan Ashworth, Justice of the Peace for the County of Lancashire, and Secretary of the Rishton Weavers' Association, found themselves at a hearing of the Blackburn County Police Court, on Wednesday September 28th. 1932.

In the first case, against Thomas Sanderson, who was summoned "for unlawfully and persistently following operatives with a view to compelling them to cease work," Mr. H. Backhouse, defending, said that the summons should have been withdrawn due to the dispute having ended. Indeed it seemed to him "a great mistake on the part of the police or anyone else to go forward with these summonses."

Obviously Supt. Pagett disagreed and proceeded to address the Court:

"On Sept 21st. work was in progress at Daisy Hill Mill, Rishton, and three of the men employed there lived in Spring St., other two residing in Stourton St."

"The mill ceased work at quarter to five, and when the men left the mill they were confronted with a large crowd of people shouting and booing in Henry St. On going into Spring St. the men were followed by a crowd of 100 who had detached themselves from the main body. The crowd were shouting 'blacklegs' and 'lazy-----'."

"When they got on Spring St., the defendant Sanderson was seen at the head of the crowd. In Clifton St. defendant was spoken to by P.C. Waring, in answer to whom he said he was going home. The crowd continued to follow the operatives, with defendant at their head. Defendant did not go home, but crossed Commercial St. and followed the operatives to the vicinity of the Conservative Club. Here there were other policemen seeing the men safely home, and they stopped the crowd there. Defendant waved his arms and shouted to the crowd to 'come on'. The operatives got home."

"P.C.Waring said that at the time he was on duty in the vicinity of Daisy Hill Mill. He saw the operatives leave the mill, and when they went into Henry St. there was a very large crowd of people. About 100 followed the operatives into Spring St., acting in a very rowdy manner. He knew defendant, who was at the head of the crowd. Defendant did not go home as he said, and after passing Commercial St. he was still at the head of the crowd. When he spoke to defendant later, the latter said 'I stopped to speak to my daughter on the corner.'"

"Cross-examined by Mr. Backhouse, [P.C. Waring] denied that defendant pointed out his two daughters. [However] **He admitted that defendant never interfered with him or any of the other officers or operatives.**"

"Harry Towers, a weaver, of 41, Stourton St., Rishton, one of the operatives at the mill stated......'They seemed to be after us for going to work.' 'I was not afraid for myself, but for my parents.' He did not know the defendant and had never spoken to him."

"James Towers, weaver, of 41, Stourton St., corroborated, and said he could not say why the crowd was following them home. He was not influenced at all by the crowd."

"I was afraid,' said Thomas Joseph Clarke, another of the operatives, who resides at 75 Spring St., Rishton......He did not go straight home because he did not want a crowd of people round his door."

"Mr. Backhouse: 'You were terrified?' - 'Well, I was and I wasn't, but I was not going to be intimidated by the crowd.' In answer to further questions, witness said he did not know defendant and had never spoken to him."

"Alfred N. Chaddock, a weaver, of 74, Spring St., Rishton, said......'The object of the crowd in following them was because they did not like them working. They stopped his union pay, so he went in again.' Answering Mr. Backhouse, witness said he knew defendant by sight and he saw him in Henry St."

"Frederick Almond, of 44 Spring St. another of the operatives, said he did not know defendant."

"**Mr. Backhouse said no attempt was made to speak to any of the operatives. Defendant had nothing whatever to do with them. 'You can't stop people following a crowd, that is not persistent following.' It was not persistent following to be one of a crowd, and as there was no other summons against the man he submitted there was not sufficient evidence against him.**"

"The magistrates, however, decided that there was a case to answer.

"Defendant, in evidence, said he was not an official of the Weavers' Association, nor had he acted as picket. He had nothing whatever to do with it, beyond the fact that he was a weaver by trade. He knew none of the operatives who had been in the witness box."

"On the day in question he was standing at the old Post Office corner talking to two men - Messrs, Walton and Eagles. He saw a crowd coming down from the mill. There were a number of persons surrounded by police and the crowd followed. He was going to the Conservative Club, and along with the two other men he followed amongst the crowd. He was never within forty yards of the weavers who had been working."

"When he reached the Conservative Club he saw his two daughters talking to their aunt, and he put up his hand for them to wait for him. Walton left him and said he would go home. He was talking to some men when three police officers and a sergeant went up to him. When about five yards away P.C. Waring said 'Come here I want you.' Witness said 'If you want me, come here.' When he asked the constable what he wanted him for P.C. Waring replied 'For inciting two young women to follow the crowd.' Defendant pointed out that the two young women were his daughters, and told the police to go and ask them."

"In answer to Supt. Pagett defendant denied that he was spoken to by a constable before he got to the Conservative Club. The statement that he was at the head of the crowd was a falsehood. He had gone into the town to get something for tea, and later to see a man at the Conservative Club."

"Arthur Eagles, a weaver, of 15, Brook St., Rishton, said he met Sanderson and stood with him and Mr. Walton at the old Post Office corner. When the crowd came down from the mill they got jostled, and they walked along behind the crowd. It was not true to say that Sanderson at any time headed the crowd, and the defendant was not spoken to by an officer prior to reaching the Conservative Club."......

"Defendant's other companion, Henry Walton, weaver, of 117, Spring St., said he was with Sanderson until they got to the Conservative Club, and during that time the defendant was not spoken to by an officer."

"Whilst witness [Walton] was going home an officer went up to him and asked him for his name and address. Witness said 'Well, you want a case, but if you want my name and address I will give it to you.' He never asked why the officer wanted his name and address; he just gave it him for quietness."

"Defendant's daughter, Josephine Sanderson, said she was never in the crowd and was talking to her aunt. She saw her father put up his hand and shout that he would not be long. The police never approached her to ask if she was defendant's daughter, although they passed her."

"Mr. Backhouse said the prosecution appeared for some reason to be endeavouring to follow a case which was decided some years ago. In that case there was a crowd of people who became disorderly, and it was held that a person who was with that crowd was entitled to be convicted for following. There was an essential difference, however, and that was that in the case mentioned the person who was persistently following started by stopping people coming out of the mill and talking to them. He was a picket. On the evidence there was no doubt that no such thing happened in the present case."['Observer' October 1st. 1932]

The 'Observer' was not a fully paid up member of the weaver's cause, and therefore it is fair to assume that it's reporting of these events was objective. Anyone reading the report today could only assume that a not guilty verdict was reached; there being no evidence whatsoever to suggest Mr. Sanderson was guilty. However, the magistrates took no notice of Mr. Backhouse, Mr. Sanderson, Mr. Walton, Mr. Eagles, Josephine Sanderson, or indeed any of the prosecution witnesses, none of whom pointed the finger at the accused. They found him guilty and "bound the defendant over for six months in the sum of £5, and ordered him to pay £1..19s. witnesses' expenses."

Following the magistrates extraordinary decision, Mr. Backhouse, who also appeared for Mr. Ashworth, declined to have his second case heard by the magistrates on the bench that morning. He intimated that he wanted to go to the Quarter Session and the court was adjourned.

Jonathan Ashworth duly appeared at Blackburn Police Court on Monday October 3rd., on three summonses alleged to have occurred outside Daisy Hill Mill, Rishton, on Thursday, September 22nd. He was summoned for persistently following three cotton operatives from the mill, with a view to compelling them to cease work; for besetting the approach to Daisy Hill Mill; and for following the operatives from the mill in a disorderly manner. He pleaded 'Not Guilty' and elected to be tried at Preston Quarter Sessions.

"Supt. Pagett, outlining the case for the prosecution, said that on Sept. 22nd., work was in progress at Daisy Hill Mill, and the three men whose names were mentioned in the case were employed at that mill. It was arranged for the men to leave work at 4-45 p.m., but some time before that a crowd of two or three thousand people had assembled in the vicinity of the mill."

"Defendant was at the corner of Ashworth St., which is at the entrance to the mill, and there were also about 18 pickets. The majority of the workpeople left the mill in two motor cars. It was thought then that the people would go away, and the police waited in the hope that the crowd and defendant would go away and allow the workers to go home peaceably. The crowd, however, did not disperse, and seeing Henry St. was blocked, the mounted police, who were in reserve, had to be called out."

"Eventually the three men had to be brought from the mill, and this was a signal for Pandemonium, the people yelling and booing at the top of their voices. The defendant and the pickets remained at the end of Ashworth St. As the mounted police moved down the street the operatives followed, and immediately behind them was the defendant at the head of a large crowd of people."

"In Henry St., he [Supt. Pagett] spoke to the defendant, but he continued to follow the operatives to the Canal Bridge. Here the mounted police wheeled and faced the crowd, and the men were allowed to go home without further molestation."

"When he heard defendant shout 'Come on, follow up,' said Supt. Pagett, one of the mounted police went up to him, and said, 'I consider you are responsible for the crowd becoming hostile to these men, and unless you stop I will report you.' Defendant replied, 'Oh, we'll see.'......"

Fred Entwistle, winding master, 4 Wheatfield St., Rishton, who had commenced work at the mill on Sept. 12th., gave evidence for the prosecution. Mr. Backhouse then asked him:

"Do you agree with me that the main demonstration was against the importation of police? - No, on the contrary."

"Witness, who said he had lived in Rishton 40 years, admitted that he had never before seen mounted police in demonstrations. The defendant never spoke to him."

"Mr. Backhouse: Did one of the horses of the mounted police go on the footpath amongst the women and children? - I don't know whether it was on the footpath."

"Didn't Mr. Ashworth protest against this? - I saw him protesting."

"Was it a fact that women and children were taken from under the horses' hoofs? - I can't say."

"Did you go to work the following morning? - I did."

A second prosecution witness, Charles D. Trengove, labourer, 52 Hermitage St., Rishton, who was also working at the mill on the day in question, corroborated the evidence of Mr. Entwistle. However, he added that he did not see the defendant anywhere after seeing him at the end of Ashworth St. A third witness, Joseph T. Bithell, 52 Hermitage St., Rishton, said he had been working at the mill and had been afraid of the crowd, but nothing further is quoted of either witness. ['Observer' October 4th. 1932]

"Sergt. Knowles said ....He saw Supt. Pagett speak to Ashworth, but subsequently the latter continued as before, following the operatives about 150 to 180 yards."

"Mr. Backhouse: Did Mr. Ashworth go up to the police officer and protest that the officer was on the footpath? - [Sergt. Knowles] I saw him go up to him, but I don't know what transpired."

Further evidence was provided by P.C. Simmonds and P.C. McMillan, but they didn't add anything new to the story so far.

"Mr. Backhouse submitted that there was not a single witness, with the exception of the extraordinary police witnesses, who said that Mr. Ashworth took the slightest part in the affair. Merely to be in a crowd accidentally or out of curiosity was neither persistent following or disorderly following. What evidence was there that Mr. Ashworth followed in a disorderly manner? Was it following in a disorderly manner to protest to a police officer on a horse who went on the footpath into a crowd of women and children? The mounted policeman was the only person who said one word to Mr. Ashworth, and Mr. Ashworth denied that he ever uttered a word."

"As I said at the proceedings last week." added Mr. Backhouse. "I consider it would have been for the better to have withdrawn the summonses. Each time I hear a witness I come more and more to that conclusion. Mr. Ashworth is a Justice of the Peace and is far more likely to be assisting in keeping the peace than breaking it. You don't find a single syllable said against Mr. Ashworth until you come to the last two or three police witnesses. The people who came out of the mill had not one word to say against him."

The Bench incredibly decided, against all the evidence, that there was a case to answer and so Mr. Ashworth was committed for trial at the Preston Quarter Sessions. The hearing took place at Preston on Wednesday and Thursday, the 12th. and 13th. October.

Mr. Ashworth faced 4 counts - intimidation, besetting a cotton mill, following a person with two or more persons in a disorderly manner, and watching a cotton mill. However, when the case commenced, the prosecution withdrew the charge of intimidation, and the following day the counts of watching and besetting were withdrawn. This left 'persistently following a person with two or more persons in a disorderly manner in the street,' as the only count upon which the case proceeded. I do not intend to repeat the evidence already given at the earlier trials, but I will relate any new evidence that was presented.

When one blackleg was cross-examined by the defence counsel he rather naively stated that he didn't think his actions in commencing work at the mill - where he was not usually employed - was likely to cause ill feeling. He was apparently surprised when the crowd shouted 'blackleg', 'dirty rats' and 'take them and drown them'.

Mr. E.G. Hemmerde for the defence said:

"They could not blame Mr. Ashworth for the fact that crowds gathered. Mr. Ashworth had, after consultation with his president and vice-president, gone down there to try and keep the situation in hand, and to the best of his ability he did so."

"Mr. Hemmerde referred to it as 'a deplorable case against a leading trade unionist, which should never have been brought.'"

"Defendant, in evidence, stated he had been in the weaving trade for forty years. When the strike commenced pickets were appointed and given their instructions for peaceful picketing. So far as he knew those instructions were carried out. When the operatives from the other mill commenced work at Daisy Hill Mill there was a good deal of local feeling. Prior to the day in question the relations between the police and the crowds had been quite happy. He heard on the Thursday morning that extra police had been drafted into the town, but so far as he knew he could see no need for them."

"When he arrived in the vicinity of the mill the crowd was cheering and booing, and they all seemed happy. There were several men near him, and when Supt. Pagett approached him he told those who were pickets to split up. Subsequently the mounted police came on the scene, and they seemed to add greatly to the excitement. He never urged the crowd to 'come on,' and never had any conversation with P.C. Wiggans."

"When the mounted police commenced to move down the street one of them [Sergeant Rooke] turned his horse on the footpath amongst the women and children. People went to him [defendant] and complained, and he went on the footpath and told the officer that he would report him for taking his horse on the footpath. The officer made no reply and rode away. 'I had to pull two children from under the horse as it was leaping up,' he added; and went on to say that he walked down behind the horse to see that it did not happen again. Further down the street Supt. Pagett went up to him, and said, 'Mr. Ashworth, I shall book you for interfering with the police in the discharge of their duty and inciting the crowd.' He [defendant] thought he was alluding to him remonstrating with the mounted policeman."

"Defendant stayed there for a few minutes, and when he turned the corner at Edmondson's chemist shop the mounted police were across the Canal Bridge. He never went any nearer the bridge than Mr. Trengrove's painter's shop."

"He and the President and Vice-President of his Association went in the opposite direction to see Mr. B. Ainsworth, [Conservative] chairman of the Rishton District Council, in reference to the mounted police. A Special Council Meeting was held to protest against the importation of police."

"In answer to Mr. Jalland, [Prosecuting] defendant said he could not say whether the crowd followed him or not. He was surprised to a certain extent to hear that the three operatives were terrified."

"Robert Gildert, President of the Rishton Weavers' Association, corroborated defendant's evidence, and said that Mr. Ashworth instructed the pickets to walk about in twos. It was when the mounted police entered Henry St., that the booing started......Defendant did not go any nearer to the bridge than Trengrove's shop."

"Benjamin Ainsworth, cinema proprietor, High St., Rishton, Chairman of Rishton District Council, said that on the afternoon in question defendant and Gildert visited him to protest against the importation of police. Previously he [witness] had spoken to Supt. Pagett in reference to the same matter, and on the same evening a special meeting of the Council was called to see if steps could not be taken to obviate a recurrence of trouble."

"Miss Harriet Barnes, a nurse at Queen's Park Hospital, Blackburn, said she saw the crowds and the mounted police. 'I saw a mounted man mount the pavement, and women and children were in danger.' The crowd was very well behaved at the time, and this action was greatly resented by the crowd."

"James Ratcliffe, of 40 Hermitage St., Rishton, vice-President of the Rishton Weavers' Association, and Thomas Sharples, of 52 Parker St., Rishton, gave corroborative evidence, and both declared that defendant never went to the Canal Bridge. Sharples said the statement by P.C. Wiggans that a conversation took place with Ashworth was not true."........

"Charles Clayton, 19 Lord St., Rishton, who was one of the pickets......saw Supt. Pagett speak to Mr. Ashworth, and Mr. Ashworth told him [witness], and a friend to go about in twos and keep moving. He saw the mounted police arrive, and one of them went on the footpath. The pickets' instructions from Mr. Ashworth were quite clear."......

"John W. Banks, 104 Hermitage St., corroborated, and cross-examined by Mr. Jalland, said he saw the defendant pull two children from underneath a horse which had mounted the pavement."

"Fred Taylor, 40 Station Rd.,Rishton, also spoke to seeing a mounted policeman mount the pavement at a point where there were women and children. In answer to Mr. Jalland, witness said the horse was on the pavement for about five yards."

"Thomas Ratcliffe, of 12 St. Charles Rd., Rishton, said when the operatives left the mill he walked down to Parker St., over the Canal Bridge with Charles Trengove, whom he knew. He never saw the defendant at all, and heard no conversation between P.C. Wiggans and defendant. P.C. Wiggans was on his left the whole of the way, and he never saw him speak to anyone. "......

"George Hoyle, 24 Knowles St., Rishton, denied that defendant said 'come on,' or that he was spoken to by P.C. Wiggans. 'I saw the mounted police mount the footpath and I pulled a child from under the horse ridden by P.C. Wiggans and put it in a back street. I subsequently followed the horse down the street,' he added. He saw defendant at Edmondson's corner and afterwards saw him going in the opposite direction to the bridge. Mr. Ashworth never went nearer the bridge than Trengrove's shop."

"This completed the case for the defence."......

"Addressing the jury, Mr. Backhouse declared that there was not the slightest scrap of evidence directed to the charge of following in a disorderly manner. With the exception of P.C. Wiggans, the police evidence, including that of Supt. Pagett, had been a direct flat contradiction to that. Whatever might have been the attitude of the crowd, he hoped they were not going to blame Mr. Ashworth for that. As soon as the Superintendent spoke to Mr. Ashworth the latter asked the pickets to split up."

"'People have a perfect right to picket peacefully, provided they don't do it in such a way as to frighten operatives. They have a perfect right to try and persuade operatives not to go back to work if they like,' said Mr. Backhouse. They had heard that there was a general resentment in the town against the importation of police. It was not suggested that anyone had the right to control the police except the Chief Constable of the County, and acting under him, Supt. Pagett. What he did say was that the District Council, as representing the people of Rishton, were entitled to protest if they thought it was not being done properly, and they would be failing in their duty if they did not protest when the people had asked them.'"

"If one of these policemen does a silly, tactless act like riding on the footpath amongst a crowd he must expect a magistrate who is present to protest. It is a very unfair thing that he finds himself here after he has made that protest, charged with something totally foreign to what he was doing."

"Mr. Backhouse went on to say that the only scrap of evidence directed to proving that Mr. Ashworth was doing anything disorderly, was the evidence of P. C. Wiggans, who said defendant started shouting 'Come on.' The astounding thing was that Wiggans was the only person of all the witnesses who heard or saw anything of the kind."

"'I ask you to say that the police have exaggerated their evidence in this case,' he concluded."........

"After an absence of an hour and a half the jury returned, and the foreman asked for the Act to be read over, as some of the jury were not satisfied. A copy of the section of the Act relating to the case was accordingly handed to the jury, who again retired."

"On returning after a further half hour's retirement the foreman said the jury could not all agree, and consequently the bench retired to see what could be done in the matter."

"On returning, Sir James Openshaw said in view of the very serious case.....they were of opinion that the case should not be tried at Preston again but at the assizes."['Observer' October 15th. 1932]

The trial in Manchester began on Monday, November 21st. During that day all the evidence for the defence and the prosecution was heard again. It was on Tuesday that the two sides and the Judge, summed up and left the decision to the jury.

In his speech for the defence Mr. Hemmerde stated the following with regards to evidence dealing with Mr. Ashworth's protest to Sergeant Rooke:

"When you have got all that mass of evidence can you have any doubt whatever that Mr. Ashworth was justified in the step he took in going to remonstrate with the officer who was on the footpath?" he said."

"The Supt. gave them no word of detail as to what defendant was doing. The only person who said he was doing anything was P.C. Wiggans, who said that defendant shouted 'Come on, follow up.' The curious thing was that no one else seemed to have heard that. The defendant also flatly denied having a conversation with P.C. Wiggans. If Wiggans did speak to him he did not hear him."

"From the corner of Edmondson's chemist's, went on Mr. Hemmerde, there was no evidence that defendant was following up to the bridge, although there was a lot of police evidence to say he was seen there. They had heard on the evidence of Entwistle that looking round he saw Ashworth down by Edmondson's, and there was a mass of evidence to say he did not go any further. That, he submitted, disposed of following entirely in High St."

"Why should not the evidence of ten or twelve people who all said Ashworth never went down High St., supported by that of Entwistle and the Chairman of the Rishton District Council, be believed, asked Mr. Hemmerde. He submitted that the whole idea of following in High St. completely broke down on that evidence. In Henry St. they had no definite suggestion that defendant was doing anything wrong."

"Rishton is a peaceful little place, and obviously there was resentment about the importation of police, because the Chairman of the Council has told you that he rang up Supt. Pagett in regard to the matter as a consequence of people complaining to him. There was evidently a strong feeling against the importation of police, and I suggest that it is the secret of the whole thing. It is not for you to decide whether the police were necessarily brought or not, but I suggest to you that Mr. Ashworth's whole attitude on that day was as proper as it possibly could be."

"Do you think," he went on, "that you would ever had heard anything of this case if Mr. Ashworth had not remonstrated with the mounted officer? I suggest to you that all Mr. Ashworth did was his duty as a man responsible for order. From the moment he remonstrated with Sergeant Rooke he was evidently a marked man. Then we know how five summonses were taken out charging [him] with every conceivable offence, and four were dropped, leaving the little one of following."

"If you are going to accept uncorroborated evidence of the police when there must have been dozens of people round who might have been called, if you are going to put police evidence on a pedestal by itself, if you are going to approach criminal cases in that way it won't be long before you find the 'frame-up' in this country. The police evidence is no more entitled to be believed than other evidence, and I ask you to say you are absolutely dissatisfied with the evidence so far as it says Mr. Ashworth went up to the canal bridge in High St."........

"Mr. Justice Lawrence, summing up, said the statute under which defendant was charged had been on the Statute Book since 1875 and all they had to do was to see whether the facts from the case brought it within the words of the Statute beyond all reasonable doubt. Something had been said about other charges, but that was a matter with which they had nothing whatever to do."

"It seemed to him that it didn't make very much difference whether the horse's front or back feet went on the footpath. The police in the exercise of their duties had to clear the streets on occasion, and it was for that reason they were mounted on trained and quiet horses. It seemed to him that with an experienced officer like Sergeant Rooke the danger was very little. They might think defendant was in a very excited state and thought something dangerous was going to happen, when it was not really going to happen at all.".....

"It is for you to consider," said the Judge in conclusion, "which of the stories you believe."

"After an absence of 75 minutes, the jury returned a verdict of "Guilty".....

"Mr. Hemmerde said a number of similar cases came forward at Preston and every one was treated leniently there. He would like to ask His Lordship in that case to treat this man of excellent character with the greatest possible leniency."

"His Lordship: None of these charges were against a Justice of the Peace?"

"Mr. Jalland [Prosecution]: They were not, your Lordship."

"Passing sentence on Ashworth, the Judge said 'You are a person who has been appointed a Justice of the Peace and have taken oath to observe the law and maintain it. I think, therefore, that an offence of any sort in your case is more serious than in the case of another person. The sentence, therefore, I pass upon you is imprisonment for one month in the second division.'"

"On hearing the foreman of the jury say 'Guilty' Ashworth bowed his head and stood gripping the dock rail. He leaned back as if staggered when Mr. Justice Lawrence passed sentence. He opened his mouth, but no sound came, and he seemed dazed."

"An officer assisted him slowly from the dock, and as he did so two men sitting behind the dock burst into tears."['Observer' November 26th. 1932]

Obviously this crass example of class warfare had to be countered. Even the normally docile weavers leadership had to get up off their backsides and protest against this injustice. To let this action by the ruling class go by without a determined fightback would mean that other union leaders in the future could end up behind bars. The same issue of the 'Observer' reported that the Central Committee of the Weavers' Amalgamation had stated the following:

"The recent judgement given at Manchester Assizes by which Mr. J. Ashworth, J.P., Secretary of the Rishton Weavers' Association, was sentenced to a month's imprisonment in consequence of action taken in the recent dispute, has aroused considerable feeling and resentment among district associations of the Weavers' Amalgamation."

"Weavers' throughout the county are amazed that a district secretary of Mr. Ashworth's character and influence has been sentenced to a month's imprisonment for carrying out his duties as a trade union official. So far as we can learn, his actions were of a peaceful character, and his main intention was to assist the police in carrying out their duties as helpfully as possible."

"The Central Committee of the Weavers' Amalgamation have had this matter under consideration during the last two days, and are contemplating taking actions in order that the responsible authorities might have their attention called to the sentence."

The Central Board of the Northern Counties Textile Trades Federation at their meeting in Blackburn on Friday November 25th., passed a resolution expressing the opinion that the sentence was excessive in view of the high character of Mr. Ashworth.

Also on Friday, speaking in the Labour Hall Haslingden, Mr. Andrew Naesmith said:

"In the last two or three days class legislation had been responsible for sending to prison for one month a man whose character was beyond reproach and one of the most inoffensive individuals it was possible to meet in a day's march."

"Jonathan Ashworth,...... will be in a prisoner's garb; he has thrown off his civilian clothes and will have to conform to prison regulations; he will not be able to receive any visitors or to get any letter that arrives before seven days have expired."

"Jonathan Ashworth had only done what thousands of men

and women were doing in Haslingden during the Syke Mill Dispute. It made one's heart cringe when they knew that under the Trades Dispute Act and the Trade Union Act of 1927 either trade union official or trade union members could be subjected to heavy penalties for such alleged breeches of the law."

"They could not lie still in face of that aspect of legislation. They had to recover the rights and liberties of the working class organisations. There were many more things in social and economic life that they must keep in front of their eyes. If they relaxed their efforts they would make it even more difficult for those who were coming behind."

A petition signed by 2,834 Rishton people was placed in the hands of Mr. Andrew Naesmith on Monday morning November 28th. The petition was only opened on Saturday at the Weavers' Offices in Cliff St. Throughout Saturday and Sunday crowds of people visited the offices in order to sign it. As the 'Observer' stated:

"The fact that the population of Rishton is only about 7,000 is an indication that the majority of householders in the town have signed."

The petition stated:

"This case is one which the advisor to His Majesty might fitly recommend a revision of the sentence or immediate release from prison,......"

Support also came on the Sunday afternoon from a mass meeting of engineering workers held in the Labour Hall, Accrington, where the following resolution was carried unanimously:

"That we, representing the whole of the branches of the A.E.U., Accrington District, strongly support the Amalgamated Weavers' Association in their protest against the imprisonment of Mr. Ashworth." ['Observer' November 29th.1932]

On Tuesday November 29th., the petition together with a similar document prepared and organised by the Weavers' Amalgamation, was taken to the Home Secretary [Sir John Gilmour] in London, by Mr. Naesmith, Mr. Hindle, President of the Amalgamation, together with the solicitor in the case.

On the same day, a meeting of the Rishton Trades and Labour Council, of which Mr. Ashworth was the President, passed a resolution of total confidence in Mr. Ashworth. Mr. Gildert presided and several other speakers, including Mr. W. Howson, the Accrington Labour Party Agent, spoke of Mr. Ashworth's self sacrificing spirit.

On Saturday December 3rd., to the delight and satisfaction of everybody, Jonathan Ashworth was released from Strangeways Gaol on the instructions of the Home Office, after serving 12 days of his one month's sentence. The 'Observer' reported the event as follows:

"It was to Mrs. Looms, Mr. Ashworth's niece, at whose residence he stays in Rishton, that the first intimation of his release came...... Early on Saturday afternoon a telegram reached her from her uncle saying that he was at Victoria Station, and that he was coming to Rishton at once."

"Mr. Ashworth's wife also received a telegram on Saturday afternoon which said, 'Coming home at once.- Dad'."

"As soon as the news was received the President of the Rishton Weavers', Mr. R. Gildert, was informed, and he, along with Mr. Ashworth's son-in-law and another friend, rushed to Blackburn by motor car to meet Mr. Ashworth. On arrival in Blackburn they discovered that Mr. Ashworth had departed for Rishton, and thereupon they chased back towards Rishton and overtook the bus in which he was travelling. When about a mile from Rishton they noticed Mr. Ashworth in the bus and signalled to him. He immediately alighted and was received with much enthusiasm. The four travelled to Rishton by car, and the news of their arrival spread like wildfire."

"Very shortly after Mr. Ashworth's arrival at his niece's house, people commenced to call to see him, and soon there was a queue to congratulate him on his release and to give him a hearty handshake. Mrs. Ashworth, who had been waiting at Rishton railway station expecting her husband by train, joined him at the home of her niece, and there was an affectionate reunion, along with their two daughters. People crowded outside and cheered everytime they caught a glimpse of Mr. Ashworth through the windows."

"When Mr. Ashworth arrived in Rishton on Saturday afternoon one of the first persons to congratulate him upon his release was Coun. B. Ainsworth, J.P. Chairman of the Rishton Urban District Council, who, it will be remembered, was one of the witnesses for the defence during the trial of Mr. Ashworth. Another was the Rev. T. McLoughlin, secretary of the Great Harwood Free Church Ministers' Fraternal, upon whose behalf he prepared a petition appealing to the Home Secretary for a remission of the sentence of imprisonment."

"As Mr. Ashworth was going to the Empire Cinema, Rishton, where a reception had been arranged for him on Sunday afternoon by the local Textile Trades Federation, hundreds of people lined the route, and when he arrived at the cinema, which was crowded, there was an outburst of cheering, and the singing of 'He's a jolly good fellow.'"

"Throughout the meeting Mr. Ashworth was affectionately referred to as 'Jonathan,' and at intervals fresh bursts of cheering broke forth."

"Mr. Andrew Naesmith, J.P. said.....All the time that Mr. Ashworth had been incarcerated their thoughts and prayers were with him, and he would make it clear that Jonathan's character had not in any way been belittled. Indeed, some of them regarded him with greater respect than they did three months ago. Jonathan had been through the valley of the shadow, and come back a purer, stronger and more courageous man than ever."

"There had been three ways in which the Amalgamation could deal with the matter. One was to appeal to a higher court, another to petition the Home Secretary, and the third to raise the matter in the House of Commons, and organise intensive propaganda throughout the county. They chose the middle course, and he was bound to say that Sir John Gilmour gave them a patient hearing and was humanely disposed towards them. They decided to present a petition to the Home Secretary and they tried to get employers in Blackburn and Rishton to sign the petition, but these expressed reasons why they could not do so. His colleagues in Rishton, however, got to work and secured 2,800 signatures in the township, while in addition there were 38 supplementary petitions of district associations of weavers."

"Mr. R. Gildert, President of the Rishton Weavers' Association, said that no doubt all who saw the incident of September 22nd., out of which the case arose, would be of the opinion that Mr. Ashworth was innocent. The action that he took on that occasion of looking after children was one that might have brought him a medal, but in trade disputes a different view was taken of things. It was a great shock to hear of the sentence but the sequel was greater. Union officials in times of stress were compelled to take a stand and fight for the rights of the workers, and sometimes they had to suffer. Sometimes the sledgehammer hit them hard, and it had hit their friend Jonathan."

"Rousing cheers burst out when Mr. Ashworth rose to reply. Evidently speaking under the stress of great emotion, he said he did not know anything of what was going on until he was released. The first intimation was when a warder told him to collect his things together and see the Governor, who had told him he had received instructions from the Home Secretary that he was to be released at once. The Governor gave him no reason why he was to be released......"

"It was all right to laugh and talk about being in prison, but there was a different feeling when one was there. No one knew the feelings he went through. He had been suffering in mind for two months before the Manchester trial, and he put on as brave a front as he could. On top of that, when he went to Manchester he was in the dock for a whole day, and the following day he was placed in the dock again for the summing up of the judge and the jury's decision. When the sentence came of a month's imprisonment it put the finishing touch on it. I broke down, and I am not ashamed of saying it,' he added."

"Mr. Ashworth tendered his heartfelt thanks to all who had taken part in the efforts for his release during the last twelve days......" ['Observer' December 6th. 1932]

The 'Observer' Editorial joined in the great welcome back extended to Mr. Ashworth saying:

"It is not in the least surprising to know that congratulations have poured in upon Mr. Jonathan Ashworth J.P. since his release from prison on Saturday......One can readily appreciate the joyous demonstrations that have taken place in Rishton during the weekend, and the congratulations extended to Mr. Ashworth from such a wide area."

Mr. Ashworth had a weeks rest at his home in Blackpool and returned to Rishton and work on Monday December 12th.

1933

THE EMPLOYERS' EFFORTS TO GET AN EARLIER START TO THE DAY

On Saturday January 14th., the 'Observer' reported that the Accrington Cotton Employers Association had written to the Textile Trades Federation, announcing that after a ballot of their members, the starting time of 7.45 a.m. would remain in force. This issue had been a further worry to the operatives since Tuesday November 25th. 1932, when at a meeting between the employers and the trade unions held in Accrington Town Hall, the employers had indicated that they preferred the earlier start which had been adopted by 7 or 8 rogue firms in the district.

This had been a strange position for the employers to take because one of the rogue firms, Stanhill Ring Spinning Mill, Oswaldtwistle, had informed the

'Observer' on November 12th. 1932, that the extension of hours involving the 6.00 a.m. start, had been ended and that the firm had decided to revert to the 48 hour week with a starting time of 7.45 a. m.

Maybe the employers had taken note of the moderate Mr. Emmett, when he stated at the Accrington Weavers' Half Yearly Meeting on the 6th. December:

> "There is nobody anxious to create a strike but certainly we cannot fall in with the employers' suggestion of an earlier start." ['Observer' December 10th.1932]

This followed up his statement made to the press issued after the November 25th. meeting in which he warned the employers that if they couldn't fall in with the 7.45 start the Federation would give notice to abrogate the agreement on hours within the Accrington District. ['Observer' November 29th. 1932]

However, the wayward employers failed to adhere to their Associations ballot result and continued to maintain the earlier start. The Accrington and District Textile Trades Federation received a letter from the Employers' Association stating that they had advised all their members to fall into line, but that this had had little effect. The Accrington Federation then decided to invite the Church and Oswaldtwistle Federation to a conference in order to organise joint action on the issue. ['Observer' March 11th. 1933]

This issue became part of the overall campaign against the employers refusal to operate the Midland Agreement. This was carried on during the whole of 1933 and 1934.

THE COTTON CRISIS CONTINUED

The minutes of the Great Harwood Weavers' Association state that Messrs. Green Bros., and Birtwistle and Fielding Ltd., were not observing the More Looms Agreement. Indeed their anger was such, that the following resolution was carried and forwarded to the General Council Meeting of the Weavers' Amalgamation.

> "That it is the opinion of the Council that our representatives on the More Looms Joint Sub Committee should not attend any more meetings until existing agreements are applied to our better satisfaction." [Minute Book January 12th. 1933]

On Thursday, January 19th. 1933, the more-looms-system was introduced at Peel Mill, Accrington, on a small scale, [48 looms with 8 weavers] although it extended the system later. The mill contained 900 looms of 40 inches width and 300 of 36 inches.['Observer' January 21st 1933]

In the week commencing Monday, January 30th., Messrs John Bury and Company's Union Mill also started the 6 loom system on 48 looms. Oak Vale Mill and one of W.F. Chambers', Accrington mills had been running a 6 looms system for some time. ['Observer' February 4th. 1933]

The Great Harwood Weavers' Quarterly Report, presented at the British School on Wednesday March 8th, contained the following:

"Birtwistle & Fielding's are determined to go their own way and are not applying the More Looms Agreement in a single instance. It is high time the Government reviewed the Report of the Economic Advisory Council's Committee which was presented to Parliament in July, 1930. Of all the conclusions and recommendations in that Report, only those which have necessitated a sacrifice by the Operatives have been applied. On page 26 of the Report we find: "We are confident that the organised Operatives and Employers of Lancashire will embark forthwith upon the serious consideration of the measures essential to the recovery of their trade. If however, this hope is disappointed or if any section proves recalcitrant, we think it right to place on record our considered view, that it would be the duty of H.M.Government themselves to confer upon them any necessary powers." We believe the dishonouring of agreements alone, however limited, is ample reason why the Government should act upon the recommendation of the Report quoted above."

The slogan of the meeting, printed in bold lettering on the Report was:

"Workers of the World unite, you have nothing to lose but your chains, and you have a World to win." Karl Marx

The management of Antley Manufacturing Company's, Providence Mill, Church, started to pay wages based on the 6 looms-to-a-weaver price list, to weavers employed on 4 looms. A mass meeting of the operatives expressed disgust and forwarded the matter to the Weavers Amalgamation.['Observer' April 8th.] The Cotton Employers' Association met with the firm, but their discussions did not immediately alter the situation. ['Observer' April 22nd.] However, the Company retreated on this issue shortly afterwards, but adopted a further policy of confrontation later in the year.

This occurred on Monday, October 30th., 1933, when the joint Textile Federations of Accrington, Church and Oswaldtwistle, met to consider the imposition of a 10.18 % wages reduction at both the Company's Church mills, Providence and Albion. Only a sparsely attended shop meeting, indicated that the Company won the day. ['Observer' November 4th. 1933]

The Accrington Weavers' Half Yearly Report stated:

"During the past few months a number of our members have had some experience of what is known as the more-looms-to-a-weaver system, and there seems to be only one opinion, that it is a bad, inhuman and degrading system, that sooner or later will have very serious effects on their physical well-being." ['Observer' May 27th. 1933]

At the Half Yearly Meeting, held on Tuesday, May 30th 1933, Miss Worsley, presiding, said that:

"at places in the vicinity there had been attempts to put into operation, more-looms prices on narrow cloth. The Amalgamation felt that it was only by some kind of Parliamentary action, or by amendment to the particular clause that this could be stopped." ['Observer' June 3rd. 1933]

The Church and Oswaldtwistle Weavers' Half Yearly Report stated:

"So far as the six-loom agreement goes, we in this area have not had a big change-over. Only one firm has decided to change, and so far as the operatives are concerned it is certainly not to their advantage. The benefits which were predicted would result from the introduction of this system have not shown themselves, and the abuse of the agreement which we suggested would arise has certainly taken place....."

"It would appear..... that the time has arrived when the employer and operative who will not honour agreements must be saved from themselves. The only sensible way to do this is by having agreements legalised so that the offenders may be brought to heel....."

"Whilst we do not suggest that the legalisation of agreements will recover lost trade, it will at least have the effect of keeping all employers and operatives on a straight basis....." ['Observer' June 17th. 1933]

At Higham's, Woodnook Mill, Accrington, a four shift system was started on 60 new automatic looms by agreement with the union. The shift system operated as follows:

A shift of women	7.30 a.m.	12.00 noon
A mixed shift	12.00 noon	4.30 p.m.
A shift of men	4.30 p.m.	midnight
A shift of men	midnight	7.30 a.m. ['Observer' August 5th. 1933]

THE MASS DEMONSTRATION IN GREAT HARWOOD

The Great Harwood Weavers' Association were having great difficulty maintaining the observance of agreements in the township. They were even considering expelling all their members employed at Clayton Street, Delph Road and Premier No. 3 Mills, who were breaking the agreement. This culminated in a Special Meeting of the Association on June 29th. 1933, which was attended by Hindle, Naesmith, and Bates from the Central Committee of the Amalgamation. The Minute Book states:

"1. That the Secretary apply for a local Federation Meeting at the earliest convenient date.

2. That the Secretary inform the Blackburn Employers Association that we are willing to cooperate in the publication of a joint manifesto upon the observance of the agreement.

3. That the Secretary write to the surrounding District Weavers' Associations, inviting their views upon the advisability and practicality of a Joint Demonstration in Great Harwood."

Favourable replies were received and noted at a meeting held on July 19th. The demonstration was discussed further on July 31st., August 4th., and August 16th. The Sub-Committee charged with organising the event composed of the President, Mr. Peter Williamson, Mr. Seed, Mrs. Hallworth, Mr. Bibby, Mr. Wolstenholme and five subscription collectors. The event ended up costing the Great Harwood Weavers' £40.. 12s.. 3d. which they thought was money well spent.

The demonstration took place on Saturday 26th. August 1933, and was a mile in length. Its route was from the fairground to the Agricultural Society's showground. Thousands lined the streets, in what were ideal weather conditions.

A band headed the column, behind which were members of the Weavers' Amalgamation's Central Committee. Next came the Central Committee of the Northern Counties Textile Trades Federation, followed by the District Weavers' Associations of Blackburn, Clitheroe, Rishton, Church and Oswaldtwistle, Clayton-Le-Moors and others. A further band followed and the rear was brought up by the members of the Great Harwood Association.[Blackburn Times, September 2nd. 1933]

The meeting on the showground was addressed by Mr. J. Hindle J.P., President of the Weavers Amalgamation, Mr. Andrew Naesmith J.P. Secretary, and Miss A Loughlin a member of the T.U.C. General Council.

The Great Harwood Weavers' Half Yearly Report published November 2nd 1933, described the event and its result as follows:

"The outstanding event of the last six months was our splendid

Demonstration against Breaches of Wages & Hours Agreements, which was held on August 26th. Aided by the splendid weather and the magnificient support by Blackburn and the surrounding District Associations we were able to stage one of the largest and most impressive events of its kind that have ever been held in the area. We believe it did much to prevent the spread of private arrangements for wage reductions between employers and operatives which were imminent at that time. If it could have been followed up immediately by similar Demonstrations in other parts of the County, it would have stimulated the spirit of loyal Trade Unionism in the hearts of the Weavers and Winders throughout Lancashire. Our Demonstration received wide publicity and this put our problems and difficulties in the forefront of the news, so that every reader of the newspaper in the County was made aware of the determination of the Weavers' Associations to fight for the honouring of agreements. It was the last call to employers to voluntarily come into line and combine to eliminate unfair competition. They have failed to respond and our efforts are now directed to obtaining legal sanction to the agreements we negotiate on your behalf."

".....We believe that the need is urgent and the time is ripe for Government control and so have prepared a scheme of Cotton Control which is being submitted to the Employers' Associations. If we get their support, and we hope we shall, there will be a joint approach to the Government with a request for legislation to implement the scheme. In broad outline the scheme provides for a Cotton Control Board composed of Employers and Operatives with powers to issue licenses. No Firm will be able to run without a license, which will be withheld from Firms who do not observe wages and hours agreements negotiated by Trade Unions and Employers' Associations. The Board will be empowered to re-organise the industry from the buying of raw cotton to the selling of the finished cloth, to cut out unfair competition, to close redundant mills and to control production. By these means we hope to place the trade on a secure foundation upon which we can firmly direct our efforts to combat foreign competition and, we believe, regain much of our export trade and enable better wages to be paid."

THE DEATH OF MR. PETER WILLIAMSON, PRESIDENT OF GREAT HARWOOD WEAVERS'

Mr. Williamson of Heywood Street, Great Harwood, was 73 years old. He had been appointed President in 1900, having previously been a member of the Committee. He left a widow and three daughters.[Blackburn Times, September 30th. 1933]

The Great Harwood Weavers' Half Yearly Report stated:

"His name has appeared at the foot of these Reports for over 30 years, and during the whole of his service to this Association - as Mill Representative and as President - his judgment and his actions were determined after asking himself the question 'Will it be in the interests of the Union and the Members generally.' Never have we known him complain of his own trials and tribulations, but he was ever ready to take up the cudgels on behalf of anyone who went to him with a complaint of injustice or harsh treatment.....His loyalty and honesty of purpose was beyond question. His lifetime of service to his class is a splendid example to his younger comrades in the movement........"

"The photograph which appeared in the press on the occasion of our recent Demonstration, has been enlarged and hung in the office.[Hyndburn Trades Council is interested in locating the whereabouts of this photograph.] Also a marble pedestal and vase will be placed on his grave as an everlasting tribute to his fellowship with us."

THE COTTON CRISIS CONTINUED

In Clayton-Le-Moors, Canal Mill closed down on Friday August 18th. 1933, causing a further economic disaster in the locality. This left only the newly established Spajaard's Mill and the small Claymore Manufacturing Company's Mill, running in the township. ['Observer' August 26th.1933]

On Monday, September 25th. the Weavers' Amalgamation met the Employers in Manchester and insisted that until the wages agreement was uniformly observed, no further discussions would take place on any proposed extension of the more-looms scheme. ['Observer' September 26th. 1933]

The Employers disregarded the Weavers objections and submitted proposals to their district associations for a further cut in wages of 1s..7d. in the £1. This caused Mr. Emmett to say:

"It is no use the Employers' Association wasting time trying to get us to agree to another reduction in wages or anything else so long as they themselves will not observe the last wages agreement. The first thing to be done is to secure legal compulsion to wages agreements.

There should be legal force just as there was, for instance, under the particulars clause, which required that a weaver must be supplied with particulars of the cloth being woven."

The article went on to say that the Central Committee of the Weavers' Amalgamation had passed a resolution calling for direct Government intervention in the industry and would be organising a campaign throughout the County against any interference with wages. ['Observer' October 21st.1933]

On Tuesday November 7th., a Mass Meeting of over 3,000 operatives took place in King Georges Hall, Blackburn, following a torchlight procession through the town. A further 1,000 people attended an overflow meeting in the Overlookers' Hall. It was the first of a series of demonstrations held in the cotton centres. Mr. Naesmith used the occasion to launch a vigorous attack on the employers fixation with cutting wages. He demanded the establishment of a Cotton Control Board. ['Observer' November 11th. 1933]

600 operatives gathered in Oswaldtwistle Town Hall on Wednesday November 22nd. to protest against the breaking of the Midland Agreement by the employers. Mr.H. Potts of Accrington presided and was supported by Mr.G. Porter and Mr.W. Hughes Chairman and Secretary of the Oswaldtwistle Weavers' Association, Mr.J.R. Emmett J.P. of Accrington Weavers', Councillor Hope of Clayton-Le-Moors, Mr. Whittam of Haslingden, and Mr.A. Barker of Skipton.

"Mr. Whittam said: "So far as Japanese competition went, or over-capitalisation, or whatever the cause of the precarious position of the industry, no employer or manager had the right to enforce conditions in any mill which they would not like their wives or children to undergo."

Mr. Barker said: "If the employers said that wages had got to come down in order to meet competition, then they could not at the same time demand that their high salaries and social status should be maintained."

Referring to a meeting the Unions had held with Lancashire M.P.'s at the House of Commons on November 16th., he went on to comment that their elected representatives could only see the problem of Japanese competition and had closed their eyes to the more important solution to the situation, namely a thorough reorganisation of the industry. Mr. Barker said:

"It was futile to imagine any improvement so long as they allowed the conduct of the industry to remain in the hands of the people who had always mismanaged it. Do not imagine that because they made money years ago the industry was carried on efficiently. Nothing of the kind. Nobody with any sense at all believed that. There had always been room for reorganisation in the industry, and it was reorganisation within the industry that they as officials of the operatives' unions were pressing for, believing that by reorganisation they would have a chance to meet competition on fair and equitable lines."

"There is vast room for reorganisation, and as the people who have been trying to conduct it for a generation have mismanaged it, bring in the State. Let us have statutory control, let us have Government interference, let us make it so that those parties who trade on the innocent and the economic position of many of our people - let us make it impossible for them to carry on that nefarious work. Let us say to the pirates 'You must adhere to recognised agreements or shut down.' If a man breaks the law he lands in gaol, and I want to make it so that employers who break the law will do likewise."['Observer November 25th. 1933]

LOCAL AUTHORITY SUPPORT FOR GOVERNMENT INTERVENTION IN THE COTTON INDUSTRY

Oswaldtwistle U.D.C., containing only one Labour representative, decided at its March meeting to support a resolution organised by Darwen Council, that urged the Government to grant financial assistance to the textile trade by means of a subsidy. ['Observer' March 26th.1932]

Twenty months later Oswaldtwistle U.D.C. decided to give their support to the campaign of the cotton unions against the breaches in the wages agreement. All local authorities in Lancashire had been asked to support such action by passing resolutions stating that they:

"view with great regret the appalling state of the cotton industry. We are deeply concerned at the poverty and distress due to the continuous unemployment and the low earnings of the workpeople, who in many cases are unable to pay their rents and rates, whilst our poor rate is gradually increasing. Owing to the breaches of joint agreements that are occurring, the disorganised condition of the industry, and the serious undercutting of the price market, we urge the Government to institute some form of statutory control that will give stability and confidence to those employers and operatives who are desirous that agreements should be honoured. Continuance of the present state of affairs can only result in increasing difficulties for us as local administrators; and that copies hereof be forwarded to the Prime Minister, the President of the Board of Trade, and the Minister of

Labour."

Oswaldtwistle resisted adopting the resolution submitted, but framed and passed the following:

> "That this Council is of opinion that one of the principal causes affecting and retarding the recovery of the cotton industry is the breach, or non-observance, of the agreements arrived at between employers and operatives, and is of the opinion that where agreements have been so arrived at between accredited representatives there should be some means adopted by which agreements so made are legally binding and enforceable."

The same newspaper reported that Church U.D.C. also supported the resolution, but decided to strike out the words: "We urge the Government to institute some form of statutory control" and substituted instead, "We urge the Government to consider what method will give stability and confidence." ['Observer' December 2nd.1933]

On December 4th. Accrington Town Council adopted the resolution compiled by the Textile Trades Federation; ['Observer' December 5th 1933] and this was further given support by Clayton-Le-Moors U.D.C. ['Observer' December 9th 1933]

The report of the events in the Accrington Council Chamber caused the following letter to be written, which attacked the more reactionary elements that surfaced during the debate:

> "Sir, - I have read with interest the reported discussions in the Accrington Town Council meeting on the resolution moved by Coun. G. Kilshaw.
>
> During the discussion, both Coun. G.E.Slack and Ald. Barlow offered their opinions. With Ald. Barlow I have no desire to quarrel: he is an old man who of late years has suffered much. Age, with its growing limitations, is entitled to commiseration, if not tolerance.
>
> But with Coun. Slack it is a totally different matter. No man on the Council displays more audacity which is oft times mistaken for courage. The colossal nerve of the man in giving expression to these words.
>
> "Why was the cotton trade in such a state of chaos at this moment.....because, not merely for weeks or months, but for years, the trade union leaders in the cotton trade would not face a situation which was indeed a crisis. Month by month procrastination - an ineptitude and a lack of leadership which was indeed tragic; a trembling fear all the time of the left-wing people in Barnoldswick and Nelson"
>
> reminds me of the quotation from Goldsmith:

> "And still they gazed and still the wonder grew,
> That one small head could carry all he knew."

The self-assurance and smug complacency which ascribes our industry's difficulties to trade union leadership is one that cannot go unchallenged. I ask Coun. Slack to make good his charges on the public platform, or in writing. I have not much time for debate or newspaper correspondence, but I will gladly devote some time to this matter. Coun. Slack is so often guilty of making outrageous observations on a variety of subjects that he has little knowledge of, that it is time the bluff was called."

Yours, Andrew Naesmith, Sec. Amal. Weavers' Assoc."
['Observer' December 9th 1933]

Slack, of 'Sunnycroft' Beech Crescent, wrote a reply on the 16th. December, which ended:

"What I have said, I have said - I have nothing to withdraw, nothing to modify."

I have no doubt that, at the time, Slack was regarded as the most vociferous spokesman of the employing class in the district; a man who could always be relied upon to defend the actions of that class no matter what. Indeed I feel sure that he would have enjoyed reading this paragraph; it would have been how he would have liked to have been remembered. His name still came up in conversations I had with older Labour councillors/aldermen [Wallace Haines, Michael Walsh and Bill Ridehalgh] during my three years on Accrington Borough Council 1971-1974.

THE COTTON CRISIS CONTINUED

At the Half Yearly Meeting of the Accrington Weavers' Association on December 5th., Helena Worsley, President, used the occasion to stress the need for a revival in membership. She said:

"They had only 60% of the people working in the mill members of the Association, and there was 40% who did not care a hang what the Union did, and were prepared, generally speaking, to accept lower wages. If only they could get some of that 40% in the Union they would be able to handle these things much better than they did to-day." ['Observer' December 9th. 1933]

1934

It was reported that of the 13 mills still operating in Church and Oswaldtwistle, a half were not working in accordance with the Midland wages agreement. ['Observer' January 13th. 1934]

On the 15th January, Helene Mill, Accrington, which employed 212 people, began operating the 6 loom system under the Midland agreement. It was arranged so that no workpeople were totally discarded. All operatives were employed two weeks out of three, in order that they never actually ran out of unemployment insurance benefit. This meant that they never came under the 'Means Test'. ['Observer' January 13th] However, within the month, the matter had been put in the hands of the Weavers' Association and the Textile Trades Federation, because of complaints by the operatives. ['Observer' February 10th.] Nothing came of the ensuing discussions and so the 6 loom system continued. ['Observer' February 20th.1934]

At Wheatfield Mill, Rishton, the firm had posted a notice stating that they were reducing wages by 2s..6d. in the £1. The employees took part in a ballot vote and unanimously decided to interview the company and ask them to withdraw the reduction, failing which they were prepared to go on strike. ['Observer' January 16th.] It is unclear whether, or not, a strike took place, but the Mill had closed down by July, at which stage the Rishton District Council were organising public meetings to encourage the purchase of shares in a new company. ['Observer' July 14th 1934] The Council were unsuccessful and the Mill was sold in November, for other commercial usage. ['Observer' November 6th.1934]

On February 15th., Britannia Mill, Great Harwood, one of 9 idle mills in the township, was sold. It had previously employed over 250 people. ['Observer' February 17th.1934]

Canal Mill, Clayton-Le-Moors, was sold piecemeal and was demolished soon afterwards. ['Observer' February 17th.1934]

Steiner's Hagg Dye Works, Accrington, which employed 60 operatives closed down. ['Observer' April 7th.1934]

On April 25th., representatives from the Communist Party, and the National Unemployed Workers' Movement, handed in a letter to the Great Harwood Weavers' Association asking for the committee to receive a deputation with a view to holding a joint Public Meeting. It was resolved:

"That, as we cannot co-operate with the associations named, for any purpose, the deputation be not received." [Minute Book]

On June 2nd. notices were posted outside Wellington and Victoria Mills, Great Harwood, [nearly 800 operatives] stating that a ballot of workers would take place on Saturday June 9th., regarding a proposal to cut wages. The Weavers' Association quickly organised their own ballot, in which an overwhelming majority voted against accepting a wage cut. Faced with this fact, the Church Street Manufacturing Company withdrew their notices. ['Observer' June 12th.1934]

The 'Observer' September 15th., reported that Mr. Jonathan Ashworth J.P., Secretary of Rishton Weavers' Association, was making steady progress following a serious illness which required an operation.

On September 26th. the Great Harwood Weavers' Committee heard that of 72 weavers attending a shop meeting of Palatine Mill workers, only 8 voted in favour of accepting the firms proposals for implementing wage cuts. [Minute Book] This eventually led to 250 operatives coming out on strike on Tuesday October 9th. However, the firm withdrew its demands and work resumed on Wednesday at noon. [Minute Book]

On Monday November 12th. Park Mill, Accrington re-opened after being closed for 12 weeks. ['Observer' November 13th.1934]

PRESENTATION TO MR. ARTHUR DAWSON.

A large gathering took place at the Co-operative Assembly Rooms, Oak Street Accrington, on Tuesday night, November 27th. 1934, when the Accrington branch of the National Union of Textile Workers made a presentation to their area organiser Mr. Arthur Dawson, who had been with them for 14 years. Mr. Michael Walsh, President of the Accrington branch, occupied the chair and explained that they were there to honour Mr. Dawson prior to his departure for Halifax. The reason for this, was that, his area of responsibility had extended to include Lancashire, Halifax, Bradford and Scotland.

Mr. Ledwick, Secretary of the Accrington branch, said that above everything else they would remember Mr. Dawson for what they knew as the 'labour supply arrangements'. In effect this meant that the union secured for their members any vacancy that arose within the industry locally, while at the same time providing the employer with men capable of doing the work.

Mr. Arthur Shaw J.P., General Secretary, presented Mr. Dawson with a grandmother clock in oak, with Westminster chimes.

Coun. Kilshaw said:

> "Arthur Dawson had many fine attributes. The chief of these he regarded as his indomitable courage. Arthur Dawson did things which most of them thought twice about and then left undone. They could never forget his capacity for work, the enthusiasm he brought into his work, his loyalty, devotion, comradeship, and that eloquence which simply swept them on. He believed Accrington was losing its

best and most accomplished orator, and whilst he wished him well he regretted his departure." ['Observer' December 1st.1934]

THE DEATH OF MR. WILLIAM HUGHES.

The Secretary of the Church and Oswaldtwistle Weavers' Association, Mr. William Hughes, died on Saturday 8th. December, at the Manchester Jewish Hospital where he had undergone surgery. He had been in bad health for some time, but continued to work until three weeks before his death. He was only 48 years old, and had resided at 31 Knowles Street, Rishton, with his wife.

He had served on the committee of the Church and Oswaldtwistle Weavers' Association before becoming President. In 1919, he was appointed Assistant Secretary and Insurance Clerk. In 1929 Mr. Hughes succeeded to the position of Secretary.

"His term of office being coincident with one of acute trade depression and the breaking of wages agreements, he had had many difficult situations to deal with, and his duties caused him considerable anxiety." ['Observer' December 11th. 1934]

THE NEW WAGES AND HOURS AGREEMENT.

In his annual report to the Weavers' Amalgamation in Manchester, on Saturday May 19th. 1934, Mr. Naesmith passed comments on a Government Bill [Cotton Industry Temporary Provisions Bill] that had commenced its readings in Parliament. He stated that it was designed to provide machinery by which agreements, reached between unions and employers, could be made enforceable by law.

"It marks a step along the road towards removing chaos and unfair labour conditions and will tend to control unscrupulous individuals from stealing an advantage from those who endeavour to carry out both the letter, and the spirit of an agreement." ['Observer' May 26th. 1934]

On the 28th. June, 1934, the Bill became an Act. However, this did not mean that the agreements already in existence, were enforceable by law. In discussions between the Weavers' Amalgamation and the employers, the operative's representatives had urged that these existing agreements be brought under the provisions of the Act. The employers in reply demanded a further 2s. in the £1 reduction. Mr. James Bell, Vice President, of the Amalgamation said:

"We find your present suggestions altogether unacceptable to us, as they mean a further substantial reduction from the wages of the operatives who are now working under the rates fixed by agreement. They also, in effect, justify the action of those who have not honoured agreements by bringing wage rates down to their level instead of lifting them up to the standard of the honourable employers." ['Observer' July 10th.1934]

Hopwood says:

"No progress could be made with the employers, and the dilemma was reported to the General Council, who considered the situation in July 1934. District Associations were circularised, and the problem was discussed again in August, when the General Council authorised the Central Committee to continue joint discussions in an effort to secure agreement on wage rates to be legalised, the terms of any agreement to be submitted to the General Council for approval or otherwise."

"Armed with this authority the Central Committee did not at once proceed to use it, as contact with the employers was known to involve reductions in wages, and probably a revision of the More Looms List, as well as the Uniform List and Coloured Goods List. It was felt, however, that a continuation of the existing situation would be against the best interests of the Amalgamation and its members, and talks were reopened with the employers in September, 1934."

"A joint sub-committee was appointed, and proposals and counter-proposals were sent backwards and forwards, without any tentative agreement being reached. The operatives' representatives suggested that the disagreement should be submitted to the Conciliation Committee, but the employers would not agree."[21]

Further joint meetings took place lasting well into October. Eventually, the General Council at it's meeting of November 17th. decided to submit the whole position to a ballot vote of the members. The question on the ballot paper, which followed an explanation of the negotiations up to date, was:

"Are you in favour of giving the Central Committee full authority and power to conclude a new agreement, for submission to the Minister of Labour to make it legally enforceable." ['Observer' 24th. November,1934]

The Great Harwood Weavers' Half Yearly Report of November 1934, urged their members to vote unanimously for the approval of a new agreement.

The Church and Oswaldtwistle Weavers' also agreed to recommend the acceptance of the agreement at a special meeting held on November13th. ['Observer' November 17th.1934]

Mr. J.R. Emmett and his Accrington Executive advised their members to give an affirmative answer to the question. They were very upset when weavers from Nelson, Skipton and Colne, visited Accrington, Church and Clayton-Le-Moors, to distribute leaflets at mill gates advising members to vote against the agreement. Mr. Emmett said:

> "We very much resent people coming from other districts to influence our members, and feel very strongly about it. We regard it as an act of disloyalty to us and to the Amalgamation." ['Observer' November 27th. 1934]

The Nelson, Colne and Skipton Associations issued a spirited reply, which included the following statement:

> "We are not concerned with loyalty to a large body of employers and operatives who have ridden rough-shod through all agreements during the past few years, but we are deeply concerned about those who have remained loyal members of their trade unions."

> "Again we reiterate our statement on the leaflet - which has been stated to be untrue - that all cloths of the uniform list will be subject to a wage cut of at least 1s..1.5d in the £1, and as cloths become finer or are made with art silk, high reeds, etc, the severity of that reduction will be increased." ['Observer' November 27th. 1934]

The Accrington Weavers' held a meeting at the Co-operative Assembly Rooms, Oak Street, on December 4th. to discuss the proposed new agreement and how it would effect Accrington. Apparently it meant a couple of mills in the town having to pay considerably more and it also put an end to people paying money out of their wages as share capital. In addition it also guaranteed the 48 hour week. ['Observer' December 8th. 1934]

The result of the ballot, declared on December 15th. showed that out of 104,185 papers issued 89,369 were returned:

| In favour | 56,924 |
| Against | 28,195 |

This led to further meetings with the employers over the next month, which where known as Revision Joint Meetings.

Hopwood continues:

> "As a result of these protracted and wearying negotiations the way was now clear for an approach to be made to the Minister of Labour for the machinery to be set in motion under the new Cotton Manufacturing [Temporary Provisions] Act, 1934, and in accordance with the provisions of the Act a Board of Inquiry was set up, under the chairmanship of Dr. Hector J. W. Hetherington, [Vice-Chancellor of Liverpool University], with two other nominated members, and a panel of Assessors from each side of the industry. This Board of Inquiry held

preliminary meetings and on 13th May, 1935 the Board received evidence from objectors to the new proposed List. These objectors were cross-examined by the Amalgamation representatives upon the panel, and the proceedings lasted for a whole week. There were 18 objections, the majority from individual firms, and there were objections from our Nelson and Colne Weavers' Associations. The objections fell into five categories: [1] The geographical limitations of the Act itself; [2] Local Disadvantage allowances which were contained in the new List; [3] Applicability of the agreement to rayon weaving; [4] Reductions in weavers' wages in the Nelson and Colne areas; [5] the agreement would retard progressive methods in weaving."

"The Report of the Board of Inquiry was published on 15th. June 1935, and summarised the circumstances leading up to the new agreement, dealt with the points raised by the objectors, and made recommendations to the Minister. The Board recognised that the new agreement had defects but they had no reason to doubt that it was a notable improvement on what had gone before and upon the then existing chaotic situation in the industry. The Board agreed that the fundamental necessity was to make an Order bringing the new List into force."

"The Minister of Labour acted upon this advice, and the first Statutory Order on textile workers' wages was made on 27th. June, 1935, by Order No. 602, the new wage agreement to operate from the 15th. July, 1935." [22]

The new legalised agreement caused an outcry in the Nelson area. Over 5,000 people gathered to protest, and the meeting demanded that the Amalgamation Executive secure massive wage increases, to compensate them for their losses due to the agreement.

Alan and Lesley Fowler state:

"The growing opposition to the new Act and the wage reduction helped to ensure the election of a new Labour M.P. [for Nelson] at the General Election, Sidney Silverman."

"The Nelson resolution became the basis of the Amalgamation's campaign for an advance of 15% in 1936." [They got 7.5%]......

"Industrial peace in the industry and the new consensus between employers and Union had been bought at the expense of the Lancashire Weavers." [23]

Andrew Bullen agrees with the above sentence when he states:

"The price of peace, however, had fallen less heavily on the employers who had begun the undermining of agreements than on the operatives, the wage cut being bitterly resented by some Amalgamated Districts." [24]

THE DEATH OF MR. JONATHAN ASHWORTH J.P.

In the early hours of Christmas Day, the Rishton Weavers' Secretary died at the home of his daughter, Mrs Helm, 119 Stanhill Lane, Oswaldtwistle. He was 61 years old. News of his death was apparently not unexpected, due to the illness which had overtaken him in September.

The Church in School Street, Rishton, was crowded for the funeral, at which Mr. J.W. Sunderland read from the scriptures. Blinds in most of Rishton's houses were drawn, as a mark of respect for the man who had been their Weavers' Secretary since 1923.

Representatives of weavers' organisations from over 30 Lancashire textile towns attended the funeral. The Weavers' Amalgamation was represented by Messrs. J. Hindle J.P. President, of Burnley, A. Naesmith J.P. Secretary, of Accrington, and Alderman Luke Bates J.P. of Blackburn. ['Observer' January 1st.1935]

CONCLUSION

The tragedy of the situation was that Capitalism had failed the Lancashire operatives. Machinery stood idle, unemployment queues grew, and even the producers of raw cotton were ruined because it couldn't be sold. In primitive societies, poverty due to plenty was unimaginable, but under private ownership it was the end result of the system. Each new labour saving technique led to increased productive capacity, which other nations then employed and the effect was mass unemployment worldwide. It also meant that employers put every effort into reducing the wages of their employees that remained.

"The cotton manufacturers and the mineowners fix their eyes only on their own industry. They do not see industry all over the world as a whole and when they want 'to regain their markets' by pushing down wages or increasing productivity of labour through improved machinery and scientific management they do not realise the implications of the fact that exactly the same arguments are being used, and exactly the same steps are being taken by their rivals and by the employers in other industries."

"In the world of to-day the market cannot expand to keep pace with the increase in the world's productive capacity since the wage earners who form the mass of consumers in the advanced countries, and the peasants in the more backward countries receive a continually decreasing share of the total income. Hence under our system of production it is inevitable that the more wealth the world is able to produce, the more difficult it becomes to sell it, although the majority of mankind are without the first necessities of life." [25]

For over a hundred years the British cotton industry had yielded immoral profits, but had never in its history paid a living wage to its workforce. At the outset it relied on the slave labour of pauper children, and then flourished on the backs of the appallingly low paid women workers. Even during the period under discussion the mainly sweated female operatives still maintained thousands of shareholders, brokers, merchants and other City spivs, in the manner to which they had grown accustomed.

The Chapter shows, without any fear of contradiction, that the capitalist bosses of Lancashire's cotton industry carried out a premeditated, evil class war against their operatives. This caused a series of defensive strikes, demonstrations, petitions and other forms of action by the workers. The result was the longest and most viciously fought class battle of the inter-war years.

The main reason for the Capitalists embarking on this course of action was the over-capitalisation that had occurred after the First World War. This was highlighted in an article in the Financial Times, of December 31st. 1926, [26] which stated that 142 mills with a pre-war value of £6,048,000 were sold during 1920 for £49,503,000. There was also the promotion/marketing costs of £3,126,000 to be added, which brought the total paid to over £52 million. In other words the mills had cost over eight times more than they had pre-war. The most important aspect of these transactions, was that a large proportion of the purchase price was raised through bank loans and overdrafts. The first legal priority of such mills, was to repay the yearly interest due to the banks, which in effect became a reckonable part of their production costs. [27]

Stone Bridge Mill in Oswaldtwistle was sold for £80,000 by the Vine Spinning Company in 1920, but could only be sold for £1,400 in 1933. ['Observer' June 17th. 1933] This provides a useful example, because if a mill previously valued, at say, £10,000 had normally paid a 10% dividend to its shareholders, only £1,000 profit was required at the end of the year. However, if the same mill suddenly had a share value of £90,000 it required a profit of £9,000 per year to pay a 10% dividend. The mill owners in many cases were in a position of negative equity and were faced with high interest payments to the banks. Indeed the money owed the banks often exceeded the actual [1927-1934] value of the mill. In order to maintain their high lifestyles:

"many directors have sought at all costs to keep their mills going in order to retain their salaries or fees, and to this end have put off the evil day of collapse by piling debt upon debt without scruple." [28]

In addition to the tremendous extraction of money from the industry by the banks, there were all the opportunities that had always been available for rich pickings by the various middlemen - 'cotton broker, yarn agent, cloth agent, packers, shippers etc'.

In a paper read to the Athenaeum Textile Society in 1928, it stated:

"1. There is the great disadvantage of a commodity passing through many hands. At each stage there are separate overheads and an attempt at separate profits.

2. In Lancashire's organisation there is the problem of certain key sections forming themselves into price rings and holding the other sections to ransom. Certain sections are more interested in a high rate of profit than in a large turnover.

3. The burdens of bad trade are very unequally distributed."

Freda Utley goes on to say:

"In so far as 2 is concerned it is well known that the percentage now taken by the exporting merchant is much higher than pre - War. The latter has been satisfied to export less and charge more.

"Finishers' charges and profits have been maintained at a very high figure owing to the monopoly position of a few very big firms." [29]

These gross mistakes caused by free market Capitalism, caused the mass unemployment, poverty and suffering of the ordinary workers of Lancashire. The operatives were innocent, the owners were guilty.

The only reason the employers wanted to cut wages, increase hours and give the operatives extra looms, was to give themselves a higher profit margin. These proposals could not have any appreciable effect on the shop price, which was required if any increase in trade was to take place. Manufacturers sold cloth to the merchants by the piece, but the consumer bought the cloth by the yard. Now it so happened that the weavers wages per yard, in December 1930, were between a halfpenny and a penny. Therefore, the weavers were caused all the stress and suffering of the next four years, without the employers harsh policies having any chance of altering shop prices for the consumer. [30]

The propaganda from the employers side was that they had to enact harsh policies against the workers in order to capture world markets and to increase home consumption. However, they were not daft; they knew that this would not happen but it was an excellent ploy to increase their profits.

In addition to the over-capitalisation just discussed, Britain's adherence to the Gold Standard, from 1925 to September 1931, at the pre-War parity of £1 = $4.87 could only be described as lunacy. Such a rate was at least 10% too high and therefore we lost long established export markets to our growing foreign competitors.

The Wall Street Crash of 1929, led to a World Slump. As one commentator said: "when America sneezes, the rest of the world catches pneumonia." Between 1929 and 1933 the United States imported 70% less than they had previously, which caused economic havoc worldwide. [31]

Faced with these overwhelming trading difficulties, there is no doubt that the cotton industry had to modernise. Weaving mills full of, in some cases, machinery fifty years old, had eventually to install automatic looms. Spinning mills needed to invest in more up to date ring frames. The industry under capitalism had already seen a dramatic number of permanent mill closures. Eg. in Great Harwood and particularly Clayton-Le-Moors. Free market economics could not help the situation.

The right-wing union leaders had no clear answers formulated that would cure the cotton crisis. They had not demanded the nationalisation of the industry, but had wanted some form of Government intervention and control, in order to put a stop to the anarchy which prevailed.

Unfortunately the 1934 Act did not produce any increase in trade. In fact 1938 witnessed the worst trading position since 1850. Unemployment in the industry returned to over 30%. At the outbreak of the second World War membership of the Weavers' Amalgamation had dropped to 95,000. The Act had merely benefited the employers at the expense of the workers.

The Communist Party denounced the Act for securing the position of the employers and the union bureaucrats, whilst totally disregarding the demands of the militant rank and file.

The Weavers' Amalgamation's executive, the Central Committee, was totally in the hands of the full time district officials, who had only got their jobs due to their ability to understand the complicated Price Lists and not through their dedication to the class struggle. During this period the monthly General Council meetings of the Amalgamation, which were more representative of the feelings of the operatives, frequently rejected the executive's proposals. As Bill Whittaker says:

> "Rarely did the Amalgamation give effective leadership to any mill-based campaign. Too often the leaders joined in to divert, behead and immobilise the action. As one right-wing official told me, rather crudely, many years ago: 'First we mother them, then we smoother them'."

"All the efforts and solidarity of the weavers was betrayed and defeated. The cotton workers of the early 1930's were every bit as determined and united as the miners of today [written in 1985], but they had no effective leadership."

"With different leaders concerned to lead their members in struggle, some glorious pages would have been written in working-class history."[32]

Margaret McCarthy stated that as far as Accrington was concerned local Communist leadership was non-existent, and had to be brought in from outside.

"Ernie Woolley was our principal importee, turned out to be a very popular energetic and rousing leader."[33]

In North East Lancashire as a whole however, the relatively small numbers of Communist Party members and importees led a valiant campaign. Twelve Party members were arrested on trumped up charges, just in order to get them out of the area temporarily.

"Harold and Bessie Dickinson served three months each, Rose Smith also served three months. Ernie Wooley six months, [hard labour] Tommy Coughlin, Trevor Robinson, Maggie Nelson, Bertha Jane, Mick Jenkins and others, served varying sentences."[34]

Jim Rushton, from Earby, was fined £40 which the people of the township raised in two weeks. Margaret McCarthy herself was also arrested and fined 5s. These people have to be admired for their devotion to the cause. It is obvious that the wages and conditions of the cotton operatives would have been much worse, if it hadn't been for Communist Party activists and Labour Party sympathisers organising them to thwart the evil ambitions of the employers and the ruling class in general.

REFERENCES

1. Hopwood, E. 'A History of the Lancashire Cotton Industry and the Amalgamated Weavers' Association'. Pub. Amalgamated Weavers' Association 1969. p. 121
2. Ed. Tracey, H. 'The British Labour Party' Vol.3 Pub. Caxton Pub. Co. Ltd. London. 1948. p.288
3. Bullen, A. 'The Lancashire Weavers' Union'. Pub. Amalgamated Textile Workers Union, 1984. p.50
4. ibid. p. 51
5. Fowler, A and L. 'The History of the Nelson Weavers Association'. Pub. Burnley, Nelson, Rossendale and District Textile Workers Union. 1984. p.54

6. McCarthy, M. 'Generation in Revolt'. Pub. Heinemann Ltd. 1953. p. 151
7. Fowler. op. cit. p. 60
8. ibid. p. 62
9. ibid. p. 63
10. Bullen. op. cit. p. 56
11. Dutt, R.P. 'India Today'. Pub. Gollancz Ltd. Left Book Club. 1940. p. 329
12. ibid. p. 333 to 337
13. Utley, F. 'Lancashire and the Far East'. Pub. George Allen and Unwin Ltd. 1931. p. 321
14. Swann, S. 'Politics of Labour in a Lancashire Mill Town: Accrington Between the Wars'. Dissertation M.A. Sheffield University. 1988. p. 14
15. Rothwell, M. 'A Guide to the Industrial Archaeology of Accrington'. Pub. Rothwell 1979. P. 20
16. Rothwell, M. 'A Guide to the Industrial Archaeology of Oswaldtwistle'. Pub. Lancashire County Council. 1978. p.9
17. Swann. op. cit. p. 13 and 14
18. Hopwood. op. cit. p. 121
19. Bullen. op. cit. p. 59
20. Ed. Fowler, A. Wyke, T. 'The Barefoot Aristocrats: A History of the Amalgamated Association of Operative Cotton Spinners'. Pub. Kelsall, G. Littleborough 1987. Article by Alan Fowler 'Spinners in the Inter-War Years'. P. 174 and 175
21. Hopwood. op. cit. p.115
22. ibid. p. 116
23. Fowler, A and L. op. cit. p. 85 and 86
24. Bullen. op. cit. p. 61
25. Utley. op. cit. p. 19 and 20
26. Jenkins, M. 'Cotton Struggles 1929-1932' Marxism To-Day. February 1969 p. 51
27. Utley. op. cit. p. 46
28. ibid. p. 51 and 52
29. ibid. p. 54
30. Jenkins. op. cit. p. 53
31. Stewart, M. 'Keynes and After'. Pub. Penguin books 1975. p. 169
32. Whittaker, B. 'North West Labour History Bulletin No. 10. 1984/85. Review of the History of the Nelson Weavers and the Lancashire Weavers Union. p. 61
33. McCarthy. op. cit. p. 55 and 56
34 Jenkins. op. cit. p. 55 and 56

Chapter Three

The Engineering Industry, Brick Manufacturing and Mining.

I have already described the actions of the local Amalgamated Engineering Union, the General and Municipal Workers Union and the Miners' Federation branches, towards the Trades Disputes and Trade Unions Act of 1927. This Chapter comments on the many other events that affected their members interests.

THE ACCRINGTON & DISTRICT ENGINEERING ALLIED TRADES FEDERATION.

This was the local organisation of the Confederation of Engineering and Shipbuilding Unions, whose area organiser was based in Bolton. In 1926 the Allied Trades, together with their full time officials, had negotiated with the Blackburn & District Engineering Trades Employers' Association on the issue of a £1 per week pay claim locally. However, it was usually the Confed. that negotiated nationally with the Engineering Employers' Federation on issues of pay. The Allied Trades could negotiate with the Employers locally and put out propaganda on the following issues:
a] Working conditions
b] Compensation agreements
c] Holiday arrangements [Wakes weeks], both with the Employers and the local Educational Executives
d] Works buses

e] Agree to resolutions to be forwarded from local branches of trade unions to the Confed.

f] Agree to resolutions to be forwarded from local trade union branches to the Accrington TCLP

The Allied Trades met on a monthly basis and the number of delegates to its meetings were fixed in proportion to the numerical strength of the various unions that were affiliated. Unions belonging to this body at this time included the AEU, GMWU, National Union of Foundry Workers, Amalgamated Moulders' Union, National Union of Sheet Metal Workers, National Engine Men & Firemen's Union, Amalgamated Grinders & Glaziers Society, and others.

I obtained most of the above information from Mr. Frank Maddrell, of Oswaldtwistle, in an interview held in May 1985. Frank was the Secretary of the Allied Trades from 1950 until it ceased to exist around 1953.

THE AMALGAMATED ENGINEERING UNION.

Accrington was part of Division No.11; the AEU being split into 26 Divisions, each having an Organising District Delegate who acted as a full-time official. The ODD for No.11 Division was Alderman Samuel Frith of Oldham, whose area covered Wigan through to Oldham and stretched northwards to Colne.

Due to the depression the number of Divisions was cut to 20 on the 1st. of January 1931, and Accrington became part of Division No. 9. In the election for the ODD for No.9 Division Accrington had a candidate, Bro. J.R. Cressey, who came a bad third to the victorious Sam Frith.

Incredibly, Accrington, which was split into 9 branches, with over 2,000 members did not have a full-time District Secretary. Its District Secretary was Bro. G.K. Chalmers who worked on the shop-floor at Howard and Bullough Ltd., the largest employer in the town. The branches and shop stewards elected representatives on a yearly basis to the District Committee which met every week. The positions of District Secretary and District President were also up for re-election yearly.

1927

At their meeting, January 20th. 1927, the District Committee of the AEU had to accept the situation, that the management of Howard and Bullough Ltd had the right to refuse reinstatement to anybody discharged for smoking during working hours. [Minute Book] The firm of Howard and Bullough were the largest employer in Accrington by the 1920's, with their various buildings dominating the towns industrial landscape. At its peak the firm employed nearly 6,000. [1]

The Minutes of the AEU-DC of June 2nd. 1927, detailed the following event. The shop steward in the Fluted Roller Dept. No.2, Joseph Walsh appeared before them in order to explain why an unofficial stoppage took place in his, and Dept No.1, on Friday May 27th. resulting in the discharge of a non-unionist named Evans. The Minutes read as follows:

"1. Sometime since Evans was discharged for bad work.

2, The foreman reinstated Evans.

3. Immediately on reinstatement Evans adopted a provocative attitude, both by word and deed towards the AEU members in this dept. Pushing, Tripping, Insults, Challenging to Fight and Rushing the work.

4. On Friday May 27th. Evans culminated the above by Striking Bro. Eastwood on the jaw.

5. The Management have protested against the stoppage of work, and threatened to restart Evans.

6. Our Members have informed the Management that they will immediately cease work again if Evans is restarted.

7. The Management have called a Meeting of the Works Committee for 10 am. Thursday June 9th. and agreed to postpone reinstatement pending this meeting.

8. Members in this Dept. feel that the firm are adopting this attitude for the purpose of splitting the solidarity of the members. [Membership in the 3 Fluted Roller Depts. is approx. 80%]

After full discussion the following resolution was carried, as the firm rules that any workman striking another during working hours shall be instantly discharged.

E7/23. That the Works Committee at Howard and Bullough be advised 'Not to Agree' to the reinstatement of Evans."

At the Works Committee Meeting the Management requested that the workers representatives leave the matter in their hands. Evans must not have been allowed back, because there is no further mention of the case in the copiously written minutes.

In 1924 national negotiations began for a pay increase of 20s. / week, but by 1927 nothing had been achieved. The Engineering Allied Trades Movement decided to instruct districts to make local demands for wage increases; nothing came of this, but it did cause the employers to reopen national bargaining at which they offered a 2s./ week increase to plain time-workers. This was accepted by a 2 to 1 majority of the combined votes of the unions affiliated to the Engineering Allied Trades Federation. The AEU members were not satisfied with the result but accepted that it was best to take the offer. [2]

The Accrington AEU-DC appeared to dislike the way in which a combined vote with other unions had been arrived at. [Minute Book. July 1927] The voting figures for the Accrington GMWU were 622 for and 98 against accepting the 2s./ week offer. [GMWU Minute Book July 14th. 1927]

In reference to the continuing strained relationship with the local GMWU, the AEU-DC instructed their delegates to the Engineering Allied Trades Federation, to vote against Joint Meetings for Propaganda Purposes. [Minute Book August 11th.]

On September 15th. the AEU-DC decided to send a letter to the Accrington Labour Party, "on the obnoxious attitude displayed towards our delegates by the Secretary and President". This correspondence generated discussions for a further three DC Meetings. [Minute Book]

1928

The AEU members at Howard and Bullough had been complaining for many years about the high handed way they were forced to do piece work. At the January 4th., Works Committee Meeting, they finally won some concessions on the issue, namely: 1] It was agreed that Foremen would no longer be able to compel workmen to commence work on piece work, where the price was in dispute. 2] The shop stewards were to have the right to inquire about the piece price for any job in their department. 3] Shop Clerks were to have lists of all piece prices for the men's use. [Minute Book January 5th 1928]

It was reported that the membership of the Accrington AEU stood at 2,427. [Minute Book January 12th.1928]

The DC at it Meeting, 23rd. February, accepted the recommendations of a sub-committee that had been set up for propaganda purposes to increase membership. Its proposals were:

"Open Branch Meeting, March 5th. Lecturer D.B. Lawley. Subject 'Jack London's Works'.

Open Branch Meeting, March 26th. Lecturer A.L. Williams.

Special Meeting, March 28th. Lantern Lecture. 'Teeth in Relation to Health'

Smoking Concert to be held in April."

Mr. Lawley had previously given lectures on China to the GMWU members at two meetings in January. Indeed, the GMWU bought a copy of his book 'The Hustling Hobo' at its February 2nd. Meeting. He was obviously a local resident at the time, but seems to have disappeared from the limelight after this lecture.

A Mass Meeting of all engineering apprentices was held at the AEU Rooms at 10.30 am. on Sunday June 10th. as part of a campaign to get 100% membership amongst apprentices. A sub-committee was set up to organise Sports and Social Events. This recommended a cricket match between the Howard and Bullough Apprentices of the Spindle and Flyer Dept. and those employed in the Fountain Street Depts. This was held on July 4th. at Bullough Park. On July 8th. the Apprentices Cycling Club held its first run. [Minute Book]

Disagreements with the other unions in the Engineering Allied Trades Federation led to the DC recommending, at their August 16th meeting, that their affiliation should be terminated on December 31st 1928. This was restated and approved at their meeting of September 6th. [Minute Book]

The Apprentices Committee were encouraged to send two members to the Quarterly Meeting of Shop Stewards and an application for a football pitch at Bullough Park for the use of apprentices matches was forwarded to the Town Clerk. [Minute Book December 6th.1928]

Following their grudging acceptance of the 2s. / week increase in 1927, the Engineering Joint Trades Movement put in a demand for a national 8s. / week increase, but this was met with a flat refusal by the employers. Mr. J.T. Brownlie, President of the AEU, stated that it was not the inability of the employers to pay such an increase that prompted the refusal. He said:

> "It is a matter of power.....we are not as powerful as we hope to be; one day, we will be powerful and will control matters in a manner that will be beneficial not only to those who are engaged directly in the industry but will be beneficial to all members of the community." [3]

1929

The April edition of the AEU Journal reprinted leaflets of the Communist Party and the National Metalworkers' Minority Movement which had urged the membership to vote for a slate of left-wing candidates for past elections to the National Executive etc. The article went on to condemn this practice and proceeded to fully comply with the TUC witch hunt of Communist Party activists. This anti-democratic policy led to the temporary expulsion of many C.P. members from the union.

An application was made to the Directors of Howard and Bullough Ltd. to provide full facilities for workmen to leave the works in a clean and presentable fashion. When these wash basins had been provided, the DC wanted 4 minutes before the end of a shift to be allowed for washing after abnormally dirty working conditions, and 2 minutes for all other workers. [Minute Book April 21st] On May 9th the DC heard that the response from the management, at the Works Committee Meeting, had been one of failure to agree. [Minute Book]

Nationally, the engineers were aware that failure to secure increases in wages was not due to the weakness of their case, but to their loss of membership and the disillusionment existing after the sellout of the General Strike. In an effort to provide a focus of hope, and a rallying point, the 1929 National Committee adopted the 'Engineers Charter', which called for:

"1. £4 a week as a national minimum wage.

2. The establishment of a 44-hour week.

3. The abolition of systematic overtime.

4. Shop stewards in every shop and a factory committee in every factory.

5. The Union's right to control the numbers and conditions of employment of youths and apprentices.

6. Payment for all Statutory Holidays.

7. Payment for periods of sickness after 12 months' service in one firm.

8. Every metal worker a Trade Unionist." [4]

Jeffreys emphasises that the Charter was received with enthusiasm by the membership.

Samuel Frith, in his Report published in the August edition of the AEU Journal, stated that he attended a Central Conference with a case from Accrington that concerned youths employed as machinists at Howard and Bullough Ltd. Apparently the firm was sacking them as they reached the age of 21, because they did not want to pay the adult wage. He said:

"These youths are only paid the apprentice rates during the time up to 21 years of age, and we hold that if youths are not serving apprenticeship to a skilled trade then they ought to receive much more than the apprenticeship rate during the whole time from them starting, to becoming 21 years of age. We further claim that from their time of becoming employed they should be taught the workings of the department, so that they cannot be placed in the position of, as the firm states, only being used to lad's jobs. Especially would I say to parents who have boys working at this firm: Make sure if your boy does commence to work at the firm that you have a thorough understanding of what your boy is to become before you allow him to start. This, I believe, is one of the best means of stamping out this system which seems to have been so prevalent in the past."

The distribution of a Communist Party leaflet, entitled 'Howard and Bullough Worker', appeared to particularly irk the DC. Apparently it contained comments about their actions at that time, which probably concerned their response to the treatment of apprentices by the Howard and Bullough management. [Minute Book April 25th. to June 20th.1929]

Mr. G.K. Chalmers, District Secretary, was presented with an English Dictionary and a briar pipe, at a gathering attended by over 100 officials and members in the AEU Club Rooms. This was in recognition of his 10 years service as District Secretary ['Observer' December 14th.1929]

1930

Mr. J.T. Brownlie, President of the AEU, paid a visit to Accrington, during which he attended a social gathering on Saturday 25th. January and addressed a private Mass Meeting of members in the Labour Hall the following morning. Part of his speech printed in the 'Observer' is reproduced below:

"Some people were very apprehensive as to what was going to happen in the near future. He knew that the present system under which they lived whereby they had to compete with each other to obtain employment and sell their labour for a wage left much to be desired. In consequence they were compelled to live in dwellings that in many instances were not fit to house pedigree pigs. The working people, the women of this country were now for the first time possessed of political power. He could not for one moment believe that the working people of this country were going to use their political power for returning people to the legislative institutions of the nation to carry on the present competitive system, whereby the few enjoyed all the amenities and luxuries produced by the many, and the many were compelled to live a life of hardship." ['Observer' January 28th.1930]

Unfortunately, the working-class did not behave in the manner predicted by Mr. Brownlie. They continued to vote for representatives of the ruling class and perpetuated their own misery for many years to come. During the last 18 years, the descendant of these oppressed workers of the 1930's, again voted into power the class enemy and the resulting poverty and degradation was predictable. The Conservative working-class voter has a lot to answer for.

Bro. Samuel Frith wrote of attending a meeting of Accrington No. 2 Branch in January in order to present an Award of Merit to one of the oldest officers of the branch, Bro. Regan. He was one of those old stalwarts who belonged to the society when it was dangerous to be a member. He had seen the membership grow from 70 to 2,300. during the whole of that time he had been active in his branch. Frith said:

> "One of the finest tributes paid to an official that I have heard for a long time was, that at the last election of a sick steward, one of the members moved Bro. Regan because it was better than medicine to the sick members to see Bro. Regan's face." [Feb. 1930 AEU Journal p. 25]

The AEU Cycling Club was inaugurated and had its 'first run' to Downham on Saturday 1st. March, leaving the AEU Rooms at 1.00 pm. [Minute Book]

The AEU's non-membership of the Allied Trades Federation continued, but a Joint Meeting did take place in the AEU Rooms, April 13th., between the AEU, Amalgamated Moulders, and Ironfounders. The following resolutions were adopted unanimously:

> "A. That in the event of the local Association of the Engineering Employers Federation failing, at any future period to observe the customary holidays for the Engineering Trades in the Accrington District, the Societies represented at this Joint Meeting shall immediately meet together with a view to obtaining a 'Joint Local Conference' on the Holiday Question."

> "B. That the above Societies shall elect 'three representatives' for each organisation, who shall form a joint sub-committee to deal with questions of a general character, the decisions of this sub-committee to be subject to ratification by the parent bodies."

> "C. ....G.K. Chalmers, shall act as the Convener and Secretary to the sub-committee."

> "D. That the undermentioned Societies be asked to appoint representatives to form a Joint Works Committee for the firm of Lang Bridges Ltd. Societies: AEU, Ironfounders, Sheet-Metal Workers, Pattern Makers."

This was, undoubtedly, a devious move by the AEU. to sideline the GMWU. The Lang Bridges works employed around 400 in 1910 and at its peak employed 1,000. [5]

The above took another turn when at the July 3rd. DC. it was decided that a letter be written to the local branch of the Sheet-Metal Workers Society informing them that the AEU were not connected with the Allied Trades Federation, and therefore a Works Committee for Lang Bridges would be set up without GMWU representation. [Minute Book]

Questionnaires were sent out to shop stewards at Lang Bridges respecting the formation of a Works Committee in November. However, the result of the stewards survey caused the DC to defer action pending a revival of trade.[Minute Book]

Meanwhile, Mr. George Kidd Chalmers, District Secretary, of 17 Robert Street, Accrington, had been appointed a Justice of the Peace. ['Observer' May 3rd.] In the July AEU Journal the result was declared in an election for a place on the National Executive. Eight members were originally nominated and in the second ballot Bro. Chalmers lost out to Bro. Sam Bradley. The result was:

>Bro. S. Bradley   4,609 votes
>Bro. G.K. Chalmers   2,939 votes

After the General Strike, the Mond-Turner talks; discussions between the T.U.C. and a group of industrialists led by Alfred Mond, were strongly resisted by the AEU nationally. At the 1928 T.U.C. the President J.T.Brownlie attacked the General Council for discussing industrial matters with a group of industrialists who represented nobody but themselves. He followed this up at the 1929 TUC by demanding that the talks cease. When the talks continued the AEU felt that they had to support the following resolution moved at the 1930 T.U.C., which called for:

> "opposition to the false cry of industrial peace and to the policy of collaboration with the enemies of labour, who are vigorously and ruthlessly attacking the standard of living of the working class at the very time they are conferring with the General Council, and instructs the Council to put an end to such conferences forthwith, as they are a serious menace to the interests of the working-class movement."[6]

A series of socials and concerts were arranged for the winter months in order to develop fellowship in the movement. On Wednesday 1st. October, at the AEU Club, songs and duets were given in 'a pleasing manner', and Bro. Chalmers J.P. gave a talk on:

> "Unemployment, speaking on the fallacies of withholding trade, over-population, over-production, the loss of world markets, the cheap living and competition of other nations and world causes." ['Observer' October 4th.]

The Socials continued, with a convivial gathering held on Wednesday November 5th. The Concert was of a 'very high tone', and Bro. J.R. Cressey gave a very interesting lecture on 'the commercial life of an insect'. ['Observer' November 4th.]

A Mass Meeting of members took place on Sunday morning 9th. November, at the AEU Club, in order to hear their new National President, Mr. W.H. Hutchinson. Also in attendance were Sam Bradley, of the National Executive Council; Alderman Sam Frith; George Hale, Burnley District

Secretary; J.W. Charnley, Blackburn District Secretary; and Mr. G.K.Chalmers presided.

"Bro. Chalmers stated that although their membership was well over 2,000 in the Accrington District, they had lost some, and he appealed for the support of all present to try to regain their lost members."

"Bro. S. Bradley said.....One of their worst [problems] was the effect of non-unionists, who were not only impeding their own cause, but were a menace to society."

"Bro. W.H. Hutchinson, National President, gave a stirring address.....[in which] he expressed the view that the non-unionists were responsible for much of the conditions they were forced to accept."

On Sunday November 30th. Mr. Tom Snowden MP. addressed the Shop Stewards in the AEU Rooms. In his address he defended the policy of the minority Labour Government, saying that they were not responsible for the industrial depression.

The third in the series of concerts was held in the AEU Club on December 3rd. with Bro.R.O. Jones, the ODD of Liverpool, the speaker.

1931

The Shop Stewards Quarterly Meeting, January 11th. forwarded the following resolution to the Prime Minister, Mr. Tom Snowden MP, and the T.U.C.:

"That this meeting of shop stewards and other local officials call upon the Labour Government to support the Trade Unions in their fights against the Employers encroachment on the workers wages and conditions, particularly in the present struggles in the mining and cotton industries." [Minute Book]

The attack by the employers caused the DC. to rethink its attitude towards the local Allied Trades Federation. At their meeting of February 12th. the Secretary was instructed to attend the next Allied Trades meeting, although with a watching brief only. On February 19th. Mr. Chalmers reported back on his observations of the meeting held on February 16th. and was instructed to go to a further meeting on February 25th. and to support a joint letter of protest against the demands of the Engineering Employers. [Minute Book] This letter is reproduced in the section on the GMWU.

Although the Secretary attended a further meeting of the Allied Trades on March 25th., the DC passed the following resolution on March 26th.:

> "That this Committee in view of our disaffiliation from the Allied Trades Federation cannot agree to participate in any Mass Meeting arranged by that body."[Minute Book]

On Saturday 28th. March, a Social was held at the AEU Rooms on Blackburn Road, at which the local officials and their wives had a hot-pot supper and heard addresses by Bro.W.H. Hutchinson, National President and Sam Bradley from the National Executive. This was followed by a Mass Meeting of members in the Labour Hall on Sunday morning, at which the honoured visitors surprisingly injected a breath of militancy on those present. The meeting involving a healthy discussion lasted for 3 hours. ['Observer' March 31st.1931]

The 'Observer' June 6th. reported that the Employers' Federation had issued an ultimatum to the workers, that they would impose their proposals on July 6th. which :

> "include a readjustment of the rates and the periods for overtime on day shift, night shift and the two and three shift systems. The employers have adhered to their original demand that piece work prices and bonus or basis times for payment by results shall by reduced to 25% over the ordinary time rates, excluding war bonus. The 47 hour week is not to be touched."

On Sunday June 7th. the Shop Stewards meeting at the AEU Rooms passed a resolution urging their Executive to resist to the utmost any attempt at increasing hours of labour or reducing wages. ['Observer' June 9th.]

Edmund Frow joint founder of the Working Class Movement Library in Salford, wrote in Labour Monthly, June 1931, in a prophetic article entitled 'The Attack on the Engineers':

> "The present situation has features in common with the situation during the war years. At that time the Trade Union leaders did nothing to fight for or protect the engineers, but entered into an agreement with the Government in order to chain the workers to the war machine."

> "During this period the rank-and-file workers showed a good understanding of what was required. Throughout the industry, the workers threw up a new unofficial rank-and-file organisation which led them in struggle - the Shop Stewards and Workshop Committee movement. This movement embraced all workers irrespective of grade or Trade Union on the basis of their mutual interests against the employers."

> "When the big slump came after the war, the employers, with the assistance of the Trade Union leaders were successful in victimising

many of the leaders of the Shop Stewards' movement, partly as a result of the unclarity of the militants as to the next steps to be taken in the changed situation that arose."

After a meeting of the Engineering Union Executives held in London on June 17th. the following resolution was agreed to:

"That this Conference expresses regret at the employers' decision to impose the conditions contained in the statement made to the Trade Union representatives on the 4th. June. Further, that steps be taken by the Negotiating Committee to reopen negotiations with the employers, and report the result to a further conference of Executives."

At meetings held on June 19th. and 20th. amended proposals wereoffered by the employers with which the Negotiating Committee agreed. On June 23rd. the union Executives met in London with delegates from 32 organisations being present. After discussions the following resolution moved by the GMWU and seconded by the Sheet-Metal Workers was put to the vote:

"Having considered the recommendation of the Negotiating Committee this Conference is not prepared to accept the terms submitted."

Unfortunately the resolution was defeated by 38 votes to 61, the terms being, therefore, accepted by the meeting. The AEU Executive then reluctantly decided to accept the new terms as agreed by the Joint Conference of Trade Union Executives.[7]

The editor of the AEU Journal said that:

"We can certainly appreciate the feelings of our members who are called upon to make a sacrifice, particularly so, having in regard to the fact that the old conditions were only obtained after many years of unceasing effort. We wish, however, to make it perfectly clear that the acceptance of the employers' terms was no more satisfactory to the officials than to the membership generally."

"We recognise that our action will be adversely commented upon in many quarters. That, of course, we are accustomed to....."

"The concessions agreed upon will, we hope, result in safeguarding the rates of wages of those not engaged upon any system of payment by results for, we feel sure, everyone will agree the standard rate of our time workers is far too low."[8]

Bro. G.K. Chalmers had the job of explaining the agreement to the Shop Stewards Quarterly Meeting held on Sunday July 5th. ['Observer' July11th.] These were [reduced overtime rates from time and a half to time and a quarter and the hourly night-shift rates from time and a third to time and a sixth, and cut the basis of piece-work prices from 33% over time rates to 25%, with proportionate reductions in existing piecework prices]

The AEU Journal, August 1931, printed articles from the Daily Worker and leaflets from the National Minority Movement - Metal Section, as evidence to take disciplinary measures against members who had put their name to them. The Daily Worker article stated:

> "In spite of the determination of the rank and file of the workers in the engineering industry not to accept any worsening of the present conditions, the officials of the Trade Union concerned have deliberately flouted the decisions of the workers. They are begging Sir Allan Smith to meet them again in order that they can come to a mutual settlement with a view to avoiding a lockout on 6th. July"

> "In London, Sheffield, Glasgow, Manchester and Newcastle, and other large industrial centres where engineering workers are engaged, strong resolutions have been passed against any worsening of conditions, and against any further negotiations on the employers proposals. Now the leading officials step in and attempt to arrive at a settlement over the men. This inevitably means the acceptance of the principal proposals of the engineering employers."

> "We warn all engineering workers that they are facing the most serious situation in their history. At once, the action of the leading officials must be repudiated, in every factory and Trade Union branch throughout the country."

The members who put their names to this article were dealt with under Rule 21 of the AEU. This in effect meant that they were all [including Edmund Frow] expelled from the union, except the only full-time official involved, Jack Tanner, who apologised. This was a draconian measure that only showed that the union at this time was basically undemocratic. A Members Rights Movement was then set up to get the men reinstated. In 1932 this organisation printed a regular paper called the 'Monkey Wrench'. [9]

James Jeffreys who wrote the official history of the AEU for its 25th. Anniversary states:

> "There is little doubt that had the lead been given the membership would have been prepared to face the hardships involved in strike action, but the Executive Council would not risk a major dispute, which they considered could not possibly be carried through to a successful conclusion in view of the widespread unemployment, declining membership and the strain upon the funds." [10]

At the Accrington Shop Stewards Meeting, Sunday August 9th., it was stated that all arrangements had been made for a 'Back to the Unions' Campaign, to be held throughout September. This included the distribution of leaflets to claimants at the Royd Street Labour Exchange on Friday August 14th. and 21st. Bro. Lamb, National Organiser was drafted into the district for a few day to help in the campaign. He appears to have done a good job because the DC, September 17th. has the following comments:

> "That in future, when the Organising District Delegate is in the district on Compensation Cases and business other than conference work, he be instructed to hold out door meetings at various works gates, and Bro Frith be informed of this decision, to continue the propaganda work done by Bro. Lamb, National Organiser......"

> "That this DC express to E.C. their entire satisfaction, and appreciation of the work done in this district by Bro. Lamb." [Minute Book]

He reciprocates the praise in his report published in the October, AEU Journal, when he said:

> "Credit is due to the Accrington DC for the attention which has been given to preparatory arrangements for an organisation campaign. Such were admirable in their conception and events proved the wisdom which had been exercised."

1932

Throughout 1932 the Union took certain actions in relation to the 'Means Test', but this will be discussed in Chapter 4.

A Social Evening was held for apprentices and youths, on January 6th.; around 100 responded. Prizes to the value of 25s. were given in the form of vouchers to be spent on books, or tools, to help them in their work. Bro. Ald. S. Firth J.P. of Oldham, O.D.D. addressed them on the benefits of organisation. ['Observer' January 12th.1932]

At the Shop Stewards meeting on Sunday morning January 10th., Bro. Herbert Rothwell, District President, said that no one would regret the passing of 1931, as it had been one of the worst they, as an organisation, had gone through. ['Observer' January 12th.1932]

A Mass Meeting of members took place on Sunday morning, January 17th., at which Bro. Sam Bradley of the National Executive gave an address. He said:

> "The cure for much of the unemployment in the engineering industry was a shorter working week, as they were now able, owing to the development of machinery, to produce at a much quicker rate. The decrease of the spending power of the worker was a suicidal policy, and

he believed that with a rally back to the ranks by non-unionists they would be able to resist any movement in the direction of wage reductions." ['Observer' January 23rd.1932]

The death of Bro. Ald. S. Frith J.P. of Oldham, who had been the area's ODD since the AEU came into existence in 1920, was reported to the Shop Stewards Meeting on February 7th. ['Observer' February 13th.] Bro. Frith had been Oldham's first Labour Councillor, first Labour Alderman and first Labour Mayor. [AEU Journal March 1932] Tom Blackburn took over as the ODD.

The 'Observer', March 26th. reported that an educational visit had been made by AEU members to Howard and Bullough's Works, and that the incredible number of 233 people had applied to take part. ['Observer' March 26th.1932]

The DC, on September 1st. sent a letter to the Prime Minister and the local M.P., requesting increased facilities of credit to increase British exports to the USSR. This was further taken up by the Shop Stewards at their meeting on Sunday 4th. September, when they passed the following:

"That we, the Accrington District Shop Stewards of the AEU, representing over 1,500 trade unionists engaged in the textile machinery industry, strongly urges the Government and the Exports Credits Guarantee Department, to give the most liberal guarantees to firms requiring same for the purpose of accepting and completing orders for manufactures and supplies, required by the authorised representatives of the USSR and thus encourage the largest number of workers being employed in the metal, engineering, electrical equipment, textile machinery and other trades. This meeting of Shop Stewards urges it to be imperative in the interests of the workers' livelihood, that the freest possible schemes of credits should be sanctioned in order to enable the largest number of workers possible being employed on useful work, instead of forcing them on the unemployment insurance funds and eventually handing them over to the tender mercies of the Public Assistance Committee."

The meeting then listened to a lecture by Mr. J.Crispen from the National Council of Labour Colleges, on 'The World Crisis and the Present Cotton Dispute'.['Observer' September 10th.1932]

Support for the Weavers was expressed at the DC meeting of September 1st and 8th. The minutes of September 22nd. state that the local T.U.C. Cotton Relief Fund had raised £70 in its first week. [Minute Book]

At a Mass Meeting in the Labour Hall, November 27th., a resolution was carried unanimously, in support of the protest organised by the Amalgamated Weavers against the imprisonment of Mr. Ashworth, the

Secretary of the Rishton Weavers' Association. [Minute Book]

The November, AEU Journal, warned branches that copies of the 'Monkey Wrench' had not to be sold at meetings, and that if any member participated in its distribution they would be liable to be dealt with in accordance with rule. This seemed a silly decision, after the expelled members it [Monkey Wrench] had been set up to support, had been reinstated by the Final Appeals Court of the AEU in July 1932. [11]

The Accrington DC at its December 22nd. Meeting, strongly protested against the imprisonment of Bro. Tom Mann, and appealed to the Home Secretary and Prime Minister for his immediate release. [Minute Book] Tom Mann, 76 years old, was an ex-General Secretary of the AEU. He had been arrested, due to his position as Treasurer of the National Unemployed Workers' Movement. It was a totally fabricated charge and the old man had to spend 2 months in prison from 17th December 1932 until February 1933.[12]

1933

The National Executive were still pursuing their campaign against the Communist Party in the AEU Journal, February 1933, when they warned branches and DC's not to place Communist Party, and Minority Movement correspondence before members for discussion. Failing to observe this instruction rendered the secretary involved being dealt with in accordance with the union's rules.

At the Shop Stewards Meeting of March 5th., Bro. J.R.Cressey opened the proceedings by making reference to the Anniversary of the death of Karl Marx. He said that Marx, more than any other, was the founder of modern Socialism. As a mark of appreciation of his life and work the Stewards rose and stood in silence. ['Observer' March 11th.1933]

A Mass Meeting of members took place on Sunday morning, March 12th., to discuss the new National Health Insurance Act. ['Observer' March 14th.1933]

At the Shop Stewards Quarterly Meeting, Sunday 9th. April, Mr. Chalmers said their membership was around 1,800 and went on to say that there were over 700 youths who were not enroled in their ranks. He appealed to the stewards to approach these youths to try and enrol them. ['Observer' April 11th.] The meeting also agreed to accept the DC's programme supporting the 'Back to the Unions' campaign, which involved 5 months action to get back late members and enrol non-unionists. The campaign was to run from April 9th to October 1st. [Minute Book]

On May 10th. Mr. Herbert Walsh J.P., of 66 Garbett Street, Accrington, died at the age of 49 years. He had been a prominent member of the AEU, having been a DC member and branch official for 16 years. He had also been a member of the Accrington Labour Party Executive Committee for 15 years and was Vice Chairman on his death. He had been employed at Howard and Bullough's, in the Fluted Roller Department, for about 32 years. ['Observer' May 13th.1933]

The DC at its May 18th. meeting, tendered their thanks to all who took part in the Funeral of the late Mr. Walsh, and expressed satisfaction regarding the large number who paid this last tribute of respect. [Minute Book]

Sadly, another member of the DC for several years, Mr. Samuel Foster Brigg, of 94 Ormerod Street, Accrington, died on June 14th., aged 56 years. He was also a leading shop steward at Howard and Bullough Ltd. and a union delegate to the Accrington Labour Party, to which he was Auditor. Mr. Brigg had also taken an active part in the Accrington Discussion Class, formerly occupying the position of President. He was also an active member of the Accrington and Church Co-operative Society. ['Observer' June 17th.1933]

The DC June 15th. sent a letter of condolence to his widow and son. The DC and all members were invited to walk in the funeral procession. [Minute Book]

The DC, September 27th. discussed the discharge of Bro. Higham, shop steward at Lang Bridges Ltd. The full time official was brought in and after investigation the DC were of the opinion that Bro. Higham had been victimised for his activities as a shop steward. At the DC, Meeting, November 8th., it was stated that after union pressure, Bro. Higham had been reinstated and had kept his position as shop steward. The Executive Council ordered that he be paid his full wages for the time he was suspended at the firm. [Minute Book]

1934

It was reported to the DC that 158 new members had been made during the visitations to non-unionist campaign, March - December 1933. [Minute Book January 31st.]

The DC continued to pursue a campaign that excluded the GMWU and held a joint meeting with the Amalgamated Moulders, and Ironfounders on March 8th. at which they discussed the elimination of non-unionism. This committee met again on April 26th., May 6th. and November 29th.[Minute Book] but it must have been meeting on a more regular basis during this period.

The DC of March 14th. sent a £2 donation towards the TUC Austrian

Workers Relief Fund.[Minute Book]

In addition to the joint meetings with the Moulders and Ironfounders, the DC also sent delegates to the Labour Party 'Back to the Unions' campaign meetings, which were held throughout the year.

Tom Blackburn ODD's report for Division No. 9 in the AEU Journal, June 1934 stated:

> "On May 3rd. I attended an interesting function at which the Order of Merit was presented by Bro. Sam Bradley E.C. to Bro. G.K. Chalmers J.P. The affair was exceptionally well attended and the speeches testified to the high regard in which Bro. Chalmers is held by the members in the Accrington district."

On Friday August 3rd. Bro. James Henry Cosgrove, of 17, Fairclough Road, Accrington, died at the age of 49 years. He had been a member of the DC since 1925 and a shop steward in the cast-iron roller department at Howard and Bullough's since 1920. He was an accomplished step dancer and prior to the First World War toured the halls of Canada and the United States. A contingent of workmates and fellow members of the AEU preceded the cortege to the cemetery. ['Observer' August 11th.] The DC conveyed its deep sympathy to his wife and stood in silence to his memory at its meeting of August 8th. [Minute Book]

Jeffreys says:

> "The sacrifices made by the workers [in 1931] did not bring any immediate alleviation of the depression. Unemployment among AEU members until December,1932, remained as high as 25% and membership continued to fall until it reached its lowest level of 190,695 in August, 1933."

> "In the last months of 1933 the process of gradual recovery began. The numbers of unemployed slowly declined, although they remained in the following five years over the million mark. In the engineering industry, recovery was largely conditioned by preparations for war. From 1935, more and more members of the AEU were absorbed into the munitions industry, and along with the drop in the number of unemployed came a steady increase in recruitment to the Union." [13]

THE GENERAL & MUNICIPAL WORKERS UNION.

The Accrington GMWU had a full time Branch Secretary, Mr. W.A. Lambert. It held an Annual General Meeting in July each year, at which Officials and a Branch Executive were elected.

In addition to this, the organisation required sub-Committees, due to the varied industrial work carried out by its local membership. The majority of its members were employed in the engineering industry, mainly at the town's largest engineering works, Howard & Bullough Ltd. For this section, a monthly meeting took place of the Engineering Shop Stewards Committee.

The vast majority of the employees at the town's brickyards [Accrington Brick & Tile Works, Altham; Huncoat Brickworks; and Whinney Hill Brickworks.] were members of the GMWU and therefore they had a separate Clayworkers Shop Stewards Committee meeting each month.

1927

The Quarterly Meeting of the GMWU, January 20th, delegated 7 of their members to attend a Conference on 'Workers Control in Industry', at the Co-op Rooms, Accrington, on February 12th. [Minute Book] The GMWU had a membership of 1,700. ['Observer' February 5th.1927]

After a discussion on the 'Back to the Unions Campaign, the GMWU Branch Committee, May 5th., decided to pay existing members 3d. for each new member recruited. [Minute Book]

The Branch decided to print 1,000 handbills inviting their members to join in the Labour Party Procession and Field Day on August 13th. [Minute Book July 7th.]

The Annual Rally took place in the Town Hall, Accrington, on Saturday November 26th, at 7.00 pm. Will Thorne M.P. General Secretary, together with Charles Dukes J.P., District Secretary, attended. Admission was 6d. and 1,000 tickets had been printed. [Minute Book]

1928

The Members Quarterly Meeting, January 19th., requested the Engineering Allied Trades to take up the matter of non-unionists. [Minute Book]

Arising out of a report of the Engineering Allied Trades Meeting, a discussion took place on the employers refusal to make any advance regarding a claim for a 8s. increase / week. The following suggestion was agreed:

> "That our Union along with the other Labourers Unions should press for an advance for our members irrespective of the Craft Unions, and if this failed Nationally, then local and district efforts should be instituted. Also that if the Allied Trades were not prepared to join in an

active campaign on 100% Trade Unionism, then Bro. Harrison [Full Time Organiser] be asked to visit Accrington on a weeks campaigning. [Minute Book May 10th. Engineering SS]

Three weeks later on May 31st. the Clayworkers Shop Stewards Meeting were informed that the Clay Industry employers had given notice of a 6s. / week reduction in wages. The meeting agreed to urge all non-members to join the union and fight this piece of class warfare. A Mass Meeting was arranged for September 12th. On September 25th. it was reported that the union had rejected the employers application for the reduction and that the matter had been adjourned. The Shop Stewards received a letter regarding the issue on December 27th. and again on May 23rd. 1929. On June 27th. 1929, they finally received a letter stating that the employers had withdrawn their claim for a reduction. On hearing this they passed the following resolution:

"That this meeting of Representatives of the Clay Workers, is of the opinion that the prosperous condition of the Industry warrants a claim for an increase of wages to those employed therein, and therefore calls upon the Union Executive to bring the matter before the Workers Side of the J.I.R.C. of the Clay Industry, with a view to a claim for 6s. / week advance for Adults with proportional advances to Boys and Youths. [Minute Book]

Returning to 1928, on October 20th. the GMWU held their Annual Rally in Accrington Town Hall. The speakers were the Rt. Hon. J.R. Clynes MP. and Mr. Chas. Dukes J.P. Admission was 6d. and the assembled audience were entertained by the 'Imperial Opera Singers'. Clynes stated that "the Accrington Branch membership was the best of any branch in the country." [Observer' 23rd. October 1928]

1929

At the Quarterly Meeting, January 17th., the membership stood at 1,820. [Observer January 26th 1929]

The claim for a 6s./ week advance was again mentioned at the Clay Shop Stewards Meeting of July 25th, when the branch sent a further letter to their negotiators pointing out that the membership were "still of the opinion that the prosperous conditions warrants the claim being pressed forward." [Minute Book] They got a letter in reply stating that such action was indeed taking place.

At the Clay Shop Stewards August 22nd. Meeting, a discussion took place on how to put pressure on the employers to establish closed shops. This theme was continued at the Branch Committee, September 5th., in which the question of non-unionists was addressed. It was agreed that the Engineering Shop Stewards carry out a full census of their workshops and then to encourage non members to join. [Minute Book]

The 6th. Annual Social took place at the Labour Hall, Accrington, on Wednesday October 30th. It was regarded as being a very satisfactory affair. [Minute Book]

Non-unionism reared its ugly head again at the Branch Meeting held on November 7th., when it was agreed that:

> "Two members be engaged to visit [non-unionists] homes and that they should work 2 nights per week of about 2 hours each evening and that the Contingent Fund be asked to pay them 2s.6d. each per evening." [Bros. G.E. Holman and H. Hayhurst were engaged for this job. Minute Book]

The Engineering Shop Stewards, on November 14th., congratulated their Branch Secretary, Councillor Lambert on his elevation to the Aldermanic Bench of Accrington Borough Council.

On December 19th. the Clay Shop Stewards heard that the management at Enfield Works had stopped men from smoking during working hours and that certain men had been laid off as a punishment. It was resolved that the Secretary send a letter of protest to the firm. [Minute Book]

1930

Bro. Porter, attended and gave a short address on the wages claim, to the Engineering Shop Stewards Meeting, February 20th. He promised to take up the following matter:

> "It was resolved, that in the opinion of this meeting a move forward on behalf of the lower paid workmen might be made by the consideration of asking for a local Conference with the employers on the matter." [Minute Book]

At the Branch Meeting, May 1st., Bro.W. Riding gave a brief report of a mutiny of representatives of various unions called together by the Allied Trades Federation to discuss an advertising scheme for propaganda purposes. This caused the Branch to ask its Secretary to request the Accrington Trades and Labour Party to convene a special meeting of industrial representatives for the purpose of securing greater industrial organisation amongst the non-unionists of the town. [Minute Book]

Alderman W.A. Lambert, District Secretary, 7 Craven Street, Accrington, the first Labour Alderman, was appointed a Justice of the Peace. He had been Secretary for 15 years. For several years he had been Secretary of the Trades Council before that body became amalgamated with the Labour Party. ['Observer' May 3rd.1930]

At the Quarterly Meeting, October 22nd. a protest was sent to Accrington Borough Council due to their decision to erect the proposed new Police and Fire Station in stone. The members were of the opinion that it should be built in brick and thus find employment for local labour. [Minute Book]

The Annual Social took place on Wednesday October 29th. [Minute Book]

1931

At the Quarterly Meeting, January 7th., the members extended to the Accrington Miners, their thanks at the repayment of the £100 loan made to them during the Miner' Lockout of 1926.

At the Engineering Shop Stewards February Meeting, Bro. Harrison, Dist. Org., gave a report of the conferences that had taken place with the employers. The demands of the employers would have further reduced the meagre livelihood of the workers. The meeting resolved to adopt the suggestion:

"re the Allied Trades movement, and further to suggest to our District Office the presenting of a circular or handbill setting forth the employers proposals with suitable explanatory wording as to what those proposals meant to the workers in the industry and that a sufficient number be obtained so that each member be supplied." [Minute Book]

The 'Observer' reported that the various unions affiliated to the local Engineering Allied Trades Federation were taking a determined stand against the employers demands upon the workers in the engineering industry. Alderman W.A. Lambert, President, and Mr. E. Entwistle, Secretary, had sent the following letter to the Chairman of the unions Negotiating Committee:

"The members of the Societies in this district most emphatically protest against the proposals as stated by Sir Allan Smith at the meeting held in London on January 30th. last, when speaking on behalf of the Engineering Employers Federation, and calls upon the Executive Committee of the various Societies to resist those proposals to the uttermost."

They also sent a letter to Sir Allan himself which ended:

"And that we are to inform you that our members are demanding that those proposals be resisted to the uttermost by the

Executive Committee of the various unions affected, as in their opinion the sacrifices already made by them have so far shown no stimulant to trade." ['Observer' March 14th.1931]

On April 29th. the Accrington and District Engineering Allied Trades Federation held a Mass Protest Meeting in the Labour Hall, but unfortunately there was only a meagre attendance. I presume that a boycott by the AEU had taken place. However, the meeting presided over by Alderman W.A. Lambert, was addressed by Mr.H.N. Harrison, of the GMWU, and Mr. Brown, Secretary of the Woodcutting Machinists' Society. Mr. Harrison said:

> "I am giving no secrets away when I say that inside our own Council meetings we have definitely made up our own minds that we shall resist the proposals wherever we can." ['Observer' May 2nd.1931]

At the Clay Shop Stewards Meeting of June 25th., discussions took place regarding the settlement arrived at with that industry's employers. The unions had agreed to 2s. per week reduction for men, and no reduction for women and those under 21. It was resolved that Bro. Porter should be informed that:

> "the men were not satisfied and that this meeting strongly protests against any settlement having been arrived at before consulting with the men concerned by ballot or otherwise."

The meeting also extended to Bro. Fred Riding, Assistant Secretary, their warmest sympathy and regrets at hearing of his severe accident. They wished him a speedy recovery to full health and strength. [Minute Book]

The Engineering Shop Stewards Meeting, July 16th., heard a report of the agreement made with the employers. [Already discussed in the AEU section] The meeting did go on to address the inter-union difficulties locally when it resolved:

> "That this meeting call upon the District E.C. to arrange for Area Conferences to be held of Engineering Branches to consider and discuss the future policy of the Union in regard to working conditions with other unions." [Minute Book]

The GMWU obtained new premises at 2 Stanley Street, Accrington, which were officially opened by Bro. H.N. Harrison District Organiser, on Monday evening September 14th. He said that "there was no branch in the whole district which was more efficiently managed than the Accrington Branch." ['Observer' September 15th.]

The Annual Concert took place on November 4th., making a loss of £2..17s..3d. [Minute Book]

1932

At the Annual General Meeting, July 13th., it was stated that the Membership amounted to 1,561.['Observer' July 23d]

The distribution of propaganda leaflets was discussed at the Branch Committee of August 4th., when it was decided that two members be paid 2s. each to give them out at the Labour Exchange and at Accrington Stanley's practice match on August 13th. It was also agreed to distribute 5,000 GMWU football fixture cards, covering the games to be played by Accrington Stanley, Blackburn Rovers and Burnley. [Minute Book]

At a Special Joint Meeting of the Branch, the Executive, and the Contingent Fund Committee, in September, it was decided to make a grant of £20 to the T.U.C. Cotton Dispute Fund. [Minute Book]

At the Members Quarterly Meeting, October 20th., the Secretary, Alderman Lambert, tendered his resignation. This was accepted with regret and many speakers expressed the hope that he would have a long and comfortable period during his retirement. It was recommended to the National Executive that Bro. Fred Riding take over as Secretary. [Minute Book]

1933

Alderman Lambert was presented with a gold watch suitably inscribed, a framed photograph of himself, and a handsome supper set for Mrs. Lambert, at the Members Quarterly Meeting held in the Co-operative Rooms, Oak Street, Accrington, on January 19th. The money for these gifts had been raised by collections amongst the membership. Bro. Carter, President, thanked him for his splendid 15 years service as Branch Secretary.

Bro. Lambert, replied in happy vein and declared his appreciation of the spirit which had prompted the presentation of such gifts. He also very graciously handed back to the chairman the photograph to be hung in the branch office for all time. [Minute Book]

Bro. Walter Gregory, who was my next door neighbour in Craven Street, during the 1950's and 60's. presided over the Members Quarterly Meeting held on April 20th. I never ever saw him without his pipe, in which he smoked black twist. Anyway it never did him any harm, he lived an active life well into his 90's. The Secretary's Report touched upon the deepening depression and the serious growth of Fascism in Europe. An appeal was made for greater strength and vigilance to combat same. The meeting also carried the following resolution unanimously:

"That this meeting of the Accrington Branch of the GMWU, protests against the imprisonment of the 27 leaders of the Trade Union and Peasants Movement in India, charged in the Meerut Conspiracy case, and realising that the purpose of this trial is to deprive Indian workers of their rights to organise, demands their immediate release."

It also passed a further, resolution:

"That we send a resolution of protest to the acting Prime Minister, and Member of Parliament for the Division, against putting on the embargo against imports from Russia." [Minute Book]

At the Clay Shop Stewards, May 25th., it was stated that all the yards were extremely busy, with Whinney Hill extending their plant. This encouraged a discussion on whether or not to put in a claim for an advance of 6s./ week nationally. An amendment was then put to ask for 6s. advance locally, which was carried. [Minute Book]

At their next meeting, on June 22nd. the Clay Shop Stewards heard that their national negotiators had put in for the following concessions from the employers:

"1. An advance of 2s./ week, minimum rate 48s for 48 hours.
2. Boys and Youths Agreement by Joint Sub-Committee to be ratified.
3. One week's holiday with pay."

Bro. Porter the full time official was present and he heard those in attendance give strong arguments in favour of going forward with a local claim for 6s. Bro. Porter would not move from the national proposals outlined above, which left the members present feeling let down. [Minute Book]

At the Engineering Shop Stewards Meeting, August 10th. it was reported that the Directors of Accrington Stanley Football Club had refused to allow the Branch to renew its contract to advertise by hoardings on their ground. Keen resentment was shown. [Minute Book]

This matter carried on at a Special Committee Meeting held on August 17th. After further discussions, the Directors had offered the union the possibility of paying a rental of £2..10s. for the first season and £4 for subsequent seasons. However, the meeting resolved that 30s. was the maximum they were prepared to pay, and that a deputation should meet with the Directors to discuss the matter further. The posturing of the Union paid off, because at the Committee meeting of September 7th. the Secretary told those present that the Directors had accepted their 30s. offer. [Minute Book]

The September 7th. minutes also state that:

"Situation between the AEU and ourselves. The secretary informed the meeting of the activities of the AEU in pressing certain of our members into their organisation on the grounds that they would not get work at various places unless they were members with them. Certain action to deal with this situation was outlined and endorsed."

This was further discussed at the Engineering Shop Stewards Meeting of September 14th., when the Secretary reported the poaching of GMWU members by the AEU. He suggested intensive propaganda against same. [Minute Book]

The Clay Shop Stewards, at their September 28th. Meeting, heard that the employers had rejected their wages claim for 2s./ week extra, at a time when the yards were very busy. [Minute Book]

With regards to the situation in the local brickworks the December 28th Clay Shop Stewards Minutes state the following:

"Many complaints were given of the need for a revision of the existing agreement in the industry owing to the drastic changes in production and transport and after a long discussion, the following matters were decided upon: For Bro. Porter and representatives to discuss with the firms with a view to a reclassification of jobs, also that certain other men be brought up to standard rates.....It was also resolved after long Discussion that Bro. Porter send in to the local firms a request for holidays with pay."

1934

Will Thorne MP. one of the oldest of the pioneers of the 'new unionism' finally gave up his position as General Secretary, his place was taken by Charles Jukes, J.P. who was well known in GMWU circles in the Accrington area.

The Clay Shop Stewards, January 25th. Meeting heard that the Accrington Brick and Huncoat Brick Companies had refused their claim for one weeks holiday with pay. [Minute Book]

The members employed in the brickyard were apparently not pleased with the service they were getting from their full time district official, Bro. Porter. The above minutes state that at their next meeting they would discuss forging a policy common to all present when meeting and dealing with Bro. E. Porter.

Bro. F. Hudson opened the discussion at the Clay Shop Stewards February 22nd. Meeting, the minutes stating the following:

"The chief points in Bro. Hudson's remarks were that we should tabulate accurately all data in each case of presenting grievances for Bro. Porter to take forward when necessary. That the shop stewards must be united and agreed on all matters when Bro. Porter is present. A useful and valuable discussion took place on this matter and the basis laid for a strong policy in the future."

On the 22nd. March the Clay Shop Stewards were informed that with regards to their 2s. claim in wages, the employers had not turned up in force at the meeting and therefore they could not arrive at a decision. The meeting resolved that: "Bro. Porter be urged to press the claim to the end in spite of the difficulties of the employers side." [Minute Book]

The Engineering Shop Stewards Meeting of April 12th. listened to their guest speaker, Mrs. Rushton a local woman who had been part of the Lancashire Women's contingent on the Hunger March to London, but more of this in the next Chapter. At the end of the meeting it was unanimously decided to call for the unconditional release of Comrades Tom Mann and Harry Pollitt who had been arrested for sedition in regards to their work with the unemployed. They did eventually get bail and when their trial came up on July 3rd. at Swansea they were found not guilty. The whole case was yet another piece of class warfare by the establishment.[14]

All the meetings at this time emphasised the dangers inherent in Fascism and urged 100% union membership as a strong deterrent. The local Labour Party had organised special conferences to combat Fascism and reports back were heard at the Engineering Shop Stewards Meeting of May 10th. Reports were also given of Labour Party special meetings for the 'Back to the Unions' campaign. [Minute Book] These meetings continued into the summer.

Impatience with the progress of their pay claim, caused the following to be written in the Clay Shop Stewards Minutes of June 28th.:

"On the wage claim a long discussion took place on the method adopted by Bro. Porter of securing names and addresses to support this claim, resentment be expressed at the seemingly weak idea. Also strong arguments were expressed for prosecuting the claim locally with vigour." [Minute Book]

When discussing the 'Back to the Unions' campaign at the Executive Committee Meeting, July 5th., it was resolved that Fred and William Riding be the GMWU's delegates on its executive and for them to oppose any move to have the political party's agent [Mr. Howson the Labour Agent] made its secretary. [Minute Book]

At the AGM, July 19th. resentment was again expressed of the unfair methods adopted by other unions in efforts to wean members away from the GMWU.[Minute Book]

The Clay Shop Stewards finally got Bro. Porter to attend their meeting on August 22nd. The Minutes read:

"Bro. Porter addressed the meeting at great length on the

difficulties to be overcome in the task of securing a restoration of the wages cut imposed in 1931, mentioning, bad organisation of employers and men, partial prosperity only in the trade in different parts of the country, and other factors. The representatives replied with vigour to all the points raised and were emphatic in demanding that this area, owing to good organisation and trade, ought to be took into consideration and the increase sought here irrespective of other areas."[Minute Book]

The matter seems to have been finalised at the Clay Shop Stewards Meeting of February 28th. 1935. Bro. Porter's Report of the Clay Council, February 20th., disclosed the early restoration of the 2s. to adult wages. [Minute Book]

At the Executive Meeting December 6th. the Chairman of the Branch Bro. H. Carter tendered his resignation together with his Shop Stewardship, owing to a severe breakdown in his health. The Executive recognising all the circumstances, resolved to accept the resignation with deep regret and placed on record their highest appreciation of the long services he had rendered to the branch and the union, especially his 17 years as branch chairman. He had also been the GMWU's chief Shop Steward at Howard and Bullough Ltd. [Minute Book]

List of educational lectures at the various GMWU meetings.

Engineering Shop Stewards

Jan. 13th. 1927. Bro. W. Howson 'What is the meaning of the Labour Party'
Feb. 10th. 1927. Coun. R.I.Constantine 'The work of the Town Council'
Mar. 10th. 1927. Bro. W. Holman 'Study is it worthwhile'
May 12th. 1927. Bro. R. Dawson 'Literature'
Oct. 13th. 1927. Bro. R. Dawson 'My impressions of the week-end school at Nelson.'
Dec. 8th. 1927. Mr. George Lunt 'My visit to Russia'
Jan. 12th. 1928. Mr. D Lawley 'China'
Feb. 9th. 1928. Coun. R.I. Constantine 'A newspaper'
Mar. 8th. 1928. Bro. W. Riding 'The universe'
Apr. 12th. 1928. Bro. W. Brotherton 'Problems of industry'
Sept. 6th. 1928. Bro. H. Harrison ' Propaganda'
Nov. 8th. 1928. Mr. Tom Snowden 'Prospective Labour Candidates address'
Dec. 13th. 1928. Bro. W. Riding ' The future of leisure'
Jan. 10th. 1929. Bro. W. Holman 'The need for education'

Feb. 14th. 1929. Bro. F. Riding ' Three weapons of the workers'
Apr. 11th. 1929. Bro H. Carter 'Rationalisation'
Sept. 12th. 1929. Coun. Constantine 'Some reflections and experiences of a magistrate'
Oct. 10th. 1929. Bro. R. Dawson 'Personality'
Nov. 14th. 1929. Bro. C. Powell 'Trade unionism and the future'
Dec. 12th. 1929. Bro W. Riding 'Unemployment'
Feb. 20th. 1930. Bro. Porter 'Wage claim'
Mar. 13th. 1930. Bro. W. Holman 'Art'
May 8th. 1930. Bro.T. Mercer 'Holidays with pay'
Jun. 12th. 1930. Bro. F. Riding 'Unemployment Insurance'
Jul. 10th. 1930. Bro. F. Riding 'Unemployment Insurance cont.'
Aug. 14th. 1930. Mr. Lawther 'Unemployment'
Sept. 11th. 1930. Coun. Constantine 'Education'
Oct. 9th. 1930.Mr. Webb 'Unemployment'
Nov. 13th. 1930. Bro. W. Riding 'Why am I here'
Dec. 11th. 1930. Mr. W.T. Whittaker [Lib. Assoc.] 'Free trade and unemployment'
Feb. ? 1931. Bro. Harrison [Dist. Org.] 'Report of Conference with employers'
May.7th.1931. Bro. W. Riding 'Organisation'
July 16th. 1931. Bro. Harrison 'Recent reductions'
Aug. 13th. 1931. Mr. Tom Snowden MP. 'General' + Bro. Dawson 'Organisation'
Sept. 10th. 1931. Coun. Constantine 'Review of Tolpuddle Martyrs Book'
Oct. 8th. 1931. Mr. Holmes [Chief Constable] 'Crime Psychology'
Nov. 12th. 1931. Bro. W. Brotherton 'Reforms'
Dec. 10th. 1931. Mr. Humphries 'New Unemployment[Anomalies] Act'
Feb.11th. 1932. Mr. Singleton Borough Librarian 'Libraries'
Mar. 10th. 1932. Mr. Hindle Borough Sanitary Inspector 'Your Health Dept'
Apr. 14th. 1932. Mr. G. Lunt 'Russia'
Sept. 8th. 1932. Bro. Dawson 'Means Test Protest Committee'
Oct. 13th. 1932. Coun. Baron 'A day in the life of a miner'
Jan. 12th. 1933. Bro. W. Brotherton 'Works Welfare Schemes'
Mar. 9th. 1933. Mrs. M. Brotherton 'India and the Lancashire Cotton Trade'
Apr. 6th. 1933. Mr. Wright Robinson [NUDAW] 'Support the Co-op Movement'
May. 11th. 1933. Mrs. Boardman 'A visit to the USSR'
Oct. 12th. 1933. Mr. Bill Haworth 'Democracy and Dictatorship'
Nov. 9th. 1933. Mr. J. Crispin 'Working Class Education' N.C.L.C.
Dec. 14th. 1933. Mr. J. Crispin 'From Feudalism to Capitalism' N.C.L.C.
Jan. 11th. 1934. Mr. Walsh 'The Industrial Revolution - Growth of Trusts' N.C.L.C.

Feb. 8th. 1934. Mr. Knight 'The Growing Surpluses; Imperialism' N.C.L.C.
Mar. 8th. 1934. Mr. Knight 'The Problems of the New Order: The USSR' N.C.L.C.
Apr. 12th.1934. Mrs. Rushton 'Unemployed March to London' [By Accrington's Rep.]

Clayworkers Shop Stewards

Oct. 27th. 1927. Bro. R. Dawson 'My impressions of the week-end school at Nelson'
Nov. 24th. 1927. Mr. George Lunt 'My visit to Russia'
Jan. 26th. 1928. Mr. Crewe 'Football and its laws'
Feb. 23rd. 1928. Mr. D. Lawley 'China'
Apr. 26th. 1928. Bro. L. Wright 'A visit to Gibraltar and Spain'
Jan. 24th. 1929. Mr. Tom Snowden 'Prospective Labour Candidates address'
Mar. 21st. 1929. Bro. F. Riding 'Three weapons of the workers'
Apr. 25th. 1929. Bro. H. Carter 'The Turner-Mond Conferences'
Feb. 27th. 1930. Bro. J. Crewe 'The shop steward, his duties and position'
Mar. 27th 1930. Bro. Carter 'The Shop Stewards agreement in the engineering industry'
Apr. 24th. 1930. Bro. F. Riding 'Reasons why trade unions were born'
May 22nd. 1930. Bro. A. Holder 'A few reflections on life'
July 9th. 1931. Bro. Porter 'Recent reductions'

These lectures had been a feature of the Engineering Shop Stewards Meetings since 1922, and of the Clay Shop Stewards since 1926. It was unfortunate that they ceased to function when they did, because they did provide the opportunity for ordinary union members to develop their self confidence and debating skills, at a time when many had left school at 11 or 12 years of age.

THE ACCRINGTON, ALTHAM & RISHTON BRANCHES OF THE LANCASHIRE & CHESHIRE MINERS' FEDERATION.

Accrington, Altham and Rishton, each had branches of the Lancashire and Cheshire Miners' Federation [LCMF] and delegates were sent to the monthly meetings of that body, which were held at the Miners' Offices in Bolton. Accrington branch covered the collieries owned by Messrs. George Hargreaves and Company at Scaitcliffe, Broad Oak, Huncoat and Calder; Altham branch covered Moorfield and Whinney Hill pits owned by the Altham Colliery Company; and the Rishton mine, owned by Messrs. P.W. Pickup Ltd. comprised Rishton branch.

All three branches were part of No. 2 Panel which also included Burnley, Hapton Valley, Bank Hall, Cheapside, Deerplay, Cliviger, Rossendale, Little Lever, Rose Hill and Darwen. Each Panel annually elected a representative to serve on the LCMF Executive Committee.

The LCMF was a constituent member of the Miners' Federation of Great Britain, to which it sent elected representatives to sit on the National Executive Committee.

1927

A feeling of hopelessness must have prevailed at the close of the 1926 dispute, with absolute poverty being a fact of life in every miners family. Those fortunate enough to be given their jobs back had the prospect of further reductions in their wages on July 4th. 1927, when the Lancashire & District settlement of December 1926 came into force. This agreement provided for a reduction on the 1911 rates from 46% to 32%. This meant a cut in weekly wages by as much as 6s.

On Monday July 18th. after the reductions had come into effect, 60 drawers employed at Huncoat and Calder Pits, Accrington, unofficially struck work in protest. At Whinney Hill and Moorfield Pits, Altham, a number of youths took similar action. ['Observer' July 23rd.1927]

By Monday, August 1st. the drawers were back at work having accepted some minor concessions. ['Observer' August 2nd. 1927]

Politically, the local branches had voted at the April 23rd. Monthly Conference in Bolton against the affiliation of the Communist Party to the Labour Party, although the Conference narrowly voted in favour of such action. The Accrington Branch appear to have then reacted in a naive manner by proposing the following resolution at the Monthly Conference of May 21st. which was defeated:

> "Seeing that there are so many different opinions with different political organisations connected with labour, and that this has weakened our resistance to the capitalist system, we feel it to be essential, in the interests of the cause, that all labour political sections should fuse into one party, ie. the National Labour Party. If this is carried , to be moved at the Annual Conference of the Labour Party."

On Saturday, August 13th, Mr. Harry Smith, President and Councillor

Baron, Secretary, headed the Accrington Miners' contingent in the 8th. Labour Party Procession through the town.

1928

On Sunday January 15th. at 3 pm. Mr. A.J. Cook, Secretary of the Miners' Federation of Great Britain, together with Mr. J. Tinker M.P. addressed a Public Meeting at the Picture House, Accrington. Mr. John McGurk was in the chair and the admission was 6d. Mr. Cook kept the large audience, [the spacious building being packed to overflowing] interested for an hour and a half, 'with his passionate declamation, clever epigrams and flashes of wit.' ['Observer' January 17th.] [The part of this speech relevant to the cotton crisis has already been stated in Chapter 2.] Mr. Cook said:

"He wanted to try and create in that great audience confidence in themselves. Persons may change but principles won't; ideals go on, though individuals may betray. He wanted to raise the status of faith that they had, for he believed in human nature and that sooner or later right will prevail."

"In striking fashion he charged the audience with being responsible for the mess the country was in, in that they returned a Tory Government to power. 'To-day,' he remarked, 'Ignorance is a crime; you have no right to be ignorant.'....."

"I love art, music, love all that is best. My class have been in the past denied the best of these. By whom? By God? Where is there a man who says it is an act of God that poverty prevails? The man who dares to say it is an act of God that human beings should suffer poverty and misery is a liar. It is not written in the Old Book 'Starve my lambs' but there is the text 'Feed my lambs.' The whole teaching laid down there is brotherhood. Nature has not failed, and with the knowledge men possess we have arrived at that stage when the best of everything and sufficiency should be available for all....."

"Human nature, he affirmed, would respond to the best when the best was given to them. There were of course, exceptions. We were making human nature. A rose tree that would not grow in a London slum would bloom profusely in a country garden, and human nature was what environment made it. Hence he pleaded for economic security for the workers as well as the Cabinet minister, the naval officer, the schoolmaster, the policeman, and others in the civil service. He urged that such economic security could not be obtained for the worker under a capitalist system, and deplored the fact that certain classes who enjoyed economic security were anti-Labour, and were trying to keep down the worker......"

"The New Year has been heralded with a fanfare of trumpets; 1927 has gone, and I wish I could bury her face downward. She is here; the skeleton of 1927 has appeared in January, 1928, and the ghosts are here. We have to face them; it is no use pretending they don't exist. It is not a question of temperament or of optimism. If I thought that every man was going to get a living wage and that there was going to be plenty for all and predicted that, I should be an optimist. But I am a realist, and I am not going to allow you to be gulled. After an allusion to the coal dispute in 1926, he said: 'It is not Cook that creates crises, it is crises that creates Cooks; and the incubator is in the colliery offices. The colliery owners breed them.' But he said the worker had reached a more intelligent stage. Twenty years ago the captains of industry told the miners that they were ignorant - without heads, and he added 'They used to advertise for hands; now we take our heads with us,' a sally that aroused roars of laughter which increased when holding up his arms, he said, 'They used to want it here,' and then touching his head he added 'It is up here they are getting it. We have been changed from being mere hands to human beings prepared to demand our rights.'....."

"The meeting closed with the singing of 'The Red Flag'."
['Observer' January 17th. 1928]

The LCMF supported left-wing resolutions at this time, including one attacking the decision by the TUC to break up the Anglo-Russian Trade Union Committee. More importantly however, was their objection to the Turner/Mond talks. At the LCMF Annual Conference, January 28th., the following resolution was carried:

"That we strongly protest against the Sub-Committee of the TUC in taking part in the Industrial Peace Negotiations, without first consulting the various affiliated organisations."

At the Monthly Conference, February 25th., a further resolution was carried:

"Seeing that meetings have taken place between the General Council of the TUC and the Mond Group of employers, with a view of the bringing about peace in industry, and charges levelled at the Secretary of the Miners' Federation [Mr. A.J.Cook] for the magnificent stand he has made as a definite result of his loyalty to the rank and file of the Trade Union Movement:

1. That we demand a verbatim report of the proceedings; and

2. That we congratulate Mr. Cook on his magnificent stand and repudiation of the General Council."

The adoption of Mondism as a policy [so called, after Sir Alfred Mond, founder of I.C.I.] represented a complete surrender by the TUC to the authority of capitalist industrialists. Only A.J. Cook opposed the policy on the TUC General Council.

The 1928 TUC Conference approved a policy whereby it welcomed the rationalisation and trustification of industry and proposed the setting up of a National Industrial Council under which a system of compulsory conciliation was to be operated. This appeasement by the leadership resulted in conditions deteriorating throughout industry, with 'extensive speeding-up, breaking of piece-rates, [and the] violating of agreements.'[15]

A more militant response was called for by the Minority Movement, but this was ignored by the TUC and Labour Party leadership. Eventually this culminated in the 1931 debacle, in which Ramsay MacDonald and his henchmen deserted the Labour Party to form a National Government. Mondism, in effect, sold the working class into virtual slavery.

At the Accrington Discussion Class on Sunday March 18th., the speaker did not turn up and so Mr. Harry Smith, Accrington Miners' President, volunteered to give a talk on 'What the miners think of Mr. Cook'. Several local miners, and other trade unionists, added their appreciation of the miners' leader in the subsequent debate.['Observer' March 20th. 1928]

Altham Branch, overwhelmed by the poverty afflicting them, forwarded the following resolution to the LMCF Meeting of April 21st. but withdrew it during the discussion:

"Seeing that the British miners are confronted with a biased and callous reactionary Government, who refuse to legislate, or take any part in relieving the most distressed coal mining areas, and observing the large increasing numbers of miners, and their families who are lacking food, clothes, and shoes, and are embarrassed in financial difficulties, we beg to move that the Executive Committee of the MFGB make a special International appeal throughout the Continental coal mining areas, as soon as possible, for the above requirements, to relieve or alleviate, more or less, the most affected mining areas."

The European miners were as badly off as their British counterparts and so an appeal such as the above would not have been a productive exercise. In addition, the feeling of the meeting would have probably been against the begging nature of the proposal - the miners did have their pride.

Over the summer months the Accrington Branch campaigned to have

Dr. R.S. Ross, of Cannon Street, Accrington, dismissed from his position as Certifying Surgeon for Industrial Diseases for the District, because he was also officially the employers' doctor. This action succeeded during September. [LCMF Minute Book]

At the Oswaldtwistle Labour Party Monthly Meeting, at the Weavers' Institute, Mr. Albert Bernasconi, President, and a working miner, gave an interesting lecture on 'Some aspects of the Mining Industry'. The 'Observer' report, August 4th. stated:

"He contended that the mine owners succeeded in obscuring the real financial position of the industry and made profits by keeping the most profitable developments of the coal industry to themselves. He said that colliery companies and proprietors were financially interested in practically every phase of the coal using industry, and by selling coal at ridiculously low prices to subsidiary concerns were able to reap the profits, whilst the mines themselves were nominally being run at a loss. The remedy for this state of affairs as advocated both by the Miners' Federation of Great Britain and by the Labour Party was that the mines should be nationalised and that all coke and all by-product plants attached to collieries should be treated as part of the coal mines and should be acquired by the State along with the coal mines."

At the Accrington Discussion Class on Sunday October 28th. the speakers were Mr. Harry Smith, President of the Accrington Miners and Mr. Tom Brunton of the local branch of the I.L.P. Harry alluded to the coal dispute of 1926 and said that the miners suffered a defeat because they were not backed up and he appealed for class consciousness amongst the working people.['Observer' October 30th.1928]

On Sunday December 23rd. the Accrington branch of the Miners' Federation under the Chairmanship of Mr. Harry Smith, again welcomed their National General Secretary, Mr. A.J. Cook, as guest speaker at a public meeting in the Picture House, Church Street. Mr. Tom Snowden, Prospective Labour Candidate, joined him on the platform.

"Mr. Snowden said he regarded it as a privilege to be on the same platform as Mr. Cook. He was one of those who were proud of the fact that they had one man at least [Mr. Cook] who was prepared to have the courage of his convictions. The present was the time of the year when they preached peace and goodwill, and he supposed there was a real genuine feeling of goodwill among men and nations, but in spite of all the generosity and hospitality of people they could not have peace on earth and goodwill among men and women so long as they had a system of society that spelled poverty for millions of the people in the country......"

"Far too long they had been satisfied with palliatives. The question of poverty in the coalfields and throughout the country was not a question that required a palliative but a question that ought to receive the consideration of all men who had constructive minds, with the object of removing the cause instead of being satisfied to deal with effects......"

"Referring to Mr. Cook, Mr. Snowden asked was it not a fact that if he and Mr. Maxton and the so-called wild men of the Clyde spoke with greater fervour and earnestness it was because perhaps they felt more deeply in their hearts, and was it not evidence of their genuine sincerity for the cause of the moment? It had always been thus. He [Mr. Snowden] had been a local preacher in his better days, and had often preached about Stephen being stoned to death. Stephen lived on, but not a single man who threw a stone was remembered, and that was true to-day. When those who were stoning Mr. Cook died and were forgotten, Mr. Cook would live on......"

It was a pity that Mr. Snowden's radical socialist ideals expressed in Accrington that night were not maintained. His support for the left, in the form of praise for the actions of Arthur James Cook and Jimmy Maxton did not last, as we have seen in his appeasement to the cotton bosses already highlighted in Chapter 2.

Mr. Cook spoke for over an hour and was given a 'hearty reception'. He said:

"It was true that Keir Hardie, just like Moses, was in advance of his time, crying out in the wilderness, warning the nation in its days of prosperity against the days of adversity, but economically there were none so blind as those who would not see. Hardie he would never forget, though some men in the House of Commons to-day labelled Labour - only the label, he was afraid, was correct - would not listen to him. The Old Book was a true guide: 'By their fruits ye shall know them.'"

"He [Mr. Cook] did not care what his opponents thought of him, but he did care what his own class thought; they were the judge and jury of his actions. And leadership was very hard and difficult. Only those who had tried it knew how difficult it was to lead in the working-class movement. There were a great mass of men who did not think at all, who were satisfied with a couple of pints and the pictures. They had no right to ask him or any candidate to do what they were not prepared to do themselves......"

"Continuing, Mr. Cook said the time was coming when intelligent people would not trust somebody who deceived them, and when people became disillusioned two things happened, they either got into revolt or despair. Speaking of the economic position in the coal industry, he said that was evidence of the suicidal policy of Toryism. If the fact that the basic industry of the country under Toryism had to be subsidised by charity was not sufficient evidence of the demise of Toryism, then no inquest was necessary - it was a funeral. Why was it industry was in such a chaotic state at present? He wished people would try and understand cause instead of playing with effects......"

"He was glad the crisis had come, and someone was going to answer for it. It was not an accident, Hardie said twenty years ago that unless science was controlled the nation would be destroyed and chaos and conflict would result......"

"They the Labour Party, he continued were arriving at the stage where they were marching to power; 1929 would be a march to power. It was the power that came with the courage to use it; they could only get what they were strong enough to take. There were thousands of people in the country who said he was afraid of revolution. 'I am, and I tell you that every vote for the return of Baldwin is a vote for a bloody revolution.'"

"Concluding Mr. Cook said Liberalism had failed; Toryism had crucified and massacred the miners and he would never rest until the Eight Hours Bill was repealed. He stood for a human movement, for a constructive system, for womanhood and their boys being protected. He was a Socialist; he was spending his Christmas preaching the great gospel. Christmas without Socialism meant charity; Christmas with Socialism meant Christianity."

1929

The Annual Conference of the LCMF was held on Saturday, January 26th. Mr. McGurk, Vice-President, made the Annual Address to the delegates and to the press, as follows:

"The year we have just passed through has left us much worse off than 1927. We were led to believe by the powers that be that we had seen the end of the slump, and that the outlook was brighter than it had been for years so far as industry was concerned. But the prophets had reckoned without taking into consideration the nature and composition of the present Government. We, as miners, have never been under any delusions with regard to the mining industry, for the Government and the coal owners between them are responsible for the present position of the coal industry. The British public were warned in 1926..... Nearly 300,000 mine workers have been thrown out of employment since 1926. Under-employment is rampant everywhere in the British coalfields. What does the Government offer? Just a policy of sending round the hat - begging - charity.....The money has been sent for political purposes - to try and condemn the Leaders of the Miners' Federation in every part of the British Coalfield. But charity and such relief does nothing to solve the present problem. If we take the amount contributed to the Lord Mayor of London's Fund, together with the Government's pound for pound, it only amounts to about one week's relief in 52. To me, however well intended the British public are, we must watch very carefully what the Government's intentions are, or in other words 'Watch Baldwin,' the world's greatest hypocrite. In April this year when the 30 Stamps business comes into operation scores of thousands of our mine workers will be deprived of unemployment pay, due to no fault of their own. Their crime will be failure to get work. This Relief Fund may be used, and possibly will be used by the lackeys of the present Government, as a means of assisting the Government not to repeal that part of the Employment Act. This to me is the greatest danger of the Relief Fund. It is already on record that Boards of Guardians have been enabled to get out of their responsibilities by refusing to give our poor relief, due to our poverty stricken miners getting some measure of relief - due to a generous public at Xmas time. As I say, charity will not solve the problem. Women and children in the Coalfields are literally starving, malnutrition must be rampant......How long can this be endured? Our great hope is that in a few months time the workers of this country will have an opportunity to put our own Labour Party in power."

"Just a word with respect to the position of those who are working in the Mining Industry in Lancashire to-day, just to see what wages they are getting, and to prove the sacrifice they have made towards getting the industry on its feet. We will take the Government's own figures, supplied to them by the coal owners, therefore they must be correct. In 1920 the average earnings per quarter show that in September, £52 16s. 1d. per man was earned. In 1922, September, they had dropped to £25 6s. 4d. In September, 1924, during the period Labour was in office, they rose to £30 15s. 0d. per quarter. In

September, 1926, £27 14s.9d.; September, 1927, £26 1s. 7d. Quarter ending September, 1928, the latest return, shows the figure to be £23 16s. 8d. If we take the full sacrifice made it is just £28 16s. 1d., or a reduction in his wages of £2 4s. 3d. per week. No mean sacrifice, yet judging from the actions of some of our 'Scrooges' who own and control collieries, even this is not enough. Not withstanding our present low wages, we have the Medical Officer of Health for Sheffield advising us that even if a wage of £3 per week goes into a home where there is a family of five, this figure allows no margin at all for any minor luxuries, which are really a necessity to most. He puts the income as being £2 7s. 0d., per week whatever size the family under five. We have ample means of proving that these figures are correct, and not too high, from our own Convalescent Home at Blackpool. We know now exactly what it costs to keep a man; those figures are forthcoming every quarter. It thus proves that society has failed miserably to provide a living wage."

"May I appeal to all here to examine our position with regard to membership. In March, 1926, we had 76,339 members; at the present time we have 50,062. It is only fair and true to say that according to the latest official figures only 77,609 are employed in the industry in Lancashire and Cheshire, as against 97,582 in March, 1926. I make an earnest appeal to all who are not members to become members at once, as single-handed they must realise that they are useless in any attempt to improve their conditions. Come inside the Union and help us to secure at the end of this year a new wages agreement which will enable all mine workers to have and enjoy a standard of life worthy of the name."

"In conclusion, I would like to appeal to all workers to sink their differences and pull together for one common end. Let us all work and strive between now and the General Election to return the Labour Party to power with a bumping majority.....Let them lead the way for the socialisation and mutual co-operation for the common good of the workers of this country, instead of the present system, which is for the private aggrandisement by the rich and powerful, backed up by a reactionary Tory Government."

At the Accrington Borough Council Meeting, February 4th. the Mayor stated that the Miners' Distress Fund was up and running in Accrington to which £46 had already been subscribed. Councillor Baron, Secretary of the Accrington Miners' is quoted in the 'Observer'. [February 5th.]

"Mr. Baron said there was a lot of confusion existing and he was sorry to have to say that his opinion was that Accrington and Burnley would not be included. He approached the Mayor a fortnight ago and asked if Accrington had to be included and the Mayor replied in the affirmative, but he [Mr. Baron] told him he had information that it would not. 'There is a tremendous lot of miners distress in Accrington' added Mr. Baron 'and if Accrington miners, some of whom have been out of work for 3 years, have not to take part in any Distress Fund, then it is the intention of the Accrington Miners' to take up their own'"

The Mayor said he was not in a position to discuss the matter. The same newspaper happened to report that the Miners' Distress Fund in Rishton had raised £86 17s. 0d

On Friday February 15th. at Accrington Town Hall the Miners' Distress meeting heard that the Mayor of Burnley, the head of the North East Lancashire Divisional Committee, had designated Accrington as the centre of an area including Blackburn, Oswaldtwistle, Church, Rishton, Great Harwood, and Huncoat for the purposes of dealing with distress. Families receiving more than 5s. per head assistance after deducting rent were deemed to be outside the scheme. Only 4 cases in Accrington and 8 in Blackburn apparently came within the scale and their details were forwarded to the Chief Constable of Accrington, who had the job of sending them to Burnley for processing. ['Observer' February 16th.1929]

However, the following Tuesday 'Observer' reported the Town Clerk of Accrington as stating that:

"The Lancashire Divisional Committee were not prepared to recognise North East Lancashire as a distressed area, although they were prepared to give immediate assistance to individual cases of distress."

The Adjourned Annual Meeting of the LCMF, at Bolton, Saturday February 23rd., received a letter from the Accrington Branch protesting against their district not being included under the Lord Mayor's Distress Fund. The officials explained that two districts had been left out in Lancashire, but it had been decided that a sum of £200 should be granted to each of these districts. So really speaking, they had now been accepted for relief although they were not formally an Area Committee like other places.

The scales of relief for each family were to be:

No. of persons including the parents.	2	3	4	5	6	7	8
Net income after deducting	22/6	27/-	30/7	33/9	37/10	44/1	50/5

rent.

However, the meeting felt that it was necessary to protest and they made application to the Lancashire Divisional Committee for such areas to be included in the scheme and a District Committee established for relief of distressed miners.

A Grand Concert held in the Labour Hall, Blackburn Road, Accrington, on February 27th. raised money for the Miners' Distress Fund, admission 6d. The Chairman for the evening was Mr. Harry Smith and the Snips Concert Party provided the entertainment free of charge.

Oswaldtwistle Urban District Council established a Miners' Distress Fund according to the 'Observer' March 2nd. This was followed by Church UDC on March 9th.

It was reported to the Executive of the LCMF at their meeting in Bolton, March 2nd., that Mr. Harry Smith and Mr. J.W. Higgins had been victimised by Messrs. George Hargreaves and Co. Accrington Collieries. More details emerged at the Executive Meeting of March 16th.:

> "No. 34. Accrington. Mr. McGurk reported that he had been invited to meet the Officials of the Accrington Branch for the purpose of considering the position that the Branch finds itself in owing to the attitude of the management. At the present time the President of the Branch [Harry Smith] is still playing [suspended]. The Agent for the firm is meeting the men without the Branch Officials and getting men to agree to prices for machine gotten coal which they cannot make wages at. This also applies to the Pneumatic Picks which are now in use. The Agent, F. Whittaker, still defies the owners' side of the Joint Wages Board by only allowing twenty minutes for meals, which in itself is a violation of a clause in the Wages Agreement. In fact Mr. Whittaker, the Agent, appears to be trying to ride rough shod over the Branch Officials and the whole of the employers."

The situation was discussed again at the Executive Meeting, held on April 13th. when it was reported that Messrs. John McGurk, Harry Smith and Albert Bernasconi met F. Whittaker, on Friday, April 5th.:

> "A full and frank discussion took place regarding the position of the Accrington Branch Officials being ignored by Mr. Whittaker, himself; also the case of Harry Smith and J.W. Higgins being stopped. After a long interview it was agreed that H. Smith and J.W. Higgins should commence work again. They both started on Tuesday, April 9th.
> [LCMF Minute Book]

In the last week in May, a minority Labour Government took Office and Mr. Tom Snowden became Accrington's Labour M.P.

At the Monthly Meeting of the LCMF at Bolton, August 10th., Mr. McGurk gave his report of the 1929 MFGB Conference, including the Wages Question. Conference had passed the following resolution:

"That the time has arrived when the MFGB should take steps to secure a higher standard of life for the miner. A higher minimum rate of wages than the one we have at present, considering the time when it was fixed and the present cost of living, is long overdue, and also a return to a national wages agreement, so as to give all mine workers a living wage and a decent standard of life, such national agreement to be based on the cost of living, and contain a uniform minimum percentage guarantied to all grades of workmen in and about the mines."

"Also this Conference instructs the Officials and Executive Committee to take whatever steps are necessary to secure that the output and profits of all by-product plants be included in the ascertainments."

On Saturday November 9th. the 'Observer' published a letter from Harry Smith in which he pleaded with local people and the Co-operative Society to buy Accrington coal in preference to Yorkshire coal, which could be bought more cheaply. This was backed up the following Saturday with a further letter on the subject by Albert Bernasconi.

At a Special Conference held at the Miners' Offices, Bolton, Saturday November 16th., Mr. McGurk gave his report of the Special MFGB Conference, at which the following resolution was passed by 72 votes to 14:

"The Committee having given full and careful consideration to the position arising from the decision of the Annual Conference have urged upon the Government to repeal the Eight Hours Act, and the return to a Seven Hours working day."

"This was conveyed to the Government, and extensively examined and discussed with the Cabinet Committee, who have given assurances that the Government intend to implement their pledge to repeal the Eight Hours Act, and as a first instalment the Government proposes introducing a Bill this session, providing for the reorganisation of the production and sale of coal to be applied to every colliery in January, 1930, also a Bill to reduce the hours of working to 7.5, to become operative, on April, 6th., 1930. In the opinion of the Government this can be accomplished without any reduction in wages."

"It is resolved that the Committee while adhering to our Conference decisions relating to a reduction of hours, complete reorganisation of the industry including a National Wages Agreement, in the circumstances we recommend that the plan in general principle, proposed by the Government, be accepted, and that the Executive Committee, in conjunction with the Miners' MP's, continue their efforts to further improve the plan."

"The Committee regret that the Mining Association refused the invitation of the Government to meet in Joint Conference with the representatives of the Federation and the Government."

"That is what we are asked to vote upon before leaving this meeting to-day."

After much discussion the Lancashire and Cheshire delegates resolved, with only 7 voting against:

"That this Conference accepts the recommendation of the National Executive Committee on the Mining Situation, and our Delegates to the Special National Conference be instructed to vote for accceptancc of the Government's proposals." [Minute Book]

The MacDonald, Labour Administration, did not do what the MFGB had originally hoped for. Instead of the restoration of the 7 hour day a compromise of 7.5 hours was offered, which meant that Districts like Yorkshire who already worked such a system would gain no benefit. The legislation also aimed to regulate the supply and sale of coal production through a system agreed with the owners. At the Special MFGB Conference of November 5th., Yorkshire delegates had refused to go along with the Governments proposals and Herbert Smith, President of the MFGB and a Yorkshire man left the Conference Chair in disgust. [16]

On Sunday November 24th. Mr. A.J. Cook made his fourth appearance before an Accrington audience, at the Picture House. Mr. Harry Smith, presided and the platform included Councillors A. Dawson, and Baron. In his opening remarks, Mr. Smith said that the size of the audience spoke well for Mr. Cook's popularity with the Accrington Miners. He went on to say:

"Regarding the mining question,......at one particular time they felt they were being practically submerged in the industrial struggle, but they had recognised by the experiences of 1926 that not only had they to organise industrially, but they must also organise politically. Anybody who thought [otherwise].....must be living in a fool's paradise. A Bill was shortly to be introduced into Parliament with a view to shortening the working day, and whilst it was not all they hoped to achieve, it was a contribution towards the end......"

Mr. Cook received a warm reception and congratulated his audience for electing a Labour Member of Parliament for Accrington. He continued:

"Whatever might be said about myself, I was never afraid to put forward my point of view. I have been defeated - will be defeated again - but I have always believed, whether successful or unsuccessful, I would continue inside the movement to propagate and to put forward my own point of view. [Hear, hear.] During the last six months I have worked..... to get the whole national conscience aroused to see the necessity of a real conscious endeavour to reconstruct our industrial life......"

"I want to say here that to me the questions at issue are not personal questions, and that I honestly believe there are men, capitalists, bankers, Tories, and Liberals, who are as honest as I am, so that they have not purposely, gradually, and wilfully created unemployment for the purpose of misery. Why I say that is this, it strengthens my case that capitalism has failed because it could not succeed. Toryism and Liberalism have failed because they could not solve unemployment nor give the workers a living wage. If it could why didn't it? That is the challenge."

"How was it that in this age of great mechanical advance, scientific discoveries, and when productivity had increased beyond the dreams of even the most optimistic, that the more we produced and the more machinery there was, we got more poverty and insecurity. Machinery, mechanical invention, science, and electricity were great servants of humanity, and great destroyers unless understood and controlled by those who made them......"

"It must be admitted by all thinkers, students, and economists that the conditions in Lancashire, Scotland, and the whole of the industrial North - bankruptcy, poverty, and insecurity - were a result of capitalist ignorance, capitalist inefficiency, and lack of foresight and scientific development. He could not get himself even to believe, however, that the majority of colliery owners could be pleased at the wages the miners were receiving, at least no colliery manager, because if one wanted good work one must give good conditions. They could not get the best out of a man who had not either security or a living wage, and no man could be interested in his job if he was afraid he was going to get the 'sack' form every week. There could be no relationship between a man and his job unless he had security....."

"It was not agitators who created a revolution, but conditions......

"On the coal industry," he added, "I can assure my miner friends that we shall watch carefully every step that this legislation takes when we have accepted the proposals of a Labour Government to reorganise, reconstruct, resuscitate this vital industry, we will help to do it not in the interests of capitalism but in the interests of the miners, because we want a healthy industry. I want it, the miners want it. We have been denied the right to do it......"

Cook was giving all his support to the minority Labour Government, hoping that they would eventually 'come up trumps'. He said that Labour MP's were facing great odds and could only act for the first few months as an ambulance brigade. He continued.

"A strong trade union movement was more necessary to-day than ever, because whilst their people in the House of Commons were fighting administratively they wanted to create a backing in the country so that it would go on......"

"Miners, and I am one of them, trust the Labour Government. We shall not allow them to delay, but we shall recognise the difficulties they are up against......"

"Speaking on the Unemployment Bill, Mr. Cook confessed he was disappointed in it, and he appealed to the Government to wipe out the six day period, whilst he also referred to the rates of pay......The only way to solve [unemployment] was by rebuilding our industrial life, and it was in industry that men must find work......Mr. Cook appealed for a 100% trade union movement, and declared that through the great Labour, trade union, and co-operative movement they were going to win economic freedom.[Applause]"

1930

The Annual Conference of the LCMF took place in Bolton, on Saturday, January 25th. Mr. McGurk in his Presidential Address said:

"As industrial toilers engaged in a most dangerous industry, we are no better off than we were at this time last year..... it is nothing short of a disgrace and a scandal that they should have to labour under the conditions which exist in and about the mines, for the miserable pittance which they receive at the week-end. In no other industry in Great Britain can it be said that the wages are so low, having regard to the nature of the work our mine workers have to do. Twelve months ago our people were soothed with charity, monies, food and clothing, subscribed to by a generous and sympathetic public. The hearts of the British public were stirred by the powerful appeal made by H.R.H. the Prince of Wales, and were brought into closer touch with the mine workers' lives. The newspapers were overflowing with kindness to help the miner and his wife - but to help him to what - to seek charity and alms, rather than to help him to get what is his just right, his inherent right, a living wage......"

"The general election of last year gave the mine workers the opportunity of showing their utmost contempt for what the Tory Government had done; this contempt was reflected in the result of the General Election by the return of the Labour Party with the greatest number of members to the House of Commons, which enabled the Labour Party to form a Government. The mine workers and their wives have pinned their faith in the present Government seeing to it that they get a fair deal. The introduction of the Coal Mines Bill is an instalment to that end. No sane miner' leader will say that the Coal Mines Bill gives the mine worker anything like what he is properly entitled to; it does not give him that economic security which is his right; it only gives what a minority Government can force. It can only give him half of what the Tory Government put on, viz: half-an-hour off the present working hours....."

"Those of us who have been educated in the hard school of experience, starvation, and privation, are entitled to ask and seek the co-operation of all men and women of goodwill to assist in trying to bring about a more scientific and efficient system of selling the hard ur of the miner, so as to bring about an improvement of his itions and a better standard of life for him. National co-ordination therefore be our goal, which must seek for its end and ultimate ct the nationalisation of mines, minerals and bye-products......"

"What is it we are asking the Government to adopt? The wing is all we are asking for, and with goodwill in the industry, e figures as we put in the Amended Minimum Wage Bill, are within power of the people who own the mines at present, to pay:-

"a] An adult daywage worker shall be paid a minimum daily rate of wages of not less than 11s. per day.

b] An adult piece worker shall be paid a minimum te of earnings of not less than 12s. per day.

c] An adult surface worker shall be paid a minimum ate of wages of not less than 10s. per day.

d] A juvenile underground worker shall be paid a um daily rate of wages at 14 years of age of not less than 4s., and years of age of not less than 5s., and so on, with six monthly ces up to the minimum daily wage or rate of earnings for an adult r.

e] A juvenile surface worker shall be paid a minimum daily rate at 14 years of age of not less than 3s. and at 15 years of age of not less than 4s., and so on, with six monthly advances up to the minimum rate of daily wage provided for an adult surface worker." [Minute Book]

At the monthly meeting of the Joint Committee of Employers and Union Representatives, Monday 10th. March, held at the Queen's Hotel Manchester, it was reported that Harry Smith had been appointed as one of the workmen's representatives for the following twelve months. [Minute Book]

At the LCMF Conference of March 22nd. Mr. McGurk gave his report from the MFGB Executive Committee. They had discussed the progress of the Coal Mines Bill through Parliament and how the Government had been defeated on various Clauses. Mr. McGurk said:

"It is reported truthfully or otherwise that it had leaked out from the Cabinet that if the Government was defeated on this clause or any other in the Bill, the Government would not consider it a first class issue, would not resign or go to the country on it. This leaking out from some source or other induced the Liberals to go into the Lobby on this particular clause with the Tories and bring about the defeat of the Government......."

"Further than that we are also told that if the Government was defeated on one or two more Clauses they would withdraw the Bill. I can assure this Conference that inside the National Executive Committee last Thursday there was an extremely bitter feeling. It is suggested, but nobody can tell how truthful it is, that there are certain members of the Cabinet who do not like the Bill at all; I for one would very much like to know who they are" [Minute Book]

The Labour Government should have regarded any defeats to the Bill as a loss in confidence in their administration and resigned. If this policy had been firmly advertised to the Tory and Liberal opposition they would not have been so quick to tamper with the Bill. At that particular time, the defeat of the Labour Government over a Bill which the majority of the electorate thought of as being moderate, could not have helped the chances of the Tories or Liberals in any ensuing General Election.

On Saturday 14th. June, at the Monthly Conference of the LCMF, the following resolution proposed by Accrington Branch was carried unanimously:

"That this Federation grant £500 to the Yorkshire Woollen Workers to help them in their fight."

Harry Smith was declared elected onto the Executive Committee of the LCMF representing No.2 Panel at the Monthly Conference of July 12th. The meeting also passed the following:

> "That this Conference emphatically protests against the action of the House of Lords with regard to the Coal Mines Bill, and demands that the 7.5 hour day be inserted when the Bill comes before them again on Tuesday afternoon."

It took six months before the Labour Lord Chancellor, Sankey, introduced the Coal Mines Bill in the House of Lords on April 29th., 1930. His speech pleased the MFGB who printed his speech in pamphlet form. Sankey had stated that he still firmly believed that Nationalisation was the only solution, but that a Minority Labour Government could not propose such a sweeping solution to the industry's difficulties. He was of the opinion that working the 8 hours system had caused over-production, unemployment, and Britains remaining miners working longer hours than any of their European counterparts.

Unfortunately, the 'tread softly' approach of the Labour Government was attacked instantly by the Peers of the Realm, who during Committee carried an Amendment to permit a 'spread-over' of 90 hours a fortnight. Robin Page Arnot states:

> "The Government were aghast. The amendment wrecked their Bill: for it meant that in some Districts the miners would still be on 8 hours. Should they now withdraw the Bill? The question was turned over and over. Eventually, with a proviso that the 'spread-over' in any District must have the assent both of the Mining Association of Great Britain and of the MFGB, they reluctantly swallowed the amendment: and the Bill became law." [17]

Indeed, more details emerge from the Minutes of the LCMF Monthly Conference, 9th. August, 1930. Mr. McGurk informed the delegates, during his report from the National Executive of the MFGB, that officials of the MFGB had met with the Government, who had suggested the insertion of the words in the clause, 'the hours to be agreed between the MFGB and the Mining Association of GB.' It was the opinion of the Government that the Bill would go through if this was agreed to by the MFGB. When it came before the Executive it took a 'long, long time to come to a decision', but it was eventually accepted by 10 votes to 9. During the discussion Mr. McGurk asked that the letter be read that had been received from the LCMF. This is produced below:

> "Dear Mr. Cook,
>
> At our Monthly Delegate Conference held on Saturday last, the 12th instant, the question of the House of Lords Amendment to the Coal Mines Bill was discussed. After a lengthy discussion the following resolution was unanimously carried, which I was instructed to forward on to you:-

> "That this Conference strongly protests against the action of the House of Lords, and expresses its utmost indignation of their conduct with respect to the Coal Mines Bill. We urge the Government to stand firm, stoutly resist the Lords' Amendment on the spread-over of hours, and insist upon the retention of the 7.5 hours clause. We trust the Labour Government will accept the challenge of the Lords against democracy, and develop the issue for the total abolition of the Second Chamber."
>
> I am, yours truly,
> P. Pemberton

Mr. McGurk voted against accepting the principle of spread-over and his report was accepted. The Accrington Delegate said:

> "The Executive Committee had no right to accept the principle of a spread-over. Had the ten members who voted in favour of acceptance a mandate from their respective districts, if not it was altogether wrong?

Many more questions were asked, particularly about how the Act would work in practice, at the end of which Mr. McGurk said; 'There is only one thing certain in this world and that is death. I cannot answer conundrums.'

At the LCMF Monthly Conference, held at Bolton, 6th. September, the Chairman read a letter from the Accrington Branch, which asked for a discussion on the question of overtime and that a resolution of protest should be sent against same to the Premier, the Minister for Mines, and the Minister of Labour. The discussion duly took place with the Accrington Delegate stating:

> "The real object of the letter is to bring information out of the Delegates. We believe overtime is rampant and that men are ignoring it owing to fear of victimisation."

This coincided with a letter received from Mr. Cook, who was also asking for information regarding excessive overtime working. [Minute Book]

With regards to safety in the mines the following statistics are gleaned from the LCMF Monthly Minutes of 27th. September:

> "We were very greatly concerned about the increase in the number of accidents. In 1928 there were 983 killed and 161,036 injured; in 1929 there were 1,065 killed and 174,971 injured; an increase of 82 in the number killed and 13,935 in the number injured."

The Meeting also discussed the question of spread-over and overtime in much detail. The Accrington Delegate said:

> "With regard to the attitude of [Manny] Shinwell, [The Labour Minister for Mines] we did expect that something of a very important character had taken place. If Shinwell is not prepared to tackle the

question of overtime, what other redress have we? Something must be done inside the House of Commons to see that Shinwell does his work."
Finally, it was unanimously resolved:-

"That this Conference enters its strong protest against the action of the National Executive Committee in not calling a National Conference to discuss the question of the spread-over, and demands that a Conference be called at once in the interests of all the miners of this country."

It was also agreed that as much publicity as possible would be given to the protest.

The Coal Owners asked the LCMF to consider the question of the:

"Adoption of the 'Spread-over' principle with an 86 hours fortnight of 11 working days, which means 8 hours per day from Monday to Friday inclusive and a 6 hours shift on Saturday when the pits worked on such day."

At their Monthly Meeting, November 1st., the LCMF delegates unanimously resolved:-

"That our representatives on the Joint Wages Board meet the employers' representatives to discuss with them the provisions of Part 3 of the Coal Mines Act, 1930, and that our representatives be instructed to submit counter proposals for adoption of the seven-and-a-half hours working day with the necessary adjustment of wages to compensate the workmen for the reduction in working time." [Minute Book]

The matter was discussed at the Joint Committee Meeting with the Employers in Manchester on November 10th., where it was resolved that the question be discussed further at a meeting to be held on November 24th. [Minute Book]

In the meantime a Special Conference of the LCMF was arranged for November 22nd., where it was agreed that their representatives on the Wages Board would press the owners to adopt the 7.5 hour day without any reduction in wages.[Minute Book]

The Joint Meeting was duly held on November 24th. but it terminated with each side adhering to their original proposals. 'The owners for the spread-over, and the workmen for the 7.5 hours with percentage increases.' [Minute Book]

A Special Conference was held of the LCMF the following day, November 25th., at which it was resolved:

"That the recommendation of the Executive Committee and Wages Board be accepted, and that a ballot vote of the rank and file be taken on Thursday or Friday next week, and the results to be at the

255

Offices not later than Saturday morning."

It was also agreed that the two following questions be put on the ballot paper for members to vote upon:-

"1. Are you in favour of accepting the coal owners' proposals for adoption of the spread-over, which means present hours and conditions with a maximum of 40 hours per week for a temporary period of four months?

2. Are you in favour of accepting the hours fixed by the Coal Mines Act, 1930, which are 7.5 hours per day, and submitting our case against a reduction in wages to the National Industrial Board?" [Minute Book]

The result of the Ballot Vote was read out at the Monthly Conference November 29th.

For No. 1 - Spread-over   11,360
For No. 2 - 7.5 hours day   25,025

The coal owners terminated the existing agreement by giving one months notice and stated that they could not afford to pay the 6.55% increase to piece rate workers that the 7.5 hours day required. After much discussion, during which the Accrington Delegate moved that a ballot be taken of the coalfield before Thursday's Special National Conference, it was finally accepted unanimously:

"That we accept the recommendation of the National Conference, and that in the event of a stoppage in any District we support national action being taken by the whole of the MFGB, but before the men are called out a ballot of the whole coalfield shall be taken to ascertain the opinion of the members on this important question."

"Further, that a Special Conference of the LCMF be convened for Saturday next." [Minute Book]

At the Special Conference, December 6th., the report back from the MFGB Conference stated that the result of the vote on possible strike action was:

209 For
230 Against
100 Neutral

This caused the MFGB Delegates to agree on the following:

"That the Government recommendation be referred to districts for consideration; replies to be sent to the MFGB within a week."

Such recommendation was as follows:

"Do you agree to accept the suggestion of the Prime Minister that the Federation give the industry a chance to get its Re-organisation

Schemes of the Coal Mines Act working effectively by approving spread-over applications for a temporary period of three months without any reductions in wages, and without prejudice to the position of those districts not affected by the Act or those who have arrived at settlements on the basis of 7.5 hours per day?"

The LCMF delegates discussed the matter, taking into consideration the fact that the owners would inform them on the following Monday of the amount they intend to take off wages under the 7.5 hours a day proposals. It was finally unanimously resolved:

"That our representatives on the Joint Wages Board meet the coal owners on Monday next and ascertain from them the extent of the reduction in wages they propose under the 7.5 hours working day. Also discuss with them matters arising out of their letter dated the 5th. December, and report to a Special Conference of this Federation to be held on Saturday, the 13th. December."

The Monday meeting with the employers, held in Manchester on the 8th. December, saw the coal-owners submit the following terms for a 7.5 hour day:

"The minimum percentage below which wages cannot fall would be 23.73% on the 1911 basis rates, instead of the 32% payable under the existing agreement."

They also stated their proposals for the spread-over of hours, which were: 7 hours 48 minutes per day Monday to Friday inclusive. Saturday morning and week-end shifts to remain the same. [Minute Book]

The LCMF Conference of Saturday 13th. December, unanimously accepted:

"That we confirm the decision arrived at through the ballot vote of the members and refer our application for the 7.5 hours day without any reduction in wages to the National Industrial Board."

"That we appeal to the NEC [of the MFGB] to defer taking any decision until after the LCMF case has been before the National Industrial Board." [Minute Book]

The Board met and recommended for agreement between the owners and workers the following:

"On Monday, Tuesday, Wednesday, Thursday, and Friday the shifts for underground workers to be 7 hours 45 minutes and on Saturdays 6 hours....."

"The rates of wages, subsistence wages, custom and conditions of work, including week-end shifts, in operation in November 1930 to continue."

"The above terms to continue to 31st. March 1931, and thereafter until altered by agreement between the parties."

The LCMF Meeting of December 20th. accepted the Boards recommendations on a card vote by 820 to 168. Altham and Accrington voted with the majority, whilst Rishton voted against.

The Boards recommendations were put to a Joint Meeting of coal-owners and the LCMF at the Queens Hotel, Manchester on the 29th. December 1930, and were accepted.

1931

In January the miners learnt that their National Secretary, A.J. Cook had unfortunately had to submit to an operation for the amputation of his right leg. The LCMF's Annual Conference expressed sympathy and hoped for a quick recovery. [Minute Book]

In February a dispute took place at the Accrington Collieries with regards to surfacemen's scale of wages being reduced in breach of the temporary agreement. John McGurk, Harry Smith and James Baron met with the owners where it was agreed to revert back to the agreement and to pay arrears. However, Mr. F. Whittaker, "**intimated to the deputation that he proposed reducing the rates of other workers under the firm, and at the same time gave the President of the Branch [Harry Smith] to understand that he had not long to reign at the colliery by asking him to try and get a job away from the colliery.**" [Minute Book E.C. Meeting 14th. February]

Also in February, the Altham Miners had to resort to the threat of industrial action to stop the management imposing reductions. [Minute Book 28th. February]

The Accrington Branch members working at Calder Pit voted for industrial action by 197 votes to 16, on Thursday March 5th. However, this dispute regarding piece work prices was defused when a deputation led by John McGurk met the management. The union considered the employers revised offer to be satisfactory and therefore recommended acceptance. The meeting also agreed that Harry Smith should be found work at the coal face and he agreed to accept work on the machine face.[Probably at the Scaitcliffe Pit.] [Minute Book]

John McGurk and the Branch Officials again met with management regarding a further dispute at Calder Pit, at which a satisfactory settlement was arrived at. [Minute Book 25th. April]

A Special Conference of the LCMF on Saturday 4th. April met to discuss the recommended Wages Agreement reached between their Executive and the coal owners. By 106 votes to 12 the following terms were accepted.

"1. Hours and conditions to operate after the Easter Holidays and to continue until the 30th. June 1931.

2. Monday to Friday inclusive, seven and a half hours shifts.

3. Saturday mornings six and a half hours.

4. Week-end short shift seven hours.

5. Meal times twenty minutes.

6. Surface workers' hours as in December 1930, except on Saturday morning, when the hours will be half-an-hour longer than in December last.

7. No alteration in the present rates of wages." [Minute Book]

However, during the debate the Accrington Delegate spoke against acceptance of the above. He said:

"I move the rejection of these proposals; we were living in hopes that at least we were going to try and improve conditions of the underground workers; it is disheartening to find that the conditions of our men are being worsened. The whole trend seems to be to get North-East Lancashire levelled down to the rest of the coalfield. It is absolutely wicked talking about our men working seven hours on Saturday, his Saturday afternoon is gone when he has had his bath and a meal. I believe our men would strike against these terms. I say stop the pits to-morrow rather than accept these proposals. Any advantage is being given to the coal owners." [Minute Book]

The North-East Lancashire District argued for their previously shorter Saturday shifts at the Joint Committee Meeting with the Employers in Manchester on the 20th. April, but did not gain anything from the discussion. [Minute Book]

At the LCMF Monthly Conference, 13th. June, on a vote taken by a show of hands the Chairman declared Mr. James Baron elected to the Executive Committee, but a card vote was demanded by the Blackrod Branch, the result of which was:

    Mr. H. Twist 589 votes
    Mr. J. Baron 415 votes

At a Special Conference held in Bolton 30th. June, the following resolution from Accrington Branch was read:

"That having regard to our Delegate's report of the National Conference, we strongly urge our National Conference representative to try and use all his influence in trying to secure [if we are still to operate the seven-and-a-half hours day] the November conditions in any suggestions that may be put before the National Conference on Thursday next."

The LCMF EC recommended the following resolution which was carried by a very large majority: [including the Accrington Delegate]

> "That this Conference gives plenary powers to our Delegates to the Special National Conference, as suggested by the last National Conference, to obtain the best terms possible with respect to both hours and wages, but that they be instructed to move to extend the period of the seven-and-a-half hours day for eighteen months and the adoption of the November, 1930, conditions and customs."

At the Special Conference of the MFGB held on June 25th, the delegates "were dismayed to learn that their proposals to the Cabinet Coal Committee for a Minimum Wages Bill had never been put to the whole [Labour] Cabinet. Bitter words were uttered. S.O. Davies remarked that the Labour Government's proposals were really 'that they shall introduce legislation in the interests of the coal-owners.'" [18]

A second Special Conference of the MFGB took place on July 2nd. when the delegates had to accept or reject the 'final proposals' of the Labour Government. The proposals were:

> "Firstly, the 7.5 hour day would be continued temporarily for a period of twelve months; Secondly, during the twelve months of the 'temporary extension of the 7.5 hour day' the minimum percentage additions to basic rates and to subsistence allowances in all the 7.5 hour Districts would continue in force as minimum rates, that is to say, they would not be reduced." [19]

The delegates voted 346 to 186 in favour of their acceptance.

In the House of Commons on July 6th. the Bill was debated and this gave Mr. Ebby Edwards, the Acting Chairman of the MFGB, the chance to say:

> "Let me make it quite clear at once that this Measure does not satisfy the miners. There is nothing about the concessions in this Bill calculated to make the miners jubilant. Our claim is for a 7 hour day and a minimum wage, and hon. Members can well understand the dissatisfaction of the miners in regards to a Measure of this kind." [20]

On July 8th. the Coal Mines Act 1931 became law.

On July 22nd. 1931 at the Annual Conference of the MFGB the following resolution was carried unanimously:

> "That we press the Government to introduce a Bill for the Nationalisation of the Mines and Minerals, and in case of failure to pass such a measure, we urge the Labour Party to make Mines Nationalisation the chief plank in its next election programme." [21]

Events within the month however, were to make the above resolution meaningless. On Monday August 24th. Ramsay MacDonald resigned as Labour Prime Minister and accepted a Royal Commission to form a 'National Government' together with Tories and Liberals "in order to keep the pound on the gold standard and otherwise deal with the financial situation."

Robin Page Arnot in his history of the MFGB quotes Sidney Webb who had been a Labour Cabinet Minister at the time.

"A startling sensation it will be for those faithful followers throughout the country who were unaware of MacDonald and Snowden's gradual conversion to the outlook of the city and 'London Society.' J.H. Thomas has never been a Socialist and will probably cease, like other ci-devant trade union leaders, to be even formally on the side of the Labour movement."

"So ends, ingloriously, the Labour Cabinet of 1929-31. A victory for the American and British financiers - a dangerous one, because it is an open declaration, without any disguise, of capitalist dictatorship; and a brutal defiance of the Labour movement." [22]

MacDonald remained as Prime Minister until 1935.

The Executive Committee of the MFGB at its meeting on August 27th. resolved unanimously:

"This E.C., having received a full report of the meeting of the General Council of the TUC and the Labour Party Executive, approves of the attitude adopted by these bodies in their determination resolutely to oppose the expedients adopted by the new Government, particularly respecting Unemployment, and this Executive instructs its Mining Members of Parliament to support without fail the policy adopted by the TUC and the Labour Party."

This policy was officially endorsed by the LCMF at their meeting of August 29th. [Minute Book]

On October 5th MacDonald dissolved Parliament and on October 27th. he won a landslide victory. This was not surprising after he and his cohorts had caused such disillusionment within the Labour Movement during their 2 years in office. Unfortunately the working-class who were 90% of the population were now only represented in Parliament by 10% of the MP's, such was the scale of MacDonald's betrayal.

Meanwhile back in the Greater Accrington district, Rishton Miner's branch had requested help from the LCMF Executive in a recruitment drive. However, during these September visits by the E.C. representatives, 20 colliers and 6 detailers were given notice which was regarded as victimisation by the branch. As a result these men received strike pay for a period covering up to 12 weeks. The total amount paid was £202.. 4s. but it would appear that they were reinstated. [Minute Book 26th. December]

On the 2nd. November A.J. Cook, Secretary of the MFGB died. Ernest Bevin an opponent of Cook for many years, provided the following eloquent tribute:

> "I know of no man in the Miner's Federation who had fought so hard and yet created such an extraordinary love for himself in the hearts of miners as Arthur Cook. He was abused probably more than any other man of his generation, and yet all the time he worked and fought, guided by the highest motives." [23]

The LCMF at their November 28th. meeting agreed to a MFGB recommendation to donate a half penny levy per member on behalf of Cook's widow and family. [Minute Book]

1932

In his Presidential Address at the LCMF Annual Conference held at Bolton, 23rd. January, John McGurk said:

> "The most gratifying feature concerning the result [of the General Election] was the fact that approximately 7 million voters were not prepared to be influenced by the men who had deserted the Labour Party; I need not name them; the workers made them and made it possible for them to become great forces in the counsels of State, the workers trusted them, had faith in them until they betrayed that great trust; they have now sewn the seeds of their own political destruction. The workers were stampeded by fright into voting for the National Government Candidates; they will live to regret putting this Government in with such power. The Public Assistance Committees are now doing the nefarious work of the National Government; the Means Test with all its inquisition is a most abominable thing. I regret to have to say that even our own people, and in very great numbers, refused to believe those of us during the General Election who explained what the Means Test meant to them; they preferred to believe Archbishops and Bishops, men who are real parasites, men who have never done a day's work in their lives. I would rather at any time trust a burglar than a Bishop." [Minute Book]

John's anger at the poverty stricken sights he saw on a daily basis obviously caused him to indulge in a little poetic licence towards the end of his statement. [And why not?]

The 1932 Minute Book of the LCMF contains many pages of heated expressions of disgust at the results of the Means Test, but this subject will be discussed in Chapter 4.

The 'Observer' of May 21st. announced the closure of Whinney Hill Colliery, owned by the Altham Colliery Company. This was further bad news for Clayton-Le-Moors which had been the township hardest hit by the depression in the textile industry. Approximately 300 workmen were employed in the pit, and the management stated that as many as possible would be absorbed into the workforce of Moorfield Colliery which was roughly double the size of Whinney Hill. The pit had operated for 62 years and its last shift finished on Friday June 10th.

The amalgamation of three East Lancashire colliery companies was announced in the 'Observer' of August 13th. and was to take effect from January 1st. 1933. The three firms involved were John Hargreaves Ltd, owners of several Burnley pits; George Hargreaves and Co. Ltd, owners of Huncoat, Scaitcliffe, Broad Oak and Calder, together with nine small pits in the Rossendale Valley; and Altham Colliery Co. the owners of Moorfield. The new company was named 'Hargreaves Collieries Ltd.'

The Executive Committee of the LCMF recommended that a grant of £5,000 be made to the cotton workers to aid them in their dispute. [Minute Book]

On Sunday December 4th., Mr. Harry Smith, chaired a Public Meeting held at Accrington Labour Hall, to discuss the topic of 'The International and National Outlook in the Coalfields.' The meeting was addressed by Mr. J.A. Parkinson M.P. for Wigan and by Mr. P. Potts, County Councillor for Swinton. During the proceedings a resolution was passed calling for an international agreement and a speedy ratification of the Geneva Convention concerning mine workers conditions of employment. The resolution also urged the MFGB to press for a Minimum Wages Bill. ['Observer' December 6th.] The meeting was only one of dozens arranged throughout the coalfield.

The same newspaper also quoted Mr. John McGurk, speaking in Wigan, as saying that he "hoped, winter or no winter, labour would be withdrawn from the mines next month unless they got a fair wage. The British public must know that we are not going to stand the present conditions any longer."

1933

In his Presidential Address at the Annual Meeting of the LCMF, 21st. January, John McGurk said:

"One cannot look back on 1932 with any degree of pride with regard to the conditions of all workers. Unemployment and underemployment is still more rampant than ever......"

"Still more abject is the Government's failure to cope with this terrible problem or to promote the recovery of our trade and industry. Figures alone cannot tell the true story of this National tragedy. It can only be told by those who actually come in contact with our own people and by those of us who know the state of affairs in the homes of our people. The sombreness in the homes of weary and heartbroken mothers, fathers who tramp miles and miles every week in search of work, eventually giving up in sheer despair, hungry, clothless and ailing children."

"This problem the National Government has never tried to seriously face, except by a protectionist policy, this being the traditional expedient of the Tory Party for protecting the pockets of the rich. The reduction of Unemployment Benefit, the vicious Means Test, the policy of cuts and economies has not only reduced the purchasing power of the people, but has increased human hardship and suffering unprecedented in the annals of this country."

At the Monthly Conference of the LCMF, 13th. May, the result of the ballot of delegates for the appointment of Representative on the National Executive Committee of the MFGB was announced:

	First Vote	Final Vote
Harry Smith [Accrington]	284	491
J. Cannon	235	444
R. Newton	124	
J. Powell	108	
E. Keegan	81	
W. Nicholson	70	
S. Coucill	19	
A. Redgrave	14	

Harry Smith was therefore duly elected to the EC of the MFGB for 12 months. This was an honour that clearly showed the esteem with which he was held by his colleagues. It was also a fillip for the trade union movement in Accrington and was a matter of pride for his family and friends.

At the 5th. August, Monthly Conference, the position in Germany was discussed which resulted in the following resolution being carried:

"We demand the immediate release of Thaelman, Torgler, and all other comrades who are to be tried on the framed up charge of the burning of the German Reichstag. We believe this trial is a plot to murder them. We also protest most emphatically against the brutal treatment of the German working class leaders. To be forwarded to the proper quarter."[Minute Book]

On the 26th. August the LCMF passed the following resolution after prolonged debate:

"Recognising that the Coal Owners have now refused to guarantee even our present deplorable conditions, we demand that this Federation go forward with a campaign for the seven hour day and a National Wages Agreement, embodying wage increases for all mine workers above and below ground."[Minute Book]

However, in his Report from the National Executive Committee given at the LCMF's 23rd. September meeting, Harry Smith stated that:

"There seems to be a feeling inside the National Executive that they will do extraordinarily well if they can retain the present situation, never mind an advance in wages or reduction in hours at the present time."[Minute Book]

He further gave expression to his impressions regarding wages and conditions Nationally, at the October 28th. meeting, when he said:

"There is no possible hope of establishing a National wages agreement during the present regime of the present political party in power. We want more East Fulhams [By-Election victories], and have got to either wait for a change in the political situation or enter on a struggle to improve our present conditions. There is no possible hope as far as a National Agreement is concerned." [Minute Book]

In November, pit head baths were opened at Calder Pit. Apparently they were the first in Lancashire. ['Observer' 4th. November]

At the LCMF meeting of December 23rd., Harry Smith described his participation in the MFGB Delegation to the Prime Minister on December 11th.:

"I felt I at least ought to put a question of my own, and said: 'Excuse me, Premier, seeing that [you believe] all the suggestions of the Federation offer no solution to present problems, what is your own solution to the depressed mining conditions in the area you represent at Seaham Harbour?' He replied: 'My friend, I have already done more than any other man within the limits of the present situation.'......after that diplomatic reply, however, I went on then with a further question: 'Is it not a fact, Mr. Premier, that since the National Government came into power the conditions of the miners have considerably worsened?' His reply was: 'If your friends, the Labour Party, had been in power your conditions would have been considerably worse.'

These answers to Harry's questions were merely the tired diplomatic responses of a politician [Ramsay MacDonald] who had lost all enthusiasm for improving the lot of the common man and whose only objective in life was to enjoy the personal riches and lifestyle coming from his position as Prime Minister, a job he had no intention of giving up easily.

Harry Smith ended his Report as follows:

"I felt that the deputation was absolutely futile. There is no hope whatever so far as the MFGB is concerned with the present Government; and as far as the owners are concerned, there was never any hope. The only hope we have is in the strength of our own organisation."[Minute Book]

1934

In his Presidential Address at the LCMF Annual General Meeting, 20th. January, John McGurk said:

"Unemployment and misery still exist on a scale never yet experienced, and the effect of this prolonged state of affairs on the health of our people, is a problem which must be the concern of all right thinking men and women....."

"Again I repeat, the wages paid at the present time to the mine workers are a disgrace and a scandal to those who own and control the mines.....The wonder to me is that the mine workers do not rise in revolt; nothing on earth would give me greater pleasure than to see this done, and the sooner they do, then the quicker they will get a better standard of living, together with economic security and justice....."

"If ever a case has been made out for the State to own and control the mines it has been made out now, for the present owners of the mines are not competent to run a tripe shop......"

"If ever a body of men deserved economic justice it is those who toil in and about mines. Let us go forward, not with fear, but with courage, and in the justice of our claim for economic security, slowly but surely we shall remove the monstrous injustice, the terrible evils and the deep-rooted iniquities which at present exist......"[Minute Book]

At the Annual General Meeting of the Accrington Miners held on the 23rd. January, a resolution was mischievously passed asking Major Procter the town's Tory MP to support an amended Minimum Wage Bill for miners, which would shortly be introduced in Parliament by Mr. Tom Cape, Labour MP, for Workington.

The President, Harry Smith, reported that all negotiations between the

MFGB and the Government had broke down, with districts being left to make their own agreements. He was then re-elected President for a further twelve months. ['Observer' 27th January 1934]

A discussion took place on the proposed Draft Agreement as to the regulations of Mine Workers' Wages in the District, at the LCMF 14th. March meeting. The Accrington Delegate moved its acceptance saying:

> "The only difference between this new agreement and the old one is this, that the owners are prepared to cancel deficiencies existing, which are in the region of three million pounds, and to cancel this each year. To recompense them for that, they want us to increase the ratio percentage in case of a surplus from 13% to 14% which will make no difference to the industry. The main reason why I support and recommend the acceptance of this agreement is on account of its short duration. Between now and the end of this year we ought to be putting our minds to steep with regard to some fresh agreement." [Minute Book]

The Draft Agreement was accepted. In Harry Smith's Report at the LCMF's April 14th. Meeting he said "if Lancashire has not done as well as we desire, it has got an agreement equal to any other county in Great Britain." [Minute Book]

At the LCMF Executive Meeting, 5th. May, John McGurk reported that two deputations within a week had met Colonel Bolton at the Accrington Colliery Offices, the point being the question of redundancy and 35 men receiving notice at Scaitcliffe Pit. The deputation asked Colonel Bolton to adopt the policy of last in first out, but he refused. It was decided that a ballot be taken of the whole of Accrington Collieries with a view to giving 14 days notice. However, it was reported at the Executive Meeting, 19th. May, that as a result of further discussions it had been agreed that the last in would be the first out. This decision was accepted by the men at a mass meeting. [Minute Book]

THE TRAGIC DEATH OF MR. HARRY SMITH, PRESIDENT OF THE ACCRINGTON MINERS' AND EXECUTIVE COMMITTEE MEMBER OF THE MINERS' FEDERATION OF GREAT BRITAIN.

On July 23rd. tragedy hit the Accrington Miners' Association, when Mr. Harry Smith died whilst working underground at Scaitcliffe Pit. The 'Observer' of July 28th. reported the sad event as follows:

> "News of the death of Mr. Harry Smith, President of the Accrington Branch of the LCMF, who collapsed and died with tragic

suddenness while following his employment at Scaitcliffe Colliery, on Monday afternoon, caused a big shock in many quarters. He was 40 years of age."

"Deceased left home in good spirits and apparently in his usual state of good health about 6.15 am. About 1.50 pm. ten minutes before he was due to finish work he complained to one of his colleagues of feeling sick, and after walking about eight yards he collapsed. Several men ran to his aid and he was taken to the surface. Dr. Ross was called and pronounced life extinct....."

"Mr. Smith resided at 1 James Street, Huncoat and leaves a wife and five children, three girls and two boys, to whom will go out a wide measure of sympathy."

"He had worked at Messrs George Hargreaves and Co. Collieries all his life, having at various times worked at Huncoat, Calder and Scaitcliffe Pits."

"Amid many manifestations of esteem and regret, the remains were interred at the Accrington Cemetery. Despite the inclement weather many sympathisers lined the route and congregated at the cemetery."

"Mr. Smith's activities in many spheres were reflected by the large number of public representatives attending, including Mr. John McGurk, President of the LCMF and Mr. Pemberton, Secretary......"

"The Accrington Labour Party was represented by Mr. W. Howson agent, Councillor R.I. Constantine JP, CC. President, and Councillor W.H. Roberts, while Mrs. Howson represented the women's section."

"Mr. Fred Constantine, Labour Agent for the Clitheroe Division and Mr. J.W. Sunderland JP, CC, President, represented the Clitheroe Labour Party."

"The committee and officials of the Accrington branch of the Miners' Federation preceded the hearse to the cemetery and amongst them were Councillor James Baron, Secretary, G. Gorton, Treasurer, A. Taylor, Insurance Secretary and Mr. William Kennedy, a former secretary of the branch."

[Miners representatives from St. Helens, Burnley, Hapton, Cheapside, Altham, Rossendale, Deerplay, and Pendlebury also attended.]

"At the graveside Mr. McGurk paid deceased a glowing tribute. 'We who have known Harry Smith,' he said, 'must realise that we have lost one of the best, in so far as in his day and generation he tried to serve the cause, to which he belonged faithfully and well. For many years he had been a representative of the Accrington Miners at our conferences at Bolton, and finished up a member of the National Executive of the MFGB.'"

"At this time last week,' Mr. McGurk continued, 'We were together at Edinburgh. He was apparently healthy and strong, and today he is gone. When I got to know, I had the greatest shock of my life. He has passed away, but the work he has done will live on. I would ask everyone to follow the example of Harry Smith.'"

"'He fought with us not only in trade union work but in the wider field of politics, he had one aim in life, and that was to leave this world better than he found it, so that those who came after him could benefit and reap the reward of the work he had done.'"

"'In extending to Mrs. Smith their heartfelt sympathy he was sure he was speaking for everyone in the Lancashire and Cheshire coalfield.'"

In his opening remarks to the LCMF Conference, 4th. August, John McGurk, included the following comments about Harry:

"One thing can be said of Harry Smith - I have known him many years and you may have noticed that we did not always see eye to eye in this Conference - he never bore any malice to any living soul. He was a great driving force and wanted to go very fast, not too fast, but his years made all the difference. If things could have moved as fast as he wanted them to, the mine workers of this country would have been in a much different position than they are to-day. Everyone will agree that the Accrington Branch has lost an extremely good Delegate, and will require a lot of filling owing to the influence he had with the owners of the colliery where he worked." [Minute Book]

The Meeting stood in silence for a few moments in his memory and condolences were sent to his wife.

The Accrington working class does appear to have lost a commanding figure with the loss of Harry Smith. At 40 years of age he should have been able to provide leadership to the local Labour Movement for a further 25 years. Indeed his prospects for gaining a national position of importance looked good. His reports back to the LCMF of the proceedings of the MFGB were thorough and well composed. His self confidence was growing with every MFGB meeting he attended. This can be seen in his cross-examining of Prime Minister, Ramsay McDonald. He also had the advantage of being liked as a person by people who disagreed with him on various issues; John McGurk being an example. His death was, however, most tragic for his wife and young family, who had to struggle through the lean years of the thirties without the main breadwinner.

At the Annual General Meeting of the LCMF, held on January 19th, 1935, John McGurk said:

> "Reviewing the past twelve months, in so far as the Mining Industry is concerned, and those who have invested their capital, i.e., the mine workers, and their capital is their labour, the return in the nature of wages is as meagre as it was twelve months ago, and in fact as it has been for many years past; whilst on the other hand, judging from the reports which appear in the Press from time to time of Public Companies, ie., Colliery Companies, the shareholders appear to be doing very well. Apart from these reports the Balance Sheets of private Subsidiary Companies come into our hands and reveal the same state of affairs. Still, the mineworker, who every day goes down the mine, risks life and limb, has to be content [so long as he will remain content] with the same miserable pittance which is called or termed wages."

Throughout 1935 the MFGB organised a successful publicity campaign for wage increases, which gained much public support. Big consumers of coal, such as ICI, volunteered to pay more for the product, on condition that the money was used to increase the miners' remuneration. In addition a MFGB ballot vote in favour of pursuing a wages claim to the extent of ceasing work, was carried by 409,351 to 29,215. These facts made the employers finally agree to negotiate, and in January 1936 the Lancashire miners were offered an increase of 1s. per shift, which they accepted. Life continued to be hard for the Greater Accrington miners, and their story will hopefully be continued in a future volume.

Average Monthly Membership of local Branches.

		Full	Half	Comp. and Strike	Sick & out of work	Grand Total of Monthly Averages
1927	Altham	721	72	2	24	819
	Rishton	219	31	4	30	284
	Accrington	545	76	3	121	745
1928	Altham	740	86	5	9	840
	Rishton	173	23	5	48	249
	Accrington	398	61	3	204	666
1929	Altham	706	76	10	12	804
	Rishton	192	26	4	40	262

	Accrington	336	34	3	84	457
1930	Altham	641	110	25	29	805
	Rishton	210	29	2	48	289
	Accrington	309	37	4	111	461
1931	Altham	656	96	29	50	831
	Rishton	213	27	5	59	304
	Accrington	280	34	1	230	545
1932	Altham	544	62	30	101	737
	Rishton	208	38	3	53	300
	Accrington	359	38	5	147	549
1933	Altham	454	36	24	66	580
	Rishton	198	58	5	55	316
	Accrington	411	49	6	99	565
1934	Altham	461	37	17	53	568
	Rishton	180	59	7	61	307
	Accrington	461	38	8	163	670

Total Membership of local mines:

1927	1928	1929	1930	1931	1932	1933	1934
1848	1755	1525	1555	1680	1586	1461	1545

REFERENCES

1. Rothwell. M. 'Industrial Heritage: A Guide to the Industrial Archaeology of Accrington'. Pub. M. Rothwell 1979. p. 30.
2. Jefferys, J.B. 'The Story of the Engineers 1800-1945'. Pub. Lawrence and Wishart Ltd. 1945. p.237.
3. ibib.p.237.
4. ibib. p.238/239
5. Rothwell. op. cit. p. 32
6. Jefferys. op. cit. p. 238
7. AEU. Monthly Journal July 1931. p.11
8. ibid. p. 46
9. Frow, E. and R. 'Engineering Struggles'. Pub. Working Class Movement Library.1982. p. 93
10. Jeffreys. op. cit. p. 241
11. Frow. op. cit. p. 91 to 94
12. Kingsford. P. 'The Hunger Marchers in Britain 1920-1940'. Pub. Lawrence and Wishart. 1982. p. 162
13. Jeffreys. op. cit. p.241
14. Mahon. J. 'Harry Pollitt: A Biography'. Pub. Lawrence and Wishart. 1976. p.

185 and 186
15. Hutt, A. 'British Trade Unionism-A Short History', Lawrence & Wishart. 1975. p. 120
16. Arnot, R.P. 'The Miners in Crisis and War', George Allen and Unwin Ltd., London 1961. p. 35
17. ibid. p. 36
18. ibid. p. 55
19. ibid. p. 56
20. ibid. p. 57
21. ibid. p. 62
22. ibid. p. 76
23. Davies, P. 'A.J. Cook', Manchester University Press. 1987. p. 185

Chapter Four

Unemployment and the Means Test.

WAL HANNINGTON & THE NATIONAL UNEMPLOYED WORKERS MOVEMENT.

The main organised pressure group involved in the battle against poverty and unemployment in the inter-war years, was the National Unemployed Workers' Movement. Wal Hannington, the Communist activist, was its National Organiser. Their continuous activities, particularly the six hunger marches to London kept the plight of the industrial poor to the forefront for two decades. Without this band of dedicated fighters, the conditions of the poor would undoubtedly have been significantly worse.

The NUWM's Charter issued in June 1924 called for the following scales of outdoor relief to be paid to a married man with two children:

Man and wife per week	£3 0s. 0d.
Two children per week	18s. 0d.
Total cost per week	£3 18s. 0d.
Annual cost	£202 16s. 0d.

The cost for the above family to be maintained in the workhouse, according to the government figures of the day, would have been £264 15s. 9.75d per annum, or £5 1s. 10.25d. per week. A convict at the same time cost the State £111 per annum. [1]

A circular was issued by the Ministry of Health on May 5th. 1926, stating that scales of relief should be kept within a scale of 12s. for a wife and 4s. for each child up to a maximum of 32s. [£1 12s.] per week. 'The suggested scales were considerably lower than those already in force in many Poor Law Unions.' [2]

I will take up the story with the establishment of the Labour Government in May, 1929. Wal Hannington's book outlines the main points, which I will reproduce at this stage. Having presented this information, I can then narrate the events as they occurred locally.

"The establishment of the second Labour Government in May, 1929, raised big hopes amongst the unemployed for improvements in their conditions. It was not a majority government and subsequently the workers' criticism of its omissions and weaknesses was met by its apologists with the plea that it was a government only in office and not power....."

"It may be said that any change in policy on the part of the [Ministry] designed to benefit the working class would be challenged in the House of Commons. Quite true, but a government ready to meet that challenge would rally the whole working class behind it, and would come out of the conflict strengthened, not weakened......"

"One might say that the characteristic of the 1929 Labour Government was that of proving that capitalism was quite safe in the hands of the Labour administration. It was upon this rock that the Labour Government was wrecked in September 1931. Had they given leadership and inspiration to the workers in the fight against the bankers and against capitalism generally, the results of the 1931 General Election would have been altogether different. Labour would have gone back in power with a mighty working-class backing....."[3]

"One of the burning questions,.....amongst the unemployed when the 1929 Labour Government came in, was that of the mass disqualification of claimants at labour exchanges by the 'not genuinely seeking work' clause......"

"The official figures, issued in the Ministry of Labour Gazette, of the disallowances by local insurance officers under this clause for the twelve months immediately preceding the 1929 Labour Government totalled 285,685."

"There were a number of other injustices which the unemployed naturally expected the Labour Government to tackle, and immediately following the formation of the Government the NUWM prepared an unemployed charter. This charter contained twelve points, which were briefly as follows:

1. Raise the benefit scales of the unemployed.
2. Remove the 'not genuinely seeking work' clause.
3. Restore to benefit all unemployed persons who were disqualified under the previous government's administration.
4. Make benefit continuous during unemployment; no disqualification unless suitable employment at trade union rates has been offered and

refused.

5. Abolish the six days' waiting period; benefit to operate from first day of signing.

6. Introduce national plans of work schemes at trade union rates and conditions.

7. Abolish all test and task work under the Boards of Guardians.

8. Guarantee full trade union conditions for all unemployed transferred under the industrial transference scheme.

9. Give the lead for a general shorter working day without wage reductions, beginning with the mining industry, and government establishments and government contracting firms.

10. Introduce a system of adequate pensions for all workers over the age of sixty, in order that they can retire from industry.

11. Raise the school-leaving age to sixteen, with government maintenance grants.

12. Repeal the Guardians Defaults Act, and establish a national scale of relief, not lower than the unemployment insurance benefit scale.

"Here was a charter of elementary demands, which every worker would at least expect a Labour Government to consider. The unemployed movement conducted a national campaign, and found tremendous support for the charter......" [4]

"[Labour] back-benchers in the House of Commons began openly to express their dissatisfaction with the policy of the Minister of Labour, and when members wanted to know whether the government was going to end the 'not genuinely seeking work' clause, Margaret Bondfield replied to the effect that the clause was considered to be a necessary protective qualification for the unemployed insurance scheme. She proposed, however, that additional machinery for the examination of claimants should be set up in the form of Boards of Assessors."

"The unemployed movement claimed that this simply meant an additional inquisition and would not remove the injustice. These boards were not established until November 1929; in the meantime heavy disallowances of claimants under the 'not genuinely seeking work' clause continued......" [5]

"The establishment of Boards of Assessors involved an additional investigation of claimants disallowed under the 'not genuinely seeking work' clause by the local insurance officers, before they went before the chief insurance officer for endorsement. The unemployed claimed that it was not new committees of inquiry that were wanted but the complete abolition of the clause that was robbing thousands of unemployed of their benefits every week."

"The NUWM led a nation-wide campaign for a boycott of the Boards of Assessors. Many big protest demonstrations took place. The struggle became particularly intense in Yorkshire and Lancashire where angry demonstrations were held outside the labour exchanges against the administration of the new Boards; in several places these demonstrations resulted in clashes with the police....."

"Our agitation had the effect of considerably modifying the administration of the Boards, and, when the new Unemployment Insurance Act came into operation in April 1930, this machinery was scrapped."

"The unemployed also had grave cause for complaint against the Ministry of Health. The policy pursued by Mr. Arthur Greenwood not only staggered the unemployed but seriously alarmed many of the local authorities with Labour majorities. He opposed an established scale of relief, and instructed the local authorities that each case must be treated on its merits. This meant that the extent and amount of relief was entirely in the hands of the Guardians and their relieving officers, and the applicant had no right to claim a definite scale. The Minister also insisted upon test work being performed by able-bodied applicants, and he threatened to remove Boards of Guardians for discontinuing to recover relief debts incurred by the miners."

"The term 'test and task work' relates to local schemes of work operated under the authority of the Guardians, on which recipients of poor law relief are compelled to work on roads, parks, sewerage, wood-chopping, stone-breaking, etc., in return for which they receive no recognised wages, but a scale of relief......"

"Refusal to perform test and task work not only means that relief to the applicant can be stopped, but that the local authority has the power to prosecute the applicant who can be imprisoned on a charge of refusing to maintain his family......"[6]

"With the advent of the Labour Government in 1929 we fully expected that the pernicious system of task work would be strongly discouraged if not completely abolished. But [this was not to be] [7]

"An anti-working-class policy was also pursued over the question of relief debts. During the lock-outs of the miners in 1921 and 1926, many of them had been driven to apply for relief. It was granted in many cases for the dependents, but the miner himself had to accept the relief on loan and give an undertaking that it would be paid back.

The total amount of debt in many mining areas ran into many thousands of pounds. The miners' wages were beaten down so low that following the lock-out of 1926 it was impossible for them to keep up payments......"

"The Boards were compelled to recognise how difficult it was for the miners to pay the debts out of the starvation wage which they were receiving. They realised that the repayment of the money meant taking the bread out of the mouths of men and their families, who had already been reduced to starvation." [8]

"The result was that many boards of guardians during 1928 and 1929 discussed the question of liquidating the remaining debts and making no further effort to enforce payment. This line had met with resistance from Tory Ministers of Health, but the local authorities expected a change of attitude under the Labour administration; but what did they find?....."

"The Minister of Health threatened to surcharge the guardians if they did so, and compelled them to rescind their resolution and to continue to collect the debt......" [9]

"The whole policy of the Labour Government can, I think, be summarised as follows. First, it was based on the belief that any substantial reduction in the number of unemployed depended solely upon the ability of British imperialism to defeat its rivals in the struggle for world markets; therefore the government devoted itself openly to help the recovery of British capitalist industry."

"Secondly, it believed that, in order to effect this recovery, there must be an intensive drive for improving the organisation and equipment of British industry and for lowering the cost of production. Accordingly, wherever the employers were prepared to adopt measures of rationalisation, the government would help them to get credit on favourable terms by pledging government support for loans......"

"The whole policy led to a rapid increase in the number of unemployed. By December 1930 the number of registered unemployed had reached 2,643,127, under the pro-capitalist policy which the Labour Government was pursuing. Mr. MacDonald attempted to excuse the increase in the number of unemployed by referring to the crisis which was sweeping the world."

"The failure of the government to abolish the 'not genuinely seeking work' clause and remove numerous other grievances which were driving more and more unemployed into desperate poverty led to the NUWM deciding at the beginning of February 1930 to organise a national march to London......" [10]

"In this march there was a special women's contingent from the derelict textile areas of Lancashire and Yorkshire. This was the first time that women had undertaken a hunger march in Britain, and it was significant that it should happen under a Labour Government, with Margaret Bondfield as the Minister of Labour......"[11]

"The continuous rise in the number of unemployed and the increasing insolvency of the unemployment insurance scheme led to the Labour Government appointing a Royal Commission on Unemployment Insurance, which received royal warrant on 9th. December, 1930. A criminal court judge, by the name of Holman Gregory, was appointed chairman of this commission, much to the astonishment of the unemployed, and, out of the remaining eight members of the commission, only two of them were known to have any sympathies at all with the Labour movement."

"Yet it was to such a commission that the Labour Government entrusted the task of making recommendations for the future of unemployment insurance. Towards the middle of 1931 the Minister of Labour began to press the commission for its report and it responded with an interim report in June 1931. This recommended wholesale disallowances of claims in respect to four sections of the unemployed - married women, part-time workers, casual workers, and seasonal workers, estimated to secure a saving of £5,000,000 in the unemployment insurance scheme."

"In the House of Commons on 22nd. June, during the debate on unemployment, Miss Margaret Bondfield said, 'The Government agree in principle with the recommendations of the royal commission and we propose to place before the House proposals to give legislative effect substantially to these recommendations.' This statement was followed up by the introduction of the measure known as the Anomalies Act, under which hundreds of thousands of unemployed were subsequently to lose their benefits."

"Two months later, following the royal commission's interim report, the Special Economy Committee that had been appointed by the Labour Government, with Sir George May as chairman, also issued its report. This report, coupled with that of the royal commission, played an important part in the events which brought down the Labour Government in August 1931. The economy commission recommended 10% cuts in all benefits of the unemployed, and similar cuts in the wages of civil servants, teachers, police and the armed forces. They also recommended heavy reductions in health services, maternity and child welfare expenditure, making a total saving of £96,000,000......"

"At the end of July 1931, when this special report was issued, the number of registered unemployed stood at 2,713,350, The report of the economy committee was a signal for an outburst in the capitalist press, which demanded quick and drastic measures against the workers. The cabinet met and began to draw up its plan of attack......"

"The fact that the Labour Government was about to launch an economy campaign at the expense of the working class immediately drew forth nation-wide protests from the workers' organisations, and particularly the unemployed, who were to bear the greatest brunt......"

"In the cabinet a division of opinion developed; eight out of the twenty-one ministers stood out against the economy cuts, particularly that in the benefits of the unemployed. Messrs. MacDonald, Snowden and Thomas began to negotiate with the bankers, and it was soon very apparent that the bankers were running the show. The press developed a violent campaign designed to show that the Labour government had landed the country into a state of bankruptcy. The growing opposition of the workers throughout the country drove more of the cabinet ministers into the ranks of the opposition, and finally on 24th. August, 1931, the cabinet completely split and the government resigned. "

"It was truly an ignominious end for the Labour Government. The vested interests which they had so faithfully served now kicked them out of office, whilst in the mouths of the workers a nasty flavour remained over the pro-capitalist policy which they had pursued. Had they been true to working-class principles, repudiated the economy proposals, stood together and fought their enemies in the House of Commons on defence of the workers' standards, demanding that the deficiencies in the capitalist system should be made good by the capitalists themselves and not at the expense of the workers, we should have seen an entirely different situation and one in which the whole working-class would have rallied to their support." [12]

1930

By 1930 the local government apparatus for dealing with Poor Law matters in the Greater Accrington area consisted of the following committees. The Lancashire County Council had a Public Assistance Committee [PAC], which controlled the activities of the district PAC's [still referred to as the Guardians], which in turn controlled the local PAC's [locally referred to as the Relief Committees].

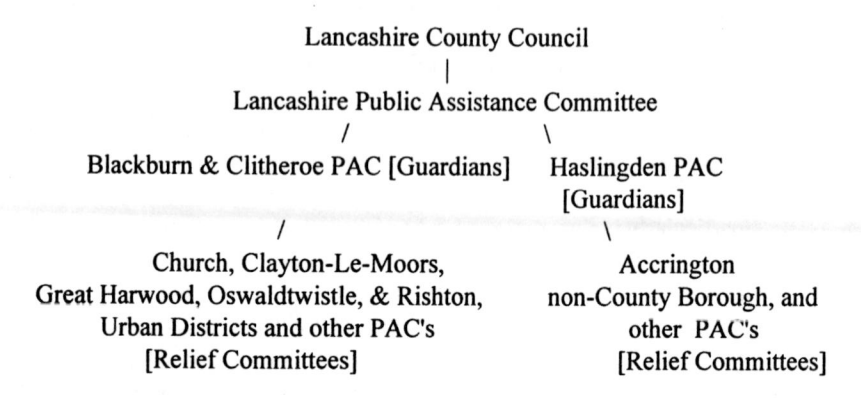

```
                    Lancashire County Council
                              |
                Lancashire Public Assistance Committee
                      /                    \
  Blackburn & Clitheroe PAC [Guardians]    Haslingden PAC
                                            [Guardians]
                  /                              \
       Church, Clayton-Le-Moors,              Accrington
  Great Harwood, Oswaldtwistle, & Rishton,   non-County Borough, and
      Urban Districts and other PAC's          other PAC's
          [Relief Committees]                [Relief Committees]
```

NB. Blackburn County Borough was not part of the Blackburn & Clitheroe Division. Being a County Borough, it was a County Council in its own right and as such controlled its own PAC programme.

MARGARET McCARTHY & THE 1930 HUNGER MARCH TO LONDON.

The first reference to Hunger Marches appears in the 'Observer' of April 15th., 1930, under the heading 'Scottish Hunger Marchers At Accrington - Speeches on the Market Ground.' Strong speeches were made attacking the Labour Party, who it was stated had refused to give them a sixpence to help them on their way. They also attacked the institution of the Monarchy and the tactics of the police. Local Communists gave supporting speeches and a meal was taken at a dining room at Bull Bridge. The marchers then set off to Burnley and when they reached Huncoat further speeches were made outside the Griffin Pub.

Oswaldtwistle's Margaret McCarthy relates her activities on this march in 'Generation in Revolt'. She had only a few months before returned from a three month stay with her friends in the German Communist Party. At this time, she was living in rooms in Burnley, devoting herself entirely to agitation against the more-looms dispute and organising the unemployed. Indeed, she was the secretary of the Burnley branch of the NUWM. She says:

"Some indication of the type of problems we attempted, apart from the general one of agitating against unemployment itself, was in the relief we obtained for Burnley's unemployed women, who were being dealt with in a shameful way. The Women's Labour Exchange used then was a totally inadequate place, with a narrow doorway."

"Through this single door each signing day, 2,000 women passed in and out in the morning and the same again in the afternoon. The confusion was indescribable, and the delays intolerable......"

"We had this altered by demanding and obtaining the opening of an additional Women's Exchange at the Westgate School, and at the Mount Pleasant School for the men....."

"Against this background, the call came for another hunger march to London; but on this occasion it was resolved to include in the march, for the first time, a women's contingent. However, to avoid any possibility of scandalous gossip which would injure the purpose of the march, it was resolved that the women should hold their march separately, down the East route to London, while the men proceeded down the West way." [13]

The marchers assembled and demonstrated in Burnley on April 20th. 1930, and made their way to attend the May Day rally in Hyde Park. In addition to her job as steward for half of the contingent, Margaret was reporting the events to the 'Daily Worker.' An example of the appalling treatment given to the marchers as they proceeded to London is described by Margaret as follows:

"The local organisation in Sheffield had arranged for us to spend the night in the workhouse, and the Deputy Town Clerk had agreed that we should not be treated as casuals. After an evening meeting, therefore, we had entered the workhouse leaving huge crowds outside who quietly dispersed. When all was still and we were preparing to turn in, we were advised that we were to submit to 'casual' treatment and be bathed and searched, and it was made clear that there were sufficient forces in the institution to compel us to submit. To this there was no alternative but to march out into the streets again, rather than have the Press report our humiliation next day. So out into the night we marched. Crowds collected round us at the Town Hall and threw money to us, but the police drove them off. There was no doubt about the Sheffield authorities determination to make our overnight stay unpleasant."

"That night we remained out in the open, tramping from street to street, keeping on the move to give the police no excuse for any action......So out in the rain we stayed, reporting the position to huge crowds of Sheffield citizens in the morning, and sleeping on the bus to Luton, where we spent the night in a church, and were charged very heavily for the privilege." [14]

In stark contrast to their harsh treatment in Sheffield, the friendly members of St. Albans Labour Party, 'indignant at the behaviour of the Sheffield authorities [were] eager to make it up to us.' Their time spent in St. Albans was the highlight of the march.

After the Hyde Park demonstration they stayed in London for over a week, addressing meetings and agitating generally.

THE ATTITUDE OF MR. TOM SNOWDEN MP.

The 'Observer' May 24th., printed a letter under the nom-de-plume of 'An Elector'. The writer stated:

"What the man in the street wants to know is where does Tom Snowden stand about unemployment to-day, not last year, next week, or sometime else. We are not getting hot and bothered about whether he prefers to fight a Tory or a Liberal at the next election. He can satisfy himself that he will have to fight, because there are thousands of men and women in this division who twelve months ago voted for Tom Snowden as the representative of the policy of 'Labour and the Nation.' These voters are not concerned with how many companies he is chairman of, but they want to know why they 'must be starved into submission.' They did not vote for Tom Snowden expecting to be told a year later that the employers in the woollen industry under a Socialist Government would be allowed to 'starve people into submission.' They will not vote again for such a policy. Let Tom Snowden tell us at once what he has done. After the election he said 'when he got into Parliament he was going to urge upon his leaders one thing - they had to keep faith with the promise that they were going there to fight for the downtrodden and for the unemployed man and woman.'......'He was a great believer in simple truths.' Yes and so am I. Let us have a few about the promises of the Labour Party to deal with the unemployed, and particularly what Tom Snowden has done."

Those were strong words, and those interested in politics would have expected an equally strong reply from Tom Snowden, but they did not receive one. Instead he wrote back to the 'Observer' on June 7th. saying that he would not correspond with an alias in their letters page.

At the Accrington Labour Party, Annual Field Day, on July 12th., Councillor Constantine, President, said:

"As far as he was concerned he hoped the Labour Party would

institute a very bold policy and attempt to grapple with this great problem [unemployment]. He knew they were in the minority, and he knew they might be defeated, but at any rate they might make the attempt and put into operation such measures as would very substantially reduce the number of the unemployed."

"They knew there was only one solution for the problem, and that was the application of Socialist principles to industrial life."

These sensible words of Constantine's were not listened to by Snowden, who minutes later, according to the 'Observer', said the complete opposite:

"Coming to the unemployment question, Mr. Snowden said they were not responsible for industry; the Labour Party was not responsible for commerce."

His audience must have wondered what they were listening to. If what Snowden had said was true, then they had all been wasting their time in trying to build up the Labour Party and the working class movement over all those years. The truth was that the Labour Government was responsible for the running of industry and commerce, and in 1930 it was the duty of the Labour Government to interfere on the side of the working class. The economic situation was deplorable when the Government took office and it was now many times worse. Surely, a bold attempt to improve matters for the workers by introducing Socialist measures, was worth a try. Alternatively, taking up some of the ideas emanating from John Maynard Keynes, would have at least shown that the Government was thinking of creative policies to overcome the problems which it was facing. But, no, the Labour Government was behaving ostrich like, ignoring the problems that it faced, and betraying the hopes and aspirations of the working class. Unfortunately, Accrington's mill-owning Labour MP., Tom Snowden, appeared to have sided with those who saw no solution to the crisis. It was obvious at this stage that he would lose at the next election.

On August 9th. 1930 the 'Observer' printed an article by Snowden entitled 'My First Session. A Parliamentary Survey. Again on unemployment he said:

"Every man and all parties are baffled by the rising [unemployment] figures......The constructive part of the Labour Government is to be found in the £95,000,000 work schemes, which will provide 380,000 persons with work for one year. This I know, is poor satisfaction to the cotton operatives and engineers of Lancashire."

In Accrington work was provided for around 50 men, for two years, to convert the towns open ashpits to ash bins.['Observer' November 29th.] There were over 14,000 unemployed just at the Accrington Labour Exchange, plus over 7,000 at Great Harwood, Rishton and Clayton-Le-Moors. The area now covered by Hyndburn Borough Council had an unemployment figure of over 21,000. The Labour Government's scheme only touched the surface of the problem.

UNEMPLOYMENT CONTINUED.

The GMWU Engineering Shop Stewards meeting passed a resolution calling attention to the large number of applicants for unemployment benefit being struck off, under the clause "not likely to secure work in an insured trade," which in their opinion was a most effective substitute phrase for the old "not genuinely seeking work" clause. This they said was defeating the purpose of the Labour Government's Act of 1930. [Minute Book, October 9th.1930]

The GMWU Members Quarterly meeting, of October 22nd., protested against the Borough Council's decision to erect the new Police and Fire Station out of stone. The meeting was unanimously in favour of the local brickworks providing the building materials and thus giving much needed work to those laid off. [Minute Book]

The Great Harwood Weavers' Association condemned the Employment Exchanges for forcing offers of domestic service work upon their female members. They held that the refusal of such an offer should not prejudice the right to receive further Unemployment Benefit. The reality of the situation however, was that unless the applicant could prove that the offer of the job was not 'reasonable,' benefits were suspended for six weeks. [Half-Yearly Report, November 2nd.1930]

1931

The Admissions and Repayments Sub-Committee, of the Haslingden Guardians, which covered the Accrington area, and which only had a minority of Labour members, unexpectedly decided to cancel the amounts outstanding to 24 cases of relief given during the 1926 coal dispute and to a further 59 cases given during the 1929 cotton strike. The amounts varied from £12 0s. 6d. to £19 15s. 0d. ['Observer' April 4th. 1931]

The Great Harwood Weavers' Association reported that during the previous twelve months, their Secretary had appeared before the Court of Referees supporting members in 457 cases under the Unemployment Insurance Acts. [Half-Yearly Report, May 4th.1931]

The GMWU Branch Committee most emphatically protested against the proposals contained in the interim Report of the Commission on National

Insurance Benefits. [Minute Book June 4th.1931]

When the Cabinet split and the Labour Government resigned on August 24th., Tom Snowden sent a message to the Accrington TCLP saying that he did not agree with the actions of MacDonald, and Philip Snowden, and he would be supporting Mr. Arthur Henderson and those that had left the Cabinet. The reduction in unemployment benefit appeared to have been the final straw as far as Snowden was concerned. ['Observer' August 29th. 1931]

The two cuts in benefit announced by the Government were as follows. The first was to take effect from October 1st.. Under this order, the rate of benefit for an adult male dropped from 17s. to 15s. 3d; for a wife from 9s. to 8s.; for an adult female from 15s. to 13s. 6d.; only the 2s. rate for children was left untouched. If we take the example of a man, wife and two children, their income would be cut from £1 14s. to £1 11s. 3d. per week.

The second order to take effect from October 8th., brought in the means test. This isolated claimants eligible for benefit as of right from those who had run out of benefit. Unemployment benefit was now limited to 26 weeks per year and in order to obtain such benefit each claimant had to have amassed at least thirty contributions in the preceding two years.

These regulations immediately excluded over half of the registered unemployed men. These unfortunate souls were to have a new relief entitled transitional payments which would only be given after a means test at the hands of the local poor law guardians, i.e. the Public Assistance Committees.[PAC] This meant that hundreds of thousands of men who had never ever imagined having to submit themselves to the poor law, now had to face that humiliation. Many of them were middle-aged skilled workmen who had always paid contributions and who regarded unemployment benefit as a right. In addition, unemployed married women became subject to the Anomalies Regulations and by the end of the year 134,000 of them had been disallowed benefit. [15]

The Great Harwood Weavers' Association Executive Committee, on October 7th., received a letter from the local 'Council of Action' [which would appear to have been Communist controlled] asking the Committee to receive a deputation "to put forward proposals for a United Demonstration against the National Government and economy drive." The Committee resolved that whilst in sympathy with the principles involved, in the opinion of the Committee no useful purpose could be served by receiving the deputation. [Minute Book]

TOM SNOWDEN'S BELATED CONVERSION TO THE CAUSE OF THE UNEMPLOYED.

At his selection meeting, held on Sunday 11th. October, Tom belatedly criticised the composition of the various committees and commissions that had been appointed during the period of the Labour Government. It was, he said,

"Their unmistakeable duty to trust each other as members of the same party, before appointing men with whom they had nothing in common."['Observer' October 13th. 1931]

Later that day, Tom opened his election campaign at the Palace Cinema, Accrington, where a full attendance heard him say the following on the Means Test:

"Mr. Snowden then indicated what the new means test for the unemployed at the end of 26 weeks would mean. This investigation into means would prejudice those who had been careful in regard to their savings. If, at the end of 26 weeks' benefit, there was to be anything at all it ought to be something in the nature of a flat rate, determined irrespective of whether people had a certain amount of money. Men and women had made their contributions and were entitled to some benefit. In pounds, shillings and pence it was going to be more costly to administer the new scheme than the old. There were going to be plenty of officials to look after the officials." ['Observer' 13th. October 1931]

On October 23rd. Tom Snowden led an unemployed deputation of four men and two women to see the Mayor of Accrington. They were followed in procession by over 200 local unemployed. After the meeting, which lasted forty-five minutes, Mr. Snowden who was accompanied by Inspector Todd, of the Accrington Police Force, walked back to Ellison's Tenement at the head of the demonstration. The first issue discussed had been the unemployed's request for the free use of a room for them to meet. The Mayor promised to receive a deputation on this issue the following Monday, if the Council agreed. The second point had been in regard to benefits, but this was now an issue for the Public Assistance Committee, who would now have to administer transitional relief. When addressing the crowd Snowden warned the unemployed:

"That they would not like what was going to happen to them...... It was up to the unemployed to be organised, not as a political party, but as a properly constituted body for voicing their protests intelligently. If the Government could find money for wars they could find money for the unemployed to live." ['Observer' 24th. October 1931]

On October 29th., Major Procter, the Tory Candidate, gained a record majority of 12,622, over Tom Snowden. Tom's late and reluctant support for Accrington's working-class could not wipe out the memory of the two years in which he had so faithfully supported MacDonald's traitorous leadership. Two years in which the cotton workers, the miners, the engineers, and the unemployed had seen their standard of living plummet, and in which the capitalist class had been unaffected. Tom only had himself to blame for his loss, but it was Accrington's workers and unemployed who had suffered and who would continue to suffer under the new National Government.

The Great Harwood Weavers' Association reported that their Secretary had appeared before the Court of Referees supporting members in 231 cases, during the previous six months. These included test cases covering a large number of other members. The Association had interviewed the PAC and the UDC. They had asked every organisation in the township, Clubs, Societies, Churches, Ministers of Religion, and Trade Union Branches, to write letters of complaint to the Prime Minister. In addition they had distributed 6,000 postcards containing a resolution of protest, which they hoped had been posted to the PM. [Half-Yearly Report, November 5th. 1931.]

COMMUNISTS MARCH TO MOORLANDS.

The Communist Party organised a march on Thursday afternoon, November, 12th., to the offices at Moorlands, headquarters of the Haslingden Guardians Committee, of which Accrington was part. A deputation of eight was appointed and a procession was formed in which were carried 'fantastic banners.' Accrington people made up part of the demonstration. The 'Observer' reported:

> "[At Moorlands] the deputation submitted requests that the Guardians Committee should abolish the means test; that their officers should not visit the homes of applicants for transitional benefit; and that they should make good the 10% reduction in the amount of unemployment benefit."

The Clerk to the Guardians stated that their part was simply to carry out the rules and regulations laid down for them and went on to explain the new scales which were:

> "15 shillings for a man; 8 shillings for a wife; 7 shillings per head for each adult dependant over 21 years; 5 shillings for each adult dependant between 16 and 21; and 2 shillings per head for others - subject to the total amount not exceeding £2 5s. per week." ['Observer' 14th. November 1931]

NUWM DEMONSTRATION IN GREAT HARWOOD.

In Great Harwood on Thursday night, November, 12th., noisy scenes took place at a demonstration which took place after the Urban District Council refused to meet a deputation of unemployed, or to accede to their request for a meeting on the Town Hall Square, at which a member of the council could give reasons for the Council's refusal. The 'Observer' reported:

"After a time the crowd which gradually grew bigger and bigger, made a hubbub, some being inclined to force their way into the Town Hall, banging the doors, and clamouring for admittance. There was much shouting and booing. The police were called in from outside areas, and finally the crowd dispersed."

"A letter from Mr. J. Kay, secretary of the NUWM, addressed to the Chairman of the Council, was read at the Council Meeting. It stated:

"As a result of our meeting on the 10th. instant, I have to inform you that a deputation representative of local unemployed will wait upon you to-day at 7.45 pm. to place the following demands before you:

"1. That the Lancashire Public Assistance Committee refuse to operate the means test.
2. That a free room be placed at the disposal of the unemployed, the same to be used for recreation, and transactions of business relative to claims for benefit.
3. That all unemployed workers children be provided with free footwear.
4. That free feeding for children of the unemployed is made compulsory.
5. That a 25% reduction in all rents of working class dwellings be made, to take immediate effect.
6. That the Council go forward with more relief schemes, the same to be worked on a strict rotary system."

The Council declined to see the deputation and sent them the following letter in reply:

"I have to inform you that the Council have carefully considered the request stated in your letter. The members fully realise and sympathise with the difficulties you raise, but as they have no power to deal with these questions they feel that no good purpose could be served by receiving a deputation."

After three hours of noisy demonstrations, the crowds dispersed shortly after 10 o'clock.['Observer' November 14th.1931]

THE MARCH FROM GREAT HARWOOD TO CLAYTON-LE-MOORS.

On Tuesday 17th. November, the Great Harwood NUWM asked the Clerk to Clayton-Le-Moors UDC, for permission to hold a meeting on Barnes Square that afternoon. They were refused and so they applied to the police, who told them that if a meeting was attempted they would be moved on. After lunch 500 marchers from Great Harwood duly arrived in the township. They walked up Whalley Road as far as Church Lane, and then turned round into Atlas Street, eventually making their way to the Recreation Ground where a meeting was held. The intention of the day's activity was to encourage the unemployed of Clayton-Le-Moors to organise themselves to protest against the means test. ['Observer' November 21st.1931]

THE MARCH FROM GREAT HARWOOD TO RISHTON.

On Thursday, November 19th. a similar march took place from Great Harwood to Rishton. Mr. J.W. Sunderland, Secretary of the Great Harwood Weavers' Association addressed the crowds before they set off. 'Great numbers of people lined the streets' to welcome the marchers. A carnival atmosphere existed with the processionists singing popular airs. A meeting was held at which the unemployed of Rishton were urged to unite with them in their organised opposition to the means test. ['Observer' 21st. November 1931]

The same newspaper printed the following letter sent by the Great Harwood UDC to the Prime Minister and to their MP Sir William Brass. [Great Harwood was in the Clitheroe Parliamentary Constituency]

"I am instructed by the Great Harwood Council to call your attention to the present methods of applying an Order in Council imposing the means test in this district."

"The operation is unequal, and in many cases reduces the standards of living to the scale of outdoor relief of the Public Assistance Committee. There are more unemployed persons in proportion to the population here than elsewhere, and this is the very worst time of the year to impose these additional hardships, which are causing considerable dissatisfaction."

"Public meetings are being regularly held on the town square, addressed by persons who are organising demonstrations, and strong feeling is being shown. There is a possibility of disturbances of the peace, and the Council respectfully request that immediate attention should be given to this very urgent matter."

It is important to point out that the Labour members were in a minority on the Council and so it was the Governments own supporters who were showing their grave concern at the situation. They offered, in a covering letter to the County Public Assistance Committee, suggestions to alleviate severe hardship. When household income was being ascertained they wanted the following items excluded:

"Health insurance up to 10 shillings, income from any subsidiary occupation up to 7s..6d. per week, disability and widows pensions, and small savings up to £100."

Mr. J.W. Sunderland was present, by invitation, at the meeting of the UDC and made a strong protest against the means test.

At the Accrington TCLP monthly delegates meeting Councillor T. O'Connor J.P. gave a report on the work being done by the Public Assistance Committee which was extremely busy at this time. With regards to transitional payments, he said it would be found that:

"Many people who thought they were qualified to receive payment would be either completely knocked off, or their payments would be considerably reduced." ['Observer' 21st.November 1931]

NUWM DEMONSTRATION IN ACCRINGTON.

The 'Observer' December 1st. reported that 3,000 people had gathered on Ellison's Tenement, Accrington, the previous afternoon, to take part in a demonstration organised by the local branch of the NUWM to protest against the means test. After speeches a deputation was elected to visit the PAC.

"A procession was then formed, and proceeded via Union Street to the Peel Street side of the Market Ground. 'Work or Full Maintenance' and 'Down with the Means Test - Not a Penny Off the Dole' were the inscriptions in red lettering on two large white banners..... On arrival at the Market Ground there was a crowd of between three and four thousand."

The deputation went off to see the PAC with their demands for the abolition of the means test and the crowds were then treated to speeches given by two young women, who were 'vehement' in their denunciation of the hardships inflicted upon the unemployed. The deputation returned saying that their protest would be read at the next meeting of the Committee and meanwhile they would continue their campaign. The orderly crowds then dispersed.

Also on November 30th., the Lancashire PAC met in Preston, where an unsuccessful attempt was made by the Burnley Board of Guardians to increase part of the scale of out door relief. They wanted the allowance of 8s. for the second adult in a family raised to 10s. and the present 2s. allowance for a child increased to 3s. Mr. R.I. Constantine, the newly elected first Labour Mayor of Accrington, in moving the Burnley request, said:

> "Some people unemployed for years, had got down to the bone in clothes and furniture, and parents were unable to provide enough for their children. Many towns had to feed their necessitous school children, and if they had to pay 2s. 6d. a week for a child in that respect, how was it possible for parents to keep children for a week on 2s.?"

['Observer' 1st. December 1931]

NUWM MARCH FROM GREAT HARWOOD TO ACCRINGTON - ARRESTS MADE.

A further demonstration against the means test took place in Accrington on December 1st. at which two arrests were made. The 'Observer' reported the events as follows:

> "Demonstrations against the means test were promoted on Tuesday by the Great Harwood branch of the NUWM, and after a meeting had been addressed in front of Great Harwood Town Hall, a large crowd joined in a procession to Accrington with the intention of taking part in the Accrington demonstration. The processionists, who numbered about 200 were accompanied by a jazz band, and a number of them carried banners with inscriptions in red letters demanding 'Work or Full Maintenance' and the abolition of the means test."

> "On arriving at the borough boundary at Altham the processionists were met by a contingent of the Accrington Borough Police, under the charge of Chief Constable Holmes and Inspectors Todd and Sharples, and the leaders informed that as the procession was unauthorised, it could not be allowed to proceed through the borough, ..."

> "The crowd became restless and efforts were made by the band, which headed the procession to drown the discussion between the police and the leaders of the unemployed. The processionists found their way out of the difficulty by furling their banners and walking on the footpath."

> "By the time the demonstration approached the railway arch in

Whalley Road the procession had to some extent been re-formed, and the efforts of the police to break it up by diverting the marchers into Meadow Street led to some lively scenes, and a certain amount of scuffling in the course of which a man and woman from Great Harwood were arrested. Subsequently they were released on bail."

"Meanwhile the processionists who had been diverted into Meadow Street crossed over into Maudsley Street, and into Whalley Road again, while the larger section made their way down Castle Street and along Hyndburn Road to the Tenement, where the meeting organised by the Accrington unemployed was in progress."

Later a Great Harwood deputation went to the police station where a large crowd assembled. This resulted in the marchers agreeing not to re-form into a procession until they reached the borough boundary at Hyndburn Road, Church. The Procession then made its way back to Great Harwood. ['Observer' December 5th. 1931]

UNEMPLOYMENT CONTINUED.

At the Half-Yearly Meeting of Great Harwood Weavers' Association, on December 2nd., held in the British School, a good attendance passed the following resolution unanimously:

"That this Meeting .....approves the action taken by the Committee in protesting against the means test and in endeavouring to secure the withdrawal of the Order of Council. That the Committee be instructed to proceed further with such efforts as they deem likely to be successful. That a strong protest be sent from this meeting to the PM., Minister of Labour, Minister of Health, the local MP., the County PAC, and the local PAC." [Minute Book]

On Thursday December 3rd. at the Clayton-Le-Moors UDC Meeting, the demands obtained on Monday from a deputation of unemployed, comprising Messrs. James A. Procter, George R. Tierney, Leonard Shaw and Clarence Duckworth, were considered. The demands were:

"That the Council take steps to abolish the means test.

That all the unemployed's children be provided with free meals and footwear.

That the UDC take an active part in reducing rents by 25%.

That the Council supply the unemployed with a free room to hold meetings."

The anti-Labour Council replied saying that the first three points were out of their control. The unemployed knew this to be the case, but it was effective propaganda work under the circumstances. Their response to the fourth request however, showed their class hatred for the townships poverty stricken citizens, when they decided to inform the deputation that:

"Having regard to the fact that the Council are custodians of a public institution handed down by persons embracing all sections of the community, they did not see their way to grant the request." ['Observer' 5th. December 1931]

The NUWM was reported to be attempting to set up a branch in Oswaldtwistle and Church. A number of persons from the locality joined in the procession organised by the 'aggressive' Great Harwood Branch, which marched to Blackburn.

"Twelve months have elapsed since the provision of dinners for necessitous scholars commenced in Church and Oswaldtwistle. An Average of 70 children are feed six days per week under the direction of Mr. Norman, the school attendance officer." ['Observer' December 5th.1931]

At the Haslingden Guardians Annual Meeting, held on December 2nd. the NUWM's deputation to the Accrington Relief Committee was discussed and it was agreed that a group of 8 should be received and allowed to put their case. The result was that by 18 votes to 10 the Committee rejected a proposal that they should refuse to administer the means test. Support for the resolution was forthcoming from Accrington's Labour Councillors A. Dawson and T. O'Connor, and from the Conservative S. Tetlow. An interesting fact to come out of the discussion was provided by Coun. O'Connor who pointed out that "under the old Board of Guardians the scale for a child under 16 in 1916 was 3s 6d., in 1918 - 4s 6d., and in 1921 - 10s. 6d. From 1928 to 1930 they allowed 36s.[£1 16s.] for man and wife and three children." However, a resolution was unanimously adopted expressing the opinion:

"That the recently adopted scale of out-relief is still below subsistence level particularly where applicants for relief or transitional benefits are responsible for excessive rents, and urging the County Committee further to consider the matter with a view to its increase." ['Observer' December 5th.1931]

On Monday, December 7th., at the Accrington and Church Co-operative Society monthly meeting, members protested against the means test and agreed that the Society would not divulge information on members savings etc. to the PAC unless subpoenaed by a court. ['Observer' December 8th.1931]

At the Rishton Trades Council meeting, December 8th., Mrs Fish pointed out that the scale in Preston [covering the Lancashire County Council area] was 23s. 3d. for man and wife and 2s. for each child, but in Blackburn [County Borough] the scale was 2s. higher in the first case and 1s. in the second.

The half-yearly report of the Rishton Weavers' Association complained about the means test and in particular:

> "To deprive parents of benefits because they have children working, or some other members of the family are working, is gross injustice. We must agitate and protest until these grave scandals are removed." ['Observer' December 12th.1931]

GREAT HARWOOD DEMONSTRATOR'S COURT CASE.

On Wednesday, December 9th., the case against Richard Rutter and his wife Edith, of 36 Haywood Street, Great Harwood, who had been arrested during the unemployment demonstration on December 1st., took place at Accrington Police Court. He was charged with three offences, the conducting of an unlawful procession, conduct likely to cause a breach of the peace, and with an assault on the police. However, during the proceedings the first two charges were dropped. His wife was charged with obstructing a police constable in the execution of his duty. Both pleaded not guilty. The 'Observer' of December 12th., reported the following:

"P.C. Bernasconi said he was in company of P.C. Smith on Bull Bridge. He went to defendant and said, 'I am going to report you for conduct likely to cause a breach of the peace.' He said, 'You're what!' At the same time he struck witness in the left ribs with his elbow. P.C. Smith then took him into custody and he became very violent. The male defendant said it was untrue that he banged the constable in the ribs."

"Witness said the woman defendant came to the assistance of her husband, and attempted to free him. She caught hold of P.C. Smith's right hand and attempted to force herself between him and Rutter. Both were taken into custody, locked up, and afterwards bailed out......"

"Defendant said he was walking down the middle of the street. He would give P.C. Bernasconi his due - he was very nice with him - but P.C. Smith forced his arm behind his back, and it was that he objected to. As they went along he asked his wife to take his watch and chain. He appealed to Sergt. Cunliffe that it did not require them to shove his arm up his back and told them he would go to the Police Station quietly."

"Mrs. Rutter said the police had her husband's arm in his back.

He shouted to her and asked her to take his watch and chain, which were in danger of falling to the ground. The constable told her it would be alright, and put it in her husband's pocket again. He then said, 'You are under arrest,' and that was all she did."

"The defendant called several witnesses. A man at the back of the Court declared that a list of witnesses had been sent to the Court by registered post, but the Clerk said it had not been received."

"Herbert Owen, unemployed, of 214 Queen Street, Great Harwood, said he was not in the procession, but he saw Mr. Rutter on Bull Bridge, and he did not assault the police."

"Eleanor Jakeman, 6 Castle Street, Accrington, also said defendant did not use violence. The constable did it to him; he had his hands in his back."

"Mary Bibby, 23 Castle Street, corroborated."

"The magistrates retired, and on their return the Mayor announced that the Bench had decided that the case against the man was proved, and they ordered him to pay the cost of the proceedings. [4s.] In regard to the case against the woman they found the charge not proved, and dismissed the case."

UNEMPLOYMENT CONTINUED.

The GMWU Engineering Shop Stewards had as their guest speaker, the manager of the Labour Exchange, Mr. Humphries, who gave a description of the new Unemployment Anomalies Act. [Minute Book, December 10th.1931]

The 'Observer' December 12th., also printed the following letter from Labour Councillors, Dawson, Roberts and O'Connor, attacking Conservative Councillor Tetlow:

"Coun. Tetlow, while a member of the [Accrington Relief] Committee voted against the undersigned on every occasion when we proposed an increase over the scale."

"We have consistently opposed in committee the calculation of disability pensions, war pensions or widows pensions being regarded as part of family income and Coun. Tetlow just as consistently voted against us. We have constantly opposed in committee the concept of family grouping, which has meant, in effect, that every unit of the family is regarded in turn as head of the family, which concept has meant in effect that father must maintain mother and the family, or mother must maintain father and the family, brother must maintain sister, or sister must maintain brother, parents maintain adult children, or adult children must maintain parents, which ever suits the purposes of the regulation."

"We also have been tempted to resign, but have preferred for the present to remain, with the object of giving better treatment to our unfortunate citizens than Preston has decreed. We therefore suggest that if Coun. Tetlow really disagreed with the scale, that when he was on the committee he should have voted with those of us who have tried to ignore it, and that he should have remained to give his support to those of us who are pursuing and are prepared to pursue this policy, instead of leaving us to be voted down by those members of the committee who will vote for the miserable scale without regard to the miseries they inflict on their fellow citizens."

On December 14th, Clayton-Le-Moors' NUWM, held a social and supper in the Co-operative Assembly rooms, with the intention of raising money to provide a Christmas treat for the children of the unemployed. About 300 people attended. ['Observer' December 22nd.1931]

NUWM MARCH FROM GREAT HARWOOD TO RISHTON.

At Rishton on December 15th., 50 police were on duty, when a large body of NUWM members proceeded from Great Harwood to the township. The PAC were meeting with a deputation of Rishton's unemployed at Hanson's Mill, where the PAC's offices where situated. The Great Harwood crowd surrounded the building and refused to disperse. At that point Supt. Pagett called on his men and the demonstrators were moved on, but only to the other side of the Canal Bridge. After a while the police called out the available strength of the police division and cleared the road. The marchers then gathered at the bus terminus to await the arrival of members of the PAC, but the police again moved them on. ['Observer' December 22nd.1931]

COMMUNISTS MARCH TO MOORLANDS.

On December 16th., Communists from Accrington, Bacup and Rawtenstall joined up with their Haslingden comrades to march to the PAC's offices. The procession contained three hundred people and there was an accompanying crowd of several hundreds. Twelve, or so, managed to slip inside the premises and presented themselves as a deputation to the committee, which would report to the full Guardians Committee. The deputation won no concessions and eventually left. The 'processionists left for their respective towns but in demonstrative mood.' ['Observer' December 19th. 1931]

UNEMPLOYMENT CONTINUED.

Conservative controlled Church UDC, on December 17th., after an interesting discussion on the reduced scale of benefits, passed unanimously a resolution of protest. Copies where to be sent to the Prime Minister, the Minister of Labour and Major Procter MP. Their one representative on the Guardians Committee resigned.

On the same day Conservative controlled Rishton UDC, who had no representative on the Guardians Committee, could find no volunteer to take up the position. ['Observer' December 19th.] The local PAC must have been made up of appointees from Preston, although Mrs. Fish, from Rishton Labour Party, appears to have been a co-opted member.

At the Conservative controlled Oswaldtwistle UDC meeting, held on December 24th., their representative on the PAC, Mrs. Harrison stated that she had resigned her position. No one volunteered to take her place. The meeting also passed a resolution against the administration of the means test. ['Observer' December 29th. 1931]

On New Year's Eve, the Lancashire PAC debated the means test for two hours. Even Mr. G. E. Slack, the right-wing chairman of the Haslingden Guardians was aggrieved at the situation saying:

"Remember in dealing with applicants for transitional payments we are dealing with a class of person very different from the average applicant for poor-law relief. In industrial areas they were dealing with thousands of cases; his own sub-committee had between 5,000 and 6,000 cases"

The meeting eventually passed the following resolutions:

"1. That, as in the opinion of the committee, the Order in Council requires that the same scale should be applied in the case of applicants for transitional payments as in ordinary relief cases, and, in view of the problems raised they recommend that a sub-committee be appointed to consider and make recommendations upon the revision of the existing scale and regulations." [unanimously]

"2. That in the meantime Guardians' Committees and sub-committees be expected to conform generally to the scale of allowances and regulations for the administration of public assistance in determining amounts of unemployment insurance transitional payments, without being required to report departures therefrom in those special individual cases in which exceptional circumstances exist." [17 votes to 15]

"3. That for the present, and in lieu of the requirement that all such departures be reported, the several Clerks to Guardians Committees be instructed to advise the PAC of any unreasonable departure not in keeping with the spirit of the regulations or of any consistent course of action contrary thereto." [16 votes to 9] ['Observer' January 2nd.1932]

1932

At the Clayton-Le-Moors UDC meeting January 4th., letters were read from the Clerk to the Guardians Committee of the Blackburn and Clitheroe Section of the Lancashire PAC, pleading for the Council to nominate absolutely anybody it could think of, to act on the Committee. With Councillor Joinson having just resigned, the UDC found it impossible to nominate anyone, and so the position remained vacant. The meeting also carried the following resolution:

"That the attention of the Minister of Labour be drawn to the hardship created by the operation of Regulation 4ii of the Unemployment Insurance [Anomalies] Regulations 1931, and urging him to amend the regulations so as to provide that any decision as to whether a person can reasonably expect to obtain insurable employment in the district shall be arrived at on the assumption that conditions of trade are normal." ['Observer' January 5th. 1932]

Also on January 4th. at the Accrington Town Council Meeting, Councillor Robinson resigned from the PAC, and was replace by Alderman Barlow. This gave Coun. Dawson, Labour, who was still on the PAC, the chance to make a political speech, in which he said:

"We want to know whether you [the Town Council] will give us some backing in trying to break down these pernicious regulations which are being utilised for starving thousands of people in Accrington." ['Observer' January 5th.1932]

Later that day the Oswaldtwistle Co-operative Society held its Quarterly Meeting at which the President, Mr. H. Hurst, condemned the means test and expressed his sympathy with those who had gone through the experience. ['Observer' January 5th 1932]

There was a good attendance at the Clayton-Le-Moors Labour Party, on January 5th., when they passed a resolution against the means test and its application. Copies were sent to the Prime Minister and Major Procter MP. ['Observer' January 9th.1932]

At the Haslingden Guardians Committee Meeting, Councillor Dawson moved and Councillor O'Connor seconded, a proposal that a deputation of the unemployed should be received, but only two other members of the committee voted in favour. ['Observer' 9th. January -article corrected as above in the 'Observer' January 16th.1932]

At the Blackburn and Clitheroe Area Sub-Committee of the Lancashire PAC, held at Blackburn on January 7th., the resignations of the Oswaldtwistle, Church, and Clayton-Le-Moors representatives was announced. With the sanction of the County Committee and the Minister of Health, it was stated that the Act was now being administered in those districts by the Clerk, Mr. W.I. Bentley.

Mrs. Fish, Rishton, protested against a statement made by Major Procter MP., who had inaccurately stated in a speech in the Division, that the Committee had full discretion in administering the Act. She said that he 'knew perfectly well that they were not only tied down by the Order of Council, but also by the scale adopted by the Lancashire PAC.' ['Observer' January 9th.1932]

The same issue of the 'Observer' quoted from the Clayton-Le-Moors Weavers' Association's Quarterly Report:

"The conditions under which the unemployed workpeople have been existing have been greatly aggravated by the Unemployment Anomalies Act, and by the Means Test. Under the Anomalies Act a great number of married women are being deprived of unemployment benefits..... In the cotton trade areas....it has always been customary for women to go to work in the cotton mills after marriage. In fact it would have been impossible to staff the mills in normal times without the married women. It is a great hardship that women, who would undoubtedly have been working if work was available, should now be deprived of unemployment benefits."

On January 12th., the 'Observer' Editorial, 'Observ[er]ations,' felt obliged to write the following:

"My Oswaldtwistle correspondent, writes 'Are the unemployed of Oswaldtwistle, Church, and Clayton-Le-Moors receiving the same benefits as the unemployed of Accrington?' From enquiries I have made I can state definitely that they are not, and that they are being less generously treated by comparison. Abundant evidence can be presented in proof of that statement and as the allowances come from public funds it is high time that steps were taken to remedy the grievances of the unemployed of the three townships."

"The first grievance is in regard to allowances for rent. In Accrington, the unemployed applicant for transitional benefit who lives in a house for which he pays a rent of 10s. is allowed 5s.and his unemployment pay is increased by that amount.......in the districts.....no such allowance is made......"

"In Accrington allowances are made in respect of the weekly sums paid for insurance and for trade union contributions. In the three townships no such allowances are made."

"Surely these facts are a call to the members of the Guardians Committee of the three townships to resume the administration of the means test and to determine that the unemployed of their area shall be treated at least as generously as the unemployed of Accrington......Let our representatives resume.....and not leave the administration of the means test entirely to officials."

On Thursday, 21st. January, at a meeting of Church UDC, it was reported that the situation was perceived to be so serious in the Blackburn and Clitheroe Guardians area, that a meeting of local authorities involved, had been held in Blackburn. Church, Clayton-Le-Moors, Great Harwood, and Oswaldtwistle were represented from the Greater Accrington district. The recommendations coming from the meeting, and which the Lancashire PAC, refused to receive were as follows:

"a. Where two families live in the same house, the case for each family should be taken separately.

b. Adult members of a family who are boarding should be considered for income at board rates.

c. Wages of sons-in-law, daughters-in-law not to be included in a family income.

d. After obtaining the income actually received by a family, the transitional payments to be assessed in accordance with the scale of payments as recommended by the meeting.

e. That the Order be interpreted to mean that amounts of transitional payments shall not be based upon out-relief scale, but upon the needs of the applicant, providing such payments do not exceed the amounts payable as ordinary Unemployment Insurance benefit.

f. Increases in scale payments were recommended as follows:- Man and wife 25s., plus maximum rent allowance of 10s. per week. Four shillings in respect of the first and second child, and 3s. for each additional child under 16 years of age. Ten shillings for young persons aged 16 to 20 inclusive. Adult man 15s. 3d. with rent and rate allowance, if householder. Adult woman 13s. 3d., with rent and rate allowance, if householder.

    g. Savings or investments in possession of applicant or his wife, or both, up to £100 to be ignored. Over £100 to £250 - 5 % to be assessed as income. Over £500 applicant not to be considered to be in need. Savings of members of family who are not applicants to be ignored.

    h. Disability pensions to be ignored. Special consideration to be given to war dependants' pensions. Widow's pensions - 50% to be ignored. Workmen's compensation claimants and equivalent to be ignored. Other pensions to be considered as income of recipient and not of family.

    i. 10s. of each person's earnings to be ignored.

    j. Applicants appearing before the Committee to be allowed trade union representation." ['Observer' January 23rd.1932]

The above recommendations did not come from a meeting of Socialists, all the local UDC's were controlled by supporters of the National Government. The actions of the National Government were therefore viewed, by at least some of its supporters in the local industrial areas, as being too harsh. The Lancashire PAC however, with representative from more rural areas, showed no compassion and continued to adopted the hard line Government regulations.

The Lancashire PAC at its meeting in Preston, January 25th., did hear the report of their own special sub-committee on relief scales. This did suggest that able bodied single persons should be relieved according to circumstances, but at a lower rate than unemployment insurance benefit. It was also proposed that the allowances for children aged 12 to 16 should be raised from 2s. to 3s. Councillor R.I. Constantine, Accrington, voted in favour of the proposals, but Councillor Slack, Accrington, opposed them. The proposals were defeated. [Observer' January 26th.1932]

At Accrington Town Council Meeting, February 1st., Councillor Tetlow, Conservative, withdrew his motion which read as follows:

> "That this Council do urge the Government to take from the PAC's and their Guardians Committees the onus of deciding transitional payments by way of the means test, and place the same entirely in the hands of the Ministry of Labour.

The discussion on the subject could not be discussed due to the motion being withdrawn. ['Observer' February 2nd.1932]

The Accrington TCLP, had Mr. Charles Roden Buxton, as their guest speaker at the Town Hall, Monday 1st. February. Councillor Dawson chairing the meeting, spoke of the means test as 'pernicious in principle.' ['Observer' February 6th.1932]

On Thursday 4th. of February, a deputation from the Accrington Textile Trades Federation, comprising of Mr. Hughes, Oswaldtwistle Weavers, Mr. R. Armistead, Warehousemen, Mr. H. Potts, Cardroom Workers, and Councillor Hope, Clayton-Le-Moors Weavers, had an interview with the Parliamentary Secretary to the Minister of Health, in London, to discuss the anomalies and hardships arising out of the regulations governing the application of the means test. No comments were reported after the one hour long meeting. ['Observer' February 6th.1932]

On Wednesday February 3rd., the Haslingden Guardians Committee, had the following figures, up to the end of January, presented to them: ['Observer' February 6th.1932]

Given full benefit	992
Given partial benefit	3,594
Given nothing	4,106
Total applicants	8,602

The 'Observer' reported that a batch of applications for transitional benefit, supported by the Accrington PAC, had been turned down by the Lancashire PAC in Preston. In the County's opinion the Accrington Committee had been too generous in dealing with applicants who possessed minor resources. This was the first time that Accrington's interpretation of the regulations had been questioned. ['Observer' February 13th.1932]

At the Co-operative Assembly Rooms, Oak Street, Accrington, February 18th., a meeting, under the auspices of the Accrington TCLP, was held to discuss the means test. Representatives took part from trade unions, working men's clubs, co-operative societies, ex-servicemen, and a few religious bodies, the room being 'fairly full'. The address was given by Mr. J.W. Sunderland, Secretary of Great Harwood Weavers and the chair was taken by Councillor Dawson. The following resolution was carried unanimously:

> "That this meeting,......emphatically protests against the submission of applicants for transitional benefits to a means test based upon Poor Law standards, and calls upon the Government to introduce legislation which will have as its object the removal of the stigma of pauperism from people who satisfy the conditions of being normally available for and seeking insurable employment." ['Observer' February 20th.1932]

During his opening remarks Councillor Dawson quoted from the Manchester Guardian:

> "To the effect that while the average of cases turned down by

the PAC was 16 % for the whole country, the average for Lancashire was 31%, and the average for the Haslingden Union was higher than that for Lancashire...... 'This,' he said, 'meant that the districts where unemployment was heaviest suffered most, while residential districts escaped, which was only another way of saying that the poor had to pay.'"

On the 29th. February, at the Accrington Town Council Meeting, the public seats in the Council Chamber were all occupied an hour before the start and large numbers were unable to gain admission. The reason for such crowds was the fact that Councillor Dawson had given notice of his intention of moving the following resolution:

"That this Council enters its emphatic protest against the submission of applicants for transitional benefits to a 'means test,' based on Poor Law standards and calls upon the Government immediately to introduce legislation the object of which will be to provide assistance to those who satisfy the condition that they are available for, and are endeavouring to secure, employment in an insurable occupation, the administration of such benefits to be vested with the Ministry of Labour."

However, the public were to be denied their right to hear the debate, because Councillor Tetlow, Conservative, rose and proposed that the Council go into Committee and discuss the topic in private. At this Councillor O'Connor, Labour said that Councillor Tetlow's attitude "was childish," especially since Tetlow had run away from discussing the matter a month earlier. Unfortunately for the public, the Council voted by 14 votes to 12 to discuss the matter in private, where it was passed by a large majority. The attitude of Tetlow and his colleagues did not endear them to the people expelled from the public gallery, or Accrington's unemployed. ['Observer' March 1st.1932]

Even the 'Observer' was not amused, saying, "for many reasons this is to be regretted, as from all accounts the discussion was of a very high standard." In fact, so eager where they to give the public a taste of the debate, they allowed Councillor Dawson, Labour, to write two full columns in the March 5th. issue of the paper, in which he gave an account of the proceedings from his point of view.

The Accrington AEU District Committee heard a report of the proceedings of the Joint Trades deputation to the local PAC on February 29th. [Minute Book March 3rd.1932]

Also on the 29th. February, the Lancashire PAC Meeting was the scene of yet another animated discussion on transitional relief. The Central Relief Sub-Committee had recommended that the scale of payments be increased by the substitution of 3s. for 2s. in the case of the first three children under 16 years of age. This was rejected by 18 votes to 14. ['Observer' March 1st.1932]

On Wednesday, March 2nd., the Haslingden Guardians' Committee again discussed transitional benefits and the County PAC's attitude on claimants' assets. After much debate, the Committee passed the following resolution unanimously:

"That this committee was of the opinion that the method now adopted in dealing with cases of transitional payments where assets are taken into consideration is acting with undue harshness in this area, and requests the PAC of the County to reconsider the decision." ['Observer' March 5th.1932]

At the No.5 Area Guardians Committee [Blackburn and Clitheroe] meeting held on Wednesday March 2nd., a resolution was carried unanimously, protesting against the attitude of the PAC and suggested that assets of £100 should be ignored when calculating payments. ['Observer' March 5th.1932]

The Accrington TCLP held a public meeting in the Labour Hall, on Sunday evening, March 6th., at which Councillor Dawson challenged Major Procter MP. to debate with him in public the topic of the means test. Procter did not take him up on the offer. ['Observer' March 8th.1932]

On the 16th. March, at the Lancashire County Council Meeting, there was an unsuccessful attempt to remove Councillor R.I. Constantine, Accrington, from the County PAC. The situation arose when the County was re-appointing three non-County Borough representatives onto the PAC, one of whom was Councillor Constantine.

Mr. George Tomlinson, Farnworth [later to become Rishton Weavers' Secretary and eventually the Minister of Education in Attlee's post-war Government] supported Councillor Constantine. However, Councillor Slack, Accrington, accused Constantine of "throwing mud" and hoped that he would not be re-appointed. Constantine survived by 37 votes to 36. ['Observer' March 19th.1932]

At the No. 9 Area Education Committee at Rishton, March 21st., outspoken comments were made by representatives of all political parties against the miserly 2s. allowance for children under the means test.['Observer' March 22nd.1932]

On March 30th., the Lancashire PAC rejected a call to increase the scale of outdoor relief for children from 2s. to 3s., by 28 votes to 11. ['Observer' April 2nd.1932]

The 'Observer April 16th, reported on the work of the National Unemployed Association, Accrington branch, a moderate grouping. They had set up a bureau to give advice for means test cases. Mr. J. Cuthbertson, president,

said:
> "Since January we have dealt with about 250 cases.....and 75% of the cases have had a successful issue.....We render these services without any question of creed or political belief."

The Accrington AEU District Committee on April 21st., heard a report of a conference of all local associations held to discuss ways to protect claimants against the vicious operation of the means test. This conference had taken place on April 19th. and was followed up by another on April 25th. A sub-committee was formed from the delegates and this continued to meet, at least once a month, until Spring 1933. [AEU Minute Book] The GMWU was represented by Bro. R. Dawson, who remained their delegate throughout. [GMWU Minute Book, Branch Committee May 5th.]

At Accrington Town Hall, on May 23rd., a meeting of 116 men and women representing 60 different organisations in the Accrington area, took place to discuss the means test. The idea for such meetings Countywide, originated from the Mayor of Darwen, who chaired the meeting, in place of Councillor Constantine, [first Labour Mayor of Accrington] who had been very seriously ill in hospital. The meeting agreed unanimously to set up a District Committee consisting of two representatives from each organisation attending that evening. ['Observer' May 24th.1932]

On Thursday May 26th., Oswaldtwistle UDC received a deputation of unemployed workmen, who complained about the recruitment arrangements for engaging men on the sewerage reconstruction work scheme; part of the government's work creation programme. The men were supposed to be taken on for an eight week period and then replaced by other unemployed men on the register. The deputation was angry that certain individuals were receiving privileged treatment by being kept on for, in some cases, 24 weeks. The Council agreed to the mens' demands, except for a limited number of key tradesmen. ['Observer' May 28th.1932]

At the Lancashire PAC, Monday May 30th., a memorandum was presented to the meeting of an interview that had taken place with a Joint Deputation from the LCMF and the United Textile Workers Association, regarding transitional benefits. The deputation had complained that they were receiving a lower scale than applied in neighbouring county boroughs. They accepted that the PAC could not pay more than unemployment benefit but submitted that a distinction could be drawn between ordinary Poor-law cases and transitional payments. The 'Observer' stated:
> "The deputation also raised questions relating to the method of applying the public assistance scale, and contended that the expression used in the Order in Council 'shall make such inquiries and otherwise

deal with the [transitional] cases as if they were estimating the need of an unemployed able-bodied person who had applied for Public Assistance' was not intended to mean other than the form of inquiry, and that it was wrong for the PAC to construe the phrase as meaning that the scale of assessment and scale of benefit should be that of the Poor Law scale." ['Observer' May 31st.1932]

The PAC debated the report but decided to maintain their interpretation of the regulations.

In Accrington, Monday 13th. June, a meeting took place of the Council, recently formed to deal with injustices and anomalies created by the means test. It was held at the Cannon Street Baptist School. The Rev. A.W. Wardle, presided, Miss Helena Worsley [Weavers] was Secretary, and the speaker was Mr. G.K. Chalmers [Engineers]. Representatives of various trade unions, churches, political parties, working mens clubs, and womens guilds were present. It was arranged for an Executive of 15 to be elected under the Chairmanship of the Rev. Wardle. ['Observer' June 18th.1932]

The 'Observer' July 9th. reported that 382 recipients received out-relief in Accrington for the week ending June 25th.

On July 29th., a meeting took place in Accrington, of the East Lancashire Joint Committee for the consideration of the application of the means test, with the Chairman of the Accrington Committee, Rev. A.W. Wardle, presiding. It was reported that a deputation had been down to London to see the Under Secretary of State, but had received no joy. They were told that applicants must be treated as for Poor Law relief, except that money paid must be in cash and not in kind. In addition they were informed that there was no chance of any changes taking place until at least 1933, when the Royal Commission would be presenting its findings. ['Observer' July 30th.1932]

The above organisation later became known as the Association of Societies for Protection against the Means Test. In the 'Observer' September 10th. it was stated they had sent a lengthy resolution to the Government, local MP's, Lancashire County Council, and the chairmen of the PAC's for the district. It included the following paragraph:

> "We would emphasise that in lodging this protest, we are voicing the wishes of many thousands of citizens of all political parties who view with alarm the imposition of undue hardships upon a class of people which has hitherto been the backbone of the nation."

It was signed by the members of the Joint Committee:

> "Miss H. Worsley; Rev. A.W. Wardle, Supt., Accrington Wesleyan Circuit; W. Fairhurst, Accrington Chamber of Trade; G.K. Chalmers, JP., Amalgamated Engineering Union, Accrington; W.

Haines, Unitarian Church, Accrington; Rev. H. Motley, Cannon Street Baptist Church, Accrington; G.F. Kilshaw, Accrington Weavers' Association; A. Waring, JP., Great Harwood UDC; G. Fox, Great Harwood Textile Warehousemen; C. Roach, Great Harwood Working Men's Clubs; J. Okell, Great Harwood Labour Party; H. Townley, secretary, Great Harwood Ministers' Fraternal; J.W. Sunderland, JP., Great Harwood Weavers' Association and Great Harwood Trades Council; L. Airey, Darwen Conservative Association; H. Smalley, JP., chairman, Darwen Liberal Association; J.K. Bailey, JP., Darwen Weavers' Association; J.C. Richardson, Darwen Trades Council and Labour Party; Mrs. Mayoh, Darwen Trades Council and Labour Party; Mrs. Flint, Society of Friends, Darwen; C.H. Haworth, Society of Friends, Darwen; G. Ashworth, Pickup Bank Congregational Church, Darwen."

Mr. Jamieson, Secretary of the Accrington Branch of the National Unemployed Association, sent a letter to the 'Observer', September 24th., stating that the Mayor, Councillor R.I. Constantine, Labour, had challenged them to get off their backsides and to demonstrate against the means test. The branch said they were prepared to organise a march to the local PAC, if Constantine would lead them. The Mayor replied:

"I cannot accede to your request to lead a deputation to the local Guardians Committee to protest against the means test. I am, every month, doing my agitating at Preston, on the PAC there, which controls the local Committee."

The above organisation appeared to be ultra moderate and friendly with Major Procter MP., Conservative, who tried to have the best of both worlds by saying locally that the Act was being wrongly interpreted by the Conservative and Liberal controlled PAC's, whilst nationally he was supporting the Governments hardline approach to public spending cuts. Constantine was right to urge them into action on their own account.

The Lancashire PAC, Monday September 26th., was annoyed that some single men had been moving out of their family home and into lodgings in order to obtain transitional relief. They therefore passed the following resolution:

"That outdoor relief shall not be allowed to persons removing into lodgings for the purpose of securing relief which would otherwise not be obtained."

The PAC also informed the Ministry of Labour that they were having problems with local Guardians Committees disregarding the terms of the Order in Council and the administration of test work. They maintained the line, that the Minister of Health had ruled that the amount of work required to be performed by able-bodied men in receipt of relief should not be varied according to the amount of relief granted. Certain local authorities had apparently stated that they would only order test work in proportion to the amount of relief paid [and rightly so]. ['Observer' September 27th.] I think that this latter point really shows the Conservative-Liberal majority, on the Lancashire PAC to be basically evil. Such an attitude cannot be defended by human beings, it was a policy of slavery.

The 'Observer' October 1st., published a letter from Mr.J. Jamieson of the Accrington, National Unemployed Association, in which he attacked the actions of the Lancashire PAC.

The number receiving out-relief in Accrington, week-ending September 24th., was 591. ['Observer' October 4th.1932]

The 'Observer' October 8th., reported that 250 Hunger Marchers had taken possession of Nova Scotia Mills in Blackburn, in order to shelter from the heavy rain, but they were evicted by the police. They spent the night at the Queens Park Institution, before setting off in the direction of Darwen. They also mentioned a contingent marching from Nelson and Colne to Manchester, where they would join up with the main demonstration.

The letters from Mr. J. Jamieson became progressively more militant. On October 29th. he demanded that the representatives on the PAC's resign, because their operation of the means test had only brought "poverty, and plenty of it, and destitution." He said that the Accrington branch would rather deal with a government official than with the members of the local PAC, and he asked electors not to vote for members of the PAC in the local elections.

The Mayor of Accrington, Councillor Constantine, figured prominently at the Lancashire PAC meeting in Preston, October 31st. He had criticised Councillor Mr. W.A. Spofforth, Chairman of the Committee, who was absent from the meeting. Apparently Spofforth had written an article attacking the way in which transitional benefits were administered. Constantine remarked that:

> "Mr. Spofforth, had been more responsible than any other member of the Committee for the harsh and inhuman way the means test had been administered by the Lancashire County Council. It appeared from the article that he had completely turned round and expressed the opposite view."

Constantine was attacked by the Conservative-Liberal majority and the meeting became very heated. Later in the meeting, Constantine was jeered from different parts of the room, causing him to say:

> "I wish you would calm those people, Mr. Chairman."

A member retorted:

> "The only way to keep the meeting calm is for you to stop at Accrington."

To which, Constantine replied:
"They let me out sometimes." ['Observer' November 1st.1932]

The Great Harwood Weavers' Association commented on the Report of the Royal Commission on Unemployment Insurance, saying that it contained recommendations for a reduction of benefits and a wider application of the Means Test. They said that whatever scheme was devised, it would be unacceptable to them "unless it provided an adequate maintenance for unemployed persons and their families." [Half-Yearly Report, November 5th.1932]

The 'Observer' November 19th., reported that 123 Accrington men were employed upon the two relief schemes, these being the construction of the new Fire Station and Police Courts, and the conversion of ashpits. In Oswaldtwistle, 66 men were employed on the new sewerage works relief scheme.

Lively interruptions took place at the Accrington and District Council for the Consideration of the Means Test, in Accrington Town Hall, on November 22nd. The hubbub occurred when Labour Party delegates questioned the chairman, the Rev. A. W. Wardle, how it was that Mr. A. Dawson was not on the platform? Mr. Wardle explained that Mr. Dawson was publicly committed to the abolition of the means test and that when the organisation was founded, with himself as leader, he had definitely stated that he would be "no party whatsoever to the abolition of the test. He had to think of every political party in the town."

Mr. Joe Robinson sprang to his feet describing the meeting as "an insult to the intelligence of the workers, and that any man who was simply out to discuss the means test was a coward."

The Mayor, Councillor Constantine, supported Mr. Dawson's right to be on the platform, but this did not happen. The following resolution was carried by a large majority of the delegates, only three voting against:

"This meeting of the citizens of Accrington and District welcomes the changes made in the means test, but still considers that many of the evils of the test remain, and regrets that there has not been a more generous treatment of applicants for transitional benefit. We deplore the tendencies which still exists to lower the status of the unemployed to Poor Law standards, the manner of calculating family income, which imposes unfair hardship upon the relatives of claimants and is injurious to the best interests of family life, and also the low standard of savings allowed by the regulations, which penalises thrift and imposes unmerited hardships upon a class of people which hitherto has been the backbone of the nation." ['Observer' November 26th.1932]

Councillor Constantine again took a prominent part in the November

28th., meeting of the Lancashire PAC. The Leigh area had protested against the disallowance of benefit to nearly 100 unmarried persons who, it was alleged, had left home to secure benefit. Councillor Constantine supported the reference back, saying:

> "He wanted to ask Mr. Spofforth, who he understood had the ear of the Prime Minister, whether the household income regulations were to be broadened. The method of arriving at the family income was worse than in the old Poor Law days when a son-in-law, stepfather, aunt, or uncle, and so on were never taken into account. To-day all who lived in a house were lumped together."

The proposal to refer the minute back was defeated and so benefit was not given. ['Observer' November 29th.1932]

Over 300 children of the totally unemployed of Accrington, took part in a Christmas breakfast on December 24th at Union Buildings Mill in the rooms of the Accrington and District Unemployed Association. Mr. J. Jamieson, secretary, said, they were thankful to the various local shopkeepers and others who had helped in the treat. He went on to say that the organisation was non-political, and that they had been able to relieve the lot of the unemployed working man in many ways. ['Observer' December 31st.1932]

1933

On Sunday, January 15th., at the Accrington AEU Shop Stewards Meeting, the President Bro. Herbert Rothwell, criticised the payment of transitional benefits through the PAC's. The data possessed by the local AEU showed that payments were altogether too small. ['Observer' January 21st.1933]

In the report of the Haslingden Guardians Committee, of Wednesday, January 25th., Councillor Lambert, Accrington, asked what was the standard sum that should be paid for a person who was in the infirmary? He had noticed that in one case it had been decided to recover the old age pension of 10s. per week and that the balance was paid by the daughter. The Clerk stated that the cost of maintenance was £1 6s 10d per week, and therefore the pension was taken and the daughter paid 16s 10d per week towards the parent's upkeep. ['Observer' January 28th.] Councillor Lambert was probably amazed at how anyone could afford to contribute in such a way.

At the Lancashire PAC, Monday January 30th., the officers had stated that the cost of outdoor relief had increased substantially. Councillor Constantine commented that when unemployment benefit and other services were cut by the Exchequer, the Tories and Liberals on the Committee were most satisfied. Now they were upset because of the effects claimants were having on the local rates. ['Observer' January 31st.1933]

On Sunday February 5th., the Accrington AEU Shop Stewards passed a resolution calling on their National Executive Council to lodge a strong protest with the Ministry of Health against Health Insurance arrears during periods of genuine unemployment, which, in their opinion was calculated to strike a deliberate and vital blow at the most unfortunate section of the community. Also the local District Committee was asked to protest "against the inquisitorial methods of the PAC's in administration of the Means Test." ['Observer' February 7th.1933]

The new headquarters for the Accrington branch of the National Unemployed Association, situated in what was formerly Union Buildings Mill, Union Street, was officially opened by the Mayor, Councillor Constantine, on Saturday February 11th. Mr. H. Taylor, president, chaired the event, and said that although only started four months ago, they had now got a membership of 150 paying 1d. per week. The Association had been formed to try to abolish the means test. The Mayor said:

> "It was not the wish of any member of the Council that the various schemes we have in hand for providing work for people have been dropped. I think the Government are now realising the mistake they made in stopping these schemes, and there are signs on every hand that these schemes will have to be resumed. The Accrington Town Council will be one of the first municipal authorities to take advantage of that....." ['Observer' February 14th.1933]

A Mass Meeting of AEU members was held in the AEU Rooms, Blackburn Road, Accrington, on Sunday morning March 12th.. Bro. Rothwell, President, announced that the meeting had been called to enable the rank and file to record their opinion on the new situation that arose under the National Health Insurance Act, regarding the arrears of unemployed members. The Secretary, Bro. Chalmers JP., explained how arrears would be charged, and gave many examples of anomalies that affected different classes of unemployment. Arrangements were apparently in place whereby members could pay any arrears by instalments, and any of the 10 branch secretaries could give information on how this could be done. A resolution was carried urging the National Executive Committee to protest through the medium of the TUC, and the Labour Party. ['Observer' March 14th.1933]

On April 8th., the 'Observer' reported that Mr. Crompton of the Adelphia Stadium, Accrington, had opened his physical training class to the unemployed on Wednesdays. The Mayor also stated that arrangements could be made for unemployed men to use the swimming baths daily between 1.30 and

2.30 pm., free of charge.

"To ask men to work for four days per week for 10s. is slavery," said Councillor Constantine at the Lancashire PAC, on Monday April 24th. This statement was in reply to the incredible suggestion by the South Lancashire Rivers Catchment Board, that the removal of mounds of earth excavated from the new cuts in the River Glaze would make suitable task work for the unemployed. They had ascertained that it would take 124 men to do the job, but the Leigh Guardians Committee had rightly declined to send men on such a scheme, saying that the work should be performed by paid labour. However, the Central Relief Sub-Committee, of the PAC, recommended that the views of the Ministry of Health should be sought on the matter. Constantine objected saying that the Board should be re-named the 'Catch-Men Board'. As usual, Councillor Slack, true to form thought that the scheme was a good idea. The meeting agreed to forward the scheme to the Ministry of Health for their comments. ['Observer' April 25th.1933]

The Accrington and District Employment Committee at its monthly meeting in the Town Hall, Tuesday 25th. April, heard a resolution, passed by the Bolton Employment Committee, requesting support for an appeal to the Government to remove the assessment of transitional payments from the PAC's and to place its administration under the control of the Employment Exchanges. ['Observer' April 29th.1933]

On Tuesday May 2nd., the keys to the Unemployed Centre in Union Street, Accrington, were handed over to the Mayor, Councillor Constantine. Due to a considerable fall in membership it had been found necessary to close the rooms down. However, Constantine, still thought that some use could be made of the premises for the benefit of the unemployed, and so he called a meeting on Friday May 5th. to discuss the formation of a Council of Service. A number of the town's 'worthies' agreed to serve on this 'non-political' committee, which had the objective of providing vocational facilities in addition to recreational amenities. ['Observer' May 6th.1933]

At the meeting of the Lancashire PAC, Monday May 29th., another sharp exchange took place between Councillor Constantine and Councillor Slack. The Ministry had advised that the task work at the River Glaze site should be carried out as soon as possible, to which Councillor Constantine retorted that it amounted to slavery. Slack thought otherwise and the Chairman, Alderman Hodgson, protested at the use of the phrase 'slavery'. Hodgson then went on to say the following monstrous comment:

> "The object of the Ministry's orders was not to be a deterrent to applicants for relief, but to prevent them rusting, to keep their minds occupied, and to keep them fit." ['Observer' May 30th.1933]

To demand task work of such a nature, however, was an act of class warfare. Men of all ages and backgrounds were conscripted into this 124 strong army of navies. The work was arduous and the payments received were paltry. Slack and Hodgson would not have endured the work for 10 minutes, it would have put their lights out. Constantine was correct when he described the scheme as slavery.

The Rev. H. Motley, issued a strong appeal in support for the Council of Service, from the pulpit of Cannon Street, Baptist Chapel, on Sunday May 28th. He said that one in three employable people in the town were without work, and he believed that it was necessary for the community to provide help in the form of occupational groups, education classes and physical training. He asked for men of ability and knowledge of practical matters, who would go and exercise supervision in the Centre, and announced that the Mayor would be making an official appeal for funds. ['Observer' June 3rd.] His heart was in the right place, but such a scheme could not hope to be successful without numerous full-time staff, paid for out of the rates, or from taxation. Indeed this was to some extent admitted by the Rev. Motley, when in a letter published in the 'Observer' July 1st., he said the following regarding the Council of Service:

"The appeal has produced no flood of willing and generous support, but a mere trickle."

LANCASHIRE HUNGER MARCH TO PRESTON.

'Hunger Marchers' from all parts of the County accompanied a deputation to the Lancashire PAC, on Monday July 24th.. Preston corporation's covered car park was used by the 'marchers' on Sunday night. Earlier, on Saturday afternoon the marchers on their way to Preston, had attempted to hold a meeting in the centre of Accrington, but the police would not permit it. Strong forces of police were on duty in Preston all week-end and the planned march down Fishergate on Monday was banned. Only the deputation was allowed to approach and enter the Council Offices. Three of the marchers, Councillor Throup of Nelson, Mr. Harker of Bolton, and Mrs. Rushton of Oswaldtwistle, addressed the full committee for an hour and ten minutes and demanded the following:

"1. Full scales of benefit for all unemployed whether married or single and full rent allowances;

2. Abolition of task work and repudiation of social centres;

3. Unconditional feeding of necessitous children, free boots and clogs, and full maternity benefit for unemployed mothers;

4. Disregard of the means test;

5. Representation for National Unemployed Workers' Movement [NUWM] and trade unions in local PAC Relief Committees;

6. A resolution from the Lancashire PAC to the National Government protesting against impending economies;

7. More facilities for trade with Soviet Russia."

The 'Observer' reported that Mrs. Rushton made a woman's appeal, paying particular attention to the children. Councillor Constantine said:

"Not only the earnestness of the deputation, but the fact that there were thousands of people outside, proved that the people were waking up to the conditions the committee had deliberately imposed on them."

The Committee decided by 21 votes to 6 to appoint a special committee to look into the marchers' demands. This was merely a delaying tactic to get the marchers 'off their backs' and out of Preston. ['Observer' July 29th.1933]

On September 25th., the Lancashire PAC considered the report of the Special Committee set up after the July demonstration. Unfortunately for the unemployed, Councillor Slack had been appointed its chairman. The report 'rambled on' using legalistic jargon and really did not come out in favour of being more generous to the unlucky mass of people on benefit. After 2 hours of debate the committee voted, by 16 votes to 14, to postpone further consideration pending the announcement of the Government's proposals on the matter. Again, the debate witnessed many lively passages between Councillors Constantine and Slack. At the start, Constantine asked for a deputation from the Lancashire Hunger Marchers' Council to be admitted as observers, but the committee would not allow it. During the debate, Constantine said:

"He did not expect anything better,......It was simple jargon that they had got in the report. He considered the sub-committee had run away from their job, and granted a few concessions without any change of heart or outlook."['Observer' September 26th.1933]

The 'Observer's coverage of the event was quite substantial. Taking into account the size of print used, I would estimate that it would cover at least 3 pages of the typical 1997 edition of the Accrington 'Observer'.

UNEMPLOYMENT CONTINUED.

An example of the condition of the job market, was the 254 applications for the position of gas meter collector in Oswaldtwistle at a wage of £2 14s. per week. Eight men were called for interview by the Gasworks Committee and they chose Mr. J. Hartley of Haworth Street, who had led the efforts to form a limited company to re-start Commercial Mill, Oswaldtwistle. The 'Observer' stated that this was "convincing proof, if such was needed, of the dearth of jobs." ['Observer' October 7th.1933]

The winter session of the Central Co-operative Womens Guild, held in the Assembly Rooms, Oak Street, Accrington, Saturday October 7th., was opened by the Mayor, Councillor Constantine. There was a large gathering of members. Constantine remarked on how the Society's sales had dropped substantially since the means test came into operation. It had, he said, "caused many decent people to be degraded and to suffer in a way they ought not to have done." ['Observer' October 10th.1933]

On Wednesday, October 18th., a large gathering watched the Mayor, re-open the Centre for the Unemployed, instituted by the Accrington Council of Social Service. The centre comprised of two large rooms, one for recreation, the other to be used as a workshop. Tools and benches had been donated by the public. It was envisaged that unemployed men could attend and construct anything they wished. A section of the workshop had been set aside for men to repair the family footwear. It was also announced that 40 to 50 new allotments would become available in the borough, mainly in Baxenden; the rents to be 7s. 6d. per year.]'Observer' October 21st.1933]

The Great Harwood Weavers' Association's Executive Committee, October 18th., refused a request from the 'Lancashire Marchers Council' for use of a room in their headquarters. [Minute Book]

Major Procter, MP., Conservative, had accused the Labour Party of bringing in the means test, and so Mr. F.G. Burgess, Accrington's Prospective Parliamentary Labour candidate, put him right at a public meeting held in the Labour Hall, on Sunday, November 5th. He said:

"That if they wanted the truth of the whole matter it was the National Government itself who instituted it by means of the emergency Act which they passed in the House of Commons when Labour was on the opposition side before the General Election. They fought tooth and nail in a minority and the National Government were entirely responsible for the means test. It was not debated in Parliament. It was done by department, by dictatorship; an Order in Council brought about the means test on the plea of national emergency." ['Observer' November 7th.1933]

At the Great Harwood Weavers' Association's Executive Committee, on November 15th., the Secretary's action in forwarding resolutions to the local MP, and the Trades Council, protesting against the cessation of National Health Insurance Benefit to unemployed persons, was endorsed. [Minute Book]

On Monday, November 27th., Councillor Constantine and 6 other members of the Lancashire PAC, walked out in protest at the Committee's decision not to receive a deputation of 'Hunger Marchers.' The marchers 300 strong had arrived from various parts of South and East Lancashire. The objectives of the march were to demand immediate provision of work schemes with full trade union rates of pay; increased relief and two cwts of coal per week, for each unemployed family; and non operation of the means test. Councillor Constantine declared that it was only "common courtesy" to receive the deputation and said the committee were being "most unfair." ['Observer' November 28th.1933]

The first concert to take place at the Unemployed Centre, Accrington, took place on Wednesday evening December 13th. The choir of Oak Street, Congregational Church presented a burlesque revuette, entitled 'Life and Laughter.' The room was full to overflowing. The 'Observer' December 16th., reported that the "weather was bitterly cold outside, and the warm interior certainly presented a most cheerful sight."

On Saturday, December 23rd., the 'Observer' reported that the supplying of mid-day meals at the Unemployed Mens Centre, Union Street, Accrington, under the scheme of the Council of Social Service, still continued. On Monday 76 meals had been provided, on Tuesday 90, Wednesday 136, and Thursday 127. Whether this was an ongoing event, or just a Christmas Special, the paper does not explain.

At the Lancashire PAC, Thursday 28th., December, Councillor Constantine was again prominent. Apparently, Sir William Brass the Tory MP. for Clitheroe, had condemned the Tory controlled PAC's scale of relief in Parliament, saying that "he hoped in the near future they would make their scale adequate." The Committee, had 'noted' the attack. Constantine said that he had looked up the word in the dictionary, and found that it meant "to heed, observe carefully, attend to," which was not what they were doing in that case. ['Observer' December 30th.1933]

The 'Observer' December 30th. carried a picture of 250 children being sat down to tea on Christmas Day, at the unemployed Centre.

1934

Clayton-Le-Moors Weavers Association were angry about an aspect of the new Ministry of Health scheme, which had become law on January 1st. This was in regards to the rule that all people who had been totally unemployed for over 2.5 years would be ineligible for medical benefit. The Association announced that this would affect no fewer than 300 of their members and so a resolution of protest was sent to the Government. The Secretary, Mr. J.W. Hope, said that the new regulations affected the township more severely than other places in Lancashire. ['Observer' January 6th.1934]

A further concert was held at the Unemployed Centre, Accrington, on Wednesday January 10th, when the 'Tonics' Concert Party, of Whalley Road Methodist Church, gave their services free of charge. ['Observer' January 13th.1934]

A football team from the Unemployed Centre succeeded in defeating a similar team from Oswaldtwistle by 6 goals to 5 at Higham's Playing Fields, Accrington, on Tuesday January 16th. ['Observer' January 20th.1934]

The 'Masqueraders,' a group of young ladies from the Wesley Church, Abbey Street, Accrington, provided the entertainment at a concert held at the Unemployed Centre on Wednesday, January 24th. Councillor and Mrs. Constantine were in attendance. ['Observer' January 27th.1934]

The Lancashire PAC met on Monday, January 29th., and Councillor Constantine stated that the out-relief figures had doubled since the National Government took office. He commented:

"They heard so often that they had turned the corner, but what corner? It was foolish talk. If the figures of the county boroughs [eg. Blackburn etc.] were taken into account, it would be found what the position really was so far as Lancashire was concerned. If the figures for unemployment and Poor Law were given side by side they would be able to judge whether or not unemployment in Lancashire was decreasing." ['Observer' January 30th.1934]

It was reported that the Blackburn and Clitheroe Guardians Committee had considered a request for concessions from the Rishton Relief Committee on behalf of people wishing to take part in a Hunger March to London. The prospective marchers had asked for boots and clothing on loan, together with an undertaking from the PAC that their dependants would be cared for in their absence. The Clerk said that the Ministry ruled that it would be illegal for any committee to supply equipment of that sort and that if dependants became destitute then the committee would have to consider whether the marcher should be proceeded against for the offence.['Observer' February 6th.1934]

At the GMWU Branch Committee meeting, February 1st., the "Lancashire Marchers to London of Unemployed," appealed for financial assistance. A donation was sent but the Minute Book does not state how much.

The Accrington AEU District Committee, on February 7th., refused to give any support to the above march, stating "that the letter from the 'Marchers' Council' lie on the table." [Minute Book]

COUNCILLOR CONSTANTINE DEFEATS COUNCILLOR SLACK IN A HEATED COUNTY COUNCIL ELECTION.

Councillor Constantine spoke at a public meeting held in the Labour Hall, Accrington, Sunday February 11th. He was in the process of fighting a County Council Election against his bitter enemy Councillor Slack. The contest was the talk of the town. In his speech he said the following informative remarks:

"Many people wondered how it came that he was contesting for a seat on the County Council. They thought he was already a member. He was a member of the Lancashire PAC. County boroughs like Blackburn, Burnley, Preston, Manchester and Liverpool controlled their own Poor Law. The Lancashire PAC had nothing to do with them; but there were another 16 municipal boroughs and urban districts over which the PAC had control. This committee was composed chiefly of members of the County Council and a few co-opted members, of which he was one. He was one of three members who represented the non-county boroughs of Lancashire..... When the findings of the PAC came before the County Council, of course, he was not there. As a consequence that was one reason why he wanted to be there."

"He might also remark that occupying the position he did, attempts had been made by one or two persons in previous years to remove him from that PAC. So far they had not been successful,......He wanted to be a member of the County Council so that he could not be removed from the PAC [except] at the desire of the ratepayers......"

"The Lancashire County Council comprised 140 members, and there were 22 Labour members......Mr. Constantine described the atmosphere at Preston at the moment as a dead weight of reaction and Toryism...... [He] said there ought to be a number of people on the County Council who were not cotton manufacturers and colliery proprietors....."

"In conclusion, Mr. Constantine said he had never entered a fight with greater confidence." ['Observer' February 13th.1934]

A further public meeting took place at the Labour Hall, Accrington, on Sunday February 18th., when Councillor Constantine was joined by County Councillor George Tomlinson, Labour, of Farnworth.

The Accrington TCLP monthly delegates meeting of Wednesday February 21st. resolved "to give all possible support to the appeal from the

Hunger Marchers Committee." ['Observer' February 21st.1934]

At the election on March 1st., Councillor Constantine had an impressive victory over his arch rival Councillor Slack; the result being:

Accrington North

R.I. Constantine, Labour   5,482
George E. Slack, Liberal   <u>3,020</u>
Majority   2,462

The spirited contest was a great personal triumph for Constantine, because the Ward was traditionally a Liberal/Conservative stronghold. Slack had represented the area for 6 years, having been unopposed in his previous two contests. At the Labour Hall following the result, Constantine addressed a crowded audience as follows:

"The electors of North Division have emphasised in no uncertain voice that the policy I have pursued for the last three or four years on the PAC meets with the approval of the great majority......"[Applause]

"The majority of electors did not agree with the callous and inhumane manner in which the Lancashire County Council administered the means test. He could now tell them that he was not talking out of his hat as they had accused him, but that the people of Accrington were behind him." ['Observer' March 3rd.1934]

UNEMPLOYMENT CONTINUED.

At the GMWU Engineering Shop Stewards Meeting, April 12th., the guest speaker was Mrs. Rushton, who gave her impressions of the "Unemployed March to London."

"She gave a detailed account of the various towns which they stayed at, and the reception accorded them, also the Great Congress proceedings in London, and their activities whilst there, ending with a passionate appeal for unity and solidarity amongst the workers to combat the growing attacks of the capitalist class."

"A few questions were asked which the speaker suitably answered, after which Mrs. Rushton was heartily thanked for her most interesting account of the march." [Minute Book]

At an inquest on the relieving officer for Rishton, under the Lancashire PAC, on Saturday April 21st., it was revealed that a warrant had been issued for his arrest on a charge of falsification of accounts. The body of the deceased had been found in the River Calder. He had been missing since April 10th.

['Observer' April 24th.1934]

At the Great Harwood Weavers' Association's Executive, April 25th., a letter was read which had been handed in by representatives of the Communist Party and the NUWM, which asked the Committee to receive a deputation with a view to holding a joint Public Meeting. The Committee resolved that, "as we cannot co-operate with the Associations named, for any purpose, the deputation be not received." [Minute Book]

After years of perseverance, Councillor Constantine and his supporters won an important issue, at the Lancashire PAC on Monday April 30th. They managed to increase the outdoor relief allowance for children from 2s. to 3s. per week. ['Observer' May 1st.1934]

On the 14th. May, the Unemployment Act 1934, became law. This will be given a thorough examination at the end of the Chapter.

Proposals to close the Employment Exchange in Rishton, met with a storm of protest. There were around 700 people signing on at the centre and the authorities wanted them to walk to Great Harwood instead. ['Observer' June 23rd.1934]

On July 7th., the 'Observer' reported some of the comments made by Accrington trade unionists at the annual meeting of the Council of the Federation of Textile Trade Unions at Southport, on July 6th. Mr. A. Dawson moved a resolution calling on the Government to appoint a committee to investigate unemployment, saying:

"Science and invention, instead of being boons and blessings to mankind, had proved in the hands of the capitalists to be most implacable enemies. Unless they adopted some new methods the unemployed army would always be with them."

Mr. Michael Walsh [a future Labour Mayor, and Alderman, of Accrington] described the resolution as, "namby-pamby and spineless." He thought the Federation had missed their road. The cure for unemployment was the reconstruction of the social order. It was futile for them to ask for the appointment of a committee to consider the matter. The resolution was carried.

A picture appeared in the 'Observer' July 14th. of the Unemployed Women's Handicraft Class, held at premises in Portland Street, Accrington. The membership stood at 45 and the women had to be signing on, to be eligible for free membership.

On Thursday September 20th., the Accrington TCLP Women's Section had Mrs. Rushton, of Accrington, as their guest speaker. She gave an account of her activities on the recent Women's Hunger March to Westminster, to protest against the Unemployment Bill. The speaker spoke of the sympathy they received en-route from religious organisations and of the meals they had received from many co-operative societies. She mentioned lobbying Major Procter MP., and went on to issue a warning in regard to Fascism, which she stated would destroy hard earned privileges won by the working class if it ever came to power. ['Observer' September 22nd.1934]

It was announced that the Unemployed Centre had a new warden, Mr. W.G. Shaw of Aitken Street, who had been a mechanic at Broad Oak Mill up to its closure in 1929. ['Observer' October 13th.1934]

The Unemployed Centre, Accrington, was officially re-opened for the winter session by the Mayor [Councillor A. Wilkinson] on Monday, October 22nd.. Councillor Constantine remarked that the Centre had received a lot of criticism, with many saying that it was no solution to unemployment, but he added: "If we give up this Centre, it won't bring nearer by one minute a solution to the unemployment problem." He thought that if properly and wisely used, the Centre could be of great benefit, but he was not unmindful of the greater problem of solving the unemployment crisis. ['Observer' October 23rd.1934]

The programme outlined, included wood working lessons, boot repairing, physical training classes, and health lectures. Allied to the allotments expansion, the committee proposed lectures on horticulture and poultry keeping. It had also been decided to provide dinners for the unemployed at one penny a time.

Elsewhere, in the paper, an extensive report of the work of the Centre during the previous twelve months, stated that from December 1933 until the end of April 1934, over 12,000 dinners had been provided. Average membership during that period was 228.

I will leave the Accrington and district developments at this point. Further local incidents will hopefully be published in a further volume covering the period 1935 to 1945. I will, however, proceed to give a national picture of the events leading into 1935.

The Unemployment Act 1934, had become law on the 14th. May. It was in three parts:

"1. the Unemployment Insurance Act proper, dealing with all unemployed claimants on statutory benefit;

2. an entirely new scheme for creating an Unemployment Assistance Board, to deal with all claimants who exhausted their statutory benefit and all able-bodied persons in receipt of poor law relief;

3. the appointment of an Unemployed Insurance Statutory Commission to inquire into the working of the Act and to make recommendations every year as to changes in amounts of benefit or of contributions or in administration."

The scales of benefit were as follows:

	s.	d.
1. Workers of the age of 21 and under 65;		
Men	17	0
Women	15	0
2. Workers of the age of 18 and under 21;		
Men	14	0
Women	12	0
3. Workers of the age of 17 and under 18;		
Boys	9	0
Girls	7	0
4. Workers under the age of 17 years;		
Boys	6	0
Girls	5	0
The rates of benefit payable in respect of dependants;		
For an adult dependent	9	0
For a child dependent	2	0

Wal Hannington in his book, 'Unemployed Struggles,' gives a clear explanation of what this new Act involved:

"The first statutory condition for the receipt of benefit was that not less than thirty contributions should have been paid in respect to the two years immediately preceding the date of application for benefit. If satisfying this condition the claimant would be entitled to draw twenty-six weeks' benefit. At the end of this period, if still unemployed, he would have his case reviewed and be entitled to receive additional benefit on the following conditions:"

"An additional three days' benefit for every five contributions paid in the five years prior to the date of his first claim, less one day's benefit for every five days' benefit received during that five years."

"In simple terms, this meant that if the claimant had been in regular insurable employment for the whole five years before the date of his claim, he would be entitled to a [further] twenty-six-weeks' benefit. The period of additional benefit would graduate downwards according to the amount of unemployment in the five years. [eg.] If he had had sixty weeks' unemployment in that five years, he would receive only eight weeks' additional benefit......The other regulations governing Part 1 of the Act did not differ much from those previously in force."

"It was Part 2 of the Act which caused a storm against the Government in the winter of 1934. There were 1,250,000 persons on transitional benefit who, on 7th. January, 1935, would pass under the control of the new Unemployment Assistance Board. The date for the transfer of the able-bodied unemployed in receipt of poor law relief under the scheme was fixed for 1st. March, 1935......"

"A point in connection with Part 2 which aroused special resentment, even before the new scales of allowances were made known, was the provision for compulsory training for the unemployed applicants under the U.A.B. in either residential or non-residential training centres."

"The drafting of the unemployed into labour camps meant that they would be removed many miles from their home towns and from their families; that they would live under semi-military discipline; that out-of-bounds areas would be laid down beyond which they must not go; they would have to perform a full week's work on road-making, land drainage systems, new sewerage schemes, afforestation, improvement of canals and bridges, etc., for which they would be paid no wages, but would receive their meals in the camp, plus 4s. a week pocket money, whilst their dependants, if any, had to exist on the scales of allowances provided by the U.A.B."

"We claimed that such a system of labour meant the creation of a new slave class in this country; a class of persons who would no longer be regarded as wage-earners, but who were expected to be content though their family life was broken up and they were compelled to work without wages."

"We claimed that this would tend to create a slave mentality, and that the ruling class would use these workers to undermine established trade union standards and conditions; that the Government would not hesitate, in fact, if it could create the right psychology amongst this mass of unemployed, to use them as an organised blackleg force, to smash any industrial struggle in which the workers were engaged. Such were our arguments against this proposed labour camp scheme which the Government had adopted from the report of the Royal Commission on Unemployment. This report had referred to a similar labour camp scheme in operation in Germany, and we therefore claimed that this meant the application of Fascist methods in Britain by a constitutional government......"

The NUWM organised many demonstrations in scores of towns and cities, throughout the nation. On the 8th.-10th. December, at the 9th. national conference of the NUWM, a resolution was carried urging united action addressed to the TUC General Council:

"To secure the fullest co-operation of all working-class organisations for action against the Act in the various localities we strongly urge the General Council of the TUC to give its support to the fight of the NUWM and to advise its constituent bodies to carry out, with the NUWM, a proposal designed to ensure mass refusals of the unemployed to enter the slave camps with the guaranteed support of all employed workers."

The TUC replied that it would not correspond with the NUWM under any circumstances. Immediately following this negative exchange, the Government released the new scales and regulations in respect of Part 2 of the Act. The new conditions shocked the country. The reductions per week in the scales of allowances were as follows:

Man and wife	2s. 0d
Single adult male, living with family	7s. 0d
Second and subsequent members of family	9s. 0d
Single female worker, living with family	7s. 0d
Subsequent females living with family	8s. 0d
Youths, 18 to 21 years of age	6s. 0d
Girls, 18 to 21 years of age	5s. 0d
Boys, 16 to 18 years of age	3s 0d
Girls, 16 to 18 years of age	1s 6d

The Government had, however, cunningly tried to give the impression that they were being generous to the children, to whom they gave the following increases:

	s.	d.	
Between 11 and 14 years of age	2	6	a week increase.
8 and 11	2	0	
5 and 8	1	6	
Under 5	1	0	

Immediately following the publication of the UAB regulations, a big demonstration of the unemployed marched on the Glasgow PAC. These demonstrations took place all over the country during December 1934, and January and February 1935. Indeed the Manchester Guardian, which was unlikely to exaggerate events estimated in its issue of February 4th., that over 300,000 workers were marching in South Wales on Sunday February 3rd. The TUC's argument that the demonstrations were just the actions of a few Communists was therefore shown to be a lie. The working-class were very angry at the yet further reductions to their income and they expressed this dissatisfaction by attending the demonstrations in ever greater numbers.

On February 5th. 1935, the National Government had to retreat to some extent before this storm of protest. The Minister of Labour, Mr. Oliver Stanley, stated in the House of Commons, that the old regulations would remain in force.

Wal Hannington states:

"The Government was severely shaken and on the verge of collapse. The Minister of Labour had to admit that a blunder had been made, but he tried to hedge by stating that 'the new regulations were sound in principle, but the grievances were due to the rigidity in administration and the mistakes inherent in a large and new measure.' News leaked out that the UAB's original scales had been rejected by the Government as too liberal. When the government had to answer this charge, it twisted and squirmed in an effort to avoid its responsibility. Scenes took place in the House of Commons when demands were made that the government should publish the facts and show who was responsible....."

"I think it is unquestionable that, had the official leaders of the TUC and the Labour Party clearly identified themselves with the great struggle which was raging and given leadership in the struggle, the government could have been overthrown at a moment when it was thoroughly discredited and could no doubt have been replaced by a strong Labour government, pledged to a policy of protecting and advancing the standards and conditions of the working-class."

"The NUWM continued the struggle against the government, long after the scales had been restored, with the demand that the whole of Part 2 of the 1934 Unemployment Act should be repealed. 24th. February [1935] was again a national day of demonstration for the complete repeal of the Act; in towns throughout the country unemployed and employed workers marched side by side under the slogans of 'Down with the Slave Act.'....."

"Such was the character of the agitation that continued against the government. For more than fourteen months the government was afraid to lift the stand-still order and make another attempt to reintroduce the scales and regulations for the full operation of Part 2."

"On 4th. July, 1935, the Unemployment Insurance Statutory Committee recommended an increase in the child dependant's allowance for all claimants drawing statutory benefit under the unemployment insurance scheme. It meant raising the allowance from 2s. to 3s. a week. The Government was preparing for a General Election in November 1935, and they deliberately held back the information concerning the extra shilling to the children until a few days before the election, then announcing that the increase should come into operation as from 31st. October, 1935."

"There can be no doubt that the persistent agitations conducted by the NUWM in respect to the children's allowance was responsible for the decision which led to the increase, small as it was." [16]

The TUC and Labour Party leadership throughout this period, even after the debacle of 1931 and the establishment of the National Government, refused to take a militant stand against the evils of the capitalist system. The wealth of the capitalist class increased tremendously during this period of misery and depravation. There had been over a doubling of estates assessed at over £1,000 for estate duty, since the war. [17] On the other hand, however, the NUWM dominated by the Communist Party persistently kept the plight of the unemployed, and under employed, to the fore. Locally, as I have shown in this Chapter, the NUWM, particularly in Great Harwood, stirred the citizens into action. Hundreds, and at times thousands, of them took to the streets to show their anger. I believe that the 'powers that be' have never given anything to the 'lower orders' out of good hearted human decency. All improvements gained over the years by the working-class have come about by organised actions of strength. Every improvement in the social services such as health and education have only come about after prolonged action by the workers. Equally, it is the case that in periods such as the inter-war years, standards previously won had got to be defended by strong united action. This was the job that the NUWM gave itself, and the activists both locally and nationally deserve our whole hearted admiration for their efforts at this time.

However, one of the policies of the NUWM was that the Labour Movements' representatives should resign from the PAC's, and let the capitalists take the full blame for the peoples misery. This was a revolutionary policy which, if adopted by the Labour members of PAC's, would have brought even harsher attacks on the unemployed. Eg. The benefits paid by the Accrington Relief Committee, which contained some very vociferous Labour members, were significantly greater than those paid out by the Church and Oswaldtwistle Committee which contained no working-class members. Hopefully, according to this strategy, the unemployed would become so angry at their pitiful condition that they would finally attempt to overthrow the whole capitalist system. This aspect of the NUWM's policy was however, with over 60 years hindsight, an over simplification of the situation.

The actions of Labour members such as Councillors Constantine, Dawson, and O'Connor, in continuing to remain members of the various PAC's, brought the evils of the system much more before the public. Every time they protested at the PAC and Council Meetings about the means test, it was reported in great detail in the 'Observer'. These reports contained the comments of the Tory and Liberal majority, which were always monstrous in their contempt for the working-class. The treatment of Councillor Constantine at County Hall by the rural Tories was utterly disgraceful. Reading the reports of the proceedings one gets the idea that they would have gladly murdered Constantine if they could have got away with it, and all because he was rightfully speaking up for the working man. I am glad that the likes of Constantine stayed at their posts. Constantine and Dawson also demanded the right of the deputations of the NUWM Marchers, to be allowed into meetings to plead for a more sympathetic approach from members. The TUC General Council could have learnt a lot from the progressive humanitarian attitude of these two gentlemen.

The lack of national action on a large scale by the Labour Party and the TUC in particular, was a dereliction of duty. Although the various hunger marches were organised by the NUWM, they could have easily taken them over for their own ends because of their more highly developed organisation. The handful of activists of the NUWM were vastly out numbered by the rest of the labour movements full and part-time officials. The trouble was that the leadership just did not want to be associated with anything that might be considered militant, instead they appeared to be wanting to appeal to the reasonableness of the middle-class and hoping for a compromise with capitalism. That approach did not work because even with things as bad as they were, they lost the 1935 election. This sort of craving for respectability was to be seen again under Kinnock, Smith and Blair. There is no doubt that the Labour leadership of the 1980's and 1990's has done nothing to give hope and encouragement to the unemployed and the low paid. Their leadership qualities have been abysmal.

REFERENCES.

1. Hannington, W. 'Unemployed Struggles 1919-1936'. EP Publishing Ltd. 1973. p. 124.
2. Ryan, P. 'The Poor Law in 1926' in Morris, M. [Ed] 'The General Strike.' Penguin Books, 1976. p. 365.
3. Hannington. op. cit. p. 201.
4. ibid. p. 202 & 203.
5. ibid. p. 205.
6. ibid. p. 206 & 207.
7. ibib. p. 208.
8. ibib. p. 209.
9. ibib. p. 210.
10. ibib. p. 211.
11. ibib. p. 212.

12. ibid. p. 216 to 218
13. McCarthy,M. 'Generation in Revolt'. Heinemann Ltd. 1953. p.150 to 152
14. ibid. p. 153 & 154
15. Kingsford, P. 'The Hunger Marchers in Britain, 1920-1940'. Lawrence and Wishart Ltd. P. 134
16. Hannington. op. cit. Pages 298 to 320
17. ibid. p. 321

CHAPTER FIVE

THE POLITICAL SITUATION.

1927

ACCRINGTON TCLP AND THE ILP

CHARLES RODEN BUXTON.

Charles Roden Buxton had first stood as the Labour candidate in Accrington in 1918 and had become the town's first Labour MP at the General Election of 1922. He lost the 1923 and 1924 General Elections, although he increased his vote on each occasion. The reason that he lost was due to a compact between the Liberal and Conservative Parties locally, that endured until 1945. Under this, they agreed not to put a third party into electoral contests in the Division and they asked their supporters to vote for the candidate endorsed by both parties. So in effect the Labour candidate was opposed by only one anti-socialist candidate throughout that period. However, this agreement did not apply to the UDC elections.

Buxton was a nominee of the Independent Labour Party and he made good socialist speeches until he compromised his position during the Miner's Lockout. In February 1926 he had accepted the position of Parliamentary Adviser to the Labour Party and had in October & November 1926 left his Labour Party duties locally and nationally, in order to accompany Ramsay MacDonald on a recuperative holiday to North Africa.

On his return he had been influenced by MacDonald and his associates in London. With regards to the 1926 dispute the line he adopted was that the TUC General Council had done all that it could for the miners' cause and he then limited his speeches to worthless sentimental utterances about the miners' "great demonstration of endurance, courage and determination", when what they really wanted was supportive action and money.

The only people to blame for the miners' defeat were the General Council of the TUC and the leadership of the Labour Party. Buxton outwardly appeared oblivious to this fact, inwardly he was probably behaving like an ostrich by placing his head in the sand and hoping the awkward situation facing him would go away.

Eventually Buxton according to the 'Observer' of January 29th. 1927, transferred his candidature from the ILP to the Trades & Labour Party. The members of the Accrington branch were told that the Divisional Council of the ILP were unaware that the change had been made until it had become a fait accompli. However, he still continued to speak at meetings organised by the Accrington ILP right up to his departure to become MP for Elland, Yorkshire.

Eric Jones comments on the Accrington ILP as follows:

> "The more idealist or committed socialists usually became involved in the ILP initially.
>
> "The ILP had their rooms behind and above shop premises at [87 Back] Blackburn Road. The large upstairs room had a stage or platform in it and housed a piano, and was used for general meetings, dances, concerts, theatre performances and other social functions. The smaller downstairs room was much more cosier with its fireplace, easy chairs, billiard and other games tables, soft drinks bar and was essentially the Club Room where ILP'ers would gather every evening."
> [1]

Alice Haines wrote me a letter on the 10th April 1996, in which she said:

> "The ILP was more cultural than the Labour Party. On Sunday afternoons we had talks on Poetry, Art and Music; and Wallace and I, Norman Marshall and D. Horabin formed a small Dramatic Society..... We decided to do Shaw's "O'Flaherty V.C." and Miss Wigglesworth wrote to Shaw asking him to waive the Royalties. He wrote back refusing, saying he was a member of the Writers' Trade Union and couldn't waive the fee etc. - A nice letter if I remember."

The contents of this letter to Shaw, somehow became known to the national press. Alice continued:

> "Later St. John Irvine, the Drama Critic of the 'Sunday Observer', wrote an article about amateurs wanting to perform plays without paying royalties. He didn't mention the Accrington ILP, but mentioned Shaw complaining."

The leading lights in the Labour Party nationally were members of the ILP, but at the ILP Annual Conference in Easter 1926, the grouping moved to the left, by electing James Maxton as it's Chairman. In his presidential address he said:

> "I am glad the Movement has adopted the Socialism-in-our-time policy..... The main factor in the process - the creation of the will

to Socialism - is well within our control, and just as we struggled in the war days to develop the will to peace against terrific odds and with many factors operating that we could barely influence, so we can struggle now to develop the will to Socialism."

"This does not imply a static view of Socialism or the conception that Socialism is a mechanical thing which is achieved on a certain day and remains unchanged thereafter. But it does mean that there will be a definite point of time at which private capitalism and its ravages will be decisively subordinated to the welfare of the common people and that from thence onwards life will return to everybody a daily increasing dividend of material comfort, happiness and freedom."

"The more the Labour Party becomes absorbed in the responsibilities of Parliamentary life and the more the responsibilities the Labour Party has to undertake, either as the official opposition or as Government, the more will the tendency be for them to be entirely taken up with the immediately practicable which always creates a tendency to lose sight of the ultimate ideal. The ILP's duty is to keep the ultimate ideal clearly before the working-class movement of the country. Political success for the Labour Party is a certainty, but political success is itself a poor end unless, behind the Parliamentary majority, there is a determined revolutionary Socialist opinion. It will be part of my duty to try to make as far-reaching as possible this feeling which I believe is the feeling of the Party." [2]

WORKERS' CONTROL.

The underlying principle of 'Socialism-in-our-time' was the theme of a Special Conference organised by the Blackburn and Nelson ILP Federation, held in the Co-operative Assembly Rooms, Oak Street, Accrington, on Saturday February 12th. 1927. Its title was 'The Problem of Workers' Control in Industry' and it was introduced by Mr. Manny Shinwell, ex-Minister of Mines in the Labour Government. The chair was taken by Andrew Naesmith. Mr. Shinwell commented:

"For what purpose were the trade unions to re-build 'their shattered organisations?' Was it for the purposes of collective bargaining within the limits of capitalist industry, of extracting extremely moderate concessions from the industry of a 5% increase in wages, or alternatively of resistance to a 5% reduction in wages? If that were the sole end and purpose of trade unionism in this country, we might as well have no trade unionism at all. [Hear, hear.]"

"He conceived the purpose and end of trade unionism to be the preparation of the workers for the task of participating in the administration of industry, and if trade unions were not prepared to undertake the task, then the edifice erected by the trade unions was of very little value to the working classes....."

"There were certain trade union officials who ventured the opinion that workers' control of industry could be dove-tailed into the existing capitalist order of society, but he had yet to see a scheme sufficiently satisfactory in its details to justify acceptance. They could not apply the principle of industrial democracy or workers' control where the interests of parties conflicted....."

"In other words the idle shareholder who was the owner of the capital had interests which were diametrically in opposition to the interests of both manager and worker."

In his concluding remarks, Manny said the following, which was received with much satisfaction by those present:

"In a wise, well ordered State they would ask whether a person was performing necessary functions and rendering social service; if so, obviously that person was entitled to all that the State could provide in the way of material consideration. He did not want industrial workers to be paid on the capacity of the industry but to receive consideration on the capacity of the community to provide it."

"Having decided that the objective of trade unions was ownership of industry by the State with a share of control in industrial administration by the workers, then it was the plain duty of trade unions to take the necessary steps to educate the people in that direction. He would like to see trade unions all over the country who accepted this point of view set up committees of study for this purpose, and that men and women should come together and thrash out the question as to 'How we should run the factory when the time comes.'" ['Observer' February 15th. 1927]

At the Accrington ILP.-AGM, it was decided that a policy of militant socialist propaganda and education covering the whole division would be embarked upon.

"The spirit of the meeting throughout was expressive of the determination of the members to bring more and more before the public the conceptions of social service and organisation for which the ILP stands." ['Observer' March 12th. 1927]

Being part of the Labour Party, or the Independent Labour Party [ILP], or indeed the Communist Party, tended to mean that you had a hectic round of socials and meetings to attend. For instance at a Labour Party Social, held under the auspices of Peel Park and East Wards, in the Co-operative Assembly Rooms, Oak Street, Accrington, on Wednesday February 9th. 1927, an audience of over 400 attended. Councillor Constantine presided and a humorous sketch entitled 'Foiling the Reds' was given by the ILP Dramatic Group. ['Observer' February 12th. 1927.]

UDC ELECTIONS.

Labour movement candidates:
Church:
Harry Smith, Labour. 3 Albert Street. Machinist.
Walter Turner, Labour. 303 Dill Hall Lane. Blacksmith.
Joseph Colbourne, Labour. 244 Dill Hall Lane. Joiner's Labourer.
Peter Henry Holmes, Labour. 4 George Street.
Oswaldtwistle:
Immanuel: Albert Bernasconi, Labour. 19 King Edward Street. Coal miner.
Foxhill Bank: William Henry Greenwood, Labour. 204b Union Road. Grocer & Baker.
Rishton:
William Stairs, Labour. 25 Grange Street. Weaver.
Mary Holden, Labour. 105 Spring Street. Weaver.
John William Banks, Labour. 104 Hermitage Street. Weaver.
Herbert Crossley, Labour. 64 Chapel Street. Weaver.
Clayton-Le-Moors:
Frank Butterworth, Labour. 68 Burnley Road. Coal miner.
Harry Edmundson, Labour. 31 Victoria Street. Restaurant Keeper.
Margaret Alice Kennedy, Labour. 28 Whalley Road. Married Woman.
Great Harwood:
North: James E. Edmundson, Labour.
South: Alfred Hayhurst, Labour.
East: Thomas Dobson, Labour.
West: Frank Marsden, Labour.

The Elections produced the following limited Labour victories:
Oswaldtwistle: Mr. W.H. Greenwood, Foxhill Bank Ward. 20% of the contests.
Church: Mr. Peter Henry Holmes & Mr. Walter Turner. 50% of the contests.
Clayton-Le-Moors: no victories.
Rishton: no victories.

Great Harwood: Mr. Thomas Dobson. 25% of the contests.

Guardian Elections took place in Peel Park and West Wards in Accrington, which resulted in Mr. T. O'Connor, an insurance agent, winning for Labour in the latter. ['Observer' 23rd. 1927]

OSWALDTWISTLE'S FIRST LABOUR CHAIRMAN.

On April 28th. Oswaldtwistle UDC voted in it's first Labour Chairman, Councillor William Henry Greenwood, a grocer of Union Road. He had the distinction of being the only Labour nominee ever to be elected on to the UDC. After leaving elementary school, he had worked in a weaving shed, but then he moved to the Oswaldtwistle Co-operative Society grocery department. He subsequently set himself up in the grocery business. A founder member of Oswaldtwistle ILP prior to the First World War, he was by 1927 the typical moderate, saying:

> "He hoped..... each member returned would taboo politics in the Council Chamber and in the administration of local affairs." ['Observer' April 30th.1927]

It would appear that he had lost his enthusiasm for radically changing society in favour of the working-class and had adopted a more 'middle of the road' approach to politics.

ACCRINGTON TCLP CONTINUED.

The atmosphere of Labour political meetings, however, was one in which radical socialist speeches were the norm. Take for example, Mr. Charles Roden Buxton's eulogy on Accrington Market Ground on Sunday July 10th:

> "The Labour Party had taken a distinct line, which anyone could understand. They did not believe in the revolutionary up-turning of national life, but in the constitutional revision and the constitutional development of national life. They believed in the gradual conversion of their country in its industrial and political systems into a Socialist Commonwealth, with equal rights for all in which national wealth would be distributed, not by confiscation, but by measures which would see that all in the various branches of national life would get their fair share for their labour. It would not be done by revolution, but it would be done rapidly and constitutionally. With that ideal and aim in view they could go forward in their work, realising that they could bring the

national life onto a higher level, both internationally and imperially and nationally, and it was only the Labour Party that could effect that result." ['Observer' July 12th.1927]

On Saturday August 13th. 1927, the Accrington TCLP, held their 8th. Annual Demonstration, followed by a sports day in a field off Sandy Lane. It was estimated that over 5,000 people took part, the procession taking over 30 minutes to pass any given point. The route of the march began at Ellison's Tenement, along Hyndburn Road to Park Road to Blackburn Road, thence on to Abbey Street and Sandy Lane. All the branches had a tableaux on top of a lorry. Other organisations taking part were the ILP, the Accrington Weavers, Accrington Miners, National Union of Railwaymen, National Union of General Workers, the Amalgamated Engineering Union, National Union of Foundry Workers, the Sheetmetal Workers Union, Woodcutting Machinists Society, National Union of Clerks, Amalgamated Grinders and Glazers Society, and the Amalgamated Moulders' Union. ['Observer' August 16th. 1927. p.5]

On Saturday August 20th. it was reported that the Accrington TCLP had completed the purchase of 'Parkside' Blackburn Road, for use as their headquarters. It had formerly been the residence of the late Sir George Macalpine and since the War had been used as the local headquarters of the Medical Board of the Ministry of Pensions. It was the home of the Labour Party until the mid-1960's. The building then became Platt's Club.

ACCRINGTON BOROUGH ELECTIONS.

The Labour candidates were:
North: Mr. William Riding, Labour.
South: Mr. Herbert Walsh, Labour.
East: Mr. Arthur Dawson, Labour.
West: Mr. C. Burke, Labour.
Peel Park: Mr. J. Bradley, Labour.
Central: Mr. James A. Coulton, Labour.
Higher Antley: Mr. Charles Myall, Labour.
Spring Hill: Mr. W.H. Roberts, Labour.

In the Elections, Labour only managed to win one seat out of eight. The winner being Mr. W.H. Roberts. in Spring Hill Ward.

Mr. Tom Brunton, one of Accrington's socialist pioneers spoke at the Discussion Class on Sunday October 30th. It was a reply to the Communist Party's attack on the Labour Party the previous week. Tom later became the President of the Accrington Labour Party and spent the last years of his life as a

Communist. He said:

"He would say a thousand times that the Labour Party was not wrong, but abundantly right. It had declared that Socialism was its ultimate objective, and no working-class party which was aiming to the best of its ability to that objective could go wrong." Mr. Blair please note. ['Observer' 1st. Nov. 1927]

THE RUSSIAN CONNECTION.

At the Accrington TCLP-Annual General Meeting on Wednesday May 18th 1927, the following resolution was passed, and was sent to Mr. Hugh Edwards MP [Lib. Accrington] and the Prime Minister:

"That this meeting send a vigorous protest to the Government for the unscrupulous action taken by the police in raiding the Russian Trading House of ARCOS Ltd, and we claim the action as being unjustified so far and a grave danger to amicable trading between the two countries involved, and can only end in making British diplomacy look ridiculous in the eyes of other countries." ['Observer' 21st May.1927]

Special Branch had raided the Russian trade delegation in London on May 12th. Nothing of importance was found, but trading and diplomatic relations between the two countries was broken.

Much interest was taken in the Soviet Union at the time. The 'Observer' of October 8th. reported Mr. Charles Roden Buxton's speech at the Picton Hall Liverpool, in which he gave his thoughts on his recent trip to Russia.

Mr. Arthur Dawson, Organising Secretary of the National Union of Textile Workers, based in Accrington and Labour Candidate for East Ward in the November Council Elections also visited the Soviet Union and his observations were published in the 'Observer' of November 29th.

Miss Margaret McCarthy, of Oswaldtwistle, also visited Russia, accompanying the delegation that included Mr. Dawson. ['Observer' December 20th.] This was an enormous delegation of British trade unionists, invited to Moscow to participate in the 10th Anniversary of the Revolution. Margaret stated in 'Generation in Revolt' that "attached to the big adult delegation was a youth delegation of which I was one, the only girl."[3]

Tom Mann had seen the delegation off from London on October 29th. Margaret described some of her fellow passengers as follows:

"Will Lawther, then a young, laughing, handsome man, was leader of the adult delegation..... Shapurji Saklatvala [Communist MP for Battersea] a kind humorous man..... spent a lot of time with us." [4]

Margaret attended the great international youth gathering, at which Bukharin, leader of the Comintern was the main speaker.

"Most fascinating for me were the receptions, where we met among the guests figures of world fame: Krupskaya, Lenin's widow, Clara Zetkin and Madame Sun Yat-Sen; the Indian revolutionary Manabendra Nath Roy; the Russians, Lozovsky, Melnichansky, Rykov and Bukharin." [5]

Whilst in Moscow she became ill, but she had many visitors including "William, the son of Karl Liebknecht."

After returning to Lancashire she said:

"I began my platform career that December in 1927 on dark, cold, damp evenings in the Accrington Market Place, telling the world about Russia, and soon I was touring the Lancashire towns on a Messianic mission of bringing the truth about the Soviet Promised Land to the Lancashire cotton operatives." [6]

Mr. George Lunt, Treasurer of the Accrington TCLP, visited Russia as a private individual in the latter part of 1927, and he spoke about his excursion at the Accrington ILP meeting of January 14th.1928.['Observer' January 21st.1928]

1928

ACCRINGTON TCLP CONTINUED.

Mr. Levi Fish who presided at the Rishton ILP meeting held at the Primitive Methodist School on January 24th, informed the audience that the Rishton branch, one of the strongest in the area, had acquired the house "Westwood", for their headquarters. He stated that the rooms were now the centre for the spreading of Socialism. The guest speaker, Mr. C.R. Buxton said:

"The great fight was between Toryism and Labour, or between Capitalism and Socialism..... He had not changed or wavered since the first day he came to Rishton: he had put forward the principles of peace and socialism when they were very much less popular than today..... Underlying the Labour policy, they had war against war and war against poverty. Those two ideas comprised the great aims and ideas of the Labour Party....."

"Mr. Buxton went on to speak of the distribution of wealth. Everything Labour did, he said, was tending to better the conditions of the workers. The great underlying evil of the country to-day was the bad distribution of wealth. It was a fact that of the whole national income of the country one half went to one-tenth of the people, and the other half had to be divided amongst nine-tenths of the people. That was a great injustice and entirely opposed to any principles of justice and fairness."

"Labour had now a practical policy in the surtax..... [This would be] placed on those who were receiving their incomes from property..... but even then only if they had more than £500 a year."

The surtax idea was very gradualist, £500 per year equated to five adult workers annual wages in Rishton. Such a tax would be viciously attacked by the wealthy and if it had come into operation it would not have significantly redistributed wealth within the community.

Whilst circumstances were looking up for the ILP in Rishton, events were turning against them in Accrington. Mr. W. Brotherton, Secretary, explained to the 'Observer', February 18th., that financial responsibility due to a decrease in the membership of the institution compelled them to terminate the tenancy of their present rooms. He went on to say:

"Although the effects of Mr. Philip Snowden's resignation from the National body had influenced members of the ILP and in some quarters it was thought that the work of the ILP had come to an end, they in the Accrington branch were convinced that there was still vitally important work for them to do. The only suggestion which was considered practical for the present was that the E.C. would have to meet at the house of some member, and when a branch meeting was necessary then rooms would need to be hired for that purpose."

Maintaining his commitment to socialism at this time, Mr. Brotherton had the following letter published in the 'Observer' of March 3rd:

"Speaking on internationalism at Haslingden as reported in the 'Observer' of Saturday last, the Rev. R. Guy Ramsay said "the modern Socialist Sunday Schools were no help to the cause of world brotherhood."

"Here are a few of the precepts of the British Socialist Sunday Schools.
1. Love your schoolfellows, who will be your fellow workmen in life;
2. Make everyday holy by good and useful deeds and kindly actions;
3. Do not think that those who love their own country must hate and despise other nations or wish for war, which is a remnant of barbarism;
4. Look forward to the day when all men and women will be free citizens of one fatherland living together as brothers and sisters in

peace and righteousness.

"The declaration repeated at the school each Sunday runs:
"We desire to be just and loving to all our fellow men and women, to work together as brothers and sisters, to be kind to every living creature and so help to form a new society, with justice as it's foundation and love it's law."

Perhaps Mr. Ramsay will tell us how teaching based on these maxims is no help to the cause of world brotherhood."

At the ILP meeting held in the Labour Rooms, Warner Street, Accrington, on the 12th. March, Mr. R. Catterall, Treasurer, was able to report that they had left the old rooms free from debt and had a workable balance, which enabled them to make a £5 donation to the Accrington TCLP's building fund. Mr. Sam Hinchliffe, President, pointed out the need to continue in existence locally and "for keeping Socialism a vital issue." ['Observer' March 17th. 1928]

UDC ELECTIONS.

The Labour movement candidates:
Church:
John Barker, Labour. 31 St. James Street. Machinist.
Henry Smith, Labour. 3 Albert Street. Machinist.
Oswaldtwistle:
Immanuel: Albert Bernasconi, Labour. 19 King Edward Street. Coal miner.
Foxhill Bank: John Jones, Labour. Colwyn View, Sunny Bank Drive. Railway Passenger Guard.
Clayton-Le-Moors:
Frank Butterworth, Labour. 68 Burnley Road. Coal miner.
George Reginald Tierney, Labour. 14 Church Lane. Coal miner.
Rishton:
William Stairs, Labour. 25 George Street. Weaver.
John William Banks, Labour. 104 Hermitage Street. Weaver.
William Mercer Bolton, Labour. 1 Clifton Street. Cotton spinner.
Great Harwood:
East: W. Slynn, Labour. Weaver.
West: G. Doughty, Labour. Weaver.
    The Labour Party's success in the Elections were disappointing:
Church: Mr. Harry Smith. 25% of the contests.
Oswaldtwistle: no victories.

Clayton-Le-Moors: no victories.
Rishton: Mr. William Stairs. 25% of the contests.
Great Harwood: no victories.

In the Guardian Elections, the results of which were announced in the same newspaper, Mr. Levi Fish was unopposed in Rishton and Mrs. Ada Mathers won one of the two seats in Great Harwood. Elsewhere Labour failed to win any seats. ['Observer' April 3rd. 1928]

A By-Election took place in East Ward, Accrington, due to the elevation of the two anti-Socialist ward councillors to the Aldermanic Bench. This resulted in a further Labour defeat, with two Liberals being elected. ['Observer' April 14th. 1928]

In April 1928 the ILP moved their meetings to the Stanley Supporters Club Rooms, in School Street, Accrington, which according to the 'Observer' attracted large audiences.

THE DEPARTURE OF MR. BUXTON.

On May 1st. a great political surprise hit Accrington when Mr. C.R. Buxton announced that he was leaving Accrington to contest the Elland constituency in the West Riding. Apparently, Mr. Ramsay MacDonald and Mr. Arthur Henderson had pressed Buxton to accept the invitation from the Elland CLP. Accrington Labour Officials expressed their sorrow at losing his services. The 'Observer' gave the following brief background history of the man:

"Born in 1875, Mr. Buxton is the son of Sir Thomas Fowell Buxton, Bart., who was at one time Governor of South Australia. He was called to the bar in 1902. Mr. Noel Buxton, ex-Postmaster General, is a brother. Educated at Harrow and Trinity College, Cambridge, Mr. Buxton was a frequent speaker on political, and social questions at the Union, of which he was at one time president. From 1903 to 1908 he was principal of Morley College for working men and women in South London..... and was also first president of the South London branch of the Workers' Educational Association....."

"In 1906, Mr. Buxton stood for East Hertfordshire Division in the Liberal interest, and in 1908 for the Mid-Devon Division, being elected for the latter in January 1910, only to be defeated in December of the same year. He was adopted as Liberal candidate for Central Hackney in 1912, but in 1916, on account of his labour views, the Liberal Association executive resolved that they could no longer consider him as their candidate. It was then that he threw in his lot with the ILP."

"Mr. Buxton's first appearance in Accrington was in the summer of 1917, when he spoke at the meeting on the Accrington market ground in favour of peace by negotiation. Later he was adopted Labour candidate for the division, so that his political connection with Accrington has lasted over 10 years."

"Mr. Buxton has travelled much in various parts of the world. During 1897 and 1898 he acted as private secretary to his father, who was Governor of South Australia, and during this period took opportunities to visit New Zealand, India, Siam, China and Japan. Later, after a breakdown in health, he spent 6 months on a cattle ranch in Texas, living the life of a cowboy..... He has covered on foot large parts of France, Italy, Germany, and Austria. In the Balkan States, Mr. Buxton has taken particular interest, and he has made himself an acknowledged authority on their affairs. He was one of the founders of the Balkan Committee. During the War [1914-1915] he went on a political mission with his brother Mr. Noel Buxton MP., with the object of securing the adhesion of Bulgaria to the side of the Allies; in the course of this an attempt was made on their lives by a Turkish assassin [October 1914] and he was shot through the lung."

"Since the war Mr. Buxton has worked without ceasing for the reconstruction of industrial life both in this country and throughout Europe, and for the uniting of the working classes of all countries in the International Socialist movement....."

"In 1904 Mr. Buxton married Miss Dorothy Jebb. [Sister of Eglantyne Jebb, the founder of the Save the Children Fund in 1919] Both Mr. and Mrs Buxton are members of the Society of Friends. Mrs. Buxton frequently accompanied her husband on his visits to Accrington, and has been closely associated with him in his political work...... He is the author of many publications." ['Observer' May 1st.1928]

It was a sad day for all of Buxton's friends and supporters in Accrington. The man was a genuine Socialist who devoted his life to the betterment of the working-class. The constituency really was lucky to have had the benefit of his services over such a long period of time.

Mr. Buxton opened Rishton ILP's new headquarters 'Westwood' on Saturday May 5th. The premises comprised of a large detached house which was only just off the main road. There were two fairly large rooms downstairs, well suited for small meetings and upstairs there was a meeting room and billiard room, in addition to a bathroom and two little box-rooms. Apparently the interior decoration was "very tasteful."

Mr. George Tomlinson, of Farnworth, the future Labour Minister of Education and former Rishton Labour Councillor, presided.

Mr. Fish said of Buxton:

"I feel that he has well and truly laid the foundations and has made so many Socialists in the Accrington division."

Mr. Buxton said:

"We consider things from the point of view of spreading our ideals and our principles and above all spreading the great, the uplifting and inspiring doctrines of Socialism and of internationalism for which we stand."

"Now if we have done something - and the previous speakers evidently think we have - to make Socialists and to make internationalists..... if we have imparted the faith and strengthened the convictions of ourselves and our friends who have had these beliefs for many years - if we have deepened our political life and our intellectual life and even our spiritual life in the work we have done by putting forward Socialism and internationalism, and true Labour principles, then, I say, we have done something that undoubtedly is well worth doing, and we shall always think with satisfaction of the work we have done in the past ten years quite apart from any personal success in an election." [Applause]

....."He beseeched them never to forget that feeling about politics which they had acquired in the past ten years. He hoped they would remember those words, cherish them and spread the principles, raising the ideals of those about them to the highest point, and it would make what they had done ten times worthwhile." [Applause] ['Observer' May 8th. 1928]

Mr. Charles Darwood, was aged 76 years when he wrote a letter [dated 21st. December 1978] to Ken Slater, the then AEU District Secretary. It included the following:

"I can give you some of the excitement down there when Mr. Charles Roden Buxton came amongst us to put up for Parliament..... He became the first Member of Parliament for the Labour Movement in Accrington. Looking back I have never known such excitement anywhere when the result came through. Mr. Buxton was a quiet spoken and very intelligent person, of sallow complexion, wore thick [rimmed] glasses which were very rare in those days."

Roland Hagan, who was the Secretary of the Accrington Workers' Education Association, for an incredible 60 years, mentioned to me a comment made by Councillor Constantine regarding the differing attitudes to publicity between Buxton and his Liberal opponent Edwards, particularly with regards to the religious aspect. Constantine said at a meeting:

> "There he was [Edwards] at Oak Street Congregational Church, fawning over the large Sunday congregation, whilst Buxton had set off very early to walk over Hambledon Hill to the Quaker Meeting House at Crawshaw Booth [Rossendale]." [7]

Buxton's walk would have been at least 10 miles there and back, over high open moorland. Apparently Buxton stayed at the commercial hotel in Willow Street, Accrington, run by Wallace Haines's father. Wallace had to give him a call early every Sunday morning that he stayed with them. [8] Wallace Haines was later to become the President of Accrington TCLP and a Mayor of Hyndburn.

Victoria de Bunsen quotes a letter that Buxton wrote to Eglantyne Jebb in the thick of one of the Accrington campaigns:

> "All our friends are working like Trojans. We have crowds of working-class people [and a few others] giving their time and energy to making the Labour cause prevail, without the least hope of personal reward for themselves. This is the fine side of an election. And many people are raised by it above themselves - that is they forget for the time being their own interests and merge them in the interests of their cause - of the welfare of all other men and women and of the unborn generation too. I tried to say this at the end of my speech last night, and to beg of them not to lose all that afterwards..... I shall not be the least downcast or depressed if beaten. I want to use all the remainder of my life for getting something done in the way of decent government - better distribution of wealth and opportunity at home, and better relations with foreign peoples, and particularly the helpless 'native races'. I think I can do this more effectively in Parliament..... But if I don't get in, I shall still pursue the same course as far as circumstances allow..... Yesterday [Sunday] was about the biggest strain as far as I was concerned. I had five meetings and all big and important, causing a sense of responsibility which adds somewhat to the effort of speaking. The night was a record they say in Accrington, for we not only had 1,000 people in a Picture Palace, but two 'overflow' meetings of about 900 and 500 respectively! However, I prepared well for this, for I started early after breakfast that morning and walked for one and a half hours across the high moors, alone to a place called Crawshawbooth, where there is a little old seventeenth-century Friends Meeting House - got there in time for a real good meeting - a strengthening one, though only a dozen or

so Friends were there - and then walked back again in time for dinner. The solitude of the moors and the morning worship stood me in good stead for the rest of the day." [9]

There is no doubt that qualitatively speaking, Charlie Buxton was the most outstanding and sincere parliamentary candidate that this constituency has ever had.

THE OPENING OF THE BLACKBURN ROAD LABOUR HALL.

On Saturday June 16th. 1928, the Rt. Hon. Arthur Henderson MP for Burnley and Mr. Buxton, performed the opening ceremony for the Labour Party's new headquarters on Blackburn Road, Accrington. The 'Observer' described the building as follows:

> "The offices of the Party, committee rooms and a billiard room equipped with a full-size table, occupy the ground floor, and the upper storey has been converted into a spacious assembly hall with a seating capacity of over 300. The new Labour Hall has been artistically decorated."

The purchase price of the property and the alterations cost in total £4,400. They had £1,600 left over from their previous bazaar and £215 raised through an appeal, leaving them a debt of £2,600. Today that would be the equivalent of taking on a £1/4 million mortgage.

The glorious weather allowed the speeches to be made outside in the grounds, where a large gathering of supporters awaited the invited guests. Councillor Constantine presiding, stated that sometime in the future they hoped to build an extension that would create a hall capable of seating 1,300. [Nothing came of this wish however.] He went on to say:

> "I hope that now we have got here, this hall will be the centre of all democratic and progressive movements in this town, and that from it an influence will radiate."

Henderson in his speech made the following statement that was to prove very prophetic:

> "Given power..... as far as he was concerned.... he would frankly give up if they had not given effect not merely to some of the more superficial proposals dealing with land monopoly, monopoly in industry, the inequalities and injustices of the present industrial system. If they had not introduced more of goodwill, comradeship, equality and a fairer distribution of the fruits of industry they would deserve the

most bitter retribution the electorate could mete out to them."
Buxton contributed £100 to the building fund, and in his address said:
> "The thing that mattered was the ideals for which they stood, and politics so regarded was not a mere game, and was not a mere question of tactics, one party ousting the other." ['Observer' June 19th. 1928]

If only the present Leader, his Cabinet and others, who hold power in today's Labour Party, would take note of the attitudes expressed at this and other events held at the time, and alter their policies accordingly.

Those ideals enthusiastically expressed 'for free' by a handful of activists after their hard day's work, had been accepted by a highly significant number of the electorate in the Division, in not much more than one generation. The present Labour leadership by comparison, appears to have now nothing in common with the likes of Buxton and the members present at the above events, but everything in common with the views of the class enemy. I do not believe this view to be an exaggeration.

MR. TOM SNOWDEN SELECTED.

Mr. Tom Snowden, a worsted manufacturer of Bingley, was chosen at a selection conference in the New Labour Hall on Saturday June 23rd.

Originally there were three candidates, namely: Alderman A Robinson, JP., of Liverpool; Mr. W.J. Tout JP., secretary of the Todmorden Weavers' Association and former MP for Oldham; and Mr. Snowden. Alderman Robinson withdrew from the contest before the meeting took place. Mr. Snowden was the surprise winner by 42 votes to 32. Apparently the textile trade unions had expected more support for Mr. Tout.

The 'Observer' described Mr. Snowden as a native of Cowling, the home town of his distinguished relative, the Rt. Hon. Philip Snowden. It continued:
> "He began work as a weaver when 10 years of age, and was afterwards a warp twister but left his native village 20 years ago to commence business as a worsted manufacturer. His residence is at Rosemont, Bingley, and his family consists of wife, son and daughter.....
>
> "He was secretary to the [Cowling] Wesleyan Methodist Sunday School, and was a local preacher, and another position he held was that of Secretary to the local Co-operative Society..... For a long number of years he has been a member of the Bingley UDC, which he

has served as Chairman..... For 9 years, he has represented the district on the West Riding County Council, and he is Chairman of the Grammar School and a governor of Giggleswick Grammar School. He is a Justice of the Peace for the West Riding, and deputy chairman of the Bingley bench....."

Snowden had unsuccessfully fought 3 previous Parliamentary Elections; Skipton in 1922; and Central Sheffield in 1923 and 1924.

"Mr. Snowden joined the ILP when he was 20 years of age, and has been a member of the Labour Party since its formation. He is also a member of the Workers' Union....."

"It may appear strange that the Accrington Labour Party should have chosen an employer as their candidate. "But," says Mr. Snowden, "If the principles of the Labour and Socialist movement were right and just when I was a weaver, they are right now when I employ weavers. A good cause is never wrong....."

"He is a member of the Independent Order of Oddfellows, Manchester Unity." ['Observer' 26th. June 1928]

He next visited Accrington on Wednesday July 4th, when he met with the Executive Committee and briefly addressed members who had attended a social gathering in the Labour Hall. On Thursday he visited some of the local trade union secretaries and in the evening addressed an audience of some 250 members of the Womens' Section, again in the Labour Hall. ['Observer' July 7th. 1928]

However, all did not run smoothly with Tom's selection. On Wednesday July 11th., Accrington TCLP received a "rude surprise" when it became known that Bingley TCLP had taken exception to Tom's name going forward as Prospective Labour Candidate for Accrington. Indeed they had passed a resolution with a view to taking steps to bring about his withdrawal. The 'Observer' reported the background to this as follows:

"Mr. Snowden had resigned from the Bingley branch of the ILP following which the Bingley TCLP had passed a resolution calling upon him to resign his position on the West Riding County Council and the Bingley UDC."

"This was followed by a later resolution that the facts of the relationship between Mr. Snowden and the Bingley TCLP should be forwarded to the National Executive of the Labour Party."

"Mr. Hubert Smith, Secretary of the Bingley TCLP, now declares that Mr. Snowden's adoption as Prospective Labour Candidate raises a vital issue as to whether a man can sit as an Independent on any public body and at the same time run as an Official Parliamentary

Labour Candidate."

"It would appear that Mr. Snowden's former comrades on the Bingley TCLP are bent upon doing their utmost to bring about the withdrawal of his candidature for Accrington by bringing pressure to bear on the National Executive and if necessary upon the Accrington TCLP." ['Observer' July 14th. 1928]

Tom Snowden wrote a letter to Mr. Howson, the Accrington Labour Agent, giving his explanation of events, and this was forwarded to the 'Observer' for publication as follows:

"There is a point upon which I think I ought to inform you without delay. About 18 months ago I resigned from the local ILP - it only applied to the Bingley branch - because of local domestic trouble. The local TCLP is manned and influenced by Communists, in fact, the secretary is a pronounced Communist, and stood as such at the last UDC election."

"Things came to such a pass that our local Labour MP, Mr. Wm. Mackinder, had a public meeting to repudiate them. This will give you some idea of the sort of people they are. I told them long ago that I should have nothing to do with them, and I shall not under any circumstances. Seeing that I have become Labour candidate for Accrington, they are now trying to intimidate me. They threaten to write to the national party. This does not concern or bother me in the least, and you at Accrington must not take the matter seriously. As a matter of fact in the Communist section two railway men are chiefly responsible, and the railway branch have decided not to re-nominate them, so steps are being taken in the right direction."

"Personally I have decided to resume my activities with the Bingley Labour Party so long as they keep within the constitution of the Labour Party. This is distinctly understood between Mr. Mackinder and myself. But I will not have anything to do with them so long as their secretary, Mr. Hubert Smith, declares himself to be a Communist, or until he repudiates his association with them. In any case things will make themselves right because I have nothing to fear from either our local people or the general public."

"It is purely a domestic affair and has nothing to do with the [national] Labour Party. At this moment I occupy every position of trust and confidence in public affairs. My only point is that it might get into the Accrington local press and be misunderstood."

"It won't in the least interfere with my enthusiasm and devotion to Accrington. I am not made of the stuff that is easily perturbed; in a sentence, I shall mind my own business and get on with my job." ['Observer' July 14th 1928]

LABOUR PROCESSION AND FIELD DAY.

The above event was held on Saturday July 14th. At the head walked a row of girls in white and red holding the words 'Trades & Labour Party'. They were followed by the Howard & Bullough Band and the large banner of the Accrington Labour Party, behind which walked the Executive Committee.

In their wake came 300 children, behind who, marched the St. John's Ambulance Pipe Band. The Women's Section with their banner were well represented and they were followed by the ILP with their banner. These were then followed by a succession of tableaux from all the various wards in the Parliamentary Division.

The remainder of the procession comprised all the various engineering trade unions with their respective banners. These were headed by the Accrington Old Band. The National Union of Textile Workers were next, followed by the Accrington Miners'. The Miners' were positioned before the Accrington Ladies' Athletic Club. Next came the Accrington Weavers' Association led by the Read and Simonstone Band.

Finally members of the Assurance Agents' Society and the Clarion Cycling Club brought up the rear.

The March ended at a field off Burnley Road, beyond the reservoir, and the thousands taking part heard speeches from Mr. C.P. Trevelyan MP. for Newcastle and Mr. Tom Snowden. Snowden's speech contained the following paragraph:

> "I only belong to one brand of Socialism and that is the Socialism which Keir Hardie promulgated in his own day, which means the socialisation of the means of production and distribution, and if you like, exchange. [Hear, hear.] I am not ashamed of that at all, because it is a fundamental basic foundation upon which we can lay a new social order, so therefore why should we be ashamed of it? I don't mind being called a full blown Socialist."

THE MAXTON / COOK INITIATIVE.

At the ILP monthly meeting held at the Stanley Supporters' Club, on Friday July 20th, there was some controversy concerning the Maxton / Cook Manifesto. After a discussion, the resolution proposed by Mr. David Bussel that the branch should give its support to the manifesto, was defeated. The meeting also accepted Mr. Tom Snowden as a member.

Jimmy Maxton and Arthur Cook had drawn up a manifesto setting forth the basic aims of the Labour and Socialist Movement which called upon the workers to carry out a frontal attack on Capitalism. The manifesto was in the following terms:

"For some time a number of us have been seriously disturbed as to where the British Labour Movement is being led. We believe that its basic principles are: [1] An unceasing war against poverty and working-class servitude. This means an unceasing war against Capitalism. [2] That only by their own efforts can the workers obtain the fullest product of their labour."

"These basic principles provided the inspiration and the organisation on which the party was built. They were the principles of Hardie and the other pioneers who made the Party. But in recent times there has been a serious departure from the principles and policy which animated the founders. We are now being asked to believe that the party is no longer a working-class party, but a party representing all sections of the community. As Socialists we feel we cannot represent the views of Capitalism. Capitalism and Socialism can have nothing in common."

"As a result of the new conception that Socialism and Capitalism should sink their differences, much of the energy which should be expended in fighting Capitalism is now expended in crushing everybody who dares to remain true to the ideals of the Movement. We are convinced that this change is responsible for destroying the fighting spirit of the party, and we now come out openly to challenge it. We can no longer stand by and see 30 years of devoted work destroyed in making peace with capitalism and compromises with the political philosophy of our Capitalist opponents."

"In furtherance of our effort, we propose to combine in carrying through a series of conferences and meetings in various parts of the country. At these conferences the rank-and-file will be given the opportunity to state whether they accept the new outlook, or whether they wish to remain true to the spirit and the ideals which animated the early pioneers."

"Conditions have not changed. Wealth and luxury still flaunt themselves in the face of the poverty-stricken workers who produce them. We ask you to join in the fight against the system which makes these conditions possible."

Yours fraternally,

A.J. Cook,
James Maxton." [10]

Cook and Maxton had been the greatest opponents of the 'Peace in Industry' Campaign, which Sir Alfred Mond of the employers and Mr. Ben Turner on behalf of the TUC, were the leading propagandists. Maxton published a pamphlet against the Turner / Mond talks, which contained the following:

"The Mond Proposals may be divided into two categories: [1] the sugar-coating of the pill and [2] the pill itself. The sugar-coating of the pill is contained in the resolutions of trade union recognition and victimisation. A great deal has been made of the fact that the employers in the Mond Conference have declared in favour of the recognition of the Trade Union Movement. Those who extol this declaration as a great victory for the working-class forget that it is a recognition on the basis of the Trade Unions Act."

"At the end of a long period of class struggle when workers' wages have been severely cut and the Trade Unions Act has been placed on the Statute Book to prevent the workers resisting wage cuts, the employer turns to the manacled trade unions and graciously condescends to recognise their existence and negotiate with them. And trade union leaders have the audacity to hail this as a victory for the working-class."

"The resolution on victimisation is an empty resolution. No group of employers have ever declared in favour of victimisation as a principle. They have always carried out victimisation under the guise of cutting down their staff, and even with the existence of the present resolution they can continue to do so."

"The central feature of the Mondist policy is the acceptance of Capitalism..... Those who favour this policy say in effect, 'Let us put aside these impossible schemes of nationalisation and working-class control, these flashy futilities about speedy realisation of Socialism, and let us help to make capitalism more efficient. We will not, of course, repudiate Socialism in words, but in our-day-to-day activities we will be influenced, not by Socialist policy aiming at defeating the capitalist class as a preliminary to the realisation of Socialism, but with a policy of co-operation with the capitalist class in raising industry under capitalist ownership to a higher degree of efficiency.' Naturally, the capitalists do not mind anyone holding fast to Socialist ideals or catch-words as long as these ideals and catch-words are not a guide to everyday action." [11]

Mr. Philip Snowden, who had resigned from the ILP in late 1927 was the guest speaker of the Accrington TCLP's Town Hall meeting on Thursday September 13th.

ACCRINGTON BOROUGH ELECTIONS.

The 'Observer' started the ball rolling by writing the following in it's Editorial column 'Observ(er)ations.'
"Why, after so many reverses at the polls, the Socialists should seek to put retiring members who have served the town well and faithfully to the trouble and expense of an election is by no means clear. There can be little doubt that the attack will be decisively beaten off by the preponderating body of Liberal and Conservative voters in the Wards. Socialism can make no great appeal to the electorate in a progressive and well governed town like Accrington." ['Observer' October 23rd.1928]

The Labour candidates were:
South: Herbert Walsh, Engineer, 66 Garbett Street.
East: William Riding, Machinist, 206 Haywood Road.
West: Cornelius Burke, Engineer, 45 Hyndburn Street.
Peel Park: Michael Walsh, 75 Oswald Street.
Central: Herbert Victor Podmore, Textile Worker, 28 Pilot Street.
Higher Antley: Charles Myall, Engineer, 54 Hopwood Street.
Spring Hill: William Arthur Lambert, Trade Union Secretary, 7 Craven Street.
[Observer' October 27th.1928]

The Labour Party were victorious in West, Central and Spring Hill. The new Council comprised 19 Liberals, 8 Labour and 5 Conservatives. ['Observer' November 3rd.1928]

ACCRINGTON TCLP CONTINUED.

On Thursday November 8th, at the Clayton-Le-Moors, Labour Party meeting, Mr. R.T. Howson who had held the Presidency for many years, was presented with an umbrella and tobacco pouch by Mrs. Kennedy.

At the Discussion Class on Sunday November 7th., Mr. Bill Brotherton, was given the chance to reply to the previous Sunday's speaker, Mr. F. Bright, Communist, as well as delivering a talk on 'The Coming Election. What Party should the Workers Support?' He said:
"The Labour Party was a Socialist Party in so far that it sought to win for the workers by hand and by brain the full fruits of their

labour, with as basic and equitable distribution as it was possible to make, and coupled with that the fullest system of self-government that the mind of man could conceive."

"The Labour Party sought to obtain power in Parliament, believing that Parliament was the supreme authority in this country, and vested in Parliament was the greatest power in the State....."

"The Labour Party stood for revolution by reason and not by force."

He hoped for a Labour victory at the coming General Election and added to this by saying:

"Supplementing the Labour majority in Parliament they must also have their local councils and boards of guardians manned with Labour men and women who would seek to administrate upon humane lines rather than on reactionary lines as at the present time. They must also supplement the Parliamentary weapon by the full strength of the trades union weapon, and the organised co-operative movement."
['Observer' November 17th. 1928]

1929

THE UDC ELECTIONS.

Labour movement candidates:
Church UDC.
Samuel Potts, Labour, 46 Elmfield Street, Engraver.
Walter Turner, Labour, 306 Dill Hall Lane, Blacksmith.
John Robert O'Connor, Labour, 32 Commercial Street, Cotton yarn worker.
John Barker, Labour, 31 St. James Road, Machinist.
Oswaldtwistle UDC.
Immanual Ward: John Jones, Labour, Colwyn View Sunnybank Drive, Passenger guard.
Foxhill Bank Ward: Thomas Clitheroe, Labour, 246 Union Road, Painter and decorator.
Rishton UDC.
John William Banks, Labour, 104 Hermitage Street, Cotton weaver.
Henry James Earnshaw, Labour, 1 Norfolk Street, Iron moulder.
William Mercer Bolton, Labour, 1 Clifton Street, Cotton spinner.
Great Harwood UDC.
East Ward: Arthur Waring, Labour.

West Ward: Thomas Henry Seed, Labour.
Clayton-Le-Moors UDC.
Joseph Hardy, Labour, 5 Waterloo Street, Coal miner.
George Reginald Tierney, Labour, 14 Church Lane, Coal miner.
James William Hope, 1 Albert Street, Trade Union Secretary, [Clayton Weavers']. Mr. Hope was not a Labour candidate - he stood as an Independent.
Results.
Church - Mr. O'Connor won one of the four seats and Mr. Turner by coming 5th. gained election for one year only.
Great Harwood - Messrs. Waring and Seed were successful.
Clayton-Le-Moors - Mr. Hope won as the Independent Trade Unionist.
In Rishton and Oswaldtwistle the Labour candidates suffered defeats. ['Observer' March 26th. 1929]

An election took place during the same week for Huncoat Ward Accrington, where the Labour candidate, John James Barnes, of 24 Burnley Lane, Huncoat, a shop assistant was defeated by Mr. Fred Whittaker, Manager of Hargreaves Collieries. ['Observer' March 30th.1929] Huncoat Labour Party had been very enthusiastic in their electioneering, even holding a Public Meeting with guest speakers Alderman Dobbie, prospective Labour candidate for Clitheroe and Mrs. Cooper JP of Nelson. ['Observer' 26th. 1929]

PRESENTATION TO MR. BUXTON.

This took the form of a Public Meeting held in the Palace Picture House, Accrington, on Sunday March 10th., at which Mr. Tom Snowden and Mr. Buxton both spoke. Councillor Constantine presented Mr. Buxton with the following books:
"Poetical Works", by Robert Bridges.
"Poetical Works", by Lord Byron.
"Ethico"
"Shakespearian Tragedy"
Two Volumes of "English Diaries", by Arthur Ponsonby.
All the above were inscribed:
"Presented to Mr. C.R. Buxton MA. by Accrington Trades and Labour Party in appreciation of the very valuable services rendered during his 10 years connection with the Party." ['Observer' March 12th. 1929]
Mr. Buxton speaking at the ILP Annual Conference, in Carlisle joined in the dispute within that organisation by saying:

"The ILP is getting more and more disliked..... If we don't alter our policy we shall be out of the main stream. In my opinion the function of the ILP should be entirely to abandon its connection with Parliamentary candidates and Parliamentary work and legislation and the day-by-day administration of affairs, leaving it entirely to the Labour Party and concentrating on the work of making Socialists and with the work of general propaganda for Socialist principles." ['Observer' April 2nd. 1929]

Buxton who had ceased to be an ILP approved parliamentary candidate in 1927, had obviously maintained his membership of the organisation. He disliked the splits within the movement and thought that the main objective was to win the next election. In the meantime, he wanted the ILP to quietly curtail it's role by concentrating on converting the British people to Socialism. The question he did not answer, however, was how did the Labour Party, as it then was, cope with the people that the ILP converted? A similar question could be put to Tony Blair today.

THE GENERAL ELECTION.

The 'Observer' Editorial opened the campaign by saying:
"Politically the situation in the Accrington Division is not without its difficulties, both for Mr. Edwards and for his Liberal and Conservative supporters. But the fusion of the two Parties for the purpose of fighting the election has at least the one outstanding merit of ensuring that the seat shall not be captured by the Socialists..... The Socialists will spare no efforts to reverse the verdict of the last two elections, and it behoves all who realise the peril which lies in Socialism to do their utmost to ensure that such aims and ambitions are frustrated." ['Observer' May 4th.1929]

In answer to this provocative statement, Tom Snowden and the Accrington TCLP orchestrated an excellent campaign. On Sunday May 5th. public meetings were held at the Empire Picture House, Oswaldtwistle at 3 pm. and at the Palace Picture House, Accrington at 7 pm.; where in addition to Tom Snowden, Alderman Mrs. Kathleen Chambers of Bradford spoke in his support.

Between then and election day, Thursday May 30th., public meetings were held almost on a nightly basis across the constituency. The town halls of Accrington, Oswaldtwistle, Clayton-Le-Moors; various picture houses; many schools; and Ernest Street Baptists rooms Church; were utilized to the full.

Guest speakers included Charles Roden Buxton, the Rt. Hon. Arthur

Henderson, the Rev. H.I. James [formerly of Cannon Street Baptists Church, Accrington], and Ramsay MacDonald himself.

The result was:	Tom Snowden, Labour.	25,336
	J. Hugh Edwards, Liberal.	23,110
	Labour gain. Majority	2,226

MR. RAMSAY MacDONALD'S VISIT - RECOLLECTIONS OF THE TIME HE LIVED IN ACCRINGTON.

The visit took place on Tuesday May 21st. when a crowd of over 5,000 assembled on Ellison's Tenement to see MacDonald at 1.15 pm. Prior to his arrival they heard speeches from Coun. R.I. Constantine, Mr. Andrew Naesmith and Mr. Snowden. He had come to Accrington from Burnley and after his short stay travelled on to Blackburn. Mr. MacDonald was accompanied by Lord Arnold, Mr. Arthur Henderson and Mr. A. Greenwood. The 'Observer reported:

"Mr. Tom Snowden said..... Mr. MacDonald was a statesman and he was a man who could be trusted. He [Mr. Snowden] regarded that meeting as an augury of the future. He had never known at any election such a feeling of resentment as was being shown by the present electorate, from one end of the country to the other.[Hear, hear.] Now, why is that? It is easy to explain, that you men are not only toilers but you have begun to think, and immediately the men and women of this country begin to think instead of sub-letting it to those who give you playing fields and other things, we shall have an alteration, and a drastic alteration. [Hear, hear.]" ['Observer' May 25th. 1929.]

In extending his thanks to Mr. Macdonald, Tom said to the audience:

"I want you to send me to Parliament and if you do I won't let you down..... I will be a loyal supporter for everything that stands for the good of this Parliamentary borough of Accrington." [Applause.]

Snowden should have been reminded of the above when the Weavers' of the constituency were treated in such a disgusting manner during and after his short reign as MP.

Mr. MacDonald's remarks concerning his former residency in the borough, were reported in the 'Observer' of May 25th. This fact is not well known in Labour History circles and so I will reproduce the article in full:

"Mr. Ramsay MacDonald lent a homely touch to his brief visit to Accrington on Tuesday by recalling, doubtless to the surprise of very many of his hearers, that he was no stranger to the town, and that for a brief period in his youthful days he lived in Accrington. He aroused the interest of his audience by mentioning several names - "my friend Johnny Pilling, one of the most human and delightful old boys I have ever met in my varied life; Townsend, an old friend of mine; and an old greaser, Sutcliffe -." Before Mr. MacDonald could finish the sentence there was a shout of "Here he is." and Mr. Sutcliffe, a grey-bearded veteran, was pushed through the crowd to the platform and clasped warmly by the hand by the Socialist leader."

"The second name mentioned by Mr. MacDonald was, as many would readily guess, that of Mr. A.T. Townsend, J.P. Mr. Townsend recalls that Mr. MacDonald's stay in Accrington was brought about by the Rev. Mordaunt C. Crofton, who some forty years ago, was curate in charge of St. Peter's, Accrington, and was closely interested in the Christian Socialism movement of that day. From St. Peter's, Mr. Crofton went to St. Stephen's College, Bristol, and it was there that he came into touch with young MacDonald, then about nineteen, who was taking a two years' course of study at the College."

"With a view to the young student gaining some knowledge of industrial conditions in the North of England and combining this with a seven weeks' holiday, Mr. Crofton wrote to Mr. 'Johnny' Pilling, then foreman of the millwrights' department at Howard and Bulloughs, asking if arrangements could be made for MacDonald to stay in Accrington. It was readily agreed that he should stay with Mr. Pilling's brother, Mr. Andrew Pilling, of Richmond Street, who was also employed at Howard and Bullough's, and, like his brother, was connected with St. Peter's. Mr. Crofton also wrote to Mr. Townsend regarding the proposed visit of his protege, knowing as he did that both had kindred interests in social and economic questions. Mr. Townsend was at that time working at Howard and Bullough's and Mr. 'Johnny' Pilling was his foreman."

"During Mr. MacDonald's stay in the town he attended in company with Mr. Townsend several meetings of a semi-private character at the old Altham's Cafe, where the premises of Messrs. J.W. Bridge now stand, and also at the Workman's Home, now the Rechabites Hall, Abbey Street. They had several long walks over the hills together, and spent much of the time discussing social and industrial questions. Mr. Townsend remembers Mr. MacDonald as a strong, healthy youth, with black, curly hair. After leaving St. Stephen's College he became a free-lance journalist, and did not enjoy too many of fortune's smiles. During that period of his early career he wrote to Accrington inquiring if he could get a job at Howard and Bullough's, but it was realised that he had had no training and it was thought that the work would be scarcely congenial to him. Just about that time he received an appointment as secretary to an MP., and this started him upon the career which led to the Premiership and leadership of his Party."

"Mr. Townsend holds the impression that Mr. MacDonald was not quite right in describing Mr. Sutcliffe as a 'greaser'. He believes he was in charge of a travelling crane. Mr. Sutcliffe was a former secretary of the local branch of the S.D.F., and now resides at 79. Marlborough Street, Burnley."

Alice Haines in a letter dated 15th January 1995, said that she was present at the Tenement Meeting, and added that Mr. Sutcliffe lived on Lower Antley Street, Accrington, prior to moving to Burnley. His son Mr. A. Sutcliffe, became a prominent member of the AEU, District Committee and won West Ward for Labour in the 1945 Borough Elections.

ACCRINGTON TCLP CONTINUED.

On Saturday June 22nd. at 7.30 pm. the Labour Party held a Grand Victory Celebration in Accrington Town Hall. The Harry Howson's Concert Party provided the entertainment and Mr. Tom Snowden MP gave a speech. Admission cost 6d. The newly elected MP also attended victory functions at Rishton and Oswaldtwistle.

The amount that each candidate could legally spend on election expenses was £1,137. Labour spent £477..19s..10d. to the Liberal/Conservative's £795..6s..0d. ['Observer' July 2nd. 1929]

On Saturday June 29th the inaugural meeting took place of Clayton-Le-Moors, Young Labour League, at the home of Mrs. Parr. 25 members later enjoyed a ramble under the direction of Miss Phyllis Parr and Miss J. Heys. ['Observer' 6th July 1929]

THE LABOUR PARTY FIELD DAY.

This took place on Saturday July 13th and was again favoured by ideal weather. 5,000 children and adults had a 'delightful time' at the event, which was held in a field off Burnley Road. The Accrington Old Band played musical selections throughout the afternoon and evening. Speeches were made by Councillor Constantine and Tom Snowden MP. Snowden said:

"That they would benefit common humanity; not the few but the many, and because of that the present Labour Government was charged with a great responsibility of establishing upon the Statute Book of the country legislation of such a character as would benefit mankind and give confidence and trust to the people. And he believed they would do it." [Applause]

Tom's confidence in Ramsay MacDonald and his Cabinet would be tried and tested during the next twelve months or so.

THE LABOUR PARTY TRIP TO BINGLEY.

On Saturday August 24th., 500 Accrington Labour supporters descended on Bingley, in two specially chartered trains. These picked up at Rishton and Church departing at 12.50 pm. and 1.58 pm. Mr. Tom Snowden MP having welcomed them at the station on their arrival, took his guests on a grand tour of Bingley, which included a trip around his mill. Tea was provided in the Co-operative Hall, Bingley, in two sittings. The party arrived back in Accrington at 11. 10 pm.

THE ACCRINGTON BOROUGH ELECTIONS.

The Labour candidates were:
North: Samuel Turnell Pilkington, Labour, 249 Burnley Road, Manager.
South: Richard Ingham Constantine, Labour, 'Rodenhurst' Laund Road, Wholesale Stationer.
East: Arthur Dawson, Labour, 31 Avenue Parade, Trade Union Secretary.
West: Thomas O'Connor, Labour, 103 Ormerod Street, Assurance Agent.
Central: William Howson, Labour, 2 Mather Avenue, Secretary.
Peel Park: Michael Walsh, Labour, 75 Oswald Street, Stoker.
Higher Antley: James Baron, Labour, 45 Perth Street, Coal-hewer.
Spring Hill: John Lord, Labour, 5 Primrose Street, Locomotive Engine Driver.

All eight candidates were successful; including Sam Pilkington who incredibly knocked George Slack, Liberal, off the Council in North Ward.

ACCRINGTON'S FIRST LABOUR ALDERMAN - MR. W.A. LAMBERT.

At the Town Council meeting November 1929, four Aldermanic seats were up for election, which had formerly been held by the Conservative / Liberal alliance. The result of the ballot amongst the councillors, [aldermen were not allowed to vote for the aldermanic bench] was 12 votes each for the retiring aldermen, Bury, Rawson, Sudall and Wilkinson, and 12 votes each for Lambert and Roberts, the Labour nominees. However, Mr. Fred Whittaker the representative for Huncoat voted unexpectedly for Bury, Rawson, Lambert and Constantine. This meant that with 13 votes Lambert had been elected, as the first Labour alderman for the Borough. The Mayor had to give his casting vote in order to chose the fourth alderman, and this resulted in Mr. Sudall losing his seat.

'Observerations' said:
"It was a development such as had apparently never been anticipated by Liberals, Conservatives or Socialists......"

"Had the Labour group on the Council known how Mr. Fred Whittaker was going to vote, we may be pretty sure that they would have added Councillor Constantines name to those of the two Councillors for whom they voted. Had they done so, Alderman Wilkinson would have been 'out' and Councillor Constantine would have been an alderman." ['Observer' November 12th 1929]

Mr. C. Myall was returned unopposed in Spring Hill Ward for the Labour Party in the By-election caused by Mr. Lambert's elevation to the Aldermanic bench.

ACCRINGTON LABOUR PARTY'S BAZAAR.

This took place over a four day period in Accrington Town Hall. Each Ward organisation ran a stall, and concerts were held every evening in the Court Room. On Wednesday 27th, November, the event was opened by Alderman Kathleen Chambers of Bradford. On Thursday it was opened by Mr. Tom Snowden MP. Friday was 'Ladies Day' and this was opened by Lady Cynthia Mosley MP., wife of Sir Oswald. On the final day, Saturday, the Labour Party welcomed back Mr. Charles Roden Buxton MP. for Elland. ['Observer' November 30th. 1929] The event raised the incredible net sum of £1,430. ['Observer' 2nd. December 1933]

1930

UDC ELECTIONS 1930.

The Labour Movement candidates were as follows:
Oswaldtwistle.
Foxhill Bank: William Henry Greenwood, Labour. 204b Union Road. Grocer.
Immanuel: Walter Stirling, Labour. 27 Stanhill Street. General worker.
Church.
Peter Henry Holmes, Labour. 4 George Street. Insurance agent.
Francis Joseph Duffey, Labour. 15 Canal Street. Textile Worker.
Clayton-Le-Moors.
Henry Edmondson, Labour. 31 Victoria Street. Restaurant keeper.
Margaret Alice Kennedy, Labour. 28 Whalley Road. Housewife.
Joseph Finch, Miner. 35 Earl Street. Coal miner.
Joseph Hardy, Miner. 5 Waterloo Street. Coal miner.
Rishton.
Thurston Bradshaw, Labour. 9 Chapel Street. Cotton weaver.
Henry James Earnshaw, Labour. 1 Norfolk Street. Moulder.
Great Harwood.
North: George Henry Fox, Trades Council. Trade Union Secretary.
South: Thomas Tickle, Trades Council. Railway Clerk.
East: William Slynn, Trades Council. Weaver.
West: John Chambers, Trades Council. Insurance Agent.
Mr. Holmes was successful in Church; Mr. Greenwood in Oswaldtwistle; Mr. Edmondson in Clayton-Le-Moors; but all the other candidates were defeated.

ILP.

The 'Observer' Editorial kept up its mischievous snipping at the Labour movement by writing the following:

"One of the Four Socialist Group was speaking at Birmingham on Saturday. It was Mr. James Maxton who described members of HM's Ministry [The Labour Cabinet] as guilty of 'sin' and 'treachery'. Mr. Philip Snowden and Mr. J.H. Thomas were singled out for special abuse. And the Prime Minister [MacDonald] himself did not escape castigation. ['Observer' April 22nd.1930]

The following week it again passed comments, this time on the ILP Conference at Birmingham, stating:

"One speaker declared that in 10 months, Mr. Thomas had done more for British Capitalism than the Tory government did in five years..... The chief interest of the proceedings lies of course in the indication which they give of a coming split in the Labour Party. When these things are being said by the Government's 'supporters', while the most brilliant defence of Mr. Snowden's Budget is made in the House of Commons by Mr. Lloyd George [Liberal], interesting developments seem probable." ['Observer' 29th. April 1930]

NEW BOROUGH MAGISTRATES.

From the Labour side the following were appointed to the bench: Councillor T. O'Connor, 103 Ormerod Street. He had 22 years service on the Board of Guardians and was Chairman in 1921-22. He was first elected to Accrington Borough Council in 1919 but was defeated after his first period of service. In November 1926 he was re-elected. He was a worshipper at Sacred Heart RC. Church and was a member of the Knights of St. Columbia.

Alderman W.A. Lambert, 7 Craven Street. He was the senior Labour representative on the Council and the first and only Alderman. For several years he was Secretary of the Trades Council before that body became amalgamated with the Labour Party. He had been Secretary of the General Workers' Union in Accrington for 15 years.

Mr. G.K. Chalmers, 17 Robert Street. He had been District Secretary of the Accrington AEU since 1919. Prior to that he was branch secretary from 1913 - 1919.

Mr. Alfred Rowkins, 129 Higher Antley Street. He had 11 years service on the Haslingden Board of Guardians and 12 years service on the Board of Management of Accrington Victoria Hospital. He had been a railwayman for 40 years, the last 26 years as a passenger guard. He was Treasurer of the local branch of the NUR and was a former Chairman. He worshipped at St. Peters Church and had been a member of the Independent Order of Rechabites for 52 years.

MR. TOM SNOWDEN'S DEFENCE OF THE GOVERNMENT.

This took place on Sunday May 4th., at a Public Meeting held in the Palace Picture House, Accrington. Mr. Snowden MP said:

"It must not be assumed that the Labour Government was satisfied. They were very much dissatisfied. With the best will in the world this Government was not able to present to the House of Commons a definite, clear cut policy of constructive Socialism. Rightly or wrongly, the Cabinet felt that it was better to patch and palliate than to endeavour to get their Socialist programme through this present Parliament and know at the very outset that they would be defeated....."

"If he felt that was the beginning and end, and that they could not put a definite constructive alternative policy before the country, then he would say the Labour Government had failed. He knew that the people of this country preferred work to unemployment benefit and until they could put their definite policy of constructive Socialism into operation it was their bounden duty to see that men and women had the best and most decent life they could....."

"Mr. Snowden, in conclusion said that the critics both within and without had no right at the present time to criticise the sincerity of the Prime Minister or the Chancellor. He had a great admiration for Jimmy Maxton. He believed he was a sincere a man as ever lived, but he thought his policy was a most misguided one. The difficulties of the Prime Minister were big enough as it was. Mr. Snowden ended with a visionary appeal for the new social order, when in the absence of that haunting fear of poverty, which menaced old people especially, there would be neighbourly love, beauty, and nobility, which would enable them to see those beauties of life they were unable to enjoy while keeping their faces to the grindstone." ['Observer' May 6th. 1930]

ACCRINGTON NUR'S PRESENTATION TO ITS SECRETARY.

Councillor Lord who had spent 20 years as Branch Secretary, was presented with gifts by Mr. J. Marchbank of London, at a Public Meeting held in the Kings Hall, on Sunday afternoon May 18th. The Chairman for the meeting was Tom Snowden MP. All transport workers and Labour representatives were welcome. Important statistics emerging from the meeting were that in 1909 the branch had 163 members and in 1930 this had increased to over 400 members.

THE LABOUR PARTY FIELD DAY.

This was held on Saturday July 12th. during glorious weather. It was convened in a field off Burnley Road. "The children, who predominated, had a happy time, romping over the grass and competing in the many games provided for them." The Accrington Old Prize Band played throughout the afternoon. The speakers were Mr. Tom Snowden MP, and Councillor Constantine. The contents of their speeches, mentioning the cotton crisis and unemployment have been included in previous chapters.

ACCRINGTON BOROUGH ELECTIONS.

Labour candidates were as follows:
North: William Morris Sproul, Labour. 'Arcady' Poulton Avenue. Railway Signalman.
South: Joseph Edward Greenwood, Labour. 36 Royds Street. Secretary.
East: Henry Smith, Labour. 1 James Street, Huncoat. Coal Miner.
West: George Farnworth Kilshaw, Labour. 27 Garfield Street. Trade Union Assistant Secretary.
Central: William Alex Haines, Labour. 36 Willow Street. Clerk.
Peel Park: Herbert Henry Parsons, Labour. 3 Yorkshire Street. Postal Worker.
Higher Antley: Herbert Walsh, Labour. 66 Garbett Street. Textile Machinist.
Spring Hill: William Henry Roberts, Labour. 46a Charter Street. Gentleman.

Again the 'Observer' showed its political preference in no uncertain terms:

> "In 7 of the 8 wards, the Socialists are engaged in an endeavour to capture seats hitherto held by 5 Liberals and 2 Conservatives. It would be no good thing for Accrington and its ratepayers were they to succeed. All over the country, Socialist control of municipalities has meant reckless expenditure and soaring rates."
> ['Observer' October 25th. 1930]

It then went on to praise the qualities of the Tory and Liberal candidates. Meanwhile the Labour municipal candidates, together with Tom Snowden, presented themselves to the electorate at a public meeting held in the Labour Hall on Sunday October 26th at 7 pm. Their undoubted enthusiasm for the cause did not however, receive the approval of the electors. Labour lost all seven seats in which there was a contest. Their only victor was Councillor Roberts, in Spring Hill, where he was unopposed. The local activists had received the wrath of the electors, who had been influenced by the miserable performance of the Labour Party in Government. The new council was 13 Liberals, 6 Conservatives, 1 Independent, and 13 Labour.

1931

On Wednesday 21st. January, the General Management Committee of the Accrington TCLP passed the following resolution:

"The Accrington TCLP views with alarm the attacks now being made on the workers' standard of living in the railway, cotton, and mining industries....."

It also called on the Government and particularly the Prime Minister, Ramsay MacDonald, to give:

"all possible support to the workers' cause and the workers' efforts to resist the attacks being made upon them by the employers."['Observer' January 24th.1931]

MR. JAMES MAXTON MP'S VISIT TO ACCRINGTON.

The Accrington branch of the ILP organised a public meeting in the Co-operative Assembly Rooms, Oak Street, on Friday February 27th. Mr. Tom Brunton, President, chaired the meeting at which Mr. Maxton MP was the guest speaker. Admission was by ticket, which cost 4d., and the attendance was described by the 'Observer' as 'large'.

Tom Brunton in his opening remarks stated that the Chancellor of the Exchequer, Mr. Philip Snowden, had said "We shall have to economise." He [Tom Brunton] wondered that the words did not blister Philip Snowden's tongue, when he thought of the working classes.

Mr. Maxton stated quite openly that his purpose there that evening, was not to appeal for votes for the Labour Party, but to get men and women to join the Socialist movement and to struggle for Socialism. He went on to say:

"The ILP had come under steady fire because they had regularly and persistently criticised the Labour Government. They had been accused on that account of disloyalty. He denied that charge."

"His first loyalty was to Socialism and to the working classes. [Hear,hear]. He had never been disloyal to them. It was the duty of Socialists to stimulate the people of this country to demand Socialism and compel the Labour Government to deliver Socialism. [Hear,hear.]. The happenings of the present time, the condition of the people, the steady deterioration of the industrial and commercial life of the country, even with the Labour Government in office, were not arguments against Socialism, but arguments for Socialism. One could accuse this Government of many things. One could say that it was not wise leadership for the Labour Government to take office in a minority position. Without the power to change capitalism substantially they would be held responsible in the public eye for all the evils of capitalism. [Hear, hear.].''

"One might say that the Government had not used the splendid opportunities to propagate Socialism and denounce capitalism. One thing could not be laid against them, and that was that they had tried Socialism as a remedy for all the troubles of the day. Whatever responsibility might be placed on the shoulders of the Labour Government, no responsibility for the existing conditions of this country could be laid at the door of Socialism because there had been no application of Socialist principles to the solution of the present difficulties."

"They had reached a stage in industrial development in which this world and the people of this world were capable of producing goods at a greater speed and in greater quantities than ever before. And every day some new device, some new invention of engineering skill, some new discovery of science, some new idea for better organisation made production at greater speed and in greater quantities more easy still. To-day, in the midst of plenty and confronted with the possibility of greater abundance still, they faced these facts not with joy and confidence in the future, but with terror in their hearts. One would have thought that they would have looked forward to greater quantities of the material things of life and steadily diminishing working time and a reducing expenditure of energy being called upon from each of them for their material needs. That ought to be the result of greater abundance and greater ease of production. Socialists told them that that was as it ought to be.[Hear, hear.] The difficulties of to-day arose not because the genius of man had been wrong not because the skill of man and the hand and brain of man had been misdirected, not because Nature had been stupid in her abundance of resources. The difficulties of to-day arose simply because while men had put their brain power and their body power into discovering newer and better methods of production, up to date no serious thought had been given as to how, when they had produced their goods in abundance, they were going to distribute them fairly amongst the people.[Hear, hear.]."

"The function of the ILP was to shout into the ears of this nation, to din into their ears that the only problem that needed to be looked at and faced up to and tackled at the present time was not the problem of production but the problem of distribution. [Applause.]"

"Each party admitted that the problem was one of over production, but each party, having said that the problem of this country was one of over-production, turned its back on that theory and began to provide devices for producing more."

"The Conservatives when in power had two great big Acts of statesmanship to further their policy. One was de-rating and the reorganisation of local government, and the other was the Electricity Act. Both were directed towards the end of producing more goods to cope with the problem of over-production. The Liberals' great scheme was the great development loan - that the country raise some hundred million pounds for developing roads, docks and harbours, and extending the telephone system so that more goods might be produced! What had the Labour policy been? To co-ordinate and rationalise essential industries so that they might be able to produce more goods!"

"Let him say that he was quite in favour of these measures, which were quite good, but as cures for the present evils they had nothing to do with the case; they were wasting the time of the nation; they were breaking the heart of the nation; taking all the joy and hope out of the life of the people. If those who made for greater production or speedier production left the question of distribution untouched they would make for full, utter national ruin."

"A large proportion of the members of the present Government had had some record of service to Socialism and had spoken from platforms or walked in processions with a banner over their heads with the words "Socialism is the only hope of the workers." Now they come forward to the ILP and say, "Socialism in our time is impossible." If it was true that Socialism was the only hope of the workers and if it was also true that Socialism in their time was impossible, if they put these two statements together and drew the logical deduction it meant that if there was no hope for Socialism in their time there was no hope for the worker in their time. He rejected this absolutely."

"They were bound to be on the very threshold of the solution of mankind's difficulties. If they asked him why he said this so confidently he would reply that it was a matter of faith. And faith was not an easy thing to argue about. The history of mankind had shown that mankind had always solved its problems up to now. It was impossible to believe that what primitive men with their limited opportunities could do they would fail to do with the advantages they had got. But for the solution of any problem the first thing necessary was to face up to it honestly and fearlessly with clear and unclouded eyes and admit above all that it was their problem."

"To those who said that Socialism in our time was a foolish

dream and that it was something for the dim and distant future, he said that was cowardice - intellectual and moral cowardice -and it was trying to shove on to the shoulders of unborn grandchildren responsibility that they ought to shoulder. [Applause.]"

"The plan which had a moral sanction behind it, which had a religious sanction behind it, which had got fair play and sportsmanship behind it was to guarantee to every human being within the land a decent living income - [Hear, hear.] - and make the organised State responsible for seeing that into every home every week there came an income that would provide all the needs of that home and give to the persons who made up the family circle the assurance of being able to live healthily and take pleasure in life. It might be said that that was a very difficult thing to do, and he was not prepared to say that it was an easy thing to do. But he wanted to remind them that to do anything else was a difficult and complicated task. To let things go drifting to disaster created even bigger difficulties and more complications."

"Teachers and policemen and MPs and Cabinet Ministers and the King were all valuable, but from the point of view of getting the things without which they could not do for twenty-four hours they were secondary in importance and they were all being carried on the backs of the real wealth producers. [Hear, hear.] It might be impossible for the coal trade or the railways to pay a living wage. But what could be proved was that the total wealth of the nation combined, if it paid his living wage, could also pay the living wage of the workers in the various industries that produced wealth. [Hear, hear.]"

"Anything that stood in the way of the whole of the people getting a decent opportunity had got to be forcibly and firmly removed. They in the ILP came to them and asked them to make their fight centre round a determination for a living wage for all with the power of the State behind and the State in a position to guarantee it. To do that the State must become the responsible owner, controller and director of the essential things of their industrial and commercial life. It must become controller and director of our import and export trade. If it did that they would proceed along the road that led to liberation for the whole of the people, to all the nation playing their part of the work of the world, having a fair and reasonable share of the wealth of the world, so that the world ceased to be a great prison house for humanity in which they looked out through the bars with eyes of hatred at the men in the other cells. [Applause.]"

"Replying to questioners, Mr. Maxton said he made no

indictment against the Labour Government that he did not make against the whole working class movement because the policy of the Labour Government, if not dictated by the working class movement, had certainly received approval by the working class movement at every stage. If they were going to get a change of policy and get a Labour Government that was going to act towards the end for which the Labour Government was brought into being it would not be by merely a change of heart at the top, but a change of heart right through. The trade union method had got to be revised and brought up-to-date. Instead of being the instrument of snatching the best out of its own industry it had got to be regarded as the instrument for a whole social change." ['Observer' March 3rd. 1931]

In direct opposition to the Labour leadership, Maxton argued that the ILP should not relegate itself to being a mere Socialist education society. He maintained that it had a continuing duty to:

"Devise methods, plans and schemes for the achievement of Socialism." [12]

Maxton and his friends openly opposed the moderate 1928 Labour Party programme, "Labour and the Nation." He said:

"I have sat and watched a Tory Government for four and a half years trying to run Capitalism...... and they have been unable to make any impression on any one of the outstanding problems..... A Labour Government cannot run Capitalism any more successfully than Baldwin and the others." [13]

When the result of the 1929 Election was known, Maxton wanted Labour to remain in opposition and to let a Tory / Liberal coalition Government take the flack for rising unemployment. He could see that, [after the experience of the first minority Labour Government in 1924] taking office under such circumstances would result in Labour being blamed for the inevitable economic crisis. Much better, he thought to remain in opposition and build an active militant Socialist movement ready to take over after a future election.

Maxton's attitude proved to be correct, Labour took office, the world depression got worse and unemployment grew to unprecedented levels, as Chapter 3 has described.

Mr. Tom Brunton, Chairman of the Accrington ILP spoke on the "Economics of a Madhouse", at the Discussion Class on March 8th. He said:

"They did not seem to have persuaded the working classes as yet that they were living in a madhouse..... If one could see the [world] as a spectator instead of a participant one would think that the subject was intensely simple of achievement. All they required in the way of sustenance, housing, recreation, literature and the rest, they could have successfully accomplished - in a limited fashion he agreed - some hundred years or so ago. The developments of the last two hundred years had been of such a character not only in variety but also in intensity that they could now produce wealth in such very surplus abundance that why they did not feed themselves, clothe themselves and house themselves would at times look to be a nightmare to one outside the show....."

"So easily were they duped and misled....."

After 11 months of a Labour Government, Tom said:

"He saw nothing looming ahead but utter, unpierceable blackness...... The only shaft of light there was for the working classes was to seek a way out and pursue it...... Liberalism, he declared, had no hope for the working classes. As soon as the Labour Party, with all their weaknesses and inefficiency and their vagueness and lack of the devil-may-care, brought in the Trades Union Bill to restore conditions filched by the Conservatives, the Bill was destroyed by the Liberal Party."

"Socialism was the one hope of the working classes, the only certain hope. The others were blind alleys." ['Observer' March 10th. 1931]

On Thursday May 7th. at the Accrington Labour Party, Women's Section meeting, Mr. Terry McCarthy, brother of Margaret, spoke on the subject of 'The ILP Living Wage Proposals.' The 'Observer' reported his contribution as follows:

"The real problem was one of lack of co-ordination between production and consumption owing to restraints imposed by capitalist social order. The ILP suggested redistribution of national wealth to enable stagnant surpluses to be consumed. This was a necessary stage in the commencement of the application of Socialist Policy. Mr. McCarthy outlined the ILP programme and appealed for support and consideration." ['Observer' May 9th. 1931]

COUNTY COUNCIL ELECTIONS.

There were no contests held throughout the entire Division, due to the Labour movement failing to produce a single nominee. The Conservative and Liberal candidates were elected unopposed. ['Observer' February 28th. 1931]

UDC ELECTIONS.

Labour movement candidates:
Oswaldtwistle.
Foxhill Bank: John Richard Cressey, Labour. 2 Whewell Row. Textile Machinist.
Clayton-Le-Moors.
Henry Edmundson, Labour. 31 Victoria Street. Restaurant Keeper.
John James Hutchinson, Labour. 39 Willow Street. Green Brick Setter.
Joseph Hardy, Miner. 5 Waterloo Street.
Great Harwood.
Mr. Tom Tickle and Mr. G.H. Fox.
Church and Rishton Labour Parties failed to nominate candidates. ['Observer' March 14th. 1931]

The results were extremely disappointing, with no Labour victories within the entire Division. ['Observer' March 31st. 1931] However, with the appalling national leadership of Ramsay MacDonald and Philip Snowden it was to be expected.

THE CRISIS.

The minority Labour Government had taken office in May 1929 dependant upon Conservative and Liberal support. Baldwin's Government had budgeted for a surplus of £4 million, but instead, the new Labour Chancellor of the Exchequer, Philip Snowden, found that by the time of his first budget there was a deficit of £14.5 million and the unemployment insurance fund had accumulated a debt of £36 million.

International trade had gone from bad to worse, following the Wall Street Crash of 1929, and this had resulted in industry slowing down and unemployment rising. Britain was also on the Gold Standard at the time, at a rate that was 10% too high, therefore making it virtually impossible for the country to export any goods. The May Committee on the state of the economy, reported to the Cabinet in July 1931, that the country faced a deficit of £120 million and recommended cuts of £96 million. In August 1931, Snowden, rather than tackling the problem in a Socialist, or even a Keynesian manner, decided to follow the advice of the Governor of the Bank of England. This was to impose additional taxation of £81.5 million and to make savings by cutting unemployment benefit, social services and teachers salaries by 10%. The minority Labour Government fell and a National Government, under the former Labour leader Ramsay MacDonald, was established. [14]

The effects of the above, on the Accrington TCLP, are dealt with below:

Mr. Tom Snowden MP., in a message to Councillor W. Howson, agent to the Accrington TCLP, said that he did not agree with the attitude taken by Mr. MacDonald and Mr. Snowden, and that he would support Mr. Henderson and the others who had left the Cabinet in disgust at the appeasement to the capitalist enemy. Tom stated that " he was definitely against a reduction in unemployment grants." ['Observer' August 29th. 1931]

Tom spoke at considerable length on the political situation at a meeting of the Clayton-Le-Moors Labour Party, held in the township's Co-operative Assembly Rooms, on Saturday evening August 29th. The 'Observer' reported the event as follows:

"Remarking that the Prime Minister and the Chancellor had done things which the Labour Party, with practical unanimity, had disapproved of, Mr. Snowden went on to describe the events of the past fortnight, and to the proposals put before the Cabinet for conferring with the other two orthodox political parties on the difficulties of the situation. That submission did not appeal to the majority of the Cabinet. They felt they had an obligation to a wider sphere, viz, the Trade Union Congress, to the Labour Party, and to the Parliamentary Labour Party. That was a very important point in the issue at stake. The Labour Party had condemned autocracy and said that democracy ought to be supreme....."

"Having regard to the fact that the trade union movement had had a great responsibility for the formation and sustenance of the Labour Party, and seeing that this was a question which affected the workers and democracy in general, in spite of the urgency which the PM and the Chancellor claimed, the majority of the Cabinet thought there ought to be consultation with these bodies. The consultations took place, and the TUC Executive and the Labour Party Executive at once, and with unanimity, took exception to the policy they were invited to pursue, viz, to take part with either the Conservative or the Liberal Party in the formation of a National Government."

"The Labour Party and the TUC had good reason, for taking that view," proceeded Mr. Snowden. "The workers of this country have regarded the orthodox political parties as being not merely the traditional enemy of the Labour and the Socialist movement, but by almost every act and deed of the past they have, on essentials, been diametrically opposed to the principles and policy and the action of our movement, and they had no confidence in their ability to redress the wrongs as they exist at the present time, and no confidence whatever that they could give expression to the point of view of our party......"

"The situation had arisen substantially through the report of the May Committee appointed by the Government to go into the question of national expenditure....."

"With regard to the recommendations of the May Committee there was almost, complete disagreement [from the TUC and the Labour Party]......"

"Mr. Arthur Henderson made it abundantly clear that in the proposals which were submitted.... in the main, the only thing that had to be attacked was the social services of this country....."

"It was a strange thing that they had always to begin with the workers first..... Why didn't they start with the rich?....."

"Not for the first time we were asked to make sacrifices for our country. During the war they were asked to make sacrifices for their country and sacrifices were made in human-kind. Now we were confronted with a financial difficulty and we were asked to make sacrifices for the well-being of the nation from the small and inadequate income the workers had to be content with. "Well, we are not having it." said Mr. Snowden emphatically. "We formed an Opposition..... We are not having the social services of this country sacrificed to the calf of gold."

"Mr. Snowden proceeded to argue that from the point of view of sound economics it was not good to reduce the unemployment pay of the workers. One of the reasons we were suffering from bad trade to-day was not because we could not produce, but, because of the lack of purchasing power of the community at large. Another reason why unemployment pay should not be reduced was that a hungry democracy was likely to be a menace to the country. He did not think this had been taken into consideration as much as it might have been. If the people were ill-fed and lacking social services, it might cost the country far more in other respects......"

"Labour members had had a sorry time during the past two years. They had not had a majority in Parliament, and he had had to say "Yea" and "Amen" to lots of things he did not like. On many matters they had had to compromise, but there were certain things on which they were uncompromising and this was one of the things on which they could not compromise....."['Observer' September 1st.1931]

The Accrington TCLP Executive, were addressed by Tom Snowden on Wednesday, September 2nd. The meeting unanimously adopted the following

resolution:
> "That this EC having heard Mr. Snowden explain the various points relating to the political crisis, unanimously approve of his attitude and the line of action he has taken, and pledge themselves to give him their wholehearted support." ['Observer' September 5th. 1931]

The National Government belatedly came off the Gold Standard in September and in October called a General Election. Tom Snowden was again adopted as Labour Parliamentary Candidate at a delegate meeting held in the Labour Hall, Accrington on Sunday October 11th. He said that it was Philip Snowden's and Ramsay MacDonald's duty, and those who had jumped ship and supported them, to have discussed the whole situation with the Labour movement. After all, these traitors would not have occupied the positions they did without the backing of the Labour movement in the past.

He went on to denounce the constitutions and the composition of the various Commissions and Committees, appointed to deal with problems occurring during the Labour Government's term of office.

Later that day in the Palace Cinema, Accrington, Tom opened his campaign to a full and lively attendance. Councillor A. Dawson presided. Councillor Dawson attacked the Liberals and the Conservatives for putting one nominee forward as the National candidate. He asked the question, "What right had the Liberal and Tory parties to assume they were the true patriots?" He hoped that the workers would not be taken in by this sentimental appeal to nationalism.

Tom decided to praise the qualifications of the Labour Party's new leader, Mr. Arthur Henderson. He said:
> "It would be generally admitted by fair-minded men and women in all parties and in other countries that if there was one man in this country who had succeeded in filling an office of great responsibility it was ...... Mr. Arthur Henderson, at the Foreign Office. [Applause.] He believed Arthur Henderson gave a broad and correct interpretation of the policy to which men and women would heartily subscribe who were never members of the Labour movement, in regard to the question of peace, the League of Nations, and above everything to the Disarmament Conference to be held in February of next year."

Tom also brought up one of the most strikingly obvious alternatives to cutting unemployment pay and the salaries of the teachers.
> "The Prime Minister ought to have referred to the loanholders, whose interest the Chancellor of the Exchequer had been awaiting a favourable opportunity to convert to a lower rate. That conversion apparently had to be voluntary, but they could use compulsion when it

came to the unemployed, the police and the navy."

This last point was detailed in an ILP pamphlet, published in 1932, entitled "The Jugglers of Finance are Bleeding the Nation White." I will precis the document at this point, because it is a central part of the debate and shows without any doubt how the working-class was swindled.

The History of a Great Swindle.

"In July, 1914, it was apparent that war in Europe was inevitable. The first casualty in this country was **the banking system and the gold standard.**"

"Large withdrawals of cash took place from the banks in the week ending July 29th, 1914. A panic set in amongst the bankers. They have never more than a small portion of money in their vaults and tills to meet all demands that can be made legally upon them......"

"**Thus on August 1st, 1914, the Governor of the Bank of England appealed to the Government to save the banking system of the country......**"

"Asquith and Lloyd George replied immediately. They promised to introduce legislation to meet the situation. Monday, August 3rd, 1914, was a bank Holiday. Tuesday, Wednesday and Thursday were declared to be special bank holidays. **On Thursday, August 6th, the Currency and Bank Note Act was passed through all its stages and received the Royal Assent. On Friday the banks opened and the public were given a new money. They were given pieces of paper declared by the Government, in the name of the people of this country, to be money.**"

"**The banks had failed and the people provided them with the money which they are popularly supposed to look after.**"

"**The only money the banks had, was money supplied by the State.**"

But What Happened Next.

"In November, 1914, the Government went to the bankers, who had only the money the Government had made for them, and asked for a **loan of £350 million pounds** to carry on the war."

"Let Mr. Frederick Temple, author of 'War Finance and the Worker,' published in 1916, tell you what was his experience:-

"When the war broke out at the beginning of August, 1914..... the Capitalist banking system hopelessly broke down, a moratorium was declared, and it would never up to now, have been able to fulfil its obligations to its creditors had not the State come to its succour by providing it with legal tender paper money. The State was the one big thing."

"Therefore, when about two months later, the State proceeded to apply to the bank for a loan of £350 millions of money, the spectacle was enough to make the gods laugh..... of course, the Bank of England had not got it. So the directors said, 'We will make an issue to the public.'"

"Subscriptions began to dribble in, but although the Press did its best, and suggested that the loan would be subscribed two and three times over, **those inside knew better, and it soon became apparent that the bank, in order to save its face, would have to adopt some new expedient, and this it did. It issued circulars to city firms and business men, which contained a truly remarkable offer. One of these offers came to me. It set out that if I filled in an enclosed form of application for a portion of the War Loan it would lend me the whole of the money [knowing that it had not got it]. Had I applied, say, for £20,000 of War Loan, I should have had to put up no margin, no money, no securities. It would cost me a penny stamp for the covering envelope and no more. Those who availed themselves of the offer were charged 3% for the accommodation. The State will ultimately pay them 4% and the taxpayers will pay this 4% to the State - this being the only real part of the transaction......"**

"This was a clear creation of credit and nothing more nor less than the writing up of figures in the books of the banks....."

This Continued All Through the War.

The second War Loan was issued in June, 1915. The receipts were £592,479,544......By the time the third War Loan was raised they were still bolder. The book, 'British Finance,' previously referred to, states:-"

The banks publicly advertised that they were prepared to grant loans not only to existing customers, but to strangers, to enable them to subscribe to the War Loan, provided the applicants were in a position to pay off the advances within a reasonable time."

"What does this mean?

"If you or I had secured a portion of the War Loan we should have drawn from the Government, **for patriotically lending our name to our country in its hour of need,** interest at 5.5%. The banks would have charged us '1% below bank rate varying' - that is 4%. We would patriotically pocket the difference. "

"If at the end of the two years we went to the bank and confessed our inability to repay the loan, they would say, **'It doesn't matter in the least. We have the War Loan. We draw all the interest now for ourselves.'**

"No wonder the receipts from the third loan were nearly a £1,000 million pounds....."

"The fourth, or Victory Loan, of June, 1919, was raised in the same way. Of this the banks took the sum of **£111 millions** in direct subscriptions......"

But How Have The Finance-Jugglers Fared.

"As the standard of life of the community has fallen, as prices have fallen owing to the banks withdrawing and refusing money, to industry and commerce through their policy of deflation, so has the **return on the fixed income derived from these gilt-edged securities risen.**"

"**To-day the moneylenders are drawing from the tax-payers a sum which will buy twice as much as it would in 1920.**"

"**Every decrease in the standard of living of the workers has been accomplished by more wealth for the moneylenders.**"

"[In 1931] it appeared that they had pushed deflation and the cutting off of money from industry to such a point that their system was collapsing. **They could not get enough in from the tax-payer to pay, not the 'dole' of the unemployed man, as they said, but the £300 millions 'dole' they draw in interest, on this fictitious debt.**"

"Therefore, [they say] we have to **economise**. The '**dole**', **wages, social services, have to be cut......**"

"**One thing is certain: the power of the moneylenders must be broken. ..... The financial system is bleeding the nation white. To save yourselves you must end it. Join with us in your fight. SUBSTITUTE SOCIALISM FOR CAPITALISM.**"[15]

As far as the workers were concerned, many [particularly those who took no interest in politics,] were unaware that since 1920 - **in wage-cuts alone they had suffered a loss in money almost equal to the capital of the National Debt.**

The above article on war loans is backed up by the National Government's Budget of 1931, which showed the following expenditure:

Out of every 20s. [£1]:-

           For War

	s.	d.
To war debt	9	2 1/2

Army, Navy and Air Force	2 11
War Pensions	<u>1 4 3/4</u>
	13 6 1/4
For Social Services	
Education	1 3 1/2
Old Age Pensions	0 11
Widows' / Orphans' Pensions	0 1 1/4
Health and Housing	0 6 1/2
Unemployed	0 6
Other Services	<u>3 1 1/2</u>
	6 5 3/4

"Every year £350 million is paid out as interest and sinking fund to those patriotic bondholders who lent their money during the war at 5% and who have already received since the end of the war not less than £4,000 million in interest. Yet the War Debt still remains." [16]

THE GENERAL ELECTION CONTINUED.

Tom's campaign continued. On Tuesday, October 13th, a large attendance welcomed him at Rishton's, Primitive Methodist School. Mr. Bill Brotherton supported him. On Wednesday, October 14th, he addressed a crowded meeting in Accrington Town Hall, in which he was supported by Mr. A. Greenwood, the Minister of Health in the last Labour Government. On Thursday, October 15th, a good attendance awaited him at Clayton-Le-Moors' Town Hall.

His meetings the following week were:
Saturday, October 17th, Accrington Town Hall, with Mr. Arthur Henderson. Labour Party Leader.
Sunday, October 18th, Palace Picture House, Accrington. and the Market Place.
Monday October 19th, Oswaldtwistle Town Hall and Baxenden Wesleyan School.
Tuesday October 20th, Accrington Town Hall and Rishton Primitive Methodist School.
Wednesday October 21st, Clayton-Le-Moors Town Hall and Ernest Street School Church.
Thursday October 22nd, Accrington Town Hall and Holy Trinity School Oswaldtwistle.
Friday October 23rd, the Church School Belthorn, St Oswalds Knuzden and St Mathews School Stanhill.

Sunday October 25th, Empire Picture House Rishton, Palace Picture House Accrington and the Market Ground Accrington.
Monday October 26th, Oswaldtwistle Town Hall, Ernest Street School Church and the Palais-de-danse Accrington.

At the Sunday Meeting October 18th, at the Palace Cinema, Mr. Gordon MacDonald, MP for Ince in the last Parliament, who had previously spoken to the Accrington Discussion Class in the King's Hall, addressed the meeting. The appearance of "Snowden and MacDonald" together on the same platform excited some amusing comments.

The topic of religion always reared its ugly head in Accrington election campaigns, particularly the attitude of the Roman Catholic clergy, headed by the Jesuit Father McAvoy, Parish Priest of the Sacred Heart, Accrington. The Conservative Party also often played the RC card to much success over the years. At Oswaldtwistle Town Hall on Monday October 26th, Tom Snowden had to reply at some length to the message in Saturday's 'Observer' from Father McAvoy SJ, in reference to Paddock House RC School. He had been accused of not getting a grant for the school.

"I would be the last person to deprecate or insinuate that Father McAvoy has not done a very great deal for that school, and I would be the last to infer that he did not make a supreme effort to get, not only recognition, but also a grant, but I am going to point out one or two simple facts."

"Father McAvoy has admitted from a public platform in the Parliamentary Borough that during the membership of Mr. Hugh Edwards he tried to get recognition. Neither Hugh Edwards nor the Tory minister, in the person of Lord Eustace Percy, would give the slightest ear of consideration to the proposal. I was invited to this school, and after being satisfied, I spent months on the matter. I have a letter now asking me if I would get an interview which had been refused by the Tory ministers. What Father McAvoy did not tell you was that Tom Snowden went with him to the ministry."

"It was not done in a week, he went on. In an interview with Sir Charles Trevelyan and Mr. Morgan Jones, he [Mr. Snowden] told them he wanted it done, and finally the Labour minister granted to Paddock House School what the Tory Minister refused.[Applause.] ['Observer' October 27th.1931]

In the main, the Catholic working-class of Accrington voted Labour, however, anti-Labour sermons by Father McAvoy and his fellow priests did significantly affect the Labour vote. Michael Walsh a Catholic Labour Party local government candidate during this period and an active trade unionist, used to earnestly plead with atheist Bill Brotherton to 'keep his head down' during election times, as this would be counter productive in gaining Labour votes.[17] During the 1959 General Election my Headmaster at Holy Family RC Secondary School, Accrington, brought the Conservative candidate round to every class and told us all, in no uncertain terms, to tell our parents to vote for him. The Labour majority dropped to below one thousand. Although, this power to affect election results is less today, it did prove significant in the 1983 election when the Catholic Tory won by only 20 odd votes.

Philip Snowden, the Chancellor, intervened in the campaign by sending the following letter to the 'Observer':

11 Downing Street
Whitehall SW.

"Sir,

I am sorry that Tom Snowden should have the discredit of the most cowardly attack which has been made in this election. You report him as saying:- "The Chancellor dare not go into the country and face the electorate. If he cared he could have gone into Colne Valley or any other constituency and fought an election."

He made that disgraceful statement knowing full well that I have not recovered from the effects of a serious operation which make it impossible for me to travel and take the platform.

I am sure every decent-minded man and woman in Accrington will resent such a cowardly attack, and feel that a person who can make it has no claim either to respect or confidence.

With best wishes for the success of the National Candidate.

I am etc,

Philip Snowden

This epistle from Snowden shows him to be undoubtedly the class traitor that his ex-comrades believed him to be. A man with all those years of robust electioneering behind him should not have been seen to be publicly upset at Tom Snowden's comments. [One almost feels like saying 'didums do'.] His last sentence in which he encourages people to vote, [in Accrington's case] Conservative, and therefore for the class enemy is deplorable. ['Observer' October 24th.1931]

The General Election took place on Thursday October 29th. and the result was a terrible defeat for the working class. The Tory propaganda plus the ex-Labour leadership's totally inept record in Government had won the day for the nation's oppressors.

Major H.A. Procter. Conservative.	30,799
Tom Snowden. Labour.	<u>18,177</u>

Majority.   12,622

John S. Clarke, adventurer, archaeologist, antiquarian, councillor, editor, gun-runner, historian, horseman, journalist, lecturer, lion-tamer, magistrate, Member of Parliament, poet, revolutionary, secretary, zoologist, a leader of the Socialist Labour Party, spokesman for the shop stewards' committees at the time of World War One, and a man who "did many good deeds in an extremely naughty world," [18] wrote humorous epitaphs for the politicians of his day. In the midst of the 1931 crisis, Ramsay MacDonald received the following verse in his morning post:

> Here lies Ramsay Mac,
> A friend of all Humanity,
> Too many pats upon the back
> Inflated Ramsay's vanity.

> The Blarney Stone he oft times kissed,
> But departed in his glory:
> For having lived a socialist
> He died a bloody Tory.[19]

He was in more vitriolic mood when he composed a further verse for J.H. Thomas, the railwaymen's union leader, and Cabinet Minister, who left the Labour Party along with MacDonald and Snowden.

> This sour, unconsecrated ground
> The traitorous corpse encloses
> Of J.H.T. - an unclean hound
> Whose soul in hell reposes!

> Reposes? Yes, while others howl
> On white-hot grids connected -
> No fiend will burn a thing so foul
> For fear he gets infected!
>   N.U.R. [20]

At the Accrington TCLP Women's Section meeting on November 12th, Mr. Tom Brunton, speaking on 'The Result of the General Election', said that:

> "The defeat of the Labour Party was not due so much to the national crisis as to the spineless policy of Government when in office. In future the Labour Party would have to face the facts, and by propaganda and education prepare the minds of the people for a great fight." ['Observer' November 14th 1931]

DEATH OF MR. J.C. BREARE. SECRETARY OSWALDTWISTLE LABOUR PARTY.

Mr. Breare died on Sunday night, October 25th. in the Victoria Hospital. The deceased of 4 Dale Street, was only 29 years of age. He reportedly was a 'zealous worker in the Labour cause', being Secretary of the Oswaldtwistle branch for 8 years. He apparently had been employed for a time at the Oswaldtwistle Labour Exchange; more recently however he had been the assistant to Mr. Howson the Labour Agent. He had passed the examination enabling him to become a Labour Party agent and this was obviously his ambition, which was sadly not to be. ['Observer' October 27th. 1931]

ACCRINGTON BOROUGH ELECTIONS.

The Labour candidates were:
South: Herbert Walsh, Labour. 66 Garbett Street. Textile Machinist.
East: Ellen Dawson, Labour. 31 Avenue Parade. Housewife.
West: Cornelius Burke, Labour. Hyndburn Inn. 314 Blackburn Road. Licenced Victualler.
Central: Herbert Victor Podmore, Labour. 26 Pilot Street. Textile Worker.
Higher Antley: Alfred Rowkins, Socialist. 129 Higher Antley Street.Railway Guard.
Spring Hill: Charles Myall, Labour. 54 Hopwood Street. Engineer.['Observer' October 27th. 1931]

Again, the national situation did the above candidates no favours and all lost, including Charles Myall in the former Labour stronghold of Spring Hill. ['Observer' November 3rd. 1931]

ACCRINGTON'S FIRST LABOUR MAYOR - COUNCILLOR CONSTANTINE.

Constantine's nomination was moved by the senior member of the Council Alderman Rawson and seconded by Alderman Waddington with Alderman Lambert supporting. Ald. Lambert said:
"When Mr. Constantine was representing the borough, he would be able, by his affability and manner, to conduct himself in a way that would bring honour to the community of which he was the chief magistrate." ['Observer' November 10th. 1931]

Richard Ingham Constantine was born in Helmshore and was a lifelong Wesleyan and teetotaller. He arrived in Accrington two years after his marriage around 1897 and eventually became a wholesale stationer in Bank Street. He was a member of the Social Democratic Federation in 1905 and later the ILP and the Labour Party, first standing for the Council in 1909. Eventually he was elected for South Ward in 1919, and only had twelve months absence from the Council up to his death on Friday May 5th 1953. He was made an Alderman of the Borough and he served for many years on Lancashire County Council. The chance to be Accrington's Parliamentary candidate was offered to him on various occasions, but he always refused saying that his time would be better spent at the local level.

I believe that during his early career he was truly a man ahead of his time and I think we must remember that in 1931 he had already given 26 years service to the Labour cause. The situations which feature him in this volume show his opponents in the Lib / Con coalition, who outnumbered him and his colleagues so dramatically both on the Haslingden Board of Guardians, the PAC, the County Council, and the Accrington Town Council, to be bullying, pompous buffoons, all apparent believers in the master and men philosophy of life. Maybe it was this cold, uncaring, repressive attitude of the representatives of Accrington's ruling class which instilled in him the fortitude and determination with which to attack, in his own mild mannered and at times humorous way, their dominant and evil hold of power. [21]

MAXTON AND THE ILP'S DISAFFILIATION.

Maxton said, after the fall of the Labour Government and the establishment of the National Government:
> "To me their failure was due to a complete lack of faith in Socialism..... and their lack of belief in..... the working classes to achieve Socialism..... I firmly believe that out of the defeat that at present faces the working classes in their effort for Socialist liberation, out of the schism and faction will develop speedily a new political Socialist movement of the working class which will be strong enough in faith, in morale and in personnel to achieve success where its predecessors failed." [22]

On the other hand, Arthur Henderson and the official Labour and TUC leadership, emphasised the attacks made by Maxton and his colleagues, as being responsible for the debacle. The Labour Party's catastrophic defeat had brought the differences between the Labour Party and the ILP to a head.

The ILP continued to debate this relationship and three distinct groupings emerged: those who wished to unconditionally accept Labour's standing orders; the conditional affiliationists; and those that wanted to make a complete break by disaffiliating. Maxton supported the latter; maintaining that to stay within the Labour Party meant "creating in the public mind that the capitalist system in all its essentials must be preserved at all costs." He argued that keeping Labour Party membership would stop the ILP from abiding by its principles.

In July 1932, at a special ILP conference, disaffiliation was carried by a huge majority. Maxton said:

"I shall try within five years to unite the working classes without any imposition from above by non-Socialists. I shall make it a real unity of revolutionary forces." [23]

Looking at the situation after 60 years, I agree with the analysis, that "it was the integration of the Labour Party into mainstream party politics which led to disaffiliation." [24]

Maxton, [and who can blame him] thought that the collapse of Capitalism was imminent. Over-production coupled with a lack of wherewithal to consume on a world-wide scale, pointed in that direction. However, we can now see that Capitalism managed to stagger from one crisis to another, whilst at the same time the working class failed to achieve the heights of class consciousness required for a Socialist revolution to take place.

The 1931 General Election resulted in the ILP being reduced to three MPs. William Knox writes:

"The 1930's were to prove to be a fascinating period in Maxton's political development as he struggled with the problems of leading a small party, which, although larger than the Communist Party of Great Britain, faced the prospect of marginalisation and the task of developing a form of Socialism free from Social Democratic and Stalinist defects in the socially and politically devastating atmosphere of Fascism, unemployment and war.[25]

TOM SNOWDEN'S SPEECH AT RISHTON.

This took place at a Labour Party gathering in the Rishton Co-operative Rooms on Saturday evening, November 28th. He maintained that to get over 18,000 votes still showed that Socialism was close to peoples hearts in the Accrington division. A question was put to him, asking if he could guarantee that their present leaders in the future would not give them away? He said: "If there was one man that can be trusted, it is Mr. George Lansbury." [Lansbury had just been made the leader of the Labour rump in Parliament] Mr. Snowden went on to say:

"That the movement was greater than any of its individual members, and he believed that the principles of the Socialist movement were the only principles that could redeem mankind, which could bring peace and plenty. In standing firmly by the movement one had peace of mind, a sense of having done the right thing, irrespective of honours and responsibilities."['Observer' December 1st. 1931]

The meeting was of a social character and was the first of a series of 'get togethers'. The evening saw a selection of songs, and dancing, plus a piece of theatre. This latter, took the form of Mr. Wallace Haines and Miss Alice Snowden, of Accrington, acting the famous quarrel scenes from Sheriden's 'School for Scandal.' The two players eventually married, with Alice becoming an Alderman and Mayor of Accrington, and Wallace becoming Mayor of Hyndburn.

ALICE AND WALLACE HAINES.

Alice Haines in her letter of February 6th 1995 explains the events happening to her shortly after this night in Rishton:

"I am the Alice Snowden, who represented Cunliffes Mill, until I left the industry when I married..... The Weavers' Union were very kind to me. They sent me to Bangor University, for two weeks amongst other members from various branches to study 'Cotton Economics.' As a result, Andrew Naesmith put my name forward to some women's organisation who sent working class girls to Brynmawr College in the USA for twelve months. I came in the last three and Bertrand Russell's first wife, was my chaperon in London. I didn't get it but I was promised a chance in 1933. I got married instead."

Alice also wrote the following:

"My family were very distantly related to Philip and Tom Snowden, who happened to be cousins. My great grandfather was a handloom weaver at Cowling and the Snowden family, uncles, great uncles, had an annual pilgrimage to Cowling."

ACCRINGTON TCLP'S SALE OF WORK.

The event took place in the Labour Hall, on Wednesday and Saturday,

December 16th and 19th respectively. On Wednesday, Mr. Andrew Naesmith opened the proceedings, whilst on Saturday, Mr. Tom Snowden was the guest speaker. The ceremonies were presided over by Mr. H. Holgate, an Oswaldtwistle schoolmaster. Due to the Depression, the amount raised did not measure up to previous bazaar type functions held by the Party. However, £156 was raised for the building fund. This was the equivalent of around 75 weekly wages and so in todays money this would be worth £15,000. ['Observer' December 22nd.1931]

1932.

The 'Observer' reported that Councillor A. Dawson, had temporarily replaced Councillor Constantine as President of the Accrington TCLP, due to the latter becoming the Mayor. [Observer' January 2nd. 1932]

With regards to choosing a Prospective Parliamentary Candidate, the Accrington TCLP announced that August 30th. 1932 would be the final date for receipt of nominations. ['Observer' January 23rd. 1932]

On Monday February1st., Charles Roden Buxton spoke in Accrington Town Hall on 'The Problems of Empire.' ['Observer' February 2nd. 1932]

NEW MAGISTRATES.

It was announced that the following Labour nominees had been appointed to the magistrates bench:-

Mr. J.W. Sunderland. Secretary of the Great Harwood Weavers', whose activities have already been documented in earlier chapters.

Mr. R.T. Howson, who had been the President of Accrington TCLP prior to the election of Councillor Constantine. He had for 18 years been the Secretary of Great Harwood Miners' Association, when that area had working mines. He had also been a delegate for 25 years to the monthly meetings of the LCMF, serving for 2 years on its Executive Committee. Over the years he had attended a number of TUC and Labour Party Annual Conferences. For 26 years he had been on the Board of Clayton-Le-Moors, Co-operative Society, and for the last 4 years had acted as Secretary. From that position, he had become a member of the North East Lancashire Executive of the Co-operative Associations, and was Chairman of its Hours and Wages Board. He had also given 9 years service as a Councillor on the Clayton-Le-Moors UDC. ['Observer' February 23rd.1932]

Mr. William Brotherton was the guest speaker at Clayton-Le-Moors

Labour Party's March 1st. meeting. He spoke of "the betrayal of the Labour cause by the action of some leaders of the Party." ['Observer' March 5th.1932]

UDC ELECTIONS.

Labour movement candidates:
Church: No candidates.
Oswaldtwistle: No candidates.
Clayton-Le-Moors:
Thomas Carter, Labour. 41 Grange Street. Retired Secretary.
Henry Edmundson, Labour. 31 Victoria Street. Restaurant Keeper.
Joseph Hardy, Labour. 5 Waterloo Street. Coal Miner.
Margaret Alice Kennedy, Labour. 28 Whalley Road. Married Woman.
James William Hope, Secretary Clayton-Le-Moors Weavers. 1 Albert Street.
Rishton:
James Moorhouse Tattersall, Trades Council. 12 Blackburn Road. Solicitors Clerk.
Great Harwood:
North: Herbert Walmesley, Socialist. Twister & Drawer.
South: J.W. Sunderland JP., Socialist. Trade Union Secretary.
    Frank Wilcock, Unemployed Workers' Candidate. Motor Body Builder.
East: Arthur Waring JP., Socialist. Insurance Agent.
    Alf Ainsworth, Communist.
West: T.H. Seed, Socialist. Weaver.
    Richard Rutter, Unemployed Workers' Candidate. Labourer. ['Observer' March 19th. 1932]
    Mr. Tattersall failed to be elected in Rishton by only 16 votes. The Weavers' Secretary, Mr. J.W. Hope, was elected in fourth place at Clayton-Le-Moors. In Great Harwood, Arthur Waring was Labour's only victory. ['Observer' April 5th. 1932]

THE MAYOR'S ILLNESS.

The 'Observer' April 26th., reported that the Mayor, Councillor Constantine, had undergone a major operation for a perforated duodenal ulcer at a Manchester Nursing Home. On May 21st. the same newspaper carried an advert, thanking all those who had made enquiries about his health, and stating that he hoped he may be worthy of the esteem and affection shown towards him.

THE LABOUR LEAGUE OF YOUTH.

On Thursday April 28th, the League was addressed by Councillor Howson, on "The Philosophy and History of the Labour Party." Mr. Brunton presided. ['Observer' April 30th. 1932]

On Thursday May 19th, Mr Brunton "expressed great satisfaction at the growth of the League" and said that they had now had 20 educational lectures. The speaker that night was Mr. George Lunt, who gave an interesting talk about his visit to Russia. ['Observer' May 21st. 1932]

Mr. Tom Brunton gave a lecture on "The Class Struggle" at the June 2nd meeting.

On June 7th, Messrs. W.A. Haines and N. Marshall were the leading speakers at a meeting held in Clayton-Le-Moors, Town Hall, which had the intention of re-starting a Labour League of Youth in the township. Officers and a committee were formed. ['Observer' June 11th. 1932] In the same paper, it was reported that a Mr. H. Skinner had presided over the Accrington, June 9th, meeting of the League.

Alice Haines in a letter dated 10th April 1996 stated the following:

"Norman Marshall went to the ILP with his father in the early 1920's. He was a moulder at Bullough's which he hated, and in the early 1930's his parents bought him a grocers shop in Wellington Street. He left it later and worked at Luptons as a warehouseman.....From 1945, he took charge of the General Election literature distribution, which was then done centrally at the Labour Hall. Norman organised [this up to and including] the General Election of 1964. He never took any official position in the Party..... He remained a family friend until he died suddenly in the 1970's."

Marshall Tomlinson was another active member of the League of Youth, and Alice had this to say about him:

"Marshall was a weaver in Haslingden, who came down to the ILP in Accrington. He was a devout Shavian, a good chess player, a member of the Accrington Chess Club. He was a great reader and had a marvellous library.....a great character."

"Norman [Marshall] and I stood [as witnesses] for Sallie and Marshall's wedding at Haslingden Registrars Office in 1935."

"I am afraid I cannot remember much about Marshall's debates. These would have been at the ILP and the Accrington Discussion Class."

Alice thought that Harry Skinner went on to become a Secretary of West Ward.

The Labour League of Youth held a joint meeting with the Accrington Womens Section on Thursday October 13th. when Mrs. Boardman of Samlesbury gave an account of her recent visit to the Soviet Union. ['Observer' October 15th. 1932]

Mr. Bill Haworth, appealed for all young people to do some constructive work for the League of Youth, at the Oswaldtwistle Labour Party meeting of October 26th. A good gathering had heard Mrs. Boardman speak on her "Impressions of Russia." ['Observer' October 29th. 1932]

On Tuesday December 13th, the inaugural meeting of the Oswaldtwistle Labour League of Youth, was held at the Weavers Institute. Mr. R.C. [Bob] Campbell, presided over a good attendance. A speech dealing with youth and the present situation was delivered by Mr. Terrance McCarthy, who was on vacation from Ruskin College Oxford. An Executive Committee was appointed, together with the following officials: Mr. R.C. Campbell, President; Mr. H. Bailey, Secretary; and Miss Bernasconi, Treasurer. ['Observer' December 17th. 1932]

THE ILP.

The ILP advertised a meeting on the Market Ground, Accrington, for Sunday afternoon, June 12th, which was to be addressed by Mr. Fenner Brockway. ['Observer' June 11th. 1932]

At the Discussion Class on Sunday October 2nd 1932, Miss Judith Todd B.Sc. of Preston, a member of the ILP, spoke on the ILP controversy. The 'Observer' gave it a lengthy report. ['Observer' October 4th 1932]

ACCRINGTON BOROUGH ELECTIONS.

The Labour candidates were:
East Ward: Arthur Dawson. 31 Avenue Parade. Trade Union Secretary.
North Ward: William Morris Sproul. 'Arcady' Poulton Avenue. Railway Signalman.
South Ward: Richard Ingham Constantine. 'Rodenhurst' Laund Road. Wholesale Stationer.
West Ward: Thomas O'Connor. 103 Ormerod Street. Insurance Agent.
Central: Harry Smith. 1 James Street, Huncoat. Coal Miner.
Peel Park: Michael Walsh. 75 Oswald Street. Stoker.
Higher Antley: James Baron. 45 Perth Street. Coal Miner.

Spring Hill: John Lord. 5 Primrose Street. Engine Driver.

Mr. O'Connor, Mr. Baron, Mr. Lord and Mr. Constantine were victorious.

THE NEW PROSPECTIVE LABOUR CANDIDATE - MR. FREDERICK GEORGE BURGESS.

Mr. Tom Snowden remarked to an 'Observer' reporter prior to the selection conference held at the Labour Hall, Accrington, on Saturday December 17th, that he was prepared for an adverse vote.

The contest was between Tom and Mr. Frederick George Burgess, of London, who was nominated by the NUR and supported by the AEU. Tom had the backing of the Miners' Union.

After both men had addressed the 80 delegates, a ballot vote was taken which resulted in Mr. Burgess being victorious by a margin of 2 to 1.

Mr. Burgess was a native of Kent, who had been active in the trade union movement for 30 years. He was a former activist in the Social Democratic Federation and had helped to establish his local Labour Party. With regards to education, he was connected with the original Ruskin Hall movement.

In 1918 he fought Maidstone, for Labour, gaining over 6,000 votes. He finally made it to Westminster in 1929 when he became the Labour MP for York, a seat he lost at the last election.

He was well known in the Labour movement as a writer and cartoonist, working under the nom-de-plume of 'Battersea Bowser.' His contributions could be read regularly in the 'Railway Review' and 'Social Democrat.' Apparently, he supplied the first poster cartoons used by the Labour Party. An effective public speaker, he regularly used his own cartoons as illustrations to his talks. ['Observer' December 20th. 1932]

Tom Snowden, who had been a conscientious 'middle of the road' MP, was obviously dejected at not being re-selected. However, his lack of militancy during the cotton dispute and his constant excuses for the actions of the Labour Government meant that he had exhausted the goodwill shown towards him after taking over from Charles Roden Buxton.

1933.

Mr. Burgess gave his first speech in the constituency, at a public meeting held in the Labour Hall on Sunday January 29th. He said:

"The ruling class..... had been living as parasites upon the nation. The objection to them was the same objection as that of the student when the professor spoke about the flea. 'The flea is a very nice interesting insect,' said the student, 'what I do object to is the way in which it gets it's living.'"

He went on to say:

"We preach the class war, friends, but they [the ruling class] have been practising it, and nothing but Socialism will eliminate it."

He maintained that it was possible for everyone to live a full and complete life, but this would only come about when men and women determined that they would not put up with the present system any longer. ['Observer' January 31st. 1933]

DEATH OF MR. BERT J. LEE.

Mr. Lee of 101 Dale Street, Accrington, was a well known local railwayman and trade unionist. He died on January 24th, aged 47 years. He had been connected with the NUR for 25 years.

When the conciliation machinery was set up on the railway in 1921, he became a member of the local District Council. Later he became its secretary and from that position served on the wider body of the LMS, Sectional Council for the No.3 Area, which covered the whole of the Lancashire and Yorkshire lines. He had spent 9 years on the latter body.

He had attended and spoken at many NUR Annual Conferences. His name had been submitted by many branches as a candidate for the NUR's Presidency later in the year.

For some years he had been a member of the Trades Council and had unsuccessfully contested two municipal elections. He was also a frequent contributor to the debates of the Accrington Discussion Class.

He left a widow, two daughters and one grandchild. ['Observer' January 28th. 1933]

MAJOR CLEMENT ATTLEE MP SPEAKS IN ACCRINGTON.

The Deputy Leader of the Labour Party, Mr. Clement Attlee MP and Miss Mary Carlin of the Transport Workers' Union, spoke at a public meeting organised by the Accrington TCLP in the Town Hall, on February 11th.

Mr. Attlee said:

"When science had gone so far ahead that machinery was rapidly putting people out of work, what was the Government's remedy? Their remedy was to send the British representative to Geneva to oppose a reduction in the hours of labour. 'I think one of the first bits of building we have to do is to build a bigger asylum,' commented Major Attlee." ['Observer' February 14th 1933]

On Monday February 27th, Mr. Charles Roden Buxton returned to Accrington in order to present a Lantern Lecture in the Town Hall, held under the auspices of the TCLP. The subject was a description of his tour of East Africa. ['Observer' February 28th. 1933]

THE UDC ELECTIONS.

Labour movement candidates:
Oswaldtwistle:
Immanuel: Mr. William Haworth, Labour.13 John Street. Operative textile machinist.
Foxhill Bank: Mr. William Henry Greenwood, Labour. Union Road. Grocer.
Clayton-Le-Moors:
Joseph Finch, Labour. 35 Earl Street. Coal miner.
Ernest Nuttall, Labour. 14 Melbourne Street. Miner.
Rishton:
James Moorhouse Tattersall, Labour. 12 Blackburn Road. Solicitor's Clerk.
Robert Gildert, Labour. 6 Harwood Road. Weaver.
Great Harwood:
North: George Henry Fox, Trades and Labour. 12 Thorn Street. Union Secretary.
East: John William Sunderland, Trades and Labour. 29 Arthur Street. Union Secretary.
Alf Ainsworth, Unemployed Workers' Movement.
South: F. Wilcock, Unemployed Workers' Movement.
West: R. Rutter, Unemployed Workers' Movement.
Church: No candidates. ['Observer' March 18th. 1933]

In Oswaldtwistle Mr. W.H. Greenwood was returned unopposed. At Clayton-Le-Moors both Labour candidates were elected, having come third and fourth in the poll. The two Labour nominees in Rishton were also elected in second and fourth position. In Great Harwood, Mr. Sunderland the Weavers' Secretary was victorious. ['Observer' April 4th. 1933]

CLAYTON-LE-MOORS' LABOUR PARTY PRESENTATION.

On Tuesday April 25th, Clayton-Le-Moors Labour Party, held a victory celebration in the Town Hall, at which a presentation was made to their retiring president, Mr. Harry Edmundson. He had been forced to stand down due to the continued indisposition of his wife. He was given a pouch of tobacco and a pipe. ['Observer' April 29th. 1933]

RISHTON LABOUR PARTY RALLY.

The 'Observer' of June 17th, reported the events at a Labour Party Rally held in Rishton at 'Westwood'. Councillor J.M. Tattersall was the speaker. Sports were indulged in during the afternoon, whilst in the evening a social and dance took place at the Co-operative Rooms. Cross's Orchestra provided the music for dancing.

Mr. Burgess spoke at a large number of open-air meetings throughout the constituency during July and August.

ACCRINGTON BOROUGH ELECTIONS.

Labour movement candidates.
Spring Hill: Mr. William Henry Roberts. 46 Charter Street. Gentleman.
Central: Mr. Harry Smith. 1 James Street, Huncoat. Miner.
Higher Antley: Mr. John Harling. 347 Willows Lane. Draper.
East: Mr. Michael Walsh. 59 Limefield Street. Stoker.
North: Mr. William Howson. 2 Mather Avenue. Secretary.
South: Mr. Roger Carter. 6 Dunnyshop Avenue. Machinist.
West: Mr. George Farnworth Kilshaw. 27 Garfield Street. Trade Union Assistant Secretary. [Observer' October 28th. 1933]
Mr. Roberts and Mr. Kilshaw were the only successful candidates.

THE LABOUR PARTY BAZAAR.

This took place in Accrington Town Hall and was held over four days. On the afternoon of Wednesday November 29th, the Rt. Hon. F.O. Roberts, Minister of Pensions in the 1929 Labour Government, opened the proceedings, together with Mr. Burgess. After his speech, Mr. Roberts played a couple of tunes upon an ordinary handsaw, producing the notes by means of a fiddle bow. He then took up a violin and led the audience in singing 'Daisy,' 'Lift up the People's banner,' 'Old folks at home,' and winding up with 'The Red Flag.'

On Friday the event was opened by Mr. Charles Roden Buxton. ['Observer' December 2nd 1933]

On the final day, Saturday, Mr. J. Marchbank, General Secretary of the NUR, opened the proceedings. The 'Observer' reported the proceeds to be £662. ['Observer' December 5th. 1933]

OSWALDTWISTLE LABOUR PARTY LEAGUE OF YOUTH.

The Oswaldtwistle Labour Party League of Youth Headquarters was opened by Mrs. Boardman of Samlesbury, on Saturday November 18th. It occupied a position on Higher Peel Street. It was built of wood and was intended to serve as both the League's and the Oswaldtwistle Labour Party's official premises. The ceremony was presided over by Mr. R. C. Campbell. Bob said:

"These youths' sections were springing up all over the country as a protest against the present conditions under which youth had to get its existence. They were banding themselves together with such force that they hoped to have an effect in bringing about greater success in their progress towards Socialism."

After the singing of 'The Red Flag', Mrs. Boardman unlocked the door and declared the first Labour building in Oswaldtwistle open. She was then presented by Mr. Campbell with a copy of the Fitzgerald edition of the 'Rubaiyate of Omar Khayyam." ['Observer' November 21st. 1933]

The League held its first Annual Meeting on Thursday December 21st, at their new headquarters. Mr. Bob Campbell presided over a large attendance. The Secretary reminded those present that only 12 months previously, they had only 16 members and no meeting place, but now they had wonderful premises and a membership of 82. ['Observer' 23rd. 1933]

1934.

On Sunday January 14th, Mr. Ernest Marklew, Labour candidate for Colne Valley spoke along with Mr. Burgess at a public meeting held in the Labour Hall, Blackburn Road. Mr. Marklew was renewing his acquaintance with

Accrington after many years. He last spoke in the constituency in support of Mr. Dan Irving, the Socialist Candidate prior to the First World War. He said:
> "He doubted whether the workers took 30% of the wealth they created, yet wealth was being produced at such a rate that if it were divided equally each household would receive £500 per year." ['Observer' January 16th. 1934]

THE COUNTY COUNCIL ELECTIONS.

I have already commented on Councillor Constantine's victory, in Chapter 4. The results for the Hyndburn area were as follows:

Accrington North.		Church & Oswaldtwistle.	
R.I. Constantine Lab.	5482	Wm. Metcalf Lib.	2777
George E. Slack Lib.	3020	J. Read Con.	2654
	2462	Mrs. M.E. Boardman Lab.	2220
			123

Great Harwood
J.W. Sunderland Lab.	2546
H. Whitehead Con.	2542
	4

Mr. William Brotherton chaired a Labour League of Youth meeting, held in the Labour Hall on Sunday, March 4th, when Mr. Will Nally of its National Advisory Council was guest speaker.['Observer' March 6th. 1934]

THE UDC ELECTIONS.

Labour movement candidates:
Oswaldtwistle:
Foxhill Bank: John William Hill, Labour. 18 Paddock Street. Operative Baker.
Church:
Richard Rawlinson, Labour. 22 Victoria Street. Locomotive Fireman.
Majorie Haworth, Labour 12 Victoria Street. married Woman.
Clayton-Le-Moors:
Joseph Hardy, Labour. 5 Waterloo Street. Coal Miner.
Margaret Alice Kennedy, Labour. 28 Whalley Road. Housewife.
Edmund Pickup, Labour. 7 Alexander Street. Clerk.
Rishton:
Thurston Bradshaw, Labour. 9 Chapel Street. Weaver.
Tom Hayhurst, Labour. 7 Howard Street. Clerk.
Great Harwood:

North: George Gardner. National Unemployed Workers' Movement.
South: W. Hothersall. Trades Council.
East: W. Slynn. Trades Council.
   S. Stott. National Unemployed Workers' Movement.
West: R. Rutter. National Unemployed Workers' Movement. ['Observer' March 10th. 1934]
Unfortunately none of the above candidates were elected.

MR. MANNY SHINWELL AT ACCRINGTON.

On Monday March 26th, Mr. E. Shinwell, ex-Minister of Mines in the last Labour Government, spoke at the Accrington TCLP meeting along with Mr. Burgess. This was held in the Co-operative Assembly Rooms, Oak Street. Mr. Shinwell said:

"The Labour Party sought, as always, to advance the claims of the working classes for a higher standard of life, and after a close analysis of the existing system they had arrived at the definite conclusion that Socialism could not be achieved unless by replacing private ownership in industries where it had admittedly failed, by public ownership in the national interest." ['Observer' March 31st. 1934]

NEW MAGISTRATE - MRS. SUSANNAH HOLGATE.

The 'Observer' June 30th, reported that Mrs. Susannah Holgate, of 42 Fielding Lane, Oswaldtwistle, the wife of Mr. Heywood Holgate, headmaster of Hippings Wesleyan Day School, had been appointed as a J.P. She was described as "an ardent advocate of Socialism." A native of Oswaldtwistle, she was well known in her youth as a soprano vocalist, under her maiden name of Miss Cissie Brierley.

A CHURCH AND OSWALDTWISTLE LABOUR PARTY PICNIC.

An enjoyable picnic to Salmesbury Cottage, the home of Mrs. Boardman, took place on Saturday July 10th. Mrs. Boardman had formerly resided in Oswaldtwistle and had been connected with the Labour movement for many years. She had in the past stood in the County Council elections on the Labour ticket. Bob Campbell told me that she was the wife of the Manager of

Blythes Chemicals, of Church, but I have not seen this documented anywhere. Over 80 person took part in the picnic. ['Observer' July 17th. 1934]

MR. MICHAEL WALSH.

Mr. Michael Walsh was chosen to represent the Accrington TCLP at the Labour Party Annual Conference at Southport, which was due to begin on October 1st. ['Observer' September 22nd. 1934] At the Accrington Borough elections on the 1st November, he failed to gain election in East Ward by only 7 votes.

Sadly, his wife died on Saturday November 17th. She had been ill for only a few days and was only 42 years old. "Of a jovial disposition, she was greatly esteemed and very popular." She left four children, three girls and one boy, the eldest being thirteen. ['Observer' November 20th. 1934]

ACCRINGTON TCLP CONTINUED.

Mr. Manny Shinwell paid a further visit to Accrington, on Sunday September 30th. He said:
> "They of the Labour Party, were Socialists first and last, and all the time, and why? Because Capitalism could no longer function in the interests of men, women and children of this country.... In these circumstances the Labour Party were asking them to dedicate themselves to the cause of Socialism." ['Observer' October 2nd. 1934]

On Thursday October 4th, Mr. Burgess was supported by Mr. Hugh Dalton, at a meeting in the Labour Hall. Sir Stafford Cripps was the guest speaker, with Mr. Burgess, at the same venue on Saturday October 13th. Sir Stafford said:
> "They were agreed on the fundamental thing that they wanted a Socialist State..... [However] The people had got to show that they were determined to face up to the risks which were entailed in making a direct onslaught upon Capitalism. If they could create that spirit and feeling in their ranks they would create what they had got to create and that was a new hope for the people of this country." ['Observer' October 16th. 1934]

On Sunday October 14th. Mr. Andrew Naesmith and Mr. Burgess spoke at a public meeting in the Labour Hall.

OSWALDTWISTLE UDC BY-ELECTION.

Mr. William Henry Greenwood, Labour, had resigned and moved to Blackpool. This caused a By-election in Foxhill Bank Ward. John W. Hill, the Labour candidate failed to gain election by 57 votes.

ACCRINGTON BOROUGH ELECTIONS.

Labour movement candidates:
East: Michael Walsh, Labour. 59 Limefield Street. Stoker.
West: Herbert Parsons, Labour. 57 Tremellen Street. Store-keeper.
Central: Wallace Haines, Labour. 44 Portland Street. Bookbinder.
Peel Park: Herbert Potts, Labour. 24 Avenue Parade. Trade Union Secretary.
Higher Antley: John Marshall Harling, Labour. 347 Willows Lane. Draper.
Spring Hill: Fred Mills, Labour. 95 Rawson Avenue. Railway Shunter.
Labour were successful in having Wallace Haines, Herbert Potts, Fred Mills and J.M. Harling elected to the Council.

THE OSWALDTWISTLE CLARION CYCLING CLUB.

Bob Campbell told me, during an interview in the mid-1980's, that he had founded the Oswaldtwistle Clarion Cycling Club in 1924. It's motto was "Be in time and fear not." At various times it had a membership of over a hundred.

They held some of their first meetings in Oswaldtwistle Library and had a notice board on the wall of a cycle shop in Union Road. During the period 1924 to 1929 the Club was involved in distributing the Labour Party's propaganda literature throughout the township. In the summer months it was a regular occurrence for them to organise cycle rides to Blackpool, where they could find accommodation for 9d. per night. Bob always stayed at number 4 Coope Street.

Prior to the building of the Labour Party Institute in Higher Peel Street, in 1933, the Clarion met in premises in Tattersall Street, where they used to organise Potato Pie Suppers in order to raise funds.

With regards to the new Institute, Bob stated that the land had been sold to them cheaply by Abel Bury an anti-Socialist Councillor. Doctor Farquar apparently bought a number of house plants to brighten the place up a bit. The building had hot and cold water and was capable of holding over a hundred people. In addition; "them that liked a drink could walk across the road to the 'New Inn.'" [26]

Mention has been made of the club taking part in the Labour Party Annual Procession, but little evidence remains of its activities. However, the 'Observer' of April 7th, contained the following advertisement:

Clarion Cycling Club.

35 members of the Church and Oswaldtwistle Clarion Cycling Club set off on Good Friday for a camping holiday in the Ribble Valley.

On Sunday there will be a camp fire rally at Downham.

To meet at the Labour Party Headquarters, Higher Peel Street. Oswaldtwistle. at 8.45 am.

Information from John Flegg. C/O Oswaldtwistle Labour Party

Mr. Flegg reported that 37 members had cycled from Oswaldtwistle to the Downham rally, and that they had met up with over 700 of their comrades. ['Observer' April 14th. 1934]

On Sunday April 22nd, 32 members from Oswaldtwistle cycled to Glasson Dock under the leadership of John Flegg. ['Observer' April 28th. 1934]

Having got the above publicity the Club would appear to have carried on their activities throughout the summer but no further use was made of the 'Observer' as a means of creating further interest.

THE FASCIST THREAT.

Lecturers had appeared at the Discussion Class and other public platforms denouncing the ideas and actions of Mussolini and Hitler over the previous decade. However, the threat posed by these evil doctrines had been coming more to the fore in the early thirties.

On May 11th, 1933 a Miss Noble had addressed the Accrington TCLP, Womens' Section on the political dangers of Fascism to the Labour movement. She said:

"Believers in democracy must utilize every weapon at their disposal to fight the growth of Fascism in this country." ['Observer' May 13th. 1933]

On October 29th, a Mr. E. Parker, gave 'The Case Against Fascism' at the Discussion Class. On Sunday November 26th, 1933, one of Sir Oswald Mosley's main propagandists, Mr. Moir, spoke at the Discussion Class on 'The Case for Fascism'. He arrived 40 minutes late, which together with his non-attendance the last time he was booked to speak, did not go down well with those present.

Mr. Harry Smith, President of Accrington's Miners', said that Hitler had scrapped the trade union movement in Germany and done away with the ballot box. ['Observer' November 28th.1933]

An anti-Fascist letter was published in the 'Observer', December 30th, from Mr. Marshall Tomlinson, a member of the Labour Party League of Youth. Mr. William Brotherton wrote a similar letter, entitled 'Socialism and Fascism', which was published on February 24th. 1934. The following day a Fascist speaker appeared at the Discussion Class. Again the speaker was late and so a Mr. Bonner of Rising Bridge spoke in an anti-Fascist manner until his arrival. ['Observer' February27th. 1934]

On Sunday, March 18th, a further debate on Fascism took place at the Discussion Class. Mr. A.C. Miles of Manchester, wearing a blackshirt gave the case for, whilst Mr. A. Leacey of Blackburn, "condemned it root and branch." ['Observer' March 20th. 1934]

In the Labour Hall, Accrington, on Sunday March 25th, Mr. F.G. Burgess and Councillor G.F. Kilshaw spoke at length on the dangers of Fascism. Mr. Burgess said:

> "Citing the example of Tom Mann, that a man was not now free to express his opinions. The danger was that Fascism was not so much blackshirts - that was merely a theatrical expression of the idea in the minds of some people. What they had got to watch was the Fascism which existed in the minds of the National Government today."

['Observer' March 27th. 1934]

On the 14th. March, Mr. John Lancaster, of Lion Street, Church, wrote an anti-Fascist letter to the 'Observer'.

Mr. Burgess again took up the subject at the Accrington TCLP, Womens' Section, meeting of April 26th. He said:

> "The danger today was not from the Mosley group, the 'Mickey Mouse people'; but from the tendency of the present Government to introduce legislation upon Fascist lines. Mr. Burgess,.....instanced the Sedition Bill, as striking at the very root of individual liberty in giving power, hitherto unknown in this country, to the police to search houses of political suspects. [of the Left]....."

> "Fascism would perpetuate the exploitation of the workers, whilst Socialism sought to abolish it." ['Observer' April 28th. 1934]

A good anti-Fascist letter from someone writing under the nom-de-plume of 'Ecce Signum' appeared in the April 28th 'Observer'.

On April 29th, an Anti-Fascist Protest Meeting was held in the Labour Hall, Accrington. Mr. Andrew Naesmith, presided and Mr. A.A. Purcell J.P. Secretary of the Manchester and Salford Trades Council, was the principal speaker. The following resolution was adopted unanimously:

> "That this meeting of delegates representing the democratic

organisations within the Accrington Parliamentary Borough, views with grave alarm the growing activities of Fascist forces in this country. It is apprehensive of the tendencies displayed in recent legislation by His Majesty's Government. It calls upon the existing working class organisations to be alive to the menace and to unitedly take such action as will preserve the rights of free democratic organisations." ['Observer' May 1st. 1934]

At a public meeting held in the Labour Hall, Sunday May 6th, Mr. Burgess made a further attack on Fascism.

The Accrington branch of the British Union of Fascists, held a propaganda meeting at the Kings Hall, Accrington, on Sunday May 13th, with a speaker from London, a Mr. A. Broad.

"The rather small audience took a lively interest in the proceedings, and after the address the speaker was called upon to answer a fusillade of questions, both written and verbal."

Mr. William Brotherton, asked several questions some of which resulted in sharp exchanges. This resulted in Mr. Brotherton being spoken to by a Fascist steward, but the incident passed off without anything untoward happening.['Observer' May 15th, 1934]

Mr. Burgess attacked Fascism again, at an open-air meeting on Accrington Market Ground, on Sunday June 3rd, at which Mr. Michael Walsh presided. ['Observer' June 5th. 1934] He again appeared at the same venue on Sunday June 24th, where he "addressed a large crowd of people." Mr. Wallace Haines occupied the chair. ['Observer' June 26th. 1934]

The Accrington Workers' Education Association branch had protested to Major Procter the Tory MP, against the contents of the Incitement to Disaffection Bill. Mr. Roland Hagan, its Secretary, wrote again to him stating the WEA's objection "to any attempt on the part of the government to interfere with individuals in their ownership of books and pamphlets." ['Observer' June 17th. 1934]

On Sunday July 22nd, Sir Oswald Mosley opened the Accrington branch, British Union of Fascists,' headquarters, in Jacob Street.

"Sir Oswald made an inspection of the premises while the local Blackshirts, numbering about 25, including three women, stood in a row at attention....."

"When the ceremony was over the local members of the movement gathered round their leader, and with great fervour shouted in unison "M-O-S-L-E-Y, Mosley," and then "Two, four, six, eight, whom do we appreciate followed by a vociferous "Mosley." The Fascist leader was not on the premises for more than ten minutes."

['Observer' July 24th 1924]

The officer commanding the Accrington, BUF, was Mr. William Hodgson, locally known as 'Bronco Bill,' who later in the year was involved with the death of a Mr. Joseph Hurley.

At a well attended open-air meeting on Accrington Market Ground, Sunday August 26th, Mr. Burgess said:

"In the House of Commons he noticed that when reference was made to Mosley and the Fascists some Tory members cheered."

He went on to outline the failure of Capitalism and ended by saying:

"Fascism had no remedy, because it was merely a new capitalistic government aiming to keep the workers perpetually in a state of ignorant servitude. Its rule was by force and machine gun. Al Capone and Dillinger, the American gangsters, were mere babies at their business. They dominated and intimidated only a small portion of the American population, and for once America had to give second place to the political gangsters of Europe. In Europe they were dominating not merely a section of the population but whole nations, as in Italy and Germany. Political salvation could not come to us from such a source."

"If they wished to reconstruct society upon a scientific basis they must do it themselves, hence the appeal of the Labour Party, the party composed of workers themselves. They appealed to all the workers to unite, before it was too late to bring about a needed change by peaceful and constitutional methods." ['Observer' August 28th 1934]

During the latter part of 1934 no specific meetings were organised of an anti-Fascist nature, although mention was made of the Fascist threat during speeches made on many other topics. The debate was of course to continue throughout the 1930's and this will hopefully be covered in the future, in a sequel to this volume.

MR. BILL HAWORTH.

During this period, Bill was serving his political apprenticeship, which culminated in his election as Communist Convenor of Howard and Bullough's Works' Committee. A position he held throughout the 1940's and early 1950's. Ken Slater, the former AEU District Secretary, said of Bill and his family:

"Bill was in many ways a remarkable man, from a remarkable family, from Oswaldtwistle. There were four brothers. Tom who I never knew well, because he died young. He was a full-time organiser for the Chemical Workers' Union. Jim who I met on one or two occasions who became the Member of Parliament for the Walton Division of Liverpool during the period 1945-50..... Jack who lived in Haslingden, very loyal to the Labour Party, a very likeable man in many ways. Bill of course became the Convenor at Howard and Bullough Ltd. He was a very well educated man who could get on a platform and speak with great effect on any of half a dozen subjects at very short notice and without notes. He was one of the best educated working men that I have ever met." [27]

Bob Campbell, speaking about Bill's activities during this period, said:

"Billy Haworth was a cracker. He was a good organiser, not a big head, very level headed and very progressive in his ideas."

"Whilst Bill was a member of Oswaldtwistle Labour Party, he had a rostrum made by the local joiner in Simpson Street. It cost £2 and was kept at 286 Union Road, Bill Starkie's house. Bill Starkie was at one time the President of the Oswaldtwistle Weavers' Union." [28]

In 1927 Bill lived at 13 John Street, Oswaldtwistle. During the Spring of that year he had four letters published by the 'Observer,' in which he attacked government policy on Education. In May, he presided at a Labour Party open-air meeting on Accrington Market Ground on the topic of "Russia." He was an Executive Committee member of Accrington TCLP and active in the Workers' Education Association.

In October 1928, he chaired a meeting of the ILP., held in the Stanley Supporters' Club, which was addressed by Mr. Andrew Naesmith on the "Cotton Trade Difficulties." In December 1928, he progressed to the position of speaker when he gave a talk entitled "The Call of Democracy." This was followed by "The Hope of the Future," in January 1929, and "Democracy," in February 1929, all at the ILP meetings.

The WEA congratulated Bill "who has taken up studies at Manchester University." ['Observer' October 8th. 1929] I think that this must have involved some kind of part-time diploma in the social sciences.

On February 1st. 1931, he spoke at the Accrington Discussion Class on the subject of "Sexual Reform." The following month, April 30th, he spoke at the Accrington TCLP, Womens Section, on "Modern Psychology, the emancipation of women, and the decline of organised religion."

In the 'Observer' of May 30th,1931, the WEA announced that a Wireless Discussion Group had recently been formed and Bill was the leader of the "Unemployment" Course. He "gave an interesting lead to the discussion which followed the lecture. The number of listeners attending was about twenty."

He returned to the Accrington TCLP Womens Section, on February 18th, 1932, when he lectured on "Certain People of Importance," in which he outlined the works of many well known people, including H.G. Wells, Bertrand Russell, J.S. Huxley and B.S. Haldane. On September 22nd, 1932, the ladies were again entertained by Bill, when he gave an address on "Revolutionary Poets." "Mr. Haworth read several poems written by minor poets including those of Joe Corrie and F.C. Boden," and then discussed the merits of their work. ['Observer' September 24th. 1932]

In March 1933, he stood for election in Immanuel Ward, in Oswaldtwistle UDC. The result was:

N. Ball	Con.	574
A. Walsh	Lib.	549
W. Haworth	Lab.	321

During 1933 and 1934 he was active in the organising of the Oswaldtwistle Labour Party, League of Youth and was Secretary of the Oswaldtwistle Labour Party Branch.

His story will hopefully unfold in a further volume .

CONCLUSION.

Past writers on the history of the Labour Party have commented on its wide programme that allowed "persons with diverse political philosophies ranging from near-Communism to near-Toryism" to be fully paid up members.[29]

This was the Labour Party's Achilles heel, in that right-wing neo-Tories were members and held positions of high office. By their actions during both the General Strike and the 1931 Crisis, MacDonald, Snowden, Thomas and others, showed that they had no right to have held membership during that period. The Labour Party Constitution clearly stated in Clause Four that it was their duty:

> "To secure for the workers by hand or by brain the full fruits of their industry and the most equitable distribution there of that may be possible upon the basis of the common ownership of the means of production, distribution and exchange, and the best obtainable system of popular administration and control of each industry or service."

The traitors who left to establish the National Government with the workers' class enemy, the Tories and Liberals, had obviously disagreed with the above for a number of years, and as such should have resigned and joined the opposition a decade before.

R.H. Tawney wrote an article in the Political Quarterly during 1934, in which he castigated MacDonald and company as follows:

"The objective of a Socialist Party, and of the Labour Party in so far as it deserves the name, is simplicity itself..... It is to abolish all advantages and disabilities which have their source, not in differences of personal quality, but in disparities of wealth, opportunity, social position, and economic power. It is, in short, a classless society..... "

"Side by side with action of a strictly economic character, such as the transference to public ownership of foundation services; the establishment of machinery to bring the support of capital to industry under public control; the creation of a permanent Planning Department; and such other measures of the same order as may be adopted, must go a policy for the improvement of education, health, and the system of local government, which themselves, it may be remarked, are matters not irrelevant to economic prosperity."

"Quality of support is as important as quantity. The way to create it is not to encourage adherents to ask what they will get from a Labour Government, as though a campaign were a picnic, all beer and sunshine. It is to ask them what they will give. It is to make them understand that the return of a Labour Government is merely the first phase of a struggle the issue of which depends on themselves."

"Who will believe that the Labour Party means business as long as some of its stalwarts sit up and beg for social sugar-plums, like poodles in a drawing room? It will not do. To kick over the idol, you must first get off your knees. Either the Labour Party means to end the tyranny of money, or it does not. If it does, it must not fawn on the owners and symbols of money. **How can followers be Ironsides if its leaders are Flunkies ?** [30]

REFERENCES.

1. Jones, Eric. "The Origins & Nature of the Organised Working-Class Socialists in Accrington: 1850-1945". Ruskin College Thesis 1978/79. p. 51.
2. McNair, John. "James Maxton: The Beloved Rebel". Pub. George Allen and Unwin Ltd. 1955. p. 153 & 154
3. McCarthy, Margaret. "Generation in Revolt." Pub. Heinemann. London 1953. p. 103
4. ibid. p. 105-106
5. ibid. p. 113
6. ibid. p. 119

7. Interview between Mr. R. Hagan and myself, April 1985.
8. Interview between Alice and Wallace Haines, and Eric Jones, April 1978.
9. de Bunsen, Victoria. 'Charles Roden Buxton: A Memoir.' Pub. George Allen & Unwin. London 1948. p. 56 & 57
10. McNair, op. cit. p. 171 & 172
11. ibid. p. 177 & 178
12. Knox, William. "James Maxton". Pub. Manchester University Press. 1987. p. 78
13. ibid. p. 80
14. Tracey, H. [Ed] "The British Labour Party. Vol. 3." Pub. Caxton, London, 1948. Article by J. Vernon Radcliffe "The Rt. Hon. Viscount Snowden." p. 229 & 230
15. Tait, Fredrick. "The Jugglers of Finance are Bleeding the Nation White." Pub. ILP. London. 1932. p. 5 to 15
16. Rust, William. "Down with the 'National Government!' Pub. CPGB 1931. p.5 & 6
17. Interview between Alice Haines and myself, May 1985
18. Challinor, Ray. "John S. Clarke - Parliamentarian, Poet, Lion-Tamer." Pub. Pluto Press 1977. p. 85
19. ibid. p. 10
20. ibid. p.76
21. Ainsworth, Jim. "Accrington 1926" Pub. Hyndburn Trades Council 1994. p.27 & 28
22. Knox. op. cit. p. 96
23. ibid. p. 99
24. ibid. p. 101
25. ibid. p. 106
26. Interview between Bob Campbell and myself January 1985
27. Interview between Ken Slater and myself January 1985
28. Bob Campbell op. cit.
29. McHenry, D.E. "The Labour Party in Transition 1931-1938". Pub. George Routeledge. London. 1938. p. 233
30. Tawney, R.H. "The Choice Before the Labour Party." Pub. in "The Attack and other Papers." Pub. Spokesman. 1981. p. 52-70

CHAPTER SIX

THOUGHTS ON SOCIETY'S IMPROVEMENT.

Hyndburn Trades Council has the ultimate aim of producing a complete history of its activities, but in addition it wants to bring before the public of North East Lancashire the thoughts and ideas that encouraged its founders.

These ideas are as relevant today as they were a hundred years ago. If only working-class people would take an interest in their movement they would see how the ruling-class together with the connivance of certain Labour politicians have managed to maintain a system of exploitation over the last two hundred years.

It is a century since Robert Blatchford, of the 'Clarion', was enthusiastically putting forward the principles of Socialism in his newspaper, books and pamphlets. The difference between then and now however, is that Blatchford was relatively successful in his efforts to inform the working class of the advantages of Socialism. He was working against a background of a two party [Liberal & Conservative] capitalist electoral game that led the workers to believe there was no alternative to the existing system. Socialist ideas were new and untried but their continual promulgation, touched on in this volume, eventually resulted in the landslide Labour victory of 1945. Unfortunately the leadership of the Labour Party did not determine to maintain and increase the knowledge and interest of such ideas, and so we now find ourselves having gone backwards to a situation not unlike that faced by Blatchford.

In his writings he explained economic theory using simple analogies in a common sense way. It was this ability to effectively write about the realities of late Victorian Britain and the necessity for Socialism that resulted in the success of his publications. 'Merrie England' published in 1893 sold over 700,000 copies in a few months, eventually selling over one million. In his preface to Blatchford's autobiography, A.M. Thompson wrote:

> "A year before its issue there were not 500 Socialists in Lancashire; twelve months after there were 50,000. A census taken at the time in a North of England Labour Club showed that forty-nine

members out of fifty had been 'converted' by 'Merrie England'. As the Manchester Guardian lately said: "For every convert made by 'Das Kapital', there were a hundred made by 'Merrie England'."

Blatchford's ideas of the 1890s were correct and are just as relevant to today. He was an exceptional communicator using the media of his day; the Socialist movement should be looking to using new technology for getting its message across in a similarly effective way in the 1990s. In the meantime I will highlight his ideas as outlined in 'Merrie England'.

The Conservatives foolishly maintain that avarice, the passion for riches, the incentive of gain, is the only constant element of human nature. They are so convinced of this fact, that they develop economic and philosophical theories based entirely on this misconception.

Human nature is very complex and the desire for progress, and a love for the rest of human kind is forgotten, in Tory theories and actions. My acquaintances, friends and colleagues would instinctively prefer love to hate, light to darkness, and good to evil.

Apart from an unbalanced minority, almost everyone would save a fellow creature from death and suffering, if this could be done without personal cost or risk. Many people would even chance their own life in such circumstances.

Usually only a lunatic would wantonly murder, destroy necessary food stocks or poison the water supply. However, evil people may do such things if there are some personal advantages to be had. Therefore, it is obvious that people often do good for its own sake, and that a minority will do evil in the hope of gain.

The Tories though, believe that greed is the chief motor of the human heart. Blatchford however, believed the "love of approbation" to be "a hundred fold stronger force than greed." [1] In other words he knew that the desire to get praise or admiration was a stronger motive and that this was part of a desire for progress, and a love for your fellow man.

People have died, suffered imprisonment, and torture, for the sake of religion, for the sake of political ideals. Not many would do that for money. "Men will fight for money, but they don't want to die for it." [2]

It is truly amazing that the adherents of Thatcherism persist in the belief that greed is the motive power of humanity. As Blatchford said 100 years ago, the unfettered;

> "rights of individual enterprise is anarchy.....the basest and the vilest have the advantage, for the vile man and the base will fight with less ruth and fewer scruples."

> "So much for the survival of the fittest. So much for Laissez

Faire [The Market Economy]. The man who accepts the Laissez Faire doctrine would allow his garden to run wild, so that the roses might fight it out with the weeds and the fittest might survive." [3]

Thatcherism states that there is no such thing as society - there is only individualism. This to all thinking people is a nonsense. As Blatchford said;

"You may have wondered why.....the apostles of individualism should be so strangely blind to the danger of leaving private enterprise uncurbed. But you need not wonder about these things, for Individualism is a relic of savagery, and its apologists would be agitating for the return of the good old individual right of carrying a stone club and living by promiscuous robbery and murder, were they not convinced that the law of supply and demand, although a more cowardly and brutal weapon than the cannibal's club, is infinitely more deadly and effective....." [4]

He went on to state the following, which was a truism if ever there was one. "A mob of antagonistic individuals is a chaos, not a society." [5] Only in this sense is Thatcherism correct. If only Labour leaders had emphasised this gaping hole in Thatcherism at the time, it might have struck people that the Government was talking absolute nonsense. He further stated:

"Society, is a union of people for mutual advantage......Individual liberty is what we all desire - so far as it is possible to have it. But it is not possible to have it in its complete form, whilst we live in communities. By living in communities, men get many advantages. It is not good for man to be alone. For the advantages that society gives us, we must make some sacrifice....."

"A state of Socialism would give us all as much liberty as we need. A state of Individualism - of anarchy - would give some of us more liberty than it is wise and beneficial we should have." [6]

"If it had not been for interference with the liberty of the individual and the freedom of contract in the past the lot of the workers would have been unbearable....."

The world's first industrial capitalists of Victorian Britain, were eventually shamed by the voices of protest at the harshness of their system and had to reluctantly pass laws to stop the most glaring excesses. Blatchford says:

"Do you know anything about the Truck Act, which abolished the nefarious custom of paying wages in bad food ? Did you ever consider the effect of forbidding the payment of wages in public-houses, or the employment of climbing boys by sweeps? Have you ever read the history of the Factory Acts? [7]

"Read them.....and I think you will be cured of any lingering affection for the 'Freedom of Contract' and the 'Rights of the Individual'....."

"Now I think Individualism strengthens the hands of the rogue in his fight with the true man; and I think Socialism would fortify the true man against the rascals. I grant you that Socialism would imply some interference with the liberty of the individual. But which Individual? The scoundrel."

"Imagine a dozen men at sea in a boat with only two days' provisions. Would it be wise to consider the liberty of the individual? If the strongest man took all the food and left the others to starve would it be right or wrong for the eleven men to combine to bind him and divide all fairly? **To let the strong or cunning rob the weak or honest is individualism. To prevent the rascal from taking what is not his own is Socialism."** [8]

Sixteen years later, the above sentiments expressed by Blatchford were adopted, although in an opportune way by the capitalists themselves. In an attempt to eliminate the worst excesses of the system, Winston Churchill, in his capacity as President of the Board of Trade in 1909, took on the role of the social reformer. He established the Wages Councils, an idea that surprisingly [from today's perspective, since the Tory Government has just abolished them] had widespread support amongst Edwardian business people. At its First Reading in Parliament, he said:

"They will generally be not merely boards for the purpose of fixing the minimum rates of wages.....but boards designed to nourish.....the interest of the workers [and] the health and state of their industry."

He wished:

"To use these organisations.....to rally to the side of these minimum standards all the healthy elements in the trade, and finally.....to protect the good employers."

At the Second Reading, he said:

"Where you have no organisation, no parity of bargaining, the good employer is under-cut by the bad, and the bad employer is under-cut by the worst. Where those conditions prevail you have not a condition of progress but a condition of progressive degeneration."

"[It will be] to the credit of this country that it took a leading and prominent position in what is a noble and benign work in raising as far as possible the general level of life and wages." [9]

The Labour Party and indeed the Trade Unions should have campaigned vigorously against the disbandment of the Wages Councils. The above quotes of Churchill's should have been used to embarrass the Government from billboards in every town in the country. Demonstrations should have been held, but instead we only got a lukewarm token jesture of a campaign from the Labour establishment.

During the early 1980's, students of British twentieth century economic history, could predict where monetarism and a full blown market economy strategy would lead us.

Unemployment, in a market economy such as Britain, can achieve a state of equilibrium at three, four, or even five million, whilst inflation is maintained at a relatively low level, and profits are made that keep the City of London happy. However, the resulting social chaos and misery that is caused by this system can be seen by any objective observer. Politicians have a problem, they can continue as they are, and leave Britain to face a bleak future, or they can make changes and reverse the decline in the fabric of the nation.

Again, unemployment is not something new, the first five chapters of this book have dealt with this problem. The hard times of the inter-war years left the population bitter and resentful; so much so that the wartime National Government commissioned the 'Beveridge Report - Full Employment in a Free Society,' which was published in 1944. The preface to this all-Party Report said:

> "Full productive employment in a free society is possible.....it is a goal that can be reached only by conscious, continuous organisation of all our productive resources under democratic control.....Full employment is in fact attainable while leaving the conduct of industry.....to private enterprize.....but, if contrary to this view, it should be shown by experience or by argument that abolition of private property in the means of production was necessary for full employment **this abolition would have to be undertaken."** [10]

With regards to how this was to be enacted, the report states:

> "The Policy for Full Employment is a policy to be carried through by democratic action, of public authorities, central and local, responsible ultimately to the voters.....A large part of the execution of the programme - in health, housing, education and other fields - and the adjusting of the programme to local conditions will be a function of local rather than of central government." [11]

In the inter-war years companies were holding back on increasing output, not because of a shortage of labour and capital, but because they could not sell any more goods in an economy of three million unemployed. Cutting wages could not help either because if all wages in the British economy were cut simultaneously, overall purchasing power would be reduced and therefore people could only buy less. [12]

John Maynard Keynes suggested that the answer lay in more spending. The wherewithal to purchase any increased output was the missing ingredient. He said that anything that raised demand would contribute to lowering unemployment. How much more sensible, he thought to create incomes by planning worthwhile road and house building programmes. The confidence this would instil in business would get Britain out of its economic recession.

> "If the degradation and shear waste of unemployment was ever to be eliminated the state would have to accept explicit responsibility for achieving that objective." [13]

The Beveridge Report provided the platform from which to put the ideas of the liberal economist Keynes into practice. It was not Socialism, but it was a big improvement on what went before. The years 1945 until 1979 were the most civilized 34 years for the British working-class in the history of planet Earth. A Welfare State, together with strong trade unions and a policy of full employment ensured that everyones standard of living rose tremendously. However, serious inequalities still existed in society, just as they had in Robert Tressell's day.

Robert Tressell, who died of tuberculosis in 1911, wrote the best ever novel of British working-class life: 'The Ragged Trousered Philanthropists.' Its theme was the class-war.[14] Over the decades many trade unionists, Labour Party MPs and officials, were converted to the Socialist cause after reading this great work. Unfortunately, the vast majority have tended to forget it's message, once they achieved a postion of authority [and hence a substantial income] within the movement.

Tony Crossland, the late Labour Party right-winger, believed that the unjust distribution of private wealth could be cured just as well in a pluralist, rather than in a wholly state-owned, economy with much better results for social containment and the fragmentation of power. However, he said this in 1956.[15]

In his later book, published in 1974, he summarises an idealised Marxist view of the previous 20 years. [1954-1974]:

> "According to [the Marxists] a major transformation of power relationships has taken place in the British economy, due partly to the growing concentration of industry and partly to the growth of the multinationals. Economic power has moved sharply away from the state and the workers, towards a small oligarchy of private manufacturing firms. These firms were easily able to frustrate the efforts of the last Labour Government [1964-1970] to create or induce greater equality, faster growth, higher investment and exports, regional justice, price and profit restraint and industrial democracy."

> "Thus it is capitalist power which is, in the last resort, the

cause both of the inequalities and the poor performance as already described. The ownership of the means of production is even more obviously the dominant influence on society; the revisionist thesis, to the contrary, has been disproved. It follows that a massive increase in public ownership is required, not so much for reasons specific to any particular firm or industry, but generally to transfer this concentrated power and wealth from a small oligarchy to the people". [16]

Crossland, at the time, saw no reason to accept this view, although he admitted that events may have been acutely disappointing to a democratic socialist. However, he was wrong, the Marxist interpretation was correct. Indeed, any objective observer of the events of the post-war period could not fail to see this fact. The trouble today, after 18 years of a Tory Government, is that the post-war consensus experienced by Crossland, whereby Keynesian methods were used by all governments to minimise unemployment and to provide sufficient investment in the welfare state, has come to an end. The Tory Government broke completely away from such a policy and returned to the class warfare of the 1920s. Under such circumstances I believe that a return purely to Keynesian methods would be insufficient; they were insufficient in 1974 from my point of view.

The Tory Government's acts of class-war, included the mass shut down of the steel industry, ship building, engineering in general, and the coal mines. They told the public that the market economy would provide alternative jobs in leisure, retail and distribution, and other service industries. This claptrap of an explanation for an unmitigated disaster in the regions, together with a housing policy that was to end in tears, conned the voters of middle England into re-electing the Conservatives on a further three occasions.

In local government, the introduction of Compulsory Competitive Tendering was a further act of class-war by the government. The services defined in the 1988 Act for CCT purposes were, refuse collection, street cleaning, school and welfare catering, other catering, grounds maintenance and vehicle maintenance. In the following year, the management of sport and leisure facilities were added to this list.

The Act prohibited councils from "stipulating terms and conditions of employment, training or other opportunities and promotion," in specifications for gaining contracts. [17] Therefore, workers unfortunately transferring to private contractors would no longer enjoy local government pay and conditions.

My opinion of the Tory Government inspired policy of CCT, is that it is a narrow-minded, class-based attack on the living standards of local authority employees, that has the ultimate aim of lowering wages, imposing inferior working conditions, and increasing job insecurity, on a massive scale. This opinion appeared to be that of Frank Dobson when he was shadow environment spokesman. He won a standing ovation for his speech at the 1996 Labour Party Conference, when he said:

> "What we won't do is impoverish dinner ladies and call it 'efficiency,'.....The reality of CCT for thousands of dedicated, hard-working people is ugly impoverishment. It's not efficiency - it's exploitation. It's rotten, it's wrong and we'll end it." [18]

We can only wait and see whether New Labour carries out this pledge. All this of course, has been taking place during a period when numerous highly-paid, high profile, directors, whose actions have been detrimental to their companies' success, have received redundancy packages of as much as £1 million and in almost every case they have been offered further lucrative salaries with other companies.

The executives of the privatised utilities have seen their salaries rise from figures around the £50,000 mark, to over and above a quarter of a million pounds per year. There does not appear to be a CCT system of recruitment for them. In almost every case, bright young enthusiastic economic doctorates from Britain's best universities, would probably have offered to do their jobs for £30,000 per year or less. Indeed if we were talking high profile, important positions, such as the Governor of the Bank of England, some already successful millionaire might offer to take on the job for free, in order to gain the kudos associated with the position. It is even possible that such a person would be willing to pay a large amount of money, to secure the post.

In the case of 'fat cat' jobs, the old boy network would not allow for such a situation to occur. Unfortunately, however, these very same people, enthusiastically endorse such policies for reducing the wages and lowering the conditions of service, of people whose livelihoods were formerly looked after by Local Government Whitley Councils.

The problem nationally with such a policy is that the tax base shrinks. Less tax collected, together with social security payments to the now lower paid and the extra thousands of unemployed, just adds to the economic and social ills of the country. It is a short-sighted policy.

In education, the opting out of schools, together with Colleges of Further Education and the New Universities being forced to leave local authority control, will result in a deterioration in the service. The situation that education now finds itself in, is not dissimilar to those services experiencing CCT, in that each unit is in charge of its own budget, which shrinks every year. This will result in mass redundancies, coupled with a lowering of wages and a worsening of conditions. Experienced teachers are being made to take early retirement, in order to be replaced by novices on half their salary.

The introduction of CCT, insecure part-time work, temporary contracts, dramatic cut-backs in central government grants to local authorities, rate-capping, and the disruption caused by the Poll Tax, have all contributed to a general sense of unease within local government. The position of the workforce in the private sector is even more catastrophic, particularly in the privatised utilities. The latter's workforce have been hit by massive redundancies, wage cuts and worsening conditions. Indeed:

"After aggregating the results for all the privatised utilities, the symmetry of redistribution is almost perfect. 'Utilities plc' has sacked nearly 25% of its workforce, some 100,000 workers, since privatisation; all of these jobs could have been sustained if the cash distributed as dividends had been applied to paying wages at the average rate prevailing inside the companies." [19]

The standard of living of Accrington's working-class has plummeted disastrously since 1979, as can be seen by the following facts taken from my earlier book "Accrington 1926":

Evidence backing the claim that skilled wages averaged £100 per week in 1979 is listed below. The figures are taken from the Accrington AEU District Committee Minute Book.

Firm	Minute	Date	Wage [skilled]
Bent Sections	92/79	28/3/79	£93.99
Platt Saco Lowell	176/79	6/6/79	£97.50 Toolroom rate
Rishton Paper Mill	175/79	6/6/79	£96.35
Mastabar Mining Co.	201/79	4/7/79	£94.47[grade 8]
Machine Fabs.	224/79	18/7/79	£96.70 [skilled average]

Apparently, skilled fitters working on piece work could earn around £125 to £130 per week. Therefore taking piece work earnings throughout the district into account, an average skilled wage of over £100 per week would have been the norm at the time of Margaret Thatcher's victory.

Today, 1997, skilled engineering workers would have to be earning around £400 per week in order to have maintained their 1979 standard of living which means they have lost around £180 per week or over £9,000 per year.

If prices had only doubled, in the same way that wages have, then a pint of draught bitter in an Accrington public house should cost 64 pence, a prescription 40 pence, a terraced house in Milnshaw £12,000, and a three-bedroomed semi-detached £28,000. Unfortunately, they all cost a lot more.[20]

During the last years of the 1974-1979 Labour Government, the economic situation was not all rosy. However, people like Tony Benn were offering a constructive analysis of the situation and were putting forward socialist alternatives, to Jim Callaghan's middle of the road approach. The following statement from "Arguments for Socialism" published in 1979 is quite prophetic and startling when read in 1997:

> "1. The economic crisis which now grips the Western industrialised world is deep-seated and fundamental.
>
> 2. Monetarism cannot resolve this crisis without endangering the social fabric of political democracy itself.
>
> 3. Corporatism, or the imposition of centralised controls from the top, is equally unacceptable and unworkable."

Unfortunately Tony's 4th. and 5th. points did not come about and the Conservative nightmare visited us instead.

> "4. Democratic socialism which combines direct public investment in industry and expanded public expenditure combined with self-management does offer a real prospect of resolving the present deadlock and protecting personal freedom."
>
> 5. The debate about democratic socialism which is now in progress in Britain is also taking place all over the world and its appeal is so great that it will prevail over both capitalism and communism." [21]

Tony went on to describe 'Democratic Socialism' as follows:

> "The Labour Party has worked on the basis that the investment gap must be filled by public investment, with proper public accountability and public ownership, and that only public expenditure can convert human needs into economic demands able to command resources and help restore full employment. Indeed we believe that the nation can earn its living efficiently and profitably only if there is a new balance of wealth and power in favour of working people. And to avoid corporatism creeping in as a by-product of these public initiatives we have been working for a wider and deeper accountability of power through greater democratic control by Parliament of government and of finance and industry and of the institutions of the Labour Movement itself." [22]

Unfortunately, since Tony wrote the above paragraph, many socialists have been expelled from the Labour Party, or left in disgust at the pro-capitalist statements and policies of the Labour leadership. This has left the working-class of Britain defenceless and their future looks very bleak. This theme was taken up by myself in a letter to the Accrington 'Observer' praising the activities of the late Ken Slater, ex-AEU District Secretary and a former Hyndburn Trades Council and CLP. Secretary:

"The Hyndburn trade union and Labour movement has lost its most sincere and active member with the death of Ken Slater.

For over half-a-century Ken was at the front of every socialist campaign mounted within the borough and the country at large.

Over the last decade he was very active within the Campaign for Labour Party Democracy and through this connection gained election to the national Constitutional Committee of the Labour Party.

Any active Socialist facing expulsion could depend on the support of Ken when the case reached this committee. He knew that their only crime was to fight for the ideals of the Labour Party, which appear to have been jettisoned by the present party leadership.

Over the last five years, the party establishment has rejected 'collectivism' and 'socialism,' replacing these concepts with 'individualism' and 'the market.'

Its reasons for this change of policy were that it mistakenly believed the working-class had been transformed and was basking in affluence in Thatcherite Britain. Unfortunately, this is a false assumption.

The working-class has had to adapt to changes in occupational terms over the last decade. But it is still in existence and will not disappear under the present system. The following three points are still true aspects of working-class life:

* The source of it's income is still the wage / salary or social benefits, or indeed both.
* The level of it's income places this group into the lower and lowest income groups.
* It's power and influence at work and in society is negligible.

The above criteria shows that the working-class constitutes around 70% of the population nationally, and in Hyndburn this figure would rise to 90%.

This class, to varying degrees, continues to bear the brunt of exploitation and subordination. It is certainly not suffering from affluence. It is of course true that many employed workers are not suffering acute depravation. They have become home owners - or rather mortgage owners; car owners - through bank loans; and some even have shares in newly privatised companies [although most have quickly sold them.]

However, to believe that this means affluence is surely an abuse of language. The well-paid and middle-class commentators who have celebrated the Thatcher years would if they had to endure it, view such affluence as a catastrophic decline in their standard of living.

Increased access to household durables does not alter the fact that the condition of the working-class has become worse over the last decade. There has been a deterioration in the 'collective.' Social services, covering health, education, and transport; these factors are of crucial importance in defining the living conditions of the majority of British people.

Insecurity is another factor affecting the workers. Unemployment is, of course, a bad episode to live through, but thousands of people in Hyndburn are in employment and suffer the indignity of low pay.

Ken Slater fought all of his adult life to improve the lot of the common man and believed it to be the duty of the Labour leadership to lead this fight.

However, over the last few years, the Shadow Cabinet has been suffering from the sickness of moderation which causes it to devise policies which are weak and uncertain. It also compels it to devote a lot of time and effort into trying to expel Socialists from the Party.

Ken Slater spent the last years of his life giving support to Socialists within the Party and advocating a Socialist solution to Britain's problems.

He will be sadly missed." [23]

If we accept the Labour leadership's revisionist nonsense, then we are going along with the idea that the directors of multi-national companies with their headquarters in Tokio, New York and Munich, together with international bankers, have a God given right to determine how our economy operates for eternity.

The privatisation of the public utilities has been and will continue to be a disaster for the British people. We must remember that one of the main reasons that the Tories did not raise much of an outcry about their Nationalisation in the late 1940's, was because they were bankrupt industries. Capitalism had failed disastrously. The British tax-payer and the workforce built up the utilities only to have them stolen, by the descendants of those capitalists, forty years later when they were successful operations.

We must also remember that Rover and Rolls Royce would not be with us today but for the Government's help when they were bankrupt in the 1970's.

The Financial Times wrote in November 1919 that:

"When your private concern reaches the dimensions of Lever Bros. it is difficult to tell it from a public body, except that it is not popularly controlled and that it is primarily occupied with making profits for its shareholders."

As I said in 'Accrington 1926', think about the situation this way - if you work for a large capitalist firm, you are really in a similar position to that of the peasant in a third world country, who works the land of an absentee landowner. Eg. Samoza and his family in old Nicaragua. It is highly unlikely that any of the shareholders have ever visited the factory, and it is possible that they don't even know the product produced. How can such a system be justified ?

Socialists hold the high moral ground in their quest for a socialist society. Millionaire shareholders only show themselves as being leeches on society.

The majority of people would bring back hanging and racist ideas are prevalent amongst the population, but it's not the job of the Labour leadership to take up such repugnant ideas and make it their policy. Thankfully they have still not gone down that path. But it is because they say that society accepts Thatcherite capitalist ideas, that they are ditching Socialism. What's the difference between hanging, racism and the ideas of the latter sentence, they are all vote winners when no one is stridently putting forward a Socialist alternative.

In my opinion it is the job of the Labour leadership to promote the Socialist ideas of their founders. Alright, adapt them to the conditions prevailing today, but don't hoist up the white flag of surrender and leave the working-class to continue to suffer under capitalist exploitation for ever and ever.

It is the duty of the leadership to speak out daily in support of Socialist policies. They should be the vanguard of the working-class, having the ultimate aim of consigning capitalism to the dustbin of history. These ideas may not be in the mainstream in 1997, but it is the job of the leadership to change peoples perceptions of the world, just like Blatchford, William Morris, Karl Marx and others did a century ago.

The tactics of New Labour may have won them the General Election, but their policies will not improve the position of the working-class. Only a Socialist set of policies, designed to put into practice ideas contained in the old Labour Party's Clause 4, will do that. Socialists have a hard job ahead of them, but the Socialist solution is the only answer to Britain's and indeed the world's problems.

REFERENCES.

1. Blatchford, Robert. 'Merrie England.' Pub. The Journeyman Press, London. 1976. [First Pub. 1893] p. 52
2. ibib. p. 54

3. ibib. p. 61
4. ibib. p. 76
5. ibib. p. 77
6. ibib. p. 78
7. ibib. p. 79
8. ibib. 80
9. Hansard.1909
10. Beveridge, Lord. "Full Employment in a Free Society." Pub. George Allen & Unwin Ltd. 2nd. Ed. 1960. p. 23
11. ibib. p. 36
12. Donaldson, Peter. "Economics of the Real World." Pub. Penguin / BBC 1975. p. 28
13. ibib. p. 31-32
14. Tressell, Robert. "The Ragged Trousered Philanthropists." Pub. London Panther 1967. p. 272
15. Crossland, Anthony. "Future of Socialism." Pub. Jonathan Cape. London 1956. p. 497
16. Crossland, Anthony. "Socialism Now." Pub. Jonathan Cape. London. 1974. p. 27.
17. Sanderson, I. [Ed] "Management of Quality in Local Government." Pub. Longmans. 1992. Article by Mick Paddon, "Quality in an enabling context." p. 72. The information originally came from Cirrell & Bennett. "CCT: Law & Practice.". Longman 1990.
18. "Municipal Journal." 13-19 October 1995. p. 14 & 15
19. "The Guardian." November 13th. 1995. p. 15
20. Ainsworth, Jim. "Accrington 1926." Pub. Hyndburn Trades Council. 1994. p. 198-199
21. Benn, Tony. "Arguments for Socialism." Pub. Penguin.1980. p. 140-141
22. ibib. p. 147
23. 'Larkin.' Accrington Observer, May 3rd. 1991.

Appendix One.

U.D.C. ELECTIONS 1927

* = Unopposed

OSWALDTWISTLE:
St. Oswald's: Mr. W.F. Metcalf. Lib.*Foxhill Bank:
St. Paul's: Mr. R. Dawson. Con.*   W. H. Greenwood. Lab.   535
St. Michael's: Mr. A. Lund. Con.*. W. Ashworth.   Lib.   <u>414</u>
Immanuel: 121
T. Heys.   Con.   608
Albert Bernasconi   Lab.   <u>474</u>
                             134

CHURCH: **CLAYTON-LE-MOORS:**
J. Grimshaw.   Con.   822   J. Riley.   Con.   1079
E. Roberts.   Con.   756   H. Pickles.   Ind.   939
C.E. Turner.   Con.   620   J. Rushton.   Lib.   933
P.H. Holmes.   Lab.   576   <u>F. Walmsley,   Con   840</u>
<u>W. Turner.   Lab.   501</u> F. Butterworth.   Lab.   728
H. Smith.   Lab.   473   C. Waine.   Con.   714
J. Golbourne.   Lab.   452   H. Edmundson.   Lab.   665
W. Holden.   Ind.   444   Mrs. M.A. Kennedy. Lab.   633
W. Lee.   Ind.   302

RISHTON: **GREAT HARWOOD:**
A. Trengove.   Con.   1275   **North:**
T.W. Bracewell.   Con.   1231   Mrs. E. Cummings. Con.   710
R. Leeming.   Lib.   1211   J.E. Edmundson.   Lab.   <u>404</u>
<u>R.H. Kenyon.   Con.   1122</u>   306
W. Stairs.   Lab.   986   **South:**
H. Crossley.   Lab.   603   A. Stansfield.   Con.   691
Miss Mary Holden   Lab.   550   Alfred. Hayhurst. Lab.   <u>478</u>
J.W. Banks.   Lab.   539   213
R.A. Hodkinson.   Ind.   429   **West:**
                                    Mrs. G.M. Boardman. Con. 705
                                    Frank Marsden.   Lab.   <u>419</u>
                                                              286

                                    East:
                                    Thomas Dobson.   Lab.   619
                                    W. Aldred.   Con.   <u>616</u>
                                                                3

ACCRINGTON BOROUGH ELECTIONS 1927.

North: **South:**
W. Whittaker.   Ind.   1,451   C. Wade.   Lib.   1,099
William Riding. Lab.   <u>902</u> Herbert Walsh.   Lab.   <u>875</u>

		549			224
East:			**West:**		
J. Sudall.	Lib.	1,036	J.S. Harrison.	Con.	1,010
Arthur Dawson.	Lab.	<u>833</u>	C. Burke.	Lab.	<u>811</u>
		203			199
Peel Park:			**Central:**		
W.E. Woolley.	Lib.	1,000	R. Watson.	Lib.	832
J. Bradley	Lab.	<u>881</u>	James A. Coulton.	Lab.	<u>710</u>
		119			122
Higher Antley:			**Spring Hill:**		
C. Livesey.	Con.	868	W. H. Roberts.	Lab.	1,208
Charles Myall.	Lab.	<u>792</u>	J.A. Prescot.	Lib.	<u>752</u>
		76			456

U.D.C. ELECTIONS. 1928.

CHURCH:			**OSWALDTWISTLE:**		
J.Wilson.	Con.	792	**St. Paul's:**		
J. Beckett.	Ind.	758	W. Ashworth.	Lib.	613
J.Dewhurst.	Con.	722	A. Holgate.	Con.	<u>490</u>
<u>Henry Smith</u>	<u>Lab.</u>	<u>673</u>			123
J. Barker.	Lab.	604	**Immanuel:**		
W.C. Miller.	Ind.	579	Rev. J. Dodd.	Con.	661
W. Holden.	Ind.	548	Albert Bernasconi.	Lab.	<u>523</u>
					138
CLAYTON-LE-MOORS:			**Foxhill Bank:**		
E.S. Butterfield.	L/C	1,137	J. Read.	Con.	422
S. Crawshaw.	Ind.	1,048	A. Bury.	Ind.	421
R. Pickup.	L/C	1,006	John Jones.	Lab.	<u>312</u>
<u>J. Clayton</u>	<u>L/C.</u>	<u>882</u>			1
F. Butterworth.	Lab.	825	**St. Oswald's:**		
G. Tierney.	Lab.	610	T. Scholes.	Con.	531
J. Ryan.	L/C	544	A. Walsh.	Lib.	<u>419</u>
					112
			St. Michael's: A. Taylor *		
RISHTON:			**GREAT HARWOOD:**		
H.A. Airey.	Lib.	1,302	**North:**		
W. Stairs.	Lab.	1,164	J.A. Fielding.	Lib.	832
A. Smith.	Con.	1,132	C. Hargreaves.	Con.	<u>427</u>
<u>B. Ainsworth.</u>	<u>Con.</u>	<u>1,080</u>	**South:**		405
G. Knowles.	Con.	1,080	J. Bentley.	Con.*	
W. Bolton.	Lab.	691	**East:**		
J.W. Banks.	Lab.	689	W. Aldred.	Con.	648
			W. Slynn.	Lab.	505
			W. Smith.	Lib.	<u>240</u>

West:		
R. Procter.	Con.	567
J. Wyatt.	Lib.	378
G. Doughty.	Lab.	<u>297</u>
		189

ACCRINGTON BOROUGH ELECTIONS. 1928.

BY-ELECTION. East Ward: 2 vacancies caused by the elevation of 2 sitting Couns. to Aldermen.

A.E. Higham.	Lib.	1,032
J.H. Priestley	Lib.	<u>958</u>
A. Dawson.	Lab.	766
R. Dawson.	Lab.	653

Peel Park:
J.S. Snell.	Lib.	1,121
Michael Walsh.	Lab.	<u>853</u>
		268

South:
J. Laytham.	Con.	1,208
Herbert Walsh.	Lab.	<u>950</u>
		258

East:
J.H. Priestley.	Lib.	930
William Riding.	Lab.	<u>724</u>
		206

West:
C. Burke.	Lab.	944
Haythornthwaite	Con.	<u>911</u>
		33

Central:
H.V. Podmore.	Lab.	830
J. Whittaker.	Lib.	<u>727</u>
		103

Higher Antley:
B. Robinson.	Con.	890
Charles Myall.	Lab.	<u>814</u>
		76

Spring Hill:
W.A. Lambert.	Lab.	1,290
H. Bunkall.	Lib.	<u>732</u>
		558

North:
J.W. Tasker	Lib.	*

U.D.C. ELECTIONS. 1929.

CHURCH:
J.W. Kayley.	Con.	881
T. Roberts.	Con.	848
J.R. Connor.	Lab.	787
J. Whewell.	Con.	775
<u>W. Turner.</u>	<u>Lab.</u>	<u>764</u>[1yr.]
S. Potts.	Lab.	706
J. Barker.	Lab.	686
G. Westwell.	Con.	675
J. Drummond.	Con.	648

RISHTON:
R. Booth.	Ind.	1,025
Parker.	Con.	921
T. Hope.	Lib.	884
W. Edmundson.	Con.	<u>857</u>
H.J. Earnshaw.	Lab.	732
W. Bolton.	Lab.	625
J. Looms.	Con.	621
R. Fielding.	Con.	619
J.W. Banks.	Lab.	603
T. Robinson.	Lib.	557

CLAYTON-LE-MOORS:
F. Sheffield.		1,054

OSWALDTWISTLE:

J.W. Hope. Trade Unionist.		1,016
S. Tench.		867
A. Dean.		<u>845</u>
M.J. Whittaker.		648
Joseph Hardy.	Lab.	596
G.R. Tierney.	Lab.	458
C.E. Robbins.		413
G. Hodkinson		394

GREAT HARWOOD:
East:
Arthur Waring.	Lab.	698
G. McNamee.	Con.	<u>466</u>
		232

West:
T. Henry Seed.	Lab.	411
J. Shackleton.	Con.	380
J. Wyatt.	Lib.	<u>331</u>
		31

St. Paul's:
J.C. Whittaker.	Con.	881
Mrs. H. Harrison.	Lib.	<u>491</u>
		390

Immanuel:
J. Ward.	Con.	614
John Jones.	Lab.	<u>489</u>
		125

Foxhill Bank:
A. Bury.	Ind.	498
J. Groves.	Ind.	395
T. Clitheroe.	Lab.	<u>278</u>
		103

St. Oswald's: G.T. Barnes Lib.*

St. Michael's: J. Foy Con.*

GENERAL ELECTION. 1929.
Mr. Tom Snowden.	Lab.	25,336
Mr. J. Hugh Edwards.	Lib.	<u>23,110</u>
		2,226

ACCRINGTON BOROUGH ELECTIONS 1929.
March By-Election. Due to Huncoat amalgamating with Accrington.

Huncoat:
F. Whittaker.	Ind.	330
John James Barnes.	Lab.	<u>190</u>
		140

West:
T. O'Connor.	Lab.	1,044
J. O. Wilkinson.	Con.	<u>877</u>
		167

Central:
W. Howson.	Lab.	806
S. Tetlow.	Con.	<u>770</u>
		36

East:
Arthur Dawson.	Lab.	950
S. Sutcliffe.	Lib.	<u>845</u>
		105

Higher Antley:

North:
S.T. Pilkington.	Lab.	1,415
G.E. Slack.	Lib.	<u>1,372</u>
		43

Peel Park:
Michael Walsh.	Lab.	907
W. Smith.	Lib.	<u>893</u>
		14

South:
R.I. Constantine.	Lab.	1,263
W. Lightbown.	Lib.	<u>1,058</u>
		205

Spring Hill:

James Baron,	Lab.	1,055	J. Lord.	Lab.	1,292	
W. Moorhouse.	Con.	787	J. Balderstone.	Lib.	653	
		268			639	

Aldermanic Elections:

Ald. Bury	13	
Ald. Rawson	13	
Cllr. Lambert.Lab.	13	First Labour Alderman
Ald. Wilkinson	12	+ casting vote of the Mayor
Ald. Sudall	12	

By-Elections:
Spring Hill:Mr. Charles Myall. Lab. *

U.D.C. ELECTIONS.1930.

CHURCH:			**RISHTON:**		
W. Greenwood.	Con.	1,052	A. Trengove.	Con.	1,527
J. Grimshaw.	Con.	1,041	R. Leeming.	Lib.	1,212
W.C. Miller.	Lib.	918	T.W. Bracewell.	Con.	1,212
P.H. Holmes.	Lab.	902	R.H. Kenyon.	Con.	987
R. Ainsworth.	Con.	784	H. J. Earnshaw.	Lab.	790
Francis J. Duffy.	Lab.	576	Thurston Bradshaw.Lab.		684
W.R. Rigby.	Con.	517		

OSWALDTWISTLE:

St. Paul's:			**Immanuel:**		
Helena Harrison.	Lib.	669	A. Walsh.	Lib.	665
R.S. Duxbury.	Con.	658	A.E. Wright.	Con.	568
	11	Walter Sterling.	Lab.	195
				97

Foxhill Bank:			**St. Oswald's:**		
W.H. Greenwood.	Lab.	588	W.F. Metcalf.	Lib.	550
C.E. Turner.	Con.	425	H. Siddle.	Con.	511
	163			39

St. Michael's:
Robert Smalley Con. *

CLAYTON-LE-MOORS:			**GREAT HARWOOD:**		
H. Pickles.	Ind.	1,264	**North:**	
J. Joinson.	Ind.	1,127	Mrs. E. Cumming.Con.		820
W. Shaw.	Ind.	832	George Henry Fox. Trades Coun.		498
D.C.E. Robbins.	Ind.	678			322
H. Edmundson.	Lab.	588[1yr]	**South:**	
Mrs. Kennedy.	Lab.	569	A. Stansfield.	Con.	805
J. Hardy.	Miners	509	Thomas Tickle.	Trades Coun.	456
J. Finch.	Miners	493			349
F. Wilson.	Ind.	386	**East:**	
		W. Clarkson.	Con.	716

William Slynn.	Trades Coun.	<u>569</u>
		147

West:
Mrs. G.M. Boardman.		Con.	771
John Chambers.	Trades. Coun.		<u>363</u>
			408

ACCRINGTON BOROUGH ELECTIONS. 1930.

North:
G.E. Slack.	Lib.	1,730
William Morris Sproul.	Lab.	<u>902</u>
		828

East:
A.E. Higham.	Lib.	1,172
Harry Smith.	Lab.	<u>672</u>
		498

Peel Park:
A. Wilkinson.	Lib.	1,256
H.H. Parsons.	Lab.	<u>763</u>
		493

Higher Antley:
E. Moorhouse.	Con.	932
H. Walsh.	Lab.	<u>911</u>
		21

South:
O. Wade.	Lib.	1,352
J.E. Greenwood.	Lab.	<u>846</u>
		506

West:
H.G. Haythornthwaite.	Con.	1,152
George F. Kilshaw.	Lab.	<u>674</u>
		498

Central:
S. Tetlow.	Con.	699
Wm. A. Haines.	Lab.	689
R.A. Johnson.	Lib.	<u>455</u>
		10

Spring Hill:
Wm. H. Roberts. *

COUNTY COUNCIL ELECTIONS. 1931.
Accrington South: Alderman James Waddington. Con. *
Accrington North: Councillor G.E. Slack. Lib. *
Church & Oswaldtwistle: Councillor W.E. Metcalf. Lib.*
Hyndburn: Councillor T.W. Bracewell J.P. Con. *
Great Harwood: Mr. J. Washington Baron. Lib. *

U.D.C. ELECTIONS. 1931.

CHURCH:
No contest - all elected unopposed.
J. Beckett.	Ind.*
J. Wilson.	Con.*
D. Grimshaw.	Con.*
W. Holden.	Con.*

CLAYTON-LE-MOORS:
E.S. Butterfield.	990
M.J. Whittaker.	962
J.E. Clayton.	817
<u>J.R. Houldsworth.</u>	<u>760</u>

RISHTON:
No contest - all elected unopposed.
B. Ainsworth.	Con.
H.A. Airey.	Lib.
A. Smith.	Con.
G. Sanderson.	Lib.

GREAT HARWOOD:
North:
Mr. J.A. Fielding. Lib. *
South:
Mr. J. Bentley. J.P. Con. *

H. Edmundson.	Lab.	473	
J.R. Dawson.		396	
J.W. Smith.		349	
J. Hardy		285	
J.J. Hutchinson	Lab.	196	

West:
R. Procter.	Con.	685
G.H. Fox.Trades Coun.		<u>431</u>
		254

East:
W. A. Aldred.	Con.	743
Tom Tickle.Trades Coun.		529
Alf. Ainsworth.	Comm.	<u>38</u>
		214

OSWALDTWISTLE:
Immanuel:
Rev. J. Dodd.	Con.	612
J. Sharples.	Lib.	<u>537</u>
		75

Foxhill Bank:
J. Read.	Con.	670
J.R. Cressey.	Lab.	<u>355</u>
		315

St. Paul's:
A.E.Wright.	Con.	652
W. Ashworth.	Lib.	<u>617</u>
		35

St. Oswald's:
T. Scholes.*

St. Michaels:
A. Taylor.*

GENERAL ELECTION. 1931.
Major. H.A. Procter.	Con.	30,799
Mr. Tom Snowden.	Lab.	<u>18,177</u>
		12,622

ACCRINGTON BOROUGH ELECTIONS. 1931.

East:
J.H. Priestley.	Lib.	1,030
Ellen Dawson.	Lab.	<u>617</u>
		413

South:
J.S. Hargreaves.	Con.	1,480
H. Walsh.	Lab.	<u>825</u>
		655

Higher Antley:
B. Robinson.	Con.	1,038
A. Rowkins.	Lab.	<u>702.</u>
		336

Peel Park:
J.S. Snell [The Mayor] Lib.*

West:
A. Leaver.	Con.	1,041
C. Burke.	Lab.	<u>847</u>
		194

Central:
R. Platt.	Con.	1,001
H. Podmore.	Lab.	<u>823</u>
		178

Spring Hill:
R. Lancaster.	Con.	1,115
Charles Myall.	Lab.	<u>1,093</u>
		22

North:
R.A. Johnson. Lib. *.

U.D.C. ELECTIONS. 1932.

CHURCH:
No contest:
Mr. J.W. Kayley   Con.

OSWALDTWISTLE:
No contest:
St. Oswald's: Mr. G.T. Barnes. Lib.

Mr. J. Whewell. Con.
Mr. W. Clements. Lib.
Mr. John Lea. Con.
Mr. L. Grimshaw. Con. [1 yr.]

CLAYTON-LE-MOORS:
Mr. F. Sheffield.	Ind.		1,092
Mr. S. Tench.	Ind.		848
Mr. A. Dean.	Ind.		842
Mr. J.W. Hope.	Ind.		654
Mr. H. Edmundson.	Lab.		627
Mr. J. Hardy.	Lab.		481

GREAT HARWOOD:
North:
Mr. G. Wroe.	Con.		744
Mr. H Walmesley	T.&L.		588
			156

East:
Mr. Arthur Waring. Lab.		807
Mr. H. Whitehead. Con.		599
Mr. Alf. Ainsworth. Comm.		46
		208

St. Paul's: Mr. J.C. Whittaker. Con.
Immanuel: Mr. Jacob Ward. Con.
Foxhill Bank: Mr. Abel Bury. Ind.
St. Michaels: Mr. E. Yates. Con.

RISHTON:
Mr. J.R. Booth.	Ind.	1,332
Mr. J.W. Edmundson.	Con.	1,116
Mr. J.H. Sowerbutts.	Lib.	1,026
Mr. J. Taylor.	Con.	943
Mr. H. Wilson.	Con.	871
Mr. J.M. Tattersall.	Lab.	855
Mr. D.B. Young.	Con.	804
Mr. I. Baron.	Con.	754

West:
Mr. C. Hargreaves.	Con.		608
Mr. T.H. Seed.	T.&L.		468
Mr. R. Rutter.	Nuwm		145
			140

South:
Mr. S. Shepherd.	Con.		767
Mr. J.W. Sunderland.	T.&L.		589
Mr. F. Wilcox.	Nuwm		43
			178

ACCRINGTON BOROUGH ELECTIONS. 1932.

Central:
Mr. F. Arnett.	Con.	944
Mr. Harry Smith.	Lab.	815
		129

West:
Mr. T. O'Connor.	Lab.	1,114
Mr. E. Ranson.	Con.	923
		191

Higher Antley:
Mr. J. Baron.	Lab.	931
Mr. J. Bancroft.	Con.	880
		51

South:
Mr. R.I. Constantine. Lab.*

East:
Mr. A. Wade.	Lib.	882
Mr. Arthur Dawson.	Lab.	867
		15

Peel Park:
Mr. W. Smith.	Lib.	1,105
Mr. Michael Walsh.	Lab.	904
		201

Spring Hill:
Mr. J. Lord.	Lab.	1,247
Mr. G.F. Nuttall.	Con.	1,059
		188

North:
Mr. G.A. Duckworth.	Lib.	1,671
Mr. W.M. Sproul.	Lab.	881
		790

Huncoat: Brevet-Colonel G.G.H. Bolton. Mc. Con. *

U.D.C. ELECTIONS. 1933.

CHURCH:
No contest.
Mr. J.A. Sharples. Con.*
Mr. J. Grimshaw. Con.*
Mr. W.C. Miller. Lib.*.
Mr. W. Clements. Lib.*.

RISHTON:
Mr. A. Trengove.	Con.	1,548
Mr. J.M. Tattersall.	Lab.	1,070
Mr. R. Leeming.	Lib.	1,069
Mr. Robert Gildert.	Lab.	978
Mr. T. Porter.	Con.	972
Mr. R.H. Kenyon.	Con.	947
Mr. D.B Young.	Ind.	685
Mr. G. Knowles.	Ind.	310

GREAT HARWOOD:
North:
Mrs. E. Cummings	Con.	719
Mr. G.H. Fox.	T&L	526
		193

South:
Mr. A. Stansfield	Con.	753
Mr. F. Wilcock	Nuwm	178
		575

West:
Mrs. G.M. Boardman.	Con.	687
Mr. R. Rutter.	Nuwm.	466
		221

OSWALDTWISTLE:
St. Michael's:
Mr. E. Heap. Con.*
Foxhill Bank:
Mr. W.H. Greenwood. Lab.*.

St. Paul's:
Mrs. H. Harrison.	Lib.	799
Mr. H. Cox.	Con.	551
		248

St. Oswald's
Mr. D. Peters	Con.	598
Mr. W.F. Metcalf	Lib.	595
		3

Immanuel:
Mr. N. Ball	Con.	574
Mr. A. Walsh	Lib.	549
Mr. W. Haworth	Lab.	321
		25

CLAYTON-LE-MOORS:
Mr. H. Pickles	Ind.	963
Mr. J.W. Talbot	Ind.	914
Mr. Joseph Finch	Lab.	767
Mr. Ersnest Nuttall	Lab.	574
Mr. J. Johnson	Ind.	568
Mr. D. Almond	Con.	530
Mr. D.C.E. Robbins	Ind.	468
Mr. W. Shaw		374

East:
Mr. J.W. Sunderland	T&L	1,150
Mr. W. Clarkson	Con.	615
Mr. Alf Ainsworth	Nuwm.	52
		102

ACCRINGTON BOROUGH ELECTIONS. 1933.

North:
Mr. G.E. Slack.	Lib.	1,372
Mr. W. Howson.	Lab.	1,176
		196

East:
Mr. A. Higham.	Lib.	887
Mr. M. Walsh.	Lab.	758
		129

Higher Antley:
Mr. E. Moorhouse. Con. 911

South:
Mr. O. Wade.	Lib.	1,150
Mr. R. Carter.	Lab.	848
		302

West:
Mr. G.F. Kilshaw.	Lab.	1,034
Mr. G. Haythornthwaite.	Con.	888
		146

Central:
Mr. S. Tetlow. Con. 889

Mr. J. Harling.	Lab.	789		Mr. Harry Smith.		Lab.	710
		122					179
Spring Hill:				**Peel Park:**			
Mr. W.H. Roberts.	Lab.	1,433		Mr. A. Wilkinson	Lib.*		
Mr. J.E. Ritchings.	Con.	928					
		505					

COUNTY COUNCIL ELECTIONS. 1934.

Accrington North:				**Church & Oswaldtwistle:**			
Mr. R.I. Constantine.	Lab.	5,482		Mr. W. Metcalf.		Lib.	2,777
Mr. G.E. Slack.	Lib.	3,020		Mr. J. Read.		Con.	2,654
		2,462		Mrs. M.E. Boardman.		Lab.	2,220
							123
Great Harwood:							
Mr. J.W. Sunderland.		Lab.	2,546				
Mr. H. Whitehead.		Con.	2,542				
			4				

U.D.C. ELECTIONS. 1934.

CHURCH:				**RISHTON:**			
Mr. J. Wilson.	Con.	995		Mr. G. Sanderson.		Lib.	1,496
Mrs. A. Barnes.	Con.	851		Mr. A. Smith.		Con.	1,151
Mr. J. Beckett.	Ind.	798		Mr. H. Wilson.		Con.	1,066
Mr. W. Holden.	Con.	735		Mr. B. Ainsworth.		Con.	1,000
Mr. R. Rawlinson.	Lab.	512		Mr. T. Bradshaw.		Lab.	856
Mrs. M. Haworth.	Lab.	451		Mr. C. Hayhurst.		Lab.	749
Mr. W. Lee.	Ind.	441		Mr. J. Brocklehurst.		Lab.	713
OSWALDTWISTLE:							
Immanuel:				**Foxhill Bank:**			
Rev. J. Dodd.	Con.	622		Mr. J. Read.		Con.	622
Mr. J. Sharples.	Lib.	540		Mr. J.W. Hill.		Lab.	422
		31					200
St. Oswald's:				**St. Paul's:**			
Mr. W.F. Metcalf.	Lib.	779		Mr. A.E. Wright.		Con.	662
Mr. C. Whittle.	Con.	388		Mr. J. Haworth.		Lib.	593
		391		Mr. P. Longton.		Ind.	58
St. Michael's:							69
Mr. Albert Taylor *							
GREAT HARWOOD:							
North:				**South:**			
Mr. J. Fielding.	Lib.	923		Mr. J. Bentley.		Con.	784
Mr. George Gardener.	Nuwm	120		Mr. W. Hothersall.		Trades C.	547
		803					237

East:			West:		
Mr. W. Aldred.	Con.	719	Mr. R. Procter	Con.	784
Mr. W. Slynn.	Trades/C	692	Mr. R. Rutter.	Ind.	<u>424</u>
Mr. S. Stott.	Nuwm.	<u>16</u>			326
		27			

CLAYTON-LE-MOORS:
No contest, all elected unopposed.
Mrs. Kennedy   Lab.
Mr. Joseph Hardy   Lab.
E.S. Butterfield
J.R. Houldsworth
Daniel Almond

ACCRINGTON BOROUGH ELECTIONS. 1934

North: Mr. R.A. Johnson.   Lib.*
South: Mr. J.S. Hargreaves   Con. *

West:			East:		
Mr. R. Lancaster	Con.	956	Mr. J.H. Priestley	Lib.	787
Mr. H. Parsons	Lab.	<u>908</u>	Mr. M. Walsh	Lab.	<u>780</u>
		48			7
Central:			**Peel Park:**		
Mr. Wallace Haines	Lab,	874	Mr. H. Potts.	Lab.	1,110
Mr. R. Platt	Con.	<u>813</u>	Mr. J.S. Snell	Lib.	<u>1,006</u>
		61			104
Higher Antley:			**Spring Hill:**		
Mr. J.M. Harling	Lab.	923	Mr. F. Mills	Lab.	1,264
Mr. A.H. James	Con.	<u>808</u>	Mr. W. Harris	Con.	<u>988</u>
		115			276

Appendix Two.

Labour Party Officials.
1927

Accrington TCLP.
President: Councillor. R.I. Constantine. Secretary/Agent: Mr. W. Howson.
Vice - Presidents: Councillor. J. Lord. & Councillor. T. O'Connor.
EC. Messrs. Fred Riding, R. Dawson, H.V. Podmore, Harry Smith, A.E. Sargent, B.Ledwick, James Bury, J. Jaques, R. Carter, Joseph Colburn, W.H. Whittam, William Haworth, & William Davenport. Couns. Baron & Roberts. Mrs. Watson & Mrs. White.
Rep.to the Lancs & Ches. Fed. of Trades Councils & Lab. Parties: Mr. A. Nile.

Accrington I.L.P.	**Accrington Women's Section:**
President: Mr. William Riding.	President: Mrs. Holder.
Vice - President: Mr. S. Hinchcliffe.	Vice - President: Mrs. Childs.
Secretary: Mr. William Brotherton.	Secretary: Mrs. Beswick
Treasurer: Mr. R. Catterall.	Ass. Sec.: Mrs. Birtwistle.
Lecture Secretary: Miss E. Wigglesworth.	Treasurer: Mrs. Genge.
Literature Secretary: Mr. N. Marshall.	Literature Secretary: Mrs. Inman.
Subscription Secretary: Mr. E. Bleasdale.	Sick Visitor: Mrs. Pilkington.
Chief Steward: Mr. F. Thomas.	EC.: Mesdames. Jackson, Morgan, Fielding,W.H.Livesey,E. Haworth, Inman, Armstrong, Ashworth, & McQueen.

1928.

Accrington TCLP.
President: Councillor R.I. Constantine. Secretary/ Agent: Mr. W. Howson
V.Ps: Couns. J. Lord & Mr. James Bradley. Treasurer: Mr. George Lunt.
Auditors: Mr. W. Ince & Mr. Robert Dawson.
EC. Couns. Baron, Roberts, & O'Connor. Messrs. H. Walsh J.P., H.V. Podmore, F. Riding, S. Potts, F. Butterworth, A.E. Sargent, T. Riley, J. Jaques, L. Gaffney, G.R. Tierney, A. Berry, William. Haworth, W. Davenport. & Mrs. White.
Rep. to the Lancs & Ches Fed Trade Councils & Lab. Parties: Mr. Fred Riding.

Oswaldtwistle Labour Party:	**Accrington I.L.P.**
President: Mr. Albert Bernasconi.	President: Mr. S. Hinchcliffe.
Vice - President: Mr. W.T.C. Davenport.	Vice-President: Mr. W. Davenport.
Treasurer: Mr. George Lunt.	Secretary: Mr. R. Dawson.
Secretary: Mr. J.C. Breare.	Treasurer: Mr. R. Catterall.
Executive Committee: Messrs. F. Christie, A. Baldwin, J. Mercer, A.E. Sargent &	Stamp Secretary: Miss Dean. Minute Secretary: Mr. N. Marshall.

William Haworth.   Literature Sec: Mr. J. Naylor.
Accrington Women's Section.
President: Mrs. Holder. Vice - President: Mrs. W.H. Livesey.
Secretary: Mrs. Beswick. Treasurer: Mrs. Fielding. Sick Visitor: Mrs. Childs.
Literature Secretary: Mrs. A. Haworth.
EC: Mesdames. Morgan, Jackson, Eastwood, Monk, Birtwistle, Ashworth, A. Haworth, Barnes, & Miss E. Nuttall.
Social Committee: Mrs. A. Haworth, Miss M. Dunne.

1929.

Accrington TCLP.
President: Councillor R. I. Constantine.VPs: Mr. J. Bradley & Coun. J. Lord.
Secretary/Agent: Mr. W. Howson. Treasurer: Mr. George Lunt.
Auditors: Mr. W. Ince & Mrs. S. F. Brigg.
EC: Couns. Podmore, Roberts, O'Connor, Messrs. H. Walsh, J.P., J.E. Davies, Fred Riding, J.T. Davenport, S. Potts, Albert Bernasconi, J. Grimshaw, W. Cain, W. Ince, J. Barker, H. Edmundson, H. Holgate, & William Haworth. Mrs. W.H. Livesey. [+ Mr. J. Finch of C-L-M's July 1929]
Rep. to Lancs & Ches.Fed of Trades Councils & Lab Parties: Mr. Fred Riding.
Delegate to the Annual Party Conference: Mr. J. Bradley.

Accrington Women's Section.
President: Mrs. W.H. Livesey.
Vice - President: Mrs. Birtwistle.
Secretary: Mrs. Beswick.
Treasurer: Mrs. Fielding.
Sick Visitor: Mrs. Pilkington.
E C: Mesdames. Morgan, Barnes,Holder, G. Livesey, W. Rushton, Stephenson, Hollingrake, Birtwell.Miss Wigglesworth.
Soc. Com: Mrs.Haworth,Miss.M.Dunne

Oswaldtwistle Labour Party.
President: Mr. Albert Bernasconi.
Secretary: Mr. J.C. Beare.
Treasurer: Mr. George Lunt.
EC: Messrs. William Haworth, F. Christie, A. Baldwin, J. Mercer, & T. Kane.

Rishton Trades & Labour Party.
Secretary: Mr. Harry Trengove.

Clayton-Le-Moors Labour League of Youth.
Organised by: Miss Phyllis Parr & Miss J. Heys.

1930.

Accrington TCLP.
President: Councillor. R.I. Constantine.VPs: Mr. J. Bradley and Coun. Lord.
Secretary / Agent: Mr. W. Howson. Treasurer: Councillor Roberts.
Auditors: Messrs. W. Ince and S.F. Brigg.
EC: Couns; T. O'Connor, M. Walsh, H. Smith (Church),H. Edmundson (C-L-M) Messrs; H. Walsh J.P., F. Riding, J.T. Davenport, J.E. Davies, W. Cain, A. Bernasconi, J. Grimshaw, S. Potts, A. Tattersall and W. Bolton. Mrs. Slater, Mrs. W.H. Livesey and Mrs. Beswick.

Representative to the Lancashire and Cheshire Federations: Mr. J.R. Cressey.
Accrington Women's Section.
President: Mrs. Birtwistle. Vice President: Mrs. Watson.
Secretary: Mrs. Beswick.Treasurer: Mrs. Jackson.Sick Visitor: Mrs. Haworth.
Literature Secretary: Mrs. Livesey.
EC: Miss Wigglesworth. Mesdames; Rushton, Eastwood, Holder, Regan, T. Bolton, Fielding, Holmes, A. Haworth.

1931.

Accrington TCLP.
President: Councillor R.I. Constantine. [Replaced by Coun.A.Dawson in Nov. 1931, due to Constantine becoming the 1st Labour Mayor of Accrington.]
VPs: Councillor J. Lord and Mr. H. Walsh J.P. Sec./Agent: Mr. W. Howson.
Treasurer: Coun. Roberts.Auditors: Messrs; Walter Ince and S.F. Briggs.
EC: Messrs; J.T. Davenport, J. Borrow, R. Carter, J.E. Davies, W. Buller, W. Turner, T. Carter, A Cattersall, W.F. Kane, A. Bernasconi, J. Grimshaw, J. Bradshaw, Councillor T. O'Connor J.P., Mrs. Beswick, Mrs. Slater, Mrs Dawson, Messrs; S. Potts, H.E. Edmundson, J. Mercer, and T. Rankin.
Rep.to Lancs&Ches. Fed.Trades Councils and Lab.Parties: Mr.J.R. Cressey.

Acc. TCLP. Women's Section.
President: Mrs. A. Haworth.
Vice President: Mrs. Holder.
Secretary: Miss A. Noble.
Treasurer: Mrs. J. Bolton.
Lit. Sec: Mrs. W.H. Livesey.
Sick Visitor: Mrs. Haworth.
Auditors:Mrs.BarnesMrs. Boulton.
EC: Misses Wigglesworth,Iddon
Mesdames: Regan,Beswick,
Holmes,Fielding, Parsons,
Rothwell, Smalley

Clayton-Le-Moors Labour Party.
President&Treasurer:Mr. Harry Edmundson
VPs: Mr. J.J. Hutchinson,Miss P.Bibby
Auditor: Mr. J.J. Hutchinson
Sec: Mr. Tom Carter
EC: Mesdames: Richardson, Howson, Hodson,Bury,Mr.R.T.Howson,J.W.Fogg
Collectors:Mrs.Bury,Mrs.Hodson
Delegates to AccTCLP:Mr.Edmundson, Carter,& Miss Bibby.

Oswaldtwistle Labour Party.
President: Mr. A. Bernasconi.
Treasurer: Mr. G. Lunt.
Secretary: Mr. P. Cross.

Clayton-Le-MoorsLabour Party Women's Section.
President:Mrs. Kennedy.

1932.

Accrington TCLP.
President: Councillor A. Dawson. VP: Coun. J. Lord and Mr. H. Walsh. J.P.
Secretary / Agent: Mr. W. Howson.Treasurer: Councillor W.H. Roberts.
Auditors: Messrs. W. Ince and S.F. Briggs.
EC: Coun. James Baron, Messrs; James Barrow, R. Carter, J.E. Davies, Miss

Worsley, Messrs; A. Tattersall, J.J. Hutchinson, W.F. Cain, J.R. Cressey, A. Bowker, W. Brotherton, Mrs. Dawson, Messrs; W.A. Haines, C. Myall. Coun. T. O'Connor, Messrs; S. Potts, R.Campbell, Thomas, Haworth and P.Cross.
Rep. to the Lancashire and Cheshire Federation of TCLP's: Mr. J.R. Cressey.

Accrington TCLP Women's Section.
President: Mrs. A. Haworth.
Vice President: Mrs. Holder.
Secretary: Miss Noble.
Treasurer: Mrs. T. Bolton.
Literature Secretary: Mrs. Fielding.
Sich Visitor: Mrs. Holder.
Auditors: Mrs. Barnes and Mrs. Murfitt.
E C: Mesdames Regan, Woods, Slater, Birtwistle, Astin, South, Rushton, Parsons Howson, and Miss Iddon.

Accrington Labour Party League of Youth.
Officials: Messrs. H.A. Haines & N.Marshall

Clayton-Le-Moors Labour Party Women's Section.
President: Mrs. Kennedy

1933.

Accrington TCLP.
President: Mr. A. Dawson. VPs: Messrs. Brotherton & G.F. Kilshaw
Treasurer: Coun. W.H. Roberts. Auditors: Messrs. S.F. Briggs & W. Ince.
EC: Miss Worsley, Messrs. R. Carter, James Barrow, H. Winter, W. Buller, J.R. Cressey, Coun. J. Finch, W.F. Cain, T. Bradshaw, Coun. T. O'Connor, N. Marshall, C. Myall, J. Connor, S. Potts, T. Carter, T. Haworth, W. Nuttall, & Mesdames Dawson, & Jackson.
Rep. to Lancs&Cheshire Fed.of Trades & Labour Parties: Mr. J.R. Crossley.

Clayton-Le-Moors Labour Party.
President: Ernest Nuttall
VPs: Miss S. Bibby & Mr. Joseph Finch.
Secretary & Treasurer: Mr. Tom Carter.
EC: Mesdames. Kennedy, Booth, Duckworth, Taylor, Pickup, Bury, Hodson, Messrs. R. Campbell, W. Greenwood,C.Duckworth & T. Carter.
Delegates to AccTCLP:Miss Bibby,Messrs Campbell & Carter
EC.Member AccTCLP:Mr.T.Carter

Oswaldtwistle Labour Party League of Youth.
President:Mr. R.C. [Bob] Campbell
Officers: Mr. H. Bailey & Miss A. Bernasconi.

Accrington TCLP Women's Section..
President: Mrs. Holder
VP: Mrs. Sparrow
Secretary: Mrs. Jackson
Ass.Sec: Mrs. Murfitt.
Treasurer:Mrs.T.Bolton
Lit.Sec:Mrs.Scott
Sick Visitors: Holder & Murfitt
Auditors: Mrs Barnes & Scott
EC:Fielding,Riley,Howson,Iddon

1934

Accrington TCLP.
President:Coun. R.I. Constantine. VP: Coun. G.F. Kilshaw & Mr. M.Walsh.
Sec./Agent: Mr. W. Howson. Auditors: Mr. W. Ince and Mr. Charles Myall.
EC: Messrs; James Borrow, W. Buller, R. Carter, H. Parsons, W. Brotherton, James Connor, Wallace Haines, Charles Myall, Coun. T. O'Connor J.P., Coun. W.H. Roberts, A. Berry, J.E. Young, J. Smith, S. Potts, T. Carter, T. Haworth, Miss H. Worsley, and Miss D. Eastwood.

Accrington TCLP Women's Section.
President: Mrs. Holder.
Vice President: Mrs. Scott.
Secretary: Mrs. Barnes.
Assistant Secretary: Mrs. M. Haworth.
Treasurer: Mrs. Bolton.
Literature Secretary: Mrs. Scott.
Sick Visitor: Mrs. Parkinson.
Auditor: Mrs. Jackson Mrs. H. Haworth.
Executive Committee: Mrs. Woods, MrsCharles,Mrs. Howson, Mrs. M. Haworth, Mrs.Fielding and Miss Iddon.

Oswaldtwistle Labour Party.
President: Mr. A. Baldwin.
Vice President: Mr. J. Flegg.
Secretary:Mr.[Bill] Haworth.
Treasurer:Mr.R.C.[Bob] Campbell.

Oswaldtwistle Labour Party League of Youth.
President:Mr.R.C.[Bob] Campbell.
Vice President: Mr. G. Flegg.
Secretary: Mr. T. Haworth
Treasurer: Miss T.P. Campbell
EC: Messrs. W. Haworth,A.Flegg J.Flegg,H.Burke, & Mrs. Haworth.

Clayton-Le-Moors Labour Party.
President: Councillor E. Nuttall. re-elected.
Secretary: Mr. Edmund Heap. replaced Mr. T. Carter.
VP: Councillors Finch & Hardy, Coun. Mrs. Kennedy & Mrs. Worsley.
Treasurer: Mr. T. Carter. Auditor: Mr. Horace Howson.
Collectors: Mesdames. Berry and Hodson.
EC: Mesdames, M.A. Howson, Taylor, Pickup, Duckworth, Booth, Holden, Messrs; W. Greenwood, Campbell and C. Duckworth.
Delegates to AccTCLP: Messrs; Pickup,H.Howson,T.Carter,& Mrs.Worsley.

Rishton Trades Council.
President: Mr. J. Ashworth.
Vice President: Mr. J. Smith.
Secretary: Mr. T. Bradshaw.
Auditors: Messrs; J. Ratcliffe and J. Sharples.

Appendix Three.

Sir Oswald Mosley - the New Party - the British Union of Fascists.

Mosley started out in politics as a Conservative and after a spell as Independent MP for Harrow, moved across to the Labour Party in March 1924. In 1929 he won Smethwick and his wife Cynthia [Daughter of Lord Curzon] won Stoke, both for the Labour Party.

Mosley's main interest was unemployment and he was given the job of devising a practical policy for its alleviation, by the minority Labour Government. However, he was unfortunate to find himself under the direction of the Lord Privy Seal, Mr. J.H. Thomas. Thomas was really bad news - "he was economically illiterate and old." [1]

Mosley decided to ignore Thomas and produce his own policy, having discussed the situation with the economist John Maynard Keynes. He knew Thomas would be negative towards his plan and so he arranged for it to be leaked to the press. This appeared in the Manchester Guardian of February 7th. 1930. It was not a revolutionary socialist policy, it merely was "a serious attempt to rationalise transport, to modernise industry along U.S. lines, plan the export trade and so on." [2] When the Labour Cabinet indicated that they would reject the idea, Mosley resigned from the Government and began to publicly criticise them over the issue.

In December 1930, he issued a manifesto which again called for "an elaborately planned economy to be directed by a cabinet of overlords, subject only to the general control of parliament. This would stimulate exports, control imports and plan home consumption." [3] The manifesto was supported by 17 Labour MP's, including Aneurin Bevan, John Strachey, and Oliver Baldwin, together with the Miners' Secretary, A.J. Cook.

James Maxton and the ILP leadership declined to support the manifesto on the grounds that its phraseology was one of the survival of British industry, as opposed to British industry passing into public ownership.

At the end of February 1931, a pamphlet was published outlining Mosley's policy, but by the time it was circulated, he had decided to go ahead with the foundation of his 'New Party'. However, by the time of its inugural meeting on Monday March 5th. 1931, practically all of his Labour supporters deserted him. Only his wife Cynthia and John Strachey followed him into the 'New Party.'

Its first test was the by-election in Ashton-Under-Lyne on April 30th. 1931. The result, in what was regarded as a safe Labour seat, was Con. 12,420; Lab. 11,005; and New Party 4,472. The New Party had split the anti-Tory vote and the Labour activists were furious. Their reaction, upset Mosley and this caused John Strachey to comment, "at that moment British Fascism was born." In fact Mosley and his New Party carried on and contested the 1931 General Election. It put up 24 candidates, who all lost. Mosley became more and more right-wing and went on to establish the British Union of Fascists in October 1932.

Cynthia Mosley's involvement in politics ended after her efforts to launch the New Party. "Increasingly she objected to [Mosley's] involvement with fascism."[4] She died of a perforated appendix in May 1933.

John Strachey resigned from the New Party prior to the 1931 General Election. He became a leading light in the Left Book Club, and eventually became Secretary of State for War in the Attlee Government.

References.

1. Thomas, Hugh. "John Strachey." Pub. Eyre Methuen, London. 1973. p. 80
2. ibib. p. 82
3. ibib. p. 90
4. Mosley, Nicholas. "The Rules of the Game." Pub. Secker & Warburg 1982. Review in the 'Sunday Observer' 3rd. October 1982

Appendix Four
TRADE UNION OFFICIALS
Amalgamated Engineering Union - Accrington District Committee.

1927 Attendance	%	1928 Attendance	%	1929 Attendance	%
A. Holding	94	A. Holding	82	A. Sutcliffe	66
G.K. Chalmers	86	G.K. Chalmers	100	G.K. Chalmers	87
H. Walsh	96	H. Walsh	90	H. Walsh	96
E. Battersby	88	E. Battersby	100	E. Battersby	100
J.R. Cressey	98	J.R. Cressey	92	J.R. Cressey	98
J.H. Cosgrove	37	J.H. Cosgrove	90	J.H. Cosgrove	70
J. Barrow	78	J. Barrow	37	J. Barrow	17
J. Law	43	J. Law	41	J. Law	79
Stirzaker	8	Stirzaker	57	Stirzaker	79
A. Sutcliffe	96	A. Sutcliffe	27	Ashmead	2
W. Watson	84	W. Watson	57	Scott	57
Heyworth	45	Whittle	20	Pearson	2
C. Myall	14	Rawsthorne	65	Rawsthorne	9
S.F. Brigg	8	J. Bradley	37	J. Bradley	55
		Nuttall	2	A. Holding	30
				S.F. Brigg	42
				Bury	13

1930 Attendance	%	1931 Attendance	%	1932 Attendance	%
W. Prescott	50	H. Rothwell	90	H. Rothwell	100
G.K. Chalmers	100	G.K. Chalmers	100	G.K. Chalmers	100
Scott	90	W. Scott	78	W. Scott	88
J.H. Cosgrove	90	J.H. Cosgrove	94	J.H. Cosgrove	98
S.F. Brigg	100	S.F. Brigg	98	S.F. Brigg	100
Stirzaker	100	G.A. Stirzaker	96	Stirzaker	96
E. Battersby	100	E. Battersby	92	E. Battersby	88
J.R. Cressey	100	J.R. Cressey	94	J.R. Cressey	94
H. Walsh	96	H. Walsh	90	H. Walsh	77
Law	63	Law	57	Thwaites	8
		J.H. Green	10	J.H. Green	21
		Fielding	6	Fielding	58
		T. Pilkington	4	T. Pilkington	6
		S. Holden	2	Bury	2
		Donnellan	2		
		W. Goulding	4		

1933			1934	
Attendance	%		Attendance	%
H. Rothwell	90		H. Rothwell	100
G.K. Chalmers	100		G.K. Chalmers	100
Stirzaker	100		Stirzaker	98
J.H. Cosgrove	90		J.H. Cosgrove	56
Fielding	75		Fielding	83
E. Battersby	81		E. Battersby	98
Green	63		Green	12
J.R. Cressey	100		J.R. Cressey	94
J. Leigh	38		J. Leigh	88
W. Scott	92		W. Scott	98
S. Holden	54		S. Holden	83
H. Johnson	2		H. Johnson	44
Thwaites	15		Thwaites	2
Higham	4		Higham	2
Bury	6		Pearson	2
S.F. Brigg	40			

Presidents:
A. Holding   1927 until Feb. 1928
Arnold Sutcliffe   Feb. 1929 until Oct. 1929
Herbert Walsh   Oct. 1929 until Feb. 1930
William Prescott   Feb. 1930 until Aug. 1930
Herbert Walsh   Aug. 1930 until Feb. 1931
Herbert Rothwell Feb. 1931 until Feb. 1936
Secretary:
George Kidd Chalmers   1920 - 1940
N.B. The District Committee met on a weekly basis throughout this period.
Accrington AEU Shop Stewards Committee:
1930 -1933
President: Mr. J.R. Cressey **Secretary:** Mr. W.H. Stokes
Treasurer: Mr. R. Carter **Auditors:** Messrs. S.F. Briggs & J. Bamber
Membership 1929 January:

Accrington	2,200	Blackburn	1,197	Burnley	709
Great Harwood	47	Rishton	30		

These figures show how Accrington was the dominant Engineering Centre of North East Lancashire at the time. Greater Accrington had more AEU members than its two much larger neighbours combined.

General & Municipal Workers Union - Accrington Branch.
Executive Committee.

P = Possible Attendance

1926-1927 P.13	1927-1928 P.12	1928-1929 P.11	1929-1930 P.12
H. Carter 13	H. Carter 13	H. Carter 11	H. Carter 11
W.A. Lambert 13	W.A. Lambert 11	W.A. Lambert 10	W.A. Lambert 10
C. McLennon 13	C. McLennon 11	J. Colbourne 11	A. Holder 8
R. Dawson 12	R. Dawson 12	R. Dawson 10	W. Riding 11
A. Hambling 10	A. Hambling 8	W. Vernon 9	T. Mercer 11
W. Holman 12	W. Holman 11	W. Holman 11	H. Hayhurst 12
T. Johns 12	T. Johns 11	T. Mercer 11	J. Grimshaw 12
D. Smith 4	D. Smith 3	D. Smith 2	G.E. Holman 10
F. Riding 12	F. Riding 11	F. Riding 11	W. Holman 12
G.E. Holman 11	G.H. Holman 9	H. Hayhurst 11	F. Riding 11

1930-31 P.11	1931-32 P.13	1932-1933 P.12	1933-1934 P.13
H. Carter 11	H. Carter 13	II. Carter 12	H. Carter 13
W.A. Lambert 10	W.A. Lambert 13	W.A. Lambert 2	F. Riding 13
T. Mercer 10	T. Mercer 12	T. Mercer 11	T. Mercer 12
A. Holder 11	A. Holder 13	A. Holder 11	A. Holder 12
W. Holman 11	A.G. Roberts 6	W. Holman 12	W. Holman 13
W. Riding 11	W. Riding 13	W. Riding 10	W. Riding 13
F. Riding 9	F. Riding 10	F. Riding 12	J. Crewe 13
H. Hayhurst 11	H. Hayhurst 13	A. Ormerod 11	J. Hutchinson 13
J. Grimshaw 10	J. Haworth 13	R. Dawson 12	J. Seery 13
G.E. Holman 8	J. Seery 13	J. Seery 11	

1934-35 P.12

H. Carter	5
F. Riding	12
W. Brotherton	6
W. Riding	6
A. Holder	12
J. Crewe	12
J. Hutchinson	12
T. Mercer	11
W. Holman	10
J. Haworth	11

Presidents:
Harry Carter   January 1918 - January 1935
William Brotherton   January 1935 - October 1937

Secretaries:
Alderman W.A. Lambert   August 1917 - October 1932
Fred Riding   October 1932 - January 1950

Accrington Weavers', Winders' and Warpers' Association.
1927
President: Mr. J.T. Davenport   **Auditor:** Mr. J.J. Mills [Dec. 1926]
EC:[June1926]BerthaHaworth,LenaWorsley,S.Tomlinson,James Hesmondhalgh, Elizabeth A. Procter. [Dec. 1926]Maria Watson [Holme Mill], S. Kay [Industrial Mill], Alice Hindle [Fountain Mill], Lily Leacey [Broad Oak], Maggie Molloy [Alliance Baxenden], Florrie Dean [Hambledon Mill], Margaret Podmore [Helene Mill].[June 1927] Margaret McCarthy [Spring Mill], Lena Worsley, Elizabeth A. Procter [Heifer Bank], Mr. S. Tomlinson [Woodnook].
1928
President: Miss Lena Worsley **Auditor:** Mr. Henry Killingbeck [Dec 1927]
EC:[Dec.1927]Mrs.MariaWatson[Holme],MissAnnieH.KirkhamJ.P.[Victoria Mill],Mrs. Margaret Molloy [Alliance Baxenden], Mrs. Lily Leacy [Broad Oak], Alice Hindle and Mr. Kilshaw [Fountain], Mr. J.T. Davenport [Ellesmere Mill]. [June 1928] Mrs. Elizabeth A. Procter [Heifer Bank], and Mr. S. Tomlinson [Scaitcliffe Mill]
1929
President: Miss Lena Worsley   **Auditor:** Mr. John Jackson Mills
EC: [Dec 1928] Mr. John W. Kenyon, Mrs. M. Watson, Mr. S. Kay, Miss Alice Hindle, Mr. J.T. Davenport, Miss Annie H. Kirkham J.P., Mrs. M. Podmore, Mrs. L. leacy, and Mr. W. Smith. [June 1929] Mr. S. Tomlinson [Scaitcliffe], Mrs. Elizabeth A. Procter [Heifer Bank], and Mrs. G. Tipping [Highams]
1930
President: Miss Lena Worsley   **Auditor:** Mr. H. Killinbeck
EC: [Dec.1929] Miss Alice Snowden. Miss Annie H. Kirkham J.P. [Victoria], Miss Alice Hindle [Fountain], Mr. Sam Kay [Industrial], Mr. J.T. Davenport [Ellesmere], Mrs. Margaret Podmore [Helene], and Mr. William Smith [Hambledon][June 1930] Annie H. Kirkham J.P. [Chambers' Victoria], Sam Kay [Industrial Baxenden], Alice Hindle [Fountain], J.T. Davenport [Ellesmere], Margaret Podmore [Helene], William Smith [Hambledon], George Tipping [Higham's], J.W. Kenyon [Peel], Stephen Tomlinson [Scaitcliffe], Alice Snowden [Cunliffe's Union Street], and Annie Blades [Heifer Bank].
1931
President: Miss Helena Worsley   **Auditor:** Mr. J. Jackson Mills.
Executive Committee: [Dec. 1930] Miss A. Kirkham [Chambers' Victoria], Miss Alice Hindle [Fountain], Mr. J.T. Davenport [Ellesmere No.1], Mrs. M. Podmore [Helene], Mr. William Smith [Hambledon], Mr. George Tipping [Highams'] and Miss Alice Snowden [Cunliffes' Union St] [June 1931] Mr. J.W. Kenyon [Peel Mill], and Mr. Stephen Tomlinson [Scaitcliffe]
1932

President: Miss Helena Worsley   **Auditor:** Mr. H. Killingbeck
Executive Committee: [Dec. 1931] Re-elected en bloc except for Mary Scott [Helena Mill] replacing Mrs. M. Podmore.
1933
President: Miss Helena Worsley   **Auditor:** Mr. J.J. Mills
Executive Committee: [Dec 1932] Re-elected en bloc except Miss Alice Hindle and Miss Mary Scott. Mr. William Jarrett took the place of Miss Scott.
1934
President: Miss Helena Worsley   **Auditor:** Mr. H. Killingbeck
Executive Committee: [June 1934] no nominations. [Dec 1934] Mr. J.T. Davenport [Oak Vale] and Mr. William Ridehalgh [Higham's] were re-elected, but no other nominations were forthcoming.
Secretary: Mr. J.R. Emmett J.P. throughout this period.

Church and Oswaldtwistle Weavers' Association.

1927
President: Mr. A. Starkie **Auditor:** Mr. B. Birtwell
Secretary: Mr. J.T. Wolstenholme **Assistant Secretary:** Mr. W. Hughes
EC:[Dec.1926]MissC.Parkinson,Messrs.J.Ellis,B.Hartley,F.Coleman,W. Preston,A.Hall,&G.S.Ormerod.[June1927]MissA.Thompson,Messrs.A.Suter, W.H.Baron,E.Sharp,P.Spillane,W.H.Bolton,J.W.Moss,H.Hindle,J.W.Lamb.
Treasurer:[June 1927]Mr.E.Grimshaw **Auditor:**[June 1927]Mr.A.Haworth
TUC Delegate: Mr. J.T. Wolstenholme
Labour Party Conference Delegate: Mr. A. Suter
1928
President: Mr. F. Coleman **Auditor:** Mr, B. Birtwell
Secretary: Mr. J.T. Wolstenholme
EC:[Dec.1927]MissC.Parkinson[CanalMill],Mr.J.Ellis[MoscowMill],Mr.B. Hartley[Rhoden],Mr.W.Preston[Albion],Mr.A.Hall[Commercial],andMr.G.S. Ormerod[Royal Oak].[June 1928]Miss A.Suter,Messrs.W.H.Baron,E. Sharp, P Spillane, J.W. Moss, H. Hindle, J.W. Lamb, G.E. Porter, & J. Marsden.
Treasurer:[June 1928] Mr. E. Grimshaw   **Auditor:** Mr. A. Haworth
1929
President: Mr. Frank Coleman   **Treasurer:** Mr. E. Grimshaw [June 1929]
Auditor: Mr.Albert Haworth[June1929]**Secretary:**Mr.W. Hughes[June 1929]
EC:[Dec.1928]Messrs.J.Marsden,J.Ellis,B.Hartley,W.Preston,A.Hall,&G.S. Ormerod,&MissC.Parkinson[June1929]Mr.Thompson[StanhillMill], Mr.Baron[StoneBridgeMill],Mr.E.Sharp[UnionMill],Mr. P.Spillane[Rhyddings Mill],Mr. J.W.Moss[Fern Mill],&Mr. H.Hartley[Church Bank Mill].
1930
President: Mr. G.S. Ormerod   **Secretary:** Mr. W. Hughes

EC:[Dec.1929]MissC.Parkinson,Messrs.J.Ellis,B.Hartley,A.Hall,&J. Marsden.
Auditors:[June 1930]Mr. W. Abbott[12 months]& Mr. J.J. Preston[6 months]
TUC Delegate: Mr. A.R. Ratcliffe
EC: [June 1930] Miss A. Thompson [Stanhill Mill], Mr. E. Sharp [Union], Mr. P. Spillane [Rhyddings], Mr. G.E. Porter [Rose], Mr. H. Embley [Church Bank] and Mr. A.R. Ratcliffe [Three Brooks Mill]

1931
President: Mr. G.S. Ormerod **Auditor:** [Dec. 1930] Mr. J.J. Preston and [June 1931] Mr. A. Haworth **Treasurer:** [June 1931] Mr. T.F. Christie
EC: [Dec.1930] Miss C. Parkinson [Canal Mill], Miss D. Eastwood [Three Brooks Mill], Mr. J. Ellis [Moscow Mill], Mr. B. Hartley [Rhoden], Mr. A. Hall [Commercial], and Mr. J. Baldry [Rose] [June 1931] Miss A. Thompson, Messrs. E. Sharp and P. Spillane

1932
President: Mr. G.S. Ormerod **Secretary:**Mr.W.Hughes
Auditors:[Dec.1931] Mr. J.J. Preston [June 1932] Mr. A. Haworth
Treasurer: [June1932] Mr. T.F. Christie
EC: [Dec.1931] Messrs. B. Hailley, J. Baldry, A. Berry, Miss C. Parkinson and Miss D. Eastwood. [June 1932] Messrs. E. Sharp [Union], P. Spillane [Rhyddings], and W. Parr [Moscow Mill]

1933
President: Mr. George Potter **Auditor:** [Dec.1932]Mr.J.Preston [June1933] Mr. A. Haworth   **Treasurer:** [June 1933] Mr. T.F. Christie
Secretary: Mr. W. Hughes
EC: [June 1933] Messrs. E. Sharp and P. Spillane

1934
President: Mr. A. Berry   **Auditor:** [Dec.1933] Mr. J.J. Preston
Secretary: Mr. W. Hughes
EC: [Dec.1933] Miss C. Parkinson and Mr. B. Hartley

Rishton Weavers' Association.

1927
President: Mr. James Crossley   **Auditor:** [Jan.1927] Mr. J.R. Pollard
Auditor: [Aug.1927] Mr. J.H. Whittaker
EC:[Jan.1927] Mr. Baron [Bridgefield], Mr. J.W. Banks [York], Mr. W. Duckworth [Albert], Mr. R. Cowburn [Daisy], Mr. J. Conway [Victoria], Mrs. Alice Colley [Winders & Warpers], Mr. W. Harrison [Rishto], Mr. H. Walsh [Unity], and Mrs. M. Harrison [Co-opted Member] [Aug.1927] Messrs. H. Seed [Bridgefield],A. Taylor [Unity], M. Yates [Victoria], W. Fletcher [Wheatfield], J. Jolley [Britannia], and J. O'Connor [Spring]

1928

President: Mr. J. Crossley **Auditor:** [Jan.1928] Mr. J.R. Pollard and to replace Mr. Whittaker, Mr. W. Bolton. [July 1928] Mr. W. Bolton
EC: [Jan.1928]Messrs. J.W. Banks[York] C. Clayton[Bridgefield],J. Conway [Victoria],R. Cowburn[Daisy], E. Hope[Rishton[H. Walsh[Unity], W. Sutton [Britannia],Mrs. Alice Collett [Warpers], Miss Mary Hargreaves [Winders][July 1928]Messrs. J. Walsh[Bridgefield], Mr. Yates [Victoria], W. Fletcher [Wheatfield], W. Duckworth [Albert], T. Bradshaw [Britannia], J. Day [Unity], & G. Hurst [Daisy]
Delegate to TUC Annual Conference: Mr. J. Ashworth
1930
President: Mr. J. Crossley **Auditor:** [Dec,1929] Mr. Samuel Leach
EC: [Dec.1929] Messrs. J.W. Banks [York], C. Clayton [Bridgefield], H. Walsh [Unity], E. Hope [Rishton], P. Holden [Victoria], Miss M. Gillibrand [Spring], Miss Alice Colley [Warpers], and Miss Mary Hargreaves [Winders]
1931
President: Mr. J. Crossley **Auditor:** [Dec.1930] Mr. S. Leach
1932
President: Mr. Robert Gildert **Auditor:** [Dec 1931]Mr. S. Leach
EC: [Dec.1931] Mr. P. Holden [Victoria], Mr. J. Ratcliffe [York], and Miss Edith Green [Winders' and Warpers']
1933
President: Mr. R. Gildert
EC: Messrs. G. Hoyle [Victoria], J. Ratcliffe [York], and Mr. W. Flectcher [Wheatfield], were re-elected.
1934
President: Mr. R. Gildert **Auditor:** [June 1934] Mr. W. Bolton
EC: [Dec.1933] Messrs. P. Hayhurst, G. Hoyle, W. Fletcher and J. Radcliffe [June 1934] Messrs. T. Ratcliffe and T. Sharples re-elected
Delegate to TUC Annual Conference: Mr. J. Ashworth
Secretary: Mr. Jonathan Ashworth March 1923 until his death on Christmas Day 1934.

Clayton-Le-Moors Weavers' Association.

1927
President: Mrs. M. Riley **Auditor:** [Jan.1927] Mr. James Westwell
EC:[Jan.1927]Messrs.W.Fogg[Royal],G.Pilkington[Prospect],F.Bulcock [Clayton]A.Cousins[Albion],SamuelRogers[Providence],J.T.Whittaker[Albert]
1928
President: [Jan.1928] Mr. C. Duckworth. [Aug.1928] Mr. Frank Wilkinson
Auditor: [Jan.1928] Mr. J.T. Westwell
EC:[Jan.1928]Messrs.J.Fielding & C.Rodgers[Royal],C.Duckworth[Prospect],

F.Bulcock[Clayton], L.Ashworth[Albert],and E.Whittaker[Albion]
1929
President: Mr. William Fogg **Auditor:** [Feb.1929] Mr. James Westwell. [June 1929] Mr. W. Bolton
EC: [Feb.1929]Mr.ThomasKnowles[Royal],Mr.ArthurTomlinson [Commercial],Mr.JamesWhite[Albion],Mrs.Marsden[Prospect].[June1929] Messrs. F. Wilkinson and J. Threlfall[Canal] and L. Ashworth[Commercial]
1930
President: Mr. W. Fogg **Auditor:** [January 1930] Mr. J.T. Westwell
EC: [January 1930] Mr. J. Threlfall [Canal], Mrs. M. Riley [Prospect], Miss Freeston [Commercial], Messrs. D. Woods and T. Knowles [Royal]
1931
President: Mr. W. Fogg **Auditor:** [July 1931] Mr. W. Bolton
EC: [July 1931] Messrs. F. Duxbury, S. Burdekin, T. Spence and N. Catterall.
1932
President: Mr. W. Fogg
EC: [June 1932] Mr. J. Threlfall [Canal], Mrs. Taylor, Mr. G. Pilkington, Mr. James Walne, Mr. R. Greenwood and Mr. H. Robinson
1933
President: Mr. John Threlfall **Auditor:** [Dec.1932] Mr. Arthur Taylor and [July 1933] Mr. Edward Whittaker
EC: [Dec.1932] Mrs. Metcalf [Canal], Mr. James Walne [Claymore], Messrs. Ernest Duxbury, David Hallworth, Robert Greenwood and Noah Catterall. [July 1933] Messrs. Fred Bulcock, Noah Catterall, David Haworth and John Fielding
1934
President: Mr. John Threlfall **Auditor:** [Jan.1934] Mr. Arthur Taylor
EC: [Jan.1934] Mr. James Walne [Claymore], Mrs. Robinson, Mr. Harry Armitage, Mr. D. Hallworth and Mr. John Fielding
Secretary: Mr. J.W. Hope held the position throughout this period.

Great Harwood Weavers' Association.

June 1929
Mill Reps. Messrs.James Dunn[York],A.Firth[Delph Rd.],A. Loynd[Deveron], F.Marsden[Bank],J.Aspinall[Victoria],R.Wardell[Prospect],T.Slater[Premier No. 3],J. Fox[St. Huberts], J. Bibby[Record], J. Byrom[Park View].
March 1930
Mill Reps. Messrs.P.Williamson[Clayton St.],T.Wolstenholme[Delph Rd],R. Whalley[Premier No.1], H. Holden[York], W. Blackledge[Saw], J. McNamee.
December 1930
Auditor: Mr. G. Doughty
Mill Reps. Messrs. F. Hoyle [St. Lawrence], R. Whalley [Premier No.1], A.

Johnson [Deveron], L. Taylor [Waverledge], J. Brennand [Victoria], R. Connell [St. Huberts], H. Edge [Wellington], F. Harrison [Albion], E. Hothersall [York], Mrs. S.E. Hindle [Bank]
March 1931
Mill Reps. Messrs. T. Wolstenholme [Delph Rd.], P. Williamson [Clayton St.], J. McNamee [Robin Lap], H. Holden [York], W. Blackledge [Saw].
June 1931
Auditor: Mr. James Thompson
Mill Reps. Messrs. J. Bibby [Record], R. Wardell [Prospect], T. Slater [Premier No.3], R.C. Mattocks [Britannia]
September 1931
Auditor: Mr. John William Edmundson
Mill Reps. Messrs. J. Barrett [Premier No.2], W. Cooper [Palatine], T.H. Seed [Wellington], J. Wrigley [Albert]. Mrs. H. Hallworth [Waverledge]
December 1931
Auditor: Mr. John William Edmundson
Mill Reps. Messrs. A. Johnson [Deveron], L. Taylor [Waverledge], J. Brennand [Victoria], R. Connell [St. Huberts], H. Edge [Wellington], F. Harrison [Albion].
March 1932
Mill Reps. Messrs. T. Wolstenholme [Delph Rd.], P. Williamson [Clayton St.], Herbert Holden [York]
June 1932
Auditor: Mr. James Thompson
Mill Reps. Messrs. J. Bibby [Record], R.C. Mattocks [Britannia].
September 1932
Vice President: Mr. T.H. Seed
Mill Reps. Messrs. W. Cooper [Palatine], T.H. Seed [Wellington], J. Wrigley [Albert], Mrs. H. Hallworth [Waverledge].
December 1932
Auditor: Mr. J. W. Edmundson
Mill Reps. Messrs. Brennan [Victoria], Edge [Wellington],Connell [St. Huberts], Harrison [Albion], Hothersall [York].
March 1933
Mill Reps. Messrs. T. Wolstenholme [Delph Rd.], P. Williamson [Clayton St.], Herbert Holden [York], L. Barton [Deveron].
May 1933
Auditor: Mr. James Thompson
Mill Reps. Messrs. J. Bibby [Record], R.C. Mattocks [Britannia].
August 1933
Mill Reps. Messrs. W. Cooper [Palatine], T.H. Seed [Wellington], Mrs. H.

Hallworth [Waverledge]
December 1933
Auditor: Mr. John William Edmundson   **Vice President:** Mr. Harold Edge
MillReps. Messrs.J.Brennand[Victoria],E.Edge[Wellington],E.Hothersall [York].
March 1934
Auditor: Mr. Samuel Heywood
Mill Reps. Messrs. Herbert Holden [York], Jack Smith [Wellington]
September 1934
Mill Reps. Mrs. H. Hallworth [Waverledge], Mr. W. Cooper [Palatine]
November 1934
Mill Reps. Messrs. E. Hothersall, J. Brennand, H. Edge.
NB. Mill Reps served on the Branch Committee for a twelve month period.
Secretaries: Mr. William Hesmondhalgh, died March 1929. [28 years service.]
Mr. John W. Hudson, April 1929, until his death on January 1930.
Mr. J. W. Sunderland, March 1930 and after.
Presidents: Mr. Peter Williamson, died September 1933. [33 years service]
Mr. Edmund Hothersall, December 1933 and after.

Accrington & District Textile Trades Federation.

June 1927
President: Mr.J.T.Davenport[Weavers] **Sec:** Mr. J.R.Emmett[Weavers]
Treasurer: Mr. Robert Whalley [Overlookers]
Auditor: Mr. J. Kayley [Cardroom Workers]
June 1928
President: Mr.S.Holmes[Overlookers] **Sec:** Mr. J.R.Emmett[Weavers]
Treasurer: Mr. R. Whalley [Overlookers]
Auditor: Mr. J. Kayley [Cardroom Workers]
December 1929
President: Mr. R. Armistead [Warehousemen]
Sec: Mr.J.R.Emmett[Weavers] **Treasurer:** Mr.J,T.Dodd[Tapesizers]
Auditor: Mr. J. Kayley [Cardroom Workers]
1932
President: Mr. J. Dodd [Tapesizers] **Sec:**Mr.R.Armistead[Warehousemen]
Treasurer: Mr.J.R.Emmett[Weavers]
Auditor: Mr.J.Kayley[Cardroom Workers]
1934
President: Mr. Ben Mather [Cardroom Workers]
Sec: Mr. R. Armistead [Warehousemen]
Treasurer: Mr.J.R.Emmett[Weavers]
Auditor: Mr.J.Kayley[Cardroom Workers]

Church & Oswaldtwistle Textile Trades Federation.
1928
President: Mr. E. Reeder [Spinners] **Sec:** Mr. W. Hughes [Weavers]
Treasurer: Mr. G. Haworth [Overlookers]
Auditor: Mr. W. Bentley [Twisters & Drawers]
November 1929
President: Mr. E. Reeder [Spinners] **Sec:** Mr.W.Hughes[Weavers]
Treasurer: Mr. Henry Kenneford [Overlookers]
Auditor: Mr. W. Bentley [Twisters & Drawers]

United Textile Factory Workers' Association - AGM.
1928 Accrington Delegates.
Mr. J.R. Emmett J.P. & Mr. G. Tomlinson, Accrington Weavers'
Mr. J.H. Duxbury, Overlookers. Mr. R. Armistead, Warehousemen.
Mr. Edward Thornton, Spinners. Mr. Andrew Naesmith, Sec. Amalgamation.
1928 Rishton Delegate.
Mr. J.R. Pickering.
1929 Accrington Delegates.
Mr. J.R. Emmett J.P. & Mrs. M. Watson, Accrington Weavers'.
Mr. J.H. Duxbury, Overlookers. Mr. E. Thornton, Spinners.
Mr. R. Armistead, Warehousemen. Mr. Robert Kay, Cardroom Workers.
1930 Accrington Delegates.
Mr. J.R. Emmett J.P. Accrington Weavers' Mr. J.H. Duxbury, Overlookers.
Mr.R. Armistead, Warehousemen. Mr. Edward Thorn, Sec. Acc. Spinners.
Mr. Herbert Potts, Cardroom Workers.

General Union of Associations of Loom Overlookers.
1930
Accrington & District - 156 Members.
President: Mr. Stephen Holmes, 217 Avenue Parade.
Vice President: Thomas Wilson, 13 Nutter Road.
Treasurer: Mr. William Heap, 4 Limefield Street.
Secretary: Mr. James Henry Duxbury, 145 Manor Street.
Church & Oswaldtwistle - 135 Members.
President: Mr. Henry Kenneford, 54 Roe Greave Road, Oswaldtwistle.
Vice President: Mr. Chris Varley, 54 Rhyddings Street, Oswaldtwistle.
Treasurer: Mr. William Haworth, 97 Market Street. Church
Secretary: Mr. James Clark, 40 Kay Street, Oswaldtwistle.
Rishton - 63 Members.
President: Mr. H. Taylor, Parker Street.
Vice President: Mr. Thomas Tattersall, 5 Chapel Street.
Treasurer: Mr. Robert Duckworth, 76 Harwood Road.

Secretary: Mr. R. Lightbown, 32 Hermitage Street.
Clayton-Le-Moors - 49 Members.
President: George Dean, 18 Milton Street.
Vice President: Willian Sagar, 98 Barnes Street.
Treasurer: Edward Grimshaw, 8 Milton Street.
Secretary: W.T. Hindle, 12 Milton Street.
Great Harwood - 203 Members.
President: John Catlow, 15 Park Avenue.
Vice President: Henry Fowles, 62 Railway Terrace.
Treasurer: James Livesey, 53 Princess Street.
Secretary: James Edward Hopper, 31 St. Cecillia Street.

1933
Accrington & District - 124 Members.
President: Stephen Holmes, 217 Avenue Parade.
Vice President: Thomas Wilson, 13 Nutter Road.
Treasurer: William Heap, 4 Limefield Street.
Secretary: James Henry Duxbury, 145 Manor Street.
Church & Oswaldtwistle - 116 Members.
President: Henry Kenneford, 54 Roe Greave Road, Oswaldtwistle.
Vice President: Chris Varley, 54 Rhyddings Street, Oswaldtwistle.
Treasurer: William Haworth, 97 Market Street, Church.
Secretary: James Clarke, 40 Kay Street, Oswaldtwistle.
Rishton - 54 Members.
President: John Mackintosh, 59 Harwood Road.
Vice President: W. E. Carter, Parker Street.
Treasurer: Robert Duckworth, 76 Harwood Road.
Secretary: R. Lightbown, 32 Hermitage Street.
Clayton-Le-Moors - 28 Members.
President: George Dean, 18 Milton Street. C-L-M.
Vice President: Harry Leeming, 282 Dill Hall Lane, Church.
Treasurer: Richard Walne, 50 Atlas Street. C-L-M.
Secretary: Edward Grimshaw, 8 Milton Street, C-L-M.
Great Harwood - 163 Members.
President: John Catlow, 15 Park Avenue.
Vice President: Henry Fowles, 62 Railway Terrace.
Treasurer: James Livesey, 53 Princess Street.
Secretary: Richard Harrison, 15 Beaconsfield Street.

Appendix Five.

THE GOLD STANDARD.

It is essential that a brief explanation is given regarding the gold standard because it affected the period so drastically. The gold standard was a system whereby a given unit of paper currency was freely exchangeable for a given weight of gold. In international trade, countries on the gold standard had to have fixed rates of exchange between their currencies. For example, in 1913 the same amount of gold could be exchanged for £1 or $4.87.

In addition to the above, the central banks of countries on the gold standard were supposed to aim for equilibrium between the amount of gold in their vaults and the amount of money in circulation. Too little gold would mean that in a crisis the Bank of England could not sell gold to people wishing to exchange their pound notes and the system would collapse. Too much gold in the vaults would mean that the authorities were missing out on giving profitable loans to third parties, which would yield interest payments.

Britain and the USA, when both on the gold standard, had to settle their international debts between each other in terms of gold. Therefore, in a simplistic way, if Britain sold less exports to the USA than she imported from that country, the resulting trade deficit would have to be paid for in gold. This would have had the effect of lowering the amount of gold in the vaults of the Bank of England, which in turn would have resulted in a reduction in Britain's internal spending and to a fall in wages and prices. Imports into Britain would then be reduced and hopefully there would be a rise in British exports due to lower prices and because British manufacturers would have to look elsewhere for markets.

In the USA, under the above circumstances, the central banks having increased their gold reserves would expand credit, resulting in wage and price rises. Imports would then rise and their exports being more expensive would fall. In theory, the operation of the gold standard would therefore have the effect of eliminating Britain's trade deficit with the USA. In practice however, the gold standard never quite worked like this. [1]

The states of Europe and North America operated the gold standard from 1880 until the first world war and its supposed success in maintaining free trade together with low inflation became legendary in right-wing circles. However, the gold standard's acclaim was a myth, because during that period millions of British and European workers, who would otherwise have been unemployed, emigrated. In addition, the rich countries invested billions of pounds abroad in imperialist adventures to gain new markets, resulting in grievances which eventually led to the first world war itself.

In 1919, in capitalist terms, the post-war inflationary boom was getting out of hand and the government accordingly introduced a deflationary package. However, they took it to extremes. In 1918 the Cunliffe Committee had advised that Britain should return to the gold standard and the aim was to achieve this at the pre-war parity. In order for this to work, British prices had to achieve equilibrium with prices in the USA, and this could only happen if severe credit restrictions took place. In 1921 the Geddes Committee recommended excessive public expenditure cuts.[2]

Eventually, Baldwin's government, under persistent advice from the Bank of England, went back onto the gold standard in April 1925. It was Winston Churchill, as Chancellor of the Exchequer, who

"presided over the most dramatically disastrous error by a government in modern economic history." [3]

Churchill's mistake was to return Britain to the gold standard at the pre-war parity of £1=$4.87. Had Britain returned at a rate of £1=$4.40 the effect might not have been so tragic. At $4.40 to the pound the prices of British coal, textiles, ship-building and engineering products would have been in line with other industrialised countries. However, we had entered at a rate that was 10% too high and therefore long established markets disappeared to our competitors.

John Maynard Keynes wrote to Churchill asking why he had done "such a silly thing." [4] Keynes had become famous after the publication in 1919 of his book 'The Economic Consequences of the Peace.' In this he had predicted that by demanding Germany give war reparations to the allies which they could not afford, Europe would only be punishing itself. It would have been more in European self-interest to have been more restrained in its peace settlement with Germany. The Establishment ignored his analysis.

In 1925 Keynes knew that wages, already too low, had kept at their 1923 level and that they would only fall further if the government acted in a deliberately deflationary manner. Unemployment was already over 10% and he thought that to go back on the gold standard at the proposed rate was too high a price to pay, and therefore he opposed the decision.[5] He was, however, a lone voice amongst capitalist economists; the Establishment had no qualms about reducing wages further and in particular the mine-owners relished the prospects. As such, the return to the gold standard had to be one of the major causes of the General Strike, the Cotton Crisis, and the introduction of the Means test.

Churchill had got it all wrong. Companies were holding back on increasing output, not because of a shortage of labour and capital, but because they could not sell any more goods in an economy of three million unemployed. Cutting wages could not help either because if all wages in the British economy were cut simultaneously, overall purchasing power would be reduced and therefore people could only buy less.[6]

Keynes suggested that the answer lay in more spending. The wherewithal to purchase any increased output was the missing ingredient.[7] He said that anything that raised demand would contribute to lowering unemployment. How much more sensible, he thought, to create incomes by planning worthwhile road and house building programmes. The confidence this would instil in business would get Britain out of its economic recession.

> "The essence of the Keynesian message was that a totally unregulated laissez-faire, free enterprise economy, simply could not be relied upon to do the job of creating and maintaining full employment. If the degradation and shear waste of unemployment was ever to be eliminated the state would have to accept explicit responsibility for achieving that objective."[8]

REFERENCES.

1. Stewart, Michael. 'Keynes and After.' Pub. Penguin 1975. pp.56-58
2. Alford, BWE. 'Depression and Recovery ?' Pub. MacMillan 1972. p. 31
3. Galbraith, JK. 'The Age of Uncertainty.' Pub. BBC/Andre Deutsch 1977. p. 203
4. ibid. p. 204
5. Stewart op. cit. p. 61
6. Donaldson, Peter. 'Economics of the Real World.' Pub. Penguin/BBC 1975. p. 28
7. ibid. p. 29
8. ibid. pp. 31-32

Appendix Six

Useful thoughts for the Labour Party front bench.

1."Dialectical materialism is the philosophy born out of the great movement of our times - the movement of the people who labour who 'create all the good things of life and feed and clothe the world', to rise at last to their full stature. It is wholly, entirely dedicated to the service of that movement. This is the source of all its teachings, and in that service its conclusions are continually tried, tested and developed. Without such a philosophy, the movement cannot achieve unity, cannot win its battles." Maurice Cornforth, quoted in Labour Monthly Feb. 1981 p. 50

2."Labour is prior to, and independent of, capital. Capital is only the fruit of labour, and could not have existed if labour had not first existed." Abraham Lincoln, Message to Congress 1861

3."We all declare for liberty; but in using the same word we do not all mean the same thing. With some the word liberty may mean for each man to do as he pleases with himself, and the product of his labour; whilst with others the same word may mean for some men to do as they please with other men, and the product of other men's labour. Here are two, not only different, but incompatible things, called by the same name, liberty. And it follows that each of these things is, by the respective parties, called by two different and incompatible names - liberty and tyranny." Abraham Lincoln, Baltimore 1864.

4"Jarrow is an object lesson.....The profiteers, having ravaged a town or country, can take themselves and their gains elsewhere. The workers have the main stake in their homeland, for in it they must remain. They have built it, and worked for it, fought for it. On their skill and their toil has been built England's industrial reputation. They were crowded into hovels, their children starved and died, and on their sacrifice great capital has been accumulated. It is time that they planned it, organised it, and developed it so that all might enjoy the wealth which we can produce. In the interest of this land we love, that is the next job which must be done." Ellen Wilkinson MP. 'The Town That Was Murdered.' Left Book Club. 1939 p. 284

5"There are certain so-called freedoms that Labour will not tolerate: freedom to exploit other people; freedom to pay poor wages and to push up prices for selfish profit; freedom to deprive the people of the means of living full, happy, healthy lives." Labour Party Election Manifesto, 'Let Us Face The Future.' 1945

6"The economy is now completely dominated by a hundred or so giant companies whose interests cannot be expected to coincide with the interests of the national economy..... Our objective is to bring about a fundamental and irreversible shift in the balance of power and wealth in favour of working people and their families." Labour Party Programme 1973.

7."Both this and the next Labour government have to justify the support given by the trade unions. This means nothing less than a Labour government carrying out Labour's pledge to bring about a fundamental and irriversible shift in the balance of power in society in favour of working people and their families." Hugh Scanlon. AUEW Engineering Section Journal, Sept. 1974

8."Britain is enormously rich, in its natural resources, in its great industries, in the enormous talent and skills of its people. To release all these forces and unite them together is impossible under capitalism. This is why Britain is in crisis and will remain in crisis as long as the monopolies dominate in Britain." Gordon McLennan, speech at the 35th Congress CPGB. 1977

9."Tory rhetoric in recent years tended to suggest that socialism and egalitarianism had destroyed the old order beyond repair..... The workers were thought to have taken over, replacing brains with brawn.This is not quite the picture presented by the new government, which is encouragingly full of hereditary peers, self-made and hereditary millionaires, wealthy landowners, scholarly products of Oxbridge, headed by a lady who has married money. What price the great social revolution that was to have got under way as far back as 1945. The Marxist left, of course, will make great play with all this. Nor can they be blamed for doing so, since nothing could better highlight the failure of British social democracy to bring about a fundamental shift in the structure of society. But the old ruling order is still very much alive and kicking. If the present Tory cabinet represents the first results of stemming the socialist flood, what in heaven's name will be carried into Downing Street when the Tory tide proper begins to flow?" Peregrine Worsthorne, 'A Kitchen Cabinet Fit For The Ritz.' Sunday Telegraph, May 13th 1979

10."People always have been the foolish victims of deception and self-deception in poverty, and they always will be until they have learnt to seek out the interests of some class or other behind all moral, religious, political and social phrases, declarations and promises." V.I. Lenin, 'The Three Sources and Three Component Parts of Marxism' March 1913.(Collected Works Vol. 19 p. 28)

11. "When I read in the bourgeois newspapers praise of something I have said or done, I look at myself in the glass and say: 'August, you old ass, what stupidity have you committed?'" Statement attributed to August Bebel (1840-1913) leader of the old German Social Democratic Labour Party. Quoted in Labour Monthly October 1975

12. "The first of all rules in a struggle is not to do what the enemy wants you to do..... You, the English working class, have but to will it, and you will be masters of the state of society." August Bebel TUC Congress 1896

13. "We have got to mobilise the workers. We have to understand classical socialism and how this is consonant with the gospel. In a word we've got to study Karl Marx again and show that he is not a terror but a scientific philosopher and a person who still has a lot to say to us." Bishop Colin Winter, Christian Socialist, December 1980

BIBLIOGRAPHY

Trade Union Minutes:
Accrington AEU District Committee 1927-1934, can be found at the Working Class Movement Library, Salford.
Accrington GMWU Branch Minutes 1927-1934, are held at the Union Offices, Stanley Street, Accrington.
Great Harwood Weavers' Quarterly Minutes 1927-1934, are housed at the Working Class Movement Library, Salford.
Great Harwood Weavers' Branch Minutes 1927-1934; Accrington & District Weavers' 1929-1934; Church & Oswaldtwistle Weavers' 1927-1934; are all available for inspection at the County Archive, Preston.
Lancashire & Cheshire Miners Federation, Delegates & Executive Minutes 1927-1934, copies in Accrington Library.

Newspapers:
Accrington 'Observer' 1927-1934 is on micro-film at Accrington Library.
Blackburn 'Times' 1927-1934 is on micro-film at Blackburn Library.

Interviews:
Alice & Wallace Haines, interviewed by Eric Jones, April 1978.
Interviews between myself and the following:
Bob Campbell, January 1985
James Dunn, January 1985
Roland Hagan, April 1985
Alice Haines, May 1985
Ken Slater, January 1985

Local Unpublished Works, available at Accrington Library, Local History Section.
Hayward, G. 'Working-Class Conservatives in Rishton between the Wars 1918-1939.' Ruskin College Thesis 1974/75
Jones, Eric. 'The Origins & Nature of the Organised Working-Class Socialists in Accrington 1850-1945.' Ruskin College Thesis 1978/79.
Stephenson, C.D. 'Farewell King Cotton: A Case Study of a Cotton Town [Great Harwood] in Decline 1920-1940.' University of Warwick BA. 1987
Swann, Steven. 'Politics of Labour in a Lancashire Mill Town: Accrington Between the Wars.' Dissertation MA. Sheffield University. 1988
Walsh, Simon. 'Coming to Terms: The Decline of the Lancashire Cotton Industry 1913-1937: Causes and Consequencies.' Extended Essay Manchester University BA. 1986

Industrial Archaeology of Greater Accrington.
Michael Rothwell has written a series entitled 'Industrial Heritage,' published by the Hyndburn Local History Society. These are Guides to the Industrial

Archaeology of Accrington[1979], Oswaldtwistle[1976], Church[1980], Clayton-Le-Moors[1979], Rishton[1981] and Great Harwood.
Local Books and Pamphlets.
Blackburn, F. 'George Tomlinson.' Pub. Heinemann 1954
de Bunsen, V. 'Charles Roden Buxton: A Memoir.' Pub. George Allen & Unwin 1948
McCarthy, M. 'Generation in Revolt.' Pub. Heinemann 1953
Spencer, W. 'Tom Snowden.' Pub. Accrington Trades & Labour Party - Election Booklet 1929
COTTON:
Bullen, A.'The Lancashire Weavers' Union.' Pub. Amalgamated Textile Workers' Union. 1984
Dickinson, B. 'James Rushton & His Times 1886-1956.' Pub. Working Class Movement Library 1982
Fowler, A & L. 'The History of the Nelson Weavers' Association.' Pub. Burnley, Nelson, Rossendale and District Textile Workers' Union. 1984.
Fowler, A & Wyke, T. 'The Barefoot Aristocrats: A History of the Amalgamated Association of Operative Cotton Spinners.' Pub. Kelsall, G. Littleborough. 1987
Hopwood, E. 'A History of the Lancashire Cotton Industry and the Amalgamated Weavers' Association.' Pub. Amalgamated Weavers' Association. 1969.
Jowitt, J.A. & McIvor, A.J. [Ed] 'Employers and Labour in the English Textile Industries 1850-1939.' Pub. Routledge, London.1988.
Turner, H.A. 'Trade Union Growth, Structure and Policy: A Comparative Study of the Cotton Unions.' Pub. George Allen & Unwin Ltd. 1962.
Utley, F. 'Lancashire and the Far East.' Pub. George Allen & Unwin Ltd. 1931.
Pamphlets:
Ainsworth, B; Dickinson, B; Hargreaves, A; McCarthy, M; Rushton, J; Walsh, F. 'The Struggle of the Lancashire Textile Workers.' Pub. Textile Workers' Minority Movement. February 1929 18 pages.
'Women & the More Loom System.' Pub. Textile Minority Movement. 1930
'A Call to Action.' Pub. Lancashire Textile Minority Movement. 1930
'For the Workers' Charter: Fight the Eight Looms.' Pub. Textile Minority Movement 1930/31
Articles:
Bullen, A. 'Watching & Besetting: The Burnley Police and the More Looms Disputes, 1931-1932.' Pub. North West Labour History Bulletin No.5
Jenkins, M. 'Cotton Struggles 1929-1932.' Marxism Today February 1969
Rathbone, H. 'The Cotton Workers' Fight Against Imperialism.' Labour Monthly February 1928
Lee, H. 'The Cotton Lock-Out.' Labour Monthly September 1929

Lee, H. 'The Cotton Weavers' Struggle and Victory.' Labour Monthly 1931
Ainley, T. 'The Cotton Workers' Fight.' Labour Monthly 1932
A Cotton Worker.'The Struggles of the Cotton Workers.' Labour Monthly August 1932
'The Choice for Lancashire.' The Labour Magazine August 1930
Richardson, T.H.'Cotton, the Cock-Pit of Britain.' The Labour Magazine February 1932
Richardson, T.H. 'Lancashire Calls for Leadership.' The Labour Magazine March 1932

Newspapers:
'The Cotton Lockout Special.' Pub. C.P.G.B. Manchester D.C. No.1 August 14th. 1929; No.3 August 17th. 1929
'Cotton Special.' Pub. Textile Workers Minority Movement. February 1932
'The Cotton Strike Leader.' Pub. Cotton Strikers Solidarity Movement. No.1.Sept. 10th. 1932; No.2. Sept. 15th. 1932; No.3. Sept. 17th. 1932; No.4. Sept. 21st. 1932; No.5. Sept. 24th. 1932; No.6. Oct. 22nd. 1932; No.7. Nov. 5th. 1932

Almanack & Guides:
The General Union of Associations of Loom Overlookers. 1930 & 1933

ENGINEERING:
Clegg, H.A. 'General Union: A Study of the NUGMW.' Pub. Blackwell. 1954
Frow, E & R. 'Engineering Struggles.' Pub. Working Class Movement Library. 1982
Fyrth, H.J. 'The Foundry Workers: A Trade Union History.' Pub. Amalgamated Union of Foundry Workers. Manchester 1959
Jefferys, J.B. 'The Story of the Engineers 1800-1945.' Pub. Lawrence & Wishart. 1945
Kidd, A.T. 'History of the Tin-Plate Workers and Sheet Metal Workers and Braziers Societies.' Pub. National Union of Sheet Metal Workers & Braziers. 1949

Articles:
Scott, J.R. 'The Fight of the Engineering Workers.' Labour Monthly May 1930
Frow, E. 'The Attack on the Engineers.' Labour Monthly June 1931

Journals:
AEU Monthly Journal 1927-1934
The General and Municipal Workers' Journal 1927-1934

MINERS:
Arnot, R.P. 'The Miners in Crisis and War.' Pub. George Allen & Unwin. 1961
Davies, P. 'A.J. Cook.' Pub. Manchester UP. 1987
Horner, A. 'Incorrigible Rebel.' Pub. MacGibbon & Kee. 1960

UNEMPLOYMENT & the MEANS TEST:
Bruce, M. 'The Coming of the Welfare State.' Pub. B.T. Batsford, London. 1961
Hannington, W. 'Unemployed Struggles 1919/1936.' Pub. E.P. Publishing. 1973
Hannington, W. 'Ten Lean Years.' Gollancz Left Book Club. 1940
Kingsford, P. 'The Hunger Marchers in Britain 1920-1940.' Pub. Lawrence & Wishart. 1982
Paynter, W. 'My Generation.' Pub. George Allen & Unwin. 1972
Vernon, B.D. 'Ellen Wilkinson.' Pub. Croom Helm. 1982

POLITICS:
1. Addison, P. 'The Road to 1945.' Pub. Quartet Books. 1977
2. Bassett, R. 'Nineteen Thirty-One: Political Crisis.' Pub. MacMillan. 1958
3. Branson, N. 'History of the CPGB 1927-1941.' Pub. Lawrence & Wishart. 1985
4. Bullock, A. 'The Life & Times of Ernest Bevin: Vol.1 Trade Union Leader 1881-1940.' Pub. Heinemann. 1960
5. Clinton, A. 'The Trade Union Rank & File: Trades Councils in Britain 1900-1940.' Pub. Manchester UP. 1977
6. Estorick, E. 'The Biography of Sir Stafford Cripps.' Pub. Heinemann. 1949
7. Foot, M. 'Aneurin Bevan: 1897-1945 Vol.1.' Pub. Paladin. 1975
8. Hamilton, M.A. 'Arthur Henderson: A Biography.' Pub. Heinemann. 1938
9. Hutt, A. 'British Trade Unionism: A Short History.' Pub. Lawrence & Wishart. 1975
10. Knox, W. 'James Maxton.' Pub. Manchester UP. 1987
11. Lee, J. 'My Life With Nye.' Pub. Penguin. 1981
12. Mahon, J. 'Harry Pollitt: A Biography.' Pub. Lawrence & Wishart. 1976
13. Martin, R. 'Communism & the British Trade Unions 1924-1933: A Study of the National Minority Movement.' Pub. Clarendon Press. 1969
14. McHenry, D.E. 'The Labour Party in Transition 1931-1935.' Pub. George Routeledge.1938
15. McNair, J. 'James Maxton: The Beloved Rebel.' Pub. George Allen & Unwin. 1955
16. Murphy, J.T. 'Preparing for Power.' Pub. Pluto Press. 1972
17. Pelling, H. 'A History of British Trade Unionism.' Pub. Penguin. 1972
18. Postgate, R. 'The Life of George Lansbury.' Pub. Longmans, Green & Co. 1951
19. Saklatvala, Sehri. 'The Fifth Commandment: A Biography of Shapurji Saklatvala.' Pub. Miranda Press. 1991
20. Shinwell, E. 'Conflict Without Malice.' Pub. Odhams Press. 1955
21. Thomas, H. 'John Strachey.' Pub. Eyre Methuen. 1973
22. Williams, F. 'Fifty Years March: The Rise of the Labour Party.' Pub. Odhams

Press. 1950
Pamphlets:
'Class Against Class: The General Election Programme of the CPGB. 1929.'
Smith, Rose. 'Working Women and the Capitalist Crisis.' Pub. CPGB. 1932
Smith, Rose. 'Women into the Ranks.' Pub. CPGB. 1933
'Release the Class War Prisoners: Class Justice.' Pub. International Labour Defence. 1931
Rust, W. 'Down With the National Government.' Pub. CPGB. 1931
Tait, F. 'The Jugglers of Finance are Bleeding the Nation White.' Pub. ILP. 1932

Mrs Susannah Holgate J.P.
Oswaldtwistle. 1934

Councillor Mrs M.A. Kennedy
Clayton-le-Moors UDC 1934

Councillor F. Mills, Labour
Springhill, Accrington 1934

Councillor J. Harling, Labour
Higher Antley, Accrington 1934

*Councillor J.M. Tattersall, Labour
Rishton UDC 1933*

*Councillor Joseph Finch, Labour
Clayton-le-Moors UDC. 1933*

*Mr Bert Lee, Accrington
NUR. Died January 1933*

*Councillor J. Lord
Secretary Accrington NUR*

Councillor Wallace Haines, Labour Central, Accrington 1934

Charles Dukes
Later Lord Dukeston, G.M.W.U

Mr J.C. Parker J.P.
Secretary, Weavers Amalgamation
Died November 1927

Councillor George F. Kilshaw
Labour - West Ward, Accrington 1933
Ass. Secretary Accrington Weavers

Mr Jonathan Ashworth, J.P.
Secretary, Rishton Weavers,
1930

Councillor Robert Gildert
Labour - Rishton UDC 1933
President Rishton Weavers.

Mr G. K. Chalmers. J.P.
Secretary Accrington A.E.U.
1920 - 1940

Mr Herbert Walsh. J.P.
Accrington A.E.U. - D.C.
Died May 1933

Mr Samuel Foster Brigg
Accrington A.E.U. - D.C.
Died June 1933

Mr James Henry Cosgrove
Accrington A.E.U. - D.C.
Died August 1934

Councillor Constantine (seated centre) playing dominoes at the Unemployed Centre, Oct. 1934

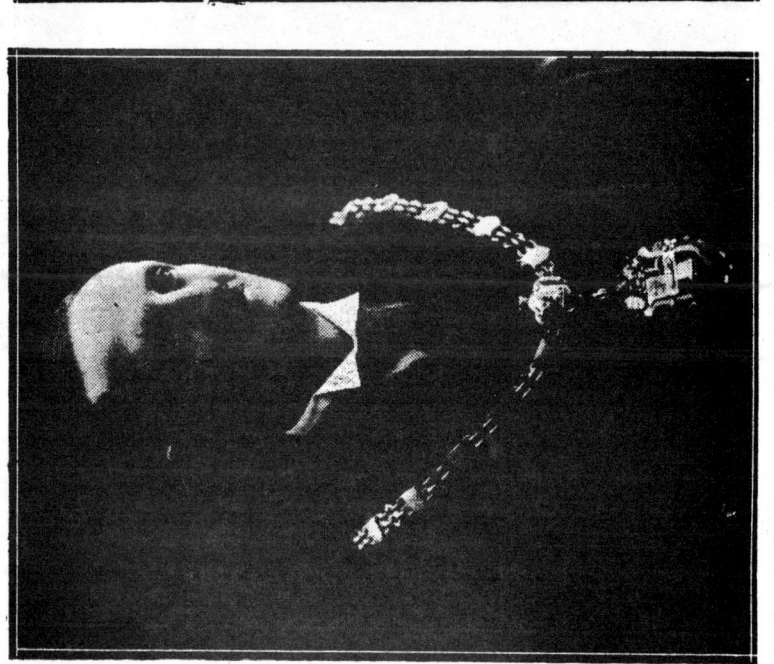

Councillor R.I. Constantine J.P. and Mrs Constantine, first Labour and Mayoress of Accrington. November 1931

Ald. W.A. Lambert, Secretary Accrington G.M.W.U. First Labour Alderman Accrington November 1929

Councillor T. O'Connor J.P. Accrington 1930

Councillor J. Baron Secretary, Accrington Miners.

Councillor A Dawson, Labour East Ward, Accrington. 1929

*Councillor S.T. Pilkington, Labour
North Ward, Accrington 1929*

*Councillor W. Howson, Secretary
T.C.L.P. Labour Central Ward
Accrington 1929*

*Mr Alfred Rowkins J.P.
Accrington N.U.R. May 1930*

"Brooklawn", High Street, Oswaldtwistle, early 1930's (L-R) Betty Ann Rushton, mother of Margaret and Terry McCarthty, Joshua Rushton, stepfather of Margaret and Terry McCarthy, Florence, American journalist and trade union organiser - communist Terry's wife, Margaret McCarthy.

A hiking weekend in the hills around Glasgow. Margaret McCarthy(4th from left) Terry McCarthy (3rd from right), Bill McKay (4th from right). Bill McKay later married Margaret, father of Morag.

Mr F.G. Burgess
Prospective Labour Candidate
Accrington.   1933

Mr Richard T. Howson J.P.
Clayton-le-Moors

Councillor W.H. Roberts
Labour - Springhill Ward

Councillor Michael Walsh, Labour
Peel Park, Accrington 1929

Councillor W.H. Greenwood J.P.
first Labour Chairman of Oswaldtwistle
UDC

Labour League of Youth headquarters opened at Oswaldtwistle, November 1933

Accrington Labour Party trip to Bingley. Mr Tom Snowden M.P. welcomes Councillor Constantine. August 1929

The new Labour Hall opened by Mr Arthur Henderson, Accrington June 1928

MARGERET BONDFIELD

Accrington Labour Party Field Day, July 1929

Ramsay MacDonald speaking on Ellison's tenement, Accrington, May 1929

Mr Charles Roden Buxton
May 1928

Councillor H.V. Podmore, Labour
Central, Accrington 1928

Councillor H. Smith
Labour, Church UDC. 1928

Mr J.R Emmett J.P. Accrington Weavers'
Secretary, September 1928

Mr J. Mills, Accrington Weavers
Auditor for 35 years. February 1929

Councillor C. Burke, Labour West Ward, Accrington 1928

Mr Tom Snowden, Prospective Labour Candidate – Accrington, June 1928

Accrington Branch Typographical Association trip to Settle, May 1927

Accrington Labour Party Dramatic Society, September 1928

Accrington Weavers' trip to Blackpool, September 11th 1928

Accrington Labour Procession, August 1927